SO YOU'RE GOING TO FRANCE!

THE TAKING OF ORLÉANS BY JEANNE D'ARC
By Jules Eugène Lenepveu

SO YOU'RE GOING
TO FRANCE!

AND IF I WERE GOING WITH YOU
THESE ARE THE THINGS I'D
INVITE YOU TO DO

BY

CLARA E. LAUGHLIN

*Author of ' So You're Going to Paris!' ' So You're
Going to Italy!' ' So You're Going to England!' etc.,
and Director of the Clara Laughlin Travel Services*

BOSTON AND NEW YORK
HOUGHTON MIFFLIN COMPANY
The Riverside Press Cambridge
1927

The Riverside Press
CAMBRIDGE · MASSACHUSETTS
PRINTED IN THE U.S.A.

TO

BETTY AND MARY CLARA LAUGHLIN

WHO QUICKLY BECAME LOVERS OF

FRANCE AND THE FRENCH

AND TO ALL THE FRENCH PEOPLE

WHO GAVE THESE LITTLE GIRLS THIS

BEAUTIFUL ENTHUSIASM

PREFACE

As this fourth book of our series goes to press, I am just back from another long sojourn in France, bringing with me the corrected proofs of this book and a greater-than-ever ardor for France as a vacation ground. Whether one goes in search of scenic beauty or of sports, of 'cures' or of comforts, of stimulus or relaxation, nowhere on earth, that I know, can he find greater variety of pleasantness, of interest, and of pastime than he can find in France. And if there is any country where he can get more for his money, I am not acquainted with it.

I heard some complaints about costs; but they were nearly all 'laid' when those making them were asked to compare the prices they paid in France with those paid for a similar grade of article or service at home.

For instance: when I landed in New York I was charged, by the hotel I went to, $6.50 for transferring a steamer trunk and sundry pieces of hand baggage from a 14th Street pier to a hotel near the Grand Central. My taxi was a dollar more. In a Paris hotel of like grade, I might have been charged as much as $2.50, but it would almost certainly have been less. A station bus for all luggage and three passengers would not have cost that much. A traveller who was charged one hundred and seventy-five francs for bringing a steamer trunk and some hand baggage to his hotel in Paris, would want redress from the War Department. I paid sixteen dollars for a night's lodging in two very small rooms — a double and a single — though it was August, and the hotel was half empty. Moreover, it is not a de luxe hotel. When I paid ten dollars for far more luxurious quarters in the most expensive hotel on the Riviera (not in 'high season' but in a season much less 'off' than August in New York), I felt that it was a very 'stiff' price. I paid nearly eleven dollars that night in New York for a very scant and simple dinner for three, of a quality that seemed to us most inferior. For that amount of money the three of us could have dined royally at a place like Foyot's, in Paris. Our usual check in a hotel reputed among the most expensive there, averaged for a dinner of three courses (and exquisite ones!) under seven dollars.

These may seem prosaic details wherewith to preface a book on a beautiful and storied land like France. But I, who am in constant, daily contact with intending travellers, know how vital a part of planning trips abroad is played by the question of finance, and how many persons have got the idea that travel is very dear, now, because it is less cheap than it used to be. Nearly everybody who goes has a fixed time to stay, and has decided upon a certain amount of money as the most that his trip ought to cost him. His problem, then, is how to get the most and best of what he wants, for his determined expenditure of time and money; and to know the relative expensiveness of different countries, as well as their charms.

The tendency in much of the old-fashioned planning which I call 'rubber-stamp' stuff, wherein itineraries in Europe are almost as much alike as tacks in a package or matches in a box, is to keep people on railway trains for a great deal more time than the travellers suspect they are letting themselves in for; to concentrate on cities (although thousands of travellers love towns and villages and country far better); to overrate the average avidity for art museums and cathedrals, and include a surfeit of things too similar; and otherwise to make of European travel a rather terrible

ordeal — anything but restful and recreative for a fresh
season's work at home. And also a very costly ordeal.

This sort of thing is foisted upon thousands of travellers
overseas, because the persons who 'do the foisting' don't
know what else there is to see; and if they *did* know ('out of
a book' as many of them only know Europe) they would
not know how to help the individual traveller select those
places most likely to give him his heart's desire.

It is my very great happiness that these little books have
helped thousands of travellers to know, for themselves,
what they want to see, and how to see it. I give direct, personal counsel to hundreds, who appeal to me, who are my
clients; but the books reach tens of thousands whom I must
counsel in these pages if I am to help them at all.

Everybody who goes abroad, goes to France; but probably ninety percent of them go only *across* France, to and
from Paris. No one could love Paris more than I do; it isn't
humanly possible! But Paris is a very cosmopolitan city —
the capital of the world! — and you must needs know it
very well indeed to get into the essentially French phases of
its varied life.

Of those comparatively few travellers who wander any
further afield from Paris than on an excursion to Fontainebleau, most of them follow one or two beaten paths which
are likewise covered by a procession of excursion cars. Not
until you have left the main-travelled char-à-banc routes in
any country can you hope to know the real flavor of that
country as it has seasoned the books you love best. Not
until you go apart from an excursion, can you hope to be
welcomed as a pilgrim and not as a 'tripper.'

France is a perfect country for 'exploration.' Her treasures are infinitely varied, and inexhaustible; the more you
wander among them, the more you want to wander, on and
on. I cannot think of any kind of delight she does not offer

— except, perhaps, jungle-hunting or seal-fishing, or beach-combing.

Living in France, for the resident and for the traveller, is not cheap, in the sense that it used to be; but it is still enough less expensive than it is almost everywhere else, to attract and hold a very great many vacationists from other European countries. If these and other travellers knew more places to go to in France, they would find sojourn there far cheaper still.

The difficulty at present is that the foreigner in France concentrates too much. There is a certain kind of visitor who *must* be at Deauville in August and wouldn't be 'caught' there in June or July or September. When Deauville, which must make its year's living in one month (not because it wishes to, but because that is the only time it can capture any business) charges him more than he thinks he ought to pay, he 'hollers.' But if he is abroad in January or February, he must, somehow or other, be packed into one of the short-season hotels of the Riviera, one of the super-de-luxe palaces which are empty by April first (when the Riviera is at its loveliest) and boarded up by May first to stay so until December. He probably complains at the price he pays. But he could have the Riviera at the same time, in the same place, in equal or greater comfort, at a third the price, if he would choose a hotel which is not chosen by all the world's biggest spenders; or he could even have that hotel at a fair price if he would go to it in April instead of January, February, or March.

When we stop competing with one another for the same hotel in the same spot, at the same moment, and then flocking off to start the competition elsewhere, there will be less ground even than there is now for talk of 'high prices.' If the places where 'inflation' exists were the *only* desirable places to be, or if they were desirable only during a very brief season, it would be different. But France is *full* of delectable places. Most of them have superior hotel accommodations. If your fancy runs to de luxe hotels but your budget does not support them, you have only to choose, for your stay at them, a moment just before the high season is on, or just after it is over. You will miss the fashion parade, but you'll get everything else, and much of it better than you'd have it in the jam. And if hotels which are excellent but not 'seasonal' nor fashionable, content you, then you may go and come entirely at your wish, and pay less than you could reasonably expect to pay for such living in a world where everything has got unconscionably dear.

And here let me say something to those persons who seem to think that bathrooms are scarce in France. They are not! They are numerous, and surprisingly elegant. One scarcely finds a hotel room without up-to-date open plumbing and a plentiful supply of hot and cold running water. And rooms with private bathrooms are no longer hard to get, even in little provincial hotels where one could scarcely expect to find them.

Beds are almost without exception luxurious. Rooms are almost invariably scrupulously clean. Here and there one finds a 'frowsy,' ill-kept hotel; but they are the exception. Here and there one finds the food a discredit to this land of marvellous eating and drinking; but the average is very high, and the best is magnificent. The national association of hotel-keepers is under supremely earnest and intelligent direction, and much is being done to meet the wishes of France's visitors. If you have any suggestions to make, I'll be glad to get them, and to lay them before the persons who may do most to get them acted upon.

A good many of the hotel men know me, and know what I am trying to do to shake travel out of a rut, to make it more *individual*, and to establish more personal contacts between travellers abroad and the people they are visiting. Many of those hotel men are keenly interested in this effort. Talk to your hotel-manager, when you can. (There is every probability that he speaks English, if you do not speak French.) Frequently he is a mine of information on his vicinity — not on 'the sights' alone, but on the people, on their problems, on industry, and on other things which will greatly help you to comprehend the life about you as you journey. The head porter always has a lot of information, always speaks English, and it is his business to tell you things you want to know. But he seldom has five consecutive minutes to give any one patron, and he tends to become brief and conventionalized — necessarily so. Managers are often busy and can't be seen for conversational purposes. But at least you can *try*, here and there. The manager who comes in contact with his guests and learns their viewpoint while giving in exchange for it his own, is developing a new type of hotel in France (and in Italy) and I heartily believe that he is making an important contribution toward that transformation of travel from 'tripping' into a fine humanistic art, which is so necessary not only to the individual traveller's joy but to that increased understanding between nations which the diplomats can only *talk* about but you and I must 'make come true.'

There is, I now realize, more of 'the power of solidarity' — of numbers and of like-mindedness — in 'us' (that is, in you and me) than in any other element travelling in Europe nowadays. What with your numerical strength (there are thousands of you always 'on the wing' over there) and your high intelligence, and your right-mindedness, I look to see you accomplish many desirable things, as the years go by. I pin more expectation to you than to the Geneva Conference!

The greatest 'liability' I see to good-will on earth and to the development of travel as a fine art and a high delight, is the ill-prepared traveller trying to digest 'a dose of *sights*' and comprehending nothing at all of the people he's living among.

I believe that We (not Lindy's 'We,' but *our* 'We'!) are accomplishing some things which should make us happy, and are going to accomplish many more. And of course it is no whit less true in travel than in any other thing in life, that those who concern themselves not only with what they're *getting* but with what they're *giving, get the most!*

Wherever you make yourself felt as a person (a friendly person) and not as a mere tourist, I'm sure you are not only doubling your own pleasure, but making things pleasanter for others who come after you. Certainly in France your out-reaching friendliness will seldom (if ever) meet with anything but a prompt manifestation of the same spirit.

I hope with all my heart that this little book (although it has had to exclude so much that I would have loved to include in it) may serve to lead you on many happy adventures.

Some day, when 'we' have become a *closer* corporation (we're a big enough one, now!) I hope to have our own headquarters in Paris and our representatives everywhere. But that means more than paying rent! It means training and maintaining an organization to do the 'so-different' thing, as we do it at Chicago and in New York. And that will take time, as well as money.

Meanwhile, I must avail myself (for your service) of the best existing organization which is small enough to give close, personal attention, large enough to have strong connections through Europe, old enough to have demonstrated its ability and reliability, and not old enough to have grown stereotyped in its methods.

I use, for those clients who come to me or write to me when their plans are a-making, any one of a score of foreign services which seems to me best to meet their requirements. But to choose one from amongst them to which I might direct you who need service over there, is not easy.

It isn't reasonable to expect that in a big office where you may cash your checks, ship your trunk, and buy a ticket to Versailles, you could *also* get the individualized attention and the first-hand, intimate information that an office can give which serves few clients on larger orders. Nor is it reasonable to expect that a man who can help you select just those parts of the Pyrénées that will give you most satisfaction in the time you have to spend there, should be available to tell you how long it takes to go to Fontaine-bleau, which any office-boy could tell you.

I'd do all my 'small shopping' in what might be called the 'department stores' of travel. Most of the big ones are good, though they tend to be crowded — to make you wait a long time and get a hurried service when your turn comes. When you want counsel on a tour (motor or rail) planned for you to meet your special tastes and purposes and take care of all your needs en route, seek it at the office of Fraser-McLean, Élysée Building, 56 rue du Faubourg St.-Honoré (a little west of rue Royale); or, call the office, tell what you want, and it may be that one of the staff can go to see you. Always, if you say, 'I am a Clara Laughlin reader,' it will greatly simplify and facilitate matters for you. For they are accustomed to executing my orders, and have much of my information on file. Moreover, they must keep some record of what they do for my readers, so I may know how satisfactory this arrangement is for you. If it doesn't give you what you want, we must try to do it some other way.

I have tried to think what could be done to facilitate the labors of those who prefer to make all their own hotel reservations after they get to Europe and as they journey along. The writing of letters is certainly a burden to the traveller. Sometimes he writes too few details when requesting reservations. Sometimes he scatters his details through a letter so they are hard to pick out.

To save labor and make things easy for the traveller and for the hotel proprietor or clerk (who may not read English handwriting too readily), I have prepared and printed some cards whereon you need only check off your requirements (one minute's work) and write your name and arrival-date. These are for any and all hotels, whichever you may choose; you write in the hotel name, and your own. A dozen or a score of these cards will be supplied you, gratis, from my Chicago or New York office, and will take up little or no room in your purse or portfolio.

All I ask of you is that in using them you regard a hotel reservation for which you have applied as a sort of contract between you and the hotel, to the extent that if you cannot use it, you will cancel it by letter or otherwise as far in advance of the time specified as is possible, and if you are delayed in your schedule, you will promptly let the manager know. A great deal of difficulty arises out of reservations being carelessly treated by the persons who asked for them. Those who do this make travel harder for themselves and for others who come after them.

I believe this simple device will save travellers a great deal of labor and of annoyance; and that if it is used, in the main, by responsible, considerate persons, who keep their word and 'play fair,' it will come — in time — to be a real help in securing for its users something of the same respect and assurance of good treatment which is accorded now to those whose reservations are made by a travel agency of prestige and perfect credit.

A request for a dozen or a score of these cards will bring them to you, gratis.

CHICAGO, *August* 20, 1927   C. E. L.

CONTENTS

ILLUSTRATIONS

SO YOU'RE GOING TO FRANCE!

SO YOU'RE GOING TO FRANCE!

I

TO MONT–SAINT–MICHEL AND BACK THROUGH NORMANDY

I

If a count could be kept, I think it would be determined that the two places in France most frequently asked about by travellers are Mont-Saint-Michel and Carcassonne.

This doesn't mean that more persons go there than to any other two places. Neither of them is easy of access, for one thing. Neither of them is a place of sojourn — like Nice, for instance, where people go to stay, for days or weeks or months. Each of them is something to look at, to take into one's book of mem'ry-pictures; to carry on into a more or less prosaic, workaday existence as a kind of 'king-for-a-day' experience: 'Once, for a night and a part of a day, I dwelt in the inmost citadel of Romance, and my imagination made me sovereign over it all.'

Not everybody expresses it that way; but there can be little doubt that this more or less describes the feeling of those who have been to these places and others like them; nor that it is the 'urge' within persons seeking to visit them.

France has scores — yes, hundreds! — of places which are little, if any, less thrilling. But of all her glory-spots those two are among the most familiar to the greatest number of intending travellers; perhaps because they lend themselves so wonderfully to pictures, and have 'been taken' so often and so successfully that almost everybody knows them instantly on sight; perhaps because returned travellers who have seen them wax more eloquent about them than about other places; perhaps because so much has been written about Mont-Saint-Michel and Carcassonne. (Certainly an astonishing number of persons seem not only to have read Henry Adams's noble book on 'Mont-Saint-Michel and Chartres,' but to have caught from it much of his fine fervor and understanding.)

At any rate, whatever the reason, thousands of people yearn to visit Mont-Saint-Michel and Carcassonne. And most of them, when they come to inquire into ways and means, find that they have, if not to relinquish, at least to defer realization of those desires.

Mont-Saint-Michel is 245 miles from Paris, and there is no direct line to it, no through train; two changes of cars must be made, and the time required for the journey is nearly 10 hours. To go there, by train, see the town and the Abbey, and return to Paris, entails a matter of three days' time, 500 miles of travel, and an expense of not less than $20 to $25. This is a good deal for one 'sight,' however glorious; and it is not surprising that many travellers feel they must forego it.

But the blessed gasoline motor makes all the difference in the world for sight-seers; and if you can command one, or a seat in one, you may have in five days a trip to Mont-Saint-Michel which will give you, to be yours forever, not only that glory-spot but something like twoscore others scarcely less glorious. That is what it means to 'motor in France' if one knows the roads, and how to 'space' the runs, and where the ideal stops are, and so on.

The places I shall include in this tour from Paris to

Mont-Saint-Michel and back are worthy of many times five days if you have abundant time for leisurely study of them. But most people haven't such time; and for them, seeking to pack a too-brief opportunity with treasure-bearing glimpses, I am writing this book.

I once sent two people out on this tour in a Paris taxi-cab; and they were transported with delight in the whole experience. To be sure, it was a 'very special' taxi, with balloon tires and an exceptionally good chauffeur, and our best Normandy courier. It cost, I think, about $250 for everything. A larger car would cost two people $100 more, but would bring down the price for four people to about $100 each for the trip. The price per person on a drive-yourself plan, without courier, might come down as low as $50 each for four in a hired car, and perhaps as low as $40 each, using less expensive hotels and less notable food, for four in their own car.

I give all these figures in the only way that one may offer prices in print — not as absolute, because they are almost sure to fluctuate from day to day; but as a sort of indication or approximation, to aid you in calculating how to spread your travel budget. If you have to ask your way, to be your own guide on the road and in towns and other sight-seeing places, you cannot hope to see as much in a short time as is possible with a courier who specializes in that section. And in my opinion it is worth a great deal to 'cover' such an itinerary in company of some one who knows it well and can answer questions about it. But there are compensations for the other way, the way of the ex-plorer who may get off the road and discover a treasure on a byway; who may not see half the places en route, but may find a Heart's Desire among them that will make him glad to forego the rest.

Any way that you can best manage to make this tour is

bound to be a good way, a superlatively rewarding investment for your time and money. It is, indeed, but a glimpse of an inexhaustibly rich section of France; but a half-loaf is infinitely better than no bread, and this glimpse is more than enough to whet your appetite for a fuller acquaintance later on.

Your start from Paris should be an early one — not a moment after eight-thirty in the morning; for your first day (if you have but five to give to this trip) is a long one and very, very full.

Out through Saint-Cloud and Ville d'Avray you go, to Versailles; and turn out of the avenue de Saint-Cloud into rue Georges-Clemenceau, keeping straight on across avenue de Paris and avenue de Sceaux till you come to rue de l'Orangerie which continues on as the Route de Saint-Cyr. And as you pass between the Swiss Lake and the south wing of the palace of Versailles, I dare say you'll be thinking of a Saturday afternoon, the last day of August, 1715, and seem to see a woman of fourscore years leaving the vast château where she had so long lived as uncrowned queen. Her husband, the mighty monarch, has lapsed into unconsciousness; the end of his seventy-two years of sovereignty is at hand; she has prepared him for it, has said good-bye to him, and is withdrawing to the girls' school she founded at Saint-Cyr and he endowed. Nearly four years more of life await her there. A little later, this morning, you are to see the beautiful estate the King gave her so that the Widow Scarron might become Madame de Maintenon. She lies in the chapel at Saint-Cyr, which is now a military school.

Beyond Saint-Cyr your way turns south toward the splendid Château of Dampierre, belonging to the Duc de Luynes. François Mansart, architect of the palace at Versailles, rebuilt Dampierre, and Le Nôtre laid out the park; but this was just after the days of that lively lady, Marie de

Rohan, widowed Duchesse de Luynes, who made so much mischief at Louis XIII's court that he ordered her to leave it, and she retaliated by marrying a personage, one of the Guises, whose wife couldn't well be asked to move. Duchesse Marie's home was in the Château de la Madeleine, above the near-by town of Chevreuse; it was there, and in Paris, that she played her intrigues against Richelieu, which Dumas utilized so breath-takingly in 'The Three Musketeers.'

The splendid park of Dampierre we do not see, and the château is open to visitors who present a card of permission from the secretary of the Duc de Luynes, only on Fridays from 2 to 4 P.M. But most of us would probably press on, past Dampierre, even if it stood open to invite us, because we have ahead of us places that we would rather see.

The glimpse we may take of the Rothschild estate at Les-Vaux-de-Cernay is not an extensive one; but I think it is worth making the slight détour for, if only to see with what exquisite taste the present proprietors have used a Cistercian prior's lodging as a residence; and how nobly the lovely, ivy-clad ruins of the twelfth-century church lend themselves to the ensemble of a twentieth-century Jewish banker's estate — or, rather, how the veneration of beauty and tradition which characterizes this remarkable family seems to take all incongruity out of their occupation of a priory, and even to make the passers-by glad that such a precious bit of the loveliness of other centuries is in the care of a family likely to conserve it for many generations. If there is anything stronger than Creed, it is Culture. And my notion of one of the things we travel for is to get a broader vision of and a deeper insight into that culture which becomes more and more gracious as it pays profounder respect to the influences of other days which made us what we are.

I have never met any member of the Rothschild family. I have no knowledge of them save as all the world has. But the impression I get as I peer, a wayfarer, at what one may see of this estate, is that the Rothschilds esteem those ruins for more than their picturesqueness, their architectural beauty; that they cherish the significance of the ancient buildings, and of this site, for their relation to the Past.

After leaving the house and grounds you will motor on for miles through fields and forest of this vast estate; and this will give you food for reflection on the evolution of society as we are constantly being reminded of it in a tour like this. I haven't any theories of political economy. I don't think I know the least thing about what's best for mankind — so I can't tell when it's happening and when it isn't. But I find it an absorbing occupation to be (as one is in Europe) constantly reminded of the overturnings and changes which go on and on in a world that sagely refuses to become settled, but leaves each generation its share of the eternal problems to work out.

The French Revolution dispossessed the Cistercian monks who had held sway here for 660 years. The French Revolution started the fortunes of the Frankfort bankers, the Rothschilds, whose descendants hold sway here now. I'm thinking of one brilliant English writer on French travel and history, who attributes nearly all recent and present troubles to the decline of the Church's power; and of another who believes that the woe of the world is increasing as the Jews wax in possessions and influence. How indignant this place must make them both! And I wonder if I'm wrong to rejoice that I can go through France without any thesis to prove; with very few prejudices to carry; and that I see in all struggle not a mere means to an end, but an end in itself: the game of Life which gives us all our opportunities to fight a good fight.

We shall, as we go forward on these journeys, have almost hourly reminders of the waxing and waning of successive social systems and religions and reforms. I find them all deeply interesting, the conflict between them exhilarating, and their contributions to our inheritance most instructive to reflect upon.

I hope I shall not disappoint you if I seem inclined to watch the world go by without feeling any responsibility for judging it.

Here, then, we are drawing near to Rambouillet, of whose fourteenth-century château only one massive tower remains, built about by the more recent portions. This domain, with its superb forest, was a royal residence until the fourteenth century when it passed to the D'Angennes family to whom it belonged for three hundred years. Its last châtelaine of that race was the famous Marquise de Rambouillet whose salon in Paris (sometimes adjourned to this château) either revolutionized French society or marked its evolution. She was the daughter of a Roman noblewoman and of the Marquis de Pisani; and when, a bride of twelve, she was taken to the court of Henry IV, she found it too much like a camp — in manners, in language, and in morals — for her taste, young though she was.

When she was nineteen, and a young mother, she began gathering about her in her own home others who shared her dislike of intrigue and coarse talk; and gradually established a new social ideal based on deference to mental and spiritual quality, on courtesy something akin to the old chivalry, and on interchange of high ideas instead of gross familiarities.

She led, and led so well that many were glad to follow. To her courage, her taste, her initiative, we owe a great deal; and as nothing remains of her Paris mansion, we cannot do better than pay our respects to her memory here in her country home.

When she first came to Rambouillet it was only a little more than half a century since Francis I had died here; and very recent were the memories of Catherine de Médicis and Charles IX finding refuge here in the Wars of Religion.

Perhaps you will care most to recall them at Rambouillet. But I hardly think so; for we shall do it much more satisfactorily in the Loire châteaux. And lest Madame la Marquise de Rambouillet seem a bit formidable to you as the founder of French salons and the reformer of French manners, I'll remind you of some of the 'folks-y' things about her which her husband's kinsman, Tallemant des Reaux, wrote nigh on two hundred and fifty years ago, but which were not printed in France till 1833 and have only just been translated into English and published in England and the United States under the title of 'Miniature Portraits.'

Tallemant probably never guessed how unpopular his 'Historiettes,' or 'Little Histories,' would be when finally they came to the light of another generation — that of the French Romanticists of Victor Hugo's early day. By that time the traditions which had grown up around the great world of seventeenth-century France made nearly everybody in it seem as Olympian as the gods and demigods of Greek mythology. Tallemant had written of them as he knew them — in nightcaps and curlpapers, so to speak. And from his nice, gossipy but not derogatory pages I'm culling for you a few of the things he says about Madame de Rambouillet, which may make you feel less trepidation in calling on her.

She was, he says, 'herself the architect of the Hôtel de Rambouillet' at Paris. 'It is from her that people learned to set the staircases on one side to allow a great suite of rooms, to raise partitions higher, and to make doors and

windows high and wide and opposite each other. So true
is this that the Queen-Mother, when she had the Luxembourg built, bade the architects go to see the Hôtel de
Rambouillet; and they were repaid for their pains. She
was the first who thought of having a room painted in any
other color than red or tan; whence the name given to her
principal apartment — the "Blue Room."'

'If her estate,' Tallemant opined, 'had been such as to
allow of great spending, she would certainly have prepared
more costly treats. I have heard her say that the greatest
pleasure she could have would have been to build a fine
house at the end of the park at Rambouillet, in such secrecy
that none of her friends had any inkling of it (and with a
little care this would not be impossible, for the place is remote enough and the park one of the largest in France, and
a good musket-shot's distance from the castle, which is
itself only an old-fashioned edifice); that then she would
have brought her best friends to Rambouillet, and next
day, when strolling in the park, would have suggested
going to see a fine house which one of her neighbors had
built some time back; "and then, after many roundabout
ways," she said, "I would have begged them to stay a few
days in this delightful place."'

You may like to think of her walking in the park and
seeing such a 'surprise palace' in her mind's eye. The
nearest she came to realizing this desire at Rambouillet was
on her last stay here when she had a cascade constructed to
surprise her son-in-law, the Duc de Montausier. But in
her Paris home she once contrived to have a magnificent
apartment built on, and furnished, without any of her
friends suspecting what was being done. And one evening,
when there was a great assemblage in her salons, a tapestry
was drawn aside and the superb new apartment was revealed. One of the three tall windows of this 'magic'

room overlooked the garden of the Hôtel de Chevreuse, next door. And all the polite world of Paris was scandalized when the Duc de Chevreuse (husband of the lively, intriguing Duchesse Marie) 'took it into his head to build some sort of a wardrobe-room, by which the garden window was blocked.' He protested that he needed the new room, to accommodate his clothes. But 'note,' says Tallemant, 'that he had forty rooms already!'

They 'squabbled' — those grand lords and ladies did! And I'm sure we feel more at home with them for knowing it.

They played jokes, too. One evening when the future Marshal de Grammont had eaten heartily of mushrooms, here at Rambouillet, some of the other guests 'got hold of his valet, and, obtaining from him all the doublets of the costumes which his master had brought with him, promptly took them in with needle and thread.'

In the morning, the Count tried on one after another of them, and when none would go on, asked: 'Have I swollen out? Can it be from eating too many mushrooms?'

Just then the bell rang for Mass, for it was a Sunday, and he was forced to go in a dressing-gown.

When his joke-playing friends saw that he was truly frightened over his condition, one of them said he knew an antidote. He wrote it out, and handed it to the Count. It read:

'Take a good pair of scissors, and unstitch your doublets.'

The Marquise did not come at all to Rambouillet in her later years, owing to her infirmity — a peculiar one which made her unable to endure sunlight in summer, and any artificial heat in winter.

'Here she is,' wrote Tallemant, 'constrained to remain almost always indoors, and never to warm herself. Necessity made her borrow from the Spaniards the device of alcoves, which are so much in vogue in Paris nowadays. The company go and warm themselves in the anteroom. In frosty weather she sits in bed with her legs in a bearskin bag, and she remarks pleasingly, on account of the great mass of head-gear which she wears in winter-time, that she becomes deaf on Saint Martin's Day, and recovers her hearing at Easter.'

To have maintained, despite such handicaps, her reputation as a very great lady whose approval 'made,' as her disapproval *un*-made, even extraordinary folk in Paris, argues either that people of her day were less averse to eccentricities of appearance and of conduct than most people are now, or that her gifts of mind and manner were great enough to make all else forgot.

At Rambouillet you will see some beautiful apartments 'done over' for Marie Antoinette; for this domain was bought and embellished by Louis XVI who had a model farm here as well as a hunting preserve. Napoleon came here not infrequently, and his rooms are preserved much as they were when he used them. And here the stupid, reactionary brother of Louis XVI, Charles X, was forced to abdicate the French throne in 1830, after having proved that a man could live through the French Revolution, the Consulate and Empire, and his brother's (Louis XVIII) Restoration, without learning anything.

From Rambouillet, your way leads on through Épernon to Maintenon. Should it chance that you have already visited the valley of the Chevreuse and Rambouillet, before starting on this tour, then continue on Route 12 past Houdan to Dreux; visit the Chapelle-Royale Saint-Louis, the burial place of comparatively recent members of the Orléans family, beginning with the widow of Philippe Égalité; and containing also the unacknowledged resting-

place of Rouzet, her humble lover whose twenty-six-year
romance with her began when they were both prisoners of
the Terror in Paris. (See 'So You're Going to Paris,' pp.
235–36.) In Dreux, whose castle used to crown the height
whereon the royal mausoleum now stands, be sure to see
the lovely Renaissance belfry, and the quaint old houses
of the Grande Rue, and to visit the Hôtel du Paradis, a
delightful inn with many treasures among its furnishings
and a fine hospitality for its guests however transient.
Then, go from Dreux to Anet, the superb château built by
Philibert Delorme, at Henry II's orders, for Diane de
Poitiers, in 1552. And you must call it Ann-*et* — not Ann-
ay. Here Jean Goujon wrought, and Germain Pilon, and
Jean Cousin; and over the main entrance, in the form of
a triumphal arch, is a copy of Cellini's Nymph of Fontainebleau for which Diane herself, 'tis said, was the model.
Anet is about twelve miles north of Dreux, and near by
Ivry-le-Bataille where Henry IV won his decisive victory
over the League under the Duc de Mayenne, that one of
the Guises who contended against Henry for the crown of
France. If you are bound for Chartres, you must return
from Anet to Dreux, whence there is a main route — 154 —
to Chartres, twenty-one miles south. Or, you can take a
'bending' road not much longer, and include on your way
to Chartres, Nogent-le-Roi which preserves its old walls
and their four gates, as well as some especially picturesque
timbered houses; then, Maintenon. Should you have seen
Chartres, you may take a small, cross-country road from
Anet to Nonancourt where Henry IV slept the night before
the battle of Ivry, and where, four hundred years earlier,
the treaty was signed by which Philippe-Auguste and
Richard Cœur-de-Lion defined their respective shares in the
Third Crusade, to drive Saladin from the Holy City.
And, seven miles beyond Nonancourt on Route 12, the

direct route to Alençon, Mayenne, Laval, Vitré, and Rennes, you will come to Tillières-sur-Avre where you will find the Hostellerie du Bois-Joly, which is unexcelled by any in France or elsewhere that I know, for charm of surroundings or quality of food. If you lunch there, you will certainly promise yourself an early return for a longer stay; for the rooms and grounds are quite enchanting, and the collection of antiques in itself worth the journey thither.

(From Rambouillet one takes Route 10 for Maintenon, a distance of 14 miles, passing through the ancient town of Épernon.)

A delightful example of a somnolent old provincial town is Maintenon. The last time I was there (which was a very few weeks ago) the friends who were with me as we drew up at the château gate were unable to believe their eyes and ears when the Town Crier came by on his round — behaving no more self-consciously than a newsboy calling 'Extrys' in a street at home; but seeming to us for all the world like somebody out of a fairy tale.

The Château of Maintenon now belongs to the Duc de Noailles of that very noted noble family into which Madame de Maintenon's niece and heiress married. (Her great-granddaughter it was who became the wife of Lafayette.) The donjon of the thirteenth-century château remains; the Renaissance portions are very beautiful; and it is characteristic that one of Madame de Maintenon's principal additions should have been a gallery uniting the chapel with the château. The unfinished aqueduct which Louis XIV began, to bring the water of the river Eure to Versailles, spans the river in splendid view from the château and, together with the reflection of the mansion's turrets and gables in the mirroring waters, makes one of the most picturesque vistas to be seen among all the châteaux of France.

I do not easily find Madame de Maintenon here. I suspect that she had not many opportunities to come here and
enjoy being châtelaine in her own domain. Louis XIV was
not an easy man to live with! Nothing, of all that has been
written about him, makes him so 'realizable' as does the
little book which Louis Bertrand wrote about 'The Love-
Life of Louis XIV,' after he had written his great book on
Louis as King. There are times, as one reads the intimate
small book, when one positively blushes as if he had been
caught peeping or listening at a keyhole! I greatly regret
that the book has not been translated into English; and
also that I may not take, here, space for more than a few
sentences from the many penetrating pages devoted to
Madame de Maintenon; but perhaps those most pertinent
to recall here are what Bertrand tells of her pathetic ruses
to escape a few of the King's continual flittings from one
uncomfortable palace to another. Madame was rheumatic
and had a delicate chest; she dreaded draughts and catch-
ing cold. The King loved fresh air and detested invalidism;
he was restless and continually 'on the go'; she desired
nothing so much as to 'stay put' and enjoy a little chim-
ney-corner tranquillity. She even got her doctor to tell the
King that she couldn't endure so much travel on rough
roads and in draughty conveyances. When she asked for
shades or awnings because the sun, pouring into her Fontainebleau apartments, was roasting her, the King replied
that shades on her windows would mar the symmetry of
the façade; those who lived in the palace of so great a king
must be glad as he was to suffer for splendid appearances
befitting his royalty. 'One must perish in symmetry!'
she wrote to one of her few confidantes.

At court she lived her life apart, having no acknowledged
position; reputed to be the power behind the throne, but
knowing herself to be very little regarded by the King in

counsels other than religious. Even in her bedroom she had no privacy; it frequently happened that after she had gone to bed under the very noses of the King and any of his ministers with whom he was taking counsel, they went on talking, six feet from her pillow. She got most terribly tired of her job, because she was not in love with the King, nor in sympathy with his passion for being a great ruler — the only real passion he ever had. And he couldn't comprehend why she wasn't completely absorbed in ministering to his glory. They 'scrapped'! That is, he found fault with her, like any bourgeois husband; but she held her tongue, and when she got her way it was without his knowing that he had granted it.

I try to see her coming here to her own house for a brief bit of doing as she chose; of going to bed when she was sleepy, and having no ministerial discussions to keep her awake; of having the windows closed and the fire hot; of 'sassing back' when some one irritated her, instead of always biting her tongue and looking placid; of telling her troubles, instead of always listening to the King's and pretending she had none of her own.

She said that Louis didn't care how much wind whistled through his corridors, so long as the doors were majestically opposite one another. I look about me, here, to see if she managed to have some of her own doors otherwise.

I hope she was able to 'swank around' here, some, and enjoy herself in her rather melancholy way. And if I had any idea of what might have been a real 'vacation' for Louis in her absence, I'd hope he had it, too. But Louis didn't know much about giving himself a rest and change. His job weighed on him quite horribly, at times; but it was the only thing in the world he really cared about, and he had no desire to forget it, even briefly, and lead another life. A colored laundress was reported to me, the other day, as having said of one of her employers who travelled a great deal: 'I dunno why that woman all de time goin' somewheres. She's gotta take herself along!'

That was poor Louis XIV's case, too; he had to take himself along — he had no other self to take. But Madame de Maintenon had! And she had this lovely place to take it to, besides Saint-Cyr. The wish, and the wherewithal to gratify it — and a terribly short tether!

From Maintenon to Chartres is twelve miles. But en route is one of the best luncheon places (or dinner, were you thereabouts later in the day) that all France has to offer: the Hôtel de la Providence, at Jouy — a roadhouse with a pleasant garden, and a kitchen scarcely less marvellous than the one at Bois-Joly, and food fit for any king, and gracious hospitality. Don't miss it!

Chartres, fifty-five miles from Paris, is built on a hill beside the Eure, stretches of which are still fringed by the ancient ramparts and spanned by old 'asses'-back' bridges. Southeast of the city stretches the great plain called La Beauce, the granary of France; and to the west lies the Perche where the magnificent Percheron horses are bred.

For the leisurely traveller, especially if he be a student of architecture or of archæology, Chartres has much to reward several days of sight-seeing. But most persons get their impressions of it in a few hours. It is the fashion in writing about travel, to lament or to ridicule this 'glimpse-snatching' manner — probably because so many travellers do a poor job of it, or get their 'glimpses mixed,' or don't 'set' them, afterwards, by reading and recalling. Certainly it can't be because the writers believe no 'glimpses' are worth while. Half the world that goes to France is still reading Henry James's 'Little Journey in France,' the sketchy record of a 'look and leave' tour he made hereabouts more than forty years ago. Much of the most delightful literature of journeying is in records of movement and not of sojourn. I know both ways of travel: the stopping for impressions, and the lingering for such acquaintance as I have with Paris, for instance, and London, and Rome and Florence. There is much to be said for each way; some places call for acquaintance if we can give them time for it; others come nearest to giving us what we desire of them, in a rather brief 'call.' I don't find it deplorable to pause at Chartres for a couple of hours. I have been there a great many times, always somewhat briefly; and I have never come away until after I had reached the saturation point in awe and ecstasy and had got more than enough to warm me and thrill me for a long time thereafter.

There has, I think, been too much written against 'glimpse-taking' without separating the right kind of glimpse from the wrong or futile kind.

I take space, here, for these remarks because I have so often gone into places like Chartres Cathedral with some one who very nearly lost all the joy of that opportunity because he was being *gnawed* by the suggestion that he couldn't 'do it justice,' or see it all.

Perhaps I'm a happy wayfarer because I know it isn't in me to do justice to Chartres Cathedral — not if I spent my life trying to do so; and because I've learned that it, and places like it, can give me an immeasurable joy in a reverent hour or two.

Please don't go there distressed by the thought of all you will probably *miss!* That's not a nicer, more praiseworthy attitude toward spiritual and mental things than toward things material.

Go to Chartres for a transfiguring hour. Transfigurations are not slow processes.

'How ill at ease,' said Napoleon, entering Chartres Cathedral, 'an atheist would feel in this place!' Most

persons who have seen it will tell you that to them Chartres
Cathedral is the most impressively sacred temple of worship they have ever been in. Napoleon was far from being
a pious person; and of those others who feel such reverence
in Chartres Cathedral, many are such as do not kneel at
this altar or at any.

One reason why this feeling smites so many visitors to
Chartres may be because of the ages upon ages through
which mankind has worshipped on this spot.

Chartres was one of the chief towns of the Carnutes, a
Celtic tribe whose territory lay between the Seine and the
Loire. It is said that they invaded Italy in the time of the
Tarquins; and we know that they fought with Vercingetorix
against Cæsar.

When the earliest Christian missionaries, sent forth by
Saint Peter himself, came here, they found a grotto in the
side of this hill and in it an altar with a statue of a Virgin
holding a Child on her knees. Such statues were common
among the Druids, whose religious rites and priestly regulations anticipated so many of those in the Christian Church.
This Virgin at Chartres may or may not have been the first
the early missionaries found in Celtic Gaul; and what they
thought of it or learned about it, we can only conjecture.
But it is believed that they were soon able to use this altar
for their own worship, and that 'before her death, an Altar
had been dedicated in Chartres to the Mother of Christ.'

This priority did much to make especially sacred the
Church of Notre-Dame de Chartres. And when Charles
the Bald, in 876, gave this church the tunic or veil believed
to have been worn by the Virgin, that relic, raised above
the ramparts of the town, was credited not only with
putting to flight Rollo and his besieging Normans, but with
converting them to Christianity.

This edifice is the fifth or sixth reared over the Druid

grotto; it was dedicated in 1260, in the presence of Saint Louis. The crypt beneath it is the vastest in France, and should be visited if possible. And if time permits, I think Chartres is as good a place as any to make the tour outside, beneath the flying buttresses — just as Amiens is, perhaps, the place *par excellence* to see Gothic splendor from a triforium, and Notre-Dame de Paris is the place to climb a Gothic tower.

But the great glory of Chartres for most visitors is its thirteenth-century glass, specially rich in blues as the glass at Bourges is in reds; and its ambulatory which has been called 'the most magnificent enclosure in existence.'

There are more than a hundred superb windows. You may be content, as I am, to revel in the beauty of their coloring and the effect they produce. Or you may like to study them as pictures and wish to decipher their stories. And, if you can hear one of M. le Maire's organ recitals in the cathedral, toward dusk, I know that you will always reckon it among your most memorable experiences.

Besides seeing the cathedral at Chartres, and some of the old houses near by, you should see the lovely, fifteenth-century Porte Guillaume, the only one surviving of the seven ancient gates; and the backs of some of the venerable houses along the Eure. For the amateur photographer, both of these, and the spiral stairway in a tower, called 'The Stairway of Queen Bertha,' are likely to yield more satisfactory results than the cathedral.

I know full well that I must seem, to some, to be slighting the cathedral when I do not call attention to the celebrated spires, and to the glorious south porch and the richness of the main portals, left over from the edifice burned in 1194; to these, and to other splendid details. But this kind of writing, so ably done by many, is beyond me. I would that every one might read, instead of such feeble

efforts as I might make, Mrs. Elizabeth Robins Pennell's
book on 'French Cathedrals'; Elise Whitlock Rose's volumes on 'Cathedrals and Cloisters of France' ('Chartres'
comes in Volume II of the pair on the 'Isle de France'), and
— of course — Henry Adams's inspiring and greatly-en-
lightening 'Mont-Saint-Michel and Chartres.'

If I were going to make pretence about anything it certainly wouldn't be about a Gothic cathedral. All I can say
about a visit to Chartres is, that when I spend an hour there,
somehow all I've aspired to be becomes nobler than before
and yet seems more attainable.

From Chartres, your way follows Route 155 through
Nogent-le-Rotrou to Alençon. Nogent-le-Rotrou is the old
capital of the Perche district, and the lordship of the town
was acquired, very early in the seventeenth century, by
Sully, the great finance minister of Henry IV. He and his
wife are (or were!) buried in a small building in the courtyard of the hospital, founded in the twelfth century. At
any rate, their tomb is there, whatever may have happened
to their bones when tombs were being violated. The castle
on the hill — the château of the old Counts of Perche —
dates in part to the first half of the eleventh century. And
there are three Gothic churches, besides the remains of an
old priory.

Fourteen miles farther on your road to Alençon, you
pass through Bellême whose mediæval counts assumed, in
1082, the title of Counts of Alençon. A gateway of the
fifteenth-century castle remains. And as you drive through
the little town you may like to recall a boy who went from
here to Paris and to fame: Aristide Boucicaut, founder of
the Bon-Marché, who was not only a great merchant but
a great philanthropist. Our Blue Guide says Henri Martin,
historian, was also a native of Bellême. But Saint-Quentin
claims Martin and all the evidence seems to be in her favor.

CHÂTEAU AND HÔTEL DE VILLE, ALENÇON

From an old print

Alençon's dukes were members of the Valois family; the first was killed at Agincourt after having with his own hand slain the Duke of York. It was here, nearly twenty years before he became the Conqueror, that William, who was then called the Bastard, became so enraged at the taunts hurled at him when he was besieging the town that he ordered the hands and feet of thirty prisoners he had taken to be cut off and thrown into the town. And on seeing these, the garrison surrendered.

The lace industry was introduced here, from Venice, by Colbert, Louis XIV's great minister. The present school is at 48 rue Saint-Blaise, and there you may buy your *point d'Alençon* where it was made.

The Préfecture, on the opposite side of the same street, is a handsome building of the seventeenth century; the church of Notre-Dame has a richly sculptured porch as lacelike as an Alençon church should be; and beside it (in the same square, and a little farther back than the church) is a mansion of 1450, in which Henry IV once stayed when he was King of Navarre and there were still several lives between him and the crown of France.

But the 'high spot' of Alençon for most wayfarers (and especially for the picture-makers) is the huge fifteenth-century gateway of the dukes' castle, one of the most imposing remains of feudal military architecture left in France, and tremendously picturesque. This is in the Place d'Armes, and is now part of the Palais de Justice and prison.

Thirteen miles northeast of Alençon is Sées (pronounced Say) whose cathedral is considered one of the best thirteenth-century Norman churches. Should it be that you have it on your list to see, and your time permits seeing it, you should spend the night at Alençon (at the Hôtel du Grand-Cerf, near the Préfecture) and go up to Sées in the morning; and, after seeing it, take the small road through

Carrouges (where there is a castle that has belonged to one
family for nearly five centuries), and there turn north to
Rânes, where there is a noble specimen of an early sixteenth-
century country château, and an unpretentious church
which Percy Dearmer, author of 'Highways and Byways
in Normandy,' said 'seems to me one of the most beautifully impressive things I have seen in Normandy.' I haven't
seen it, and I can't tell you anything of it except what Mr.
Dearmer says. The Blue Guide to Normandy doesn't even
mention Rânes; but it is on my road map. And Mr. Dearmer found it. So I think you should be reminded where it
is. And so good a guide is Mr. Dearmer (whose book on
Normandy is quite *the* classic on that section, and has given
delight and enlightenment to thousands since 1900 —
aided by Joseph Pennell's etchings) that the next time I
am thereabouts, I shall look for Rânes, expecting to like
it as well as he did.

Then, from Rânes, you could go on through La Ferté-
Macé to Domfront, which is not only a picturesque medi-
æval town, but is most exquisitely situated in the 'Norman
Switzerland.' And although I have been to Domfront,
I am sure I couldn't begin to give you so enticing a descrip-
tion of it as Mr. Dearmer does.

Entering by our road from the east, he says, 'tower after
tower of the fortification appears on our right as we go
along; the walls in between are worked into houses; the
towers themselves are all inhabited, windows are cut in
their machicolation, and chimneys project innocently from
them. At their base are terraced gardens, luxuriant with
vine and pear trees and flowers and French beans. Little
flights of steps run in and out, giving access from our road.
It is a sight such as we have not seen before, and shall not
see again.

'At the end of the road is a bank of fennel and wild

clematis; fruit trees grow below it, and beyond them lies a vast expanse of country that makes us turn our backs upon the old ramparts. . . . On the left the forest rises like a huge wave . . . on the right it dies away on the level toward the sea where Mont-Saint-Michel lies hidden, and there the setting sun comes to throw its crimson and gold, leaving the inland country in blue and opal. When the sun has gone, a white mist enfolds the rich land and the old walls regain their martial consequence in the cold glamour of the moon, looking as in the days that are past when Domfront was a terror to the country at its feet.'

It was in that castle, built about 1011, and taken by William the Conqueror, that Henry II of England received the Papal Nuncio sent to reconcile him with Becket. Short-lived, that reconciliation! And not many miles away is Avranches, where Henry was soon to kneel in atonement for having wished Becket dead — and getting his wish.

And it was at Domfront, in 1574, that Count Gabriel Montgoméry, who, fifteen years before, had accidentally killed Henry II of France in a tilt at Paris, was taken prisoner, and haled hence to Paris to be tried, and beheaded on the Place de Grève. It was as a Calvinist leader and not as a regicide-by-accident that he was condemned.

I hope you know him in the pages of Dumas's 'The Two Dianes.'

Having done these things from Alençon, you may then like to spend a night at the supremely comfortable, not to say luxurious, spa of Bagnoles-de-l'Orne, at the Grand Hôtel or the Hôtel des Thermes. Or, you may go straight on down Route 162 from Domfront to Mayenne, and there 'pick up' — just one day later — the schedule followed by those who have but five days for this tour.

Should you stay at Bagnoles for the night, you may reach Mont-Saint-Michel by way of Mayenne and Fougères;

but that would make you miss Laval and Vitré. Or, you could go more directly to the Mount by returning through Domfront (or leaving it for this section of your journey) and on through Mortain and Saint-Hilaire and Ducey. By this route you could reach Saint-Michel for luncheon on your third day out from Paris.

Now, to go back to Alençon, presuming that you have only five days for your Normandy tour, and want to make the most of them.

From Alençon you have twenty-eight miles to go to reach Mayenne. It is a long day, from Paris, and a very full one. But unless you 'make' Mayenne for that night, you'll find your second day too short for what you want it to contain. (That is, unless you're willing to forego Laval and Vitré. If you are, you could stop at Alençon the first night, and go on through Mayenne and Fougères to Saint-Michel. The hotel at Alençon is not so quietly and restfully situated as the one at Mayenne. But if those last twenty-eight miles seem too much for you, Alençon must be your first night's stopping-place.)

The guide-books call Mayenne 'a dull town with textile factories,' and that doesn't sound inviting for a night's stop. But I have twice, this year, made it the objective of a first-day-out-of-Paris run; and each time, the friends who were with me were as delighted with it as I was.

Our Grand Hotel is on the right bank of the river and very close to the river bank. Its 'front yard' is gay with flowers, and majestically presided over by a black watchdog named Porthos who seems to take his responsibilities very seriously. The last night I was there, several of us lingered quite late (very late, that is, for a provincial French town — perhaps till eleven) on the castle ramparts in the June moonlight; and we found Porthos 'sitting up for us' on the front steps when we returned. He didn't

seem to chide us for keeping him up; we rather thought he
seemed pleased with our expressions of delight in the
memorable beauty of that hour. But when he had shepherded us safe within, and the door was closed for the
night, he went off to his slumbers with the air of one who
knows he'll sleep well because his duty's done. No more
swagger's left in Porthos! One would be indelicate indeed
who seemed, in his sober age, to remember duchesses, and
amorous Madame Coquenards; although I had a feeling
that he'd have liked us to recall certain gallant fights.

Porthos, and a genial proprietor who cut his roses for us,
and excellent beds in shining rooms with plenty of running
hot water, and delicious deep *velvety* stillness, and moonlight on the river, and the best *croissants* I ever ate, are
(with other creature comforts) not the only reasons I
like Mayenne. I'm not sure that I can name the other
reasons, except to say that from a wayfarer's point of view
it's a likable town, one that leaves an endearing memory.

Pray do walk about in it a bit, after dinner; walk along
the Mayenne in both directions from the bridge; walk up
alongside Notre-Dame; and turn off, to your left, in the
direction of the castle which William the Conqueror once
besieged and took. From the foot of that great cylindrical
tower which retains its conical roof, you'll find a steep and
winding way that leads to the ramparts — now grass-
grown and tree-planted — high above the river and above
the roofs of the little, blinking, sleepy town. An hour's
reverie or low-toned converse with some friends who love
it as I do, in a place like that, is one of the reasons why
motoring in France is an ever-deepening ecstasy to me.

II

In the morning when you leave Mayenne, bear off to
your left, soon after crossing the bridge, to Aron; and

thence southeast, a bit, to Jublains, where you will find
exceedingly interesting remains of an important Roman
camp. Even if you are not eager about ruins, I'd go there,
especially if it be the season for wild-flowers. I liked seeing how the officers, exiled on duty from Rome's luxuries,
managed to do very well for themselves in Gaul. (There is
an intelligent caretaker in charge of the ruins who explains
them well.) And I greatly liked the beauty of the spot, the
wealth of bloom in the breeze-blown spaces and the seed-
sown crannies. That, and the view to eastward, toward the
lovely hills of Mayenne where Sainte-Suzanne sits girdled
by her ancient walls. It is a charming spot.

Thence, to Laval, where you meet the river Mayenne
again, and find it flowing quite proudly, and eighty yards
wide, beneath a twelfth-century bridge whose Gothic
arches make the loveliest imaginable reflections. The
Mayenne meets the just-united Sarthe and Loir at Angers,
and south of Angers they all contribute their waters to the
lordly Loire which gives itself to the sea at Saint-Nazaire,
close to where Mrs. Whitney's thrillingly fine monument
to the American doughboy stands.

The superb old Castle of Laval, founded in the tenth
century, but in its surviving form dating largely from the
thirteenth, after having served as a prison since the French
Revolution has become a museum and may be visited from
nine to five. The donjon is of the twelfth century, and its
conical roof has some of the now very rare timber-work
which antedated stone machicoulis — those holes between
wall and parapet, down which the defenders might throw
stones, melted lead, boiling oil, or what-not, upon assailants attempting to scale the walls. Adjoining the old
castle is the new castle, built about 1508 and now used as
Palais de Justice or Court-House.

I think you'll like to see the Porte Beucheresse, just

south of the cathedral, and some of the old houses in the narrow streets around the castle. Your route to Vitré is by way of the rue Joinville which becomes the rue de Bretagne; and as you pass the Place de la Hôtel de Ville, note the statue of Ambroise Paré, the celebrated surgeon whom we meet in the Dumas romances of Catherine de Médicis' court and whose most dramatic moments in fiction are those Balzac depicts in the deathbed scene of young Francis II, in his 'Sur Catherine de Médicis.' Tremendous picture! You'll recall it in detail at Orléans, and be glad to have seen Paré's statue here in his native town.

And those of us who grew up in a feeling of intimacy with King René of Anjou and his family will not leave here without recalling that his second marriage was with Jeanne de Laval, whom he courted in his best troubadour manner in this old castle of Laval.

From Laval to Vitré is twenty-two miles, a little more than midway of which you cross the border of Brittany — just beyond la Gravelle. About four miles before reaching Vitré you come to the Château des Rochers, Madame de Sévigné's Breton home.

It was an ancient château when the eighteen-year-old bride came to it in 1644, but neither grand nor gay. Its peaked turrets related it to the earlier era of Brittany's militant history, the days of Du Guesclin and the War of the Two Joans; and the dark old trees surrounding it made it both damp and gloomy enough to seem haunted with Druid ghosts. But the beautiful young orphaned heiress who came hither from extraordinary triumphs in Paris — at court and in the brilliant circles of the Hôtel Rambouillet — was not dismayed by its depressingness nor by its distance from the gay life of Paris. For she was very much in love with her husband, and here she had him to herself, far from the coquetting beauties of the capital and

from temptations to prodigal expense. But he was less
content here than she was.

Madame de Sévigné's biographers are not certain
whether her idolized daughter was born here or in Paris.
But they agree that her son, Charles, came into the world
here. Her faithless husband was mortally wounded in a
duel over another woman, and left her a widow on the day
following her twenty-fifth birthday, after having done his
best to dissipate her fortune.

She passed at Les Rochers the first months of her widowhood, with her beautiful little daughter of five and her
little son of three years; and during the next ten years,
while they were growing up, she brought them here from
time to time, to this home that had been their father's.
The daughter was called the most beautiful girl in France
— and as hardly anybody liked her, the verdict on her
beauty cannot be discounted. Her mother worshipped
her, lived for her and in her, and had boundless ambition
for her. But the daughter was cold, greedy, and self-cen-
tred, besides being lacking even in superficial charms except beauty; and although her mother had managed to repair her fortunes so as to give her daughter a large dowry,
suitors were not many nor brilliant. The one accepted
was a man who had been twice a widower, and whose estates were heavily encumbered. But he had a position as
lieutenant-governor, first of Languedoc and then of Provence, which gratified the vanity of his wife, though it
sorely taxed the finances of her mother and robbed her
brother of much that was his due.

It was to this blindly adored daughter that Madame de
Sévigné wrote nearly nine tenths of the many hundreds of
letters on which her fame rests. When they were separated,
the mother seemed to live for but one thing and that was to
share with the daughter far away everything she saw and

heard and thought and felt. Madame de Sévigné knew practically every important and interesting French person of her day; she was present at many of the most significant events of her day (which included the Regency of Anne of Austria, and the most brilliant years of the reign of Louis XIV); she had a lively descriptive style, 'an all-observant eye for trifles and the keenest possible appreciation of the ludicrous, together with a hearty relish for all sorts of amusements, pageants, and diversions, and a deep though not voluble or over-sensitive sense of the beauties of nature. With all this she had an understanding as solid as her temper was gay.' And a literary style that challenges comparison.

At what time in her life of seventy years, her forty-seven years of sojourns longer or shorter at Les Rochers (for in the last five years of her life she did not come hither at all), will you choose to imagine yourself her guest?

Suppose you choose the year 1671, when her daughter is married and living in Provence, and this neighborhood is full of gay doings to write her about, since the governor of Brittany is that year holding an assembly of Breton representatives at Vitré; and Madame de Sévigné must needs entertain him here and attend his receptions. She finds much that is amusing in the country ladies of Brittany and their efforts to live up to this occasion. So when you visit her bedroom where her intimate belongings are, and peep over her shoulder to see what she is writing to her daughter, Madame la Comtesse de Grignan, you may have a good laugh at some of her lively accounts of these ceremonious goings-on. It was in that year that the chapel was built.

Then, when you walk in the garden that Le Nôtre laid out for her, you may give yourself up to another sort of reflection. For Le Nôtre was launched upon his great career by Fouquet at Vaux — that magnificent estate which

caused the downfall of Fouquet and made Louis XIV
build Versailles to eclipse the splendors of his disgraced
Superintendent of Finance. Fouquet was Madame de
Sévigné's dear friend; she never believed him guilty of
plundering the royal treasury, and the only breath of
scandal which ever clouded her name was that breathed by
persons who believed that the letters from her, found when
Fouquet's private papers were seized, were more than
friendly.

Fouquet's disgrace and trial occurred when she had
been a widow for more than ten years. When she was here
in 1671, he was languishing in his fortress-prison of Pigné-
rol. She must often have thought of him (whether he was
her lover or only her dear friend) as she paced the paths of
this garden his protégé had made for her.

And when you go on your way into Vitré, I think you
will have a sense of intimacy with this brilliant, charming
woman, far beyond any you got in the Carnavalet, Paris,
which was so long the scene of her famed salon.

Vitré will captivate you. Before you have been there
many minutes you will be promising yourself a return
visit, or several of them, and a longer stay. The Hôtel des
Voyageurs will serve you so good a luncheon that your resolve will be strengthened. And if you go upstairs and look
at some of the bedrooms in this simple but most inviting
inn, you may find yourself engaging one, for that sojourn,
before you leave.

I hope I don't underrate your avidity for details when I
suggest that Vitré is one of the places where I wouldn't
bother with them. I'd take it as a picture, and 'make up'
anything you want to about it. Your way from the hotel
to the castle takes you through some of the most picturesque old streets you have ever seen, or ever will see. The
castle entrance is fine and stirring; the courtyard is well

worth seeing; the oriole is lovely. But I wouldn't go within the castle if I were you; it is disappointing, and I'm almost sure you'd rather have the time for the delightful streets, and for a walk beneath the ramparts, down the Promenade du Val.

Eighteen miles due north of Vitré by Route 178 is Fougères, whose castle is very much finer than that of Vitré; indeed, it is one of the most splendid feudal fortresses in France. I'm sure you'll wish to visit it; and though your interest in it may be heightened by knowing that it once belonged to that acquisitive lady, Diane de Poitiers, I doubt if you'll be half so intent upon meeting such ghosts as hers there as upon the echoing footfalls of those who once wore the collection of footwear exhibited in one of the towers. Fougères is a shoemaking and leather-tanning town, and this fascinating museum of shoes is appropriately placed. There is also interesting old furniture to be seen in the Tour Mélusine which was built in 1242 by that Hugh de Lusignan whose betrothed (Isabella of Angoulême), John Lackland of England, stole — with small resistance from the young lady! And when Hugh protested, John made him prisoner and dragged him off, captive, to England. Isabella had sixteen years in which to rue her faithlessness; when the death of King John freed her, their six-year-old daughter was betrothed to the still-unwed Hugh, then on a Crusade. But Isabella, who had always cherished a sentiment for her old lover, herself wedded him; and bore him at least eight children, some of whom played prominent parts in English history under their half-brother, Henry III.

Whether or not Isabella was much at Fougères, I do not know; but here is the tower builded by Hugh whose wedding to her was just twenty years deferred, and who may well have often wished that it had been deferred much longer.

Fougères will tempt you to linger; but you have this to consider: it is about thirty miles to Mont-Saint-Michel; and if you are to see the abbey before 6 P.M., you should reach the Mount not later than four, and as soon as you have secured your rooms at Hôtel Poulard, proceed at once up the steep and narrow Grande-Rue to the Châtelet, and await a guide to conduct you through the abbey. (It is a stiff climb, and those who find stairs fatiguing should think well before taking it.)

The first glimpse of Mont-Saint-Michel is, unquestionably, one of the big thrills in every sentient traveller's experience. I am by no means underrating it when I say I'm not sure just *why* so many people feel about it as they do. I certainly find it in my heart to wish, fervently, that fewer persons (and those principally the 'fit') were bent upon going there. What they find in it who buy all the cheap trumpery that makes it like a county fair or an East End bazaar, I can't imagine. That the lover of mediæval-ism, of the picturesque, of Gothic and ante-Gothic architecture, should make a pilgrimage to the Mount, needs no comprehending. And I suppose that of the *char-à-banc* crowds, coming from seashore resort places along the Normandy and Brittany coasts, one may dispose by remembering that holiday-makers like to go *some*where on little day-junkets, and this place serves well enough for such an objective. I dare say they find it 'odd,' or even 'amusing.' But if it could be stripped of its tawdry bazaars, rid of its horrid hawkers, washed clean of what I call its 'hot-dog' atmosphere, I believe the junketers would find it too dull even for a *char-à-banc* call. So I am ardently in favor of the plan to cut away the artificial causeway by which steam cars and motor-cars puff up to the very base of the Mount and to the mediæval gates of the tiny town, robbing the place of its island character, making it far too easy of

MONT-SAINT-MICHEL
From a print published in 1779

access, and keeping it overrun with 'trippers.' I hope to
live to see the day when this monument of the past can be
approached only by boat, and when it offers nothing for
sale except food and lodging for those come from a distance, and perhaps pictures of its own loveliness.

How the money-changers are to be driven from this
temple, I do not know. Perhaps some multi-millionaire
with a reverent spirit might buy all the houses and dedi-
cate them to quiet folk, with no merchandizing permitted.

I only know that I quite passionately resent the desecra-
tion of this place. And when I make my plaint I am not
forgetting that the Middle Ages, to which Mont-Saint-
Michel belongs, were characterized by tawdry bazaars and
mob-movements to places of repute which most of their
'trippers' had small ability to appreciate. I am only wishing that *this* stronghold of the Middle Ages might hold out
against twentieth-century besiegers as it held out against
besiegers in the past — admitting within the gates only
those with the password.

But until such a day dawns, we must take the Mount
as we find it, and expel the desecrations in our own way by
refusing to let them bother us.

As you leave Fougères to make the last stage of your
journey toward the Mount, 'what o'clock is't' in the long
ages past during which men have made pilgrimages thither?

I wonder!

Perhaps you are padding up that road with Cæsar's
legionaries, when the great dark forest of Scissey covered
what is now the Bay of Cancale and stretched away to
where are now the Channel Islands, and you call the tree-
clad peak Mons Jovis, although the Gauls have a different
name for it.

If you're a later Roman, you'll find the tides coming
higher and higher each time, up the fresh-water streams

that run to meet the sea, and overrunning the low ground around Jove's mountain; so that at high tide access to the Mount is cut off.

It may be that you're a Frankish wayfarer of the very early eighth century, come here to gaze at waters swirling above the tree-tops that your father knew, and two eminences only left rearing their crests above a submerged wood: a bigger eminence called Mount Tomba and a smaller called Tombelaine.

Missionary hermits are living on them, you hear. Well! perhaps they have their way of exorcising and keeping themselves safe. But as for you, nothing could induce you to linger in such a place. Although it may be that, as you take your way homeward through Avranches, you'll be told how Bishop Aubert of that place had gone to Mount Tomba to meditate, and Michael, the Prince of the Armies of the Lord, appeared to him and told him to build there a sanctuary in his honor.

Perhaps you also hear, later, that two monks who were sent by Aubert to Monte Gargano in the Kingdom of Naples, where a famous apparition of Saint Michael had taken place, brought back with them a piece of the scarlet veil he had left and a fragment of the marble on which he had stood; and that as the monks returned through France with these relics, miracles were wrought by them.

And, of course, after that, the place became a shrine for many pilgrims.

The other day I heard of a man who has travelled much and read much, and who said, impatiently, 'Why tell tales about *relics* to twentieth-century people?'

Poor man! I'm sure there are a great many people living *in* the twentieth century (whether *of* it or not) who venerate relics and believe in their efficacy; and the fact that I don't happen to would never make me feel entitled to scoff at those who do. If I were going to feel superior to any one, it would be to the man, supposedly intelligent, who sees nothing in a story of sacred relics but 'bunk' which ought not to be repeated.

For, unless we understand what the possession of relics believed to be miracle-working meant to a church or a shrine in mediæval times, we shall never come within a million miles of comprehending the spirit which gave to the world many of its most glorious works of human achievement.

Whatever it was that Saint Louis brought back from his first Crusade, believing it to be the Crown of Thorns, it is venerable because his desire to house it worthily made him build the Sainte-Chapelle. Whatever it was that Philip of Alsace gave to Bruges, believing it to be a vial of the Precious Blood, it is worthy of our reverence because around it worshipping generations built up superb edifices, filled them with heavenly pictures, endowed them to learning and benevolence, and were stirred to take the Cross — and lead the way for the Renaissance.

Please don't *ever* sniff at relic-tales! What you believe about the relics is no concern of mine. But that you realize what belief in their efficacy wrought is essential to your appreciation of many of the loveliest things you'll see.

Saint Michael may not seem important to your present scheme of things. But it isn't so many years since very matter-of-fact men of your acquaintance and mine were ready to believe he had something to do with the Miracle of the Marne.

So, don't approach Saint Michael's Mount looking at it with the eye of a surveyor, or even of an architect (which latter is a noble eye to travel with!), but try to see it first as men did who felt a daily need of Saint Michael.

And when the Norsemen, or Normans, began to ravage

this coast, see the terrified people from along the shore flee to the sea-girt rock for refuge and found the little town beneath the skirts of Saint Michael's convent.

A little later on our journey we shall be recalling how marvellously those pagan Norse pirates became the Frenchest of the French and the most ardent of the Christians. But at Saint Michael's Mount let it suffice to remember that half a century or so after the monks fled from the first of the invading pagans, a Norse Frenchman, now become Duke of Normandy, became incensed because the restored monks were not strict enough in their piety; so he replaced them with twelve Benedictines of austere life.

Being — as I think you know — a person of very simple mental processes and easily confused by trying to correlate too many impressions, I have for myself a habit of trying to concentrate in each place on one or two of its significant phases or features.

And for my own purposes I think of Mont-Saint-Michel principally as an abbot's fortress-town sufficiently typical to help us understand many others in those ages when the human groups were mostly of three sorts: the abbot's group, protected by his monastery; the count's group, protected by his castle; and the bishop's group, in the walled town.

How definite is your impression of feudal society? If it isn't a pretty clean-cut conception that you have, I urge you by all means to make it so; for your enjoyment of Europe depends on that at least as much as on any other one thing. And nothing could be simpler nor pleasanter than acquiring such a conception. You can get it in one fascinating book called 'Life in a Feudal Barony,' by William Stearns Davis, of the University of Minnesota; or in Funck-Brentano's 'The Middle Ages.'

It once happened that a man (the head of a big indus-

trial plant in a university town) to whom I made this suggestion got so absorbed, in the course of reading those two
volumes and perhaps a few more of a short list I'd given
him, that he entered a course on Mediæval History in the
local university. You may not go that far; but I know
you'll be very, very glad for what you know of Davis's
book, which is published by Harper's, delightfully illustrated, and obtainable anywhere, and of Funck-Brentano's,
which is translated into English and published by Putnam.

In case you don't read this suggestion until you are
where you can't get these books, let me make a brief summary of a few points about that great feudal system which
wrought so much ill and so much good and which was
probably the only conceivable system which could so well,
on the whole, have served society in those days.

Conceive it just as a repartitioning almost without end.
A man (from the king down) owned, then, just what he
could defend against others who might desire it. About the
only way to get any income out of large estates was to
'farm them out' in smaller parcels.

'Here,' says king to duke, 'is a nice big duchy for you.
Have a good time with it, and don't bother me. But I
expect so-much of all you can wring out of it; and when
I need fighting men, you're to come, at the head of so-
many.'

(There were other stipulations; but that was the gist of
them all.)

'Here,' says the duke, in turn, to a number of barons, 'is
a nice fat barony for you. Have a good time with it. But
mind you don't forget to pay me my share on all you can
make it yield you. And when I need fighting men, you're
to come, at the head of so-many.'

Imagine *that*, as a gist of the system. Almost immediately, of course, it was complicated by further subdivi-

sions, and by marriage settlements and inheritances, and by seizures and forfeitures, and so on. But the main feature of it all was that practically every one who had anything had it in some such relation with the one immediately above him; and that one had his larger share from some one else to whom he was likewise bound; and so on, clear to the top. There wasn't much property that didn't have many changes of ownership, except the property that belonged to the Church: to the religious orders, or to the bishops' dioceses. Property bestowed upon or bequeathed to the Church usually 'stayed put.'

It might, indeed, happen that a great overlord like the Duke of Normandy, could dispossess one religious order from an abbey like Mont-Saint-Michel and install another; but only with the sanction of the Pope, who could always, if not pleased, launch that terrible excommunication which might involve not only the high-handed seigneur but his terrified subjects.

So, what an abbey like this of Saint Michael's Mount got was likely to be 'for keeps.'

And as sinful sovereigns and seigneurs, when they thought of 'squaring themselves' for misdeeds, usually did it by giving or bequeathing properties to a monastery, and as these properties might be (depending on the dowries and conquests of the donor's family) anywhere this side of Jerusalem, the abbot of a very famous monastery like this of Saint Michael's Mount was lord over a great domain much of which he might never see. He had great riches, great temporal power, and great responsibilities.

He had in his keeping not only the education of youth, but the development of scholarship among the learned, the multiplication of books, the systematization of such science as the world then knew.

He had a big community of men to govern. (How

many monks there were, habitually, at Mont-Saint-
Michel I don't know. But at Vézelay there were eight
hundred, at Clairvaux seven hundred. There must have
been several hundred, most of the time, on this Mount by
the sea.) And in governing them he had a much larger
purpose to fulfil than merely to maintain an orderly institution and keep its endowment growing apace with its
needs; he had also to make his community an example of
well-ordered, useful, disciplined life, in a rather chaotic,
tumultuous, ill-ordered world. His monks must teach the
people of his domain agriculture and many manufactures, and thrift; respect for law and order, and benevolence; how to live, and how to die.

The abbot must be an entertainer on a great scale; he
must furnish hospitality to all who came, from the most
wretched mendicant to the most puissant noble or sovereign.

He must distribute alms — enormous quantities of food
to the hungry and of clothing to the naked. He must
provide doctoring for the sick as well as spiritual minis-
tration.

He must administer justice, not in his monastery alone,
but in his realm. And in an abbey like this of Saint Michael's, he must needs be an able soldier; for if ever there
was an arm of the Church militant in this world as well as
for the next world, it is here. Abbots not infrequently led
their 'quota' to war. But the abbot of Saint Michael's
seldom had need to *go* to war. It came to him, often and
insistently. The Prince of the Armies of the Lord was none-
too-militant a patron for this community of Benedictines
on their crag above the sea.

So rich was this abbey by the time its Duke William of
Normandy went overseas to become William the Conqueror that its abbot was able to fit out a fleet of six vessels to bring back the victor and his retinue.

William gave the Abbey richly of his spoils; but he was a dictatorial benefactor, and insisted on the election of his own chaplain as abbot.

I shall not take space here to tell you 'which part of the abbey was built *when*,' as that is all in your guide-book (either your Blue Guide — 'Normandy' or 'Northwestern France' — or in the little local guide you should buy; for if its English is funny, its facts are good and its pictures and maps are excellent); nor to comment on its architectural wonders which have so many times been superbly described by great writers.

All I can hope to help you do is to come here with your mind intent not only on the beauty and picturesqueness of this much-sung place, but also on its significance — on the part it played in that past which wrought for us as we are working for those to come.

It may be that you are eager to see Saint Louis here, or to stand by, in the Salle des Chevaliers (that Saint Louis knew) when Louis XI inaugurates the Order of Saint Michael. I hope you are!

But whatever you do, let me entreat you to spend an hour or two, or more, on the ramparts after dark, musing on many things. And if you can, get a small boat (about sunset) and see the Mount from the north side, where the last remnant of the Scissey forest still clings to the seaward front of the rock; and no causeway's in sight — and no postcards!

You will, I think, find few persons on the ramparts after nine o'clock or so. They're gone, in their *char-à-bancs;* or if they're stopping for the night they're down in the shops and cafés. Those who are on the walls with you are probably reverent souls, like yourself, and silent. I don't suppose anybody would contend with you as to what you should think of, standing there in the velvety night, just as many centuries away from that day's perplexities as you care to be; the important thing is to think deeply and feelingly enough about something that matters much to you, so that you get a tremendous perspective on it — as if you had viewed it from a great distance and got a new valuation on it, a whole new *sense* of values!

At the end of his noble and beautiful book on the Middle Ages, M. Funck-Brentano pays this tribute to them, in heralding the Age of World-Discovery and of the Renaissance: 'A new world shines in a clear dawn; but its splendor will not efface the fecund beauty of the centuries of Philippe-Auguste and Saint Louis, to which in all history there is only to compare the century of Sophocles, Phidias, and Pericles.'

Philippe-Auguste and Saint Louis were both great benefactors of this abbey. Few structures of the many which have come down to us as reminders of all they strove for are so typical of their centuries as this.

We shall, I hope, as we go on our way through France and through these so-modestly-offered pages, be more and more conscious of the great Human Epic, so long-begun and so far from finished; and see ourselves more and more in our relation to it. Mont-Saint-Michel profoundly impresses the sentient soul. And it is eminently such a place as we like to associate with the beginnings or the more vital rebirth of our strong feeling for the Past.

III

You will eat well at the Poulard, and sleep comfortably though not luxuriously, and you may even have the celebrated omelet again for breakfast, on payment of a supplement small indeed for food so distinguished. Perhaps you will have been out, at the base of the rock, in the freshness of early morning, and a hearty breakfast will be specially relished by you.

Soon after breakfast you should be en route back to Pontorson on your way to Avranches, twenty-one miles from the Mount. There you will mount to the *plate-forme* where the cathedral stood till it was pulled down in 1799 because it threatened to collapse. There you'll see the spot where Henry II knelt before the Pope's legates and swore that he had neither ordered nor desired the murder of Thomas à Becket. So he was absolved.

Then, to the terrace of the Jardin des Plantes, for the glorious view of Saint Michael's bay, with his abbey that he commanded good Aubert of Avranches to found.

And now, your way to Caen must be determined by whether you would rather see Granville and Coutances, with its noble cathedral, or Vire and Falaise.

The student of architecture will probably feel that he must not miss Coutances, which is thirty-five miles from Avranches.

In that case, he will come first to Granville, which the inhabitants (who do a thriving 'seaside' business) like to call 'the Monaco of the North' — its situation on a rocky promontory being, indeed, not unlike that of the Riviera resort; but with that, and having a casino, the resemblance ends; which is not to the discredit of Granville.

I doubt if Granville will long detain the tourist with too-little time for Normandy.

Leaving there, by Route 171, he will have the sea in sight for about five miles, and then nothing of especial note until he gets his first distant view of Coutances whose cathedral spires dominate the country for miles and serve as loved landmarks to the ships at sea.

Coutances Cathedral is certainly one of the most beautiful Gothic churches in Normandy, and some connoisseurs place it high among all the cathedrals of France. And it is with no disparagement to it, nor to Notre-Dame-de-Saint-

Lô, that I omitted them from what seemed to me (all view-points considered) the ideal five-day Normandy Tour. Having Chartres and Mont-Saint-Michel, Bayeux and Caen, Jumièges and Rouen, in five days seemed to me as much Gothic and Romanesque ecclesiastical architecture as the average individual can 'take in' in that space of time. It was my guess that most of us would prefer Vire and Falaise to Coutances and Saint-Lô. But those who cannot bear to omit Coutances may have that, and a good visit at Bayeux, and still get to Caen not too late to see something of her attractions that evening before dinner.

As for the rest of us, we'll take Route 176 out of Av-ranches, to Villedieu-les-Poëles, celebrated these dear-knows-how-many years for its hand-beaten copper pans and kettles. And there we'll 'pick up' Route 24b for Saint-Sever and Vire. The former has an interesting old abbey church with some good very early stained glass. But if you are thinking more of luncheon than of glass, I've no quarrel with you. I love old glass, but not so much when I'm hungry.

Vire itself is no town to slight. You will probably lunch at the Hôtel Saint-Pierre whose proprietor is renowned as a chef. He will serve you bountifully; but when I become lyric about food in Normandy it is not of Vire I'm thinking. Perhaps it would taste better in a more attractive dining-room. Perhaps one's recollections of Vire would be fonder if there were no *andouilles* mingled with them — *andouilles* being a kind of head-cheese or sausage made of many things anatomically interesting but gastronomically of limited ap-peal. The Norman is a lusty feeder, and he not only stom-achs *andouilles* (which is almost a *pun*) but esteems it. You may side with him rather than with me. And if you do, I shan't mind.

But before you leave Vire, be sure you've done justice to

its thirteenth-century Gothic gateway above which soars a lofty belfry. I agree (as usual) with Mr. Dearmer when he says that this belfry-gate 'is alone worth coming to see.'

Snatch what glimpses you can of the quaint old streets near the gateway; never mind the church unless you're a glutton for churches; and get on to the terrace beside the ruins of the castle, and look down, from the western side of the rocky spur on which the castle stands, toward Les Vaux de Vire, the little valley whose name, corrupted into 'vaudeville' is known the wide world round, because — even before the time when Villon the Vagabond made deathless songs in Paris taverns — Olivier Basselin, who had a fuller's mill here, sang songs in praise of hard cider; and these drinking rhymes, of very convivial sort, became popular and came to characterize a sort of entertainment which was — well! let us say *informal*. There was hereabouts in Olivier's day an association of 'boon companions' who drowned their grievances in the flowing bowl of apple-juice that was probably become apple-jack; and when sufficiently saturated not only sang songs but executed dances, cracked jokes, did 'stunts,' and set forth a variety of merriment for themselves and onlookers, which, when its like was desired for stated repetitions, could only be simulated by a 'variety troup.'

If you want to feel as Olivier must have felt, experiment (at Caen, to-night, after dinner) with Calvados, the liqueur made of apple-juice! But do it cautiously, I pray; and be sure some one is with you who knows where you lodge and is willing to learn vicariously of Calvados.

Olivier lived in the first half of the fifteenth century, full three hundred years and more after Henry I of England (who was William the Conqueror's youngest son), having seized the Crown of England, came over and snatched Normandy, too. Normandy had been left to his eldest brother, Robert, and England to the second son, William Rufus; and one of the few times when they ever agreed about anything was when they agreed that whichever one of them died first should be the other's heir. When William Rufus was killed, hunting in the New Forest, England, Robert was away on the First Crusade. So Henry hastened to have himself proclaimed King of England, and then came over to take Normandy, too. Robert came back to defend his duchy, and was beaten at a battle at Tinchebray (between Vire and Flers) September 28, 1106. Henry carried him off to England and then to Wales, where he passed twenty-eight years of captivity in Cardiff Castle.

After that, the English sovereigns were masters in Normandy, too, until (almost a century later) Philippe-Auguste won it back again for France from King John.

When Olivier Basselin was singing his Vaux de Vire songs, Normandy was again a possession of England (made so by Henry V) for two-and-thirty years (1418 to 1450). Olivier was a man of thirty when the English burned Jeanne d'Arc at Rouen. And he was fifty when he went down (singing of apple-jack, perhaps!) at the battle of Formigny which practically ended the Hundred Years' War and left Normandy to the Normans for ever.

Were you a leisurely traveller, to whom time means little save to make it serve opportunity, I'd say keep on Route 24b, through Tinchebray, to see its fortified fragment of a church which was probably there when the battle was fought; and Flers, which has a picturesque old moated castle; and on to Argentan where Henry II of England uttered the wish to 'be rid of that turbulent priest' — words which may indeed have been spoken in one of his many rages and not really have been meant by him. Let us hope so! At any rate, he was so scared or so repentant when he heard of the murder that he lay here on a bed of ashes, for five long weeks, refusing to see any one.

Then you could spend the night at Argentan, at the Hôtel de la Cloche, and loiter about delightfully in the morning before proceeding to Falaise.

But those of us whose days for Normandy are all too few must take the little road which leads from Vire through Vassy and Condé-sur-Noireau and across the Orne, to Falaise, where William at a very early age began reaching out for things.

And as we approach Falaise, let us remind ourselves of a few things which we may not have taken out of our mem'ry storehouse and dusted off for use, since schoolbook days.

There is such a lot about William himself to recall that it hardly seems fair to ask you to dig up and dust off his whole ancestral line. But in case you find yourself groping for a few facts, you may be glad of the following which I've translated from the 'Histoire de Normandie,' by A. Albert-Petit, a work which has been honored by the French Academy and very largely bought by the French public.

'Who were these Normans?' he asks, speaking of those hardy and far-faring Northmen who spread all over kingdom-come in the ninth century.

They were Scandinavians, whose countries were composed of an infinity of little states perpetually at war. Concubinage was practised, but the children of the concubines had no right to the paternal possessions. They, and the victims of the unending feuds and seizures, had to live somehow; and it was considered 'unworthy of a free man to acquire by sweat what he might have got by fighting.'

At first, these defrauded and dowerless ones fought at home for booty. Then, the little states of Scandinavia banded together into big states under powerful chiefs who made laws against predatory adventurers, and were able to enforce them.

Whereupon the adventurers had to go farther afield. The Swedes tended to the Slav countries, to which they gave the name of Russia, and where they established at Novgorod, in the person of one of their number called Rurik, a dynasty which ruled in Russia for eight centuries.

The Norwegians and Danes turned their prows toward the ocean; the Danes descending upon England and the Germanic countries of Charlemagne's crumbling empire; and the Norse setting upon Scotland, Iceland, Greenland, 'and finally arriving in America five centuries before Columbus'; and then, in larger companies and better organized, they invaded France.

We must not, Albert-Petit says, imagine them as 'miserable pirates, clad in skins' and fighting hit-or-miss, so to speak. In their tombs are found rich stuffs heavily brocaded in gold, and jewels which show that the splendors of Constantinople were not foreign to them. Their armor was artistically encrusted — even their horses were sumptuously saddled and harnessed.

Their boats were simple transports, not battleships; 'because, contrary to general belief, the Norsemen did not know how to fight at sea.' The type of boat principally used for the invasion of France carried thirty-two rowers, was about seventy feet long, had both ends curved high and richly decorated with sculptures, and transported from sixty to seventy men who raised a tent to shelter themselves at night. They were excellent navigators.

When they took the French watercourses for their invasions of the interior, they ordinarily divided themselves into two bands, one in boats on the river, and the other following the banks mounted on stolen horses.

Each chief was followed by his men, but he also con-

sulted them. If he didn't agree with the other chiefs, he
quit, and his men quit with him. They 'played square' in
the division of the booty, and they punished resistance
cruelly. If a Norseman was killed by one whose possessions
he was seizing, two of the French must die in expiation. In
general, they took few prisoners (except those who might
be good for ransom) and they left little behind them, 'not
even a dog to bark at them.' Monasteries were their special
objectives, because of their treasures. Nuns were violated
before being massacred. Relics were profaned. Not only
were the pagan invaders contemptuous of Christianity, but
they had a measure of zeal for proselyting, and gave immunity to those who would forswear the Christian religion. On
the other hand, when the strife was going against him, a
Norseman was always willing to purchase immunity by being
baptized. Some of them were baptized twenty times!

These were the ancestors of William the Conqueror. Why
France and her 'do-nothing' kings offered them so poor a
resistance is another story that we'll recall in another place.

What we have mainly to get in mind as we approach
Falaise is that in 911 a Norse band, led by a chief named
Rollo, besieged Chartres and were driven off by the citizens
with the aid of the Virgin's Veil. Rollo lost 6800 men. And
after that he decided to be baptized — at least once. And
the King of France, unable to dislodge the Norsemen,
thought best to come to terms with them. If Rollo would
embrace Christianity, why not grant him that northern
part of France which he had so ravaged that there was
practically nothing left of it but the soil, and make him a
vassal of the French crown?

Rollo was willing; but he and his men couldn't live on
that soil, fertile as it was, until they had repaired their own
ravages. Everybody was willing to be baptized. But how
were they to maintain themselves? So the King of France

agreed that they should continue to pillage the coast of Brittany; because Brittany at that time was practically 'none of his business.'

So there was a great baptizing at Rouen in the beginning of 912, and Rollo was given the name of Robert and became the first Duke of Normandy. Keeping the lion's share for himself, he divided among his followers enough land to keep them busy developing it into revenue-yielding property.

So quickly did these Norsemen adapt themselves to their new country that in the very next generation after Rollo, the Norse tongue was no longer spoken at the court of Normandy.

And so strict were the laws made by the bandits-of-yesteryear that flocks needed no guardian, ploughs were left all night in the furrows, houses had no locks, and a bracelet of Rollo's hung for three years on a tree in the forest and no one dared touch it. Rollo (or Robert) not only punished theft swiftly and pitilessly, but he indemnified the loser. Any one who, in making a sale, misrepresented the quality of what he sold, or charged too high a price for it, was reckoned a thief and punished as such.

Normandy speedily became the best-policed part of France. And its social structure was the first in France to foreshadow the bettering conditions of times to come.

The Norsemen (now Normans) married daughters of France and raised hordes of young Frenchmen. And from this stock sprang many of France's greatest glories, much that made the Middle Ages splendid and significant.

Rollo died in 933. Ninety-four years later (1027) William was born, destined to be known as the Conqueror, but only one of the conquering Normans of the eleventh century.

They were always ready to 'pick up and go' — those descendants of the far-faring Norsemen. And as the stiff laws of the Norman dukes made it too hazardous to 'get rich quick' at home, the only way an adventurous and ambitious younger son could hope to establish himself comfortably in life was to go where the laws were less strict or less powerfully enforced.

And they were numerous — those younger sons! For concubinage did not at once die out, the habit of 'new wives for old' was strong, and in one way and another each Norman seigneur had a good many more sons than he could provide for. Some of them became monks; 'but the majority counted on their ingenuity and their sword to make themselves a place in the sun.'

One poor country gentleman named Tancrède de Hauteville had twelve sons. 'It is not surprising,' chuckles our Albert-Petit, 'that they conquered Italy.' No! nor that Normandy contributed so heavily to the First Crusade, although it was but thirty years since she had undertaken the Conquest of England.

Now, here you are, approaching Falaise with its castle sitting superbly on a high crag above the quaint, quiet town.

Duke Robert of Normandy, the sixth to hold the title but only of the fourth generation after Rollo, was called 'the Magnificent' and also 'the Devil'; the latter, however, was a title without reproach; it was in combat and in gallantry that Robert was 'a divvil.' Jules Janin, whose portly book on Normandy with its wealth of illustrations is a great favorite of mine, saw in Robert the Devil the prototype of Richard the Lion-Hearted. He must not be too much confounded with Robert the Devil, the folklore tale from which Scribe made the libretto for Meyerbeer's opera; but his career probably contributed something to the gradual growth of that legend, and it furnished a number of more veritable stories about him, many of which make us think that Robert would have been an interesting person to know — but not too well.

I can't find out how old Robert was when William was born. But he was not the Duke of Normandy, nor even the heir-apparent, when he brought pretty Arlette the tanner's daughter up to this castle and made her the mother of William.

The story is that Robert, standing in a window of his castle at Falaise, saw Arlette washing linen at a public wash-trough far below; and sent for her to come up on the castle crag and keep him company.

It wasn't this structure in which Robert lived with Arlette; but Robert's castle may have had a window in the same place. At any rate, there is the tannery, and the wash-trough beside it; and as you look from the spot whence Robert is said to have espied Arlette, you can only marvel at the range of his vision. For, if you had to choose an Arlette from the present group at the trough, you would feel that binoculars were none-too-good an aid.

When you get to Bayeux, to-morrow, I hope you will buy a book sold there, which is called the 'History of William the Conqueror, Illustrated by Reproductions of Queen Matilda's Tapestries.' It is printed in French and in English; and no matter how easily you read French, I beg you not to slight the right-hand pages where the English translation is.

They tell us that Robert 'had very good eyesight,' and that his 'heart had never given him any trouble' until he saw Arlette.

'She was not of princely lineage, certainly, but he had found out that her parents were highly esteemed citizens, and that she even had an uncle who was a very holy man, a hermit. He therefore decided that he was quite justified in opening his heart to her, full as it was of love.' So he 'sent to fetch the bewitching Arlette, asking her to come to the castle, with all due state, as the daughter of a most respected citizen.' And yet they called him a 'divvil'! He even sent her his palfrey to make the ascent, and an elaborate outfit for the expedition.

'With a brilliant escort,' says our chronicle, 'she was taken to the castle in broad daylight.' Nothing clandestine about Robert, it would seem. And 'she completed the happiness of her lord and master by allowing him to admire her blued eyes and to revel in her sweet smile,' so that 'at the end of three seasons, towards the time when the milk-white lilies bloom and the pinky lilacs scent the air, a young prince was born.'

That time of milk-white lilies and pinky lilacs was in 1027.

Albert-Petit says that Robert's father died in 1026. Janin says he died in 1027. I'd like to know what the prospects were, while those lilies and lilacs bloomed, of the 'blued-eyed' Arlette's lusty infant who is reputed to have begun clutching the straw of his pallet before he was an hour old. At any rate, bastard though he was — and so called — those prospects improved rapidly. When William was a year old his father was Duke of Normandy; and as the handsome and hardy youngster grew, he learned his first lessons of chivalry and of sovereignty in a court which gave princely asylum to the King of France (during a revolt raised by his mother, Constance, in favor of her youngest son) and to Baldwin, Count of Flanders, fugitive from the designs of his own son — that son who was to become William's father-in-law; and to the exiled king of England and his family — young William's cousins.

Robert put King Henry of France back on his throne. What he did to settle the Flanders squabble, I don't know. But in 1034 he seems to have been in need of new worlds to conquer, or to discover; so he set out on a magnificent pilgrimage to the Holy Land, followed by the richest and most splendid nobles of his court — superbly armored, mounted on huge Norman horses, accompanied by a great retinue, glittering with jewels, scattering largesse to the gaping onlookers and throwing kisses to the pretty ladies.

I think you will like to imagine them setting forth. Whether it was from Falaise that they departed, or not, I cannot say. But we can picture it so; and young William, seven years old, with his 'blued-eyed' mother, watching them go. Was Arlette desolated? I wonder! Robert must have been difficult, at times; but his story indicates that he must also have been interesting; and I believe ladies like to be interested, even at the price of some stressful intervals.

Robert never returned. I'd love to linger over some of the stories told of that gorgeous pilgrimage; but I know I mustn't.

William was recognized by him as his heir, and presented by him to the King of France, before he left. And William was only eight years old when word came from the East that he was now Duke of Normandy. Then (or earlier) Arlette married a knight of another part of Normandy, and occasionally had the young Duke with her in her new home where, presently, he had two little half-brothers. But he used to come to Falaise at times, and I'm sure you'll have a pretty mental picture of him as a lad caracoling through the streets of this little town and up to the castle on the crag. Even when he was a child, discerning persons had begun to feel that he was remarkable.

Falaise has many other associations, but I doubt if any of them has a bit of success in getting itself recalled by the average visitor. In spite of the obvious impossibility of this being the castle structure that Robert the Devil and William the Conqueror knew, it is their crag, and their town. And

I'm sure we are content to let it be theirs, and to have met them there — as it were.

And, having seen the beautiful view from the height from which William got his first glimpse of a world he was to play a great part in, let us be on our way up to Caen (a little over twenty miles north on Route 158) where William lies buried — or, rather, where his place of sepulchre is.

Caen is on the Orne about ten miles from the Seine estuary.

It is an abbey-town; that is to say, a town which grew up about two famous abbeys William the Conqueror and Matilda his wife built near a castle which was a favorite residence of theirs. They built those abbeys to conciliate the Pope, who, after they had been married, decided that they should never have been wed, as they were cousins in the third degree or thereabouts. Building and endowing the abbeys, and giving alms in other towns of Normandy, somehow made it all right with the Pope. And I'm sure that you and I have no quarrel with His Holiness for making William and Matilda put some of their abundant means into succor for the poor and more of them into the splendid architecture of the Abbaye aux Dames and the Abbaye aux Hommes. Even at that, their children had too much left to quarrel over.

You have probably read, many times, the story of William's courtship. But, lest its outlines may have grown faint in your memory, I'll retrace them here.

Matilda's paternal grandmother was William's aunt — his father's sister Eleanora. (Another sister, you'll remember, was Emma, who, as I reminded you in 'So You're Going to England,' page 86, besides being the wife of two kings of England — Ethelred and Canute — was mother of two more, stepmother of a third, aunt of a fourth, and related by marriage even to Harold.)

Matilda's father was descended both from Charlemagne and from Alfred the Great. Indeed, Matilda was a daughter of no mere 'hundred earls,' but of most of the very blue blood in Christendom. She was beautiful and learned and virtuous, and talented and industrious and rich. It is not to be wondered at that William aspired to her hand. But it took him seven years, we're told, to get it.

There were many kinds of obstacles to the union, but not the least of them was Matilda's disdain. She 'would not have a bastard for her husband.'

This was repeated to William, who was infuriated by it as he always was by any reference to the stain upon his birth; and he mounted his horse and rode in hot haste to Count Baldwin's castle in Lille. There he strode to Matilda's presence, seized her by her long tresses, dragged her by them about the chamber, struck her repeatedly, and flung her on the ground at his feet. Then he left the castle, sprang to the saddle, spurred his steed, and was away.

Of course Matilda's father avenged this assault, and William retaliated for the vengeance; and they kept it up until Matilda decided that she liked William and would accept him for a husband. And so they were wed, with much pomp, at the Castle of Eu which William had just taken from the supporters of one who set his rival claim against William's for the Duchy of Normandy.

Not long after this marriage (some accounts say before it) William crossed the Channel to pay a visit to his cousin, Edward the Confessor, who was childless and whose heir William was more than willing to be. At Edward's court William found almost as many Normans as he had left behind in his own; and there were 'Norman prelates in the bishoprics, Norman lords and soldiers in the fortresses, Norman captains and sailors in the seaports. Normans everywhere.' Edward, son of a Norman mother, had spent twenty-seven years of his life in Normandy, and it is probable that his choice for his successor was the young Norman Duke. But Edward was married! His wife thought her brother, Harold, should be king when Edward was dead; and she 'talked Edward over' to her way of thinking.

In 1065, Harold set sail for Normandy to find out 'how the land lay' with William and his pretensions to the English crown. His voyage was a tempestuous one, his ships were driven far out of their course, and the hurricane blew them ashore on the coast of Ponthieu not far from that Castle of Eu where William had been married, but in the domain of the Count of Ponthieu. This nobleman seized Harold and imprisoned him in his Castle of Belrem. Nor would he listen to any proposition for ransom. But William who was the Count's suzerain, heard of Harold's plight and demanded his release and that he be brought by his late jailor to the Castle of Eu, where William awaited them.

There William received Harold and his suite with honors, and thence conducted them to Rouen; where, amid splendid feastings and hunts, he offered Harold the hand of his seven-year-old daughter, Adelize. Also, William invested Harold with knighthood, to make him a vassal of the Norman fief. Then they set out for Brittany, to give Harold an opportunity of showing his knightly prowess against William's cousin, Duke Conan of Brittany. In the river Couësnon which separates Normandy from Brittany, at Mont-Saint-Michel, some of the party were engulfed in the swift-rushing tide, and Harold rescued them.

After their victorious expedition into Brittany, as they were returning through Bayeux, William convoked a great council of the high barons of Normandy, to be held in Bayeux Castle; and there he induced his new vassal, Harold, to swear that he would help him obtain the English throne.

Soon after Harold's return to England, Edward the Confessor died — and Harold allowed himself to be proclaimed king by a Saxon archbishop not empowered by the Church to anoint sovereigns.

The Normans of England sent a messenger to William, who was then at Rouen, to tell him of Harold's action.

William appealed to the Pope to authorize an expedition against Harold, and to his barons to support it. To-morrow you shall see that expedition sail.

Just now you are approaching Caen, the city of spires, 'the Norman Athens,' and I daresay you are to spend the night at the Hôtel d'Angleterre. Don't forget that one of the best restaurants in France is here: the Chandivert, housed in a lovely old François I mansion, the Hôtel de Than. It is expensive — but memorable! (You will find it close to the Church of Saint-Pierre, and a minute's walk from your hotel.) If you think you wouldn't like 'Tripe à la mode de Caen,' remember that you are also in the country of 'Sole Normande,' and of those omelets such as have almost overshadowed all the other glories of Mont-Saint-Michel.

William's abbey for men is on the western edge of Caen, and Matilda's abbey for women is on the eastern edge, Between them, at the northern edge, lies the castle, and a little south of it, the Church of Saint-Pierre.

I'd go first to Matilda's abbey, wherein she is buried, and where at the dedication ceremony her little daughter Cecilia was taken into the convent, of which she became the second abbess. To enter the choir and transepts apply to the concierge of the Hôtel-Dieu (or hospital) whose chapel for the nursing sisters is there. And if you have time, follow the rue de Calix, when you come out, to the Manoir des Gens d'Armes, a curious old embattled manor-house.

Then come back by rue Basse, where the old town walls

used to be, to the Church of Saint-Pierre (which I'd enjoy mainly from without, if I were pressed for time) and past the Bourse which used to be the Hôtel d'Escoville; it was built in 1537 and has a dormer window which has been called the 'most magnificent which ever came from the imagination of an artist.' This mansion was the home of a Mæcenas of Caen in the seventeenth century, and a brilliant centre of the literary world of that great day.

Cross rue Saint-Pierre and turn up rue Froide, beside the Church of Saint-Sauveur, to rue de la Monnaie in which are two fine Renaissance mansions. And if you continue, after returning to rue Froide, to rue Saint-Sauveur, and turn west in it, you will soon come to William's abbey, and to his empty tomb.

These are, with some of the old houses in the rue de Geole, skirting the west side of the castle hill, the principal 'sights' of Caen.

As for the ghosts of Caen, they are many; but I shall not pretend to you that I meet many of them in my strolls there. One, and one only, flits, soft of footfall, before me up each quaint old street; and it is not William's, nor Matilda's; it is that of a rather sturdily built girl, blue-eyed and chestnut-haired; a girl with the air and the look of brooding reflectiveness; a girl who talks so little that her friends think her 'strange,' but who reads devouringly — reads not romances and other things appropriate to her years, but tales of old Rome and Sparta, and pamphlets hot from the presses of Paris and Bordeaux. Charlotte Corday!

It was at the beginning of June, 1793, that eighteen of the Girondin leaders, after Marat had compassed their downfall in the Revolutionary government, came to Caen with the intent to make it headquarters of a counter-revolutionary march on Paris. On June 18th, Barbaroux, the Mar-

ST.-PIERRE DE DERNETAL, CAEN
From a print published in 1821

seillaise who had summoned the Reds of the Midi to march on Paris the year before, again called upon his townsfolk and on other Frenchmen to advance on Paris, to protect the unity of the Republic, to assure the liberty of the National Convention, to punish the enemies of freedom.

I wonder at what place in Caen, Charlotte read that iron-gray placard? I wonder if that very day she formed her resolutions? We know so very little about her!

Édouard Herriot, in his book 'Dans La Fôret Normande,' devotes the last hundred pages and more to what he calls 'A Knife for Forty Sous,' a study of Charlotte and Marat which is interesting *per se*, but doubly so as the offering of a man who has played and is playing the part in contemporary affairs played by Herriot. (Elsewhere we shall have occasion to dwell on his remarkable biography of Madame Récamier.) But if he would have us believe that 'Marat still awaits an impartial judge,' he does not bring us much closer to Charlotte.

The birthplace of Charlotte, south of Lisieux, is some distance from here. It is much as it was in her day. But in Caen itself, if there is any place specially associated with her, save the Abbey and other public buildings, I do not know it.

IV

There is an old Norman proverb which says: 'If you wish to be happy, go between Caen and Bayeux.'

I wish you to be happy, in my company, so I am taking you between them not only once, but twice; we are going to Bayeux and back, but by different roads.

Let us go by the great highway between Paris and Cherbourg, which is Route 13; and cover our seventeen miles quickly. For, pleasant as is the pastoral country through which we're passing, it is hard to loiter with Bayeux beckon-

ing us; we shall make our pace more leisurely and reflective
when we are leaving Bayeux behind.

Bayeux is a place to linger in; a place one leaves re-
luctantly, no matter how long one has been able to stay.
I am almost sure that you will mark it for a sojourn at
some time when you want a delicious rest for body and
spirit, a re-creation.

It was a Gallic town, and the Romans must have thought
more than passing well of it, for they named it *Augusto-
durum*. But I doubt if your interest in it will go farther
back (I know *mine* doesn't!) than Harold's coming there
with William in 1065.

The bishopric of Bayeux was so rich in revenues that
William had given it, sixteen years before, to his half-
brother Odo (or Eudes), then only thirteen years old. (Odo
was Arlette's son by her lawful union with the Knight of
Conteville.) Odo's only excuse for being a bishop seems
to have been that he 'needed the money.' But that was a
quite usual reason in those times — and later. He was
distinctly a warrior and a schemer for worldly power. Of
the cathedral he rebuilt there are few remains. Of the
castle where William and he staged Harold's oath, there is
nothing left. But a strip of cloth has survived from his day
to this: the so-called Bayeux Tapestry. It is really an embroidery and not in any sense a tapestry — that is, not
even like needle-point. It is a strip of coarse linen, twenty
inches wide and seventy-seven yards long, on which are
embroidered in colored threads fifty-eight scenes in the life
of William the Conqueror, from that in which Edward the
Confessor is represented as sending Harold to Normandy
to tell William that he is to be the next king, to that in
which Harold is killed at Hastings and his army cut to
pieces.

I'm not sure that it is possible, when your car halts in

the rue de l'Évêché on the south side of the cathedral, to make yourself go at once into the Old Palace of the Bishops, now the Town Library, to see the embroidery before you make acquaintance with the cathedral. But if you succeed in doing it, I think you will be glad. For one thing, the embroidery is of surpassing interest — few pieces of fabric, if, indeed, any in the world, can vie with it; not just because of its antiquity and the possibility that Queen Matilda may have had some part in its embellishment, but because of the way it re-creates for us (crude as its drawing and design are) a great period of history on which we have, else, exceeding scant documentation. You will, of course, buy the reproduction of it, printed in the colors of the original; and I trust that on many an occasion, in the days to come, you may find yourself with it outspread before you, and an eager young story-lover bending over it from beside each knee. It is an enthralling picture-book as well as a price-less document. An hour with it is one of the best-possible aids to the enjoyment of your trip in Normandy.

And what shall I try to say of Bayeux Cathedral? It stands very high among the churches I love best; but I'm sure I can't tell you why. It produces an effect on me which I can in nowise describe; but if I *could* describe it, what would be the use? I have a veritable collection of books on French cathedrals; I have one learned book exclusively about Bayeux Cathedral. I read them with what I hope I may believe to be pretty fair intelligence. I'm not ignorant of architectural terms. I can read stories in stones as well as most people. But descriptive writing about architecture doesn't 'get me anywhere at all' unless it is sublimely done — beautiful words piled upon beautiful words with the effect of poetry or music; or illuminatingly done, as Viollet-le-Duc does it, for instance, making it richly interpretative of the mortal life and immortal soul that expressed itself in stone.

I shall not apologize again in these pages for my inability to write on the architecture of churches. I only beg you to believe that it is my reverent awe which stays my hand, and not any lack of admiration.

Of Bayeux I am able to say this much: that even if you are not an enthusiast about old churches, I think you should see Bayeux. And if you see it on a sunny morning, I believe you will come away from it carrying memory-pictures of a kind of lovely lightness which is not radiance, but something serenely soothing. The appeal is not to our mysticism, as at Chartres, where we feel how insupportable life would have been without the Presence in those shadowy spaces beneath the jewelled windows. At Bayeux Cathedral, as in the delicious old slumbering streets about it, I get an impression of thousands of persons who have found life, on the whole, a pleasant and fairly placid experience.

I hope you will not be too hurried to loiter a bit in those old streets. When you leave the cathedral, by the west portal which faces rue Bienvenue, note the fine sixteenth-century house at number 6 in the latter street. Then turn into rue des Chanoines, and up rue Bourbesneur, number 10 in which is a strikingly picturesque mansion. Now turn north, along the west side of the Place Saint-Sauveur, in the rue du Général-de-Dais, past the statue of Alain Chartier and toward his birthplace.

Alain is called 'the father of French eloquence.' He was born about 1392 (a year later than Charles of Orléans, and forty years earlier than Villon), of a family which attained distinction in his generation, at least, whether it had enjoyed any before or not. Alain's eldest brother became Bishop of Paris, and another brother was notary to the King. Alain was closely attached to the Dauphin, afterwards Charles VII, and was sent to Scotland, in 1427, on the mission which negotiated the marriage of little Princess Mar-

garet of Scotland with the Dauphin, afterwards Louis XI.
There is a pretty story of this Princess kissing the sleeping
Chartier, long afterwards, on 'the precious mouth out of
which have come so many fine words and virtuous sentiments,' and you may believe it if you like; for though some
authorities say that Chartier died in 1430, six years before
Margaret came to France, others declare that he lived till
1449. I hope that the latter are right, not only on account
of the kiss (which must have pleased poor Alain when he
heard about it, because he was the ugliest man of his day),
but also because that would mean that he lived long enough
to see some justification of his ardent belief that 'the cause
of France, though desperate to all appearance, was not yet
lost if the contending factions could lay aside their differences in the face of the common enemy.' (Sounds quite contemporary — doesn't it?)

What you probably know best of Chartier's is his poem
'Belle Dame sans Merci,' which was translated into English
about 1640. But he was also a vigorous prose writer and expressed himself in no halting terms against the abuses of
power in his day. In the fifteenth and sixteenth centuries
he enjoyed an immense renown, and young gentlemen were
required to learn by heart, each day, a portion of his Bre-
viary for Nobles.

You will find Alain's birthplace at the corner of the street
which bears his name and rue Saint-Malo, a little to your
left after you have turned in to rue Saint-Malo from rue du
Général-de-Dais.

Retrace your steps, then, in rue Saint-Malo, till it becomes rue Saint-Martin, with its many quaint houses including the much-bepictured one at the corner of rue des
Cuisiniers. Just before the street changes its name you
pass (number 4) the Hôtel du Fresne with a fine timbered
façade. And you must not fail at least to look down rue

Franche when you pass the corner. If, then, you go on through rue Saint-Martin and turn back toward the cathedral, you will have had a very fine glimpse of Bayeux, and an impression of the quiet, aristocratic, and ecclesiastical life which has characterized this lovely old town for ages. And if you buy a bit of precious lace, reproducing some famous old pattern, from the little shop opposite the southwest angle of the cathedral, I am sure it will always recall to you a background wherein old lace must have played its dignified part on many an occasion of provincial state such as these old houses knew through succeeding generations of France's story.

Now, when you know you must go (and if you are to have Jumièges Abbey at its greatest glory-time, you should leave Bayeux soon after eleven — which means that you should have started from Caen soon after eight), go out by rue Saint-Jean, which is a continuation of rue Saint-Martin, and take the road for Cruelly which bears to the left soon after you leave Bayeux. Creully has a castle which Percy Dearmer calls not the greatest nor the grandest in Normandy, but the prettiest; and I think you will agree with him. I doubt if you can get in, but the view from without is enough to make Creully a memorable little town for you.

If you want to see a notable country-house of the early sixteenth century, take the Caen road out of Creully for three kilometres and look for a signpost that says 'Fontaine-Henri.' Indeed, whether this interests you or not, I think you would better return to Caen; because, though you could go on to the coast and follow it to the mouth of the Orne, at Ouistreham, which is the scene of the last act of the Hundred Years' War and has a noted twelfth-century church, I'm sure you are thinking longingly of luncheon and had best get on at a fair pace toward Trouville. (And here let me remind any reader who may be making first acquaintance with this little 'method' of mine which so many travellers have approved, that in making up a day's programme, or a journey's, I am no more slighting the places and things I leave out than an orchestra director is slighting the pieces he doesn't play, nor a gourmet is slighting the dishes he doesn't order. I am trying to present a 'balanced' and feasible feast for folks who must hurry. I make no pretence of doing anything more.) Trouville is twenty-seven and a half miles from Caen by road; and you will want a stop of at least three quarters of an hour at Dives-sur-Mer. So, unless you get back to Caen before noon, you may find your resolution to lunch at the Sole Normande, Trouville, deserting you in favor of some nearer but less delectable place.

Your route from Caen goes to Bénouville, then turns to your right, for Cabourg, and continues along the coast through Dives-sur-Mer, where you must not fail to see the famous Hostellerie Guillaume-le-Conquérant (or William the Conqueror Inn), and the church with its list of William's principal vassals and other fellow adventurers across the Channel; and also the ancient and picturesque market.

You will find the inn most engaging, and you may decide to stop there for luncheon. Its reputation for many years was that it charged fantastic prices for indifferent services. I have heard recent reports of reform. Perhaps you would like to see if they are true. Certainly you could not find, anywhere, a more picturesque spot in which to lunch. And although William's ghost was a very old ghost before this inn existed, there are a great many other famous personages associated with it, including the arch-enchanter Alexandre Dumas. Any place his bulky, woolly-headed ghost walks is a place dear to me — and to you, I dare say.

When Edward the Confessor died and Harold assumed the Crown of England, he did so as the leader of a sort of nationalist movement: 'England for the Saxons'—Harold's father having been a great Saxon noble and leader of the 'home rule' party. So Harold not only repudiated his oath to maintain William's cause, but did the same with his oath to wed William's daughter. A Norman marriage would never do for a Nationalist leader!

William appealed to his fellow rulers, and the Pope. The Pope was having trouble collecting Peter's Pence from the the English clergy, so he sent William his blessing and the banner of Saint Peter to insure his victory. As for others, whom he must take with him, not only to have their aid, but to keep them from following their own purposes in France while he was away, William got them by promising to share with them the rich spoils of conquest.

All the hardy adventurers of western Europe responded to his call, to the number of some fourteen thousand knights and forty to fifty thousand foot-soldiers. To convey this army and its equipment across the Channel, some seven hundred boats were necessary. Six months sufficed to build these boats and complete preparations, including the mobilization of that army. The whole Norman coast resounded with this vast making-ready. Harold can hardly have needed spies to tell him what was going on; it must almost have been audible across the Channel.

But when all else was ready, the wind was not. Although it was August, the weather was cold and rainy; and when the departure was taken, from Dives, the fleet was blown northeast instead of northwest, and had to wait a whole month at the mouth of the Somme. During this wait (which Jules Janin likens to that of Agamemnon at Aulis), William's army grew impatient and then discouraged. William could feel victory eluding him. Every day he went to the church at Saint-Valéry to pray for a favoring wind; and when he came out, he scrutinized the weather-cock on the belfry to see if his prayers were being answered. Instead of offering up his daughter as propitiation, following Agamemnon's sacrifice of Iphigenia, William observed the custom of his day and caused the reliquary of Saint Valéry to be carried in solemn procession around his murmuring army. Its effect was all that could have been hoped for: the men's zest and courage were reanimated, they heaped the shrine with precious gifts and the sails swelled with the favoring breeze; the Pope's flag, white, striped with azure blue, floated at the mast of William's ship, the Maura, which Matilda had presented him, and with that ship leading the way, the fleet was off for England — September 27, 1066.

The delay had been providential for William; because Harold, knowing of it, had hastened north to meet a Norse invasion led by one of his own brothers, Tostig, who was married to Matilda's sister and 'in the plot.' Harold was able to repulse this invasion, near York; but ere he could regain London, William had landed at Pevensey, near Hastings. William stumbled and fell, as he was debarking. But, born leader that he was, he turned what might have seemed to his followers an evil augury by crying, 'See, seigneurs! By the splendor of God I have seized England with my two hands ... and that which I have grasped, I will by your good help maintain.'

An excellent psychologist was William; for after having encouraged his followers to belief in his destiny, he persuaded the country-folk of southern England to believe that the comet which was then terrifying them was sent by Heaven to notify them of the coming of their new king.

I dare say we mustn't let William engross us further. But he dominates Dives to-day almost as completely as in those summer days of 1066. And as for me, I always love to reflect upon those whose eternal flame of enthusiasm has to keep rekindling a kind of damp, reluctant world.

After Dives come Houlgate, and then Villers-sur-Mer, both pleasant seaside places. Then Deauville and Trouville, separated only by the river Touques. The 'high season' at these places is in August; the races are at Trouville the first fortnight of August and at Deauville the second fortnight; the latter are fashionably attended. The Sole Normand is the restaurant I like best thereabouts; in it you will find food not surpassed in France — which means, not surpassed anywhere. Of course you'll have 'sole normand'; and I am able to testify that a certain beefsteak I once had there ranks near the top among all beefsteaks I've ever eaten. Also, the American cocktails are notably good, and the French wines (of course) superb.

From Trouville to Honfleur, the route is charming, with the ivy-clad church of Cricquebœuf midway. And before you descend into Honfleur, you'll pause at the Chapelle Nôtre Dame-de-Grâce — partly to see the little church that mariners love, and partly to enjoy the fine view from that height.

Honfleur is a picture-town, just such as one would select to weave romances about. One hardly knows whether it seems most like a lovely stage setting, or an animated picture exhibition, or the illustrations of an enticing story. Many a bold seafarer set sail from there, including one, De Gonneville, who sailed thence to the South Seas in 1503; and Champlain, who set forth from Honfleur for Canada, a hundred years later.

From Honfleur, you should take Route 179 for Lisieux, if you want to go there. You enter Honfleur by the rue des Capucines; follow that street as far as it goes, and on your left you'll find the Church of Sainte Catherine with its picturesque belfry. Close by, facing the harbor, is the

Lieutenance, all that's left of the sixteenth-century castle of the King's lieutenant of the port. Continue past it, toward the Hôtel de Ville, and turn south along the eastern edge of the Basin, rounding into the rue de la République which leads out toward Lisieux. Midway you pass through Pont-l'Évêque where the cheese is made which was famous enough, seven hundred years ago, to get itself mentioned in some of the scant poetical writing of that day. Camembert, a much more modern product, originated in the village of that name which is a little farther south of Lisieux than Pont-l'Évêque is north of it.

I used to like Lisieux much better before it became such a famous place of pilgrimage. I loved the serenity of its old streets with their quaint timbered houses; and I liked musing in its cathedral (the oldest Gothic church in Normandy) on the remorse of Bishop Cauchon who was transferred to this bishopric the year after he had hounded Jeanne d'Arc to the flames, and who built this Lady Chapel — 'tis said — in expiation.

But Lisieux, nowadays, belongs to the pilgrim throngs come to pray at little Saint Theresas' shrine. And if you don't care for pilgrims, I think you would do well to go straight from Honfleur to Pont-Audemer; and then, if you have more time than you need for Caudebec and Jumièges, take the road up from Pont-Audemer through Quillebœuf to Lillebonne, and thence to Caudebec.

The 'Little Flower of Lisieux,' canonized in 1924, was a Carmelite nun who entered that austere order at a very early age. She was born at Alençon, but was a member of the Carmelite sisterhood at Lisieux, where she died, in her early twenties, of consumption. She was very, very pretty; and from her childhood she seems to have been determined not to let her beauty turn her thoughts to worldly things. Of course, her taking the veil caused comment; and her deter-

mination not to seek admiration, but to hide herself from the
world, was something to talk about, in an age somewhat
weaned from saintliness. When the seeds of disease threatened death, little Sister Theresa said that she was going
where she could serve more. And when she was gone
Thither, her lovely young body lay, as the Carmelite custom is, in the robes of her order, on an open bier, for all to
see. She was so beautiful, and so good, that many came.
The scent of many roses, the flickering of many tapers,
enhanced a solemn scene. Of those who prayed beside her
bier, some declared themselves miraculously blessed. After
her interment, her grave was much visited, and miracles
were besought there. During the late War there was great
devotion to Sister Theresa on the part of the soldiers, thousands of whom believed ardently in her efficacy to keep them
from harm. And so greatly has the cult of the gentle little
Carmelite grown that in 1924 she was declared a saint; and
now, Lisieux has practically become her shrine. Her de-
votees say that she manifests her presence by the scent of
roses. In the chapel that has been built to her memory, you
may see a wax effigy of her lying in state as she did before
her funeral; and all about it, supplicating pilgrims, some of
them in the direst need of aid.

Should it chance that some one with you wants to visit
Saint Theresa's shrine, and you do not want to, you may
spend the time looking at the old houses in rue Aux Fèvres,
the Grand-Rue, and rue de la Paix; and in the cathedral.

Pont-Audemer is twenty-three miles from Lisieux; it is a
picturesque little town with a very fine church and a quaint
inn, and many claims to celebrity. Its eleventh-century
castle was destroyed by Du Guesclin in the early fourteenth
century with the aid of the first cannon used in France.
About that same time Pont-Audemer furnished the King
of France (Charles V) with a very noted cook who wrote

the first cookbook in the French language. And Pont-Audemer claims to have invented the sausage.

It is only thirteen miles from Pont-Audemer to Lillebonne, and then ten more to Caudebec. You can shorten the distance to Caudebec a little by taking the Bourneville road; but it is a great pity to be so close to Lillebonne and not see it — with its ruins of a Roman theatre dating back to Hadrian, and its castle, founded by William the Conqueror; it was at Lillebonne that he assembled his vassals and his peers and got them to pledge their support for his invasion of England.

Caudebec is a lovely old town whose principal industry seems to be having its picture taken; and many persons have agreed with Henry IV who said that its church was the prettiest chapel in his kingdom. And though there were doubtless, in his day, many streets more picturesque than the rue de la Boucherie at Caudebec, with its thirteenth-century house of the Templars, there are not many in France that surpass it now.

A little more than half a mile from Caudebec on your road to Jumièges are the very beautiful ruins of the ancient Abbey of Saint-Wandrille, founded as the Abbey of Fontenelle, in 648; and refounded by the grandfather of the Conqueror. About the early history of the abbey you will probably care less than about its quite recent history as the home of Maurice Maeterlinck. Against these lovely settings his 'Pelléas et Mélisande' was sometimes privately enacted; and in these exquisite surroundings he may have written 'The Blue Bird' and 'Monna Vanna.' The cloisters are especially beautiful, and the great hall was a twelfth-century refectory.

Five and a half miles farther on your road to Rouen, you come to Jumièges whose abbey was founded just after that of Saint-Wandrille.

You should get there at six o'clock or thereabouts of a long day, so that you may spend at least an hour and a half therein before going on your way to Duclair for the night.

I regard a sunset hour at Jumièges Abbey as one of the most idyllic experiences that all Europe has to offer; and whatever must be sacrificed between Bayeux and Jumièges to make your arrival betimes at the latter place, I pray you to do it cheerfully.

The abbey ruins are within private grounds, and everything that taste, reverence, and wealth can do to keep their setting perfect and preserve the storied stones is done with the utmost care.

This loving work of conservation was begun in 1852 by Aimé Lepel-Cointet, whose daughter-in-law, Madame Eric Lepel-Cointet, has carried on the noble task in a way which makes us all who love these glorious monuments her debtors beyond our power to express.

A recent visitor from the United States came near closing the gates of this property against all who ask to see the abbey; in the visitors' book he wrote: 'We'll own this, too, when we want it.' If, at any time in your travels abroad, it seems to you that your appreciative and friendly spirit is not too quickly met by an answering friendliness, be patient; it may be that your fellow countryman just preceding you was of the sort who does such things as the above. The very discerning among your hosts will instantly distinguish that the resentment he has aroused should not show itself to you; but some people are a little slow — or it may be that the thrust given has opened an old wound.

It is the sheer beauty of the ruins that will engross most of us. Here we have a loveliness that moves us almost to tears, and certainly to an ecstasy which seeks no expression — knowing that there is none adequate.

But of the stories that have attached themselves to

Jumièges there are two concerning which I think you may like a little detail.

One is the legend of the Énervés, whose burial place will be shown you in the nave of Saint Peter's Church.

The tale is that they were the sons of Clovis II and his saintly queen Bathilde; that Clovis, wishing to go on a pilgrimage to the Holy Land, left the royal power in the hands of his elder son, under the regency of the Queen; that at first the young prince was obedient to his mother, but finally rebelled against her and involved with him in his revolt his younger brother, excluding their mother from all authority. When Clovis started homeward, they raised an army to prevent his return. He sought to reconcile them to his fatherly and kingly rule, but they would have none of him. So he fought, and conquered; and when the rebellious sons were brought before him and their mother to be judged it was she who ordered them hamstrung. 'The young princes,' legend says, 'endured the punishment courageously, and henceforth, dwelling in their father's house, had no other thought than to expiate their fault by fasting and prayer.' And when the King saw his sons trying to rise up and falling down helpless while other youths enjoyed themselves, he was very sad. But Bathilde bade him have faith in God. And soon the young princes asked to become monks.

'In what monastery shall we put them?' Clovis said.

And Bathilde recommended that they order a boat built, large enough to carry them, under cover, and a single servitor and supplies. Thus, without oars or steering-gear, they were set adrift upon the Seine, and came to this place, where a holy hermit lived. He took them in and gave them shelter. And when the King and Queen heard where their sons were, they gave the hermit many lands and enabled him to found this abbey wherein the hamstrung princes lived and

died in the midst of a rapidly growing community of monks
recruited from their father's ranks of nobles.

The facts are that Clovis II died when he was twenty-
six and his children were infants; he never went to the Holy
Land; his three sons reigned after him, and they were never
monks and never hamstrung. The two princes buried in the
Church of Saint Peter at Jumièges are a Duke of Bavaria
and his son who were defeated by Charlemagne and became monks in this monastery.

The legend was born in the twelfth century, under the influence of the Crusades and the troubadours; and so popular did it become that in the thirteenth century there was
erected to the memory of the Énervés the superb tomb
whose remains you will find in the musée. If you visit the
musée at Rouen you may see there a painting, by Lumenais,
showing the helpless princes drifting down the Seine. So
much stronger is a good story than a mere fact!

The other story about Jumièges, which even our soberest
guide-books pass on to us as history, is that the abbey was
'a favorite resort' of Charles VII and Agnès Sorel, and that
the latter had a manor-house near here named Manil-sous-
Jumièges.

This is crediting them with a great deal of temerity in
their choice of trysting places; for Jumièges, like the rest of
Normandy, was under English rule from the battle of Agincourt (1415) to 1449. It was in November of the latter year
that Charles VII entered Rouen as its master. He left that
city on November 28th, moved on to Caudebec, and thence
to the siege of Harfleur which capitulated to the French on
New Year's Day. On January 5, 1450, Charles came to
Jumièges whilst his troops laid siege to Honfleur.

Agnès Sorel, 'Dame de Beauté,' who had been his acknowledged mistress for five years, during which she had
borne him three daughters, was again expecting mother-

hood when, in the summer of 1449, she stirred the sluggish King to drive the English out of Normandy. He set out from Chinon on August 6th, and Agnès took up her residence at Loches. In January, after Charles was settled at Jumièges, Agnès came to join him, and was lodged in the manor-house of Mesnil belonging to the abbey domain. There, at the beginning of February, she brought into the world her fourth daughter, who lived but a few days. And on the 9th of February, Agnès died of puerperal fever.

Charles caused her heart to be buried in the Chapel of the Virgin of Notre-Dame Church in Jumièges Abbey, and her body to be interred in the Church of Notre-Dame at Loches. In both places he raised superb tombs to her memory. The one at Loches you shall see; of the one at Jumièges nothing remains but the black marble slab, recovered from the doorstep of a house in rue Saint-Maur at Rouen, on which the inscription remains quite legible: 'Here lies the noble damsel, Agnès Sorel, in her lifetime Dame of Beauty, of Roqueferrière, Issoudun, and of Vernon-sur-Seine; pitiful to all, she gave largely of her means to churches and to the poor, and died on the ninth day of February in the year of grace 1450. Pray God for her soul. Amen.'

A week after her death, Charles moved nearer to the siege of Honfleur.

The monks of Jumièges were dispersed in 1790. The village curé was offered the abbey church as a parish church, but refused it; and in the winter of 1792–93, the abbey became a barracks lodging four hundred soldiers. In 1795 the methodical demolition of the buildings commenced. From that time on, with an interval of only four years during which a Paris banker was proprietor, the destruction went on, year after year, until the Lepel-Cointet family came into possession, with their wealth of taste and reverence as well as wealth of means. The choir of Notre-Dame had been blown up, and the ruins served as a quarry for the building operations of the countryside.

What we have lost is undoubtedly calamitous. But what has been preserved to us through this beneficent family is second in loveliness to no other abbey ruins that I have ever seen. I shall probably never have other opportunity than in these pages to express my gratitude to the Lepel-Cointets. And they may never see this little book. But what of that? The expression of gratitude is not primarily for the benefactor — is it? It is for ourselves, too — a vent for our surcharge of emotion.

From Jumièges your way leads through the afterglow (I hope!) to Duclair, some five miles nearer Rouen; and there, in Hôtel de la Poste, on the very edge of the Seine, you may spend the night in one of the most delightful of French provincial hotels, without any sense of anticlimax after the ecstasy of Jumièges. This hotel claims the honor of having first introduced to a grateful world the pressed duck à la Rouennaise which has since made the fame of restaurateurs like Frédéric of the Tour d'Argent at Paris. At any rate, its cooking is superlatively good, its cellar is likewise, it has a great many exceptionally comfortable bedrooms with private baths, and if weather permits you may dine on a balcony which almost overhangs the Seine and watch seagoing ships slip downstream toward Havre. I was there last June, with the first of our Normandy tours, on such a night as few other nights in all my memories surpass in idyllic qualities: roses of unbelievable size and beauty, in greatest profusion; memorable food and wine; silver moonlight on the Seine, and the black bulk of cargo ships, showing tiny red and green lanterns, moving down the shimmering stream so close we could almost have thrown a rose on board. Stillness, perfume, ineffable delight! Every recollection of it is precious and soul-restoring.

Next morning you should reach Rouen by nine o'clock
(it is only ten miles); though, if you are a lover of architecture, you will probably start an hour earlier from Duclair, and take the river road instead of that which crosses
the top of the Seine loop, so as to see the beautiful abbey
church of Saint-Georges-de-Boscherville, founded by Raoul
de Tancarville, chamberlain to William the Conqueror,
about the time of the Norman Conquest. This church is
not in ruins, and it has not been so much restored as most
churches of its great age. It is one of the finest Romanesque churches in all Normandy.

Rouen is for most of us primarily the place where Jeanne
d'Arc was burned. And if you have her story vividly in
mind there (perhaps from a recent re-reading of Mark
Twain's book about her, or Andrew Lang's) you are probably intent on seeing, first of all, the places associated with
her. Or it may be that you have just freshened up your acquaintance with Shakespeare's 'King John,' and your
mind, as you approach Rouen, is full of those scenes Shakespeare makes so piteous, wherein young Prince Arthur of
Brittany pleads vainly to save his eyesight and then his life.
Perhaps you have been reading Elizabeth W. Champney's
'Romance of the Renaissance Châteaux,' and are most eager
to see the famous tomb of Cardinal Georges d'Amboise; or
that of Diane de Poitiers' husband. Some among you will
hasten to stand where the heart of the Lion-Hearted Richard lies. Others will want to find Corneille here — the father
of French tragedy — and some will be intent upon the
Chevalier de La Salle — or upon Gustave Flaubert.

Not knowing which is your paramount interest, I am
offering you a few suggestions which are time-conserving
and include most of the principal 'sights.' As for doing anything like justice to Rouen in a few paragraphs, or in three
hours, we know — of course — that we're not attempting

it. Mr. Theodore Andrea Cook, author of 'Old Touraine' and 'Old Provence,' is author also of a scholarly book on 'Rouen' which is one of that invaluable series 'The Mediæval Towns,' dear to so many thousands of travellers. And there is a most helpful volume called 'Walks in Rouen,' by J. H. T. Perkins.

You will probably enter Rouen from the north; and just south of the line of boulevards which now replace the old ramparts, you will find the Tour Jeanne d'Arc, close to where rue Jeanne d'Arc unites with the Boulevard de la Marne.

It was hereabouts that the old castle of Rouen stood; and the tower that Viollet-le-Duc restored was its donjon, built by Philippe-Auguste after he had expelled King John of England from the Duchy of Normandy as punishment for John's blood-guilt in the murder of poor young Arthur.

I suppose the castle of earlier days, where William the Conqueror heard that Harold had been crowned King of England, and where John, either with his own hands or those of his assassins, did young Arthur to death, must have been greatly enlarged by Philippe-Auguste, not only because he was an ardent builder, but because it would be in keeping with all that he undertook to do for the power and prestige of the Crown of France, if he made an example here of how much more puissant was a French King with none above him than an English King who was also the French King's vassal.

As Duke of Normandy, John had been, in the feudal lien, answerable to the King of France for the death of Arthur. Doubtless the punishment of this crime was only an excuse for Philippe-Auguste to annex Normandy to his possessions; but the fight that he was making to raise royal power above the feudal rivalries was in the line of progress, and I think every student of history is glad he ousted John, and sorry

ROUEN

From an old mezzotint

that John's descendants, with all the great task they had in
hand for themselves and for posterity, could not have been
satisfied to.stay on their own side of the Channel and work
at it.

I'd think a bit about Philippe-Auguste, at that donjon
tower in Rouen; especially as the savants tell us it was not
in this tower that Jeanne was imprisoned, though some of
her examinations may have taken place in this one, and
probably did; because, though two centuries divided them,
Philippe and Jeanne worked very much to the same great
end: the prestige of France.

And then, if I could take some of my brief Rouen time for
a wonderfully good and interesting collection of pictures,
and one of the greatest collections of ceramics in Europe,
I'd go on down the rue Bouvreuil to the Square Solferino,
on the east side of which is the Musée.

Rue Jeanne d'Arc which skirts the west side of the square
will lead you to rue Rollon which runs, west, into the Vieux
Marché or Old Market-Place, where Jeanne d'Arc was
burned on that May day of 1431.

It has been suggested to me, by a friend whose ideas
about books I have extraordinary reasons to respect, that
in the case of a few outstanding characters like Jeanne
d'Arc, what you may find most helpful in this little volume,
this companion of your travels in France, is a complete outline of her story in one place, instead of fragments of it here
and there in the places where parts of it occurred. So I
shall make that outline, for the refreshing of your memory
regarding all you've read of her, in our chapter that includes
Domrémy; and to it you may turn, here and elsewhere,
when we have reminders of her.

Here, we shall not recapitulate; we shall only stand with
bowed heads and uplifted hearts, recalling a sacrifice which
did more than any other in all the history of humans striv-

ing toward the Divine to benefit mankind by moving them
to tender and noble emotions.

From the southwest corner of the old market-place runs
rue Corneille at number 4 in which were born the brothers
Corneille — Pierre and Thomas — the latter twenty years
after the former; the house wherein they first saw the light
of day is long since demolished, but it was in this close proximity to the scene of Jeanne's death that they grew up —
these dramatists of history — although in their day and
until much later the scene of her martyrdom was believed
to be in the near-by Place de la Pucelle, whither you must
go to see the Hôtel de Bourgtheroulde, finished in 1532,
whose sculptural decorations (on the parts within the courtyard) are the most magnificent of their sort in France. One
range of panels depicts the Field of the Cloth of Gold and is a
contemporary representation of it as Matilda's embroidery
is of the Norman Conquest. Above the windows of this
wing is a series of pictures in stone illustrating the Triumphs of Petrarch: 'Love Conquers the World,' and
'Modesty Conquers Love' (these are gone); then, 'Death
Conquers Modesty,' and 'Fame Conquers Death'; 'Time
Conquers Fame,' and 'Eternity Conquers All.'

From the Place de la Pucelle, turn up rue de la Vicomté
to rue de la Grosse Horloge which leads, beneath the fourteenth-century belfry and clock-tower so dear to etchers,
painters, and all lovers of the picturesque, and past the
superb Palais de Justice, one of the finest public buildings
in Europe, to the cathedral.

I believe you will enjoy the Palais and the belfry scarcely
less than the cathedral; and in the great Salle des Pas-
Perdus of the Palais, I think you will like to recall a most
dramatic scene which used to take place there.

It seems that 'once upon a time' Rouen was ravaged by
a gargoyle, a dragon who devoured several persons every

day; and because the Bishop of Rouen, Saint Romain, with the aid of a condemned criminal, drove the monster into the river, King Dagobert decreed that on Ascension Day, every year, the chapter of Rouen Cathedral should have the privilege of releasing a condemned criminal.

The first proceeding was when four canons and four chaplains came to the Parlement, sitting here, to be formally invested with the right of searching the prisons, where they were scrupulously left alone with each condemned prisoner in his cell, and each was invited to tell his story.

At eight o'clock on Ascension Day morning, the chapter of the cathedral met and voted to which doomed man they would extend their privilege. Then they sat down to a fine dinner (dinner was early in those days — not later than 10 A.M.) while the members of Parlement, dressed in their red robes and escorted by soldiers, marched to the Palais and assembled in this room, where the mass of the prisoner was sung. After this, Parlement dined. And when they were all replete, the chosen prisoner was brought in, and knelt, bareheaded, before the lawmakers who were to decide whether the canons had done well to elect him. When Parlement approved, all the bells of Rouen rang joyously, and the reprieved was led away to confess, to be decently habited, and to be acclaimed by the great multitudes, not of the city alone, but from far places, to whom this was one of the finest dramas in the world.

'And what,' asks Mr. Dearmer, 'could be more dramatic than this scene? The murderer snatched from the gallows ... the smiling ecclesiastics, happy in their work of mercy ... the vast crowd delirious with a touching enthusiasm; above it all, the bells clanging out in the bright May sunshine. And how gorgeous was the setting as the procession started back for the cathedral, along the path that pikes and halberds made for it; first the charity children, then the

clergy with the reliquaries and banners of the thirty-two
parish churches of Rouen; the crosses and incense and
torches, and the first processional dragon; the trumpets
and cornets and clarions; the sub-deacon and deacon, and
the canon who was to sing the great Mass, and the archbishop in his cope and mitre; and then after a little gap the
second dragon, which was the popular "gargoyle" and
sometimes had a live sucking pig stuck in its awesome jaws;
and then the hero of the day, crowned now with flowers. . . .'

This ceremony was held for the last time in 1790.

On Ascension Day, 1431, the slip of a girl in the castle
prison of the English regent at Rouen was probably the last
of all the condemned whom any canon would have thought
of snatching from death.

At the end of rue de la Grosse Horloge is the west front
of the cathedral, in which you will find the tomb of Rollo,
erected three hundred years after his death, but commemorating him whether it contains his bones or not; and, contemporary with his tomb, an effigy of Richard Cœur-de-
Lion whose heart was interred in the predecessor of this
cathedral; also the very fine tomb Diane de Poitiers erected
to the memory of her husband, Louis de Brézé, who was
seneschal of Normandy, and the tomb of the two cardinals
Georges d'Amboise. The elder of these was that eminently
capable relative of Louis XII of whom the King used to
say, when urged to action on most things, 'Let George do
it.'

You will delight in the library stairway, of course, and in
the stained glass, and in the choir stalls. And you must on
no account fail to walk completely around the cathedral on
the outside, for many of its greatest beauties are in the
north and south transeptal portals, the picturesque Cour
d'Albane on the north where the cloister used to be, and

the former palace of the archbishops wherein Jeanne d'Arc was sentenced to death.

The Church of Saint-Maclou, which, with its bow-shaped front, is so familiar to you in pictures, is just behind the former archbishops' palace. Be sure to skirt the southern side of Saint-Maclou, on rue Eugéne Dutuit, and back of the east end to the cloister. And when you come out of the cloister (now a school yard), go north in rue Victor Hugo to rue d'Amiens, and then turn left to the Place des Ponts de Robec and the beginning of the rue Eau de Robec, a most picturesque old street skirting a sluggish stream. North of it is Saint-Ouen, considered the most perfect example of Gothic architecture in existence.

North of Saint-Ouen is what used to be its famous abbey and is now the Hôtel de Ville.

These are the principal 'sights' of Rouen. But Rouen is in itself a sight, and a fascinating old town to wander in. There are dozens of things I'd like to recall here; but I know we must not linger for more than one — perhaps; and that is a bit for which I am indebted to Albert-Petit, who says that in the old court of accounts in Rouen, an institution ancient in William the Conqueror's days, the accountants found that a checker-board cloth on the table was quite an aid in making calculations; and from that comes our word 'exchequer.'

Older even than this accountancy is the crypt beneath the church of Saint-Gervais, which you probably will not visit. This crypt is reputed to be the oldest Christian building in France. What took me to it, on the one occasion when I went thither, is that in the Abbey of Saint-Gervais, William the Conqueror, wounded at Mantes, was brought to die. Thence he was carried down the Seine to Caen for burial.

Should you be a fortunate traveller with no need to

hurry, you may spend at least three days at Rouen, and spend them not only most profitably but also most comfortably if you go to the Hôtel de la Poste, whose genial proprietor, M. Lebrun, is President of the Association of French Hotel-Keepers and runs a house in keeping with his position. Whether you are motoring or travelling by train and making local excursions from a few centers, you will do well to consider this hotel as headquarters for several days.

From Rouen your way leads southeasterly to Boos and thence to Les Andelys — twenty-three miles. If you leave Rouen at noon, you ought to be at the Hôtel du Grand-Cerf in Grand-Andely before one o'clock. The American wife of the French proprietor here is a Wellesley College girl and a charming hostess.

The Andelys are two little towns about half a mile apart. Little Andely is a comparatively modern affair, no older than the twelfth century; but Grand-Andely was a walled town under the Gauls, a place of some importance under the Romans, and in the very early years of the first French dynasty was the site of a famous convent founded by Queen Clotilde, wife of Clovis.

Soon after the death of William the Conqueror, Andely, on the border between France and Normandy, began to play an important rôle in the struggles between the kings of France and England, until — under Richard Cœur-de-Lion — it was agreed that Andely should belong to the Archbishop of Rouen, should not be fortified, and that neither king should reckon it in his domain. Thereupon Richard bargained with the Archbishop, and got Andely for himself, and built Château Gaillard!

After your luncheon at the Grand-Cerf you will wish to make an inspection of that picturesque inn which was the mansion of an important family under Francis I, and became a public hostelry in 1749. Then see the Church of

Notre-Dame; and if you haven't time for all the stained glass, concentrate on the eleventh and twelfth windows of the south aisle, depicting phases of the story of Sainte Clotilde: the murder of her father, Chilperic, by Gondebaud; the imprisonment in a monastery of the victim's family; his widow (Clotilde's mother) thrown into the Rhône; Clotilde's sister sent into exile; Clovis giving the engagement ring for Clotilde to Aurelian; Aurelian, disguised as a beggar, giving the ring to Clotilde; Clotilde given by Gondebaud into Aurelian's care, to be taken to Clovis; and her arrival at the palace of Clovis. Then, Clotilde praying in her oratory; Clovis promising her that if he wins the battle of Tolbiac he will embrace her Christian faith; the battle of Tolbiac, in which Clovis crushed the Roman power in Gaul; Clotilde instructing Clovis in her religion; the baptism of Clovis at Reims; Clovis giving alms; Clotilde building a church at Andely; and the miracle of Clotilde at the fountain of Andely.

The story of Clovis is one of the 'mile-post stories' in French history which we must have well in mind on our journeyings through France. These windows will recall to you the splendid murals of the Panthéon at Paris whose flaxen-haired Clovis has probably for you as for me vivified all mental pictures of that Frankish chieftain who became the first King of France.

The Fountain of Sainte-Clotilde is near the church. The story is that when she was building her abbey here, the workmen grumbled because they had no wine to drink; so Clotilde prayed that for them the waters of this spring might have the strength and taste of wine; and her prayer was granted. This miracle caused the Well of Sainte-Clotilde to become a place of pilgrimage, famed for its healing; especially on the 2d and 3d of June, the anniversary of Clotilde's death; ofttimes the number of pilgrims on those days reached twenty thousand; and the attendant ceremonies were splendidly impressive.

Do you recall the spires of Sainte-Clotilde's Church in Paris, as you see them from the Place de la Concorde, looking southward? When this church was threatened by Prussian bombs in 1870, the curé, whose family had once lived in Andely, vowed that if his beloved church escaped destruction he would each year lead a pilgrimage of his parishioners to Sainte-Clotilde's Well, to join with the multitudes worshipping there — some of them in petition and many in thanksgiving. And, each year since 1872, Sainte-Clotilde's of Paris has had its representation of clergy and laity in the impressive ceremonies here.

Where the Hôtel de Ville stands, there was, until sixty or seventy years ago, a mansion of imposing size and sort, which belonged, three centuries ago, to a local dignitary whose two daughters married the brothers Corneille — Pierre and Thomas. Thomas lived here a great deal, and died here; he is buried in the Church of Notre-Dame d'Andely. 'The grand Corneille,' as French writers frequently designate Pierre, died in Paris and is buried there in the church of Saint-Roch.

All that is left of the mansion which often sheltered 'the French Shakespeare' is the staircase tower, or tourelle, which leads to the museum and library. The museum has a superb canvas by Poussin, who was born near here: 'Coriolanus conquered by his mother's prayers'; three paintings depicting scenes in Clotilde's life; and — among other things — a portrait painted by Charles Chaplin in 1849 and 'given to the museum by the widow of the artist.'

Petit-Andely, which most American girls would describe as 'simply adorable,' is a place to dream in, and to dream about. But all we may permit ourselves, here, is a mere reference to its church, and a fraction of all we'd like to

Henry II, first of the Plantagenet Kings, died at Chinon on July 6, 1189. Two weeks later, his son Richard had himself crowned Duke of Normandy, at Rouen; and not until September 3d did he receive consecration as King of England.

It was characteristic of Richard (I hope you know him as Maurice Hewlett revealed him to us in 'Richard Yea-and-Nay') that when he came into sovereign power he treated much better those who had resisted him in his unfilial attempts against his father than he treated those who had allied themselves with him in disloyalty to King Henry.

Scarcely had he come into his kingdom than Richard began making plans to go on the Third Crusade. At Vézelay, in another chapter, you shall see him with his hosts, meeting Philippe-Auguste with *his* hosts, and the two monarchs leading their great following down the valleys of the Saône and the Rhône. There, and elsewhere, we shall have more to say of Richard as a Crusader and as a captive. He and Philippe had not grown any fonder of each other whilst they were travelling together; and after their expedition was over, they were on very bad terms indeed.

When Philippe-Auguste heard that Richard was released from captivity, he wrote to Richard's wretched younger brother, John: 'Look out for yourself, the devil is loose.'

When 'the devil' (who prided himself on his descent from Duke Robert the Devil, and was wont to say, 'From the devil we came, to the devil we shall return') got back to Normandy after four years' absence, he realized that only by a very determined effort could that duchy be defended against the French King. So, disregarding the treaty he had just made, which gave Andely to the Archbishop of

Rouen and forbade its fortification, Richard 'swopped' with the Archbishop and got Andely in exchange for Dieppe; then proceeded to design and under his personal supervision to erect this castle which closed to the King of France all the lower reaches of the Seine, and gave to the King of England a most disquieting advantage over the near-by territory of his suzerain.

When Richard saw his castle completed, within a twelve-month, he cried, 'How beautiful she is, my daughter of one year!' And when Philippe heard about her, he swore to take her — which he did, from King John, when the castle was but seven years old, and Richard had been in his grave four years. Then Normandy was lost to England for more than two hundred years. (I hope you've refreshed your memories of 'Ivanhoe' recently; and if you've gone on, and re-read 'The Talisman,' I'm sure you're glad.)

Of the history of Château Gaillard under the French Kings, the phase best-known in story is that which gave Dumas the theme for 'La Tour de Nesles.'

Philippe-le-Bel (the Fourth), who sent the Templars' head to his fiery death (see 'Paris,' p. 126), had three sons, each of whom became King of France in turn, and none of whom lived to the age of thirty-five. Their infamous sister, Isabella, the 'She-Wolf,' Mortimer's paramour and her husband's murderer, denounced her three sisters-in-law as having paramours. Think how this must have shamed and shocked Isabella!

Two of the unhappy girls were shut up in Château Gaillard, charged with having as lovers two brothers named D'Aunay. These young men were tortured, and it was pretended that they revealed their guilt; whereupon they were 'drawn and quartered' at Pontoise. Marguerite, daughter of the Duke of Burgundy and wife of Louis X, is believed to have been strangled; at any rate, she died here after a brief imprisonment. Her cousin, Blanche, wife of Charles who became Charles IV, was only eighteen years old when brought to Château Gaillard; she stayed here seven years. Then her husband succeeded to the throne, and demanded of the 'captive' Pope, at Avignon, a divorce, and got it on the ground, not of broken marriage vows, but of 'relationship' — having suddenly remembered that his wife's mother had been his godmother. Blanche took the veil, and died soon afterwards. Her sister Jeanne, married to the middle one of the three brothers, was an heiress whose possessions must not be alienated, and could not be inherited by her husband, who was willing to be her heir. So she, after a short imprisonment in another place (in that Château of Dourdan which I hope you may see on some of your trips south from Paris), was taken back to her husband's side, presented with the Hôtel de Nesle on the south bank of the Seine in Paris, and lived there in her widowhood and until her death. This is the remote and only connection of 'the Tour de Nesles' with the story of poor Marguerite, dead at Château Gaillard. But for millions of readers the tale will always be as Dumas wrote it, and not as scant records hold it. Is there any one who would have it otherwise?

Leisurely travellers who need not get back to Paris at the end of five days should spend the night at the Grand-Cerf, and go over to Gisors next morning and see the imposing ruins of its splendid castle; then, nine miles nearer Paris, on Route 14, see Saint-Clair-sur-Epte where Normandy was born, so to speak; for there, in 912, Charles the Simple, King of France, ceded to Rollo the Norseman that great duchy you have been visiting these days past. If you go to Saint-Clair, your way into Paris will be via Pontoise. Or you could easily go on, twenty miles, from Gisors to Beauvais, one of the loveliest old towns in France with the great-

est Gothic choir in the world, and thence in to Paris before
nightfall. Going in from Les Andelys, you take the road
for Gaillon, and there strike Route 180, which leads through
Vernon and Mantes (where William the Conqueror got the
fall from his horse which caused his death at Rouen; where
Philippe-Auguste died and his heart is buried; and where
Henry IV came a-courting Gabrielle d'Estrées) and Saint-
Germain-en-Laye.

In the event of your having stopped the night at Grand-
Andely and *not* going to Gisors, you could turn 'Peggy's'
nose toward Louviers, a most delightful old town with a
fifteenth-century inn (also the Grand-Cerf), many lovely old
houses, a church with an exquisite south porch, and gardens
even around the factories. Thence, to Évreux, where there
is another Grand-Cerf, an exceptionally beautiful cathedral, a fine fifteenth-century belfry, and much else to reward the visitor.

And if I were at Évreux, within twenty-three miles of
Beaumont-le-Roger, I never, never could forego a visit to
that fascinating old town — unless I were bent upon lunching at Bois-Joly. In this case, I'd try to forget even about
Conches, but would make proper haste down Route 154,
something less than twenty miles from Évreux to Nonancourt, and then run west a little way on Route 12, to Til-
lières, where Bois-Joly is. Thence, by Dreux and Houdan
and Versailles, in to Paris.

Now, if you cannot take a motor of your own for Normandy, nor a Clara Laughlin Motor Tour of it, and haven't
a whole summer for cycling over it as some of our fortunate
English cousins have, how may you do it by train in a few
jumps?

I'd say, direct to Mont-Saint-Michel, by way of Granville. Then to Caen for your next centre, and trips out from
there to Bayeux, Falaise, Dives, and Deauville. Then, from

Honfleur across to Havre; and thence by boat or train to Rouen; and from Rouen in to Paris.

This cannot be done in five days without a great deal of sacrifice to the making of 'connections.' Six would be better for it; and seven days better still if you want to make any part of the journey from Havre to Rouen by boat.

II

TO MONT–SAINT–MICHEL BY WAY
OF BRITTANY

I

SHOULD it happen that you can make but one brief trip in the direction of Mont-Saint-Michel, and that you would rather see more of Brittany — its rugged coasts, its picturesquely garbed people, its artist-haunted spots — and less of Normandy, I'd suggest that when you leave Paris, you follow the route of our first chapter, as far as Nogent-le-Rotrou, and then continue on Route 23, forty miles, to Le Mans. Or you might follow it as far as Alençon, and then take Route 138 to Le Mans; this will add thirty miles to your day's run.

In the event of your being so fortunate as to make two tours to the 'Emerald Coast,' I'd suggest that for this one you leave Paris by the Porte d'Orléans. Traverse the whole length of boulevard Raspail to the Place Denfert- Rochereau (named for the gallant defender of Belfort in 1870), where a copy of Bartholdi's 'Lion of Belfort' stands; and there take avenue d'Orléans, leading southwest to the Porte.

Three miles beyond the Porte, on National Route 20 (which you follow all the way to Orléans, seventy miles), is Bourg-la-Reine. As you go along its Grande-Rue (or Main Street) you are doubtless thinking of the happy days Camille Desmoulins spent in the house and garden at number 36, which was the suburban property of his young wife's family, the Duplessis (see 'So You're Going to Paris,' p. 34), and of Condorcet, the great philosopher (see 'So You're

Going to Paris,' p. 292), who died in prison here at number 49 Grande-Rue.

Three miles from Bourg-la-Reine (but not on your direct route) is Sceaux, where Colbert had his magnificent château at which, in a later day than Colbert's, Voltaire was a frequent guest; and near by is Robinson, where holiday-makers eat up among the branches of the giant chestnut-trees and enjoy the belief that they are behaving like Robinson Crusoe.

Your Orléans route takes you through Longjumeau and Montlhéry, where the donjon of the robber barons' famous old stronghold still stands guard over Gallo-Roman tombstones of a remoter past.

On you go, through Arpajon, to Étampes, also with a gigantic donjon and the residences of two ladies whose charms made them famous: Anne de Pisseleu, whom Francis I made Duchess d'Étampes, and Diane de Poitiers, who is said to have enjoyed his favor before she entered upon that of his son, Henry II.

On leaving Étampes, look, on your left, for the leaning tower of Saint-Martin's.

I can't promise you much to see on the rest of the way (about forty miles) to Orléans; for you're travelling across the great granary of France, the plain or plateau called the Beauce, and while much about it must be interesting to agriculturists from the granaries of the United States, it is not what could be called 'a scenic route' nor one rich in places of historic interest. The road, however, is an excellent one (if it is in good condition; and I think it usually is) and good time can be made on it. If you left Paris at 8.30, you should be at Orléans before 11.

Entering by the Paris road, you soon come to the Place Gambetta on which is the Grand-Hôtel et Hôtel Saint-Aignan. You might like to 'put up' there, or at the

Terminus, facing the railway station, a 'block' east. But
unless you have a preference for a hotel as against a restaurant luncheon, I'd drive straight down rue Bannier to the
Place du Martroi with the Jeanne d'Arc Monument in it;
and I'd lunch in the Restaurant Jeanne d'Arc there.

Should it be too early for luncheon, do your sight-seeing
first. Pass around the Jeanne d'Arc Monument, studying
the ten bas-reliefs which tell the story of her life: show her
hearing the voices at Domremy; leaving Vaucouleurs to go
to Chinon; before Charles VII at Chinon; entering Orléans;
leading the assault on the Fort de Tourelles; attending at
the coronation of Charles at Reims; wounded at the wall of
Paris; taken prisoner at Compiègne; in prison at Rouen; and
at the stake.

Then, enter rue Royale, running south from Place du
Martroi and follow it as far as rue du Tabour, in which,
close to rue Royale (number 13), is a delightful house of the
early sixteenth century in which is installed the Musée
Jeanne d'Arc, containing an interesting collection of objects inspired by the veneration in which she is held. At
number 35 rue du Tabour, now a convent, is the house in
which Jeanne lodged while at Orléans, and the nuns are
most courteous in permitting visitors to enter. Back of
the convent is the Church of Saint Paul, enshrining the
Chapel of Notre-Dame-des-Miracles, where Jeanne d'Arc
thanked God for the victory at Orléans.

Up rue de la Hallebarde, leading back toward the Jeanne
d'Arc Monument, is the Musée Fourché with a notably
fine collection of art works, including Raphael's 'Madonna
della Rovere,' one of Rembrandt's many portraits of himself,
and the Pourbus portrait of Eleanora de Médicis.

South from the post-office, facing rue de la Hallebarde,
runs rue Notre-Dame-de-Recouvrance, at number 28 in
which is a house that Francis I is supposed to have built for
the Duchesse d'Étampes.

If you go to see this, I suggest that you continue to the end of the street, and eastward along the quai to the Pont George V, from the middle of which is the justly celebrated view of Orléans which you have probably seen in many pictures. On the south bank of the Loire, east of this bridge, is the cross marking the site of the Fort des Tourelles. If you 'grew up,' as some of us did who are very fortunate, on stirring pictures from history, you will easily visualize the scene of Jeanne's victorious assault upon this entrenchment of the English; will see her leading, banner in hand, and her troops following, on scaling-ladders against the walls.

When you leave the bridge, retracing your steps to the quai, follow rue Royale north a very little way and then turn to your right, to the Place du Châtelet out of which, to the north, runs rue Ducerceau containing (number 64) the house of the famous architect Ducerceau, of the Louvre. This street continues as rue Sainte-Catherine, leading to rue Jeanne d'Arc. At your left, as you follow rue Sainte-Catherine to rue Jeanne d'Arc, is the historical museum, in a house built about 1530. For the student of archæology there is much here of greatest interest; and the same is true for the student of architecture and of furnishings. On the opposite side of rue Sainte-Catherine is the picture gallery, with an exceedingly fine collection of paintings and a few fine bits of sculpture — very well worth a visit, if only to learn how well-provided with notable art a provincial French city can be.

Rue Jeanne d'Arc leads to the cathedral. If you must slight many things in Orléans, I'd say that among them might be the cathedral. But whatever you must miss, do not let it be the Hôtel de Ville, to reach which I'd continue up rue Sainte-Catherine after it changes its name to rue Saint-Pierre, ending at Place Saint-Pierre. There I'd turn east (right) toward the Hôtel de Ville. But if I loved a fine courtyard, I'd wander a few steps up rue Sainte-Anne (north) to number 11, and have a peep at that; then on to the Hôtel de Ville, which used to be loaned for the royal residence when royalty came to Orléans.

The statue of Jeanne d'Arc, in front, is by the Princess Marie of Orléans, a daughter of King Louis-Philippe, France's last King. But it is not of the Maid of Orléans that I would have you think primarily here. It is of another girl who made much history, and died (a sad woman) on the scaffold, and has kept many tears flowing for her ever since: Mary Stuart.

And to get the full passion and poignancy of the tremendous drama I would have you seem to be witnessing, in that room wherein the Mayor of Orléans now performs the ceremony of civil marriage, you must refresh your memory a bit concerning the Guises and their house of Lorraine from which Mary Stuart was descended through her mother.

When the vast empire of Charlemagne was divided amongst his three grandsons, and their nephew, the oldest, richest, and best-developed part of it went, naturally, to the eldest, Lothair, whose share was much of Italy, Provence, Switzerland, Alsace, and (roughly) a great 'fat' streak running up the Rhine and the Scheldt to what is now Belgium. On the east of him was the portion of his own brother, Louis 'the German,' the beginning of Germany as known in modern history; and on the west of him was the portion of his half-brother, Charles 'the Bald,' the beginning of modern France. This Kingdom of Lothair, or *Lothario regnum*, was soon split in many pieces; but its name, corrupted in time into Lor-raine, has come down to us. The Dukes of Lorraine, who interest us in the fifteenth and sixteenth centuries, claimed descent from Charlemagne

CATHEDRAL OF ORLÉANS
From an old mezzotint

(not, indeed, through Lothair, but through Charles the Bald) and held themselves very superior to the Kings of France, who were descendants of Hugh Capet, 'an upstart.' (Charlemagne himself having been the same sort of upstart, from a grandfather who was a bastard, two hundred and seventy years before Hugh Capet!) The Duchy of Lorraine did not (as you shall recall at Nancy) become a part of France until late in the reign of Louis XV. Its dukes were kept in close alliance with the French throne by marriage and other means; the pretensions of this family to that throne for themselves were formidable only in the sixteenth century, after the death of Henry II; and then it was not the Dukes of Lorraine who made the pretensions, but the cadet branch of the family, the Guises, descended from the second son of Duke René II. This branch inherited all the fiefs that came to René through his French forbears, and was naturalized in France, where it was prolific in progeny (eight to fourteen being the number of children many of the members of the family had, through five generations) and tireless in political upheaval for about a hundred years.

The first Duke of Guise had twelve children, one of whom was the mother of Mary, Queen of Scots, and two others were among the principal actors in the drama you are about to witness; they were Francis, the second Duke of Guise, and his brother Charles, Cardinal of Lorraine. Their young niece, Mary Stuart, Queen of Scotland, was Queen of France now — wife to the feeble little heir of Henry II — and the boy King was so enamoured of her that he was like putty in the hands of her uncles. And those uncles were the implacable enemies of the boy's mother, 'the Florentine,' Catherine de Médicis — as also was her young daughter-in-law, Queen Mary (Stuart).

Most histories make it almost inevitable for us to think of Catherine, niece of a Pope, as an ardent Catholic. Recent research reveals her as ardent about nothing at all except power. She had been mortified and 'kept down' throughout her husband's lifetime. She was still despised and suspected in the reign of her eldest son. And because the Guises were intensely Catholic, Catherine inclined to throw in her lot with the only faction that formidably menaced them, which was the party of the great nobles who were more or less Protestant — some of them more, and some of them less — headed by the Bourbons and the Montmorencys, and intent upon delivering king and kingdom out of the hands of the Guises.

If you please, you are to shut your eyes very tight (as children do) for a moment after you have entered the Hôtel de Ville; and then you are to open them again and 'see with your imagination' — and no less an aid shall you have than Balzac, from whose incomparable picture of that scene I want you to witness, I am making a digest. If you are a 'prepared' traveller you have his 'Catherine de Médicis' in mind, as one of the best possible books to read before coming to the Loire; but in case you have not had time to do this, I'm drawing on it for you.

At Amboise, in a later chapter, we shall recall the failure of an attempt made there against the Guises, and the welter of blood-letting that marked the Guises' reprisals. This happened almost at the beginning of young Francis II's short reign, and about twelve hundred opponents of the Guises were removed from further troublesomeness. But there were too many left, including the leaders. So, to get the survivors in their power, the uncles of the young Queen have called an Assembly of the States-General (the first in fifty-four years!) to meet in Orléans in December, 1560. Nobles, clergy, and elected commoners compose 'the States-General'; and as it is sure to contain many who hate the Guises, the latter have brought to Orléans, to protect themselves and overpower their enemies, an armed force so formidable that Orléans is like an entrenched camp.

To insure the attendance of the Prince de Condé (younger brother of Anthony of Bourbon, who is King of Navarre by his marriage with its Queen, Joanna; and whose son Henry is destined to become Henry IV of France), the boy King, instigated by the Guises, has sent Condé a letter which reads:

'My cousin, come in all security; I give you my royal word that you can do so. If you have need of a safe conduct, this letter will serve as one. Your good cousin and friend, François.'

So Condé, and his party, including his brother, the King of Navarre, have arrived in Orléans.

The little King, and his immediate court, have established themselves in the mansion of one Groslot, the richest man of Orléans, who is also chief justice of the law courts. And this room in which you stand is the King's chamber; next to it is the great hall.

When the Bourbon Princes enter, the Cardinal of Lorraine at once makes his intentions clear: he remains covered, though the King of Navarre stands bareheaded before him.

Francis, the little King of France, chides the Bourbons, and *not* the Guises; and Condé says:

'It is not the King so much as the Messieurs de Guise who now address us.'

'Adieu, Monsieur!' cries the little King, crimson with anger.

And when the Bourbon Princes, dismissed, seek to leave the royal presence, their exit is barred by officers of the Scottish guard.

Both brothers are conducted to prison — but not to the same prison.

To avoid being in Orléans when the Guises take Condé's

life, the little King insists on sailing down the Loire; but at
the moment of embarkation, a cold wind gives him so sharp
an earache that he is obliged to return to the Groslot palace
— which he is never to leave. An abscess in the head
causes him excruciating agony. Ambroise Paré, the famous
surgeon (whose statue is at Laval), says he can cure the
King by trepanning; he has three times performed this
operation successfully, and is confident that with it he can
save the life of the frail little King.

Think of the situation for Paré! He is a Huguenot. To
save the King, to prolong his life, is to assure the death of
Condé, the continued power of the Guises, the continued
persecution of Protestants. Yet Paré is too great a surgeon
and too pious a man to let any consideration but his duty
have weight with him.

'I shall save the King,' he declares, 'and God will save
France.' But even as he speaks, one of his servants comes
to tell him that the scaffold is being erected for Condé's
execution on the morrow.

Word of the young King's desperate condition has gone
abroad. I shall imagine that somehow or other you have
got into the Groslot mansion, and into the King's chamber.
It is hung with tapestry, the floor is covered with a carpet,
and the wood ceiling is painted with blue arabesques on a
gold ground. The torches scarcely illumine it, and you with
difficulty make out the vast four-post bedstead with its
silken curtains, and the little King, pale and shrunken, his
pinched white face scarcely showing on his not-whiter pillow. His young Queen sits close to that pillow, and near
her is her uncle, the Cardinal of Lorraine. Another in the
little group by the bedside is the King's mother.

Outside, in the great hall, several men of importance are
discussing all that's hanging in the balance. And as they
talk, a messenger arrives to tell that the great Constable

Anne de Montmorency is on the march to save Condé, his kinsman by marriage.

As the night wears on, the sufferer in the great bed sleeps; the young Queen prays; the Cardinal urges his brother, the Duke of Guise, to declare himself King of France.

In the morning, there is a great gathering in Groslot's house. Everybody knows the battle that is on.

Ambroise Paré, examining the King's head, says that if an operation is not performed immediately, the King will die.

'Cut the head of my son as though it were a plank?' Catherine cries. 'I will not permit it.'

'But, madame, if there is no other way to save him?' says Mary Stuart, weeping.

'You wish the death of your son,' says the Duke of Guise boldly.

Catherine appeals to the Chancellor to forbid Paré's operation.

Paré stretches his arm over the livid little King whose eyes are already sightless, and says, 'I claim to be sole master of this case; I shall operate.'

'Save him,' urges the Cardinal, 'and you shall be the richest man in France.'

'Go on!' cries the young Queen.

'I cannot prevent it,' says the Chancellor; 'but I shall record the protest of the Queen-mother.'

Then Guise calls the Secretary of State, appoints him Chancellor of France 'in the place of that traitor' (the great de l'Hôpital), and orders the latter's arrest. Then, 'Go on, Ambroise.'

But it was not to be. There are hasty steps in the great hall; a voice of command. The Constable of France has arrived, and he fears not to stay the surgeon's hand.

There are swift, furious words. And then ——!

'It is now too late,' the surgeon says; 'the suffusion of the brain has begun.'

'Your reign is over, gentlemen,' says Catherine to the Guises.

'Ah! madame,' screams the young widow, 'you have killed your own son!'

'And you,' Catherine answers her, unmoved, 'will go to reign in your Scotland. I am regent *de facto*.'

And, leading little Charles IX by the hand, she quits the house of death — leaving defeat and despair behind her, and rolling her first triumph like a sweet morsel under her tongue.

So engrossed is every one with the change in his own position and prospects that, three days after the King's death, his body still lies forgotten in Groslot's house.

I have taken a goodish bit of our hard-pressed space for this episode; because it seems to me not only intensely dramatic in itself, and interesting because of many of the personages concerned in it, but illuminative of much that you see in this section of France. At Blois, for instance, your attention will be fixed upon the murder of the Duke of Guise by command of Henry III; that Duke was the son of this one who struggled to preserve the life of little Francis II, and his assassination was by command of Francis II's brother. And when recalling Henry IV's fight for the throne, against the League and the Duke of Mayenne, you will (I think) find it made somehow more vivid to you by harking back to this deathbed scene; because Mayenne was the second son of this Guise who ordered Condé's arrest and the King of Navarre's; and Henry IV, whom he sought to displace from the throne of France, was son of that Antoine de Bourbon, King of Navarre, whose life would almost certainly have been taken, here at Orléans, could the life of little Francis II have been saved.

CATHERINE DE MÉDICIS AND HER LADIES VIEWING THE DEAD
AFTER ST. BARTHOLOMEW
By E. Debat-Ponsan

When you leave Orléans, by the route for Ormes, you have eighty-five miles to go before reaching Le Mans, but nothing that need detain you on the way. At Épuisay, nearly fifty miles west of Orléans, you 'pick up' Route 157, the highway from Blois to Le Mans.

If your 'Peggy' has anything at all equivalent to wings, she ought to cover the distance between Orléans and Le Mans quite comfortably in two and a half to three hours. And if you reach Le Mans by 4.30, I'm sure you'll be glad of every minute from then till nightfall.

Your hotel at Le Mans is probably the Hôtel de Paris et du Dauphin, on avenue Thiers; if you enter by rue Nationale, you will find avenue Thiers crossing it after you have passed the gardens of the Préfecture (on your right).

It may be, however, that, instead of going direct to your hotel, you will drive at once to the cathedral. For, whether you are avid of churches or not, this is the section of Le Mans that is sure to give you a thrill of some sort. My suggestion is that you keep straight on, through Place Thiers and across Place de la République, and still on, through rue du Cornet and across Place de l'Épernon. Then, to your right, into rue des Bouchers, and to your left, into the Grande-Rue. As you pass up this picturesque old street you have, on your right (at number 67) the beautiful house, more than four centuries old, called the 'House of Adam and Eve.' And after seeing this, turn to your right into the Place Saint-Pierre, where the Hôtel de Ville is, then across this Place into rue des Ponts-Neufs, and turn, left, into rue des Filles-Dieu. This will bring you to the west side of the Place des Jacobins, where stands something gleaming white and new which will make your pulse leap to a quicker beat! Landowsky's monument to Wilbur Wright.

I have many deep interests in Le Mans, for its beauties

and its associations; but here I choose, henceforth, to pay my first tribute. How that monument of the birdman, with aspiring arms upraised, may be regarded by critics of sculpture, I do not know. But if it be any part of the mission of sculpture (as I, probably benightedly, imagine it to be) to produce emotion, then this must be rated high among successful monuments.

It was in December, 1908, that Wilbur Wright made from Le Mans a flight of seventy-seven miles in eighty minutes. More than three years before this, he and his brother Orville (graduates of a bicycle-repair shop, like Henry Ford) had flown more than twenty-four miles, near their home town of Dayton, Ohio, at a speed of thirty-eight miles an hour; but in spite of this demonstration of the practicability of flight in heavier-than-air machines, they could enlist no government nor private financial support in America. So, in 1908, Wilbur went to France. On September 21st, he won the Michelin prize, by a flight of fifty-six miles. (On the field of his first French flights, seven miles from here, in the direction of Paris, is another monument to him, erected by the French Aero Club.) Wilbur Wright died in 1912, at the age of forty-five. He lived to see aviation recognized as a science instead of an insanity; but not to know anything of the tremendous part it played in the Great War. To his gallant persistence we pay our homage; and to France's encouragement of his genius we render our gratitude profound. The links that bind France and America in the short history of aviation are many, and notable, and it was supremely fitting that their strength should manifest itself in the French rejoicing over Lindbergh's triumph.

From this Place des Jacobins you get also the most superb view of the cathedral. If your zest for cathedrals is not great, you may feel that you have got the greatest glory of this one when you have looked up at its superb apse soaring above this square so splendidly one does not need excessive imaginativeness to feel that these flying buttresses all but flap their wings.

But if you are even in a small degree a lover of architecture, I think you ought not to miss a closer acquaintance with Le Mans Cathedral, whose choir 'ranks with the most sublime works of French genius, and is as inspiring as Amiens, as perfect as Reims, and as "religious" as Paris.'

Some of the finest old stained glass in France is in the nave; there are at least two tombs of great interest; some of the magnificent tapestries may be on view. There are many reasons for pursuing your acquaintance with Le Mans Cathedral. The enthusiastic history-lover would consider an hour in this edifice, especially in the nave, one of the high privileges of a journey overseas. He would certainly whisk himself back, nearly eight centuries, to a christening there, at which a lusty infant probably kicked and squalled when christened Henry for his grandfather, the King of England. I suppose Geoffrey of Anjou was present at the font. And I wonder if he believed then, or at any time, that this youngster was his son. (The baby's mother was she who had been Empress Matilda of Germany and had tried to be Queen Maude of England on the death of her father, King Henry I, William the Conqueror's youngest son.) Whether 'Grandpa' Henry was at the christening or not, I do not know; but he certainly came over for some of the feasts and rejoicings in connection with it; and before he came, he summoned what proved to be his last Parliament, to take the oath of fealty to this baby son of his daughter and heiress. What he guessed, or knew, of the paternity of little Henry is a mystery. Not the gossips, only, but the respected chroniclers of the time as well, declared that Matilda's baby was not the son of her second husband, whom she despised and had married against her will, but of her cousin Stephen, even then engaged in his plotting to steal her throne. However, here in this Romanesque nave is your earliest chance to meet him who is to be Henry II of England, on whose trail you will find yourself 'camping' pretty much all over France. This native city of his became part of the dower of his daughter-in-law, Berengaria of Navarre, who lived here and near here for many years of her long widowhood. It was she who got from Philippe-Auguste permission to order parts of the ramparts torn down to make room for the building of this glorious Gothic choir.

When I was a very young person, I 'set out' to write a history of Berengaria. Goodness knows *why* — there being no one of whom I knew less. But I distinctly remember that I began it, and that discouragement soon settled down upon the task. There is, indeed, very little to be said about the good lady — Queen of England who was never *in* England — and the only reason I can think of why I should have singled her out for my first effort at biography is that she was the wife of the Lion-Hearted Richard, shared his Crusade, and probably wept at his captivity. However, I've always been glad that I made that childish attempt; it has given me (though it went no further than a few faltering paragraphs) a very folksy, proprietary feeling for Berengaria. And when I stand beside her tomb in the south transept of Le Mans Cathedral (whither it was removed in 1672 from the near-by Abbey of Espan, of which she was the foundress), I feel as if I were paying my respects to the remains of one who holds no secrets from me!

The Charles of Anjou, Duke of Maine, whose fine tomb is in the choir, was a brother of René of Anjou, the troubadour king, and brother-in-law to Charles VII; he died childless, and left Maine to the French Crown, then worn by his nephew, Louis XI.

When you leave the cathedral by the fine old Romanesque door of the west front, and step into the Place du Château, you are in the heart of the old Le Mans that Matilda knew and where her red-headed, freckled, peppery youngster got some of his first impressions of the world on whose stage he was to play so energetic a part.

This part of town is rich in picturesque old houses, and somewhere hereabouts there's said to be (I've never seen it) a fragment of the third-century Roman wall. If you get that far back in your explorations, you'll probably like to know that Le Mans has some historians who claim there was a bishopric here immediately after bishoprics began to be, and that it was visited by Saint Peter's immediate successor. The present bishop lives in the sixteenth-century house opposite the west front of the cathedral.

And though Berengaria never saw the late-fifteenth-century house at number 11 Grande-Rue which is called her house, it is almost certain that her dower-house stood on that spot. If you are interested in furniture, I hope you'll go into this house and see the reproduction of an old-time living-room.

Your way to your hotel will doubtless take you past the ancient Church of La Couture, whose beautiful porch is a work of the same period as the choir of the cathedral.

II

When you leave Le Mans, in the morning, take the Angers route (number 23) as far as Arnage, and there leave the main road for a smaller, running more directly south, to Le Lude, whose superb castle I think you should see, as it is one of the most 'satisfying' of all the French châteaux. Founded in the late fifteenth century by Jean de Daillon (whom we meet so often in Philippe de Comines' fascinating pages; he was one of Louis XI's ministers), it has some

of the features of what the French called the 'château-fort,'
or fortified dwelling, and many of the features of the François Premier palaces of three reigns later; and then — as we
half-complete the circuit of it — we get a whole façade
which might have been done for Marie-Antoinette. The
structure and grounds are superbly maintained; and so
gracious is the owner that I am almost sure you will be permitted to wander, ecstatic, on his terraces and in his grounds,
and may even be bidden within, to see some of the treasures which have been accumulating there for four and a
half centuries. I think you will feel that this is the ideal
'setting' for a hundred of your favorite romances, and will
find yourself investing them with it henceforth. The delightful little Loir (which must not be confounded with
the statelier Loire) runs through the private park of Le
Lude for over a mile, on its winding, wandering way down
from near Chartres to join the big Loire at Angers.

In the early days of Louis XIV the châtelaine of Le Lude
was an ardent huntress who cared not at all for court and
everything for the chase to which she rode with a black
wolf-hound the King had given her. She was an energetic
ruler, here in her domain which her husband seldom visited,
and noted for her chastisements of those who assailed the
virtue of women on her estate. Even after her death — so
the story runs — she came riding back, her hound baying,
her horses' hoofbeats clattering, whenever the virtue of any
lady of Le Lude was in jeopardy.

Le Lude is twenty-five miles from Le Mans. There is a
small road from Le Lude to Baugé (fifteen miles) and from
Baugé you continue to Corné and thence into Angers, com-
pleting a morning's run of about sixty-five miles which
(with only one stop) should bring you to Angers in time for
an early luncheon, which you may like to take in Hôtel
d'Anjou, on boulevard de Saumur (the friendly hospitality

of whose proprietors I cannot overpraise), or you may have heard (as I have) the charms of Hostellerie du Cheval-Blanc so sung that you feel you must go there; it is on rue Saint-Aubin, very near to the cathedral.

Coming in from Corné by rue de la Revellière, continue on the latter till it runs into rue Pasteur; then, at the Palais de Justice, turn along the Champ de Mars, on the boulevard du Palais, and down boulevard Bessonneau to the Place Lorraine, where you will find Hôtel d'Anjou, in a fine old mansion of Angers. If it is the Cheval-Blanc you seek, continue down boulevard de Saumur, past Hôtel d'Anjou, to rue Saint-Aubin, pass the Préfecture — and there you are! close to the Tour Saint-Aubin, belonging to the ancient abbey of that name.

Either before lunch or after, you must visit the Préfecture, which occupies the abbey buildings, part of them as old as 1150 or thereabouts.

The cathedral has very fine stained glass and some of the most valuable and beautiful tapestries in Europe; and there are others scarcely less notable in the Salle Synodale, above the chapel of what used to be the bishop's palace, next door. This Hall of the Synod is one of the few remaining examples of twelfth-century architecture except those in churches and abbeys.

The musée (a very good one) occupies a mansion built in the fifteenth century by the then Mayor of Angers; and beside it (in rue Toussaint, which leads south from the apse of the cathedral) are the exquisite ruins of the thirteenth-century church of Toussaint which you must on no account miss seeing. Close by is a statue of King René; and frowning down upon you are the walls of the castle in which he was born, built about 1230, with their seventeen cylindrical towers. You may walk around the ramparts if you wish; there is little inside the castle to reward a visit.

Drive along the quai beside the castle to the Pont-Ver-dun, and cross the Mayenne (or Maine). If you are inter-ested in the teaching of Arts and Crafts, you will wish to visit the National School for such, on the other side of the river. And even if you do not care for it as a school, you can scarcely be uninterested in the buildings, which were once the Abbey of Ronceray, dating in part from the eleventh century. Near them, and now housing the Archæolog-ical Museum, is the old Hôpital Saint-Jean founded by Henry II of England.

Angers is, I think, a city of many charms, and one feels that people who live there get a great deal of quiet, sub-stantial enjoyment out of their surroundings.

When you must leave it, take the boulevards on the west bank of the river, to Place Monprofit, and there take rue Saint-Jacques for Ancenis and Nantes.

About twenty miles from Angers, on your direct route to Nantes, is Champtocé, where Bluebeard's Castle is — or, at least, one of several that he had.

Gilles de Laval, Lord of Retz, and connected with some of the noblest families in Brittany, was 'a handsome youth, lithe and of fascinating address, courageous, and learned as any clerk,' when his father's death, about 1424, left him lord of many princely domains and what, for those times, was almost unlimited power and wealth. He married Cath-erine de Thouars, with whom he had a great dowry; and at this Castle of Champtocé they dwelt in almost royal state. Gilles fought gallantly under Jeanne d'Arc at the siege of Orléans, and is credited with having been the only one of her former companions-in-arms who made an effort to save her from her fate. He became Marshal of France, and his magnificence exceeded, in some respects, that of the King himself. Five hundred persons were fed every day at this castle of his. His chapel was a marvel of splendor and was served by a large body of ecclesiastics. He loved pageantry of every sort; and he spent so prodigally that even his vast means began to dwindle, and he turned to alchemy, hoping to make gold.

He sent emissaries into Italy, Spain, and Germany to invite the most celebrated alchemists to this Castle of Champtocé; and from among them he selected two, for whom he built a magnificent laboratory. Much gold was required by these persons, but none was produced. And when Gilles complained, they told him that only the Evil One could tell him how to transmute base metals into gold. A rendezvous was arranged, in which the Devil disclosed to one of the alchemists that certain herbs growing in Africa were needed. Gilles furnished the means to fetch them — and never heard of *that* alchemist more! Then the other one told Gilles that the Devil demanded a human sacrifice — that of a young child. This was done; and when gold was still not forthcoming, another child was sacrificed, and another, until nearly a hundred had been murdered. Then the Duke of Brittany, appealed to, ordered Gilles and this fiendish accomplice, Prelati of Padua, arrested and placed on trial. They were found guilty, and then confessed. At Nantes you shall see where they expiated their horrible crimes.

On bright moonlight nights ('tis said) the hideous, half-burnt body of Gilles, circled with flames, is seen 'now on one topmost point of craggy wall, and now on another, and is heard mingling his moan with the sough of the night-wind,' while pale shapes of youthful mien flit across the space enclosed by the ruined walls.

The story of Gilles, who wore a blue-black beard, seems to have mingled with the old Oriental tale; and so, too, has another Breton tragedy called 'Comorre the Cursed.' Comorre had a habit of murdering wives.

Years ago, when I was first in Champtocé, I met a most

engaging small kitten, with whom I had my picture taken. And when it became my delight, some time after that, to tell nursery tales and hist'ry tales to ladies of tender years but lusty appetites for "'tories,' I cannot measure how my prestige with these ladies was increased by my acquaintance (photo produced in evidence!) with Bluebeard's kitten-cat.

Let me urge you to acquaint yourself well with Champtocé; it may give you, too, an enormous advantage with some one you'd dearly love to impress. Take a picture of the castle, or have one taken of you standing beneath its ruins. And enlist a kitten for the moment, if you can!

There was a time when I had, on request, to 'tell Bluebeard, but leave those *died* ladies out.' I did it — several hundred times, I think; and then I was instructed: 'You can put the died ladies in now; they don't scare me any more.' And — will you believe it? — the version I'd been telling was so much more satisfactory that we never again could raise a relish for those relicts hanging by their hair. They were tame, in comparison — although in *my* version nobody died.

And now you continue on your way to Nantes, some thirty-six miles from Champtocé.

Your hotel at Nantes is probably Hôtel de France, on Place Graslin, to reach which you must pass the cathedral and the castle, the two principal things in Nantes which you have come to see. So, unless you are one of those travellers who prefer 'getting settled' and 'freshening up' to seeing things while they are 'see-able,' I suggest that when you are passing the cathedral, you stop; and then that you see the castle before you put the car in the hotel garage. If you have left Angers by two o'clock, you should easily reach Nantes by four.

When you reach Place Louis XV, look down Cours Saint-Pierre toward the river; then cross it, and keep straight

on to Place Saint-Pierre, in front of the cathedral. The
Porte Saint-Pierre, here, stands on the foundations of the
Gallo-Roman town walls, and beside it are some remains
of the old baptistery which dates from the sixth century.

I doubt if the cathedral will hold you long. What you
have come to see is the very famous tomb of Francis II, the
last Duke of Brittany, and his second wife, Margaret de
Foix. This was ordered by their daughter, the celebrated
Duchess Anne who was twice Queen of France — first as
wife of Charles VIII and then as wife of Louis XII. (Her
successor as Queen to Louis XII was the sprightly Mary
Tudor of 'When Knighthood was in Flower.')

We shall further recall Anne at the castle. Here, it seems
to me, we may best pay our respects to a work of art which
is not only of very great beauty, but of great importance as
one of the first masterpieces of the Renaissance in France.
It is the work of Michel Colombe, about whom we know too
little except that he was of Touraine and that, though he
was full of the spirit of the Renaissance as Italy knew it, he
expressed it in a characteristically French manner. The
four fine allegorical statues at the angles of this tomb, representing Justice (Anne's portrait), Strength, Temperance,
and Prudence (with two heads), started a new style in monumental sculpture — began the replacing of Gothic religious themes with classic forms and classic virtues.

From the cathedral, turn down rue Mathelin-Rodier
(named for the cathedral's first architect) to the castle,
which, though founded in the tenth century, was rebuilt in
the fifteenth century by that Duke whose tomb we have
just visited, and who was destined to be the last Duke of
Brittany. Of the older castle, where Gilles de Retz was imprisoned, tried, and executed (boiled in oil, some accounts
say; others say burned after having been hanged), little remains; but the especially kind and courteous custodian who

acts as guide to visitors will show you the spot whereon
Gilles is believed to have met his more-than-merited fate.
That was a quarter of a century before Duke Francis II be-
gan the rebuilding of the château.

Little Duchess Anne made her advent into a world,
wherein she was destined to see much history made, in
1477, when the young Duchess of Burgundy had just acceded to the vast domains of her over-ambitious father,
Charles the Bold. So many trials and troubles had this
'poor little rich girl' of Burgundy, in the years when Anne
of Brittany was toddling about here with like prospects, that
I think I see Duke Francis shake his head, many a time,
wondering how things are going to turn out if *she* has to
take her chances against Louis XI.

Anne was but eleven when her father died; but Louis XI
had been succeeded by his son, Charles VIII, who coveted
Brittany and thought the easiest way to get it was to marry
it; which he did, when the little Duchess was fourteen. You
shall attend their wedding, at Langeais, when we go to the
Touraine châteaux; you shall see Anne widowed, at Amboise; and recall her death, at Blois, when she was only
thirty-seven.

After Anne, the next personage you'll doubtless wish to
meet at Nantes is Henry IV; to see him here, signing the
Edict of Nantes (which his grandson, Louis XIV, revoked)
about which we hear so much in history. That edict practically put an end to the devastating Religious Wars. Perhaps you would like to be reminded of 'what was in it.' It
laid down, emphatically, that Catholicism was the established and general religion of France, but that the
reformed religion should enjoy certain liberties in certain
places — about seventy-five specified towns where it was
so entrenched that to forbid it there meant to prolong the
civil strife of which Henry was so weary. All vassals of the

Crown might worship in private according to the reformed rites (but not more than thirty persons to a congregation) and the greater vassals could worship publicly.

As citizens, Protestants were admitted to all offices, honors, and appointments on equal terms with Catholics. But the reformed religion was forbidden in Paris and within five leagues thereof.

In the Château of Josselin you shall see the table on which Henry signed the Edict; and here in the Château of Nantes the guide will indicate where the signing was done. Fifty years before that signing, John Knox was a galley-slave at Nantes, having been taken prisoner by the French when they besieged Saint Andrew's Castle where the murderers of Cardinal Beaton had settled themselves after having 'settled' him.

The castle has often served as a prison for persons of note. The Cardinal de Retz, that lively intriguer with the Duchesse de Chevreuse and against Mazarin, escaped from here in 1654. Fouquet, the too-magnificent finance minister of young Louis XIV, was brought here after his sensational trial for looting the King's treasury. And in 1832 this castle was the prison of the Duchesse de Berri, daughter-in-law of Charles X, who was leading in favor of her young son an insurrection against Louis-Philippe. Number 3 in that rue Mathelin-Rodier, which runs from the cathedral to the château, is the house where the Duchess lived for five months and was smoked out of her hiding-place behind a fireback in an attic chamber.

She was a daughter of the King of Naples, was married to the Duc de Berri when she was eighteen, and widowed four years later when her husband was assassinated as he was leaving the Paris opera with her. (It was located then where the Square Louvois is, alongside the Bibliothèque Nationale.) Seven months after his death, the Duchess

gave birth to a son who is known in history as the Comté de
Chambord and whom you shall recall at the vast Château
de Chambord. She went into exile with her father-in-law
when he abdicated (at Rambouillet) in July, 1830; but soon
went to Italy where she contracted a secret marriage with
an Italian count. A daughter of this union was born in this
house at Nantes; and when the marriage became known,
she lost the sympathies of her supporters; so the Government of Louis-Philippe released her. She went to Sicily and
never again emerged from obscurity. Her death, in April,
1870, was just in time to save her from knowledge of her
son's failure to secure the Bourbon crown, after Sedan, as
Henry V. At Chambord, we'll remind ourselves *why* he
failed.

When you leave the château (by rue du Château) go
through the Place du Pilori and rue de la Marne; then keep
straight on, through Place Royale and rue Crébillon to
Place Graslin, where your hotel (de France) is — a fine old
house that dispensed a time-mellowed hospitality when
Longfellow rolled up to it in a diligence a century ago.

Do you recall his descriptions (in 'Outre-Mer') of those
diligences? — 'Ponderous vehicles which totter slowly along
the paved roads of France, laboring beneath a mountain of trunks and bales of all descriptions; and, like the
Trojan horse, bearing a groaning multitude within.' 'The
diligence stopped only to change horses, and for the travellers to take their meals; and by night I slept with my head
under my wing in a snug corner of the coach.'

This hostelry was here when the Revolution unleashed its
terrors at Nantes; and of those who were among its first
patrons and went hence across the square to the theatre,
there must have been many who were drowned in the Loire
in those 'Republican marriages' whose victims, stripped
and bound two and two, were crowded onto barges that
were pushed out into the stream and scuttled.

But this is a grewsome suggestion, when you are about to enjoy the dignity and comfort of this fine old hotel, and one of its excellent dinners.

I don't know what you'll do with yourself in the evening. You may wish to attend a performance at the handsome theatre (built in 1788) across the square from your hotel. You may wish to walk north in rue Franklin (practically alongside your hotel, and named for our very own Benjamin) to rue Scribe where the Cinéma-Palace is, and an American film is probably showing, and you can reflect on American life as presented to all-the-world-and-his-wife via Hollywood. Our books they know nothing of; our travellers seldom know enough of any other language than our own to make themselves understood. Our principal self-revelation, in the universal tongue of moving pictures, is made for us by the folk of the studios and the silver screen. One of the things we may well be about, in foreign countries, is seeing how they interpret us.

Nantes has an exceptionally fine Museum of Fine Arts and a fine Museum of Natural History.

If neither of these tempt you, perhaps the Musée Dobrée will. It is housed partly in a fifteenth-century manor-house which belonged to Duke John V, and partly in an adjoining modern mansion built in twelfth-century style. There you may see tapestries, old Breton furniture, and the like.

III

When you leave Nantes, you may feel that you want to press on to Vannes, which is about sixty-eight miles, by the direct route, number 165. But if you do, you'll miss several things worth going far to see.

I'd turn off that route at la Moëre, some twenty miles from Nantes, and go through Savenay to Saint-Nazaire.

I have a feeling (which I urge on no one else) that one does well to pass through Saint-Nazaire, if only to realize in what drear, dispiriting surroundings tens of thousands of our soldiers were set down from crowded transports when they went overseas to make the world safe to live in. But there's another reason, now, for going there; and that is Mrs. Gertrude Vanderbilt Whitney's monument to those young Crusaders, dedicated in June, 1926. With what seems to me undeniable inspiration she has put a thrill into that slender young figure, alighting on outspread eagle pinions, which I (for one) will always go far to feel. There is scarce-suspended motion in those extended wings; there is intense energy in the doughboy's figure — he is going to leap lightly from that eagle's back to the soil of beleaguered France; there is consecration in the young face beneath the tin helmet, and in the grasp of the sword whose hilt is exaggerated to accentuate the symbol of the Cross. The monument stands on a rock a few feet from shore. When I saw it, the ocean was intensely blue, and flecked with sunshine gold in all the little ripples that broke about the base of that upstanding rock. We said it was the dazzling light that made us blink — but it wasn't! For each of us, he's the One We Knew Best of All; and I think each of us must feel that exquisite justice has been done to him.

Just beyond him, as we follow the lovely curving shore, we come to Pornichet, a fashionable little seaside place with many pretty villas set in pines; and La Baule, which isn't as attractive as it used to be before it had a 'boom,' though the beach is still superb; and then, unless we are bent upon seeing Le Croisic because Browning wrote about its 'Two Poets,' or because it sent 'Captains Courageous' to fish off the Banks of Newfoundland very, very long ago, we'll turn north, at a road beyond Le Pouliguen, toward Guérande.

'Croisic, the spit of sandy rock which juts
    Spitefully northward, bears nor tree nor shrub
To tempt the ocean.'

But Browning got two poems there. And he said:

'Anywhere serves: for point me out the place
    Wherever man has made himself a home,
And there I find the story of our race
    In little, just at Croisic as at Rome.'

The first of the two poems he got here was 'Hervé Riel,'
printed in the 'Cornhill Magazine' for March, 1871. He
was paid one hundred pounds for it, and gave the money
to the people of Paris suffering through the Franco-Prussian War.

All hereabouts are the great salt-marshes, nearly four
thousand acres of them, worked by people who form a sort
of race apart from the sardine-fishers of Le Croisic and
other neighbors.

Less than four miles from La Baule is Guérande, still
preserving its early fifteenth-century walls, with ten towers
and four gates facing the four points of the compass — a
lovely old town worth (in my opinion) going a very long
way to see. Drive slowly through the town; visit the Church
of Saint-Aubin, if you like; and be sure to 'circumnavigate'
the walls on the outside.

From Guérande your way leads on to La Roche-Bernard,
where you 'pick up' Route 165, and thence to Vannes
which is believed to have given its name to Venice. At any
rate, Vannes was the stronghold of the great seafaring
tribe, the Veneti, which offered stubborn resistance to
Julius Cæsar and was subdued for him in 56 B.C. by Decius
Brutus, that one of his assassins who went to his house and
persuaded him to go to the Senate when Calpurnia's fears
had all but induced him to stay at home. The Veneti used
flat-bottomed boats which were like floating castles, for the

protection of their fighting men. But Cæsar had boats built for his men, too. And when the Veneti were beaten, their senators were put to death and thousands of the simpler folk were sold into slavery.

Centuries later, when the Roman power was dwindling all through the Western Empire, and the barbarians were swarming, great numbers of people from Britain came over here, found kindred Celts, settled among them; and as the island which had been called 'Britain' began to be called the 'Angle's Land,' or 'England,' this peninsula, which had been called 'Armorica,' began to be known as 'Brittany.'

Had you gone along the left bank of the Loire, from Nantes, and then south to Pornic, you would have seen what Dr. Herbert Adams Gibbons, that ardent lover of France and writer about her, calls 'the oldest port' among the many he describes in his 'Ports of France.' 'Nowhere else in France right by the sea,' this book says, 'will you see houses of the nineteenth and twentieth century after Christ built on foundations actually made by men who lived several millenniums before the bronze age.'

But, attractive as Pornic is, we have not been able to include it in this little journey. So you may (although Dr. Gibbons says 'since the beginning of history there has been a Nantes') indulge your love of antiquity at Vannes, the threshold of those prehistoric puzzlers, 'the Great Stones' of Carnac and vicinity. Nantes may be even more ancient; but other and later phases of her story absorb us to the exclusion of the primitive.

The hotel I know at Vannes is the Hostellerie du Dauphin in the Place de l'Hôtel de Ville, and my experience of it has been delightful. If the young couple who were responsible for its attractiveness in 1926 have not betaken themselves elsewhere, I'm sure you'll like it too. But inns do change with changing managements! For instance, in

Elizabeth Shackleton's book, 'Touring Through France,'
published in 1925, and descriptive of experiences I take to
have been of very recent date, she speaks of turning hungry
away from Vitré because of its 'forbidding frowsy inn.'
Could it have been the same Hôtel des Voyageurs whose
spotless shining chambers and highly delectable food make
me think of it as a place where I should love to make a sojourn? Quite probably! I was told in Vannes that the
Dauphin had not long been such as I found it. And with
that capable management removed, it might easily lapse.
However, the same is true of most places whose charm and
satisfactoriness depend on the varying human element. I
can promise you nothing. I can only tell you what I've
found. There is also, at Vannes, the Hôtel du Commerce
et de l'Épee which is usually ranked above the Dauphin;
but as to their relative merits I cannot report.

I think that, coming in from Nantes, you'll find yourself
in the avenue de Verdun leading into rue du Roulage. Keep
on, past the Préfecture with its fine park to the Porte-
Prison, an early fifteenth-century tower gateway of the
old fourteenth-century walls. The picture made by these
fortifications, along the brook (Ruisseau de Rohan) wherein
Vannes does much of its washing, is one of those that you
must not let your camera miss; and as morning light is
essential to it, perhaps you would best do it now.

Your Hôtel du Dauphin (if you choose that one) is most
easily reached by the rue du Mené, on your right, from the
Porte-Prison. For that matter, this is also the route to the
other hotel, the de l'Épée; both are on the Place de l'Hôtel
de Ville, in the centre of which is a dashing equestrian
statue of the Constable Arthur de Richemont, who shares
with Francis II of Brittany and his duchess that splendid
tomb at Nantes.

When you have settled yourself in your room, if it over-

looks the square (as mine did), and if you are ready for
luncheon a little before it is ready for you, you may like to
look out at the Constable and say 'Howdy-do' to him. If
he takes a fancy to you, he may invite you to be his guest
at night, for a stroll in the Vannes he knew. And if he does,
I hope you'll hasten to accept.

For your hours before dinner, there is much to choose
from. Vannes has one of the greatest collections of prehistoric remains in all Europe, housed in the fine old fifteenth-century building where the parliament of Brittany
used to meet in the days of little Duchess Anne, and before; to reach it, follow avenue Thiers, running south from
the Place de l'Hôtel de Ville to the Place de la République,
and turn to your left, to rue Noë.

There is also a small museum of Breton furniture, which
you may not want to miss; it is at number 10 rue Lecage,
behind the Hôtel de Ville.

But the environs of Vannes must not on any account be
missed; and I advise you to be off betimes for them, unless you are stopping over in Vannes for another day.

The tidal water, or inland sea, or 'broads,' called the
Morbihan, lies immediately south of Vannes; it was here,
historians think, that the Romans won their decisive naval
victory over the Veneti, who may have found a last refuge
in the island now known as the Île aux Moines. You might
like to take a steamer at Vannes and sail to the inlet of this
gulf, stopping at the Île aux Moines and passing the Île de
Gavr' Inis, or Goats' Island, where there is a famous Celtic
burial chamber which antiquarians will find most interesting.

Another possibility for your afternoon is the shore ride
from Vannes to Sarzeau and the ruins of Sucinio Castle
where your Constable de Richemont was born and where
his nephew (who was Duchess Anne's father) held prisoner

for some years that Henry of Richmond who was to become
Henry VII of England. Three miles beyond Sarzeau is
Saint-Gildas-de-Rhuis of whose abbey Abélard was once
head. He was a Breton by birth, but by education had
become almost a stranger to these parts when the Duke of
Brittany brought him here, away from the persecution of
his enemies at Paris. But the great scholar was not hap-
pier here than there.

'I inhabit,' he wrote to his beloved Héloïse whom he had
left at the Paraclete, the abbey he had founded near Troyes,
'a barbarous country where the language is unknown to me.
I have no dealings with the ferocious inhabitants. I walk
the inaccessible borders of the stormy sea, and my monks
have no other rule than their own. I wish you could see my
dwelling. You would not believe it an abbey. The doors
are ornamented only with the feet of deer, of wolves and
bears, boars, and the hideous skins of owls. I find each day
new perils. I expect at every moment to see a sword suspended over my head.'

But the trip you will probably prefer to any other is that
to Auray, Carnac, and Quiberon.

It is twelve miles on the main road (Route 165) from
Vannes to Auray, where the famous battle of Auray was
fought in 1364, with Olivier de Clisson and Bertrand du
Guesclin among the warriors. King Arthur is believed to
have built a castle at Auray. But these, and other claims
that Auray has on our recognition, have been overshadowed
for most people, by the fame of Sainte-Anne-d'Auray, two
miles away, the scene of the greatest of the Breton pardons.

A pardon is really, Anatole le Braz reminds us in his fine
book, 'The Land of Pardons,' a survival of the ancient
'Feasts of the Dead'; 'and nowhere else will you find anything so deliciously obsolete; they have remained un-
changed for over two hundred years.'

Usually a pardon has three phases: the eve; the religious ceremony; and the merrymaking. The eve is devoted to confession and prayer, the pilgrims flocking in from every direction. They come bareheaded, barefooted, and usually fasting, followed by crowds of the lame, the halt, and the blind. There is a sermon, drinking at the holy well or other miraculous source, and a torchlight procession. Next day there is the ceremony which is the distinctive feature of that special pardon — the blessing of the sea, of the boats, of the cattle, or whatever it may be — followed by the procession wherein every one wears the rich, picturesque costumes that have been handed down for generations and are kept stored in old carved chests, except on such occasions as these. And in the afternoon there is a fair, followed by dancing and drinking and courting.

Sainte Anne, mother of the Virgin, being the special patron saint of Brittany, this pardon of Sainte Anne-d'Auray is perhaps the most popular of all. It occurs in March (about the 7th) and on May 23d or thereabouts, and on July 25th.

Sainte Anne is believed to have appeared here in 1623 to a peasant, and told him that a chapel had stood here more than nine hundred years before. She commanded him to build another. This was the beginning of what has grown into a great manifestation of faith. There is a fountain whose waters are believed to cure weak eyesight; and after pilgrims have washed their eyes in a basin of water from that fountain, they ascend an imitation Scala Sancta on their knees.

At Carnac, whither you are bound, the pardon is held the second Sunday in September, and is preceded by a horse and cattle fair, and the animals are taken to the church to be blessed. This is because Saint Cornelius, the patron saint of Carnac, is the patron saint of horned cattle; when a

MENHIR NEAR BREST
From an etching published in 1840

bullock, for instance, falls sick, his owner hangs up in the stable an image of Saint Cornelius, until the animal recovers.

Cornelius, an early missionary to Brittany, was fleeing from his pagan pursuers one day, trusting to find here a boat in which to escape death. No boat being at hand, he looked back and turned his pursuers into stones.

That is one explanation of the 2800 menhirs of these Carnac alignments, two and a half miles of hoary, lichen-stained stones whose origin and purpose baffle all scholarship. It may come as near the truth as any of the other explanations. What seems most probable among them is that when a chief died here, in prehistoric times, the families of his tribe set up an avenue of monoliths in a direct line with his tomb.

This whole region bristles with these strange stones; others as strange are the dolmens, or table stones, the greatest of which are found at Locmariaquer, a little port at the inlet of the Gulf of Morbihan — seven and a half miles from Carnac.

If children flock around you at Carnac offering to guide you to the Great Stones, I hope you will accept the services of as many as your running-board will hold. They have a long, strange 'chant' about the stones, taught them by either the village priest or the curator of the Musée Miln (the archæological collection, near the church), which they intone or drone in a manner that makes their Druid ancestors seem not so very far away.

I incline to think that travellers who are not archæologists may be satisfied with Carnac for the mysterious stones, and glad to go thence straight down the narrow peninsula to Quiberon at its tip. That is, if they want a fine 'dip' in the sea. Otherwise, I should not cover those twenty miles, down and back to Carnac, but would return earlier to Vannes. If you go to Quiberon, look over toward Belle-Île, some eight miles south, where Dumas laid some of the scenes of 'The Vicomte de Bragelonne,' that stirring sequel to 'The Three Musketeers,' and where he brought Porthos to his death in the caves of Locmaria. Fouquet, builder of Vaux, owned this island at the time of his downfall, and his château is still to be seen there. There, too, Sarah Bernhardt had her summer home for many years.

As you return to Vannes, perhaps you'd like to 'brush up' on Arthur de Richemont and his times. And if you're going to make a favorable impression on him to-night when he takes you sight-seeing, I think you ought to 'dust off' your Breton history back to the days when the Duke of Brittany called in Henry II of England to help him hold his own against his rebellious nobles.

Henry was willing to do this for a price; and the price was the hand of the Duke's daughter and heiress, for Henry's son Geoffrey. The son of this union was that pathetic Arthur who should have been England's king after his Lion-Hearted uncle, and who was murdered at Rouen by his uncle John. Then Philippe-Auguste took Normandy away from the Plantagenets, you'll remember, and married the murdered young Duke of Brittany's sister to one of the Counts of Dreux, who became Duke of Brittany and founded the line which finished with Duchess Anne; though in the middle of the fourteenth century there was a bitter war of succession between rival heirs. One of these heirs was the half-brother of the recently deceased Duke John of Montfort, his mother having been the heiress of the Montforts; his son, betrothed to a daughter of Edward III of England, had been educated with Edward's sons — the Black Prince, John of Gaunt, and the others. The other heir was the late Duke's niece, married to a nephew of the French King. The English helped their claimant, and the French helped theirs. The war is known as the War of the

Two Joans, because the French King's niece was named Joan and so was the wife of Montfort. The battle of Auray, in 1364, decided the issue. The French King's nephew (Charles of Blois) was slain, and the great Du Guesclin was taken prisoner. The other Joan's son, John, was recognized as Duke of Brittany, his father having long been a prisoner of the other Joan and, dying, left the struggle to his wife and son.

This son John of the victorious Joan married Mary, the Black Prince's sister; and then married Jane Holland, the Black Prince's stepdaughter. And when he had buried his second wife and was looking for a third, there were many who, to prevent his making a third English marriage whilst France was in the throes of the Hundred Years' War with England, urged upon him a young Princess of Navarre who was a granddaughter of King John of France and a great-granddaughter of King Louis X, and might be expected to be safe from English influence. (As a matter of fact, she was destined to become Queen of England — the Queen of Henry IV!)

She was young when she was wed to the Duke of Brittany, and he was old; but she brought him a fine family, of which your friend Arthur de Richemont was the third son, born at Sucinio in 1393. The earldom of Richmond in North England was given by Richard II of England to Jane of Brittany, Arthur's aunt; and, descending to Arthur's older brother, was by him given to Arthur.

Arthur was a close friend of Louis the Dauphin who, had he lived, would have become Louis XI of France, but he died, and Arthur married his widow. Arthur was captured at Agincourt and was a prisoner in England for five years. When he was taken there, he saw his mother, the Queen-Dowager of England, for the first time in twelve years. Joanna was so eager to know if he would recognize her that she placed one of her ladies in the chair of state and took her own station among the attendants. Arthur did *not* know that the lady-in-waiting was not his mother; and Joanna could not endure the deception.

'Unhappy son, do you not know me?' she exclaimed. And she and Arthur 'burst into tears.'

After this interview, Joanna's stepson, Henry V, prevented all communication between her and the captive against whom he was specially bitter; because Arthur, as Earl of Richmond, had fought against his liege. Arthur was confined first in the Tower of London, and later in Fotheringay Castle, where, long afterwards, Mary, Queen of Scots, was to die.

While he was there, his mother was arrested, charged with witchcraft and by sorcery seeking to destroy the King; and was consigned to years of solitary confinement.

In spite of this, Arthur seems to have decided that the thing for him to do, on his release, was to 'stand in' as well as he could with his liege, the English sovereign, Henry V, who was carrying all before him. So he cast in his lot with his erstwhile captors. But he was dissatisfied, after Henry's death, with what the Regent Bedford did for him in the matter of a military command to fight against the French; so he decided to fight *with* the French against the English. He joined Jeanne d'Arc at Orléans; it was through his influence that his brother-in-law, the Duke of Burgundy, deserted the English cause and signed a treaty with Charles VII, thereby saving France; it was he who took Paris from the English; it was he who recovered for France, from England, the whole of Normandy.

For fifteen months, he was Duke of Brittany, succeeding one of his nephews, and succeeded by another who was to become father of little Duchess Anne.

After you have dined, I hope you'll cross the square in

front of Arthur's statue, and follow the rue de Mené as far
as rue Brizeux. There turn to your right, beneath the old
town walls, and go to rue des Chanoines, skirting the north
side of the cathedral. Follow this to Place Henri IV; turn
south in rue des Halles to Place des Lices, the old tournament ground. Take the turning to your left at the end of
the 'tilt yard,' which is rue Porte-Paterne. When you
have crossed the little stream, had your eyeful of 'view'
and reached the boulevard, turn right to the Place Gambetta and the Porte Saint-Vincent; reënter the walled city;
and at the beginning of your 'tilt yard' bear off to your
left, till rue Noë leads you back to rue des Halles, Place
Henri IV, and (via rue Saint-Salomon) to your hotel.

Has Arthur slipped down from his boresome pedestal and
joined you on your nocturnal ramble? I hope so; for he has
a lot to tell.

When he is most fluent, he talks something like *this* (using our manner of speech so as to be the more readily understood):

'Yes — certainly I was named for King Arthur. We
claim him here in Brittany, you know. Perhaps we got him
from the British who came over here, long ago, and became
Bretons. Perhaps he really had his associations with this
country. *I* don't know.

'You go to Josselin to-morrow, you tell me. If you go by
Ploërmel, you'll pass close to the southern edge of what
they now call the Forest of Paimpont; but it is really Broceliande — or all that's left of that forest primeval. There
are still fourteen lakes in it, and it was probably from one
of them that the arm clothed in white samite held up before King Arthur the sword Excalibur. There lived Vivien,
the Lady of the Lake — she who enchanted Merlin; who
stole and brought up Sir Lancelot of the Lake; who bargained with King Arthur for the possession of Excalibur.

... If you go to Trégastel, on the north coast, they'll tell you that the Isle of Avalon is there, offshore; you may even see the fisher-folk peering toward it through the evening haze, looking for Arthur to come forth from his long repose, and "right the great wrongs which afflict humanity." ...

'Yes, I was a child here in days that have become vivid pages of romance and history. Du Guesclin was gone, well before my day, but of course I heard de Clisson talk about him. He won his first laurels as a soldier, here at Vannes, you know — way back when my father was a boy. I can't remember my father very well — I was only six years old when he died — but I believe it was from him I first heard the story of Du Guesclin at the Rennes tournament. He was extraordinarily ugly, you know — that Bertrand du Guesclin — and had been the despair of his family because he was so ill-favored, so quarrelsome, and wouldn't learn to read or write. He liked rough combats with the peasant boys better than learning his A B C. His father used to lock him up, you know; but Bertrand was good at escaping. One day, when he was running away from home, he met a horse, mounted it, and rode it fast to Rennes where there was an athletic contest going on. Bertrand won all the championships, although he was not yet sixteen. Then he borrowed armor and a tilting horse, and entered the lists in the great tournament that was being held at Rennes to celebrate the marriage of Charles of Blois with Joan of Penthièvre — the *other* Joan, you know, who contended against my grandmother in the War of the Two Joans — and there he unhorsed the most famous jousting nobles of that day. Nobody knew who the mysterious victor was till the tourney was over. Then his father, who was present, was transported with pride and joy.

'When you get to Dinan they'll show you where Ber-

trand fought his famous duel with Sir Thomas Cantorbery.
Lancaster was there, you know. You probably call him
John of Gaunt. His son was to become my stepfather —
but he didn't even have the son then!

'Bertrand fought for the enemies of my house, and of
course I was brought up to execrate him. But I always admired him secretly. He was a great fighter; it was our misfortune that he did not fight for us. The King of France,
who was my mother's uncle, had Du Guesclin interred at
Saint-Denis, you know.

'Olivier de Clisson I can remember. He fought for us and
against us. The last ten years of Du Guesclin's life, Clisson fought with him, and succeeded him as Constable of
France. He had a muddled sort of allegiance — as most of
us did in those curious days! Clisson's father was executed,
at Nantes, when Olivier was seven years old, on suspicion
of having wished to surrender Nantes to the English. And
thereupon Olivier's mother married an Englishman and
took the boy to England to be brought up! Olivier fought
for my grandmother Joan Montfort; and then, after they
had won the battle of Auray, and Du Guesclin was taken
prisoner, and the other Joan's husband was killed, and
my father was acknowledged Duke of Brittany, away goes
Clisson to fight with the other side.

'I suppose you know how furious this made my father,
and how he tried to have Clisson assassinated in Paris. I
dare say they've shown you the place where Pierre de
Craon, with forty mounted brigands, fell upon Clisson as he
was leaving the King's Saint-Pol Palace, about one o'clock
in the morning — unarmored and escorted only by eight
valets, two of them carrying torches — wounded him
gravely, and left him for dead. (Of course you know Clisson's mansion in Paris; I believe they keep the National
Archives in it now.)

'The King (he was my mother's cousin, Charles VI) swore to avenge this assault, and was proceeding to Brittany in pursuit of Craon when he was seized, in the forest of Mans, with an attack of madness in which he killed many of his own men.

'When his uncles, who had been regents in his minority, came back into power (and Charles VI was only twenty-three when he went mad), they forced Clisson to take refuge where they could not reach him. He came to Brittany and was reconciled to my father.

'But I am going too fast. You want to know about Clisson's imprisonment in the tower here.

'My mother was married to my elderly and irascible father in 1386. Her father, you know, was a pretty bad lot; I believe you call him Charles the Bad. He lived only a few months after my parents' marriage; and one of the last dirty deeds he did was to insinuate to my father that Clisson was in love with my mother.

'Father was feeling a bit sore at Clisson, anyway; because Clisson had just married his daughter to the *other* Joan's son. And I suppose this was all he needed to carry him completely off.

'Clisson was on the eve of sailing to invade England, when my father invited him to attend a parliament here at Vannes where my father had installed his bride in the castle he had built.

'Clisson, suspecting no ill, came, and attended a grand dinner that my father gave. Then Clisson invited my father to dine with him on the following day; and my father went.

'After the repast, my father invited Clisson and two of his friends to inspect some improvements he was making at the castle. Father led them from place to place, and when they reached the entrance of the keep, my father lingered behind Clisson, who ascended the stairway alone, was seized by armed men in ambush, fettered, and cast into prison. My father had ordered that he be put to death at midnight, "as privately as possible."

'As the hours passed, my father grew less angry against Clisson, and sent for the assassin, to countermand the order. And he who had been ordered to kill Clisson, fearing my father, declared, "He was drowned last night, and his body is buried in the garden." Then my father abandoned himself to agonies of remorse. No one dared speak to him, until he came back who had been named Clisson's murderer, and told my father that Clisson was alive and ready to pay a ransom for his release.

'Part of the ransom was that Castle of Josselin which you are to see to-morrow. Clisson complained of this treachery to the uncles of the young King of France; and my father was sternly reprimanded — which made him so angry that he swore he was sorry he had not killed Clisson when he had a chance.

'My mother, you must remember, was in a difficult position in this quarrel, because Clisson's daughter was married to my mother's cousin, the Viscount de Rohan.

'When Clisson came back into Brittany, after my father's attempt to have him done to death in Paris, he knew very well that in all my father's domain there was probably not a knight or squire who would bear arms for the Duke my father against Clisson, the Constable of France. But Clisson raised a civil war against my father and despoiled him of much of his wealth — including the ill-gotten Castle of Josselin.

'My mother had, I am sure, much influence in reconciling my father with Clisson; for she knew that if my father died, there were few to whom she could turn for the protection of her infants.

'So my father dictated a letter to Clisson at Josselin; and

Clisson wrote, in return, that if my father wished to entertain him again at Vannes, he must send my brother John as hostage.

'This was hard for my mother; because if father's anger carried him to excesses, her little son would pay the penalty. But she yielded — the boy went to Josselin — and Clisson came to Vannes bringing the boy back with him. The reconciliation was effected; but it was not very real.

'My father died in November, 1399. Earlier in that year my mother first saw Bolingbroke, who was to make her Queen of England. He was exiled from England and had been at the court of France, but was asked to withdraw because the King of France's little daughter Isabel was wed to Richard, the English King. And the Duke of Burgundy likewise would not displease Richard by permitting Bolingbroke to pass through his dominions. So he came here — though my father had been married to Richard's half-sister — and my father received him affectionately, and assisted him with vessels and men to go to England and claim his crown.

'It was here at Vannes, when I was a boy of six, that Bolingbroke was outfitted for his successful invasion of England. It was here that he adopted as his symbol the blue flower which has ever since been called "forget-me-not." I've heard it said that he gave one to my mother who, three years later, became his bride.

'I was a little lad of eight when Clisson knighted my brother John, in the Cathedral of Rennes; and then John, before he was invested with the ducal habit, circlet, and sword, knighted my younger brother Jules and me.

'And when my mother was ready to go overseas to become England's Queen, her uncle, the Duke of Burgundy, came and took my brothers and me to Paris. I was a lad of fourteen when he caused the murder of his near-kinsman,

the Duke of Orléans. I grew up with his children and the
children of my mother's cousin, the King of France. And I
married Burgundy's daughter, you know, after the death
of her first husband who should have made her Queen of
France.

'Yes, I have seen a great deal of history made. There are
a great many things I might tell you — but I won't! I
doubt if it is wise to talk too much to those who have known
but one generation. If Du Guesclin and I could get together, now! Or the Constable du Clisson! — la! la!'

I hope you haven't found him too garrulous. For the
things he had to talk about are those a visitor to Brittany
has most need to know.

IV

Next day, with this evening stroll etched into your memory, you start on your way to Josselin. The route (166)
which leads to Ploërmel is not the most direct. Yet, if
your heart is set on seeing the forest of Broceliande, it is the
way you must go. The town from which the forest is explored is Mauron, thirteen miles north of Ploërmel.

Josselin is ten miles from Ploërmel on the road to picturesque Pontivy.

The superb castle of Josselin, comparable to nothing else
so much as to Warwick Castle in England, was founded
about 1008 on a site very defensible and also very holy; for
more than three centuries it had been a pilgrimage shrine of
great sanctity and renown.

The son of the founder was named Josselin, and from
him the new castle took its name. Henry II of England
destroyed it before he forced the Duke who was its owner
to give his daughter and heiress in marriage to Henry's son.
So it was the maternal ancestors of poor young Prince Arthur who lived in the older castle of Josselin. Its next suc-

cessor lasted until Clisson's day, when he rebuilt and greatly
strengthened it after he had married the widow of the previous owner.

That previous owner was Jean de Beaumanoir, the hero
of the famous Battle of Thirty which was fought on a
March Saturday in 1351. The English, masters at Ploërmel, were pitiless in their demands on the poor peasants of
the district. This so incensed Jean de Beaumanoir that he
challenged the English governor of Edward III, at Ploërmel, to combat — thirty knights on each side. The 'battle'
took place between Ploërmel and Josselin, and a cross and
pyramid still mark the site. Of the thirty Breton knights,
only three were slain. Of the 'oppressors,' including twenty
English, six Germans, and four partisans of the Montforts
(Arthur's grandmother Joan), twelve were killed and the
others begged for quarter and were carried prisoners that
night to Josselin.

Clisson died in his castle of Josselin in 1407, and is buried
in the church, close by. His son-in-law and successor began
the transformation of the fortress into the most elegant
residence in all Brittany. And through the courtesy of the
widowed châtelaine, the Duchesse de Rohan, mother of the
little Duke, we are permitted to visit the castle. A fine old
servitor, bursting with pride in the great lineage and the
true *noblesse* of the family he is attached to, shows us the
imposing dining-room with the great equestrian statue of
Olivier de Clisson, done by Frémiet; the salon, with its
superb mantelpiece; the library, with the table whereon
the edict of Nantes was signed. The reverent guide will
show us a photograph of the late Duke, killed in the Great
War; and perhaps one of the young lad who now bears the
title. It may be that we shall catch a glimpse of the duchess, in her garden, writing letters or reading. Her mother-
in-law, who died in the early part of this year wherein I

write, was a great lady. of many distinctions; her salon in
Paris was one of the most distinguished of recent years, and
her ardent interest in the arts is carried on by her daughter,
Princess Murat, whose little art exhibition and tea-room
you have probably visited in Paris — on the Quai d'Horloge and Place Dauphine, where Manon Roland grew up.
Few of the great old feudal names of France are more familiar in American and English ears than that of Rohan.
It was, you will remember, a cardinal of this family who
was mixed up in the 'diamond necklace' affair of Marie-
Antoinette. And the dearest friend of that unhappy Queen,
the tragic Princesse de Lamballe, was daughter-in-law of
the Duc de Penthièvre. One of Olivier de Clisson's daughters married a Rohan, and the other married a Penthièvre.
We shall pass through Lamballe on our way to Dinan.

I would see Pontivy, if I were you — unless you are tired
of fifteenth-century castles and picturesque old streets and
quaint houses. There is, to be sure, a new quarter which
was laid out under Napoleon (Pontivy was called 'Napo-
léonville' from 1805 to 1871), but I doubt if any one would
make a détour to see that.

If you are headed for Hennebont, going by way of
Pontivy will add about eighteen miles to your distance;
going by way of Locminé and Baud is that much shorter.

Hennebont (thirty-eight miles from Josselin by the
shorter route) is a beautifully picturesque old town which
was once defended by Arthur de Richemont's grandmother
against the husband of the other Joan. Edward III of England sent a fleet to save her and to garrison Hennebont for
her. In 1372, Du Guesclin, driving the English before him
out of France, took Hennebont and slew the garrison.

You might try Hôtel de France here for luncheon, if you
are hungry. And do see the Breton Museum in the Porte
Prison, the picturesque gateway of the thirteenth-century

walled town. Should you be interested in horse-breeding,
you will find just out of Hennebont, to the north, one of
the most important stud farms in France.

From Hennebont to Quimperlé is fifteen miles; and
should you defer lunching until you get here, you may have
your midday repast in the abbot's dwelling of the ancient
abbey of the Holy Cross whose church (replaced by a modern reconstruction) was in part modelled after the Church
of the Holy Sepulchre at Jerusalem. The abbot's dwelling,
where travellers of distinction were entertained centuries
ago, is now Hôtel du Lion d'Or.

Be sure you see the 'Abbaye Blanche,' in the old Dominican convent founded in 1255 by Blanche of Champagne,
Duchess of Brittany. In the courtyard is the funeral chapel
of Jean de Montfort, Arthur's grandfather, and his wife,
the dauntless Joan who defended Hennebont and won at
Auray. And don't miss the Pont Fleuri.

Ten miles beyond (west) Quimperlé is Pont-Aven, beloved of artists, partly for the beauty of its surroundings,
partly for the quaintness of its costumes, and partly for
Hôtel Julia founded by Mademoiselle Julia Guillou, who is
the Yvonne in Horace Annesley Vachell's 'Face of Clay.'
Hotel Julia is celebrated, and you may wish to save up
your appetite until you reach it. It can be done! I've done
it — visited Josselin, paused a while at Hennebont and
Quimperlé, and lunched at Pont-Aven. But I'm not sure
I'd do it again; I thought Julia's hotel a bit 'spoiled' by
adulation; her lobsters were good, but her waitresses were
scathing and slamming. Perhaps they've reformed! It was
sad, in a place which had won such fame for geniality.

On one of the islands called the Glenans, south rather of
Concarneau than of Pont-Aven, is a vast store-pond for
shellfish destined to be consumed at Prunier's, in Paris.
We feast on crustaceans all about here, in Brittany. But,

much as I delight in them, I enjoy them most when they are served with a sauce of welcome such as I've had, for instance, at the Hôtel de France in Saint-Pol-de-Léon, on the North Breton coast. However ——! Just ahead (ten miles) is Concarneau! (This day's run, from Vannes to Quimper, via Josselin, Hennebont, Quimperlé, Concarneau —without détours — is about one hundred and fifteen miles.)

As for me, I'd far rather spend my night at Concarneau, on the sea, than at Quimper on the river. You may feel otherwise. But I find Quimper far less interesting than when I first knew it; and its Hôtel de l'Épée reminds me very much of a resort hotel in some American town which is an excursion centre. While as for Concarneau ——! Is there any other place where one may stand in a completely walled old town which is almost an island, and look out upon a sea so colorful? The sails of the sardine fishers seem to have been dyed for the delight of painters (perhaps they were!); and their blue nets, which are much in evidence being dried and mended, while they were colored not to please painters, but to deceive the little fishes, lend no little to the picturesque effect.

You may stay at Hôtel Atlantic, facing the harbor; or at Hôtel de Cornouaille at Sables Blancs (White Sands), a watering-place just outside Concarneau. (And by the way, this name, Cornouaille, which belongs to this district, is a Breton rendering of Cornwall, and another link in the chain which binds the two Britains — or Britain and Brittany.)

If, instead of stopping to watch the fleet come in, you go on to Quimper, you will find yourself in a town which has come to be a favored centre for persons who wish to make excursions from a comfortable and interesting base.

From Quimper one may visit Locronan, which has a

celebrated pardon, 'the Pardon of the Mountain,' on the second Sunday in July, when the pilgrims make the circuit of the forest where Saint Ronan had his hermitage and the sick among them crawl under his tomb for healing.

About five miles from Locronan is the Chapel of Sainte-Anne-de-la-Palue, dedicated to the Mother of the Virgin. Brittany believes that Saint Anne was of the blood-royal of Cornouaille, and that she fled to the Holy Land to escape a brutal husband. The pardon held here on the last Sunday in August, and called 'the Pardon of the Sea,' is one of the most picturesque ceremonies one may see anywhere in Europe.

Fifteen miles from Quimper is Douarnenez, the greatest of all the sardine-fishing ports, the home of some eight hundred vessels. And there is Île Tristan, believed to have been at some time the home of that accomplished but tragedy-pursued knight whose misfortunes in love have endeared him to so many peoples. Jean Richepin bought that island some few years ago. Was it there, I wonder, that he wrote 'Le Chemineau'?

Douarnenez is pretty 'fishy' — one may as well admit; and so is Audierne, a dozen miles to southwest of it, en route to the Pointe du Raz and the Baie des Trépassés (Bay of the Dead) in which the submerged city of Ys is supposed to lie. Poetic visitors to Brittany will wish to listen for 'the bells of Ys.'

Long, long ago (according to the legend) the city of Ys was ruled by a prince named Gradlon, a pious and a prudent man who defended his capital from the invasions of the sea by constructing an immense basin to receive the overflow of the water at high tide. This basin had a secret gate, of which the King alone possessed the key.

Now, Gradlon had a 'spoiled child,' the Princess Dahut, who got so mad and merry with wine one night, when she was secretly entertaining her lover, that — in search of 'a new thrill,' like some modern spoiled children — it occurred to her 'twould be 'good fun' to open the sluice-gate.

Gradlon, mounting his horse and fleeing from the flood, tried to save his worthless daughter. They were both about to perish when a voice cried out to Gradlon: 'Throw the demon thou carriest into the sea'; and at that moment, Dahut either slipped off or was pushed off; the torrent subsided; Gradlon reached Quimper safe and sound; and Dahut became a mermaid who still combs her golden hair at the fringes of the beach, in the midday sun, and her songs are plaintive as the rhythm of the waves.

Gradlon is credited with having introduced the vine into Brittany; and before the French Revolution there used to be a quaint ceremony in his honor in Quimper, where his equestrian statue stands between the towers of the cathedral. In this ceremony, while choristers sang the praise of King Gradlon, one of their number climbed up beside the King, offered him a cup of wine, placed a laurel branch in his hand, himself drank the wine for Gradlon, but with a napkin wiped Gradlon's mustache, and then threw the golden cup into the crowd below.

Off the majestic headland, the Pointe du Raz, about five miles due west, is the Île de Sein, a Druidic burial-place associated in Breton legend with the Seven Sleepers, seven Christian youths of Ephesus who hid to escape persecution and slept here for hundreds of years.

On the way from the Pointe to Audierne is Plogoff with a church dedicated to the bishop who counselled Queen Guinevere to reject the overtures of Lancelot.

Another excursion easily made from Quimper is south and west, as the foregoing is north and west; it is to Pont-l'Abbé, a town noted for the elaborate costumes of its inhabitants; and to Penmarch, which rivalled Nantes until the failure of the cod-fishing reduced its revenues, and a tidal wave swept over it. The 'land's end,' here, Saint-Guénolé, has fine cliff scenery.

V

When you leave Quimper, take Route 170, the Brest highway. And if you make no stops for forty miles, until you reach Daoulas, I think you will not miss anything of outstanding importance. At Daoulas, you leave the main road for Plougastel; but before quitting Daoulas, you may like a glimpse of its lovely Romanesque cloisters, forty-four arches of which are still standing — and may no one ever be permitted to 'restore' them!

Plougastel has one of the most celebrated Calvarys in Brittany, whereon the Passion is represented by more than two hundred sculptured figures done at the beginning of the seventeenth century. Across the bay from Plougastel is Brest. The peninsula of Crozon, which lies south of Plougastel and separates the Bay of Douarnenez from Brest Roads, is a picturesque corner of Brittany with some imposing rock formations and 'pirate' caverns. You may motor to the tip of it at Cameret; but to do this I'd leave Route 170 at Châteaulin, about halfway between Quimper and Daoulas. There is good bathing at Morgat. On the north tip of the peninsula is the Pointe des Espagnols, where Martin Frobisher got his death-wound in helping the French dislodge a Spanish force. And from a little port near there, Joanna, Arthur de Richemont's mother, set sail for England to become its queen.

Brest has little of interest, except its castle, for the wayfarer in Brittany; but to the student of affairs it offers much food for thought. It is the greatest natural harbor and port of France. 'In one year the Americans landed nearly two million troops at Brest, from forty to fifty thousand a day, without a single accident and with virtually no delay. The Leviathan, which took many days to unload and load at other ports, discharged nine thousand men at Brest, took on water and coal, and got off in thirty-seven hours.' (I quote from Herbert Adams Gibbons's book 'Ports of France.')

When you turn west from Plougastel or from Brest, to Landerneau, at the junction of Route 170 and Route 12, you have to choose between the former, taking you to le Folgoët and then to Saint-Pol-de-Léon and Roscoff, or the latter, taking you to Landivisiau, to Saint-Thégonnec, and *thus* to Morlaix. These are the rival attractions of the two routes:

Le Folgoët has a famous pilgrimage church of the early fifteenth century, with a rood-screen or *jubé*, itself worth going far to see. Saint-Pol-de-Léon has one of the finest cathedrals in Brittany, and a beautiful Gothic chapel with a famous openwork spire. And Roscoff, where little Mary, Queen of Scots, aged five, landed in France to become the affianced bride of Francis the Dauphin, has a house in which she is said to have lodged, and a fig-tree which covers an area of over seven hundred square yards.

Whereas, Landivisiau has a most beautifully sculptured church porch; Saint-Thégonnec has one of the most elaborate of Breton Calvarys; and from a point between them one may take a small road south to Guimiliau which has one of the finest of all the Calvarys, and a church with a beautiful porch.

Whichever route you take, you may make a visit to the Castle of Kerjean, one of the finest of Breton castles and now owned by the State. It is, however, more conveniently reached from the road you would follow from Le Folgoët to Saint-Pol-de-Léon.

Unless you have a special reason for going to Morlaix by

way of Saint-Thégonnec, or must save time in getting there, I'd advise the other route. It is quite possible, leaving Quimper or even Concarneau, by 8.30 or 9 A.M., to reach Saint-Pol-de-Léon for luncheon at Hôtel de France. Ask at Lanhouarneau, soon after you leave Lesneven to turn west, for directions to the Castle of Kerjean, 'the Versailles of Brittany.'

Roscoff is only four and a half miles north of Saint-Pol-de-Léon, and there is a main road into Morlaix — seventeen and a half miles. Over it the little Queen of Scots travelled, in 1548.

Morlaix is built on the slopes of a deep valley spanned by a thrillingly beautiful railway viaduct nine hundred feet long and nearly two hundred feet high, over which runs the main line from Paris to Brest. It claims as rulers, long, long ago, the kings of Lyonesse, that legendary country off the coast of Cornwall where Blancheflor, the mother of Tristan (or Tristrem — 'Child of Sorrow'), died as she brought her son into the world.

Mary Stuart lodged in a Dominican convent which was used as a Jacobin club in the Revolution, and the *place* in front of it is now called Place des Jacobins.

A little to the right of it (as you go through the town from west to east) is the so-called Maison de la Duchesse Anne, at number 33 rue du Mur. Whether the little duchess who was twice Queen of France had or had not any association with this house, I think you ought to visit it if you love quaint old houses. And I'd see something of the Grande Rue — the 'Main Street' — of a picturesque town.

Marshal Foch has his home just north of Morlaix. It was from a peaceful vacation here, with his young son and his two sons-in-law, that he was summoned back to Nancy at the end of July, 1914. And in the happy little family circle then broken, there were soon two gaps never to be filled:

young Germain Foch, the only son, and one of his brothers-in-law.

Now, in leaving Morlaix, you have some decisions to make. (Or, rather, in planning your trip in Brittany, you must decide what you will do from here.)

If you have given yourself only a week for the tour, and you want to spend some time at Mont-Saint-Michel as well as at Saint-Malo, you should be on your way, as directly as possible, to Guingamp (forty miles) and then to Saint-Brieuc (twenty miles more) to spend your fifth night out from Paris.

Should time be no object to you, you may go north-westerly, by way of Plestin-les-Grèves with its poetic grave-yard by the sea, to Lannion (twenty-four miles), north of which is Tréguier, the birthplace of Ernest Renan, and charmingly portrayed by him in his 'Memories of Infancy and Youth.' The street on which he was born now bears his name and you may visit the room where he first saw the light and his study where he probably wrote some parts of his beautiful 'Life of Jesus.'

The cathedral cloisters here are magnificent; and in them Saint Yves, the best-beloved saint in Brittany and the only regularly canonized Breton, is said to have performed many of his miracles. He was a lawyer! A lawyer and a saint! He was born at Kermartin, near Tréguier, in 1253, and studied law in the schools of Paris. After having been an ecclesiastical judge, he was ordained a priest.

As a lawyer, he tried to get his clients to settle their differences out of court; and he defended the poor and oppressed without charging them a fee. He spent most of his income in charity; turned his house into an orphanage; gave the clothes off his back to the poor; walked beside ploughmen in the field and taught them to pray; sat on the moors beside the shepherd-boys and instructed them in the use of the rosary. The pardon of Saint Yves, on the 19th of May, is 'the pardon of the poor,' and for a whole week the inhabitants of Tréguier, in emulation of their beloved saint, give hospitality to throngs of poor pilgrims.

The saint was buried near the Château of Kermartin where he was born, about a mile south of Tréguier. During the Revolution his tomb was destroyed, but the bones were preserved and reinterred in the beautiful cathedral at Tréguier. Nearly always there are people praying at his magnificent new tomb; and on occasions, pilgrims creep on their hands and knees beneath the table-tomb which is supposed to cover what was his resting-place for nearly six centuries.

Duke Arthur's brother, who was John V, had a special veneration for Saint Yves, and built his own burial chapel here — the Chapelle du Duc.

From Tréguier I should go to Paimpol, the scene of Pierre Loti's classic romance, 'The Iceland Fisherman.'

Between Paimpol and Guingamp you must choose between the right and left banks of the river, the Trieux. About three miles north of Pontrieux, on the river midway between Paimpol and Guingamp, is the fine old castle of La Roche-Jagu; and east of Pontrieux at Lanleff is a circular church, probably built by the Templars, on the plan of part of the Church of the Holy Sepulchre at Jerusalem.

There are bits of Guingamp, along the river, which suggest Bruges; the fountain, in the Place du Centre, is justly famed; the church is a fine one; and its pardon (Saturday before the first Sunday in July) is noted for its weirdly picturesque bonfire and candle-light procession in which thousands of pilgrims participate.

From Paimpol to Saint-Brieuc by way of Guingamp is about forty-three miles. There is another route, by way of Lanvollon, which cuts the distance between Paimpol and

Saint-Brieuc to twenty-six miles; but even this gives you eighty-six miles to cover between luncheon at Saint-Pol-de-Léon and dinner at Saint-Brieuc. I'd stop, if I were not hurried, at Paimpol, for the night (or cross over, from the Pointe de l'Arcouest, to the Île de Bréhat, which has good bathing, is quaint and picturesque, and gives one lobsters that are just-caught; and go on in the morning, sixty-three miles, to Dinan.)

Those who must keep this tour to seven days should keep straight on, west, from Morlaix through Guingamp to Saint-Brieuc.

I have been only once at Saint-Brieuc, arriving on a Sunday when a horse show (or, rather, cavalry exhibition) had just concluded, on the Champ de Mars. I remember that the young couple, recently married, who kept the hotel (I am not sure whether it was the France or the Angleterre) were quite casual about things like towels, and seemed not to have the help 'in hand'; but Madame was so very pretty, one could not find the heart to protest about trifles. And I distinctly remember that the dinner was memorably good. And we liked Saint-Brieuc. There was a concert and dance in the pretty promenade, that evening. And the next morning we found some antique shops that were full of treasures at attractive prices. We felt that we liked Saint-Brieuc, and would go there again some day. I hope you may feel the same about it — and even that the pretty young Madame may have grown sterner with 'the help' about towels.

When you leave there, you have little but the country-side through which you're passing to engage your attention until you pass through Lamballe, twelve and a half miles on your way to Dinan. The Church of Notre-Dame, at Lamballe, was originally the chapel of the castle. It was consecrated in or about 1220, and the choir was rebuilt by Charles of Blois, husband of Joan de Penthièvre, who was killed at Auray; or perhaps by their son, of the same name. North of the church is a promenade where the castle used to be.

Then — on to Dinan!

VI

I hope you'll share my enthusiasm for Dinan. If you want to see Dinard, thirteen miles away at the mouth of the Rance estuary, I'd turn up to it from Pancoët before going to Dinan. Dinard is a beautiful and fashionable seaside place, with a golf course near by, with many hotels de luxe, and is a good excursion centre. But I think you'll be more charmed with it before seeing Dinan and Saint-Malo than after. It is about forty-two miles from Saint-Brieuc, and you can easily get there in time for a good morning dip before luncheon. Then, after luncheon, go down to Dinan, the old walled town wherein Du Guesclin vanquished Sir Thomas Cantorbery, in the presence of John of Gaunt. The thirteenth-century (and later) walls still have fifteen of their ancient towers; and the castle, built by that Duke John IV who was Arthur de Richemont's father, is one of the most interesting in all Brittany. Duchesse Anne, then Queen, lived here in 1507.

The streets of Dinan are exceedingly picturesque; and there is good shopping for the lover of antiques.

The ideal way to go between Dinard and Dinan is by the little river boats called *vedettes*, which land you east of the town walls and permit you to enter the walled city by the Porte du Jersual and come up the rue du Jersual, toward the centre of town. But if you go by motor, and enter by the rue Thiers, you will find yourself greeted by Jean de Beaumanoir, of Château Josselin, the hero of the Battle of Thirty; and, taking rue Georges Clemenceau you will presently find yourself at Place Foch, standing shoulder-to-shoulder with Place Du Guesclin — which I think is very nice indeed.

A 'love' of an old town is Dinan, to my way of thinking. And when you must leave it, you have something less than twenty miles to go to reach another lovely old town, Saint-Malo. You have a mileage of only about seventy-five miles to-day, and should be able to do some delightful lingering.

Saint-Malo is across the Rance estuary from Dinard; and you may cross to it by ferry or motor-launch in a few minutes, if you find yourself so fascinated with Dinard that you are willing to forego Dinan. It might be that you would like to spend the night at Dinard; cross to Saint-Malo, only for a glimpse, in the morning; and then after a glimpse of Mont-Saint-Michel, go on your way toward Bagnoles de l'Orne for the next night; and so, via Bois-Joly, into Paris. That would give you the maximum of luxury, if you chance to be hungry for that after some days of the 'quaint.' Dinard has many fine hotels: the Plage, the Royal, the Crystal, the Terrasses, the Grand, etc.; and many less expensive but still good ones. And, should you find them all full, you might go along the shore, west, to Saint-Énogat or Saint-Lunaire, which are practically continuations of Dinard and have good hotels also.

At Saint-Malo you have a similar situation: should the hotels there be full and you have no reservations, you can try Saint-Servan, south of Saint-Malo and immediately opposite Dinard; or you can go two and a half miles to Paramé, with its fine, firm beach, its Casino, and numerous hotels.

This may be the place to offer what travel experience has taught me: I practically never go a-journeying until *all* my hotel reservations are made and confirmed. I find scant pleasure in 'gipsying along' as some people tell me they like to do. I don't find it 'interesting' to put up for the

night wherever I happen to be, in whatever hotel I can get
into. I have tried that way; and, for me, its disappoint-
ments and discomforts more than outweigh its care-free-
ness and its joyful surprises. I urge my preferences upon
no one. But when people are kind enough to say that I
seem to get a very great deal of delight in travel, and ask
me for 'my recipe,' I have to give as a principal ingredient
of it the spacing and planning of my journey before I start
and the serenity of mind I enjoy because I am not forever
making and remaking plans by the way. Some people hate
a 'programme' and feel that it cripples their liberty. I have
to admit that nothing could more effectually ruin a journey
for me than discussions, however amicable, many times
daily, as, 'Shall we eat or sleep here, or try another place?'
'Shall we take this road, or that?' and so on. I'd rather do
all that discussing, over maps, before I start. I'd rather
give myself the trouble, if I want to change my schedule,
of writing or wiring all along my line of march, altering the
dates of my reservations, than be on the march without a
schedule.

But that is a matter for individual preference.

At Saint-Malo there are the hotels France and Chateaubriand, and Univers, on Place Chateaubriand, close to the
ramparts on their inner side; and Hôtel Franklin on the
beach, beside the casino. Remember that the oysters of
Cancale, near by, are famous.

The great enchantment of Saint-Malo is the walls and
the sea-view from them. The little old fortress-town itself
being such a 'sight,' such an experience, I — for one —
never think of other sight-seeing there. Nor is there much
of it to do. The tour of the walls is the 'big thrill.' The fish-
market is interesting and picturesque. A causeway leads
(at low tide, only) out to Chateaubriand's tomb on the
island called Grand-Bey.

I dare say one ought to think a good deal about Chateaubriand, here where he was born; but I may as well admit to you that I don't. I prefer to think of the Corsairs.

From Saint-Malo to Mont-Saint-Michel is thirty-three miles; and at fifteen miles from Saint-Malo, en route to Pontorson (for Mont-Saint-Michel), is Dol, a delightful old town with some lovely old houses, one of which (eleventh century) is among the oldest dwellings in France.

And ten miles south of Dol is the Castle of Combourg which belonged to Chateaubriand's father.

Should it chance that you have already seen Mont-Saint-Michel (or, if you go there this time, you can return to Dol), but have not been to Vitré or Fougères, I suggest that (if you can take one more day for this tour) you have a glimpse of Combourg, then go on to Rennes, and thence to Vitré (see Chapter I) and Fougères, and Mayenne; and into Paris as by the first day's run of our Normandy tour.

If you have covered this ground, go from Pontorson to Sainte-Hilaire-du-Harcouët, Mortain, Domfront, and Bagnoles-de-l'Orne. Then, in to Paris by Argentan and Dreux, stopping at Tillières-sur-Arvre for luncheon at the Hostellerie du Bois-Joly. To see something of the places this chapter covers, journeying by train, you could make Angers your first stop (leaving Orléans for your Châteaux trip) and get on to Nantes for the night. Then go to Vannes, and make short trips out from there. Then to Quimper, as a centre. And then perhaps to Morlaix. The Saint-Malo neighborhood is an excellent centre for excursions in every direction, including the Channel Islands. And then, from Mont-Saint-Michel you could go straight back to Paris, or go up to Caen and combine your Brittany tour with a part of Normandy.

III
THE CHÂTEAUX OF THE LOIRE

I

FRANCE has hundreds of châteaux; but the majority of English-speaking travellers, when they talk of the 'château country' mean the vicinity of which Tours is the centre; the castles of Touraine and its bordering provinces; and especially the superb royal and semi-royal residences on the lordly Loire.

A visit to these castles has come (or is coming) to be as standard a feature of nearly every visitor's stay in France as the visit to 'the Shakespeare country' is of his stay in England. Almost every tourist office runs its stated trip 'to the château country.' The Paris–Orléans railway covers the principal points of interest by auto-buses running, from April to November, out of Blois and of Tours. The region is, at times and in places, too full of trippers to be pleasurable to the æsthetic wayfarer; but it is one on no account to be slighted. See it under the best conditions you can; but make sure you see it.

A glimpse of the château country may be snatched in three days, if you take an early train to Blois (three and a half hours from Paris) spend the afternoon seeing two or three châteaux out from there (probably Chambord, Chaumont, and Cheverny) and going on about six o'clock to Tours (three quarters of an hour); then spending a day out from Tours, a half-day in Tours, and returning to Paris (four hours) on the afternoon of the third day. If I couldn't do any better, I'd do that. Four days is the average time and gives many travellers as much as they can 'take in.'

But if you can take a week for the tour, you will like it much better. And if you can make a sojourn in Touraine, you will always count it high among your most delightful experiences.

What I am going to do in this chapter is to indicate how you may spend a week there; and, if a week is more than you have to spend, help you choose, from among all the places there are to see, those which you think would give you most satisfaction.

As always, I am taking for granted that you are motoring, and that you are starting from Paris and probably returning thither. The château country can very advantageously be visited en route to Biarritz or Pau or Carcassonne; it can as conveniently be visited en route to Brittany, or combined with a Brittany-Normandy tour. If you want to do it between the Riviera and Paris, you may go from Nice to Nîmes, and Nîmes to Carcassonne; then, to Albi, to Cahors, to Rocamadour; and, via Brive to Poitiers and Tours either by way of Limoges or by way of Périgueux and Angoulême. Or, if you want to go up the Rhone Valley, through Avignon and Orange and Valence and Vienne, you may turn west at Mâcon and go via Nevers and Bourges to Tours. But, supposing you to be making the tour out from Paris:

If you have not seen Chartres, I would by all means take the route thither which is described in our Chapter I; and then follow Route 10, twenty-seven and a half miles, to Châteaudun; thence, to Orléans. Otherwise, you may go from Paris to Orléans by the route described in our Chapter II.

There isn't any reason why your 'château-ing' should begin at Orléans, and go west, if you would prefer to go to Angers and 'work' east. But as one must make a beginning somewhere, somehow, I am supposing that you have lunched at the Hôtel de la Providence, Jouy; and that about three o'clock or so you are at Châteaudun, which is a most satisfactory castle to begin your tour with. (Although it isn't really a beginning — is it? — since you've had Rambouillet and Maintenon, en route.)

The castle at Châteaudun belonged, a thousand years ago or so, to the Counts of Blois, one of whom built its cylindrical donjon, one hundred and fifty feet high. The lord of the castle who most interests us, however, is that Dunois, Bastard of Orléans, who was associated with Jeanne d'Arc's victories, and carried on most splendidly after her death. He was a son of that Louis, Duke of Orléans, who was killed in Paris by the assassins of the Duke of Burgundy. Charles, the poet, who succeeded his father in the dukedom, was he who spent those long years of captivity in the Tower of London whilst Dunois battled for the rights of the French Crown as a cousin (even though a left-handed one) of Charles VII should do. Dunois built the Sainte-Chapelle here, adjoining the ancient donjon; and to him is due that wing of the château with the very beautiful exterior staircase which may have had something to do with inspiring the one at Blois. Be sure to ascend that staircase; and to see (among other things in the rooms to which it gives access) the room wherein the Revolutionary Tribunal of this district sat, in 1793–94. In no other place in France has the actual 'set-up' of the courtroom which was the antechamber of the guillotine been so well preserved. The kitchens and guardrooms are also intensely interesting; and the view from the castle terrace is very fine.

When you get to Orléans, you may like to remember that it was Dunois who defended it against the English and held it until Jeanne came to raise the siege. He was with her at Reims. After her death he continued the triumphs she had begun. He made a triumphal entry into Paris, long held by

CHÂTEAUDUN
From an old mezzotint

the English, in April, 1436. It was he, of the bar sinister, and not his legitimate brother nor his cousin Charles VII, who was largely responsible for the victories which cleared the English out of Normandy in 1450; and after that, he went to rout them from Guienne which had belonged to them ever since the marriage of Henry II of England with Eleanor of Aquitaine. Dunois took Bordeaux from them after they had held it for three hundred years.

Of all his breed he was the only real 'he-man' who was adequate to the tremendous demands of his time; and he provided a great justification for the custom of those days which countenanced fathers acknowledging their illegitimate offspring, and providing for them even to the point of making them sharers in the upbringing of the children born in wedlock. Jean of Dunois, who was only a tiny boy when his father was killed, was brought up with the children of Valentine of Milan, the passionately devoted duchess of Louis of Orléans, who grieved herself to death within a year after his murder.

About midway on Route 155 between Châteaudun and Orléans, you pass a little to the south of Patay where Dunois aided Jeanne d'Arc in a great victory and they took prisoner John Talbot, Earl of Shrewsbury. It was at this battle that Sir John Fastolf ran; and of this incident Shakespeare made an unfair use in his 'Henry VI.'

At Orléans you have the Loire. At Châteaudun you have the Loir, which flows on down to Vendôme (twenty-five miles south) and then turns westward through a section full of interest and beauty, which I commend most heartily to the wayfarer with less pressure on his scant time than the majority of travellers have on theirs. Vendôme itself is full of charm and has many associations of interest. It was the native place of Rochambeau, who aided Washington in the capture of Yorktown. Balzac went to school here, when he was a lad of ten or eleven, and gathered the impressions which he afterwards used in 'Louis Lambert.' The Belfry of La Trinité is alone worth going far to see; and the Porte Saint-Georges is one of the most picturesque old gateways left to us in all France. I have not found enough of interest in the ruins of the castle to repay me for the climb; you might feel otherwise, but I incline to believe you'll spend a brief time to better advantage in the old town itself.

West of Vendôme, along the Loir, there is the curious so-called troglodyte village of Les Roches. I say 'so-called' because, while these cave-dwellings of Touraine and vicinity, cut into the chalky cliffs, may once have housed the sort of folks that 'troglodytes' are described as having been, their present inhabitants are decent, self-respecting French people who ought not to be looked on as a race apart or as more or less scandalously uncivilized. I hope you may have an opportunity for a 'close-up' of some of the interiors of the cave-dwellers, and see in what dignity and decorum life can be lived, even in a cave. At Troo, near Les Roches, there are also interesting 'caves.' And in this same neighborhood is the ruined castle of Lavardin crowning a commanding eminence most picturesquely. In this castle John of Bourbon is said to have died, poisoned by a letter from Louis XI.

However, you are probably at Orléans (see our Chapter II); and if you have any time at your disposal after seeing the principal sights of Orléans, let me urge you to take the road to Châteauneuf-sur-Loire, and thence, by way of Germigny-des-Prés where there is the only church in France dating back to Charlemagne, to Saint-Benôit-sur-Loire where the very famous Benedictine monastery used to be which housed the remains of Saint Benedict himself, brought thither from Monte Cassino, near Naples. The

abbey church, whose crypt has the reliquary of Saint
Benedict, is one of the finest Romanesque structures in
France and one of the few with an aisled narthex or front
porch, 'descended from' the Roman atrium. If your time
permits, go across the Loire to Sully to see its lovely moated
castle; this is where Jeanne d'Arc had her last word with
Charles VII.

When you leave Orléans (betimes on a fine morning, I
hope!), cross the Pont Georges V and take the road for
Olivet, and then watch for the right-hand fork marked
Cléry. Cléry is ten and a half miles from Orléans, and your
objective there is the basilica which Louis XI erected, in
fulfilment of a vow, to house the thirteenth-century statue
of Notre-Dame-de-Cléry, which he held in such great veneration. The mean little shambling figure of Louis, shab-
bily clad, with one or more leaden images of this Madonna
on his hat, is one of the most familiar in all pages of romance. You will be intensely conscious of it in many places
on this visit to the châteaux; and to miss Cléry, or the fragment that's left of Plessis-lès-Tours, seems to me like missing the last act of a vivid drama. I own to an extraordinary
interest in Louis XI. And if Scott, in 'Quentin Durward,'
gave me my first impressions of him, it is rather from the
fascinating pages of Philippe de Comines that I have got
most of what 'intrigues' me — as the much-abused expression is. And I seem to find it easier to reflect upon Louis,
and what he did and missed doing, here at Cléry than anywhere else.

His prospects of playing an important part in the world
were poor enough when he was born, at Bourges, soon after
the death of his crazy grandfather (Charles VI) and the
proclamation of his infant cousin, Henry VI, 'by the grace
of God, King of France and England.' But by the time
Louis was six years old, the Maid of Orléans, with the aid of

Dunois and other war chiefs, had not only seen the crown set on the head of Louis' father, but had stirred the people, exhausted by the Hundred Years' War to set an English king over them, to belief in a New France. Out of misery and chaos a great New Day was emerging.

The old feudality was ruined. 'The great feudal proprietor,' as Funck-Brentano says, summing up this reign of Charles VII, 'has disappeared. The small rural nobility draws nearer to the peasants: it is to produce those famous country gentlemen who will be one of the elements of the strength, wealth, and prosperity of our country. In the towns the higher burgesses will be recast. They also will draw nearer to the working class and will give birth to the Renaissance. Trade and industry are to receive at the end of the reign of Charles VII an unheard-of impetus. The French flag will float above all others in the ports of the Levant. The great figure of the merchant Jacques Cœur remains as a brilliant witness thereof. The "little people of the King's Council" who replace the great lords and high dignitaries of former days will have greatly contributed to this renewal by the reform of military and financial administration, of judicial organization, and even of the Church itself.'

Louis was thirty-eight when he succeeded to this kingdom. For the last six years of his father's reign, Louis had been an exile at the court of Burgundy, and there — in the opinion of Comines — he was 'benefitted very greatly, for he was forced to make himself agreeable to those of whom he had need, and this advantage — which is no small one — adversity taught him.'

Louis had not seen his father in fourteen years. He had married his second wife (this Charlotte of Savoy who shares his sepulture) in defiance of his father's formal prohibition. (Margaret of Scotland, whom he married before he was

thirteen — she who kissed, 'tis said, the sleeping poet,
Chartier — had left him a widower when he was twenty-
two.) He was unfilial; he was many things that are base
and mean. But he was a great king — the first 'modern
king' in Europe.

'He was,' to continue quoting Funck-Brentano, 'the
first king to introduce systematically commercial clauses
in the treaties, agreements, or truces which he was called
upon to conclude. He entrusted his representatives in
foreign countries with commercial missions, and wanted to
organize in London, in 1470, an exhibition of the best products of French industry, so that the inhabitants of the
aforesaid kingdom should know that the French merchants
were able to provide for them, like other nations. He favored the industries connected with art and luxury: lace,
tapestries, earthen-ware. It is to Louis XI that Lyons owes
its magnificent silk industry. . . . Louis XI encouraged the
beginnings of printing. He gave a great impulse to agriculture. Louis XI created the postal service in France.'

Modest and poor in his garments, hiding in corners, shun-
ning all pomp and show, surrounded by nobodies and sometimes by vulgar scoundrels, Louis XI showed himself none
the less a great king, 'the man necessary to end the Middle
Ages for France and lead her to the New Age.'

Let us have this in mind as we journey among the castles
which conserve terrible memories of him. A tyrant he was,
indeed, and cruel, and crafty. But the spirit of coöperation
was not in his day (and indeed it has not yet got very far in
the world), so that a man who saw things to be done must
needs do them single-handed and with what might he had.
Of Louis XI one of his contemporaries said: 'The King's
horse carries the whole Council.' It is not the best way, but
sometimes it is the only way possible.

I'm sure Louis XI was a horrid, contemptible little man.

But because he was, in spite of that, a great king, a perfectly effective tool of Destiny for the thing he was appointed to do, he fascinates me. And there are few mortuary exhibits in Europe which make me reflect so stimulatingly as that skull which the curé of Notre-Dame-de-Cléry sometimes shows to the genuinely, reverently interested visitor. A delightful man, that curé! Extraordinarily informed on the period of Louis XI, he discourses on it most illuminatingly — in English, too!

In the vault next Louis lies his lusty, trusty Tanneguy du Chastel who gave his life to guard the King's. And in a fine chapel of the south aisle is the tomb of Dunois without whose soldier skill Louis' statecraft might have availed little.

And as I come out from this church, so dominated by the bones of that mean little man, I wonder if from another Sphere he ever realized the consequences of one act of his which came near to outweighing all that he wrought for progress: 'the greatest political fault,' Funck-Brentano says, 'that a French king had committed since the divorce of Louis VII from Eleanore of Aquitaine.' That is, the actions of the King against his orphaned goddaughter, the young Duchess Marie of Burgundy, which resulted in her union with Maximilian of Austria. 'Two centuries and a half of efforts, the blood of thousands upon thousands of Frenchmen, will painfully redeem the mistake committed in 1477 by the ablest and most cunning of our kings. Perhaps the consequences of this fault still weigh on us today.'

Had he befriended and protected that young girl, instead of attacking her to dismember her duchy, France might not have been rimmed round by the empire of Charles V, Spain on the southwest, the Netherlands on the north, Germany on the east. For Charles V was Duchess Marie's grandson;

through her he had the Netherlands, through her husband, the German Empire, and through his mother (married to Marie's son and heir) he had Spain, the kingdom of his maternal grandparents, Ferdinand and Isabella.

When you leave Cléry you may, if you wish, cross the Loire to Meung, which gave France one of her earliest poets, Jehan de Meung whom Dante is believed to have visited in rue Saint-Jacques, Paris. Four miles farther downstream is Beaugency which has several things worth stopping to see; but I doubt if you'll do it, or *ought* to! The bridge over the Loire, however, you can see without stopping, and without crossing. I'd stay on the left bank (the side Cléry's on) and make the best time possible to Chambord, some twenty-two miles away, and not on the Loire, but on the Cosson.

I think that most people who know the château will agree with me that of them all Chambord-the-stupendous is the least interesting. I doubt if any one has imagination sufficient to refurnish and repeople it, even in spots. Even those who lived in it when it was a sumptuous pleasure-house and not an echoing waste seem to have had little fondness for it and to have stayed there as little as possible.

Francis I, when hunting at Amboise or Blois, often came to these banks of the Cosson, where there was a little pavilion for rest and refreshment, in what had been an old feudal manor-house tucked away in the depths of the forest. There was nothing in the site that should have appealed to the owner of Blois and Amboise; but one day in 1519 the prodigal young sovereign (twenty-five years old and in the fourth year of his reign) decided to build here, ten miles from Blois, where he had just finished magnificent renovations and additions, 'a beautiful and sumptuous edifice.' On the 6th of September in that year he signed the first letters patent for what he called the 'reconstruction' of Chambourg, thenceforward called Chambord. Perhaps he was 'showing off' a bit; for he was feeling very 'sore' that summer over the election of Charles of Austria to the imperial crown of his grandfather, Maximilian. Francis had spent a lot of money bribing the imperial electors to favor him. And when he failed (June 28, 1519) he was bitterly chagrined.

His orders for the erection of the sumptuous edifice given, he was through with it for some otherwise eventful years, and he never saw the place again until after his release from captivity at Madrid. (He was taken prisoner after the battle of Pavia, you'll remember, in February, 1525, where he surrendered the sword you may have seen at the Musée des Invalides, Paris. And from this captivity he was not released until he had signed away the greater part of what Louis XI had wrung from Burgundy; had agreed to marry the sister of his captor, Emperor Charles V; and had handed over as hostages, to be kept in Spain in his stead, his two little boys, the younger of whom was to be his successor, Henry II.)

In 1526, when he next saw this place, it was sufficiently advanced so that he was able to lodge for a few days in the northeast tower; and it was then that he probably saw for the first time, among the maids of honor of his masterful mother (who had been regent in his absence), that Anne de Pisseleu, eighteen years old, who was to remain his mistress for more than twenty years. In 1530, when Francis married Eleanor, sister of Charles V (his first wife, Claude, the daughter of Louis XII and Anne de Bretagne, had died in 1524, at the age of twenty-five, having borne seven children in eight years; she it is whose emblem, the pierced swan, you see so often in this château tour), he found for Anne a good Breton husband of the Penthièvre family, whom he made Count and then Duke d'Étampes. Francis never made any pretence of affection for his new wife. She bore him no children. And Anne, as Duchesse d'Étampes, reigned at the court of Francis until his death.

The court stayed at Chambord for twenty-five days to celebrate the King's marriage with Eleanor. Then the King was here for two days in 1532, for three days in 1534, and not again till 1539, when three days were spent here during his series of splendid entertainments for his old enemy, Charles V. After that, he was here three times — once for two days, once for three days, and once for three weeks.

Eighteen hundred workmen, we're told, were employed on this construction for fifteen years; and Francis I spent in it, all told, about two months' time. Nor did all the later kings, together, occupy it much more.

It was probably during his last stay at Chambord that Francis wrote on a window-pane his couplet about the fickleness of woman and the folly of believing in her. And this glass Louis XIV gallantly shattered in compliment to Louise de la Vallière — who was *too* constant to keep him captivated! It would seem that she, knowing herself supplanted by Montespan, called the King's attention to the lines, as if to make them say 'who's fickle *now?*'

The guide (who speaks English) will show you the room where these episodes occurred; and it is, of all the three hundred and sixty-five rooms of Chambord, the one that's easy to picture as it may have been: once, with Francis, old at fifty-one, ailing, embittered, upbraiding the Duchesse d'Étampes for being less madly in love with him than she had been nineteen years ago; and once with Louis, his great-great-grand-nephew, in 1668, thirty years of age and pretty well through with all belief in women — not because they tired of him, but because he tired of them.

Louis spent a fortnight at Chambord in the autumn of 1668, and commanded much reconstruction. It was in the

autumn following that Molière wrote and produced here his
'M. de Pourceaugnac,' one of his satires on physicians.
'What,' Louis XIV once asked Molière, 'does your doctor
do for you?' 'Sire,' Molière answered, 'we argue together,
and he prescribes remedies I never take; therefore I get
well.'

In this spirit he wrote much of the medical profession.
But at this 'comedy-ballet' done at Chambord, the audience was so obviously bored that Lulli, Louis XIV's Director of Music (acting the leading part because Molière
was ill), is said to have leaped into the orchestra smashing
the harpsichord and with this horse-play evoked uproar-
ious laughter from the King, which put every one in good
humor and carried the play through to acclaim. This (and
another Molière presentation the following year) took place
in one of the guardrooms surrounding the famous central
staircase; it was on the third story, facing the north façade,
and a 'box' for the King was contrived in the staircase.

But the great attraction of Chambord, always, was hunting, of which there was an almost infinite variety. And the
Bourbon kings, like those of Valois, were ardent hunters.
With Louis XIV it was not only the passion for the chase,
but the fever for fresh outdoor air; when he was much indoors he suffered severely from headaches and indigestion;
so, as heat, cold, and rain daunted him not at all, there was
little (short of a tempest) which made him forego his hunting. And as the King did, so must the courtiers do also.
There must have been a good many in his *entourage* besides
poor, 'creaky' Madame de Maintenon, who secretly
'cussed' his restlessness when within doors. She, poor soul,
suffered from the slightest whisper of a draught, loved
screens and firesides, loathed the incessant journeying and
hunting, and suffered as much 'incompatibility of temperature' as any goodwife ever endured; even though, after

their marriage, he was physically unable to hunt as he had been used to do.

The estate of Chambord comprises about twenty-one square miles, and is enclosed by a wall nearly twenty-two miles around. The hunting there now is the preserve of the President of France; and friends of mine go there frequently on hunting parties to shoot wild boar and other game. I don't know why; but the mere mention of shooting wild boar at Chambord seems to whisk me back even beyond Francis I — back to the old Counts of Blois who hunted hereabouts in the Middle Ages.

Perhaps I ought to go on recalling various owners of Chambord — especially Louis XV's father-in-law, the good King Stanislas, and Maurice de Saxe, a great soldier whose first claims on our interest seem to be that he was Adrienne Lecouvreur's lover and George Sand's great-grandfather — but I have a theory that if we try to 'crowd' ourselves with the stories of these châteaux we shall have only a confusion of impressions and a sad satiety. Instead, I try to get one or two extra-vivid mental pictures of each place, and then add to them through my reading, afterwards.

If you seem, as you approach the fantastic pile and see its forests of spires, turrets, chimneys, outlined against the sky, to feel the pique of Francis I when he commanded it; and, when you climb its staircase of the double spiral, to see Louis XIV sitting in one of its openings, bored to death at Molière's comedy until Lulli crashed into the harpsichord, I believe you'll come away from Chambord with a more clean-cut recollection of it than most visitors. Add to this the episodes of the couplet on the window-pane — and let it go at that! Unless you care to lengthen this short list by a little reflection on the Comte de Chambord, grandson of Charles X and son of the Duchesse de Berri, whom we recalled at Nantes. The château was bought for him by national subscription, in 1821, soon after his birth. His grandfather, abdicating at Rambouillet in 1830, tried vainly to secure the succession to the ten-year-old lad as Henry V. 'Henry V' went into exile (part of it spent at Holyrood) with Charles X. He returned to Chambord after the fall of the Second Empire, in September, 1870, and proclaimed himself King. And he might have won support enough to seat and keep him on the throne of his ancestors had he not held out, not merely for the white flag of the Bourbons as against the tricolor of the New France, but for the fatal Bourbon principle of the divine right of kings.

He bequeathed Chambord to the sons of his sister, the Duchess of Parma, from whose heirs, half Italian, half Austrian, it was confiscated during the War of 1914–18, because they had served in the Austrian army. Their sister is the ex-Empress Zita of Austria.

The guide may show you the four state carriages which were to have been used for 'Henry V's' coronation. He will certainly show you the bed made for him but never slept in by him.

Now, what o'clock is it? You may feel like lunching at the Hôtel du Grand Saint-Michel, near the château, and going to Cheverny and Moulin; thence to Blois.

Cheverny, ten and a half miles southwest of Chambord, has no history of interest to us, but is splendidly furnished and superbly kept up, and well worth a visit if you wish to see how a mansion older by a generation than the palace at Versailles, looks when appropriately furnished. Many of its treasures are regarded as among the best that France conserves of their magnificent period. And the owner is very gracious about permitting visitors daily except Fridays and Sundays.

Château du Moulin, built at the end of the fifteenth century, is one of the most picturesque places hereabouts. To photographers and painters wishful to try their skill on something less stereotyped than Chenonceaux (for instance), I heartily recommend Château du Moulin, and the reflections in its water-filled moats of its lovely 'pepper-pot' defence towers and bridge with exquisite arches. It has, also, a most interesting mediæval kitchen. It is at Lassay, about twelve miles southeast of Cheverny, a little off the main road from Blois to Romorantin. And to those who will most delight in Château du Moulin, I also commend the charming old town of Romorantin, some five miles beyond, with its wealth of sculptured-timber houses and the remains of the château, rebuilt by Francis I, wherein his little grandson, Francis II, not long before his feeble young life ended, signed an edict preventing the establishment of the Inquisition in France.

You may see these three places in an afternoon and reach Blois in good time before dinner. Or, if your time for the châteaux is short, you may omit them; go from Chambord to Blois (ten miles) for luncheon; see that château in the early afternoon, glimpse Chaumont and Amboise en route, and reach Tours for dinner and the night.

I shall assume that you are not obliged to hurry so, and that you are now turned back toward the Loire, to spend the night at Blois — either at Grand Hôtel de Blois, or Hôtel de France, both near the château.

Now, Blois (pronounced Blwah) is the place where my feeling against letting too many things crowd our memories is put to its severest test. No other castle in France evokes so many familiar and fascinating ghosts. I've tried my best to concentrate upon a few of them; but I can't. All I can do is to pass in review before you a number of them and leave you to do your own selecting.

So imagine yourself, I pray, invited to attend, this even-

ing, a gathering of the ghosts of Blois, all assembling to
honor your arrival. You need not meet them all; that
would weary you. But there are many even in the most
carefully selected list.

This handsome man, majestic of aspect and mien but
most affable and winsome, is Stephen of Blois, grandson of
William the Conqueror, and King of England for nineteen
troublous years.

Behind him — very close behind — is a lovely lady:
Eleanor of Aquitaine, just divorced (at Beaugency, which
you passed this morning) from Louis VII of France. Louis
had bored her to extinction with his austere piety; and she
had tried him sorely with her levity. Personally, they were
well quit each of the other. But Eleanor's vast possessions
have been restored to her by the scrupulous Louis; and
there are a great many gentlemen who covet them.

One of these is Thibaut, Count of Blois, elder brother of
King Stephen. Eleanor left Beaugency in the morning,
immediately after her divorce was pronounced, and rode
into Blois at eventide, accompanied by the handsome and
gallant Thibaut. As they approached the castle, Thibaut's
herald rode ahead with his banner and sounded the call.

'There was a scurrying within,' says Raimon de Loi in
'The Trails of the Troubadours,' 'and the officers of the
castle strode out to welcome their master and his guests.
Eleanor was shown to her room overlooking a garden of
roses transplanted from Jericho, and, wearied by her day
in the divorce court, was provided with a hot bath and a
massage. Thibaut was the son of a brave father and was
hospitable to excess. He did the best a gentleman of those
days could do to a wealthy heiress travelling alone: he
asked her to marry him. She refused. She may have said
she would be his sister, and she certainly intended to become his cousin as soon as she could persuade Henry of

Anjou to leave off burning cities and making widows and
orphans long enough to come down and marry her. But
Thibaut was insistent and persuaded Eleanor to spend several days with him at Blois. And who can blame her? "He
who has not known lilac-time at Blois has not yet expe-
rienced the sweetness of living," says an old French proverb; and perhaps Eleanor found the gay little city which
reflects its bright clear face in the Loire, and the early spring
days (it was March) and the sound of her own language in
her ears refreshing after the gloom of the capital. Oh, there
were parties, I have no doubt; and debates, and serenades
in the morning, clear-voiced musicians singing to the accompaniment of the guitar some new *aubade* to the rising
sun and the singing of birds.

'Then once more came the question and once more the
refusal. Perhaps Eleanor noted now that she was no longer
permitted to be alone as much as before. Perhaps she
heard orders given; or perhaps she was told simply, for this
reason or that, that it would be wise not to leave her chambers. At any rate, Eleanor disguised herself in the jerkin of
a serving-man and escaped by minutes a plot to put her into
seclusion, there to be kept until she could be persuaded by
courteous or discourteous means to marry the Count of
Blois. She left Blois by night and foiled her pursuers by
slipping down the river in a boat.'

Geoffrey Plantagenet, younger brother of Henry, was
also of a mind to acquire the vast possessions of the heiress
of Aquitaine. True, he was but seventeen, and Eleanor was
thirty-two. But his ardor to help Eleanor dispose of her
wealth took no account of that. He lay in ambush for the
much-coveted lady, intending to carry her to his donjon at
Montbazon (which you shall see, presently) and there
starve her into submission. But she evaded him, and on
May-Day was wed, at Bordeaux, to his brother Henry, who

was, in the language of his uncle of Gloucester, 'acquaint with the Queen of France some deal too much, as me weened.'

This group that's coming is one of the most interesting in history. There is Louis of Orléans, brother of the mad King Charles VI. Louis bought Blois, ten years before his murder in the streets of Paris by the assassins of the Duke of Burgundy. Here he began to collect the famous library of the Château of Blois, the nucleus of which was five books given him by his father, Charles V: two Bibles, one missal, one book entitled the 'Government of Kings,' and the 'Voyages of the Venetian Marco Polo.' With Louis is his Duchess, Valentine of Milan, the most accomplished woman of her day and the most adoring wife; she grieved herself to death, here at Blois, a year after her husband's murder, having made her children swear to avenge him. One of them was Charles, destined to be known as the Poet-Duke of Orléans; and another was Louis' child but not hers — Dunois, the Bastard of Orléans.

This younger woman with Valentine is Isabella of Valois, her husband's niece — that pathetic little creature who went to England when she was nine years old as the Queen of Richard II; was widowed when she was twelve; and at twenty was wed to her cousin Charles of Orléans. In her twenty-second year she died here, at Blois, a few hours after the birth of her infant daughter. And in his passionate grief for her her young husband wrote:

'To make my lady's obsequies
    My love a minster wrought,
And in the chantry service there
    Was sung by doleful thought.
The tapers were of burning sighs
    That life and odor gave,
And grief, illuminéd by tears,
    Irradiated her grave;
And round about, in quaintest guise
Was carved — "Within this tomb there lies
The fairest thing to mortal eyes."

'Above her lieth spread a tomb
  Of gold and sapphires blue;
The gold doth show her blessedness,
  The sapphires mark her true,
For blessedness and truth in her
  Were livelily portrayed.
When gracious God, *with both his hands*,
  Her wondrous beauty made,
She was, to speak without disguise,
The fairest thing to mortal eyes.'

Five years after her death, her husband was taken captive on the field of Agincourt, and carried off to spend
twenty-five long years a prisoner in England. While he
was away, and Dunois was administering his estates for
him, France knew the great drama of the Maid of Orléans.
He was nigh upon fifty when he was released, and the remaining years of his life were passed principally here at
Blois, where he kept a literary court of as much brilliance
as the state of letters in his day could provide: Villon came
hither, 'tis said, and others whose names have come down
to us less luminous than that of the Vagabond.

Charles married, immediately following his release, Mary
of Cleves, kinswoman of his father's murderer; and when
he was past seventy he became the father of a son who
came into the world with great prospects; for Charles's
kinsman, the new King Louis XI, had as yet no son, and
the heir to the Duchy of Orléans was also heir to the crown
of France. Louis gave his own name to the baby at Blois;
and when the poet-duke passed on, three years later, there
was still no nearer heir to Louis.

Little Louis of Orléans was betrothed, when he was two
years old, to the newborn daughter of Louis XI (that pathetic Jeanne the Lame, whom we shall more particularly
recall elsewhere) and he was eight years old before his nose
was put out of joint, as we say, by the birth, at Amboise, of
that puny person who was to be Charles VIII.

So frail was this child that Louis XI could have little certainty of raising him; and it was no part of the wily King's plan to have a feeble heir outwitted by a clever heir-presumptive. So he did everything to make the young Duke of Orléans a 'trifling' and dissipated young person.

At Amboise, where he came into the world, we shall see Charles VIII pass out of it, at the age of twenty-eight, leaving his kingdom and his wife to his brother-in-law, Louis of Orléans — Louis XII of France at the age of thirty-six. His first act as sovereign was to negotiate his divorce from Jeanne, and to secure the hand of Anne of Brittany who still held her great duchy in her own right. At twenty-five years of age, Anne was already a very severe person. She had passionately loved Charles VIII, and mourned her children by him. She was melancholy, when Louis got her, and haughty; dressed more like a nun than like a queen; loved an ascetic but shrewd life; and exacted a rigorous obedience from those about her. But by this time Louis had sown all his wild oats, and was reaping the harvest in a prematurely dyspeptic and creaky 'old age' before forty.

Their eldest child was a daughter Claude. You may see Claude, here at Blois, at almost any stage of her short life of twenty-five years. But I hope you won't overlook her as a baby.

It is December, 1501, if you please. Claude is two years old, and her betrothal is at hand. This is a very sumptuous group approaching you.

This man, who is called Philip the Fair (or Handsome), is son and heir of Maximilian, Emperor of Austria. His mother was Marie of Burgundy. His wife is Joanna, elder daughter of Ferdinand and Isabella of Spain. They have an infant son, Charles (destined to become Charles V), whom they are about to betroth to the baby daughter of the French King.

I wish we had space for the details of this ceremony as history has conserved them for us. But we haven't; all I may tell you is that it was very pompous and magnificent — and that Claude shrieks lustily and has to be removed. Poor Claude! Being born a princess was even less joy to her than to most.

If Anne of Brittany had borne a son to Louis XII, the marriage of her daughter with the future Charles V might not have been a political misfortune, however unhappy it was to her personally. But no son came in answer to Anne's almost incessant prayers. And that meant that giving Claude in marriage to Charles would be to bring the Austro-Spanish ruler over the kingdom of France, too. Yet Anne favored this union obstinately, even when Ferdinand of Spain, being told that Louis complained that Ferdinand had three times deceived him, sneered: 'The besotted fool! I have deceived him more than *ten* times!'

Louis then turned his attention upon the heir to his throne, young Francis, Count of Angoulême (descended from a younger son of Louis of Orléans and Valentine of Milan), and decided to marry Claude to that youth. Anne opposed this, and went off to Brittany to nurse her offended pride. But she came back. And it was here at Blois that she died — as Claude did, ten years later.

There is a great deal here to remind us of Louis XII and of Anne. There is the lovely east wing of the château that he built, with the beautiful and often-pictured portal surmounted by an equestrian statue of Louis — a modern one; the original having been melted down by the Revolutionists of '93, to make munitions. (To the right of this portal, in the old guard-hall, is the fireplace in which were burned, on Christmas Eve, 1588, the bodies of the Duke of Guise and his brother, the Cardinal of Guise.) On the opposite side of the Place du Château from your hotel, at the southeast corner of Louis XII's wing, is the Hôtel d'Amboise in which the Cardinal Amboise used to sit at his window and converse with the King across the way. (He it was, you'll remember, of whom Louis was wont to say, 'Let George do it.') Down in the Place Louis XII, below the château, is the charming Louis XII fountain, one of seven which Blois had in his day. The Pavilion of Anne, on avenue Victor Hugo, in her day was in the gardens of the château which then extended to the edge of the forest of Blois. To this pavilion Anne often retired to make novenas entreating Heaven for the gift of a son.

Blois is, I think, the best château in which to begin that study of architectural emblems which adds so much zest to our sight-seeing among French palaces. And may I say that I have found this a quite-absorbing pursuit for children abroad, and have been astonished at their facility in it. Knowing these emblems and the stories of their owners gives them a lively something-to-do, a competitive game of discovery and counting and recognizing, which they thoroughly enjoy.

Louis XII's emblem is the porcupine. When his father, Charles, was christened, Louis, Duke of Orléans, founded the Order of the Porcupine, bristling against foes. And if you will remind the children what need there was of 'getting one's back up' in those days before Jeanne d'Arc came to stiffen the resistance of her countrymen against the English invaders, I'm sure you'll find them interested in 'the fretful porcupine.'

The Order of the Ermine was founded by John V, Duke of Brittany, to commemorate the conquest of Brittany (see our Chapter II, p. 117); the snowy ermine was adopted as a symbol of purity. Anne of Brittany used this device; and, after 1498 — the year wherein she became Queen of France for the second time — she also used the cordon, or rope, the

emblem of an order she created. The swan, 'white among
the whites,' is the emblem of Claude — the poor baby who
screamed when she was being betrothed to the future
Charles V, and who wept most of the time she was married
to Francis I. I have heard various accounts, in Touraine,
of the arrow piercing the swan's heart; but I am afraid they
do not merit repetition. If, as the guides sometimes tell us,
the arrow represents all the anguish Francis caused his wife,
I am sure that he would have effaced her 'scutcheons in
favor of something less reproachful. The cordon around
Claude's swan reminds us that she was the heiress of her
mother, Anne of Brittany.

Francis I's emblem is the salamander which says, of fire,
'I nourish it and extinguish it' — the 'fire' Francis had in
mind being the fever-heat of love.

Besides these five emblems, you will see, at Blois, the
collar of Saint Michael, composed of golden shells. This
order, you'll recall, was founded by Louis XI at Mont-
Saint-Michel, and was for many years one of the most
coveted and prized of distinctions. You will also see the
emblem of Francis I's mother, Louise of Savoy, which con-
sists of a swan's wings, a plume made of five fleurs-de-lys on
their stems, and her royal crown.

The crowned 'L' at Blois is Louis XII; the crowned 'A,'
Anne of Brittany. The crowned 'F,' Francis I; the crowned
'C,' Claude. The crowned 'H' is for Henry II, and the
'H' and 'C,' interlaced, are for Henry II and Catherine de
Médicis.

Francis I came to the throne on New Year's Day, 1515;
and among the first things he did as king was to order re-
parations and reconstructions at the Château of Blois. So it
was here that he inaugurated his career as the greatest of
France's builder-kings. But he spent, all told, little time
here; and there is nothing about him that you need to call

to mind at Blois, except that he ordered the construction of that marvellous new wing for Claude to live in, with their babies, whilst he gallivanted about 'salamander-ing.' After his return from captivity in Spain, he used Blois as he used other châteaux of the Loire and elsewhere, as 'road-houses' for brief stops on his incessant goings and comings.

If I were you, I'd reserve most of my reflections on Catherine de Médicis and her family until you are in the château. And if you have brought with you Balzac's 'Catherine de Médicis,' I urge you to do a goodish bit of reading in it here on the 'spot' described in Chapters III–VIII.

At Amboise they don't show us much of the château. At Langeais there is just one outstanding episode to dwell upon. At Chinon there are several great episodes, but only crumbling ruins. At Loches and Chaumont and Chenonceaux we have much to see *and* to recall. But nowhere is there so much to engage us as at Blois — empty and echoing though it is. So give yourself as much time for the château as you possibly can, and to that end, see something of the delightful town before or after dinner on the day of your arrival, so you may have the whole morning for the château.

You will, I warn you, be much tempted to shop at Blois — to buy antiques and needlepoint especially. And in the town I think you'll wish to see the Church of Saint Nicholas rather than the uninteresting cathedral; and some of the old houses.

Take the street (rue Porte-Chartraine) which leads past the corner of the Grand Hôtel de Blois in the direction away from the château, and follow it a very short distance to rue Saint-Honoré. In this latter street you'll find the Hôtel d'Alluyes, built by Robertet, who was treasurer of Louis XII and Francis I. The Cardinal of Guise lived here in 1588 at the time of his murder. Be sure to see the courtyard with its splendid staircase; and if the insurance company, whose offices are now here, has not 'shut up shop' for the day, see the great hall on the ground floor and the magnificent fireplace.

A few steps farther on in rue Saint-Honoré, turn to your left, to rue Beaurevoir, where there used to be an old donjon of the Lords of Beaurevoir.

Then go down the Monumental Staircase of one hundred and twenty-one steps, descending through terraced gardens with a magnificent view. At the foot of these stairs, go around the Hôtel de la Chancellerie and into rue des Trois-Clefs where the Tour d'Argent (or Silver Tower) is, a fragment of the old mint of the Counts of Blois, demolished in 1315. In the rue du Commerce, close by, at number 28, is the quaint old fish-market, and at number 41 is a most interesting old house. Also close by, at number 18 rue Saint-Martin, is the Hôtel de Cheverny, built about 1470, which used to be called 'the little Louvre' because of the almost-royal power of its owners. If you are short of time, or tire easily, turn down rue Saint-Martin, here. Otherwise, follow rue des Trois-Clefs to rue des Juifs at number 19 in which lived Nepveu, architect of Chambord; rue des Trois-Clefs leads to rue Pierre-de-Blois, at the upper end of which is the very quaint old wooden house called Denis Papin's. Denis Papin, whose monument stands on the Monumental Staircase, was born in Blois in 1647, and the French claim for him the distinction of having discovered the power of steam; he died a quarter-century before James Watt was born. Rue Pierre-de-Blois, commemorating the twelfth-century chronicler, is rich in old houses, one of which arches the street. In every direction from the Carrefour Saint-Michel, below the cathedral, are streets to delight the etcher and the lover of the Past. If you explore them, rue du Poids du Roi will lead you back into rue du Commerce and the Hôtel de Cheverny. A step or two down rue Saint-Martin from Hôtel de Cheverny are the square and fountain of Louis XII and south of the square is rue des Orfèvres, with lovely old houses. Follow rue Saint-Lubin, past the fifteenth-century Hôtel Gaillard, now the Presbytery of Saint Nicholas's Church; visit the church; and when you leave it, follow rue du Foix west to number 65, where Victor Hugo's father spent the last days of his life.

On the 17th of April, 1864, Victor Hugo wrote from his exile's home on the Isle of Guernsey to M. Queroy, who had sent him a copy of his book of etchings on 'The Streets and Houses of Old Blois':

'Sir, I am thankful to you for having made me live again in the past. On the 17th of April, 1825, thirty-nine years ago on this very day, I was arriving at Blois. It was in the morning and I was coming from Paris. I had spent the whole night in the mail-coach. . . . The voice of the driver wakened me. "Here is Blois!" he called. . . . The sun was rising over Blois.

'A quarter of an hour after I was at rue du Foix. I knocked at a little door opening on to a garden: a man who was at work in the garden came and let me in. He was my father.

'In the evening, my father took me to a hillock which overlooked his house (Butte des Capucines); I saw from above, the town I had seen from below; the aspect was different, and though severe, more charming still. In the morning, the town had impressed me as being gracefully disordered and almost surprised, as one who awakes; the evening had softened the lines. Though it was still light — the sun had just set — there was a tinge of melancholy in the air; the twilight was blurring the sharp lines of the roofs; a few glimmering candles replaced the dazzling light of dawn on the window-panes; the contours of things underwent the

mysterious transformations of the evening; stiff straight
lines decreased whilst curves increased; there were more
bends and fewer angles. I remained there gazing with emotion. . . . In the sky blew a faint summer breeze.

'The town . . . was cut into well-balanced segments of
impressive bulk. In the receding background, the terraces
overhung each other in the most natural and tranquil
manner: the cathedral, the Bishop's palace, the dark
church of Saint Nicholas, the castle, as much a fortress as a
palace, the intersecting ravines, the ascents and descents on
which the houses seem now to climb and then to slide. The
bridge with its obelisk, the beautiful, winding Loire, the
straight rows of poplars, quite in the distance Chambord,
dimly seen with its forests of turrets, the woods through
which runs the old road called "Roman bridges" (Ponts-
Chartrains) marking the former bed of the Loire, all this
was both grand and pleasing. Moreover, my father was
fond of that town.

'You have revived it before my eyes to-day. Thanks to
you, I am at Blois. . . . Is there anything more lovely than
a kindly, witty old woman? Many of the exquisite houses
you have drawn may be compared to that old woman. . . .
How deliciously have they told over again the story of the
Past! For instance, look at this fine, delicate house in rue
des Orfevres (number 16 or number 18). . . . Here is the
Silver Tower. Here is the high dark gable at the corner of
rue de Violettes and rue Saint-Lubin. Here are the Hôtels
of Guise, of Cheverny, of Sardini . . . here is the Hôtel
d'Alluyes with its graceful arcades of the time of Charles
VIII . . . here is the pretty tower called the oratory of
Queen Anne. Behind that tower was the garden in which
Louis XII, afflicted with gout, used to ride his little mule.
. . . All those personages, along with Henry III and the
Duke of Guise and others, I have seen again in the con-

fused evocation of History, while turning over the pages
of your precious book. . . . Here is really Blois, my own
Blois, my luminous Blois — for my first impression on
arriving has remained. For me, Blois is radiant; I can see
Blois only in the rising sun. These are impressions left by
youth and love of one's native land.'

(Hugo was twenty-three when he made that visit to his
father at Blois. Victor's mother, who had been estranged
from his father for many years, had died in 1821. General
Hugo died in 1828.)

I'm sure you'll want to climb the hillock of the Capucins
toward set-of-sun. And from there you can take boulevard
de l'Ouest and avenue Victor-Hugo, back to Place Victor-
Hugo and your hotel.

In the morning, enter the castle at nine, if you can. I
should pay ten francs or so for a 'private visit,' if I were you,
even if you don't understand French and cannot get an
English-speaking guide; because you will be unhurried,
and can linger in some spots as long as you like.

Enter beneath the equestrian statue of Louis XII, facing
the Place du Château. In this Louis XII wing you visit
three great ground-floor apartments with fireplaces where
you may do some practice-work with your knowledge of
royal emblems. In the fireplace of the first, the bodies of
the murdered Guises were burned. These apartments are
reached from a fine open gallery at each end of which is an
elegant vaulted staircase.

As you step into the courtyard of the château you have,
on your right, adjoining the Louis XII wing, the Salle des
États, or Hall of the States-General, the oldest existing
part of the château except the Tour du Foix. It was the
great hall of the castle of the Counts of Blois wherein the
Counts gave audiences and fêtes, received the homage of
their vassals, and sat in justice on them. It dates from the

twelfth century, and may have been here when Thibaut entertained Eleanor of Aquitaine. Certainly it was a venerable apartment when Jeanne d'Arc was here at Blois.

Adjoining it on its other side is the great Francis I wing.

On your left, as you enter the courtyard from the Louis XII wing, is an arcaded gallery attributed to Charles of Orléans, and the Saint-Calais Chapel, built about the same time as the Louis XII wing. In the sixteenth century it was twice as long as we see it (the remaining part being only the choir of the original edifice) and was very sumptuous with treasures heaped upon it by Queen Anne and other royalties.

Passing between the chapel and the wing of Gaston of Orléans (Louis XIII's brother), you reach the Terrasse du Foix with the grand old Tour du Foix towering some ninety feet above the lower quarters of the town. Its pepper-pot crest and its crenelations were swept away by order of Catherine de Médicis to make room for an astrological observatory. We are not permitted to view the stars from it now, but we shall do well to ascend to its platform for the magnificent panorama visible from there. This tower is the most considerable bit left of the mediæval fortifications.

When you have sufficiently admired, from the courtyard, the superb spiral staircase of the Francis I wing, you will ascend it. And if you do not meet on it a thrilling press of personages brushing past you as they descend, it can only be because you are a spiritual pauper and have never entered upon your rightful inheritance through books.

On the first floor of this wing are the apartments which belonged to Queen Claude, and were occupied, later, by her daughter-in-law, Catherine de Médicis. Above them are the apartments of Francis I, of Francis II, and Mary Stuart, and later still of Henry III.

Suppose you imagine yourself to be ascending here in May, 1560, along with young Christophe Lecamus, son of the court furrier, coming to Blois ostensibly on matters of royal finery, but actually to bring letters of vast importance to Catherine de Médicis from the Huguenot leaders toward whom she was leaning for deliverance from the unbearable snubs, slights, and graver possibilities of Guise hatred.

'It is easy,' says Balzac, 'to imagine Christophe's amazement as he entered the great *salle des gardes*. . . . It occupied one third of the whole front of the château facing the courtyard,' and Christophe 'placed himself near an officer, who was seated on a stool at the corner of a fireplace as large as his father's whole shop, which was at the end of the great hall, opposite to a precisely similar fireplace at the other end.'

The guards' hall in which Christophe waited was that on the King's floor, above the Queen-mother's.

Balzac describes for us in detail, which I dare not take space to quote here, the assembling of the court on that May morning, and Christophe's admission into Mary Stuart's chamber, wherein was also, at that moment, her mother-in-law, Catherine de Médicis. See Christophe hand Catherine a bill for furs long since delivered to her. Mary Stuart appears not to be looking at them at all; but her quick glance has taken in the *bulk* of the bill, and the fact that Christophe extracted it from his bosom, whereas he had taken the bill he presented *her* from his pocket. Hear Catherine tell Christophe to come with her to her apartment's below, and she will pay him.

Francis and Mary proceed to a council. Catherine is not present, and they await her. Suddenly, Mary says: 'I will go and fetch my mother myself!'

Slipping unannounced into Catherine's oratory, she catches the Queen-mother in the very act of lifting the compromising papers Christophe has brought her, to hide them in one of the secret places behind sliding panels.

In a flash, Catherine saves herself and denounces Christophe, whose ally she had been but a moment before.

'I hold the traitors at last!' Catherine cries. Christophe is led off to prison and torture, and Catherine affects to believe that the Guises are sincere in seeming to think that she has willingly served their cause.

Now, when you have seen the Queen's apartments, and have imagined Catherine, on her deathbed, in the days just before Christmas, 1588, ascend the Staircase of the Forty-Five Guardsmen, whom Dumas keeps forever alive, to the apartments which were Henry III's in those December days more than thirty-eight years after the day when Christophe came bringing the Huguenot leaders' confidential papers to Catherine. The intervening years have been terrible indeed. There has been the death of little Francis II, at Orléans; there has been the ascendency of Catherine, dominating her weak-willed son, Charles IX; there has been the massacre of Saint Bartholomew's Eve; there has been the horror-haunted, raving death of Charles. There has been the long captivity, overseas, and the death on the scaffold, in Fotheringay's hall, of Mary Stuart. Her uncles are gone, but their claim to the throne is still strong in the three sons of Duke Francis: Henry, Duke of Guise, Charles, Duke of Mayenne, and Louis, Cardinal of Guise; and Philip II of Spain is backing and abetting them.

Henry III's brother, the Duke d'Alençon, died in 1584. Henry has no heir except the Protestant King of Navarre. The ultra-Catholic party of the League, headed by the Guises, is desperate.

Henry has summoned the States-General to meet at Blois in October, 1588. There are 505 deputies — 134 of the clergy of the realm, including 4 bishops and archbishops;

180 of the nobles; 191 members of the Third Estate, or commoners. Most of them are openly for the Guises and against the King. They have forced Henry III to declare his brother-in-law of Navarre a criminal against God and man.

On December 22d, the King announced that he would summon his Council earlier than usual next morning, because he was going on a pilgrimage to Notre-Dame-de-Cléry. And on this pretext, he kept the keys of the castle instead of turning them over as usual to the lieutenant-general.

At five o'clock on the morning of Friday the 23d, the King was dressed and ready for — something. He had ordered the Forty-Five Guardsmen to rooms above his, and had two priests celebrate the Mass in his oratory and pray for the success of his enterprise. It was not so much consideration for his dying mother's feelings as fear of what she might do to intervene that caused Henry to threaten death to any one who allowed her to learn what was going on over her head.

Guise had, however, received many warnings. The night before, at dinner, he found one in his napkin, reading: 'Take care, they are going to play you a bad turn.' He wrote on it, 'They dare not,' and threw it under the table. The morning of his death he said, of one note handed him, 'This is the ninth to-day.'

When he arrived at the Council chamber, his retinue was asked to wait. Perhaps he realized then that he was in a trap, for he was cold and asked for a fire. Then his nose bled and he sent for a handkerchief — perhaps in the hope that with it would be brought back some word of what was happening outside. But the messenger was not allowed to return. He was eating some prunes, by the fireplace, when the Council was called to order. The King was not present.

THE ASSASSINATION OF THE DUKE OF GUISE
By Paul Hippolyte Delaroche

Presently the King's secretary entered and said: 'Monsieur, the King asks for you; he is in the old cabinet.'

The Duke threw his prunes on the table, asking: 'Who'll have some?' then he went to the King's cabinet. When he came to the tapestry which hung before the door, the assassins fell upon him. He fought furiously, and the struggle lasted two or three minutes. The end was in the King's own chamber, at the foot of his bed — Henry crying, 'Finish him!'

When he was finished, Henry approached the body, and touching it with the end of his sword, said: 'My God! how tall he is! He looks even taller than when he was alive.'

In the Council chamber the scuffle and cries were heard. Cardinal Guise ran toward the door, crying, 'They are murdering my brother!' He was arrested and executed next day.

Henry descended to the chamber of his mother, who had heard the struggle above her head, and said: 'This morning I have become King of France again.'

What Catherine replied to him has been variously reported; but we know it was a warning. She knew that the end of the Guises was not yet.

And she was right. In Paris the people tore down Henry's statues and hacked his portraits in pieces. The clergy denounced him openly and refused the rites of the Church to his adherents. Four thousand children, with bare feet and lighted tapers, went in procession to the Church of Sainte-Geneviève (where the Panthéon now is) and there dashed their lights on the ground, crying, 'Thus perish the race of Valois!' City after city revolted against the King.

He called Navarre to his aid. They advanced upon Paris, where Mayenne (the last of the Guise brothers) was king in all but anointment, and were on the eve of besieging it when Henry III was assassinated at Saint-Cloud by a Jacobite monk named Clément; and with him perished the race of Valois. This was in the summer following the Guise murders — July 31, 1589.

If you like, you may extend your reveries in these apartments to include that obese termagant, Marie de Médicis, who was shut up here for the good of France and her son, Louis XIII, and escaped hence. I find her poor company — and likewise her younger son, Gaston of Orléans, who built the wing of the château that adjoins Francis I's and faces Louis XII's.

But I like to see Louise de la Vallière here, where she came, with her mother and stepfather, to live when she was in her eleventh year. It was here, probably, that she first saw the young King.

II

Blois is hard to leave. But if you are to see three important châteaux this afternoon, en route to Tours, it behooves you to get an early lunch and be on your way.

Cross the Loire at Blois, and take the left bank to Chaumont, ten miles away.

Chaumont is delightfully and satisfyingly picturesque — one of the most pleasing of all the castles to see; I hope you won't miss it. But you needn't force yourself to recall much of its history. It was rebuilt, in the reign of Louis XI, by Charles d'Amboise, brother of the Cardinal Georges to whom Louis XII was always leaving the doing of things.

When Henry II became king, he gave the exquisite château and property of Chenonceaux to Diane de Poitiers, claiming that it had never been made a Crown property by his father and was his to dispose of. This was a bitter disappointment to his wife, Catherine de Médicis, who coveted Chenonceaux exceedingly. During his reign of twelve years, she could do nothing; but on his death, Catherine bought Chaumont to exchange for it. Diane agreed to the exchange on January 4, 1560; Catherine acquired this property on March 21st, and Diane became its owner on April 27th.

If it was here that Ruggieri, Catherine's astrologer, showed her the vision of her descendants' tenure of the throne, it must have been when she came to look over the castle with a view to buying it. The minute examination to which Catherine's life has been subjected by her recent biographers shows that she never lived here — and, for that matter, neither did Diane spend much time at Chaumont.

The story of the vision is that Ruggieri told Catherine to gaze steadily into a large mirror, in which she would see the future kings of France appear and each make as many turns as there would be years in his reign; and that she saw Francis II turn once, and disappear; then Charles IX, who turned thirteen times; then Henry III, who turned fifteen times and vanished suddenly; then her son-in-law, Henry of Navarre, who likewise vanished suddenly after having made twenty turns.

It is said that she would never look on Chaumont again. The apartments and furnishings shown as hers are interesting; but it is elsewhere that you should recall Catherine.

In the eighteenth century, Chaumont was bought by Jacques Le Ray, who installed here the manufacture of terra-cotta medallions executed by Nini, an Italian. Le Ray, who was a friend of Benjamin Franklin, loaned him a house in Passy to live in, and invited him to Chaumont, in 1777, to sit to Nini. Le Ray invested heavily in colonization schemes in the United States, and his son came over to fight for us. It was this son who, when Madame de Staël was forced by Napoleon to leave Paris, placed Chaumont at her disposal. And descendants of hers now own and occupy the château.

Ten miles more downstream, on the left bank of the Loire, and you are at Amboise where there has been a castle of importance since the fifth century. It is now used by the Orléans family as an old people's home for their superannuated servants, and the visitor is admitted to the chapel, gardens, terraces, and a few supremely interesting apartments.

Amboise cherishes a tradition that Cæsar had granaries in the depths of the bold rock promontory on which the castle stands. But what we know is that in the tenth century there was built here, by the Counts of Blois, who were perpetually at war with the Counts of Anjou, a formidable donjon which changed owners a good many times before it was confiscated by Charles VII in punishment for its lord's conspiracy against his favorite, La Trémoille.

On Charles's death, his widow, Marie of Anjou, came here to live. It became the principal residence of her daughter-in-law, Charlotte of Savoy, wife of Louis XI; and it was here, on June 3, 1470, that Charlotte brought into the world her long-desired son who was to become Charles VIII. Here Charles, a lad of thirteen, was affianced to the baby daughter of Marie of Burgundy and Maximilian — a union by which it was hoped to bring France a small portion at least of the great duchy which Louis XI had alienated by his treatment of Duchess Marie. Marie died when her little Margaret was two years old, and Margaret was brought up here at Amboise by the elder sister of Charles, Anne de Beaujeu, who was regent of the realm in his minority. Papa Maximilian, looking about for a new wife, saw interesting possibilities in young Duchess Anne of Brittany, three years older than his small daughter; and they were betrothed. But before either little girl was old enough to wed, young King Charles had changed his mind: he would marry the Duchy of Brittany himself! This left

Papa Maximilian without a bride, and little Margaret without a husband.

Margaret was married, at Burgos, in 1497, to the heir of Ferdinand and Isabella; but he lived only a few months. In 1501, she married Philibert II, Duke of Savoy and uncle of the young Count d'Angoulême who was destined to become Francis I; but he died in 1504. It was for him that Margaret built the exquisite Church of Brou (at Bourg-en-Bresse, near Lyon), which I hope you may have the thrill of seeing, some day. Two years later, her brother Philip died (he who had married Joanna, daughter of Ferdinand and Isabella and sister of Margaret's first husband — also of Catherine of Aragon), and Margaret became guardian of his children and regent of the Netherlands. It was she who brought up the future Charles V and his sister, her namesake, and Eleanor who became Francis I's second queen. Margaret of Austria (as she is known in history) was one of the ablest women of the Renaissance, and I hope you'll take every opportunity for further acquaintance with her. Be careful not to confound her with that other Margaret of Austria who was Charles V's natural daughter, and also regent of the Netherlands — she who was married to Alessandro de' Medici, and then to Ottavio Farnese, Duke of Parma.

Charles VIII was married at Langeais (whither you are bound, on another day), but brought his Breton bride to Amboise immediately after her coronation at Saint-Denis, and began to rebuild, amplify, and refurnish his birthplace. The old fortress of the Counts of Blois had been built on a precipitous rock rising sheer above the Loire and attached to the hill behind it only by a narrow passage. Admirable for defence, but no setting for such elegance as Charles desired.

At the western extremity of the promontory, when

Charles brought his bride here, was the unfinished chapel which his father had begun. The completion of this little gem was one of the first things that Charles accomplished after his marriage. Queen Anne, they say, had a special fondness for this chapel, rather than for the Church of Saint Florentin which stood within the castle enclosure and within which Leonardo da Vinci's will directed that he should be buried. But Leonardo knew the little Chapel of Saint Hubert, and may have admired the exquisite sculpture above its portal as much as we do. The church he chose for his sepulture was destroyed in 1808, and more than half a century later what were believed to be his bones were discovered and reinterred here in Saint Hubert's Chapel. Whether they are his bones or not, his spirit certainly hovers about this place. If you know his portrait of himself at Florence, or his statue in Milan, you can picture him hereabouts in his majestic old age. I wonder if he wasn't homesick? The favor of kings must be a poor equivalent for 'own folks' and own country, when age has crept upon one.

I find myself treading reverently all those parts of Amboise which are shown us, because that 'darling of the gods' walked here.

Do you readily recall the lovely legend of Saint Hubert that the sculpture above the portal illustrates?

Hubert was a famous huntsman of the Ardennes to whom, on a fête day when he was hunting instead of devoting himself to more serious things, appeared a stag with a crucifix between his antlers. And Hubert heard a voice which cried, 'Hubert! Hubert! How long wilt thou spend thy time uselessly? Knowest thou not that thou wert born to know, to love, and to serve thy Creator?' So Hubert was converted, and became Bishop of Liège. Mr. Frederic Lees, whose book 'A Summer in Touraine' I commend to you as among the best I know on the châteaux, thinks that this sculpture was done by Flemish sculptors or copied from Flemish models by French workmen. The figures above it, of Charles and Anne kneeling to the Virgin, are quite modern.

Charles was not only a builder, but a collector; and among his treasures at Amboise was an armory wherein was the hatchet of Clovis (presumably the one wherewith he killed the thief of Soissons), the sword of Dagobert, the dagger of Charlemagne, swords of Charles VII and Louis XI, the armor of Jeanne d'Arc and that of Du Guesclin.

Little is left of all that he did at Amboise. But to him we owe the two great towers, masterpieces of their sort, unique in France in their majestic proportions, each of them masking a spiral ascent to the château — an ascent almost ten feet wide and ample for horsemen or even for carriages. You will delight in these, and rank them high among all your experiences of mediæval France. Pretend, if you like, that you are ascending the Tour des Minimes with Emperor Charles V and his one-time captive, Francis I — now his brother-in-law — when the interior was all hung with priceless tapestries and illumined by so many torches that it was as 'bright as noonday.' Perhaps you will like even better the view of the valley of the Loire from the battlements of that tower.

Your guide-book probably says that Charles VIII built the Logis du Roi, in which you'll be shown the Salle des États (or Hall of the States) from which one steps onto the balcony from which the Protestant conspirators were hanged. But he only embellished and increased it. The Hall of the States was the great hall of the château in the fourteenth century, and the guardroom (*salle des gardes*) below it belongs to a period still earlier.

Charles died at Amboise when he was not quite eight-and-twenty. It was Easter Saturday. He and Queen Anne came out of the château to look at some of the new constructions and to watch the game of hand-tennis being played in the moat. Charles is said to have struck his head against a doorway which will be shown you, and to have died of the effects of this blow. What probably happened was that he had a stroke of apoplexy and fell against the door. At any rate, he was apparently a well man (as well as he ever was) at two in the afternoon, and at eleven that night he was dead, leaving Anne so grief-stricken that, though she married his successor in a year, she is said to have lost 'all taste for life' when she saw Charles dead. In seven years of wedded life Anne (widowed at twenty-two) had lost four children and her husband.

After his marriage to Anne, in January, 1499, Louis XII installed at Amboise the household of Louise of Savoy, Countess of Angoulême, whose five-year-old son, Francis, was heir to the throne until such time as Anne might bear the new king a son. And to keep little Francis company the King sent hither some 'pages of honor' who included the King's nephew, Gaston de Foix; Henri d'Albret, the heir of Navarre and destined to become the husband of Francis' sister Marguerite; Charles de Montpensier, to become famous and infamous as the Constable de Bourbon; Anne de Montmorency, another future Constable of France; and Philippe Chabot, afterwards Admiral of France.

The play of these youngsters at Amboise is one of the most attractive pages in the castle's history, and one over which I'd like to linger — but dare not.

Francis was at Amboise, in 1518, celebrating the baptism of his heir, with festivities 'more splendid than had ever before been witnessed in Christendom,' when the marriage took place there of Lorenzo, the renegade young grand-

son of Lorenzo the Magnificent, with Francis' young kinswoman, Madeleine de la Tour d'Auvergne. Of this union,
a year later, was born Catherine de Médicis. And within
three weeks of her birth she was an orphan.

I shall not ask you to dwell upon the details of the horrible butchery at Amboise, in 1560, which drenched it in so
much blood that the place was shunned ever afterwards.
We'll make that story as brief as possible.

You were aware, at Blois, of the plot to thwart and tie
the Guises, and of Catherine's sudden change of front, to
save herself. You knew that the court was hurriedly moved
to Amboise because the young Queen's uncles believed they
could more surely defend themselves here.

Had we space to go into details of the plot, you should see
Catherine the inexplicable, here at Amboise, warned by one
of the plotters, tell first the Guises, her mortal enemies, of
their danger, and then tell the Prince de Condé, the leader
of the opposition, that he was discovered!

There was treachery upon treachery, and hundreds of
brave men were slaughtered, that the Guises might have
fewer enemies, not only by this thinning of their ranks, but
by the intimidation of those who might have been tempted
to rise against them. To this end, Amboise became a
shambles.

As you stand on the balcony of the Salle des États and
look down, you may like to feel Catherine de Médicis beside you, and young Mary Stuart, and the frail little King,
and the Papal Nuncio, and many more of the court; and in
the square below you may see the scaffolds, surrounded by
tiers of seats for spectators. The Huguenot nobles, whose
rank entitled them to death at the headsman's block, sang
as they awaited the end — sang a psalm which Clément
Marot had recently translated: 'God be merciful unto us
and bless us; and show us the light of His countenance.'

And with their eyes they saluted Condé, their outwitted chief, standing, helpless, on this balcony between the young Queen and him who was soon to be Charles IX.

The psalm continued to be sung by the survivors while the axe flashed and fell, until the last voice was silenced.

Later, this balcony was strung with swinging corpses which were left pendent for a long time, whilst the court, under the triumphant Guises, moved to Chenonceaux — whither you may now move also.

Ten miles southwest of Amboise is Montrichard, with a beautiful church and the remains of a very old castle. But if you are short of time, you would better take the most direct route to Chenonceaux, via Civray, which is only seven and a half miles. (Should you have a schedule of your own for these visits, you may count upon the inn at Chenonceaux — Hôtel du Bon-Laboureur — for good cheer and comfortable if simple lodging.)

I shall not try to describe Chenonceaux — nor to say why our admirable Muirhead says it ought to be spelled without an *x*. But I can tell you that, although you have heard so much about it, and have seen so many pictures of it, and have got your expectations so very high, you are not (I think) going to be disappointed.

And from the first step of your approach, up the magnificent long avenue of plane trees to the last backward look of reluctant farewell, there is so much for your ravished eyes and senses that I doubt if you will find yourself wanting to know a great deal about history.

Nevertheless, there are a few things one ought to recall at Chenonceaux.

Diane de Poitiers saw it first soon after it fell to the Crown, in 1535, to help liquidate the debts of its owner. You may imagine that calculating charmer, nineteen years older than the Dauphin she had enslaved, marking this for her own as soon as it was in his power to give it to her. She had to wait twelve years for it. And then for twelve years it was hers. But Henry cared little for the banks of the Loire, and everywhere that Henry went Diane was sure to go. So she saw little enough of her château on the Cher. She undertook expensive additions there, but they made slow progress; and it was Catherine, not Diane, who enjoyed them.

The exchange of Chaumont for Chenonceaux was effected while the court was at Amboise during the slaughter of the Huguenots, and when they left that blood-drenched, horror-haunted place to come here, Catherine entered as châtelaine, for the first time. Here she gave magnificent fêtes, in the early days of April, 1560. (Not wedding festivities for Francis II and Mary Stuart, as is so often stated; for they had been married two years.)

Catherine bequeathed Chenonceaux to her daughter-in-law, Louise of Lorraine, wife of Henry III; and many memories of her sad widowhood cling to the beautiful château.

More interesting are the memories of those distinguished men and women of the eighteenth century who came here as house-guests of Madame Dupin to whose son Jean Jacques Rousseau was tutor.

But, as I have said, Chenonceaux seems to me to be a place less for reflection than for ecstasy.

I have, however, one special little personal memory of it which I shall share with you because it is of a sort which may give you pleasure, as it gave me:

The last time I was at Chenonceaux was on the day after a holiday. The caretaker who escorted through the apartments a group of whom I was one told me that the crowds of the day before had been great, from morning till night. She was very tired. Nevertheless, she discharged her duties faithfully. Our group was a mixed one — young and old were in it; natives and foreigners; rich and poor. When we came to the chamber of Francis I, there lay on the floor a morsel of the rich taffeta curtains, burnt out of the window draperies by the suns of many summers. The caretaker stooped and picked it up reverently — reverent of its age and its associations. She talked to us about the room. When we were ready to pass on to the next apartment, she bent toward a little French girl, very plainly dressed, who stood staring, in the front row of our group. 'Take it, my child,' said the guide, handing the astonished child the rich fragment, 'and keep it, in memory of a place which has seen many great people in your country's past.'

Now, from Chenonceaux, take the road for Tours — twenty miles. You enter Tours by the avenue de Grammont. As you near the statue of Balzac and the Place du Palais de Justice, you pass on your right, the Hôtel Métropole, which is a good, comfortable house. Around the corner, to your right, on the boulevard Heurteloup, is Hôtel de l'Univers, which is more expensive, but so very, very good that if you can get in there you will not begrudge the difference in cost. Such memorable food! Such unforgettable wines! But if it is the season for Touraine, make your reservations *well* in advance; for this is headquarters of the motorists-de-luxe. The Hôtel au Faisan at number 17 rue Nationale, is straight ahead, across the Place du Palais de Justice, near the river. I have no personal knowledge of it, but it is well spoken of. Before you come to it, rue Gambetta, on your left, will offer you the hospitality of Hôtel du Croissant, which has had ups and downs of favor as a moderate-price house purveying good food. What its status may be when you get to Tours, I can't predict.

Tours, as you doubtless know, is one of the most satisfactory places in provincial France for a sojourn — not only because its French is considered the best spoken anywhere (that is to say, the general speech of Touraine inhabitants; naturally, it does not surpass the French of the Comédie Française, nor of the French Academy of Letters), but because of the many delightful excursions which may be made from there, and because of the renowned food and wine, and because Tours is an exceeding pleasant city, connected by several bridges over the Loire with a charming suburb, Saint-Symphorien, which abounds in agreeable *pensions* where families may live inexpensively and learn irreproachable French.

I am not overlooking all these aspects of Tours, in writing this chapter. I am just forcing myself to remember that for every one who may make a sojourn at Tours, there are hundreds who must see it on a rapid flight.

III

If you have a week for your châteaux trip, you may devote a day to Tours and its vicinity: a morning to the city, and an afternoon divided between Plessis-lès-Tours and Marmoutier. The principal châteaux you should see in a circuit from Tours can be visited in a day; to give two to them is better.

Suppose we imagine you to be at one of the hotels near the Place du Palais de Justice, with a day to spend in Tours and its immediate environs.

With regard to the past of Tours, I wouldn't try to review too much. There was a Gallic town where Saint-Symphorien now is, on the north bank of the Loire. When the Romans came, they preferred the south bank.

Of Gatien, who introduced Christianity in the third century, I have no knowledge. But I'm sure you'll wish to think a bit about good Saint Martin, third Bishop of Tours. It was when Martin was a young legionary of Rome, seventeen years old, swinging into Amiens on a cold day in

337, that he saw an old, shivering man with no cloak. The young soldier, who had been preparing for baptism, tore his mantle in two and gave half to the beggar. That night Martin was visited, in a dream, by Christ, accompanied by angels. And Christ was wearing the half of Martin's cloak, and saying, 'This is Martin, who gave me this cloak.'

A great man and a great influence for good did Martin become; and I should hate to leave Tours without paying my reverent respects to his memory.

Then there was Gregory of Tours, the first historian of France, who was born and bred at Clermont in Auvergne, but came to Tours in his young manhood to seek a cure at the tomb of Saint Martin — and stayed, becoming bishop here in 573. He wrote ten books of history, the first four covering the period from Creation till his own day; the last six are his record of his own times, and they are of great value and interest.

After him, there was Alcuin, born and educated at York, England, whom Charlemagne made Abbot of Saint Martin's. Alcuin made the abbey school here a great seat of learning. He was Charlemagne's teacher, and his instrument in transmitting to the ignorant Franks the knowledge of Latin culture.

I hope you agree with me that these three men who wrought so nobly for the enlightenment of France, for the history of civilization, are entitled to our respects, at Tours.

Tours was a part of the domain which Henry Plantagenet, Count of Anjou, inherited from Geoffrey, who may or may not have been his father, but was certainly his mother's husband. And it remained an English possession until Henry's wretched son, John, was deprived of it for his murder of Prince Arthur.

French royal favor made Tours very prosperous throughout the Middle Ages; and under Louis XI it was the most important centre of that silk manufacture he so shrewdly encouraged.

Now, are you in the immediate vicinity of the Balzac statue? Tours is proud of its Hôtel de Ville and its Palais de Justice, so I hope you can give them a little attention, even though they are not what you came to Tours to see. Then pass on up what has now become (by changing its name without changing its direction) rue Nationale; and as you pass Lycée Descartes, on your right, remind yourself that the great philosopher (whose statue you shall see up near the river) was born in Touraine, between Loches and Poitiers, and is, with Rabelais and Balzac, a great glory to the Tourangeaux — as the natives of Touraine are called. Descartes (1596–1650) was the first great, clear, philosophical thinker to write in a living, modern, tongue, and to hold that philosophy was *common sense* and belonged to everybody. He held that *reason* is 'the most equally apportioned thing in the world,' but the one that few persons know how to use, because they have not learned the delightful exercise which a brilliant Frenchman of to-day (Canon Dimnet) makes so alluring: 'The Art of Thinking.' Descartes trained his generation to think — taught them the formulæ — and has been one of the most considerable influences on all the generations since.

The house in which Balzac was born, in 1799, is number 39 rue Nationale. Rue de la Préfecture, at the corner of the Lycée Descartes, will take you past the Préfecture (or State House, or provincial Capitol), which used to be a convent. At the end of the street, turn to your left, and cross Square Émile-Zola; then, left again, to the cathedral. The former palace of the archbishops contains the Art Museum (which is specially proud of its two fine Mantegnas); and even if you are not picture-hungry, I think you'll enjoy the garden and the great cedar of Lebanon, and the charming terrace walk where the old Gallo-Roman wall used to be.

I think you'll find very great delight in the cathedral of Tours. Its stained glass is abundant and glorious, and the effect produced by color and line in the interior is one of exquisite beauty. And if you climb to the easternmost end of the choir triforium and look thence along the cathedral's length to the western rose, you will be richly repaid for the effort. In the first choir chapel on the right is the beautiful tomb of the four infants of Charles VIII and Anne of Brittany — one of the most touching as well as one of the love-liest tombs in all Europe.

When you leave the cathedral, make your way around its north side to the cloister of La Psalette which would repay me for a journey to Tours, though there were nothing else in the city or vicinity to delight me. See if you don't feel this to be one of the most delicious corners you have ever been in!

Prowl about the east end of the cathedral as much as you can. This is the site of the Gallo-Roman town. Then turn north to rue de la Caserne and go west in it, past the Tour de Guise, so called because the young Duke of Guise was imprisoned here after his father's murder at Blois; he was seventeen at the time of the murder and was in prison for three years. The murdered Duke had fourteen children. It was his second son, the Duke de Chevreuse, who was husband of the lively, intriguing Duchesse de Chevreuse. This tower in which young Guise was imprisoned is all that's left of the old castle of Henry Plantagenet.

Continuing westward in what has now become rue Colbert, you come, presently, to the Church of Saint-Julien, belonging to an abbey founded in the fifth century; and just south of it, in rue Jules-Favre, is the fine mansion of Jacques de Semblençay who was treasurer of Francis I, was accused of plundering the treasury, and was hanged high on

CATHEDRAL OF ST.-GATIEN, TOURS
From an engraving after a drawing by T. Allom

the gibbet of Montfaucon at Paris. Short shrift for raids on the national funds in those days!

Now, make your way back to rue Nationale, and up to Place des Arts, at the beginning of the Stone Bridge. Here you have the library and the school of fine arts, and statues of Descartes and Rabelais, and a view across the river to Saint-Symphorien.

I think I'd come back, on rue Nationale, to rue du Commerce, then turn west in that to number 35, in the courtyard of which stands the very beautiful mansion called Hôtel Gouin, said to have been built in 1440 — but I think this must be a mistake unless the façade is of a later date.

Rue du Commerce ends at Place Plumereau; and the last street running north out of Place Plumereau is rue Briçonnet, at number 16 in which is the house called that of Tristan l'Hermite, because, some one, long ago, mistook Anne of Brittany's 'cordon' in the sculptural decorations for a hangman's rope, and deduced therefrom that this must have been the dwelling of Louis XI's provost-marshal and lord high executioner. The house was built in the following reign.

The district between the river and the markets is rich in picturesque old buildings. Rue Bretonneau (the street west of rue Briçonnet) runs south toward Place du Grand Marché; and in this *place* is the charming fountain of Beaune, executed in 1510 from the designs of Michel Colombe, who did the tomb of Duchess Anne's parents at Nantes, you'll remember.

In rue des Halles are two towers of the old Basilica of Saint Martin, the third church erected over Saint Martin's tomb; and close by is the imposing new Basilica of Saint Martin, recently erected above the crypt containing his remains.

Rue des Halles will take you back to rue Nationale —

and to luncheon — and you may feel that you have glimpsed the principal 'sights' of Tours.

After luncheon, direct your 'trusty steed' down avenue de Grammont past the Métropole to rue d'Entraigues, and follow this to the Botanical Gardens; then turn north along the western edge of these, to Sainte-Anne. Close to the gardens, on this road, is the farm called 'La Rabaterie,' which is said to have belonged to that 'little, pale, meagre man,' Olivier le Daim, whom Louis XI not only trusted to shave him (perhaps the supremest trust that suspicious Louis could place in any man), but also to help him administer the affairs of the kingdom.

A short distance west and south of Sainte-Anne is Plessis-lès-Tours. There is not a great deal left of the famous château where Louis XI died, and some who go out to see what there is, are bitterly disappointed. But I wouldn't, for a good deal, have missed going. I shall probably go again, some day — although I have made several visits to Tours without revisiting Plessis-lès-Tours.

For the camera eye, there's not much. For the critical ear there's a good deal of 'bunk.' Scott, they now tell us, drew a very long bow when he wrote the descriptions of Plessis which thrilled and chilled our marrow when we were twelve or thereabouts.

I don't care! I can reconstruct Plessis to myself; and re-people it, too. And I'm sure you can!

I suppose the best general authority on the châteaux is Pierre Rain, whose 'Les Chroniques des Châteaux de La Loire' I am using for this chapter, along with many scholarly monographs on the individual châteaux and a 'five-foot shelf' of books in English — some of which are scholarly, like Theodore Andrea Cook's 'Old Touraine'; and some are kind of sweetmeaty and cloying, like Mrs. Champney's 'Stories of the Renaissance Châteaux' (liable to strange inaccuracies, too); and some are diffuse and Victorian, but on the whole quite satisfying, like Frances Elliot's 'Old Court Life in France'; some are merely superficial; and some are superficial in a way that's not 'mere': like the one whose author managed to write a whole book about this district without finding out that Louis XII was not Charles VIII's younger brother.

Pierre Rain says that curious as it may seem, the principal defences of Plessis-lès-Tours consisted of the sovereign's formidable reputation; and that he lived here with any frequency only after he had so established the royal authority in Western France that he had no fear of any attack from one of his vassals.

No one, he points out, who was possessor of Loches and Chinon and Amboise would ever have bought this low-lying place for a stronghold. Louis liked it, he thinks, because it had no memories of his father. He hated every place and every person Charles had liked. And he liked Tours, and dreamed of making it the capital of the kingdom. The wanderlust of the Valois kings was strong in him, and he stayed nowhere for more than a short sojourn (Rain says that his letters show an average of five or six changes of residence per month), but as he felt his end drawing near, he tended to stay at Plessis more than elsewhere, and lived here in company with his motley familiars, his wife and son remaining for the most part at Amboise. Sometimes he had here with him his elder daughter, Anne de Beaujeu, and her husband, Pierre de Bourbon. The younger daughter, Jeanne the Lame, and her husband, the Duke of Orléans, he kept suspiciously under his eye. But his associations were more with astrologers and sorcerers, with his barber and his hangman, his quacks and other queer cronies. Toward the end, he sent to Calabria for Saint Francis de Paul, and to Reims for the Holy Oil brought from Heaven for the baptism of Clovis. Louis, who had suffered two strokes of apoplexy, wanted his whole body rubbed with the Holy Oil; but though he were to use it all, there was not enough for such use; all that could be done was to set it on an altar in the King's chamber (that room which is preserved to this day) and pray to it.

'Stretched on his bed in a corner of this big apartment that we see to-day,' Rain says, 'lighted by five windows, he tossed in fever, occupying his moments of respite with attention to the business of his realm.'

And there, terrified and terrifying to the last, he died at eight o'clock on Saturday evening, August 30, 1483, having reigned twenty-two years. A curious instrument of progress, he was; but he left behind him the foundations of modern France.

Now, come back to Sainte-Anne, and take boulevard Preuilly to the Quais and cross the stone bridge to Saint-Symphorien. Follow the levee on the north bank till you come to rue Saint-Gatien, which leads to the entrance of the Abbey of Marmoutier, one of the oldest monasteries in Christendom, founded by Saint Martin. Some four miles beyond on the road to Vouvray is the Lanterne de Roche-corbon, a very high, narrow watch-tower of the fourteenth century soaring from a cliff honeycombed with dwellings. Vouvray, I hope you need not be told, produces a most delicious white wine. There is a Vouvray 1922 which is specially choice. And be sure to try the Vouvray mousseux, or sparkling Vouvray, on the order of champagne and much cheaper. Mr. Frederick Lees says that some five miles beyond Vouvray is the château of Jallanges which he particularly enjoyed. I have not seen it; but on his recommendation I mean to, some day.

After this you should get back to Tours early enough for tea in one of the shops on rue Nationale.

Or it might be that you would prefer to spend this afternoon seeing some of the châteaux nearest Tours, so as to make to-morrow's programme less full.

You might, for instance, in a comfortable afternoon see Villandry and Azay-le-Rideau and Montbazon, on the south side of the Loire, or Luynes and Langeais on the north side; or if you were going on to Angers and Brittany, or down to Poitiers, instead of back to Paris, I'd say that you should take this afternoon for Loches.

But on that basis of a week's tour, Paris-to-Paris, on which we started out, you would have three nights at Tours. And your second day at Tours would take you to Luynes, Langeais, Azay, Ussé, Chinon.

IV

And before you start on another day of château-ing it may be that you'll like to say to yourself something like this:

'Let me see how "straight" I'm keeping them. Of course I have my photographs or postcards of them all, which I shall keep showing and telling about and gloating over, for a long time to come. And I expect to read and read about all these places — then come again. But let me see if, before I do all that, I'm getting them jumbled, as some people say they do.

'Chambord — huge; roof a forest of pinnacles and spires; great double spiral staircase in centre; Francis I — "fickle woman"; Louis XIV, La Vallière, Molière, Lulli smashing into harpsichord to make King laugh.

'Cheverny — beautiful furnishings.

'Chaumont — that Catherine bought to make Diane take. Huge, cylindrical towers flanking gateway — superb view of Loire Valley from terrace — here Catherine

supposed to have seen vision in mirror — interesting furnishings of her time — Franklin — Madame de Staël.

'Blois — the murdered Duke of Orléans and the Poet-
Duke — Louis XII and Anne of Brittany — the beautiful
outside staircase — the fine old Hall of the States — the
rooms of Catherine de Médicis — the King's rooms overhead, where Guise was murdered.

'Chenonceaux — built over the river — dream-palace —
Diane.

'Amboise — Charles VIII — Leonardo da Vinci —Saint
Hubert's Chapel — great tower with incline — tapestries,
torches, Charles V — the massacre of the Huguenots.

'Yes — I'm keeping them distinct, in retrospect. It's a
"gorge" on châteaux. But, thank goodness, I don't have
to do all my *digesting* in a week! I have the rest of my lifetime for *that!*'

This I interject because I have so often heard my scurrying compatriots cry, at about this stage of their château-
ing: 'Why look at more? I can't remember half those I've
seen.'

Don't let this feeling dismay you. Buy picture-cards,
everywhere. With their aid, and books, on your return
home, you'll find your impressions straightening out for
you quite wonderfully; and you'll be everlastingly grateful
for every mental picture you've made. For there's all the
difference in the world — as you know — in reading and
hearing about a place we've been in as compared with a
place we haven't been in.

So start valiantly on this rather 'stiff' day of château-
ing.

Cross the Loire to Saint-Symphorien and follow the
right-bank road some seven miles to Luynes. You may not
care to make the climb to this old castle on the hill, which
came, in its venerable age, into the hands of Louis XIII's

favorite, Albert de Luynes, first husband of Marie de Rohan, who after his death became the Duchesse de Chevreuse. But I have felt well repaid for the effort.

Another seven miles, and you pass Cinq-Mars-la-Pile,
with the ruins of an old castle which belonged to Marion
Delorme's lover and Richelieu's enemy, and which was
razed to the ground after the execution of Cinq-Mars. (His
gallant, tragic figure is one of the busiest ghosts haunting
these châteaux of the Loire. And Alfred de Vigny's novel
about him is one of the books you'll read with great delight
after you have made this trip.) The square shaft which
dominates the landscape here (and like the tower at Roche-
corbon stands guard over many cliff-dwellings) is of mysterious origin and purpose; the most interesting theory
about it being that it was part of an old system of signalling
by beacon fires which flamed messages along the Loire from
Langeais to Amboise, or perhaps farther.

Fifteen miles from Tours is Langeais, which will thoroughly delight you. It is a perfect type of the mediæval
castle, built just before the dawn of the Renaissance, bringing those days when beauty and luxury began to take precedence over mere security.

It was built just after Louis XI came to the throne, and
before he had put his nobles in a state of subjection which
reduced them to plotting for ascendancy (like the Guises)
instead of fighting for it among themselves and against the
Crown as they had been wont to do.

There has been a castle and a chapel here from times
'way back. The English occupied the castle that was here
when the Black Prince was campaigning along the Loire.

The builder (for Louis XI) of the present castle was also
the builder (at the same time) of Plessis-lès-Tours. What
Louis XI wanted this one for, I have no idea; but I'm very
glad he built it — as I'm grateful for every conspiring cir-

cumstance which has kept it for us, practically without change; and for the beneficence which has furnished it in perfect keeping and left it to the Institut de France to be treasured for the future.

As you cross the moat by the drawbridge and pass beneath the portcullis, suppose you 'pretend' that you are invited to the wedding of Charles VIII and Anne of Brittany.

It is December, 1491. Ferdinand and Isabella are just concluding the conquest of Granada. Columbus is on the eve of discovering us. Lorenzo the Magnificent is nearing the end of his course at Florence. Henry VII is on the English throne. The Middle Ages are behind. The Renaissance is in almost full splendor in Italy. The Age of Discovery is at hand. A wonderful hour in history!

The young King of France is twenty years old. The young Duchess of Brittany is fifteen.

She was betrothed, at seven, to the little Prince of Wales, who was soon afterwards murdered in London Tower. The next year there was talk of marrying her to her cousin, so as not to bring any foreign consort to share her rule of the duchy. But her father, when he thought of her defenceless-ness, realized that she must have military protection; so he affianced her to a Gascon sire, forty-five years old and the father of eight children — uncouth, to boot. No sooner was little Anne sovereign in her father's stead than she repudiated this alliance, and sought one with another widower, slightly younger and with fewer children: Maximilian of Austria, King of the Romans.

In March, 1490, she promised to be his. And this betrothal was more solemn than any of the others, conforming to the Breton custom that the fiancé should, in the presence of the court, thrust his bare leg into the bed of the Duchess. This was done for Maximilian by a gallant proxy.

When the King of France heard of this, he and his coun-

sellors decided that it must not be. The ousted Gascon
(d'Albret) brought his troops to aid Charles; hoping, doubtless, that Charles would make Anne keep her engagement
with him. But when they had succeeded in bringing Anne
to terms, she declared that she would marry no one but a
king or a king's son. And after three days of discussion, at
Rennes, between Charles and Anne, he announced their
engagement — leaving his fiancée as 'high and dry' as
Anne left her father!

Anne drove a shrewd bargain. She remained mistress of
Brittany and must be allowed to reside often at Nantes.
She must have with her, where'er she went, a Breton guard.
If Charles died and left no heir, his successor must marry
her, if possible. And so on.

She was small and delicate, one leg slightly shorter than
the other, but of dignified carriage withal, and enormously
impressed with her own importance — imperious, vindic-
tive, obstinate, and greedy. Not a very agreeable picture of
a fifteen-year-old girl. And as she went on in life, her
faults became accentuated and her virtues did nothing to
soften them.

Anne probably came up the river from Nantes in a barge
made splendid for the occasion. Charles had Langeais
sumptuously prepared to receive her; and she brought a
magnificent trousseau. Her bridal gown was of cloth of
gold, heavily embossed. And she had a sable mantle of
fabulous value.

The marriage contract, minutely supervised by the
King's Chancellor and the Chancellor of the Duchess, was
signed in the great hall of Langeais on December 6th. Beside Charles stood his cousin and brother-in-law, Louis of
Orléans (later, Louis XII), recently released from prison
for conspiring against the King; and his other brother-in-
law, Peter Beaujeu, the Duke of Bourbon; likewise, the

Count of Angoulême whose son, yet unborn, would one day be Francis I. In Anne's group were many Breton nobles, among whom members of the Rohan family were prominent.

The exact date of the religious ceremony seems to be in doubt. Pierre Rain inclines to think it took place immediately after the civil contract was signed, and in the same place. The Bishop of Albi, of the illustrious House of Amboise, brother of 'George,' presided over the ceremony.

Soon after the wedding the royal couple and the court moved in to Plessis-lès-Tours, where the merrymaking took place.

Langeais gives us, thanks to the supremely intelligent care of its late owner, M. Siegfried, and the wealth he had to devote to this noble task, the best idea it is possible for us to get anywhere in France, of a castle built in the transition years between the Middle Ages, and the Renaissance.

If you were en route to Angers, I'd urge you to have a glimpse of the moated Château des Reaux at Port-Boulet, thirteen miles downstream from Langeais on this north bank of the Loire. It belonged to that know-everybody relative of the Marquise de Rambouillet, whom we recalled in our Chapter I.

But if you are returning to Tours to-night, your way doubtless lies toward Azay-le-Rideau, to reach which you cross the Loire at Langeais and continue south for a very short distance — a matter of five and a half miles or so.

This is probably the château of all those in France which most of us would choose to own and live in, if we had our pick. Yet it was, not so long ago, rented to a school; and quite recently it was bought by the Government for about $10,000! Think of it! This perfect gem of architectural loveliness, in a setting that would ravish the senses of an anchorite. It is now a Renaissance museum, but its collections are not yet important.

At Azay (built about the same time as Chambord and Chenonceaux) you need not try to 'recall' a single thing. It is a place for reveries and deep ecstasies. Wander in its gardens; see it forever admiring itself in the waters of the Indre that all but surround it; imagine yourself there with a picked company of those you'd like best to entertain — bid them to meet you, entertain them as you think they'd like, have a house-party! *That's* what Azay's for! Be its master or châtelaine for an enchanted hour. It will do you worlds of good.

If you are familiar with Balzac's 'Contes Drolatiques' you doubtless remember his description of 'How the Château of Azay was Built.'

At Saché, near Azay, Balzac wrote 'The Lily in the Valley,' using as his background the château in which he was a revered and humored guest. One of the many delightful things about Mr. Frederick Lees' book, 'A Summer in Touraine,' is his account of a visit to this château and his becoming acquainted with the record of Balzac's sojourns, kept by his host, M. de Margonne, who told how Balzac was induced to read aloud evenings, the story he was writing; and how the discussions evoked by one evening's reading would appear in the text of the story the next evening.

Balzac retired at ten, his host said, and used to set a big alarm-clock he carried about with him for two o'clock in the morning, and on rising in his little room at Saché he made a cup of coffee on a spirit lamp. When he had drunk this and eaten several slices of dried toast, he sat up in bed and, on a sort of portable desk, continued to write for hours at a stretch. When in the midst of a story he was known to continue until five in the evening, his only nourishment being coffee and toast. Then he would rise, dress for dinner, and remain with his hosts until ten o'clock.

Few of the usual pastimes or sports interested him. One day, when he tried fishing (probably at the urging of one of those friends who cannot believe that what they enjoy can be unenjoyable to others), his kind host found him sitting in deep meditation, oblivious of a large fish which was hooked and struggling at the end of his line.

Ah! but he loved — he all but worshipped — this beautiful Touraine of his.

And wasn't it strange that not only he and George Sand should be at the same time singing the praises of the Indre and the Loire, but that this one tiny section of France should also lend its beauty and its romance to so many pages of their great contemporaries, Hugo and Dumas?

En route from Azay to Chinon, you may wish to pause at Ussé, which is a beautiful château more mediæval than Renaissance, and with a wide reputation for inhospitality. Some sight-seer once, it seems, broke a vase in the castle, and all sight-seers since have paid the penalty. They don't like us, at Ussé. They permit us to see the chapel and the gardens, but they don't even pretend that they are glad we came. Considering the behavior of some of us when admitted to other people's homes, I can't say that I am critical of the owners of Ussé. But I'm the more gratefully impressed by such spirit as is shown by M. Menier at Chenonceaux — and Mr. Terry, the Cuban gentleman who was its previous owner; the Siegfrieds at Langeais; the Princesse de Broglie at Chaumont, and the Marquis de Vibraye at Cheverny; likewise by the Duke de Noailles, at Maintenon, and other gracious owners of historic homes.

Chinon is some twelve and a half miles southwest of Tours, on the Vienne. One of its traditions (which its illustrious son, Rabelais, may not have believed but which he has handed on to us) is that it was founded by Cain! Certainly it has been an ancient town for so long that one cannot blame the citizens if they get a bit excessive about their city's age.

Probably your first concern with it will be luncheon, which you'll seek (I dare say) in the Hôtel de France on the tree-planted Place de l'Hôtel de Ville. I have some cherished memories of this little hotel, where I have been many times; but they are not gastronomic. However, the last time I was there, for luncheon only — covering this route just as I am outlining it for you — the food was fair, though the charm was in abeyance. It was Sunday, and there were far too many holiday-makers. Next time I revisit Chinon I shall choose a week-day, and make sure that it is not one of the innumerable holy days when all business stops, in France, as in Italy, and everybody goes on an outing. Chinon as I came to know and love it, years ago, means dropping off to sleep in one of the front rooms of the Hôtel de France, lullaby-ed by the fountain's gentle plashing and the voices of Rabelais' townsfolk, and wakened by the symphony of the market — just such a market, doubtless, as Jeanne d'Arc found here when she came to seek the Dauphin-who-should-be-king.

Don't, after you have lunched to the accompaniment of the good red wine of Chinon, be lazy and permit yourself to be driven up the hill on which the ruined castle stands. Walk up the narrow lane leading from the *place*. If you don't, you'll miss half the impressiveness of Chinon. Climb to the castle as Jeanne did — not only for the sake of recalling her, but for the picturesqueness of that approach. And though she may well loom largest in your thoughts, as you ascend, give some thought also to a few of the others who have trod this ancient way.

Never mind Cain, nor the Romans, nor the Visigoths,

nor even the early Counts of Anjou. But I'm sure you'll
wish to be conscious of Henry II, of Anjou *and* England,
whose favorite residence this was and who died here, a rag-
ing and broken-hearted man reckoned old at fifty-six; and
of Richard Cœur-de-Lion who is reputed to have died here,
too; and of detestable King John, from whom Chinon was
won back to France after a year's siege which ended on
Midsummer Eve, 1205. A little more than a century later,
Jacques Molay, Grand Master of the Knights Templar,
was 'examined' here by the Pope's cardinals in state assembled. The 'crime' of the Templars was that, with their
international organization and their secure strongholds,
they had almost inevitably become the bankers of their
day; and the King (Philippe IV) who hunted them down
was their heaviest debtor. You will recall Molay's prophecy, as he died at the stake in Paris — and how it came
true.

When you have crossed the castle moat and rung, at the
clock tower, for the keeper, you will probably be admitted
by a woman who speaks such French as you would give almost anything to speak, and has a voice which makes you
marvel why she is not at the Comédie Française. All my
recollections of Touraine are set to the music of voices
and enunciations I have heard in châteaux. Not even the
seraphic sounds I have heard from Duse and Bernhardt and
Marlowe have lingered in my ears with more deathless
melody than the voice of a young woman who once conducted me through Loches. (On my latest visit there she
was not in evidence.) And I shall never again ring for admission into the Castle of Chinon without finding my
thoughts of Henry II's funeral cortège and Jeanne d'Arc's
arrival, hard pressed by another, out of a much nearer past.

I am almost afraid to tell you about that other! Jeanne
d'Arc is always two months past seventeen when she stands

beside you at the castle gate. But Robin, when you get there, may be a young soldier in the army. Nothing 'stays put' so briefly as a little boy! But there may be a younger brother, when you get there.

My latest visit to Chinon was on a Sunday, as I have told you. I had gone down to Touraine with four friends who had never been there before. It was early June. Writing a letter home, I found that I was saying 'millions of roses in bloom.' I felt like a youngster of that age when more than two of anything is always 'millions.' So I made myself estimate. I began reckoning the probable number of roses that were rioting over any single cottage and in each tiny garden. And then I made a guess as to how many such gardens I was seeing, all along every road; and what the figures must mount to in places like the château gardens — and I decided that millions was a mathematical and not a metaphorical expression.

Touraine, what with these and all its other glories, would have seemed a Paradise had it been less populous with 'château-ists'; but, as we dare not hope that Paradise Regained will be as exclusive as Paradise Lost, I dare say it behooves us to learn to like numbers.

And Robin was one of the cherubim. But you haven't met Robin!

We were admitted by Madame the caretaker, and presently we heard a voice — the soloist of the angel choir, undoubtedly — saying: 'Par ici, mesdames et messieurs.'

He was seven — 'goin' on eight' — we learned later; he looked like 'most any small boy. But the *sounds* he could make, when he spoke French, made me feel sure that such French is the language celestial. And the gravity of him! And the absolutely academic air with which he imparted history, and discouraged inattention on the part of any in his 'class.'

In each place where an explanation was due, he halted us. Nor would he begin until each straggler stood at attention.

'In this room, ladies and gentlemen, Henry II, King of England, died, 1189.' And so on — each syllable distinct and slow (for our easier understanding) and the dripping of them honey-sweet.

When he had said his say, he gave us a reasonable time to discuss it and to look around; then he marshalled us on to the next point. But while we looked, he — snatching a respite from his labors grave — stood on his head and otherwise bestirred himself in those acts of physical prowess which are the real issues of life for all very young gentlemen.

Suddenly righting himself from one of these, he thrust his hand into his trousers' pocket and drew it forth tragically.

'Ma poche est percée!' he wailed, in tones which I should say could never be produced by 'my pocket has a hole in it,' had I not heard Julia Marlowe make music out of the most commonplace English words.

'I should think,' I ventured to suggest to him, 'that no pocket could be of much use to you.' Nevertheless, I helped him hunt for sundry coppers that were missing.

When we got back to the gate, I was congratulating Robin's mamma on his abilities (of all kinds!) when a twin cherub appeared — Richard — and there ensued a 'discussion' (wordless, for the most part, but very animated) over the division of the spoils. Richard's mamma assured me that he was no less satisfactory as a guide than Robin.

I hope it is not selfish to wish her a large family.

Now, back to Jeanne d'Arc, who also entered the castle through this gate, late in the afternoon of Tuesday, the 8th of March, 1429.

She had reached Chinon, after eleven days en route from Vaucouleurs, on Sunday, and had gone to the house of the Widow Regnier who lived near the church of Saint-Étienne.

Up at the château, they knew she was on her way. From Sainte-Catherine-de-Fierbois, a celebrated place of pilgrimage where she stopped to pray for many hours on Saturday, she sent forward Jean de Metz and Bertrand de Poulegny with a letter to Charles (who could only be the Dauphin to her, though his father had been dead for seven years, because Charles had not been anointed, consecrated, King), saying that she knew many things of interest to him, and that to prove to him the supernatural character of her mission, she would recognize him among all the gentlemen of his court.

Unknown though the girl from Domrémy was, she was the subject of everybody's conversation. The besieged citizens of Orléans had heard of her, and her promise to help them, and begged that she be sent to them without delay.

But the counsellors of the King were not wholly selfish, inert, when they cautioned him against too-easy credulity.

Who was this petty sire of Baudricourt? What did he mean by sending a rustic to tell the King his business? What kind of country would it be if every cowherd could feel that cowherds should counsel kings? Who could guarantee that the girl was not a spy of the English?

The Archbishop of Reims, who was also the Chancellor of France, was one of those who urged extreme caution. I dare say that most of us would have done the same. But Charles had interrogated Jeanne's messengers, and was moved to either awe or curiosity by what they told him. He would see the girl!

Accordingly, on Tuesday afternoon a small escort of archers was despatched to the Widow Regnier's house to bring the young Lorrainer up to the castle. As they were climbing that ascent you've just climbed, it was nearing dusk, and the sun was disappearing behind the hills beyond the Vienne. A trooper, who crossed their path and saw Jeanne dressed like a man, jeered at her, coarsely, profanely. Probably he had heard of the farmer's lass who said she could raise the siege of Orléans.

'Ah!' replied Jeanne, turning on him briefly her searching glance, 'you blaspheme, and are so near death.' And before she and her escort had reached the castle gate, the trooper had fallen into the Vienne and was drowned. You can imagine how the tongues of Chinon-town wagged over that episode; and how it reached the castle hall ahead of Jeanne.

The Count of Vendôme came to the clock tower to fetch her. Charles and some three hundred attendants were in the low-ceiled room with its narrow, pointed-arch windows, where fifty flaring torches lighted the dramatic scene. There was access to the apartment direct from the courtyard outside by a short stone stairway; and three hundred pairs of eyes were fixed on that stairway.

She entered. She was a big, strong, well-developed girl, her bust swelling firm and round beneath her boyish blouse which reached only to her knees, her black hair cut straight off, like a page-boy's, and hanging, fringe-like, to her collar, and partly covered by a soldier's cap. She was not abashed. Her bearing was almost proud, and she swept the assembly with the glance of one who believed herself an ambassador of God, come with a great message of deliverance.

Charles had donned shabby raiment and slid in among the minor courtiers; but she went to him, unhesitatingly, and knelt before him.

'Gentle Dauphin,' she said — and they tell us, who wrote of her as they saw and heard her, that she spoke in a voice which was uncommonly lovely even in ears that daily heard the speech of Touraine — 'I am called Jeanne the Maid, and the King of Heaven orders that through me you shall be consecrated and crowned at Reims and shall become the lieutenant of Him who is the true King of France.' Then, in a lower tone, so that those standing by might not hear, she told him that she had for him a happy answer to a certain prayer he had been making to the Virgin.

So saying, she turned on her heel and left him.

You must see all this, as you stand in that roofless, floor-less chamber, open to the sky of Touraine that has looked down on so much history. See Charles, lean and knock-kneed, homely, with huge nose and sensual mouth, and troubled gray eyes gazing after the strange girl as she leaves him. What prayer does she mean? Can it be THAT one?

She must not go! Give her lodging in the Château de Coudray (one of the three which constitute the Castle of Chinon) under the care of the Governor's wife, a lady of renowned virtue. The King must consider!

You will visit the tower where Jeanne was lodged; you will climb the winding stair to the platform where her chamber was, and look upon the smiling valley of the Vienne which she so often saw through tears in those days while hope grew fainter in besieged Orléans, but Charles could not make up his mind to let her go to its relief.

He often sent for her and questioned her. And, of course, the first thing he asked her was about that prayer.

'You prayed to Sainte Catherine de Fierbois for some sign that you are the true heir of the realm and son of the late King,' she said.

He had. But what more natural, at a famous shrine, from a prince whose mother — to gain her own ends — pro-claimed him bastard? Any one might have guessed that he would pray thus. Any one might have said that the Virgin had sent him assurance of his legitimacy. Yet, because this was what Charles wanted to hear, it was what did most to convince him. Dunois, commanding the troops of the King, and feeling that Orléans was not going to hold out against the English, begged that the girl be sent. Still Charles could not decide. Suppose the girl were a witch? She must be examined, as to that, by the learned theologians at Poitiers. Jeanne wept, and protested that the delay might lost them Orléans. But the King was obdurate. To Poitiers she must go. You shall go with her, in our next chapter.

And, not to be too hard on Charles, perhaps we ought to recall a disappointment he had recently suffered. Remember Arthur de Richemont, whom you met at Vannes? When Charles was proclaimed King, six and a half years ago, he knew that his first need was an army to support his claims to his father's throne, as against those of his baby nephew, son of his sister 'Kate' and Henry V of England. And who should be a better foeman of Henry V than his half-brother Arthur whom he had kept a prisoner in England after the battle of Agincourt?

So Charles made Arthur the Constable of France and the Governor of Chinon. It was just exactly four years before Jeanne came to Chinon that Arthur was inducted, with grand ceremony, into his new office which he swore to hold 'unto death, against the enemies of France.' But Arthur was not fortunate in his encounters with the English; and he got into such disagreements with Charles's courtiers as to be accused by them of treason — whereupon Charles 'took back' Chinon, and broke with Arthur; and things went from bad to worse.

Privileged person that you are — able to look in upon any scene that invites you — I dare say you'll step to some

vantage-point for viewing the town from the castle eminence; and, turning your back upon Charles and Jeanne,
will look down upon Cæsar Borgia coming to bring Louis
XII a nice divorce, and Georges d'Amboise a handsome red
hat.

It is mid-December, 1498 — almost seventy years after
Jeanne d'Arc came hither — and he rides in splendid pano-
oply who is the Pope's son. At the head of his cavalcade
come twenty-four sumpter-mules, laden with coffers over
which are thrown rich draperies embroidered with Cæsar's
arms. Behind them, another twenty-four mules caparisoned
in the King's colors. Then, sixteen beautiful chargers, led
by hand, and having stirrups and bridles of solid silver.
Next, eighteen pages in scarlet and yellow and cloth of
gold. Then, a posse of lackeys accompanying two mules
bearing coffers draped with cloth of gold and containing
Cæsar's gifts to the French King and court. Following
these, thirty gentlemen in waiting, members of Rome's patrician families, clad in cloth of gold and silver.

Then — Cæsar! 'Mounted on a superb war-horse that
was all empanoplied in a cuirass of gold leaves of exquisite
workmanship, its head surmounted by a golden artichoke,
its tail confined in a net of gold abundantly studded with
pearls. The Duke (Louis XII had just conferred on Cæsar
the Duchy of Valentinois in Dauphiny) was in black velvet,
through the slashings of which appeared the gold brocade
of the undergarment. Suspended from a chain, said to be
worth thirty thousand ducats, a medallion of diamonds
blazed upon his breast, and in his black velvet cap glowed
great rubies as large as beans. His boots were of black
velvet, laced with gold thread that was studded with gems.'

The rear of the cavalcade was brought up by more mules
and the chariots bearing his plate and tents and all the
other equipage with which a prince was wont to travel. It

is said by some that his horse was shod with solid gold, as also were some of his mules who now and then dropped a shoe as largesse for the gaping, scrambling populace. Somewhere in the pressing throng there was probably a small boy of Chinon named François Rabelais, whose father was a publican in the town. Not much of Rabelais' life has to do with Chinon beyond the fact that here he first saw the light of day; here he learned to laugh and — probably — to know that if he made others laugh he could say things that could not be said if they bore the appearance of being serious.

Louis XII, so soon as he gets himself securely married to Brittany (and Anne!), is going down to Italy to advance his claim to the Duchy of Milan, of which his grandmother, Valentine Visconti, might be considered to have been the heiress. He wants the Pope's support, and he intends to get it by binding Cæsar to him in every possible bond, including alliance with a French wife. The bride selected is a sister to the King of Navarre, and said to be the most beautiful girl in France. She has served as damsel of honor to Jeanne the Lame, and then to Queen Anne. Her story does not belong to Chinon unless it was here that she first saw Cæsar. But have scant patience with all the carelessly handed-on drooling about Cæsar having poisoned her shortly after their marriage. She outlived him by seven years; and though they spent but four months together, she seems never to have ceased longing for his return. Cæsar was not impeccable, goodness knows! But he *was* handsome and fascinating. And probably in four short months none of the honeymoon sweetness had worn thin.

Now, as you pass out beneath the clock tower, I rather suspect that you're in a funeral procession. It is a July day, in 1189.

Who is in that shabby cart, wrapped in a mean winding

sheet, a sceptre of gilded wood in his hand, a brass ring on his finger, a crown of gold fringe made from a woman's petticoat on his grizzled red head?

This is the Conqueror's great-grandson — King of England and at one time ruler over more of France than the French King. This is Empress Matilda's son, whose christening you attended at Le Mans; whose wedding you shall attend at Bordeaux; with whom you knelt at Avranches, near Saint Michael's Mount, in penance for Becket's murder.

Where is Eleanor who brought him so great possessions as heiress of Aquitaine? She has for the greater part of these sixteen years been a captive at Winchester — shut away from jealous interference with her husband's affairs and from plotting with her sons against him.

Nevertheless, the sons have plotted. The eldest, Henry, died in the midst of an insurrection against his sire, six years ago. Then, two years ago, Geoffrey was trodden to death in a tournament at Paris — but not before he had contributed much to his father's heartbreak. Richard, the old King knows, is in alliance with the King of France, against his father. But Henry has believed John, his youngest, loyal to him.

At Chinon, a few days ago, he learned that John was deep in the conspiracy against him. And thereupon Henry first raged, then wept; and, turning his face, distorted with grief, to the wall, he died.

Of all his children, only one of Fair Rosamund's bastard sons was near him when he expired before the high altar of the chapel. And hardly was his last sigh breathed than the pillage of his effects began, even to the stripping of his body not yet cold.

There he goes to his resting-place, in the abbey church of Fontevrault. And should it be that you are en route to

Brittany, or have no need to hurry back to Tours, you may follow Henry II to his burial.

Perhaps your eye has wandered southward on your map to Richelieu, and you are wondering if it would pay you to run down there. I doubt it, as nothing is left of the château. I went there once, en route to Fontevrault; but nothing repaid me for the trip except the Sainte Chapelle at Champigny-sur-Veude, three miles north of Richelieu.

I'd take, instead, the road for Candès (at the confluence of the Vienne with the Loire), where Saint Martin of Tours died and there is a very beautiful church to his memory. And then I'd go on, about a mile, to Montsoreau where lived 'La Dame de Montsoreau' whom Dumas makes a central figure of one of his vivid romances of the Valois court. From Montsoreau it is two and a half miles to Fontevrault.

The Abbey of Fontevrault was one which enjoyed the patronage of many ladies of high estate; its abbesses were not infrequently royal, and down to the Revolution it was, as a school for young ladies of great families, the most 'select' in France. It is now a prison; but between 2 and 4.30 P.M. daily visitors are permitted to see the royal tombs and the famous kitchen.

Henry II was laid to rest here in 1189. Ten years later came Richard Cœur-de-Lion; and five years later than he, his mother, who had governed for him, during his ten years' reign, his kingdom wherein he spent but four months of all that time. Eleanor took the veil here at Fontevrault when she was eighty, and died here in 1204. Her daughter-in-law, Isabelle of Angoulême, wife of John and then of her first lover, Hugh de Lusignan, also died a nun at Fontevrault, in 1246, and her statue lies here also.

There is a road from Fontevrault to Montreuil-Bellay, whose moated castle is delightfully picturesque and has a kitchen similar to the one at Fontevrault, which Viollet-le-Duc regarded as one of the most remarkable in France. This castle, which has housed Louis VIII, Charles VII, Dunois, Louis XI, Charles VIII, Henry IV, Louis XIII, Anne of Austria, and many other notables, is a private residence, superbly furnished, and through the courtesy of its owner may usually be seen by the visitor. The collections form a veritable museum, and should be especially interesting to students of furnishings. The town walls of Montreuil-Bellay are nearly intact, and there is a fine old gate of the fifteenth century.

Ten miles north of Montreuil-Bellay is Saumur which, in the time of Henry IV, was the headquarters of Protestantism in France. To-day it is celebrated for its Cavalry School, for its sparkling white wines (you may like to visit some of the cellars), and for the manufacture of rosaries. It has a castle, not particularly interesting, which is now the town museum, containing — among other kinds of collections — the Museum of the Horse, and of harness.

But you are more likely to turn north from Chinon toward the Indre, and to follow the road that runs between the Indre and the Loire, toward Villandry, a château contemporary with Chambord, Chenonceaux, and Azay-le-Rideau, built by Francis I's secretary of state. It has lately been carefully restored, has some fine furnishings, and beautiful formal gardens.

I have not been to the Château de la Carte, near Ballan, which is six miles southwest of Tours — not on the same road with Villandry, but on the road from Azay-le-Rideau. But I mean to go there. For Mr. Frederick Lees (whose book 'A Summer in Touraine' inspires me with more and more respect, the more I realize the 'casualness' of many writers on Touraine) says that it was this road that was followed by the Saracens in the eighth century, when they

were defeated by Charles Martel in the battle that saved
Europe to Western civilization. To be sure, there wasn't
any such thing to save it to — but there was *going* to be!
And while the invading Moors were doubtless far in advance of the emerging barbarians of Europe in all the arts
and sciences, still ——! I'm glad our forbears, primitive
as they were, wrought their own destiny.

So, if the grandfather of Charlemagne, on October 10,
732, drew up here his 'wall of ice' against which the fiery
horsemen of the African plains hurled themselves to death,
I want to see the place. Mr. Lees thinks the battle took
place close to the grounds of this château, which was built
(on the site of a much older one) by that unfortunate
Semblençay, treasurer to Francis I, who was hanged at
Montfaucon.

It was the sword of the victor, Charles Martel, which
Jeanne d'Arc got at Sainte-Catherine-de-Fierbois and bore
always in battle. Charles is believed to have left it as a
thank-offering, and Jeanne to have had its location revealed to her by her Voices.

V

Now, then, for your sixth day, and the return toward
Paris!

You leave Tours as you entered it, by avenue de Grammont; and two and a half miles south, you take National
Route 143, on your left, for Loches, which is twenty-five
miles from Tours by this main road and a little farther by a
prettier route which you may pick up at Cormery.

I am not sure that you would feel sufficiently repaid for
the slight détour you would have to make for Montbazon,
which lies a little off Route 143, to the west. To the
enthusiast on mediæval military architecture, the great
square donjon of Montbazon, built in the tenth century,

is worth going far to see — though its picturesqueness is spoiled by a huge statue of the Virgin incongruously and almost shockingly set atop it. (It was here that Eleanor of Aquitaine was to have been held captive by young Geoffrey of Anjou, after she escaped from Blois.) And to the lover of seventeenth-century annals this vicinity is interesting because of that very beautiful and notoriously gallant Duchesse de Montbazon who was so passionately loved by the Abbé de Rancé, founder of the Trappists. She had brought him up with her children, and was fifteen years his senior. But he was her lover; and when death took her from him he was inconsolable.

The Montbazons, after the sixteenth century, lived not at the feudal castle, but at the Château de Couzières, a mile away on the bank of the Indre. It was here that the young abbé and she had their idyl. At this time, the slip of a girl that silly old Montbazon had married was 'a colossus' (according to Tallement des Réaux), 'with a very white complexion, very dark hair, and a great majesty of bearing.' Long ago she had said that when she reached thirty she wanted to be flung into the river. But when she was far past thirty she was still 'going strong.' The old Duke was such a fool that he shared with the Duke d'Uzès the paternity of all the malapropos remarks which furnished the wits of their day with 'funny stories.' Any inanity could always be ascribed to one or the other of these men.

Loches is in many respects the most interesting and most satisfying of all castle towns and feudal strongholds. There, more thrillingly than almost anywhere else, one enters into 'shivery' romance such as used to hold us spellbound when we were youngsters — and still does, if we haven't got stiff in our mental joints and shuffling in our spirits.

People often ask me: 'If you could see only two or three castles in France, which would you see?' And I *always* include Loches, and then consider which the others would best be; the others vary, according to what I know of the tastes of the inquirer; but I have never known any one who was not intensely interested in Loches.

Coming in from Tours by rue de Tours, drive straight ahead, to Place de la Marne, where Alfred de Vigny's statue stands, and in the background looms the Tour Saint-Antoine, which once belonged to a sixteenth-century church. Crossing the square toward the south, take rue des Moulins past the Porte des Cordeliers (part of Charles VII's fortifications) and turn, right, into Grande-Rue ('Main Street'!) with its fine old houses. Do not stop, yet, to see the Hotel de Ville and the Porte Picoys, because I dare say you'll come back to their vicinity for your luncheon; but continue up steep, narrow rue du Château, enjoying its many Renaissance mansions and particularly those numbered 10, 12, and 14, of Henry II's reign, which are the Chancellerie.

Enter the castle by the Porte du Château whose twelfth-century towers must have looked down on Henry II of England and his rebellious sons, Richard Cœur-de-Lion and John.

Now, instead of turning left, as nearly everybody does, up rue Lansyer to the Château Royal of the fifteenth century, I'd turn right, down the boulevard du Donjon, and see the donjon or keep of the old castle. The château enclosure is an extensive one, as you'll see, and measures from south to north, I should think, something like a quarter of a mile.

The last time I was at Loches I bought a copy of Edmond Gautier's 'Histoire du Donjon de Loches,' wherein more than two hundred pages of very condensed information barely suffice to summarize the history connected with this one part of the Château of Loches. So I'm sure you'll par-

don me if I seem a bit staggered to know where to begin for
you an enumeration of a few outstanding associations. I
may omit the very ones you would rather have had me include. But I can only hope not.

Loches (which is called *Losh* with the *o* not so long as in
home nor quite so *u*-like as in *money*) is the same word to
which the Gaelic tongue gives, in Scotland, a sound, not of
its vowel, but of its final consonants, which seems impossible
for other kinds of vocal cords to reproduce. Once upon a
time this place was a group of *lake* dwellings, huts built on
piles in a marsh; and in the thickly forested hill behind it
were dug caves which served as storehouses, as winter
refuges, and as retreats in case of an enemy invasion. These
caves were intercommunicating and of vast extent, and
access to them was had from the lake dwellings by a narrow
causeway which could be defended or, at need, destroyed.
Thus Cæsar found them when he came hereabouts to
winter-quarter his legions in 57 B.C. (At La Roche-Guyon,
in the Seine between Mantes and Vernon, there was a
similar construction which remained sufficiently intact to
the twelfth century for the Abbé Suger to study and describe for posterity.) And to these caves came Saint Ours,
of Cahors, with some monks, to found a monastery, about
491, before Clovis had accepted baptism and declared the
Frankish country Christian. Even then, according to Gregory of Tours, there was above the caves a *castrum*, or fortified camp, surrounded by ditches and palisades, in the
midst of which there was a mound topped by a donjon,
probably of wood.

Thus the sons of Charles Martel saw it, soon after their
father's great victory over the Moors, in 732. They destroyed it and it was rebuilt. When the Norse invasions
came, the impotent French kings could do nothing against
them except give vantage-points to doughty fighters who

might be able to defend them; one such got Loches; and through his successors it came into the possession of the formidable Counts of Anjou, of whom Foulques Nerra is the most vivid figure in the annals of this countryside. Here is Gautier's résumé of Foulques, 'whose sombre and terrible figure still stands out for us as that of a hero of marvellous legends':

'Forty-three years of combats, eleven churches and convents founded and endowed; twelve towns walled and eight castles built by his orders; a sequence of cruelties, assassinations, pillagings; three pilgrimages to Jerusalem in expiation of his crimes: — such was the life of this extraordinary man, one of the greatest figures of the eleventh century, who lived under six successive kings, covered with glory, honors, and wealth, sullied by atrocious crimes; and who was an intrepid soldier, a murderer of his kindred, hypocrite and devout, violator of monasteries and builder of churches, pilgrim austere and repentant, personifying all the greatnesses and all the vices of his time.'

Loches was Foulques Nerra's principal base of operations and he probably built this donjon that you're about to visit. On your way, this afternoon, you'll stop at Beaulieu, across the Indre, where Foulques is buried in one of the abbeys he built. So, if you are a student of ancient methods of construction, note those of the donjon at Loches, and compare them with those of the ruins over the river, where Foulques (who died at Metz on his return from his third pilgrimage to Jerusalem) was buried in 1040.

There is a 'Lady of Loches,' or Lady of the Lake-town, two generations later, of whom I think we ought to be somewhat aware here. She was the third wife of that later Foulques (grandson of Nerra, or 'the Black') who is called 'le Réchin,' or the Quarreller, who imprisoned in the dungeons here for thirty years his elder brother, Geoffrey,

and seized all Geoffrey's inheritance. A horrible person was
the Quarreller; and of the lady, Bertrade, to marry whom
he sent away his lawful wife and her son, it was said that no
man could ever find aught to say in her praise except that
she was beautiful.

The King of France found her fair and tempting when he
came to Tours and enjoyed her husband's hospitality. He
was Philippe I; and the time was a little after the Norman
Conquest of England and the preaching of the First Crusade — events separated by thirty years. Philippe had
been on the throne for some three decades; he had a wife,
Berthe, and a son who was to be Louis VI, a very notable
King of France. But when he saw Bertrade, he became so
infatuated with her that he offered her the crown of France.
Bertrade lost no time in accepting; she followed the King to
Orléans, and then to Paris, and some complaisant ecclesias-
tic was found to 'marry' them, although nothing had been
done about un-marrying them from Foulques and Berthe.

This scandal brought excommunication on Philippe and
Bertrade, and on all who served them. Nevertheless, their
adulterous union lasted ten years, and four children were
born of it. Then, the 'boycotted' King sent Bertrade home
to her Quarreller; and it is said that when Philippe came, in
1107, to visit 'them' at Angers, Bertrade kept both men in
good humor with each other and with her. This Lady of
Loches who brought such shame and misery upon France
is not a pleasant person to recall, but she's not one to be
ignored.

And now let us pass on to the days when the Count of
Anjou was also King of England, and poor old Henry, in
the last days of his life, had Loches taken from him after
a week's siege by his son Richard and the King of France.

While Richard was a prisoner in Germany, his one-time
friend and ally, but then his bitter foe, Philippe-Auguste,

acquired possession of Loches. But Richard got free; Philippe-Auguste wrote to John, 'Look out for yourself; the devil has broken loose.' And 'the devil' came to take back Loches, which he did in an assault that lasted but three hours. That was June 13, 1194.

Loches was part of the dower that Richard gave his Queen Berengaria. I'm sure you won't wish too many details of its successive ownerships; but in December, 1249, in an Egyptian camp, near the Nile, Louis IX signed a treaty by which Loches became the property of the French Crown.

Charles VII was at Loches when Jeanne d'Arc came, May 10, 1429, to announce to him the lifting of the siege of Orléans, and to urge him to follow up this success until he was crowned at Reims.

In 1440, Louis the Dauphin (later Louis XI) took refuge at Loches from the wrath of his father, against whom he had conspired, and was 'smoked out' — so to speak — escaping in disguise just before his father's forces set the town of Loches in flames.

One of the first acts of Louis XI on becoming king was to liberate from captivity in Loches the Duke d'Alençon, one of his allies in a later conspiracy against his father.

And in that same year (1461) Louis began his own use of the dungeons here by consigning to one of them a certain Pierre de Brézé, Grand Seneschal of Anjou, Poitou, and Normandy, who was set at liberty only when he consented to his son's marriage with Charlotte, one of the daughters of Charles VII and Agnès Sorel. This marriage ended in a tragedy — Charlotte and her lover being killed by the outraged husband. By a later marriage he became the father of Louis de Brézé, Grand Seneschal of Normandy, who is best known to history as the husband of Diane de Poitiers (his tomb is in Rouen Cathedral); and a curious coincidence is that an illegitimate daughter of Louis XI married Aymer de Poitiers, an ancestor of Diane's.

And while we are speaking of Diane may be the best time to recall that her father, Jean de Poitiers, Count de Saint-Vallier, was brought here a prisoner in 1523, along with many of his fellow conspirators against Francis I led by the Constable de Bourbon. Saint-Vallier was not really in the plot, but he knew about it and didn't tell — and Louis XI had made that a crime punishable with death.

So, from his dungeon here, poor old Saint-Vallier wrote to his son-in-law and to Diane begging them to use their influence to get him out.

What they did in his behalf, I don't know; but it accomplished nothing just then. He languished here for something over two months; then he was taken to Paris, tried, found guilty, condemned to 'torture extraordinary' and then to decapitation.

He nearly died of fright, and of the torture known as 'the boot'; his hair whitened in a night; and he was on the scaffold when his sentence was commuted. Victor Hugo, in 'Le Roi S'Amuse,' says that Diane bought his life with her virtue; and he makes the old man burst in upon Francis during a fête at the Louvre, denouncing him as follows:

> "'Tis true, your mandate led me to the block,
> Where pardon came upon me like a dream;
> I blessed you then, unconscious as I was
> That a king's mercy, sharper far than death,
> To save a father doomed his child to shame . . . .
> Oh, hadst thou come within my dungeon walls,
> I would have sued upon my knees for death,
> But mercy for my child, my name, my race,
> Which, once polluted, is my race no more.'

It is this play, you'll recall, which was forbidden, by order of Charles X, a second representation in France, and which comes to us metamorphosed as 'Rigoletto.' Triboulet, the deformed jester of Francis I and the pander to his vices, laughs at the woe of old Saint-Vallier; and the latter curses the jester.

'The old man's malediction,' says Hugo in his preface, 'will reach Triboulet through the only being in the world whom he loves, his daughter. This same king whom Triboulet urges to pitiless vice will be the ravisher of Triboulet's daughter.'

M. Gautier says that the history, as opposed to the poetry, of Saint-Vallier's pardon is that what moved Louis de Brézé to activity on his father-in-law's behalf was that if the execution were carried out it would involve confiscation of the old man's wealth. So valiant efforts were made to keep his head on — in a dungeon of the Bastille! He was set at liberty in 1526, but his health was shattered, and he had a nervous trembling accompanied by fever, which is still called Saint-Vallier's fever.

Now, to go back a little in the history of the donjon at Loches: You know (through 'Quentin Durward' if not through other books on those times) how Louis XI went to Péronne, in October, 1468, to be the guest of Charles the Bold of Burgundy, his great adversary, and found himself trapped and forced to sign a treaty full of humiliating terms. Louis had gone, on the advice of Cardinal Balue, a tailor's son whom he had rapidly elevated to a place in the State where he sat at the King's right hand, above all the princes and high dignitaries of the realm. When Louis had had wrung from him concessions for which even the jays and magpies in their cages mocked him when he returned to Paris, he not unnaturally suspected the counsels of those who had urged him to go to Péronne; and he began seeking ways to 'get' them.

Letters fell into his hands in which the Cardinal exhorted Louis' brother, the Duke of Guienne, not to accept other

terms than those which had been stipulated in his favor by
the treaty of Péronne. The Cardinal was arrested (as were
others; but we won't go into too many details here), tried,
condemned, his goods confiscated, and his person consigned
to one of those iron cages with which Loches is specially
associated, although it had by no means a monopoly of
them.

They were not of iron, really, but of wood, with iron
binding-strips. One of them was still at Loches in 1790,
when the Revolution demanded its destruction — although
its preservation would have been a better argument in favor
of the overthrow of kings! They were about six and a half
feet square and five and a half feet high. Balue occupied
one at Loches for three years, then was transferred to
Montbazon, and later to Chinon where he was when Louis
XI had his first stroke of paralysis and was scared into
pardoning him.

Balue returned to dignities and powers; he was greatly
honored by the Pope; after the death of Louis (who
took him back into full favor and confidence) Balue de-
votedly served the interests of Charles VIII. He died in
Rome, in 1491, and was buried in the Church of Sainte-
Praxede.

Philippe de Comines was less fortunate in the reign of
Louis' son. Louis had seduced him from Charles the Bold,
and he had served Louis well and been splendidly rewarded.

But he didn't 'get on' with Louis' autocratic daughter,
the Regent, Anne de Beaujeu, and joined a conspiracy
against her. For this he spent eight months in a cage here
at Loches; and during that time he commenced planning
his memoirs — that completely fascinating book which has
given birth to so many other fascinating books about the
outstanding personages and events of his time. He is supposed to have been the author of that inscription at Loches

which reads: 'I have sometimes repented for having spoken, never for having kept silent.'

Of all the prisoners of Loches, however, none so engage our sympathy as Ludovico Sforza, the great Duke of Milan, the husband of Beatrice d'Este. I dare say I ought not to take much space here for Ludovico since I have devoted considerable to him in the Milan portion of 'So You're Going to Italy.' But in case you have not this at hand, and your memory is not quite clear about him, let me remind you that Louis XII felt himself heir to the Duchy of Milan through his grandmother, Valentine Visconti, wife of that Louis, Duke of Orléans. who was murdered in Paris by the minions of Burgundy. To Louis XII, the Sforzas were upstart usurpers. But Ludovico's mother was a Visconti, sole child (though illegitimate) of the last Visconti Duke and married by her father to the great Francesco Sforza. However, Louis XII went after Milan, and got it, Ludovico escaping. But the French soldiery and rule were odious in Milan, and the Milanese sent to Switzerland for help, and Ludovico came back again for a short while. (All this was after the death of his young wife, Beatrice, which afflicted him so profoundly.) When the French were again victorious, Ludovico was taken prisoner by them, and eventually brought here to Loches to languish in these dungeons for many years.

Sir Theodore Cook quotes, without ascribing it, in his chapter on Loches, the following: 'An old French street (here in the town of Loches) surging with an eager mob, through which there jostles a long line of guards and archers; in their midst a tall man, dressed in black camlet, seated on a mule. In his hands he holds his biretta and lifts up unshaded his pale, courageous face, showing in all his bearing a great contempt of death. It is Ludovico, Duke of Milan, riding to his cage at Loches.' Ludovico, one of the most magnificent princes of a magnificent age, the patron of Leonardo da Vinci and Bramante and most of the other immortals of that effulgent day; Ludovico who, on a simple visit to his sister-in-law, Isabella d'Este, while he was in deep mourning, took with him a retinue of one thousand persons.

Have you read the story of Ludovico and Chevalier Bayard, the young knight 'without fear and without reproach'? Bayard, fighting with the French, was in a garrison some twenty miles from Milan, when he led a sortie of knights, one day, against an Italian garrison. The attacked garrison sallied forth to give battle, were routed, and fled toward Milan, Bayard so hard upon their heels that before he realized it he was within the gates of Milan and a prisoner.

Taken before Ludovico, he was asked, smilingly, what brought him to Milan in such a hurry. Then, when he was rested and refreshed, he was courteously sent back, under escort, to his own lines.

But Ludovico was not to be so fortunate when the tables were turned. He was first imprisoned in the Castle of Novara, near the scene of his defeat. Then taken into France, where his first prison was one (at Pierre-Encise) which Louis XII himself had occupied as Duke of Orléans and a rebel against Charles VIII. Ludovico escaped from there, but was almost immediately retaken, and put in the donjon at Bourges, where he lay for some time before he was brought to Loches. He was here for some years — probably seven.

'In the damp and sombre cell,' says Gautier, 'to which daylight penetrated only through a double-barred window, three feet square, in a wall eight feet thick, the conquered soldier, the prince who had constructed palaces, who had known the joys of supreme rank, of riches, and of the arts

— alone, without knowledge of the progress of events in the world outside, almost without light — chose, to battle against the despair which gnawed him, the most extraordinary, the most difficult occupation, the most foreign to his habits, we were about to say the most impossible in his situation — he made himself a painter! His eyes accustomed themselves to the obscurity; he obtained colors, brushes, ladders; the soldier become artist threw upon the sombre walls of his cell a composition which was bizarre, original, full of grandeur and of character.'

Gautier thinks that it was above the fireplace that Ludovico began his murals with that portrait of himself in his battle casque which I reproduce for you from M. Gautier's book; and that he used three colors only: yellow ochre, red-brown, and very dark blue.

There is much that one would like to say further about this piteous captive; but space forbids most of it. I'm sure you will, though, be glad of translations of one or two of his inscriptions; these were made by Mrs. Watts-Jones, and I have them from Mr. Lees' book.

Ludovico seems to have tried to see Louis XII, and been denied. So he painted on his prison walls these lines:

> 'I do repent, but what is that to thee?
> My heart I would have joinèd unto thine,
> But thou mad'st war upon this heart of mine.
> Naught ask I henceforth, never seek thy face,
> Since thou to me wouldst show no slightest grace;
> Yet for that bliss I strove with greater pain —
> To see thee once — to speak with thee again —
> Than o'er my foe the victory to gain.'

And this:

> 'I know well that there are many, and it is a sharp grief,
> To whom one gives their dismissal.
> Who wishes to kill his dog first imputes to him the charge
>   of being mad,
> So it is with the poor man
> That one wishes to hate.'

As his health gave way, he was transferred to a room in
the Round Tower, where he died, on the 18th of March,
1508. His captivity began on Easter Monday, April 10,
1500. He was buried, with princely honors, in the Church
of Saint-Ours, but no one knows to-day where the place of
his sepulture was. 'His ashes sleep forgotten on foreign
soil,' says Gautier, 'and not even a stone indicates to the
passer-by where the bones rest of him who was the Duke of
Milan.'

When you leave the donjon, walk up the boulevard du
Donjon and rue Thomas Pactius to the Church of Saint-
Ours which Viollet-le-Duc described as 'a strange and
unique monument in which the influences of Oriental art
are blended with the methods of construction adopted in
the north at the beginning of the twelfth century... a
monument unique in the world, perfect in its kind, and of a
savage beauty.'

Here Ludovico rests from his many sorrows. Here Agnès
Sorel lay for a long time, but now her beautiful empty tomb
is in the château, in the tower wherein she often lived.

The château, in which Charles VII, Louis XI, Charles
VIII, and Louis XII occasionally dwelt, is now the sub-pré-
fecture and occupied by the local representative of the
provincial governor. It is full of fascinating memories
among which I dare not linger, though I hope you may.

When you have seen it, leave the castle precincts as you
entered them, and retrace your steps in rue du Château
till you turn, left, to the Hôtel de Ville standing, slender
and lovely, alongside the Porte Picoys. Pass beneath this
gateway in the sturdy, fifteenth-century tower, into rue
Picoys, where you will find both the Hôtel de France and
the Restaurant du Palais, between which you may choose
for your lunching place.

After luncheon, drive down through Place du Marche

and rue Balzac, and into rue de la Porte Poitevine. Thence, turn into rue de Vignemont which presently becomes rue de la Grotte. One of the best views of the castle is to be had from this hill of Vignemont. Then take rue des Roches back to the Porte des Cordeliers, and cross the Indre to Beaulieu in whose abbey church Foulques Nerra was buried. You may not care a great deal about Foulques, but you are quite sure to care about the beautiful belfry.

Then on, part-way through the forest of Loches, to Montrésor, where there has been a fortress for many centuries and a handsome château since the fifteenth century. The present proprietor of this lovely place is a Polish nobleman, and his superb collections (which he is most gracious about permitting visitors to see) are full of things recalling Poland's history, including the solid gold plate of the Kings of Poland, worth probably two million dollars.

Straight on, now, through Nouans and Luçay, you come to Valençay, where there is a magnificent château to which visitors are not admitted except in a very few outer parts. It belonged to Talleyrand, but he did not die there, as some guide-books state.

At Valençay, you may, if your time is not limited to seven days, take Route 156 for Châteauroux (twenty-five miles) and the George Sand country. Just before you enter Châteauroux, you pass through the suburb of Déols which was an important town under the Romans, has a lovely old gateway with 'pepper-pot' towers, and a curious Roman-esque belfry with a candle-snuffer top and four little candle-snuffer domes at the corners of its square base. In the Gallo-Roman crypt of the Church of Saint-Étienne is a superb marble tomb of the third century. Twenty miles south of Châteauroux (which has a picturesque castle and an important Napoleonic museum bequeathed by General

Bertrand, a native of Châteauroux, who accompanied the
Emperor in his exile on Saint Helena) is Nohant, where
George Sand's home and tomb may be visited; and all about
Nohant are the scenes of many of her novels.

If you have a day or two for this section, see the Château
of Meillant which Charles Chaumont Amboise (brother of
Georges, the Cardinal) built with wealth he got from Milan
where he was governor for Louis XII, and recall that here
he entertained Chevalier Bayard, who was to die in the
service of France's struggle to hold Milan.   And the
Château of La Motte-Feuilly, where Cæsar Borgia's wife
lived, and died — though not by arsenic-poisoned tapestries
sent her by Cæsar as Mrs. Champney relates in her
'Romance of the Renaissance Châteaux.'

Then, see the Château d'Ars, which George Sand describes in her 'Beaux Messieurs de Bois Doré,' or Handsome Gentlemen of the Golden Wood. And the Auberge du
Point-du-Jour, or Daybreak Inn, where lived Marie, the
heroine of 'La Mare au Diable,' or the Devil's Pond. And
the picturesque mill of Angibault where she placed the action of one of her stories, 'The Miller of Angibault.' Likewise, the Tour Gazeau, of which she speaks in 'Mauprat.'
And, if possible, see Gargilesse, the tiny village she described so lovingly in her 'Walks Around a Village' that it
became frequented by painters. (This is close to Argenton,
in that granite gorge of the Creuse which will give you a
scenic effect surprisingly different from any you have had
elsewhere in this tour.)

In René Doumic's book on George Sand he has this to
say of 'Mauprat': 'During her excursions in Berri, she
had stopped to gaze at the ruins of an old feudal castle. We
all know the power of suggestion contained in those old
stones, and how wonderfully they tell stories of the past
they have witnessed to those persons who know how to

question them. The remembrance of the Château of Roche Mauprat came to the mind of the novelist. She saw it just as it stood before the Revolution, a fortress, and at the same time a refuge for the wild lord and his eight sons, who used to sally forth and ravage the country. In French narrative literature there is nothing to surpass the first hundred pages in which George Sand introduces us to the burgraves of central France.'

VI

On a seven-day schedule from Paris, I should turn at Nouans to Saint-Aignan, on Route 76, and get on to Bourges, which is fifty-five miles. Saint-Aignan has some fine old houses; so has Selles-sur-Cher, eleven miles farther on; and at twenty-four and a half miles from Saint-Aignan, there is Mennetou-sur-Cher, a perfect gem of a Middle Ages fortified town with steep, tortuous streets bordered with ancient houses, and ramparts of the early thirteenth century. Then comes Vierzon, of no special interest, and Melun-sur-Yevre, of *very* great interest, with a fine fourteenth-century gateway, and the imposing ruins of the castle in which Charles VII starved himself to death. Ten miles more and you are come to Bourges.

Julius Cæsar called Bourges the most beautiful city in all Gaul; Augustus made it 'the metropolis of Aquitaine.' It belonged to Eleanor, and through her (for a brief while) to England.

Louis XI was born here when his father was — as the English contemptuously dubbed him — 'King of Bourges,' and so poor that a shoemaker wouldn't trust him for a pair of shoes. Nor were the royalties of Bourges always well fed. They often ate in their room, 'tis said, so that no one might know how scanty was their fare.

One day a young merchant of Bourges who was getting

on very well in his little silk business ventured to offer the hungry Majesties a couple of fowls and a loin of mutton. Their Majesties were grateful, and said so to the young mercer. Charles had no idea what was to become of France. But the mercer had.

The nation seemed expiring, after fourscore years of war. Fields were abandoned by agriculture and reverting to forest growth, except around fortified towns and castles where a watchman stood on the lookout for marauding bands. Highways and bridges were so dilapidated that communication had become extremely difficult. Things were going back to the state they were in at the end of the Dark Ages. All that had been built up in six fecund centuries seemed disintegrating, permeated with decay.

But over in the marshes of Lorraine was a peasant girl hearing Voices which told her what to do to reanimate the faith and courage of her disheartened people. And here in the retreat of the uncrowned King was a young merchant with some excellent ideas about economic development and national finances.

I hope you'll find him absorbingly interesting — this Jacques Cœur of Bourges. He was not born poor, like his great contemporary and fellow mercer, Dick Whittington; Jacques' father was well-to-do, and Jacques married a well-dowered girl whose father had got a good start in life through the favor of the late Duc de Berri, great-uncle of the young King and munificent patron of the arts and of many crafts and trades.

Just how much Jacques did, following upon the gift of the chickens, to 'buck up' the feeble youth whom God had called to great responsibilities without seeming to have given him any spirit for meeting them, I don't know; but I like to think that there was some interchange of opinions between them, after Charles had said 'Much obliged for the

mutton'; and that to the despondent view Charles undoubtedly expressed, Jacques made a good, hard-headed,
high-hearted reply scarcely less invigorating than those
Jeanne was soon to make.

While Jeanne rallied the spirit of her countrymen to drive
out the invaders, Jacques extended his business, became an
importer from the Levant, and began going himself to
Damascus to do his own buying. Then he acquired a ship,
to do his own transporting — and another — and another,
till the sea was covered with his vessels and their precious
freight. He had, as time went on, business houses in all the
chief cities of France, and buyers in every important mart
of the Near East. He amassed the most colossal fortune
that had ever been possessed by a 'self-made' Frenchman;
and, what is much more interesting and more important, he
placed his country in a position to vie with the great trading
republics of Italy.

Of course Charles used such a man, in diplomacy as well
as in the finances of the kingdom that was gradually emerging from the wreckage of the Hundred Years' War. And for
some fifteen years, he loaded Cœur with honors. And then,
as might have been expected, there were people who hated
Cœur because he had succeeded, and because he had loaned
them money which they didn't wish to repay; and Charles,
who had just entered Rouen in triumph, aided by Cœur's
money and by his personal assistance — his sage counsel
and his sturdy fighting ability — listened to the poisoned
tongues. Agnès Sorel died at Jumièges, you'll recall, soon
after the taking of Rouen. A viperish court dame who owed
money to Cœur started the scandal that he had poisoned
Agnès — fair Agnès who died of puerperal fever. Charles
must have known better than to believe such an insinua-
tion. But one day when Cœur was visiting him, Charles had
his benefactor seized and thrown into a dungeon. Cœur's

wealth was confiscated and a number of charges were trumped up against him. His innocence of them all was manifest; but he languished in prison for four years, whilst the King's favorites divided his possessions amongst them.

In 1456, he escaped into Italy, where he was warmly welcomed by the Pope, then fitting out an expedition to recapture Constantinople from the Turks who had three years before taken it. Who could be more valuable on such an expedition than this man who knew so much about the Turk and about ships? So Cœur set out, as guest captain of a fleet of sixteen galleys sent to the relief of Rhodes, but was taken ill en route, and died at Chios, an island on the west coast of Asia Minor, on November 25, 1456. After his death, Charles VII seems to have repented of his abominable ingratitude and allowed Cœur's sons to come into possession of whatever was left of their father's wealth.

You will, I dare say, put up for the night at Hôtel d'Angleterre, close to the magnificent mansion Jacques Cœur built for himself in his native city. Coming in from Melun-sur-Yevre, you may as well go to the station, and take avenue de la Gare south to the Place Planchat. As you reach the *place*, look, right, along rue Gambon, where are the Maison de la Reine Blanche and the Hôtel Dieu (or hospital), two of the old buildings which make Bourges an etcher's paradise. Then, as you continue through rue du Commerce into Place Cujas, you reach the top of rue Jacques-Cœur, down which you proceed to your hostelry.

I hope that there's a tiny bit left of the afternoon, or that you have a long summer twilight ahead of you. For, if you must get back to Paris (a hundred and forty miles) by tomorrow night, you may feel that you ought to leave here by noon. And there is much to see!

Jacques' palace was completed in the year of his disgrace. Everywhere it bears his motto: 'To the valiant

heart (*cœur*) nothing is impossible.' Its west wall is part of
the old Roman town ramparts. I shall not try to describe
any of its details, nor to say anything much about the
superb cathedral, with its five portals, its double aisles and
no transepts, its thrilling flying buttresses and its splendors
of thirteenth-century glass especially rich in deep reds.
But if you have been interested in sculptural interpreta-
tions of the Last Judgment which are above one or another
of the portals of nearly all great French cathedrals, I think
you may find the one above the central porch of the west
front at Bourges among the most fascinating of all. And if
you like, as I do, to have your appreciation of such things
led happily along without intimidating erudition or be-
wildering detail, I'm sure you'll like as much as I do travelling with Louis Hourticq's 'Art in France,' a small handbook (in English) with a multitude of small-sized illustrations, and a style of writing and thinking which one wishes
were more frequently found in authoritative persons.
Hourticq did not write his book to show other learned persons how much he knew; he wrote it with a lovely zeal to
make art illuminating to a great many of us — and I think
he has succeeded. His book is published by Charles
Scribner's Sons, and is exceedingly inexpensive. See what
he says about this 'Last Judgment,' pp. 77 *et seq.*

The view of the cathedral from the public garden that Le.
Nôtre designed is one of the most inspiring and impressive
we get anywhere of a French cathedral, I think. The crypt
of the cathedral is one of the finest in France.

Rue Bourbonnoux, running north from the cathedral's
east end, has some fine old houses, including the beautiful
Hôtel Lallemant. Beyond this, in Place Gordaine and
near-by streets, are many more 'etchers' bits' (or photographers'). The Musée de Berry, in the house of Jacques
Cujas, near Place Planchat, will reward you for a visit if you

have time for it. And don't neglect the statues of Louis XI and of Jacques Cœur.

When you leave Bourges, your way back to Paris lies through the picturesque old towns of Gien, and Montargis, some of whose old houses by the waterways make lovely pictures, and Némours, and Fontainebleau. Then, Melun, and on into Paris through the Porte d'Italie by which Napoleon entered on his return from Elbe to begin the Hundred Days before Waterloo. Now, to see the châteaux without using a private motor, I'd go by train from Paris to Orléans, and visit Orléans and Cléry; then, on to Blois, and take the char-à-banc there for Chambord, Chaumont and Cheverny. Then, to Tours, and make the two circuits out from there. Or, there are many Châteaux Tours run from Paris tourist offices, most of them of three or four days' duration. My own office will gladly counsel you as to how you may see the most of what you specially desire, in the time at your command and for the money you wish to spend.

IV

ON YOUR ROAD TO CARCASSONNE

I

CARCASSONNE may be reached, en route to Paris from the Riviera or from Nîmes, in two days' motoring from Nice or one from Avignon; or in about five hours' railway ride from Nîmes. It may rather easily be included in a rail journey between Paris and Barcelona, being a long day's ride distant from either and a possible night-stop between.

But for a town of such appeal, it certainly is so placed that the average traveller in France who manages to see it — who comes home saying, 'I have seen Carcassonne!' — has done so only with considerable effort.

To those who are motoring, however, Carcassonne may be made the objective of a special tour from Paris and back to Paris, or may be included in a tour to the Pyrenees or to the Riviera.

If you go by motor to Carcassonne, and return to Paris by a different route, you enter upon a tour of such surpassing interest, such varied beauty, that even Carcassonne can be only an incident of it. And if you must choose one or two among the many possible tours in France, I should say that this one will give you probably a wider, more comprehensive view of France, especially of its scenic splendors, than any other one trip you could make in a similar length of time.

It can be made in nine days, from Paris back to Paris. It can be advantageously stretched over many times nine days if you have them to give.

You may take for your first day out of Paris the route to
Le Mans which is described on page 92, and make your
second day's run through Le Lude to Saumur, and thence
to Poitiers for your second night, Périgueux for your third,
then Cahors, Carcassonne, and so on.

Or, you may take Orléans for luncheon, and down the
Loire to Tours for your first night. Or, take Chartres,
Châteaudun, Vendôme, to Tours. Or, make Bourges for
your first night, and Limoges for your second, coming down
through the George Sand country and the Gorge of the
Creuse; then, through Brive to Cahors, or to Périgueux and
thence to Cahors.

Similarly, there are several choices of route for your return from Carcassonne, which I shall indicate when we have
got farther on.

But for this chapter I shall follow a route which gives the
most comprehensive tour possible for those who may have
to make it serve instead of the several they would like to
take.

So ―― ! Out of Paris you go, by the Porte d'Orléans,
and down along Route 20, which is really a speedway, to
Orléans for lunch and a peep at the Jeanne d'Arc Museum
and the Hôtel de Ville. Then to Blois, and on into Tours.

II

From Tours, take Route 10, which is the highway from
Paris to Bordeaux and Biarritz, as far as Angoulême, stopping at Poitiers for as many hours as you can.

Poitiers is sixty-two miles from Tours, and it is one of the
most richly interesting cities in France for lovers of the past
and of the picturesque. Angoulême is about sixty-seven
miles from Poitiers, and I doubt if it will interest you much
beyond the cathedral. This gives you a day's 'run' of a
hundred and twenty-nine miles.

It should not be difficult for **you** to reach Poitiers by eleven o'clock if you go straight through. It would even be possible, if you were to leave Tours at eight, for you to have a glimpse of Azay-le-Rideau and Chinon, and still be at Poitiers by one, see something of it, and get to Angoulême for the night. And for motorists with — let us say — a fortnight for this circuit, instead of nine days, I'd urge either Azay, Chinon, and Fontevrault, then Poitiers (for the night and next day, and the second night) by Route 147, passing through Fontevrault; or even Langeais, on the right bank of the Loire, before crossing to Azay. Or, the right bank to La Croix-Verte, then over to Saumur and down through Montreuil-Bellay and Thouars to Parthenay, and then across to Poitiers. Or, I'd go from Tours to Loches (if I hadn't seen it) and thence by Ligueil to La Haye (where Descartes was born) and five miles farther to 'pick up' Route 10 at Dangé.

Route 10 leaves Tours by the avenue de Grammont, goes through Montbazon, and twenty miles south comes to the old town of Sainte-Maure of which Benoît de Sainte-Maure was a native in the days of lively Eleanor of Aquitaine. Benoît was, in a manner of speaking, a sort of forerunner of John Erskine; with, doubtless, less conscious philosophy about bringing antiquity companionably close, but animated by the same sage instinct, he wrote a 'Romance of Troy' in some thirty thousand lines, full of castles and abbeys and lovely mediæval color and pattern. His romance begins with the capture of the Golden Fleece and comes down to the return of the Greek princes after the fall of Troy. He it was who first told the story of Troilus and Cressida, which Boccaccio and Chaucer and Shakespeare all borrowed for their own uses. Benoît was a loyal subject of Henry II, and spoke of the French as 'they.' And he was probably the author of a 'Chronicle' of the Dukes of

Normandy, in forty thousand lines, relating the great deeds of Henry II's ancestors all the way back to Rollo.

So busy was Benoît with telling about Trojans and Normans that he told us very little about himself. But we know a good deal about his kind, in his age. One of the spiciest accounts of Benoît's sort we have had recently is in Raimon de Loi's 'Trails of the Troubadours'; and Sainte-Maure is a good place to make special mention of it, because it does (self-consciously, and flippantly, but not without good scholarship) somewhat the same thing that Benoît did: presents an ancient chivalry in 'up-to-date' phraseology and psychology.

Concerning those times M. de Loi says: 'Southern France ... divided into duchies, kingdoms, and principalities ... was ruled by a large number of barons, each baron surrounded by a gay and warlike court whose business it was to protect the baron's land and to kill the baron's enemies . . . . The barons and their courts lived in fortified castles on hills surrounded by moats and capped by towers so arranged as to afford protection against attack. Knighthood was, at the beginning of the period we are wandering through, in high flower, although in a very different flower from the picture of it presented in the stories of the Round Table and the Holy Grail. The knights were not really sensitive, courteous gentlemen who devoted their lives to the rescue of kidnapped maidens or the defence of a lady's honor. Too frequently they were responsible for the kidnapping of the maidens, whom they robbed of all honor. The work of the troubadours has overcast the morals of the knights of old with a glamour which they do not in any sense deserve.

'The ladies of the castle had their first taste of marriage while very young. They were frequently betrothed at the mature age of two, married in the ripe middle age of eight

or nine, and expected to undertake the administration of a
castle when senile decay had set in — at the age of fourteen.
[This is 'smarty' and misleading.] The husband was very
heavy and exercised absolute rights. He could confine his
wife to her room for years; he could chastise her with a rod,
starve her, humiliate her in a thousand ways, even make
her a servant to his mistress. . . . Under these conditions it
is not surprising that the dreams of adolescent girls should
have turned to young squires of the court who said exquisite
things exquisitely; or that they should have been delighted
to hear poems addressed to themselves in which they,
rather than their husbands, were represented as all-powerful. Nor is it surprising that these girls should have found
means to betray their husbands, who were after all busy
men engaged in the administration of a kingdom.

'A reading of the work of the earliest troubadours shows
that the poems were written, not for the men of the Middle
Ages, but for the women; and the society described by the
troubadours when they were serious is not society as it was,
but society as they wished it might be. The tradition of the
self-sacrificing melancholy lover which has dominated lyric
poetry for the last thousand years is an effeminate tradition
based on the aspirations of unhappily married mediæval
ladies.'

'The troubadour,' M. de Loi goes on to remind us — and
this is a penetrating interpretation which makes it easy to
forgive him some of his flippancies — 'was the publicity
agent for the court in which he lived. Please remember that
there were in those days no newspapers for the dissemina-
tion of scandal and gossip. . . . Yet as commerce and industry began to flourish and life became more and more
complicated, the shrewd barons of the south of France
found it necessary to devise means whereby they could
attract to their courts a better kind of fighting-man, make

alliances with more powerful neighbors, and tell the world of the power of their swords as well as of the beauty of their wives. They found the troubadours useful in solving this problem. . . . They wandered from court to court praising the ladies, disseminating gossip, and carrying out the complicated work of free-lance journalist, advertising agent, ambassador, and warrior.'

You are now on 'the trails of the troubadours' into the south of France. What your attitude is toward the tales they told and the times they lived in, I cannot know; but I suspect that it is rather sympathetic or you wouldn't be here. Perhaps your mature intelligence smiles a bit cynically at those tales of pure paladins; but you love them for what they meant to the immature person you used to be in a time to which you look back very tenderly. You can't swallow, now, some of the 'goo' which a certain school of writers purveys about 'when knighthood was in flower'; but that's no reason for treating the Middle Ages with too much condescension. There's a point of view from which they are neither benighted nor instinct with beatitude, but full of human nature fighting its way in the world with different weapons from ours, but not essentially different desires. And out of all their shortcomings, they left the world some supremely fine things — just as we, with all of ours, shall do ere we pass on and our methods have become 'mediæval' and obsolete.

Now, journey on, along this old highway from Paris to Bordeaux which has known so many wayfarers, to Châtellerault, seat of a former duchy which was given by Henry II to James Hamilton, the Regent of Scotland, for promoting the marriage between the little Dauphin and the young Queen of Scots. If you have need of anything in the cutlery line, this is a good place to buy it, where cutlery has been made for six centuries.

(Seventeen miles west of Châtellerault is Mirebeau where Prince Arthur of Brittany was taken prisoner by King John, in 1202, and never heard of more — or, rather, no more seen except by jailers. Nor is his grandmother, Eleanor, who was present at his capture — the truth being that he was besieging her in Mirebeau Castle when taken — known to have suffered any anxiety as to what became of him. And about an equal distance east of Châtellerault is the old 'ramparted' town of La Roche-Posay, just outside of which are some celebrated mineral springs and a health resort.)

Somewhere between Châtellerault and Poitiers the great battle of 732 is generally supposed to have been fought, and that victory won by which Charles Martel, Charlemagne's grandfather, saved the rest of western Europe from the fate of Spain. Moussais-la-Bataille, some five miles south of Châtellerault, is the spot where you may indulge your grateful emotions with least likelihood of challenge — unless you've 'gone and had them' with Mr. Lees, up near Tours, at Château de la Carte.

And on your way into Poitiers, be sure to stop at Dissay (ten miles north of Poitiers) to see the lovely old castle which offers some beautiful inducements to photographers — especially on the side of the moat and the stone bridge over it.

About five miles north of Poitiers, on this route of yours as you follow the course of the Clain, is Chasseneuil, which claims to be the place where Charlemagne's son, Louis le Debonnaire, was born, ten years after Charlemagne became King and in that same year when he lost so much of the flower of his chivalry in the ill-fated expedition to Spain.

Now, here you are, entering Poitiers by the Porte de Paris, close to which are the scanty ruins of the castle

which witnessed so many historic events from the days of
the Dukes of Aquitaine to the coming of Jeanne d'Arc.

Is it clear in your mind just what was the extent of the
Duchy of Aquitania? That extent varied greatly, from
Cæsar's time on; but, roughly, it was (as it descended to
Eleanor and through her to her heirs on the throne of
England) the whole of France from the Loire to the Pyr-
énées, except in the southeast where the domain of the
Counts of Toulouse adjoined it. Do you wonder that
Eleanor was much sought in marriage?

Of the Poitiers the Romans knew, not many vestiges remain, although one of them is of extraordinary interest.
Of the Poitiers that Charlemagne knew, there is this
Christian baptistery of the fourth century, and the tomb
of Sainte Radegonde, wife of Clotaire I, who founded a
church and monastery here about 560, when the Romans
had given place to the Franks. She was a captive of war
whom the youngest son of Clovis forced to marry him; but,
revolted by his brutalities, she fled to the protection of
Saint Médard, Bishop of Noyon, and besought him to
make her a nun and give her the possible security of the
cloister.

But of the Poitiers that Eleanor knew, and her sons, and
the Black Prince, and Jeanne the Maid, there is more than
enough to make Poitiers one of the most satisfying cities
in France for the lovers of history, as for the student of
architecture and the seeker for the picturesque. If you are
to glimpse its glories, and lunch, and get on to Angoulême,
it behooves you to do some careful choosing of things to
see and planning of how to see them.

I think that if I were you, I'd turn to the left, at boulevard du Pont-Guillon, pass the castle ruins, and follow the
boulevards (the bulwarks) south, along the bank of the
Clain, to the group of buildings including the Church of

Sainte-Radegonde, the venerable baptistery, and the cathedral. The baptistery is probably the oldest Christian monument in France and is now a museum containing an archæological collection. Some antiquarians deny this edifice more than thirteen centuries or so. But nobody doubts that it was a place of Christian worship in the Dark Ages when there were not many gleams of aspiration in a pretty thoroughly barbarous Europe. If you are not enough of a student to make the old Gallo-Roman and Merovingian tombstones tell you the stories they tell to some, at least you may use the baptistery for a trysting-place with any one of a long, long line of ghosts. It was an old, old edifice when Eleanor and her second husband were building the cathedral near by. And if Eleanor did not spend a great deal of time in prayer and worship when she was young and not-so-old, she probably did more or less of it when age had brought her manifold heartbreaks from family feuds and none of the golden serenity that autumn should know.

Sainte-Radegonde was rebuilt, somewhat in its present form, before Eleanor's youth — although the main portal will give you an impression of a much later day, unless you stand well back and look up at the purely Romanesque tower.

And, by the way, as I mentioned at Blois what may be done with child travellers to interest them in architectural emblems, let me suggest here how easy it is to get even a quite young child to learn a few outstanding characteristics of old buildings. And one of the first things they lay hold upon is the round arch as distinguished from the pointed arch, and what story those arches tell. I have had great delight in setting young travellers at this 'game,' which they pursue with the same zest that they find in counting lighted Christmas trees in the windows they pass on holiday-week evenings at home, or in reading (aloud!) street-car advertising, at a time when recognizing words and learning that they have surprised us by so doing is one of the most gratifying of their experiences. If you are so fortunate as to have a very young traveller (say seven or eight to twelve, with you at Poitiers, Sainte-Radegonde's tower and doorway, compared with the tower and doorway of Saint-Porchaire, which you shall see presently, will give you an opportunity to invite comparisons.

Eleanor laid the foundation-stone of the cathedral in 1162, ten years after her divorce from Louis VII and her marriage with Henry Plantagenet, and a year before her first husband saw Pope Alexander III lay the foundation-stone of Notre-Dame-de-Paris. If you are groping your way among the meanings of architecture, a 'lesson ahead' of that young comrade, like the old district-school teachers with their pupils, you may exercise your expanding facility in Poitiers Cathedral (one of the oldest you have seen) by trying to note how it shows some allegiance to the Roman-esque traditions of Aquitaine's old churches, yet reaches out after the then new fashion of Gothic. Go around to the back, and compare this apse with the marvellous apse of Notre-Dame-de-Paris. And if apses have an appeal for you, mind you do not leave Poitiers without seeing that of Sainte-Hilaire and that of Moutierneuf (which latter, close to the ruins of the castle, was founded by William VI, Duke of Aquitaine, and consecrated by Pope Urban II in the year of the First Crusade).

Rue de la Cathédrale, which leads to the Palais de Justice, is the street in which Jeanne d'Arc was lodged — at the Hôtel de la Rose, whose site is now occupied by the house bearing number 53.

If you drive up this street, and turn to your right at the end of it, where there is likely to be a market in progress, you will find yourself at Notre-Dame-la-Grande which is in many respects the most astonishing and interesting of all Poitiers churches. The modern attempt to restore mediæval colorfulness to the interior is deplored by critics, but I have to admit that it pleases me — not for the artistry with which it is done, but because it gives me the feeling of *color* which so many old churches have lacked since they were stripped of their tapestries and banners, their gilded tombs, had their painted walls whitewashed, and much else that contributed to the mystic ecstasy of Gothic and pre-Gothic ages reduced to an intellectual supremacy of *line*. I can never forget the sunny May morning when I pushed open the swinging door of Notre-Dame-la-Grande and saw a considerable congregation of market folk kneeling in worship there. Perhaps when I go again I shall find it gaudy; shall resent it as I resent the roof of the cloisters at the Abbey of Mont-Saint-Michel — furiously, menacingly. Perhaps I was in a specially receptive mood for color because I had just come from the hard white light of the cathedral. At any rate, I'm glad to have seen Notre-Dame-la-Grande, and I think you will be. The sculptures of that fascinating façade used to be colored, too. And over that delightful old Romanesque porch on the south side of the church there used to be an equestrian statue of Emperor Constantine who is believed to have been the founder of this church. By the time you have seen it, I'm sure you will be ready for luncheon, and that the Hôtel du Palais, on the other side of the Palais de Justice, will give you a good one.

After luncheon, climb the monumental staircase of the Palais de Justice whose incredibly inappropriate modern façade (1839) masks the glorious old hall of the Middle Ages. The Roman citadel was here, and the palace of the Dukes of Aquitaine a thousand years ago. The great hall,

now used as the 'Salle des Pas Perdus' (like the great hall of
the old palace on the Île de la Cité, Paris), or public cor-
ridor of the Law Courts, dates back to the eleventh century
and was already venerable when Richard Cœur-de-Lion,
aged thirteen, was crowned Count of Poitou and Duke of
Aquitaine here, with utmost panoply, on Trinity Sunday,
1170. It was a very, very old hall when King John of
France lost the battle of Poitiers and was made captive
by the Black Prince. King John's son, the magnificent
Duc de Berri, did much to enlarge and embellish the
palace. To him we owe the exquisite Gothic mullions
above the pierced gallery and the three monumental fireplaces at the south end of the hall. Note that the arcading
on one side is pointed, or Gothic. It was in this hall that
Charles VII was proclaimed King of France; because here
the Parlement of France sat whilst Paris was in the hands
of the English. That explains why Jeanne d'Arc was sent
by Charles to Poitiers to be questioned by the Doctors of
the University who were the Court of Parlement, the while
Orléans waited for its deliverer. But does anything explain
why it took four weeks to determine whether the girl was
a witch or a spy or an emissary of Heaven? Well —! Perhaps we should have deliberated as long, on so grave a
matter.

The custodian will take you into the room where Jeanne
faced her judges (for she was on trial then, as later at
Rouen), and, if he sees that your interest is great, will
doubtless make you stand, as he made me, where he believes Jeanne stood when she made those answers which
finally convinced the cautious and the sceptical — or at
least made them feel that, while it was doubtless imprudent
to trust her, it would be more imprudent *not* to.

This room is in the Tour Maubergeon, which was the
keep of the palace. It was destroyed by the English in

1346, after their great victory over the French at Crécy, and was rebuilt by the Duc de Berri thirty years after his father's capture here in 1356.

When you leave the palais (which you will do regretfully, I am sure), walk up rue Gambetta, past the grand old eleventh-century tower of Saint-Porchaire (don't take time for the church interior) to the busy Place d'Armes, site of the Roman forum, and of the market-place of the Middle Ages. I think you should visit the Hôtel de Ville, built about fifty years ago, to see its beautiful vestibule with the Puvis de Chavannes murals representing Saint Fortunat reading his verses to Queen Radegonde, and Charles Martel arriving at Poitiers after his defeat of the Saracens; and go into the Musée Municipal (in the Hôtel de Ville) if only to see the Greek statue (fourth century) which was found in Poitiers in 1902.

Antiquarians and 'collectors' should see the Musée de Chièvres, at number 9 rue Victor Hugo, running west from the Place d'Armes, which is housed in a fine old fifteenth-century mansion and represents *one* 'Collector's Luck in France,' as Alice van Leer Carrick would say. (I hope you know of her delightful book of that title, if you are interested in antiques. And who isn't, nowadays?) This collection belongs now to the society called 'The Antiquarians of the West,' who have also their own collection (more archæological and of less general interest) in rue des Grandes-Écoles, near Saint-Porchaire.

Perhaps now (if you are planning to spend the night at Angoulême) you should get your good petrol Pegasus whinnying for his southward flight.

Drive him up rue Moulin à Vent (or Windmill Street) in which the Town Hall Minerva was discovered, for a few feet, then turn to your right into rue de la Prévoté and pass the Hôtel Fumée and — in the continuation of that same street, though called rue de la Chaîne — the Hôtel Berthelot, which belonged to a mayor of Poitiers in 1529, and stands where a Roman villa stood. Turn right, at the end of rue de la Chaîne, past the Church of Saint-Germain, because it was built in the eleventh century on the foundations of some Roman baths of the *first* century, and continue, past the School of Medicine, to rue Ruffault. Turn right, here, and drive straight on, crossing Grande-Rue, rue de la Cathédrale, and rue du Pont-Neuf, and rounding into rue de Lycée and the Place de la République. Hereabouts stood the Roman arena, built under Hadrian, more extensive than that at Nîmes, and capable of holding 52,000 spectators. The ruins were demolished only about 1857. The Hôtel des Trois Piliers on rue Carnot takes its name from three old columns of the amphitheatre, and its cellars may have been dens for the wild beasts used in the Arena.

Now, continue on rue Carnot until it becomes rue de la Tranchée, and mind that at number 1 bis, rue de la Tranchée, is an old curiosity shop you'll probably wish to see. If you have time to walk across the Parc de Blossac at the southwest corner of the old town ramparts, you will be rewarded by a very fine view.

As you leave Poitiers, much depends on what time it is and how much you must hurry. In every direction hereabouts are great temptations. To the east, on Route 151, are Chauvigny with the ruins of five castles, and Saint-Savin, with its abbey founded by Charlemagne. You could see these, and the battle-field of Poitiers, if you are en route to Limoges instead of to Angoulême for the night, although they are not on the direct route thither.

A little more than a mile outside Poitiers, leaving by the Porte de la Tranchée (near the Parc de Blossac), are the remains of a Roman aqueduct coeval with the baths (first century), and lovers of Roman ruins might go on through

Lavausseau, where there is an old Templars' commandery, to Sanxay whose Roman remains were brought to light in 1881 by Père de la Croix to whom Poitiers owes so much in an archæological way.

It was he, for instance, who discovered that the Hypogée Martyrium, southeast of Poitiers, across the Clain, contains the bones of the Christian martyrs who were persecuted in the Gallo-Roman times and were first buried in a cemetery near at hand, called 'The Field of the Martyrs,' whence their remains were gathered, in the seventh or eighth century, by a priest who desired to rest among them and in that pious purpose built himself this tomb in which Père de la Croix discovered even some of their names, preserved by the priest, in paintings and inscriptions.

Fifteen miles southwest of Poitiers, on the main road to Saint-Jean d'Angély, is Lusignan, which may lure you as it has lured me, although there is little now at Lusignan to help us re-create the proud old town whose sons ruled over Cyprus for three centuries. Isabelle of Angoulême was living at the castle here, in the year 1200, the affianced bride of Hugh de Lusignan, when King John of England, whose vassal Hugh was, came hither on a visit. At that time the forests around Lusignan provided the most celebrated deer-hunting in France; and it is supposed to have been at one of the hunts given in his honor that John saw Isabelle and coveted her. We had somewhat of their story at Fougères, in Chapter I, you will recall.

I'm not sure that you would feel repaid for going to the battle-field of 1356, near Nouaille, some seven miles southeast of Poitiers; but I am sure that before you leave the vicinity you will wish to refresh your memory a bit about that battle. Philippe-Auguste had taken Poitou from King John, you'll remember, and for almost a hundred and fifty years it was an appanage of the French Crown. Then came

Edward III of England's claim to the sovereignty of all France (his mother, 'the She-Wolf,' of whom we had much in 'So You're Going to England,' having been a daughter of that Philip IV 'the Fair,' who brought Jacques de Molay to the stake, and himself dying within the year, left three sons each of whom reigned in succession and left no heir) and his victory at Crécy in 1346, then the capture of Calais.

For some years there was a truce, whilst the Black Death ravaged both countries. Then, in 1356, the Black Prince, Edward III's son and heir, started from Bordeaux, which remained English, into the very heart of France on a gigantic plundering expedition, whilst his brother, John of Gaunt, Duke of Lancaster, harried the French King in Normandy. (The French King then was John, called 'the Good,' son of Philip of Valois, who had acceded to the throne desired by Cousin Edward.) John hurried south to intercept the marauding army of the Black Prince and caught the latter, near Poitiers, in a situation where he must abandon his spoils and retreat or stay and fight to hold them. He fought, and won, though he was outnumbered more than two to one. King John and his son Philip, a lad of fourteen, fought on to the finish in a hand-to-hand struggle whose din of clashing steel could be heard within the walls of Poitiers on that Monday, September 19, 1356. King and Prince were taken prisoner, and carried captive to England as we recalled in one of the London chapters of 'So You're Going to England.' Poitou was claimed by the English then, but was recovered for France by Du Guesclin within twenty years.

On your Route 10, for Angoulême, about five miles from Poitiers, you pass Château d'Aigne, the childhood home of the Saint-Vallier girl who is known to us as Diane de Poitiers. She was born on September 5, 1499. At six she rode and hunted with her father; at ten she was promised in marriage to the hump-backed Louis de Brézé, nearly thirty years her senior. Before she was sixteen she was married to him. She had been a wife for eight years at the time Francis I is believed to have made her honor the price of her father's life.

Vivonne, a few miles farther south, has a ruined castle which was the girlhood home of the Marquise de Rambouillet.

If you find yourself approaching Angoulême in pretty good season, I'd take a left turn at Mansle, about seventeen miles north of Angoulême, and make an effort to see the Château de la Rochefoucauld where members of that illustrious family have lived for more than a thousand years. But this will add twenty-five miles to your journey from Poitiers — so perhaps you would do better to forget about it and go straight on, entering Angoulême by the route de Ruffec, continuing down rue de Paris toward Place des Halles and the Hôtel de Ville.

The latter is interesting because it occupies the site of the castle of the Counts of Angoulême and incorporates two of the towers, in one of which was born Marguerite, the idolizing elder sister of Francis I. We shall find ourselves very frequently in company with Marguerite on our journeys, especially in the south — at Pau, where she reigned as Queen of Navarre and Queen of the Renaissance; at Cauterets, where she composed the 'Heptameron'; at Bayonne, awaiting the release of her brother, which she had negotiated, from his captivity in Madrid; and elsewhere. We might, of course, as readily associate her with several score places, north and south, for like all of the Valois she was an incessant traveller. But in many places she is overshadowed by other persons. (Who, for instance, thinks of her at Fontainebleau, where her daughter, Jeanne d'Albret, was born?)

MARKETPLACE, ANGOULÊME
From an engraving after a drawing by T. Allom

Marguerite's association with Angoulême was not long continued; her parents left here when she was about two years old and took up their residence at Cognac, where her brother Francis was born. Marguerite's father died when she was not yet four; and her childhood was spent chiefly at Amboise. But I think you will like to reflect, here in Angoulême, on her advent into the world — and on her parentage.

Her mother, who was just sixteen when Marguerite was born, was Louise of Savoy, sister of that Duke Philibert of Savoy for whose last resting-place the exquisite Church of Brou was built. Louise was orphaned when a young child, and brought up in the household of her mother's brother, the Duke of Bourbon, married to Louis XI's masterful daughter, Anne de Beaujeu, Regent of France for her little brother, Charles VIII. At the age of two Louise was affianced to Charles of Orléans, Count of Angoulême, a young man of two-and-twenty who was descended from a younger son of Louis, the murdered Duke of Orléans. Between this young man and the French Crown there stood Louis XI's son, and whatever issue he might have; and Louis, Duke of Orléans (later Louis XII), and whatever issue he might have. So Louise's prospects of a crown were not brilliant. Nor were her prospects of happiness much better; for when the Count of Angoulême at length consented to marry the young person of Savoy, he did so only on condition that he might bring his mistress to live under the same roof as his wife.

This bit of genealogy will serve you in good stead as you read French history. For, when all the heirs of Charles VIII and of Louis XII and of Francis I are swept from the chessboard of history and the House of Valois has ceased to reign in France, it will be through this Marguerite that the Bourbon kings come on; it is to be her grandson, Henry of Navarre, to whom France shall owe so much.

I wonder what you'll think of the cathedral at Angoulême? I wonder what you'll think of *me* for bringing you to Angoulême en route to Périgueux, instead of to Limoges and then down through Chalus where Richard the Lion-Hearted got his death-wound? It was the ramparts — the recollection of them toward sunset — which fixed Angoulême in my mind for a night stop: the ramparts, and the cathedral towering on them, where they overlook the sunset.

Angoulême crowns a rocky plateau whose escarpments may well have made its ancient walls seem nearly superfluous. On three sides and almost on four the natural defences rise; and where battlements once frowned above them there now are beautiful promenades — in places two hundred and fifty feet above the valleys beneath, where paper has been made for centuries.

The cathedral has some very fine features and some restorations which greatly exasperate. It was, like the cathedral at Périgueux, expensively and drastically 'done over,' under Napoleon III, by Abadie whose restorations roused such tempests of protest that we are surprised to find him — when the Second Empire is no more, and the Republic is about to erect a great memorial church on Montmartre in Paris — being entrusted with the plans for the basilica of Sacré-Cœur. How he persevered, in the teeth of all he had to encounter, passes comprehension. At any rate, after you have seen something of his labors here and at Périgueux, you can the more easily understand why he reared a Byzantine basilica above a great French city with no Byzantine traditions.

If the cathedral is closed, you need not feel deprived. Those lines of the interior, which might be interesting if they conveyed any impression of age, are hard and cold in the glaring white 'newness' which has not yet begun to soften.

I may be quite wrong, but I think the exterior is enough — and then the ramparts, which you should follow to the 'prow' of the promontory, at Place de Beaulieu. Thence, a straight-ahead course, via rue de Beaulieu, will take you to your Hôtel des Trois Piliers at the other end of the plateau, in rue de Périgueux.

III

Next morning get early on the wing, for you have a day which will, I think, delight you; and it's a long day, too.

Leave Angoulême by the route de Périgueux which begins close to your hotel and is route number 139. If I were you, I'd be early to bed at Angoulême, and up and away from there by eight o'clock. You have fifty miles to cover before reaching Périgueux, and you ought to do it by ten o'clock — unless! Unless you care more about Brantôme and Bourdeilles than about caves of prehistoric man. If you do, you shall sacrifice none of my esteem.

The family of Bourdeille is one of the most illustrious in France. It was very old and very eminent for its valor when Charlemagne was king and chose the Seigneur de Bourdeille as patron of the splendid abbey he founded at Brantôme, the which Bourdeille and his posterity were to defend against 'all who might molest the monks and hinder them in the enjoyment of their property.'

Brantôme is thirty-five miles from Angoulême, on the direct route to Périgueux; and the Château of Bourdeilles is a very little off that direct route, to the southwest.

Brantôme is full of charm and of picturesqueness. It is on an island formed by two arms of the river Dronne, crossed by a curious old 'elbow' bridge of the sixteenth century. The chalky cliffs above the monastery are honey-combed with human habitations, as they doubtless were when Charlemagne was here — and long, long before his day. And while nothing remains of the abbey he knew, there are beautiful survivals of some later centuries: a very fine belfry, and a cloister of the fifteenth century; and even the eighteenth-century building, with its marble-balus-traded terrace mirrored in the Dronne, and its embowering trees, is lovelier than any other monastic building of the eighteenth century that I have seen. Brantôme has some picturesque old houses, too, and delightful sections of its old fortifications.

It was here that Pierre de Bourdeille, Abbé de Brantôme, wrote those gallant, gossipy chronicles of the Valois court which have been the delight of almost every generation since. If I do not make myself responsible for commending his 'Gallant Ladies' to you, at least I may commend his 'Illustrious Dames of the Court of the Valois Kings' — which Katharine Prescott Wormeley translated, together with Saint-Beuve's commentaries. You are not to hold your sense of humor in abeyance as you read, nor to take all that Brantôme says as gospel. But I'm sure that he cannot fail to interest any one who likes gossip of great person-ages.

He was born at Bourdeilles, in the reign of Francis I; and passed his earliest years at the court of Marguerite de Val-ois, sister of Francis, to whom Madame de Bourdeille was lady-in-waiting.

Pierre's father was a jolly gentleman who ran away to go to the wars in Italy, and somehow fell in with Pope Julius II, who took a great fancy to him and wished to keep him in his company and have him for his guest in Rome.

'Pope,' replied Bourdeille, 'if you gave me your mitre and your cap too, I would not do it; I wouldn't quit my

general and my companions just for your pleasure. Good-
bye to you, rascal.'

And so heartily did the Pope laugh at this adieu that all
those who overheard it dared to laugh too.

Pierre, being the youngest son, was destined for the
Church, or at least for church benefices; and when he was
sixteen, the abbey of Brantôme was bestowed on him by
Henry II. A year later, the young abbé, who later was to
boast that 'none of my race have ever been home-keeping;
they have spent as much time in travels and wars as any,
no matter who they be, in France,' set off for Italy, where
he became attached to the Guises, and took to court instead
of camp life.

He was at Amboise when the Huguenots were slaughtered, at Orléans when Condé was arrested. He was of the
household of the Duke of Guise when the latter escorted his
niece, Mary Stuart, back to Scotland. Brantôme saw the
threatening reception given to Mary. Then he went, with
Guise, to London, where Queen Elizabeth entertained them
graciously.

To recapitulate the wanderings of Brantôme were to
make a travel book of another sort; but we may mention
that he fought under Don Garcia of Toledo, on the Barbary
coast; that he visited the court of Portugal, then that of
Madrid, where Queen Elizabeth of Spain commissioned
him to entreat her mother, Catherine de Médici, to come to
Bayonne for an interview — which Catherine did, Brantôme accompanying her. He went to Malta to fight off the
Sultan. And thence, 'jogging, meandering, vagabondizing,'
as he says, he reached Venice. At one time he even meditated a reconquest of Peru.

What with courts and conquests, he strove somehow to
achieve fame and most particularly fortune. But he seemed
to have been born under an evil star; in one project and

hope after another he was disappointed. Then, 'to complete the destruction of my designs, one day, at the height of my vigor and jollity, a miserable horse, whose white skin might have warned me of nothing good, reared and fell over upon me breaking and crushing my loins, so that for four years I lay in my bed, maimed, impotent in every limb, unable to turn or move without torture and all the agony in the world.'

Although he was at length sufficiently restored to do a little travelling, his life thenceforth was given chiefly to bitter reflections on 'what might have been' had this one or that one not been inappreciative.

Had his day and generation acclaimed and rewarded him as he thought it should, he would never have spent his declining years telling posterity how intimately he had known great personages, and how little he had got of all that he deserved. So his ill-fortunes have been not only our gain, but have secured to him for all time a large meed of that fame he so ardently desired.

Come into this cloister that he knew so well, and imagine that you're calling on him, hoping to find him in a humor to regale you with some of his reminiscences. Is he testy to-day? Does he refuse to talk? Ah, well! you are better off than his contemporaries — for you have his garrulities forever 'on tap.' I would that we dared linger for some of the most amusing quotations from them. But I know we mustn't. Do get his 'Illustrious Dames,' though — if, indeed, so be that you have not grown up on it, as I have.

The Château of Bourdeilles stands above this same sweet, placid Dronne, on a fine promontory inaccessible from the river and isolated from the tiny town by a deep ravine in which cowers the village street. There are two rings of ramparts, and within the inner ring are the two castles, one a feudal keep, polygonal in shape and one hun-

dred and thirty feet high, and the other a fine Renaissance
château which Brantôme's sister-in-law built to entertain
Catherine de Médici; who failed to come!

Now, on to Périgueux — unless you are one of those fortunate mortals who may take all the time you wish for a
journey; in that case, I'd strike off to the east from Brantôme by the road which leads to Thiviers, about seventeen
miles away. Because in that triangle of which Limoges is
the apex and Périgueux and Brive are the bases, and Route
21 is the west side and Route 20 is the east, there is a
wealth of interest and beauty. A dozen miles northeast
from Thiviers is one of the most picturesque of fifteenth-
century castles — Jumilhac-le-Grand — its roof fairly
bristling with pepper-pot towers. Twenty miles southeast
of Thiviers is Hautefort, a superb castle parts of which date
to the eleventh century. This was once the property of
Bertrand de Born, 'who once ruled the towers of Hautefort,' Dante says — who saw Bertrand in hell, 'a headless
trunk . . . by the hair it bore the severed member, lantern-
wise pendent in hand. . . . "Know that I am Bertrand, he
of Born, who gave King John the counsel mischievous.
Father and son I set at mutual war."' It was not John
whom Bertrand set against his father, but Henry, the elder
brother of Richard and John; he who predeceased his father.
History being so full of persons who give 'counsel mischievous' that sets at variance those who should be united,
it would be interesting to know how Dante came to select
Bertrand for the culminating horror of 'the ninth chasm.'
However —! there be few castles in France which have
achieved the immortality of mention in 'The Divine Comedy'; so I think you ought to know it when you are in the
vicinity of one.

Pompadour, the castle which Louis XV gave Madame
Étioles so that she might become Madame de Pompadour,

but which she never occupied, is also in that triangle, near
its eastern edge. And on the eastern edge is Uzerche, a
town very rich in picturesque old houses.

Périgueux is very ancient. For the student of anthro-
pology its museum is a treasury indeed; for this region is
one of the richest known in evidences of prehistoric man
and beast. For the student of Roman remains, there is
much also. For the student of architecture, the cathedral
is interesting. But for the average traveller in France, with
too little time and too much to see, I'd say that Périgueux
might be slighted in favor of all that lies beyond. For now
you are entering a region of such beauty, such allure, that
you will, I'm sure, be quite distracted to know which way
to turn so that you may miss the least.

Coming in from Brantôme by rue Victor Hugo, continue
on it till you have almost reached the statue of Fénelon;
then turn, right, into Cours Michel-Montaigne, passing the
statue of the great essayist, and the Palais de Justice. Then
the Cours narrows. Pass the statue of General Daumesnil,
and at the theatre turn, right, into Place du Quatre-Septembre (remembering that September 4th is to France
what July 4th is to us — on September 4, 1870, this Third
Republic of France was proclaimed, after the disaster to
the Second Empire at Sédan), and there you'll find Hôtel
du Commerce. If you left Angoulême at eight this morning
you are probably hungry. I'd order a 'special' luncheon:
pâte de foie gras, an omelet, perhaps with cêpes (a kind of
mushroom) or timbales with truffles; a salad, mayhap, and
a bottle of Montbazillac or Peycharmant. And, having
ordered this, I'd stroll over beyond Cours Michel Montaigne into the old episcopal city. Rue de la République
will take you into Place de la Mairie, and after you have
passed the Mairie you will soon find yourself at the cathedral which is said to have some resemblance to Saint Mark's

PÉRIGUEUX

From an engraving after a drawing by T. Allom

at Venice. Perhaps it has. At any rate, it is picturesque
from a distance, especially from across the river. And as I
said at Angoulême, it may help you to understand how
Abadie came to do Sacré-Cœur at Paris.

You may be more tempted by some of the charming old
houses which you can see by turning up rue Limogeanne
(to your left) as you pass the Mairie, and especially by the
one at number 17 rue Eguillerie with that delightful 'cat-a-
corner' doorway four-hundred-and-some years old. If,
then, you wander over to the river, on the other side of the
cathedral, you shall see some more lovely old houses on the
quai close to the Pont-des-Barris.

Driving a car in these tortuous old streets is not only
difficult but unpleasing to the populace who regard the
streets as consecrate to other uses. I'd stroll hereabouts.
Then I'd eat my luncheon (if, indeed, I had not ordered it
of the picnic variety so that I might eat it on my way, without sacrificing any time to a dull dining-room) and drive
through rue du Quatre-Septembre to rue Thiers, and along
that, crossing rue du Président Wilson, to rue Chanzy.
Turn, left, here and pass the elliptical Public Garden on the
site of the Roman amphitheatre which seated forty thousand spectators (more by several thousands than all the
present-day inhabitants of Périgueux) and the equally
vanished castle of the Counts of Périgueux. And though
you may not cross the garden, I'm sure you'll be interested
to know that the eastern egress from it is called rue des
Gladiateurs — until it changes its name to rue Duguesclin!

South of the gardens, at the end of rue de Chanzy, are
the ruins of Château Barrière which embodied some of the
Roman wall, and a tall tenth-century tower, with a twelfth-
century donjon. Photographers must not miss the Roman
arch here, with the charming vista of an old, old street beneath it.

Across the railroad tracks and a little farther south is the majestic Roman tower called La Tour de Vésone, a grand old cylinder nearly ninety feet high and more than sixty feet in diameter, one fourth clean gone, the remainder looking as if the Last Trump might resound from its curving walls. It is reverently surrounded by living green, 'set' with precious bits of Roman stone-cutting; and I think you will feel that you have seen few things more impressive.

Now, recross the tracks, take boulevard Bertrand de Born for a short distance, turn up boulevard de Vésone to Place Francheville, and at Tour Mataguerre, of the old ramparts of the cathedral city, take Cours Fénelon to the Pont-Neuf, cross the river Isle, look back toward the cathedral domes and tower, and be on your way, Route 89, toward Brive.

And now you must choose (if you have not already done so) how much time you are willing to spend underground in this valley of the Dordogne where there is also so very much to see aboveground. For students of the prehistoric, or for lovers of the curious, the caves are the thing hereabouts. Castles and cloisters and quaint old towns may be seen elsewhere; but hardly anywhere else are such evidences of our very remote progenitors just emerging from the brute; and not many other localities have so many subterranean wonder-workings of nature.

I have to confess to a strong dislike of all underground sight-seeing, or even transportation. I don't like the atmospheric pressure, or the lack of atmosphere, or whatever it is. Nevertheless, I dutifully explored sundry caves and caverns in these lovely valleys, so that I might (perhaps) be a little better qualified to counsel you. Certainly they are no place for any one with a weak heart, or with a tendency to 'nerves.' Nor are they the place for one who fatigues at all easily. We were a group of five when I visited the caves, and all sturdy travellers accustomed to much effort; but we were all exhausted by so much effort in such conditions, and most of us decided that we had seen enough of 'the bowels of the earth' to last us all our lives.

You may feel very differently about it; and if you do, I am not taking issue with you. The tremendous interest of these caves to scientists and lovers of the remote past, I can understand. And, needless to say, I deeply respect their enthusiasm for such unique evidences as they find here. I am not advising any reader to forego visiting the caves (not even the weak-of-heart) and am being explicit about it only because I find that some wayfarers read hastily (if, for instance, I say, 'Keep out of Stratford-on-Avon until about five o'clock, when the "trippers" have thinned out,' I find myself quoted as having advised people not to go to Stratford at all), and I do not wish any one to miss seeing the caves because he thinks I said they are not worth seeing. They are very wonderful. But if you get deep into one and feel that you ought not to have come, please remember that I did urge you to consider before entering them.

Now, then — ! From the route for Brive, you turn off (right) at the first turn, for Le Bugue. Should you feel that you would hate to be so close (six miles) to one of the most exquisite cloisters of which anybody ever dreamed, and not see it, turn south to Cadouin, whose church has what some people believe to be a shred of Christ's winding-sheet, brought back from the First Crusade.

If you can resist this, then go from Le Bugue to Campagne, and turn to your left along the Vézère till you come to Les Eyzies, a hamlet of some four hundred souls, huddled beneath the overhanging ledges of a great rock. Until 1868, Les Eyzies was just an ordinary little old village in a lovely river valley of France. Then some workmen, engaged in the construction of a railway embankment in the vicinity (near the village of Crô-Magnon), laid bare a small cave, nearly filled with débris, and soon unearthed five human skeletons with skulls of such unusual characteristics that M. Louis Lartet, the great archæologist, was sent to this section by the Government and made many other discoveries which convinced him that these valleys had been inhabited by a prehistoric race which he called, from the village, Crô-Magnon. The skull known as 'the old man of Crô-Magnon' carried the evidence of its antiquity in the stalagmite deposit on it from a calcareous drip from the roof of the rock — a formation that could only have been made in thousands of years.

They were big folk, their stature varying from 5 feet 10½ inches to 6 feet 4½ inches; their skulls were remarkably well developed in the frontal region, and some scientists aver that 'the Crô-Magnon women had bigger brains than has the average male European of to-day.' Further explorations revealed astounding art productions in the caves where men lived who were 'engaged in a daily struggle for the barest necessities of life, in a trying climate and surrounded by a fauna whose means of attack and defence were infinitely superior to their own.'

'The caves of France,' says Charles Hercules Read, LL.D., of the British Museum, 'bring before us a race of artists of first-rate capacity, who, for accuracy of observation, and skill in indicating the character and peculiarities of the animals around them, have never been surpassed.' This, he feels, is true not only of their drawings, but of their sculptures, which he thinks 'are on a still higher plane.'

I have read a bit, as one totally uninstructed in the science may, about these interesting beings of the dawn. And while I shall not try to epitomize much for you, because I feel so inadequate to it, there is one detail which I think may interest you even if you are a little 'cold' to Crô-Magnons.

And that is, that they seemed to have very definite ideas
about the heart as the seat of life, and the circulation of
blood in relation to health. Probably they did not know how
it circulated; but they knew that ill people got pale, and dead
people got very pale; so they seem to have colored the bodies
of their dead with a rosy pigment to simulate life-glow and,
perhaps, induce its return. In one of the 'murals' of a mam-
moth painted by a Crô-Magnon artist (not hereabouts) the
big red heart is quite accurately placed and probably fairly
proportionate.

Whether we are or are not well-informed on prehistoric
man, surely we cannot approach, in this district, the evidences of his life and struggle without deep respect for all
that these caves mean to the scholars who seek to interpret
us to ourselves through the revelations of the remote
past.

And there must be a considerable popular interest either
in the prehistoric or in the remarkable geological formations
hereabouts, because there are almost daily excursions by
motor-coach through these valleys of the Dordogne, the
Vézère, and the Beune, from July 14th to September 30th,
starting from Les Eyzies and connecting with special train
service from Périgueux. Should you be exploring this region
by train and bus, I advise coming to Les Eyzies on a Sunday,
leaving Périgueux about 9 A.M. and reaching Les Eyzies soon
after 10. Then, see the caves, and take the valley of the
Dordogne trip of five hours, including Beynac and Domme
and Sarlat. This gets you back to Les Eyzies to catch the
six o'clock train back to Périgueux.

Motoring, and going in a continuous direction, I should
take the direct road from Les Eyzies to Sarlat.

And what shall I say to you of Sarlat? You may pass
through it on its 'Main Street,' which is a highway, and
never suspect that you are in anything but a dull little

provincial town. Or, your eye may catch sight of that sign (on your left as you come journeying from Les Eyzies) which invites you to 'Visit the Old Town.' I know that a great many eyes must miss that sign — even the eyes of people who have come hither in quest of wherewith to make books.

Was it because we were peculiarly in the mood for it that we succumbed so immediately to 'the Old Town's' charm? Is it possible that wayfarers might stop there, and look, and wonder why five who came before them should have gone on their way feeling that Sarlat was 'an experience'? I don't know. I'm afraid to say much about Sarlat. We loved it so — and you may not love it at all. But I'm sure you ought to look at it — to give it a chance to charm you as it charmed us. Never mind anything in particular about it. Make your own facts and romances for it. But if you find yourself enchanted, be sure to explore also on the other side of 'Main Street,' up behind the rows of country-town shops. You can't see it from the car. You must 'park' and go afoot. And should you be hungry again, you can get a very fair meal at the Hôtel de la Madeleine.

From Sarlat, I'd go south and a little west, to Beynac, whose thirteenth-century castle and little, hill-climbing hamlet beneath, perched high above the Dordogne, is one of the most picturesque and romantic-looking sights to be seen anywhere. If you climb up to it, and ascend to the donjon roof or platform, you will be superbly rewarded by one of the lordliest, loveliest views imaginable, embracing a number of neighboring castles and, in the distance, the ramparts of Domme. But even if you only gaze up at Beynac from below, you should see it, without fail, if you are one of those whose blood still leaps responsive to suggestions of 'once upon a time ——.' Any one who can look at Beynac and not feel himself weaving stories about it has had a soul-starved youth and stored up little to carry him gallantly through the hard facts of maturity.

The Manoir de Fayrac, across the river, is furnished in fifteenth-century style; and it is probable that you could go through it, if you are interested in 'period' furnishing. (I am, of course, not supposing that any one person can make all these stops in a single day, between Angoulême and Cahors; I am leaving you to select those which appeal most to you. Merely to cover the ground in a day's run means pretty continuous moving; but those who can stop only briefly and occasionally have a feast for the eyes, if they do no more than sit in the car and turn their heads. Some readers will have more time; will spend a night at Brive, at the Hôtel de Bordeaux; or at Souillac, at the Hôtel Moderne; or at Rocamadour, Hôtel des Voyageurs; or at Vic-sur-Cère, a spa, twelve miles from Aurillac, Hôtel de la Compagnie d'Orléans. A week in this valley can be as wonderfully and delightfully spent as anywhere I know.)

And on that same south (or left) bank of the river, a little farther east, is Domme, a picturesque bastide founded in 1282 by the son of Saint Louis, but looking as if it might have been one of the towns of the Holy Land brought back by Saint Louis from his first Crusade. Domme stands some four hundred and sixty feet above the river and commands a glorious view of the valley and many of its castles.

A bastide? You'll meet many of them in southwestern France. The name occurs as frequently as Villeneuve in the north, and means the same thing: a town called into being, not by slow growth, but by command, and built all at one time, ready to be peopled; a fortified village set where some overlord felt that a fortified place should be.

Sometimes the Crown established a bastide, to defend a section of its frontier. Sometimes a great vassal built bastides (as Edward I of England did all over Guyenne and

Gascony). Sometimes a mighty abbey would erect one on a distant property. Frequently Crown, Church, and nobles would combine to create a new centre of population in a sparsely settled district.

The bastides were built on a practically uniform plan, rectangular in form, with thoroughfares running at right angles, and in the centre an arcaded square which was the town forum and principal mart. They were the 'model villages' of the twelfth, thirteenth, and fourteenth centuries, and are extraordinarily interesting. One of the best examples is Monpazier, between the Dordogne and the Lot, a little south of Cadouin where the lovely cloisters are, and some five miles from the great Château de Biron, which belonged (very late in its long, long history) to that Marshal de Biron, who was a brilliant soldier for Henry IV, but was accused, and convicted, of high treason, and beheaded in the Bastille in 1602.

Photographers, painters, etchers must needs love the bastides. So, for them, let me say that I shall try not to omit mention of any important ones on or near our routes.

A little beyond Domme is the Château de Fénelon, where the great Archbishop of Cambrai was born and where his room is shown to visitors. And at the exquisite village of Carennac, also on the Dordogne, some miles east of his birthplace, is the ancient priory where Fénelon wrote 'Les Aventures de Télémaque.' There, in the Dordogne, is an island called Calypso's. And there is, all told, a dream-place to which I heartily commend you if you have the time for it. Another reason for going there than Carennac's self, is not needed. But if it were, you have it in the near vicinity of Saint-Céré, which picture-makers must not miss; and Château de Montal, near Saint-Céré, which students of architecture must not miss, because it is one of the most beautiful examples of Renaissance architecture in all

France, rivalling the best on the Loire and — of course — much less seen. Another very beautiful Renaissance château of this vicinity is at Assier, not many miles south, on the way to Figeac.

A short distance beyond Château Fénelon is Souillac, with a church that will interest students of ecclesiastical architecture, but need not detain other wayfarers; and just east of Souillac one comes to a road that goes to Rocamadour, a place about which one hears much and from which, perhaps, one expects too much. As we approach it, viewing it from across the gorge, we get its best, I think. I would certainly go near enough to get a good look at it, if I were you. But if I had lingered en route and were now a little pressed for time or weary of limb, I'd make the distant view suffice me. This is not to say that Rocamadour is not worth a visit, nor that you might not enjoy a night there, should your schedule permit. But, being a place of pilgrimage (and having been so these eighteen centuries and more), the tiny village has, naturally, the characteristics of all communities which look to wayfarers for revenue: there is an amount of solicitation, of service pressed upon you, which consorts ill with the nature of the place. How the pious pilgrim feels about such insistence, I cannot guess. But the traveller who comes hereabouts attracted by the comparative inaccessibility (by the off-the-beaten-track-ness), and by the semi-savage natural grandeur, and by the illustrious ghosts of former visitors, is likely to want quiet for reflection and for the enjoyment of all that Nature has wrought here. I must admit that on the occasion of my one and only visit to Rocamadour, we fled (all five of us of one mind) from the importunities of the one hundred and seventy-five inhabitants, all of whom seemed bent on catering to us in one manner or another.

The story of the place is that Zaccheus, 'who climbed a

tree his Lord to see,' came hither (evidently Zaccheus liked climbing!) in search of a retreat; and that his very desire for solitude, for opportunity to pray and reflect, so advertised him through these valleys that people came to marvel and remained to worship. And, Zaccheus having changed his name to Amadour, this became Roc-Amadour or Amadour's rock, and a holy place forevermore.

Now, make your way back to Route 20, which you pick up at Paynac and follow to Cahors, a beautiful drive of about thirty miles.

As you enter Cahors, which occupies a peninsula almost encircled by the river Lot, you pass through the fourteenth-century ramparts which were erected during the Hundred Years' War, north of the older wall which Saint Didier had built there seven centuries before.

On your right is the Porte-Saint-Michel, which looks as if it might be a gateway in Jerusalem. On your left is the *barbacane* where the guard of the porte lodged, and the great square tower called La Tour des Pendus, or the Tower of the Hangings. The street by which you enter is called, between the ramparts and the avenue du Nord where the city ended until the fourteenth-century fortifications were built, the rue de la Barre. On it you come presently to boulevard Gambetta, the western boundary of the mediæval city; but first you pass Place Lafayette and the Church of Saint-Barthélemy, beside the tall, square, crenellated tower (wedged in between the church and an impertinent young building only a few hundred years old) which is all that's left of the palace of John of Cahors who was Pope at Avignon from 1316 to 1334. John XXII may never have seen this tower; but his brother and nephew built the palace on the site of their family dwelling, which was probably no mean one (for they were of a rich family), but inadequate to their position as relatives of the Pope. John gave Cahors

a university, and rich posts and benefices to his townsmen
and fellow provincials; but I'm afraid there isn't much in his
incumbency of the Holy See to entitle him to our reverence,
or even to our interest — although he was seventy-one
when elected Pope and reigned until he was eighty-nine;
years when a man might be expected to have ripe wisdom
and gentleness of spirit.

Were you to turn a very little way to your right, on the
avenue du Nord, you would see the Portal of Diane which
seems to have been part of a great Roman bath.

But you are intent, I dare say, on your quarters for the
night. So continue on boulevard Gambetta, past the
Palais de Justice (on your right) to rue Maréchal Foch, at
the corner of which and boulevard Gambetta you will find
Hôtel des Ambassadeurs, with a friendly host, comfortable
rooms, and good cheer.

After dinner, take a walk.

Walk on down boulevard Gambetta, past the Hôtel de
Ville, to rue Président Wilson; then turn, right, to the
river, passing Gambetta's birthplace (number 11) and the
Lycée Gambetta — part of which used to be a Jesuit college
until the suppression of that order in France, in 1762; and
the part of recent construction occupies the site of an old
monastery of the Cordeliers.

They do well, at Cahors, to be proud of the Italian grocer's
boy whose eloquence and statesmanship did so much for
France.

Imagine him, hereabouts, in his sixteenth year, when the
loss of his left eye must have seemed like a check on the
prospects of the ambitious young student; and when, not-
withstanding, he so distinguished himself in all his studies
that his proud papa sent him to Paris to study law. Imagine the excitement at Cahors as, beginning when he was
thirty, the news from Paris came to be fuller and fuller of

Léon. 'What do you think? Léon Gambetta has been elected to the Assembly by *two* constituencies: Paris and Marseilles!' How the cafés of Cahors must have bubbled with that news!

'Léon has attacked the Empire. . . . But, war having been forced upon France, Léon says France must be defended to the utmost. . . . Have you heard? It was Léon who proclaimed the fall of the Emperor (after Sédan) and the establishment of a new republic. . . . Imagine! *Nine* departments of France have elected Léon to the National Assembly at Bordeaux (in March, 1871) and he has chosen to sit for Strasbourg, which is about to be relinquished! He's a fighter-to-the-finish, this fiery fellow from our Cahors. . . .' And so on, with increasing pride and increasing excitement, until that last day of the year 1882, when a revolver shot, at Ville d'Avray, near Paris, startled and mystified the world. What had happened? What had Léonie Léon to do with it? He was about to marry her, 'twas said. For nearly twelve years she has dominated his life — he has not only adored her, but has consulted her on all his plans and policies; he has constantly begged her to marry him, and she has refused. Then she consents, the day is set, and — a revolver goes off, in her presence! 'Surely, Léon wouldn't ——!' He didn't! But think how Cahors must have felt while the rumors of suicide ran rife. And then, on the 6th of January, 1883, that funeral at Paris! One of the most overwhelming displays of national sentiment ever witnessed on a similar occasion.

At the end of rue Président Wilson is the Pont-Valentré, the most beautiful old fortified bridge left in France. It was commenced in 1308, and finished fifty years later. The architect, tradition tells us, was confronted with difficulties so grave that he appealed to the Devil, who promised to help him, but at the price of his soul. After this bargain

the work went forward brilliantly, the Devil executing all
orders, until nothing remained undone except the top, or
cap, of the middle tower. Then the architect (who was
doubtless a monk, as all architects then were; and the more
certainly so as all bridges were still under religious control,
though the Pontifex Maximus, or Pope, might no longer be
the Great Bridge-Builder as in ancient Rome) ordered the
Devil to use a sieve for carrying to the top of that centre
tower the water needed to mix mortar for 'setting' the last
stone.

Thus the Devil recognized that he had met his master,
had been outwitted; so he disappeared. For more than five
hundred years that stone was still lacking. Then, in 1880,
it was put in place; and, to perpetuate the legend, the stone
was sculptured to show the Devil trying to snatch it away
and claim his due.

I hope you will agree with me that this beautiful old
bridge is, in itself, worth going a very long way to see. And
should it be your good fortune to see it toward the end of a
long day's sunset, in a still faintly rosy twilight, or when the
Lot is silvered by a nearly full moon, I am sure that Cahors
will always be 'double-starred' in your mem'ry picture
book.

If you cross the bridge and walk a little to your left, you
will see the mouth from which gushes the abundant water-
supply of Cahors — more than two hundred gallons per
second — brought to it by a long subterranean river. The
Romans called this gift of the gods Divona. Long afterwards, when it became the property of the Carthusian
monks, it took their name and is still called the Fontaine des
Chartreux.

Turn back, in rue Président Wilson, as far as the post-
office, and then (right) till you come to the Allées Fénelon,
where you will find marble statues of two celebrated men of

this province (Quercy). One is Jean-Baptiste Bessières, born of very humble parents at Preissac, near here, in 1768.

The other is Joachim Murat, son of an innkeeper in a bastide between here and Gramat, now called Labastide-Murat. He was born in 1767.

In 1791, both these young fellows set out for Paris where they had obtained appointments as privates in the new Constitutional Guard of Louis XVI, then in practical custody at the Tuileries.

On the terrible day of August 10th, when the palace was stormed and taken, and the royal family fled to the protection of the National Assembly, Bessières is said to have saved the lives of several of the Queen's household, at the risk of his own. Four years later, when with the army in Italy, he attracted Napoleon's personal attention by his acts of great personal bravery. After Rivoli, it was Bessières whom Napoleon sent to Paris with the captured colors. From that time on, his rise was rapid. In 1804 he was made a Marshal of France. And in 1809 he was given the title of Duke of Istria. Three years later he was killed in battle, in Prussia, and was buried in Les Invalides. He was the Emperor's faithful and trusted friend, one of his ablest commanders, and was so humane and just that he was not only adored by his soldiers, but even loved and mourned by his enemies. Please salute Bessières!

Murat's career was, as you know, even more spectacular. He met Bonaparte in Paris in 1795, when both of them were out of a job and, apparently, out o' luck. On that October night, 1795, when the shabby, discouraged young Corsican, on the eve of going to Turkey to try his fortunes there, was so suddenly given command of the defence of Paris against the Royalist restoration movement, it was this inn-keeper's son who galloped through the night with three hundred horsemen to Les Sablons, seized a supply of guns that 'whiffed' grapeshot, and got them to the Tuileries by six in the morning, ready to rout the Royalists and leave their commemorating pockmarks on the façade of Saint-Roch's.

In 1800, Murat married Caroline Bonaparte, the youngest of those sisters for whose satisfactory settlement in life Napoleon showed so much anxious concern. And in the same year that the honor was conferred upon Bessières, Murat was made a Marshal of France — of the Empire! In 1808, Napoleon, removing his brother Joseph from Naples to Madrid, to the throne of Spain, appointed Murat to the throne of Naples in Joseph's stead. This is, I suppose, not the place for a résumé of Murat's career. But surely one may pay a tribute of pity for the pathos of his end — before a firing-squad.

Napoleon called Murat 'the finest cavalry officer in the world.' If he was not the best king in the world, it was not because he didn't try to be, but because 'the soldier was helpless before the diplomats; dashing bravery is of no value in the affair of intrigue.' And because, in his truly great dream of a United Italy, he had to further his purposes with that Neapolitan soldiery of whom canny old Ferdinand (the deposed King of Naples, husband of Marie Antoinette's sister) said: 'You may dress them in blue, in green, or red; but in any color they will always run.'

King Ferdinand 'came back' in May, 1815, and King Joachim fled to France. In September — after Waterloo — Murat, with a handful of followers (thirty, to be exact!) landed in southern Italy, in a mad effort to regain his kingdom. He was captured, court-martialled, sentenced; and in half an hour he was shot. Of the eight officers who condemned him, seven owed their commissions to him!

I think that in Cahors we must seem to be in the cafés, the shops, the homes, a hundred and twenty-odd years ago, when these boys of the neighborhood were playing such brilliant parts in the affairs of the Empire; and to hear the townsfolk discussing them.

At the end of the Allées Fénelon is the fine monument to Gambetta, erected the year after his burial; and beside it is the theatre. Turn to your left, as you enter the Place de la République (where the theatre is), and you have but a few steps to go to your hotel.

This evening stroll in Cahors (although I went farther, and followed the river from the Place d'Armes, at the south end of the boulevard Gambetta, close to the remains of the Roman bridge, to the Pont-Valentré, and all the way back again) left ineffaceable and cherished pictures in my mind — lovely nocturnes of an old city very rich in memories and very charming in her manner of relating them.

IV

Next morning, be out betimes on exploration bent, I beg of you. To lunch at Albi, and see something of it, you should leave Cahors close to ten o'clock. But if you will take your coffee at eight, and cross the boulevard soon after, rue Maréchal Foch will lead you, in a minute or two, to the cathedral. I doubt if you will find it interesting, except for its age — its nave dates from the end of the tenth century. But its cloisters are lovely and well worth an effort to see.

On your right as you face the cathedral's west front is the market-place where Gambetta's father had his grocery shop, 'Bazard Génois,' the top of its sign still visible on a house-front on the west side of the *place*.

Now, turn north from the cathedral, pass beside the Préfecture, or seat of provincial government, and find yourself in the Place Champollion, named for the founder of Egyptology, who was born at Figeac in this province. In this *place* is the charming monument to Clément Marot, born at Cahors in 1495. Clément's father was a Norman,

of the neighborhood of Caen, a poet, and historiographer to
Anne of Brittany. What he was doing in Cahors, I don't
know. But he married here; here his boy was born; and here
Clément seems to have had his education till he was about
ten, when he went to Paris, where, when he was scarcely
out of his teens, he became poet to Queen Claude. In 1519,
Clément became attached to the suite of Marguerite d'Angoulême. He was with Francis I at the Field of the Cloth of
Gold (in 1520) and celebrated it in verse. He was at Pavia,
and was taken prisoner, like his King.

Soon after his release, he was again made prisoner — this
time on the charge of heresy.

His famous translations of the Psalms appeared about
1539. He had been dead for nearly twenty years when the
Huguenot conspirators went, singing one of these Psalms, to
their death at Amboise. We wonder what Cahors said about
Marot?

We know what it did in opposition to Henry of Navarre
when he was the leader of the Protestant party.

Now, here you are, behind the Préfecture, in the Place
des Petites Boucheries (Square of the Little Butcher Shops),
around which, in the thirteenth century, were established
those money-lenders called Cahorsins or Lombards, who
had their counting-houses in all the principal towns of
Europe, loaned money to popes, kings, nobles, clergy, and
charged such usury that Dante put them deep in Hell:

> 'The inmost round marks with its seal
> Sodom and Cahors and all such as speak
> Contemptuously of the Godhead in their heart.'

One day, in 1580, King Henry of Navarre, the dashing
young wearer of the White Plume, came riding toward
Cahors with a band of seven hundred men, and hid in a
thick walnut-grove till nightfall. When the darkness
was deepest, and all the lights had gone out in Cahors,

Henry blew up the gate of the bridge of Cabessut, and hurled himself and his force into the sleeping city. The tocsin rang, and here in this *place* the inhabitants mustered to repulse the assailants.

All the rest of the night, and all of the next day, there was close-quarters and '*no* quarter' fighting in these narrow old streets. When day broke, on that battle then a few hours old, it discovered Henry, fighting desperately, covered with blood, his clothing in shreds, but his courage undaunted. House after house he took, street after street, against the most stubborn resistance. And then, when the day was won, he retired to rest in a fine residence which you shall see presently.

Now, continue up rue du Château du Roi, and on your right you have the remains of the palace of the King's Seneschal in Quercy, and the quaint old streets called rue Devia and rue du Four-Sainte-Catherine— or the Oven of Sainte Catherine. From the top of this rue du Château du Roi (which has now changed its name to rue des Soubirous) you will get a more attractive view of the crenellated tower of Pope John's palace. And if you make your way over to the Quai de Regourd, on your right, and come down the river's side to the Pont-Neuf, then cross over to the majestic ruins of the convent church of the Jacobins, you will have a picture of old Cahors with the morning light upon it which will immeasurably delight you, I am sure.

When you recross the bridge, turn to your left, behind the cathedral, on Quai Champollion, where you will find the house in which Henry IV sought rest.

With this, you will have seen the principal 'sights' of Cahors — most of which will doubtless have been having their pictures taken by one or more painters, etchers, photographers, to whom the old town is a veritable happy hunting-ground.

How shall you go to Albi?

Well, if you are a lover of Ingres, of course you will go by way of Montauban, which is his birthplace, pervaded by his memory, and rich in his works; and also (being a bastide) has an arcaded central square, perhaps the handsomest of any of the sort. Montauban is thirty miles south of Cahors, on Route 20, the grand highway from Paris to the eastern Pyrénées; and from there it is fifty-five miles to Albi.

If Ingres does not tempt you, perhaps Cordes will, and Najac.

To reach Albi this way, take Route 111 to Villefranche de Rouergue, a bastide of 1252, with a number of the most charming old houses in the world; its central square, picturesquely arcaded, is dominated by the enormous tower of the Church of Notre-Dame, pierced by the public highway; and the former Carthusian monastery, now a hospice, has a good fifteenth-century cloister. (After you have become acquainted with bastides and their arcades, see how differently you'll feel about the Place des Vosges, when you get back to Paris — remembering that it was begun by Henry IV, that child of Gascony.)

Najac, ten miles nearer Albi (on Route 122, from Villefranche), has a 'picture' which our picture-makers must not miss: a marvellous old street with, in the middle distance, a hill crowned by the cylindrical towers of a ruined castle built in 1110.

To students of architecture and of the Middle Ages, I must say — as they pass through Laguépie, seven miles south of Najac — that at Saint-Antonin, some fourteen or fifteen miles west of Laguépie, there is the oldest palace that France preserves, and the most important example of domestic architecture of the twelfth century. Originally a private mansion, it is now the Hôtel de Ville. Viollet-le-Duc restored it, and reconstructed the upper stages of the tower. The edifice looks as if it had been transported magically from Tuscany, where it would have been already venerable in Dante's day. Extremely rare, even in Italy, are examples of civil architecture of that period.

And now, at Cordes, you have a triple-walled bastide of 1222, which is one of the most picturesque small towns of France. It was named for Cordova in Spain, and I am not exaggerating when I say that it looks as if Cordova had been named after Cordes — although Cordova was probably Carthaginian and old when Cæsar took it!

In other towns of France we find here and there a house of the thirteenth or fourteenth century; at Cordes we find nearly an entire street of the Middle Ages preserved intact. The little town (about thirteen hundred inhabitants) crowns an isolated hill and seems still to hold itself aloof from the maw of our modernity. In many ways it will, I think, help you, much more than Carcassonne, to recapture the feeling of what a recent writer calls 'the greatest century' — the thirteenth.

From Cordes to Albi, take the road which leaves Route 122 and goes southeast. The distance is about fifteen miles. You enter Albi by the boulevard de Strasbourg, cross the Tarn by the Pont-Neuf (or New Bridge) and get a good view of the Pont-Vieux, built in 1035, of the amazing cathedral and the fortress beside it which was the residence of its archbishops.

When you have crossed the Tarn (whose further acquaintance I hope you are going to make, after you leave Carcassonne) you are in Les Lices (or The Lists); and on your left, after you pass rue de la République, you will find Hôtel de la Poste, where you may wish to lunch; or, you may prefer to go on to Place du Vigan, and turn down rue Saint-Antoine to the Hostellerie du Grand-Saint-Antoine, at number 15.

After luncheon (and don't forget that the Tarn is the region for Roquefort and that the white wine of Gaillac is delicious) cross the Lices (or the Place du Vigan) and walk through rue Timbal, where there are some interesting old houses, to rue Mariès, passing the former abbey church of Saint-Salvi, begun in the tenth-century, en route to the cathedral.

I believe the Cathedral of Sainte-Cécile will interest you intensely and impress you profoundly. And when we realize something of what Albi and all this part of the country had just suffered when this cathedral was built, we readily understand why the house of God was made so fortress-like.

It is easy for us to think of the eleventh and twelfth centuries as swept by the fervor of the Crusades. It is not so easy for us to remember that they also were rent by great secessions from the Church. In essence, the ecclesiastics and their scandalous practices were the cause of all the disaffection; the feeling that the Sacraments were polluted in polluted hands, and that merit rather than ordination should make a priest or bishop, was called by a variety of names in different parts of Europe, but substantially it was the same protest. Some of this disaffection was turned to a frenzy of reconsecration by the preaching of the Crusades. Some of it persisted.

In the southwest of France, the prevailing disaffection was called Albigensianism. Its adherents discarded the Sacraments, translated the Scriptures, practised extreme asceticism, and believed in the transmigration of souls.

The people of this region were not only out of sympathy with Rome, they were out of sympathy with the King of France who had just established sovereignty over them. There was a political as well as a spiritual protest in their defiance of Pope and King.

The Pope (Innocent III) ordered Raymond, Count of Toulouse, to suppress heresy in his dominions. Raymond knew he couldn't do it. So the Pope appealed to the King of France (Philippe-Auguste), who answered that he was already as busy as he could be — which was true. Then the Pope declared a Crusade, and offered to all who would fight the Albigensians the same indulgences granted to those who fought the infidels in the Holy Land. Immense numbers flocked to this Crusade — 20,000 horsemen and 200,000 foot.

The city of Béziers was one of the first points of attack. It was taken, pillaged, burned, all the population massacred — more than 40,000, 'tis said. Seven thousand were burned in one church. 'Kill everybody!' one Crusader cried. 'God will recognize His own.'

The Viscount of Béziers held out at Carcassonne — but we shall recall that when we are there.

The extermination went on for twenty years, and was stopped by Queen Blanche of Castile early in her regency for her little son, Louis IX. Simon de Montfort, son of the Count of Évreux, was the chief exterminator; and those he did not burn alive or throw into wells, he left hanging to the branches of trees above which carrion birds circled in great flocks.

This Crusade strengthened Crown and Church in south-western France; but it did not make an end of devastating warfares, nor even of religious wars. So we find this land of Languedoc (the language of *oc* for 'yes' instead of *oui*), the land of troubadours and gallantry, bristling with fortified churches, of which the great cathedral at Albi is the outstanding example.

The exterior would ill prepare you for the interior, were it not for that lacy baldaquin, or porch, by which you enter.

Within is a church like none you have ever seen any-

where. No aisles, no transepts — just a vast hall, sumptuous with color and carving, and surrounded by two-storied
chapels.

No matter how 'tired of churches' you may think you
are, I don't see how you can fail to be impressed by this
one. And for the student of architecture it is, of course, a
great experience.

The archbishops' palace, between the cathedral and the
river, now contains the musée; but if you are going on to
Carcassonne, I believe you would do best to confine your
impressions of the palace to its exterior, particularly the
garden.

Your route to Carcassonne is number 118, and the distance is sixty-five miles. If you are going to Nîmes, to-
morrow, you have a hundred and twenty-five miles to
cover; and if you are going from Carcassonne to the Gorges
of the Tarn, you have a day's journey that will necessitate
your leaving Carcassonne early in the morning — certainly
by nine o'clock.

In any case, I'd get to Carcassonne as early this afternoon as possible. From four o'clock, on to sunset, you
can see it to best advantage; and after dark you can 'experience' it.

As you go through Castres, try to have a glimpse of the
backs of the old houses bordering the Agout and beautifully reflected in its placid depths. And, if you know and
love the work of Goya, the Spanish painter, you may see
three fine pictures of his in the musée at the Hôtel de Ville.
Castres is a good point of departure for visiting the
Sidobre, a plateau whereon, æons ago, some sportive forces
of Nature heaved about great granite blocks of weird formations — one shaped like a goose, one like three cheeses
piled one atop another, one like a mushroom; and so on —
very weird, and for the geologist very interesting because

all this region hereabouts is schist, and only this one little plateau is strewn with these strange granites.

Mazamet, at the foot of the Black Mountain, is an important town in the wool industry.

And soon you come in sight of Carcassonne!

I have tried to think what it is about Carcassonne that thrills us so. Of course, it is superbly beautiful and magnificently romantic. But other places are that, without making anything like the appeal to the imagination that Carcassonne does. There isn't any personage associated with Carcassonne who has great fascination for us. There isn't any one story about it that everybody knows and loves.

It is — I think — just this: Carcassonne, as we see it, is a perfect 'setting' for anything we may like to imagine there that has to do with mediævalism; and whether it be born in us or bred in us by our reading, there is evidently something in most of us that has an affinity for the mediæval.

I can imagine a perfectly preserved city of Roman times being of profound interest to students of those times and of mild interest to the general traveller; but I can't imagine the general traveller getting 'thrills all over' at the merest glimpse of its fortifications. I can fancy a possible seventeenth-century town in which nothing seemed changed since Molière walked its streets, and Racine, and La Rochefoucauld, and Mignard, and Marion Delorme, and Ninon de l'Enclos, and Madame de Sévigné; and I can realize what that town would mean to the lovers of that century; but I can't imagine the average traveller writing triumphantly home from it: 'I have seen So-and-So!'

Contend with me on this, if you will; but I'm convinced that there's a 'hang-over' of some sort left in most of us by our mediæval forbears, which stays stronger than any of the later hang-overs that have been superimposed upon it. We know they were dirty — those Middle Ages! — and we know they were coarse, and we know they were cruel; we've no wish to live in them except in fancy; and yet, when our fancy takes us thither, we find ourselves curiously 'at home' in them. Is it our dear, blessed, transporting romancers who are responsible for this? Or is there something in us which, if it has outgrown the sanitation of the Middle Ages, has not outgrown other qualities of theirs — some good, some bad?

There's *this*, too, about Carcassonne: it is unique of its sort. If only one great Gothic cathedral had been left to us, probably we should feel about it as we do about Carcassonne.

At any rate, here we are!

You are entering from the north, across the Canal du Midi, or Canal of the Two Seas, a hundred and fifty-five miles long, uniting the Mediterranean with the Garonne. This was made in the seventeenth century (1661–81), the great days of Louis XIV, entirely at his own expense, by an engineer of Béziers named Riquet, who, 'with a magnificence truly worthy of the Grand Century, pleased himself with beautifying it by shade trees and jets of water, transforming his utilitarian achievement with many spots of majestic or of charming beauty.' There are sixty-four locks in it.

If we were not entering Carcassonne, I should offer you some reminders of the canal life of France and what a part it plays in the nation's economics. But I know you don't want it now.

You approach the Cité, the fortified hill-town of your dreams, through the Ville Basse, or Lower Town, founded in 1240 when one of the hereditary counts, leading an attempt to get Carcassonne back from the French Crown,

failed, and those within the Cité who had aided him were
banished. They begged the King (Louis IX) to grant them
leave to live within sight of the Cité, since they might no
longer live within it; and he granted this indulgence. So
here, at the foot of their Lost Paradise, they built, and
lived, and died; and here their descendants carry on. The
town is built somewhat on the bastide plan, with a central
square, and streets neatly 'criss-cross.'

I would drive straight down rue Georges Clemenceau to
the square (Place Carnot) with its tall, shady plane-trees
and its handsome Fountain of Neptune. And, just beyond
it, turn, left, into rue de Verdun, passing the library and the
musée (the latter an astonishingly good one for a small
provincial town) en route to the Place Gambetta, a pleasant little public garden. Turn south as you come to this,
and after you have skirted the west edge of the square, turn
left into rue du Pont-Vieux, leading to the *pont* of that
name, a thirteenth-century bridge in the middle of which
there used to be a stone archway marking the boundary
between the Lower Town and the Cité. The river is the
Aude, which leads an exceptionally picturesque existence
from the time it rises, high up in the Pyrénées near Font-
Romeu, till it reaches the Mediterranean between Narbonne
and Béziers.

Leaving the Old Bridge, you follow rue du Faubourg de
la Trivalle and turn right, into a road that climbs toward
the Porte-Narbonnaise, the main entrance to the Cité. You
will, I believe, have one of the major thrills of your lifetime
as you enter here, between these massive towers, beneath
the double portcullis, and make your slow, cautious way up
the narrow, winding, ancient street to the Place du Château,
cross it, take rue Porte de l'Aude for a little way, and turn
(left) into rue Garibaldi, leading to your Hôtel de la Cité, a
modern and extremely comfortable hotel between the Tour

Visigothe and the Tour de l'Inquisition, on the western ramparts looking toward the Pyrénées and the sunset.

I wish I could say more about the spiritual hospitality of this hotel whose physical comforts are so great and whose satisfactoriness to our mental pleasure (enabling us to sleep within these walls, and enjoy such a view) is supreme. One feels, there, like another in the unending succession of necessary nuisances — tolerated for revenue only — and the 'revenue' extracted is considerable, I assure you. But if M. Michel-Jordy and his staff made us feel truly welcome, I dare say no one would ever wish to leave — and that might make it inconvenient both for them and for us.

Get 'Peggy' stabled and your duds bestowed — and start out. Don't be tempted by the church now — the early morning is the time to see it — nor by the antique theatre, which you'll see better from the walls; nor by the alluring shops, which will still be selling things when you have 'seen Carcassonne.' But make your way back, up rue Garibaldi, to rue Porte de l'Aude, and turn (left) toward the west gate of the city, which is a footpath gate only. Beside it is the Tour de la Justice where the circuit of the walls begins.

You will, I think, find the guide who conducts you a real enthusiast for his job, speaking slowly and so distinctly that if you know any French at all you can easily understand him, and very ready to 'spark' with special information if he sees that you are intelligently impressed. The last time I was at Carcassonne, the guide we had waxed beautifully eloquent about the performances which are given each summer (in July) in the antique theatre, by the company of the Comédie Française, Paris.

'Imagine, Mademoiselle,' he said, as we stood above the theatre, near the Tour du Moulin du Midi, '"Hamlet," played here, on a summer night; and the ghost of his father walking on the battlements, there where you stand! Imagine "Macbeth" played against the background of these crenellated towers!'

And as he went on, I *could* imagine it! His ardor was beautiful and unforgettable. He was a one-armed man, with that look in his eyes, on his face, which one often sees in France since the War: the look of one who has so greatly suffered, it is as if he had died — died to the world he used to know — and come back, like one from the dead, with a vision we have not seen and a revaluation of life in the light of Eternity.

In case you have not enough French to understand him, perhaps I had better say a few words about the towers he shows. (He, or another, of course. I dare say there are several guides.) And perhaps you would like something a little more, and more explicit. For guides have a way of seeming to think that Goths and Visigoths are much more familiar to us than they really are.

All we need, for our enjoyment of Carcassonne, is a very few facts and a great deal of fancy. Students, who wish to comprehend it archæologically, have a well-nigh perfect aid at hand in the monograph of Viollet-le-Duc, the great architect who restored Carcassonne and so many others of France's crumbling monuments, and who wrote on architecture as fascinatingly as he practised it. His monograph, in excellent English, is available in the shops of the Cité. To it I am chiefly indebted for the 'few facts' I give those who may not care for more. Viollet-le-Duc was born in Paris in 1814. He was a deep student of Gothic art, and restored a great number of the most important Gothic and earlier mediæval buildings of France. Napoleon III was his warm friend and admirer, and generously encouraged his labors to preserve to posterity the crumbling glories of France's Middle Ages. As a writer on architecture he was not only authoritative, but fascinating and interpretative.

It is said to have been the lamentations of Prosper Mérimée, author of 'Carmen,' which stopped the spoliation of Carcassonne's fortifications by the local builders in search of cheap materials.

Carcassonne, being on the one grand highway between the Mediterranean and the Ocean, in control of the road to Spain, was an important outpost of Rome; and before the conquests of Cæsar was classed among the privileged cities of Southern Gaul; so happy that it had no history.

Then came the barbarians — first the Goths, who laid waste, and passed on into Spain; then the Visigoths, who stayed, and built — built their fortifications on the foundations of the Roman walls which the Goths had destroyed. The Visigoths were apt pupils of Rome, built a strong fortress here, and remained in possession until the Moors drove them out, in 713. When the Moors were driven out, or who drove them, we don't know. Carcassonne has no more history until 1096, the year of the First Crusade, when Pope Urban II came to bless the cathedral.

Soon after that the castle was built and the Visigoth walls were repaired. None too soon! For in 1209 came Simon de Montfort and the Albigensian Crusade; in five days' siege, Carcassonne was taken.

A few years later it passed to the French Crown, and Louis IX greatly strengthened it — so greatly that it was never again taken.

This Tour de Justice, in which you start your rounds, was built either under Louis IX or his son, Philippe-le-Hardi — probably replacing a Roman tower. The next tower, the Tour Visigoth, on Roman foundations, was rebuilt by Viollet-le-Duc in the Visigothic style. Then comes the Tour de l'Inquisition, built by Philippe-le-Hardi; and when the

bishops had done what seemed to them a day's work of
'Inquisiting,' they could step out into their garden (where
your hotel now stands) and enjoy their flowers — which
must have been quite a relief, after the poor, broken, bleeding, tortured creatures, reeking of fetid dungeons, whom
they had been 'questioning' and condemning to dreadful
death.

The Bishop's Square Tower, which comes next, straddles
both the inner and outer walls, and is one of the finest examples of the military engineering of 'the greatest century.'
Nothing is left of the Bishop's Palace; but his tower is
doubtless much as it was when the Black Prince must have
inspected it.

The antique theatre is where the cloisters of Saint-
Nazaire used to be. From the walls above it, the view toward the Pyrénées is superb.

If you can bear to go within doors, this may be your time
to 'shop.' Otherwise, I'd go back along the walls to the
starting-point, and out through the Porte de l'Aude, by the
footpath, and down that path far enough to get a good view
of the western battlements with the sunset on them. The
best time to see the eastern side of the fortifications is as
you leave Carcassonne, in the morning — and in the evening, especially by moonlight!

I like the château in the evening, too. I find it easier,
then, to feel myself attending a Court of Love there in the
thirteenth century; or in the castle when the hosts of
Simon de Montfort are swarming toward Carcassonne.

The Queen of the Court of Love (some accounts call her
Agnès, some call her Adelaide) was wife of the defender of
Carcassonne against the exterminating Crusaders; and she
was the niece of the King of France.

Perhaps one could not have a better place than here, on
the bridge over the moat of this old castle — this fortress

within a fortress — to muse on those times when a Court
of Love and sweet minstrelsy might be rudely dispersed by the arrival of a bloodthirsty army which had just
slaughtered forty thousand persons at Béziers.

Montfort sent an embassy to Count Roger to offer him
and twelve of his men safe-conduct if they would deliver up
the city.

'You may tell these priests,' Roger shouted, 'that I will
let them tear the hair from my chin and head, the nails from
my feet and hands, the teeth from my mouth, my eyes from
my sockets, that I will be skinned alive or burned at the
stake, before I will deliver up to these butchers one of my
people, be he serf, heretic, or felon, whom God confided to
my charge when he made me suzerain of these countries.
At Béziers, our city of Béziers, the rich and noble sister of
Carcassonne, not a foot is left above the soil to come and
bear us news, not a hand remains to sound the alarm.
Dead! Dead! To the very last!'

When he saw he could no longer hold Carcassonne, he
went out, under a safe-conduct whose honor he knew better
than to trust, to discuss terms with his conquerors. They
put him in chains, threw him into one of his own dungeons,
and when they had attended to more pressing matters, they
sent him some poisoned food.

The ghosts of later poets than the troubadours of Count
Roger's lady also brush past one who stands musing on that
castle bridge of Carcassonne in the quickening dusk of a
mellow night.

One of them is a native of Carcassonne who left home to
be an actor, wrote some pretty poor plays, became a
Revolutionary, voted for the King's death, and himself was
brought before the Revolutionary Tribunal. During his
trial he sang his own deathless song of the southern hills and
the simple life, 'Il pleut, il pleut, bergère, rentre tes

moutons blancs'; and on his way to the guillotine he dis-
tributed his manuscript poems to the people. It was he —
Philippe François Nazaire Fabre d'Églantine — who re-
named the new divisions of time, 'Prairial,' 'Floréal,'
'Thermidor,' 'Brumaire,' etc., when the First Republic in
its fever of abolishing also abolished the Gregorian calendar.

Another who knew Carcassonne in his youth was André
Chénier — also dead by the guillotine in 1794.

And of a later day (dead only in 1893) is Gustave
Nadaud, whose lyric, impassioned lines of the old peasant
dwelling only 'five great leagues away' and crying, 'I never
have seen Carcassonne,' have done more to carry the name
of Carcassonne far and wide than all its history.

I hope that your night at Carcassonne may be one favorable to reverie at the castle, and then to ecstasy outside the
Porte Narbonnaise. Scramble down into the outer moat,
with the battlements towering above you on one side, and
the cypresses of the Cimitière Saint-Michel pointing heavenward above the white crosses of those whose victory's won.
It may be that you will hear a nightingale singing of Love
above the hearts that now are dust.

By light o' day one may be conscious of restorations at
Carcassonne. By night, there's only poetry.

In the early morning, see the exquisite glass in Saint-
Nazaire. And I think you will be reasonably content to
leave Carcassonne, a little fearful to prolong your stay lest
there be an anticlimax.

V

But if you have an extra day to spend hereabouts before
starting on your way, let me urge you to go south along the
Aude to Quillan and Axat and — if you will make a good
long day of it — to Usson and Font-Romeu.

One of the most beautiful days you could possibly spend

would be to take Route 118, through the superb gorges
known as the Défilé de Pierre-Lys and the Défilé de Saint-
Georges; down to Font-Romeu and Bourg-Madame; thence
up to Ax-les-Thermes and on to Foix, and Pamiers, on
Route 20, and in to Carcassonne on Route 119 through
Mirepoix — the most enchanting of bastides with a central
square worth travelling many miles to see.

This would be a lusty day — two hundred miles. For a
shorter loop, go to Axat, then back to Quillan and over to
Foix (for luncheon at the Hôtel de la Barbacane), and then
to Pamiers and Mirepoix, and Carcassonne — cutting some
fifty-five miles off the day's run.

Two days for the longer run, with a night at Font-Romeu,
would be ideal. But the Grand Hôtel there and the Ermit-
age are open only between June 15th and September 30th,
and in winter (for winter sports) from December 15th to
March 1st.

Now, when you leave Carcassonne, you may be en route
to Spain, via Perpignan to Barcelona, or via the Pyrénées
to Biarritz and San Sebastian. The Pyrénées are dealt with
in our sixth chapter.

Or you may be en route to Provence and the Riviera, by
way of Narbonne, Béziers, Montpellier. Avignon (which is
undoubtedly a most comfortable place to stop while visiting Provence) is a hundred and fifty miles from Carcassonne. But if you wish to see Aigues-Mortes and Saintes-
Maries, I would stop for the night at Arles, and go thence
down to Aigues-Mortes and Saintes-Maries, up to Nîmes,
and on to Avignon. In the case of Marseilles being your
objective, take the route from Montpellier through Lunel
and Saint-Gilles to Arles; thence to Salon and Saint-
Cannat and down to Marseilles. This would be a pretty
'stiff' day, but it can be done.

But if you are returning toward Paris, and have not

many more days, my suggestion for you, en route to the north, is that, if the season be at all propitious for it, you go by way of the Gorges of the Tarn. I have entered and left Carcassonne by all possible routes except the one from Toulouse; but I know none so exhilaratingly fine as this one to Saint-Pons, Saint-Affrique, and Millau. It is a day of isolation from the world — of meeting few vehicles, seeing few people; scarcely any 'sights,' yet one continuous grandeur; good roads, superb scenery, delicious quiet; a sense of being out of the haunts of men. Should you do it in July or August, you would find the section from Millau on too *much* 'haunted,' I fear. But even at *that*, I'd see the Gorges of the Tarn.

Leave the Lower Town as you entered it, and follow the Canal du Midi for five kilometres (about three miles) to Bezons crossroads. From here, your most direct road is to turn, right, toward Caunes and Saint-Pons. But there is a most notable sight I would not have you miss if you care for castles. It is the Four Castles of Lastours which are believed to date back to the sixth century, and not one of which has ever been taken by storm. They stand atop a conical hill, each castle on its separate peak or 'needle,' in a district of savage grandeur; and are, to my mind, richly worth a détour. If you think you will be of the same mind, do not turn off at the Bezons crossroads, but keep straight on to Conques (a fine old walled town with mediæval gateways, a church with a noted apse and tympanum) and cross the Orbiel which flows through a countryside celebrated for its tiny wild strawberries (*fraises du bois*) which are shipped all over France and even to England. Presently you'll come to La Caunette, a mining town; this district being rich in iron, copper, lead, gold, and silver; and a half-mile beyond La Caunette you have your Four Castles of Lastours — ten miles from Carcassonne. Then, return to La Caunette and take the road leading east toward Caunes, with its marble quarries and its old Benedictine Abbey, and its twelfth-century church containing some very fine marbles, and its old thirteenth and fourteenth-century houses. (Caunes is a bastide.)

From Caunes, climb on, up toward Route 112, which runs toward Béziers, and follow it as far as Saint-Pons — a matter of ten miles or so. At Saint-Pons take the route for Olargues, a picturesque hill-town, and Lamalou-les-Bains (twenty miles from Saint-Pons), where you may stop for an early luncheon at the Grand Hôtel Mas in the Lower Town or the Hôtel des Thermes in the Upper Town. This is a watering-place especially frequented by persons with nervous complaints, and the season is from April to November. Seven miles before you come to it is the usual starting-point for visiting the Gorges of Héric, a frightful place which might interest a movie-director who was about to film Dante's 'Hell' and wanted 'backgrounds.'

From Lamalou-les-Bains you may go on through Bédarieux (three and a half miles) and up through le Bousquet to Lodève where you get Route 9, the highway from Béziers to Clermont-Ferrand, and thirty-five miles from Millau; or you may go up through Saint-Gervais and Camarès and thence to Saint-Affrique. I should ask advice in Lamalou-les-Bains. *Always* ask local advice! The hotel head porters (concierges) invariably speak English, and it is their business to be posted about roads. They may not have your point of view as to what is interesting and worth while, but they are bound to be better informed than almost anybody else you can ask about conditions en route. If you speak French, there is always (in nearly every town of every district that travellers frequent) the local Syndicat d'Initiative which exists to promote and serve travel thereabouts. These are all under Government direction and, collectedly, make up the system of the national department of Tourisme. It is a great system; but not yet so helpful as it should be to the traveller who speaks no French. Its representative in the United States, for some years past, M. Perret, with offices in New York, has magnificently exemplified what can be done to make the resources of this system of great value to the American traveller to France. I hope you know *well* his monthly publication, 'Le Voyageur in France,' not only printed in English, but written with the clearest understanding of what the English-speaking traveller in France wishes to know. When there are disciples of M. Perret in many Syndicat offices in frequented parts of France, the last thing (except English-speaking guides in places of great tourist interest) will have been done to make France ideal for her wayfaring guests.

When you reach Saint-Affrique you are seventeen and a half miles from Millau; and about a third of that distance you come to Saint-Rome-de-Cernon where, if you are a *dévoté* of Roquefort cheese (and who is not?), you may like to make a short détour to the village of Roquefort-sur-Soulzon and see innumerable cheeses, made of the milk of ewe lambs, ripening in caverns of the limestone rock. Something like twenty million pounds a year are made in this district and brought to Roquefort to be 'cured' in the chalky caves of this picturesque village where practically everybody is concerned in some phase of the cheese business.

Sheep are the salvation of the dwellers on these great Causses, or chalky downs, of South-Central France, where little grows except such pasturage as only sheep can live on.

Millau is a rival of Grenoble in the industry of glove-making. And I suppose it is no secret that 'kid' gloves are very often 'lamb'; though that is not to say that any one suffers thereby — except the lamb, who would probably have died for 'cutlets' and 'gigots,' anyway.

At Millau you meet again the Tarn, which you left reflecting the lovely arches of the Old Bridge at Albi. And your road (107b) takes you up along the left bank of the Tarn to La Malène (twenty-two and a half miles), at the western edge of the Causse Méjean, three to four thousand feet above sea-level.

At Malène you should take a boat and descend the Tarn as far as Pas-de-Souci; then, drive back to Malène, and on to Château de la Caze. The man from whom you engage your boat at La Malène will either drive your car back to Pas-de-Souci to meet you; or, if you are unwilling to trust him to do that, and have no chauffeur, will have a car meet you there, and take you back to La Malène to resume your journey in your own car.

This means traversing the same five miles three times. But I think you won't regret it. Downstream is the only agreeable way to go in a boat. And magnificent as you may find the Gorge from the fine road, you will miss a great thrill if you don't see it from the river level. This stretch of the Tarn is the most superb of all its scenic length. And if you can find yourself afloat on it, in a little flat-bottomed boat, 'poled' or punted by two boatmen of impressive skill, and pretty much in sole possession of those picturesque solitudes, I am sure you will look back upon that hour as one you would not have missed. Especially delightful is it when a boatman blows his horn (no metal, 'made' thing, but one that Nature 'grew' for him to make echoes with) to tell your charioteer at Les Vignes to come to Pas-de-Souci and get you. Not for a great deal would I have lost the opportunity to add that river journey, late on a glorious afternoon of May, to my mind's picture-book.

If you are a student of geology, you will undoubtedly

promise yourself a return to this district, some day, and a leisurely acquaintance with its many marvels. It might even be that on a motor tour through it, you would feel that you ought to take time to see the Grotte de Dargilan, one of the finest of stalactite caverns. To reach it, you turn east from Millau, instead of north, and follow the Jonte instead of the Tarn, for twenty-four miles. The Grotte is open from June 1st to October 1st, and the visit takes two and a half hours.

This, however, is for the exceptional 'voyageur' in France; whereas the Gorges of the Tarn may well be for many.

When you have regained La Malène, you have a mere three miles to go before reaching your Castle for the night — Château de la Caze, now serving as a hotel.

The castle was built in 1489, by a young heiress of an old family hereabouts. That was the year of her marriage; and so much more distinguished was her family than her husband's that he took her name — Alamand — instead of her taking his. The couple had eight beautiful daughters who were called 'The Nymphs of the Tarn'; their portraits are painted on the ceiling of one of the castle chambers.

The food at Château de la Caze was not good when I was there. But in every other wise our stop there was an idyllic experience.

You halt your chariot at the approach to a drawbridge beneath which flows a moat, not stagnant, like many, but fed by a magnificent spring. On the other side the castle is protected by the Tarn.

Round towers with 'fighting tops' flank the four angles of the castle, and in the centre, facing the drawbridge, is a square donjon beneath whose portcullis you pass unchallenged. Within, the hall is cobble-paved as when the seigneurs may have ridden in and reined their panting steeds as the drawbridge raised defensively on their very flanks. (I don't know, of course, that they ever did; but that is the suggestion.)

Everything has been kept as 'fifteenth-century' as possible — and feudal fifteenth, not dawning Renaissance, if we except the delightful terrace above the Tarn, on which you will probably sit to take your coffee and liqueur. A night's rest in this romantic solitude is something never-to-be-forgotten. And perhaps by the time you get there, they will have found a better cook.

Be sure to wander around, beneath the giant cedar (or perhaps it is some other sort of evergreen) which towers far above the castle, to get the view from that angle. Good photographing here in the morning.

VI

And when you must leave your 'stronghold' to sally forth on the day's adventurings, go on (five miles) to Sainte-Enimie, named for a daughter of Clotaire II who was cured of her leprosy here in a fountain.

From Sainte-Enimie to Mende is sixteen miles. And here you have a choice of routes to Clermont-Ferrand. Route 88 will take you to Le Puy — sixty-five miles. Route 107 will take you to Saint-Flour — fifty-two miles. The distance to Clermont-Ferrand is thirty miles shorter by Saint-Flour; and Saint-Flour is a delightfully picturesque old town, reached by a road with many interests — including the wonderful Garabit Viaduct which Eiffel built; it is a third of a mile long, crosses the river gorge at a height of four hundred feet, and is the first of his great feats in steel.

But I am sure that most travellers will not wish to consider any other route than that which leads through Le Puy. (*Puy* means volcanic cone.)

At Châteauneuf-de-Randon, you have the last town that

Du Guesclin captured from the English; and the monument to him, on the site of his last camp, where he died.

You should reach Le Puy, easily, in time to see a good bit of it before luncheon. And unless the cooking has changed since I sampled it, it is nothing for which to sacrifice any 'sight.' If there is any better place than the Grand-Hôtel, I don't know it — nor, it would seem, does the author of 'Le Tour de France Gastronomique,' who does not wax very enthusiastic over the gustatory prospects. I believe I'd approach the hotel management as soon as I arrived, and negotiate for some trout *meunière* and *pommes frites* (French-fried potatoes) and perhaps an omelette, which almost any cook in France can make more or less acceptably. This, for fear that the table d'hôte might be very uninteresting. The mushrooms of this vicinity are said to be excellent. And the *thrush* is an esteemed delicacy, as larks are in England; but something in me balks at eating songbirds. 'Nightingales' tongues' would never tempt me to dine with Lucullus.

However, there is one local delicacy that almost everybody will wish to patronize — and that is *lace*, which is said to employ seventy thousand women of this district. Lovers of lace should see the exhibit of it in the Musée Crozatier.

If George Sand could say 'Nothing can give an idea of the beauty of the basin of Le Puy and I know no site whose character is more difficult to describe,' what can I hope to write of it that may help you to visualize it?

Except in spots, I do not find its beauty so appealing as that of scores of other places in France; but Le Puy is undeniably *astounding*. Every traveller, no matter what he has seen, must needs class it among his most extraordinary sights.

But what will you remember longest and most pleasurably about Le Puy, along with its volcanic needles of rock topped by mediæval places of worship? I wonder! Students of the life of other days may realize here, perhaps more vividly than anywhere else, what were the surroundings of a prelate-militant when men's concepts of the way to God were matters for much blood-letting. Lovers of the miraculous will be deeply impressed by Le Puy as a place of pilgrimage. Geologists cannot fail to find the erosions of this valley profoundly interesting.

But I am sure there must be many others besides myself for whom this section of the Cévennes is chiefly haunted by one of the most enchanting ghosts in all the multitude of those who have passed but not gone. Nay — *two* ghosts! For I know he would not wish Modestine omitted from the immortals. Modestine, 'not much bigger than a dog, the colour of a mouse, with a kindly eye and a determined under-jaw'; withal, 'something neat and high-bred, a quakerish elegance, about the rogue.' Modestine, who 'had a faint resemblance to a lady of my acquaintance who formerly loaded me with kindness,' and thus increased Stevenson's horror of having to belabor her.

If you haven't his 'Travels with a Donkey' in your pack on this journey, I hope you have it in your mental pack from which you are inseparable and on which you need never pay excess carriage charges. A better travelling companion for these parts there could not be.

Le Monastier, from which R. L. S. and Modestine set forth on the morning of September 23, 1878, is about fifteen miles southeast of Le Puy. Saint-Jean-du-Gard, where these travellers parted company on the morning of October 4th, is east of Millau, on Route 107, connecting Nîmes with Saint-Flour. We who employ 'Peggy' in place of Modestine cover the distance between breakfast and dinner. But if we comprehend the spirit of the people we pass en route, it is largely because of Modestine's companion.

He was just shy of twenty-eight, then. In October of the year before had appeared his first piece of fiction, in 'Temple Bar': 'A Lodging for the Night,' that tale of Villon's Paris, followed (in January, '78) by 'The Sire de Malétroit's Door.' In May, his first book had been published: 'An Inland Voyage.' During that summer, Louis had the only job he ever held, that of private secretary to his friend Professor Jenkin who went to Paris to act as juror at the International Exhibition.

'I had many letters from Jenkin in Paris,' wrote one of Jenkin's friends, 'but none were written by the Secretary.'

The Secretary was a much preoccupied young man. He had some writing to do, and some thinking to do. He came to Monastier at the beginning of September, and did the writing. But the thinking was not yet done when he and Modestine started on their travels.

Was it finished when he and Modestine parted company? Who knows? In September, 1876, at Grez, on the outskirts of the Forest of Fontainebleau, Louis had met Mrs. Fanny Osbourne, of Indianapolis, and Austin, Nevada, and latterly of the Latin Quarter. Ten years his senior she was, and the mother of three children (one recently dead, in Paris), and not divorced from her husband; a woman well acquainted with grief. Almost from the moment of their meeting there was no question in his mind but that she was the Perfect Comrade his soul sought. But there were obstacles! Item, one husband, in California; item, two parents in Edinburgh, who could only regard this infatuation as one form of suicidal mania; item, complete lack of resources, or prospects, to encourage matrimony. And so on.

For these reasons, Louis had a great decision to make.

Therefore he and Modestine came travelling over these mountains.

And at the Trappist monastery of Our Lady of the Snows, Louis 'blessed God that I was free to wander, free to hope, and free to love.' When he woke among the pines on the white highroad to Mende, where 'night after night a man's bed, it seemed, was laid and waiting for him in the fields, where God keeps an open house,' he 'became aware of a strange lack. I wished a companion to lie near me in the starlight, silent and not moving, but ever within touch. For there is a fellowship more quiet even than solitude, and which, rightly understood, is solitude made perfect. And to live out of doors with the woman a man loves is of all lives the most complete and free.'

And as he neared his journey's end, and 'the evening began early underneath the trees,' he 'heard the voice of a woman singing some sad, old, endless ballad not far off. It seemed to be about love ... and I wished I could have taken up the strain and answered her, as I went upon my invisible woodland way, weaving, like Pippa in the poem, my own thoughts with hers. What could I have told her? Little enough; and yet all the heart requires. How the world gives and takes away, and brings sweethearts near, only to separate them again into distant and strange lands; but to love is the great amulet which makes the world a garden; and "hope, which comes to all," outwears the accidents of life, and reaches with tremulous hand beyond the grave and death.'

As you leave Le Puy and look back at it from Espaly, you get the most impressive view of it. And if you take Route 106, at Borne (instead of 102), you will come, in twenty-seven miles, to La Chaise-Dieu, where, on a bleak plateau more than thirty-five hundred feet above sea-level, stands all that is left of a Benedictine monastery of which

Richelieu, Mazarin, and Cardinal de Rohan were all titular abbots, and to which Rohan was banished after the affair of the Queen's diamond necklace.

Pope Clement VI was once abbot here, and here he lies buried — or did until the Calvinists dislodged his dust when he had been dead more than two centuries. He it was who excommunicated Cola di Rienzi; who tried Queen Joanna of Naples for the murder of her husband, and acquitted her — then bought Avignon from her.

His nephew, who became Pope Gregory XI, was a benefactor of this Abbey. (He it was whom Saint-Catherine of Siena stimulated to restore the Papal See to Rome.)

The wife of Edward the Confessor spent her last days here, and is buried in the church — far from her husband's gilded shrine in Westminster Abbey.

If you find yourself growing a little too full-fed with things ecclesiastical and architectural, you may not care to stop at La Chaise-Dieu. But should this not be your case, I am sure you will feel rewarded by the visit. The decayed, dejected little town is the very essence of desolation. And to make the contrasts sharper still, on the afternoon when I stopped there, a number of years ago, there was scarcely any one in evidence except a few half-wild village children teasing an idiot boy. To step in, out of this squalor, and find one's self in that regal choir, with those handsome stalls and the magnificent Flemish tapestries above them; and in the centre, that impressive tomb with its mitred figure whose majesty is undisturbed by changes in the world without, was to etch deep the light and shade of those contrasts.

The organist was practising, too; so the massive organ case was not voiceless. I like the cloisters. But I usually like cloisters — as you know.

The next time I am in that vicinity I shall take Route

102, and when I get to Saint-Georges-d'Aurac, some twenty-five miles from Le Puy, I shall look for the Château de Chavaniac thereabouts, where Lafayette was born. The château is now the property of an American society which cherishes the memory of our gallant young French friend and offers hospitality to those who desire it. I have just had a letter from the hostess, telling me that the rooms of the château, while furnished in the period of Lafayette's youth, have been supplied with up-to-date plumbing comforts. There is accommodation for about 18 people; and instead of fixed charges, the guests are asked to contribute as they can to the Fund which is now maintaining on the estate 350 children to whom it is giving health and education. There is also a plan, well under way, to make this beautiful place a summer camp for American boys.

Whether you went to La Chaise-Dieu or by the other route, your way to Clermont-Ferrand lies through Issoire which was a refuge of Huguenots, back in the times following the Massacre of Saint Bartholomew's Eve, and as such was destroyed, root and branch (all but the abbey church), by Catherine de Médici's youngest son, the Duc d'Alençon; and on its site a lone pillar bore the inscription, 'Here was Issoire.'

And on your left, as you reach Issoire, is a region of delightful health resorts known, collectively, as the Mont Dore, in the upper Valley of the Dordogne. The Dordogne rises on the Puy de Sancy, the highest peak of Central France (6188 feet), where two small streams, the Dore and the Dogne, unite to form the lovely stream which flows across western France to join the Gironde just below Bordeaux.

This region of volcanoes which probably became extinct in late prehistoric time is still rich in hot springs of healing

waters; in limpid lakes lying in deep old craters; in picturesque rock formations and beautiful fertile valleys. The high
mountains with their browsing herds make one murmur
'the cattle on a thousand hills are mine.' The sloping
fields make a neat patchwork of green tints — the greens
of growing grains — and the fruit trees may be (according to the season in which you come) an ecstasy of bloom
or a glory of ripening apricots, cherries, pears. (Be sure to
make acquaintance with the delicious confections of fruit
jelly known as Pâtés d'Auvergne.)

The nearest of the famous resorts to your north-and-
south highway (Route 9) is Saint-Nectaire, which is about
equally known for its fine old church and for its fine old hot
springs containing bicarbonates, iron chlorides, and other
properties curative of liver complaints and rheumatism.
The Romans resorted to them, and their baths are still
there.

About four miles beyond Saint-Nectaire is Murols,
with a grand old feudal castle crowning a commanding
height; and just beyond Murols is charming Lake Cham-
bon. (A little east of Mont Dore is the Grande Cascade, a
waterfall one hundred feet high.)

The road goes on to Mont-Dore-les-Bains, with its
waters sought by sufferers from rheumatism, and its many
hotels ranging from simple to *de luxe;* and thence to La
Bourboule (three miles) whose waters, strong with arsenic
and therefore very stimulating, attract many thousands
of persons annually. Here there are not only hotels of
every class, but three classes of bathing establishment —
sumptuous, moderate, and cheap. (Seven miles southwest
of La Bourboule is La Tour d'Auvergne, the seat of that
famous family one of whose daughters became the mother
of Catherine de Médicis.)

The season for these resorts is May 15th to October 1st.

It may be that you would rather stop for the night at Saint-Nectaire (Hôtel des Bains-Romains) or Le Mont-Dore (Mont-Dore Palace, International Palace) or La Bourboule (Métropole, Médicis Palace), instead of going on to Clermont. If your quest is architecture and historic interest, I believe you will be better satisfied to spend the night at Clermont; if it is for natural delights, you will prefer the Mont-Dore, or Royat, on the lower slopes above Clermont.

As you approach Clermont, you have, off to your left, some eight miles before you reach the city, the plateau of Gergovie, a wonderful natural defence position whereon the Gauls had a stronghold which Cæsar tried in vain to take — and was nearly captured in the attempt.

Having suffered a thousand deaths (or thereabouts) in Cæsar's 'Commentaries' because no one ever felt called upon to make me feel their interest, I have a very strong feeling about making Cæsar and the conquest of 'all Gaul' a vividly realizable story for youngsters with second-year Latin staring them in the face. And I think Clermont, with its spirited equestrian statue of Vercingetorix and its vicinity to this plateau, helps. I would that the young folks might see it, and Alésia, before they see the Mamertine Prison at Rome where brave Vercingetorix perished, after six years' imprisonment.

Is there, in English, any book which gives young readers an adequate and interesting picture of what Gaul was like when Cæsar came? The nearest to it that I know is in 'The Story of France Told to Boys and Girls,' by Mary Macgregor. But like most books on France it draws (I think) too little distinction between the Gauls and those barbarians against whom Gaul besought Rome's aid. However —— !

Here you are, entering Clermont (probably by the

avenue Vercingetorix, with the Botanical Gardens and the
University at your right), and perhaps you are thinking of
a hotel. The Grand-Hôtel on the Place de Jaude is the
largest at Clermont. The Café de Paris, on the same
square, is well spoken-of; and in the Place Royale, near the
Monument to the First Crusade, is Au Gastronome, which
Monmarché (Blue Guide) stars, and Dulac ('Tour de
France Gastronomique') ignores, and I can't tell you about
because I haven't tried it. Fruits and cheeses are famous
in these parts. Tarts are delicious. Trout likewise. They
cook chicken in red wine, to the great delight of many
gastronomes. The wines of the district are good — Chan-
turge for red, and a Château-Grillet for white, may give
you some new favorites.

What you will probably wish to see at Clermont (now a
thriving industrial city, where many automobile tires are
made — Michelin, among the rest) is Bartholdi's statue
of Vercingetorix, in the square by your hotel; the lovely
Fontaine d'Amboise (which you may see on entering, by
turning from avenue Vercingetorix, right, into boulevard
Lafayette, then up Cours Sablon, past the fountain, to rue
Grégoire de Tours; then, left in that, to Place Royale and
the Crusade Monument, and the south side of the cathedral); the fine old Church of Notre-Dame-du-Port; perhaps the glass in the cathedral; AND, Montferrand, about
a mile northeast of Clermont.

I should say that if you stay in town to-night you will
probably be more in the mood for a café and a cinema,
than for any other kind of sight-seeing.

VII

In the morning, have a look at Notre-Dame-du-Port, en
route (by the avenue de la République) to Montferrand,
which comes as near as any city in France to giving us an

CLERMONT AND THE PUY-DE-DÔME
From an engraving after a drawing by T. Allom

embalmed provincial town of the seventeenth century.
There wealth and taste created fine mansions and embellished them exquisitely and dwelt in them with the dignity
of that century when the salons were born, and the French
Academy, and the modern French theatre, and French
painting, and those French 'manners,' as we ineptly call
them, which all the world essayed to imitate.

I suppose Montferrand must have been a shade (or
several shades) too elegant and reposeful to be vital. The
aggressive always swallows the reflective. Clermont, a mile
away, seems to have been energetic, resourceful, enterpris-
ing. It was venerable, but not living on its past. So, when
Louis XV was young and Well-Beloved and had not yet
begun to think of 'After us, the deluge,' for some ex-
pediency or another Montferrand was administratively
absorbed by Clermont, and 'retired' from municipal
affairs, so to speak. I dare say her nobles were all at Versailles and thereabouts, and the burghers were not assertive
enough to maintain independence.

At any rate, there is Montferrand, like the old lady that
Victor Hugo praised when writing of Blois. And if you go
there in the right mood, I'm sure you'll hear the *frou-frou*
of rich rustling silks and the jingling of elegant swords, and
many a bit of fresh gossip about Montespan's dismissal
and what the King knew about her attempts to poison
him.

Ask, at the Syndicat des Propriétaires, opposite the
Church of Notre-Dame, for a ticket to see the old mansions.
And mind you don't miss the courtyard of the one called
La Maison de Lucrèce, or that of La Maison de l'Annon-
ciation.

One of the glories of Clermont is that it gave Pascal to
the world. The site of his birthplace is marked, opposite
the cathedral; but as he left here at seven, to live in Paris,

I think you will find him haunting other places much more satisfyingly.

If you are to lunch at Vichy, as I think you'd like to do, you have only thirty-five miles to travel before one o'clock. So you may very well consider climbing the Puy de Dôme, which I would do by way of Royat, the famous spa for arterial troubles. Follow the tramway from the Place de Jaude (where your hotel is) and at the terminus of the line I think you will find indications for your further way. The view from the summit is extensive and wonderfully fine. Up there, in 1648, Pascal made his celebrated experiments in atmospheric pressure. And when, in 1876, a meteorological observatory was erected there, a vast extent of Gallo-Roman remains were uncovered, including a great Temple of Mercury which seems to have been destroyed by the barbarians about the middle of the third century. Most of the sculptures and precious objects found have been taken to the Musée of art and archæology at Clermont; but the constructions which remain in place at the top of this mountain, over 4800 feet above sea-level, are an imposing evidence of Rome's disdain of difficulties. They had fine baths at Royat, too.

On your way north you will probably use Route 9; and in a little less than ten miles from Clermont you will come to Riom, the capital of the old Duchy of Auvergne, and much like Montferrand, in its Sleeping Beauty charm. However little time you have, I'm sure you would be sorry to miss seeing the very curious clock-tower; the beautiful inner court of the Hôtel Guimonneau, with the exquisite Annunciation sculptured on the curve of its most unusual stairway; the House of the Consuls, built in 1527; and the Sainte-Chapelle of the Palais de Justice, with its splendid stained glass and tapestries. For an architect, this is a town to linger in.

(Five miles northwest is Châtel-Guyon, another popular spa.)

Ten miles north of Riom is Aigueperse, capital of the old Duchy of Montpensier. Louis VIII, father of Saint Louis, died in the castle near here, now destroyed, in 1226, after a reign of only three years.

At Gannat, less than four miles north, you turn off to your right for Vichy, your road passing quite close to the Château d'Effiat, which was the boyhood home of the unfortunate young Marquis de Cinq-Mars whose romantic figure casts its spell over so many enchanting pages.

If you lunch at Hôtel du Parc et Majestic, Vichy, you will lunch memorably, and will probably promise yourself a return, to stay for some time, when you can 'manage' it.

Moulins, thirty-three miles north of Vichy, was the capital of the Duchy of Bourbon. The parents of Henry IV were married here. I'd see the famous triptych in the cathedral, if I were you. It was painted by a fifteenth-century artist whom we know only as 'The Master of Moulins,' and is very like the Flemish triptychs of that period — the Memlings and Van Eycks and their followers. And the side panels contain portraits of Pierre II, Duke of Bourbon, and his wife Anne de Beaujeu, daughter of Louis XI and Regent of France during the minority of her brother, Charles VIII.

(At Souvigny, nine miles southwest of Moulins, are the magnificent mediæval tombs of earlier Dukes of Bourbon, back to the thirteenth century. Ten miles beyond Souvigny, on the route to Bourges, is Bourbon-l'Archambault, famous as a watering-place since Roman times, and the capital of the Bourbonnais before Moulins. Here Madame de Montespan spent her last years in disgrace, and here she died in 1707.)

Beyond Moulins, follow Route 7 to Nevers — thirty-three miles — passing through Saint-Pierre-le-Moutier which Jeanne d'Arc took from the English in 1429.

At Nevers you are back on the Loire, which you will cross, entering the city, by the handsome bridge of many arches — fifteen, I think.

The hotel of your choice may be Hôtel de la Paix, across from the railway station, or Hôtel de France on Place Jean-Desveaux, near the Préfecture and its gardens.

If I had only a little time for Nevers, I would have an evening stroll on the quais, and a glimpse of the lovely old Porte du Croux of the late fourteenth century, not far from the west front of the cathedral. And in the morning, I'd see the cathedral — notably the apse, inside and out; glimpse the old ducal palace, now the Palais de Justice; and spend as much time as I could in the Musée, southwest of the cathedral, looking at the notable collection of faïence for which Nevers is famous.

VIII

Route 7 will take you from Nevers direct to Paris (148½ miles) in a very comfortable day's run. But if you can spend a ninth day on this tour (supposing you have not *already* spent it, somewhere en route!), I'd most certainly do it.

I'd take Route 77 to Clamecy (thirty-five miles) where I might be tempted to linger, did I not know how much lay beyond. But I'd give a thought to at least one story out of the past of Clamecy. Hither, in those days when Philippe-Auguste and Cœur-de-Lion were being stirred to go on the Third Crusade, came the Bishop of Bethlehem, driven from his see by Saladin. There was a hospital at the gate of Clamecy, which had been founded forty years before, when this vicinity resounded with Saint Bernard's preaching and preparations for the Second Crusade; and to this hospital

came the exiled prelate of Bethlehem, setting up here his
bishopric, the whole extent of which was the hospital. Until
the Revolution swept the ancient world away, there was a
Bishop of Bethlehem here at Clamecy.

Turn east, at Clamecy, on Route 151, to Vézelay —
fourteen miles — and as you approach the little old town
on its hill crest, you must be prepared to see great sights
which your camera will not photograph.

Away back in the ninth century, a lord of the south (of
Roussillon) founded on the banks of the Cure, at the foot of
this hill, a convent which the ravaging Normans soon destroyed. When rebuilding was essayed, it seemed better to
do it on the hilltop, and to replace the nuns with monks.

Then, for a hundred and fifty years or so, life went on in
the monastery without other eventfulness than was inseparable from life anywhere in those unsettled days; until,
in the eleventh century, the story 'got about' (certainly
without any hindrance from the monks) that this obscure
monastery possessed the relics of Mary Magdalen. Then,
as by miracle, Vézelay became a place of pilgrimage almost
the equal of Jerusalem, or Rome, or Saint-James-de-Com-
postella in Spain.

Every road leading hither swarmed with pilgrims; and
around the 22d of July, the day specially sacred to the
Magdalen, the crowds were so great that they had to 'lodge'
not only in the cloisters and the streets, but rented space on
the housetops where they slept on straw pallets.

What the concourse must have been when Saint Bernard
came hither to preach the Second Crusade, I dare say we
can scarcely imagine. Nor can we more than faintly imagine how tongues wagged over the 'goings-on' of that gay
lady, Eleanor of Aquitaine, the Queen of France, who 'took
the cross' here, from Saint Bernard's own hands, and
donned a sort of Amazon attire, and began practising

'daily dozens' and other preparations for a campaign —
all her ladies likewise, to the scandal of the sedate. Further, they tauntingly sent their distaffs to knights who did
not enlist — very much as certain women of 1914 presented white feathers to men in England.

Eleanor was the more fervid, not only because the
Crusade appealed to her as a great lark, a grand adventure,
an escape from the boredom of her husband's dull court,
but because she was under a cloud — so to speak. To
champion the cause of her sister, whose adulterous marriage
the Pope had annulled, Eleanor had persuaded peaceful
Louis to take up arms and wage a devastating war in
Champagne. At Vitry, thirteen hundred persons took refuge in the cathedral, and perished in it when the soldiers of
Louis burned it. Saint Bernard cried aloud what he thought
of such slaughter, nor hesitated to lay the blame for it
where he knew it belonged. So it was, as we say, 'up to'
Eleanor to make a big showing of repentance — which
she did by dolling up in Amazon attire and doing daily
dozens, and then making a sad mess of the Second Crusade
by her loads of luggage, her romantic notions, her escapades
with the enemy, and other evidences of contrition.

I'm sure you are seeing Saint Bernard preaching on the
hill slope to the assembly far too vast for any church to
hold. And Eleanor, the sinner, showing great devoutness at
this shrine of Mary Magdalen.

Now, all that dazzling glint of sun on burnished steel,
that panoply of standards fluttering in the breeze, is not
Eleanor's army, but the Crusaders of her son, Richard,
setting forth with her first husband's son, Philippe-Auguste,
on another ill-starred expedition. But isn't it a gorgeous
sight? And don't you feel as if 'Ivanhoe' and 'The Talisman' had opened up and swept you into their movement,
as they did when you were twelve?

The monks of Vézelay got too rich and too haughty. They declared themselves sovereigns, recognizing no supremacy but that of Rome. Their feudal lords, the Counts of Nevers, their spiritual lords, the Bishops of Autun and the Abbots of Cluny, could all 'go hang.' What were they to the magnates of the Magdalen's abbey at Vézelay.

Now, mark what publicity can do! — even in an age that had not dreamed of print, let alone of newspapers and magazines and all that *we* call advertising. Some one, about 1060 or so, started the story that the relics of the Magdalen were here. From lip to lip the story flew, and by every road the pilgrims came, bringing gifts.

Then, about 1280, some one started the story that those relics weren't here at all! And away went prosperity on the wings of the wind. Before the Middle Ages had passed their zenith, Vézelay had begun to be a shell of vanished greatness and to fall into decay. During the Revolution it was used as a Temple of Reason until Robespierre concluded that Reason alone was a poor control for the populace, and reinstated the Supreme Being. When, in 1840, the Commission on Historic Monuments began to discuss its restoration, the condition of the church and monastic buildings was such that it was believed the least attempt to touch the ruins could result only in their collapse.

However, Viollet-le-Duc undertook it, and in 1856 had completed the work of rebuilding the church as it was when the Third Crusade swept, glittering, away to the East.

If you are likely to find Vézelay a peak among your experiences, I advise your leaving it until late in the day, instead of arriving there in the morning. About 6 P.M. of a good long day (any bright day from mid-May to mid-August) is the ideal time to see the church. In that case, I should go east from Nevers on Route 78, to Autun, which was the Athens of Roman Gaul and now is shrunk to half

the size it then had. Only if I had a first-rate antiquarian
with me should I attempt to make much out of the site
(eleven miles southwest) of Bibracte, where the Phœnicians
taught the ancient Gauls how to build houses, and the ancient Gauls seem to have taught the Phœnicians a good deal
about working iron. But I should love seeing the College
where Napoleon and his brothers went to school, and the
room in Hôtel Saint-Louis where he lodged on his return
from Elba. I should visit the fifteenth-century house of
Chancellor Rolin; I'd see the cathedral of which Talleyrand was the bishop; I'd marvel at the two splendid Roman
gates, pay my respects to the statue of the Druid Diviti-
acus who was Cicero's friend; and take Route 80, north.
If I hadn't lunched at the Hôtel Saint-Louis, for Napoleon's sake and because it's a good hotel, I'd doubtless lunch
at Saulieu, whose Hôtel de la Poste has a reputation —
and, alas! a price. Perhaps the price has diminished. But
this is an epicure's country, and one should try the best.

Then I'd follow the pretty little river Cousin to Avallon,
and reach Vézelay between five and six. Probably I'd stop
to see the very beautiful Church of Saint-Père-sous-Vézelay
before I climbed to the Magdalen's church on the top of the
hill.

If you see Vézelay in the morning (having chosen a
shorter day's run) you should lunch at Avallon, at Hôtel de
la Poste, or Hôtel de Chapeau Rouge. Avallon is a dear little
old sleepy town of many yesterdays, none of which thrust
themselves insistently on our notice, but all of which have
combined to leave an air of decent dignity — no castle
grandeur, but a great deal of substantial consequence, and
as much Roman ancestry as anybody about. Be sure you
see the town from below, looking up at the natural defences, the escarpments of rosy granite rising sheer above
the deep valley of the Cousin. And if you have time (and

inclination) go down, some nine miles, south of Avallon, to Chastelleux where there is a castle, handsomely furnished, which has belonged to one family continuously since the Middle Ages. Near by is Bazoches with a thirteenth-century castle which once belonged to Vauban, the great military engineer of Louis XIV, who is buried in the village church — only his heart having been moved to Les Invalides by Napoleon, in 1809.

Auxerre is thirty-two and a half miles northwest of Avallon. And if you have a fondness for stalactite caverns and prehistoric remains, you may indulge it at Arcy-sur-Cure, something less than halfway to Auxerre.

The Hôtel de l'Épée at Auxerre is excellent. And so, too, is the Touring Hotel. I have done a most extraordinary amount of running around in circles, at Auxerre, looking for places. When you look at a town map, you'll see *why*. No bastide here! but a spider-web effect of little old streets some of which incline to follow the horseshoe curve of the ramparts, and some to run downhill to the river — the delightful Yonne which you have been skirting for some distance, and with which you will keep close and charmed company to-morrow till it unites with the Seine at Montereau.

You will probably cross the Yonne by the Pont Paul Bert, entering Auxerre, and enjoy that view which is an almost-classic photograph: the curving quai thick-lined with trees above whose tops the flying buttresses of Saint-Étienne's apse soar splendidly; further to your right, the majestic remains of the Abbey of Saint-Germain which was a great seat of learning in the ninth century; and in the near foreground at least one canal barge, representing the constant water traffic to and from Paris by way of the Seine, the Yonne, and the great network of French canals; while up the hill above the trees, to other tree-fringes on the old battlements, climb the streets which have seen so much history.

Keep straight on (as 'straight' as the curving streets will let you) till rue du Pont, passing the Church of Saint-Pierre — whose porte is its chief attraction — crosses rue Milliaux and becomes rue Paul Bert. On your left, a little way up this street (Paul Bert) you will find the Touring Hotel; and if you continue to the top of the street and turn, left, to rue du Temple, you will soon come, on your right, to the Hôtel de l'Épée — or Hotel of the Sword.

When I went to Auxerre I had been told how good the Hôtel de l'Épée is; and to reach it I was directed up this rue Paul Bert. Seeing a hotel which looked very inviting, and being a weary pilgrim, I halted; and without asking the name of the hotel, but taking for granted that it was 'the' one, I got a smiling welcome, an extremely comfortable room, an excellent dinner, a particularly nice breakfast in a cheery little coffee-room, and set off to explore the town, delighted with the Hôtel de l'Épée. I twisted and turned in that spider-web of streets. I think I visited Saint-Pierre (unintentionally) at least four times in my search for Saint-Étienne and the Préfecture. And after a lot of wandering and a little discovering, I found myself in front of the Hôtel de l'Épée — looking totally unfamiliar. Suspecting another front, on another street, I went in. Everything was strange — but most inviting. No, I was not stopping there. Then where in the dickens *was* I stopping? Probably at the Touring Hotel, around one or two corners. I was! Now I must go back to Auxerre, for several reasons — one of which is to see if the Hotel of the Sword is really better. But the Touring Hotel is certainly good enough.

There isn't a very great deal to see at Auxerre; but there is a great deal to think about. There is — if you like —

the saintly Bishop Germain who belongs 'way back in the
night of the early fifth century, and who belongs to English
history, too; since 'twas he who led the chorus at the Alleluia Battle on the Welsh border, near Mold, when the invading Picts and Scots were put to flight by the fervent
singing of his men. He made an heroic stand for Christianity in a day when faith could scarce be blamed for
wavering; and his memory is cherished in Auxerre not less
than that of Paul Bert, scientist and statesman, who was
Minister of Education and Worship.in Gambetta's cabinet,
and an ardent advocate of liberating national education
from religious sects, while rendering it accessible to every
citizen. Paul Bert poured ridicule on the fables and follies
of certain religious tracts which seemed to him stultifying
to what nineteenth-century intelligence in a land like
France should be. And Auxerre honors him (he was her
child) for the stand he took in his day, as she honors Germain for the stand he took in his. Among Bert's earliest
works in physiological research were those he made on
the grafting of animal tissues and their vitality. This is
interesting, I think, in view of all we've been hearing about
this, lately.

Saint-Germain was Bishop of Auxerre about 430. His
cathedral stood where the Church of Saint-Étienne stands
now. But this present church was new when there came to
it another Bishop of Auxerre who interests me profoundly
— and you, too, I hope. Jacques Amyot!

As you go through Mélun to-morrow you shall see the
statue wherewith his birthplace honors him.

He was a poor lad, with a thirst for learning which drove
him to the University of Paris. There he worked as a servant for richer students, and earned the wherewithal for his
own studies; so that, at nineteen, he was an M.A. He was a
tutor at Bourges, for a while, and then came to the notice

of Marguerite of Angoulême, who used her influence to get
him made Professor of Greek and Latin at Bourges. There
he began his work on the translation of Plutarch's 'Lives';
and there he published a translation from Heliodorus which
showed such ability, not merely in transferring a text from
one tongue to another, but in making it live again, that
Francis I, in the last year of his life, rewarded Amyot with
an abbey whose revenues enabled him to go to the Vatican
Library to study the text of Plutarch there conserved.

When he returned, Henry II appointed him tutor to the
little boys who were to be Charles IX and Henry III. If
not much can be said for his influence over them, we must
remember against what counter-influence he worked. At
any rate, they were fond of him; and each, when he was
king, showed his old tutor signal honor.

It seems to have been Charles IX who got for Amyot the
bishopric of Auxerre which he held for about thirty years.
His first volume of Plutarch's 'Lives' appeared in 1559,
before he came here; but here he continued, for some time,
his scholarly pursuits among the classics.

It is said that he advised Henry III's chaplain to refuse
absolution to the King after the Guise murders at Blois.
But the Guise partisans at Auxerre believed that he had not
done what he might have done to prevent the murders; so
they incited his people against him, his house was plun-
dered, and the old man (he was seventy-five then) was obliged to flee. When the tumult died down and he could return, his health was broken, and he was an invalid till his
death, here, at the age of eighty.

The effect of his Plutarch was simply stupendous.

'First of all,' as Des Granges reminds us in his 'History
of French Literature,' 'it was a happy idea, at a time when
human energy was displayed in every form, from fanaticism
to martyrdom, from brutality to heroism [the early years

of the Religious Wars] to choose and popularize these bio-
graphies of the greatest men of Greek and Roman antiquity. Never before had such a collection of *examples* been
offered for the admiration and imitation of modern society.
Here were men of all sorts, great captains, statesmen,
legislators, orators. Every reader could profit by the example of his choice. Here were no longer, as in the works
of poets and romancers, fabulous characters, outside the
range of humanity, but men whose faults Plutarch, a truth-
ful and conscientious historian, did not hide, and in whom
could be observed the full-blooded effort of will against
human weakness.'

Amyot not only selected well, but he wrought with great
elegance of taste and a well-nigh perfect understanding of
his time. Montaigne gave him 'the palm over all our French
writers, not only for the simplicity and purity of his language in which he surpasses all others, nor for his profound
learning ... but I am grateful to him especially for his
wisdom in choosing so valuable a work.'

Amyot's 'Plutarch,' translated into English by Sir
Thomas North, supplied Shakespeare with materials for his
Roman plays. North's translation appeared in 1580, and
the first play Shakespeare got out of it was 'Julius Cæsar,'
which was written in 1599. 'Antony and Cleopatra' did not
appear until nine years later. Then followed 'Coriolanus'
and 'Timon of Athens.'

Of the three books which are believed to have belonged
to Shakespeare, one is a copy of North's translation of
Amyot's 'Plutarch,' with a marginal note which may be in
his handwriting.

The influence of Amyot's 'Plutarch' on French writers
and political thinkers, clear down to and through the Revolution, is incalculable. I'm sure you will wish, for his
sake if for no other reason, to visit Saint-Étienne, which

used to be the cathedral, and to see the thirteenth-century Préfecture, which was his palace.

Where rue Paul Bert and rue du Temple join, the wriggling, writhing rue de Paris comes to their juncture. If you follow it till you come to rue Dampierre (on your right), and almost immediately turn to your left into rue du Quatre Septembre, you will come, presently, to Saint-Étienne and, beside it, the Préfecture. Then, rue Cauchois will lead you thence to the lovely remains of Saint-Germain's Abbey that Sainte Clothilde (wife of Clovis) built to treasure the remains of the good old Alleluia Bishop.

And before you leave town, drive along the ramparts. And while you are in it, enjoy the Chablis wine whose chief mart it is.

IX

Sens is thirty-five miles from Auxerre, and Paris is sixty-five miles more. Almost to Fontainebleau you follow the course of the Yonne.

Joigny has some lovely old timbered houses. Villeneuve-sur-Yonne is a bastide, built by Louis VII.

Now, as you come to Sens, perhaps you'd like to put on your distance-lenses (the ones that give the farthest backward view) and see an expedition setting forth for the south, something well over twenty-three centuries ago. They are going to Italy, under the command of their chief or king Brennus, to possess themselves of lands where the vines grow and wine is made; for a Tuscan, very sore against his own people because of his misfortunes, has journeyed all the way hither in search of forgetfulness, has taught these Gauls the taste of wine, and is now leading them in an expedition to make themselves masters of his old home.

Brennus went a conqueror's way, straight to the Capitol

at Rome. The walls of the Eternal City could not keep him out. He and his followers, full of vinous courage, took the city — but not the citadel on its rock. At the foot of that Capitoline Rock they sat in siege, when the city had been sacked and destroyed. At last, Brennus ordered the rock scaled under cover of darkness — and it was done; but the sacred geese cackled, the garrison was roused, and the attack failed.

Perhaps, in your 'hist'ry-book' when you were very young, you had a picture of Brennus in the Roman Forum, when, wearied of his siege, he consented to be bought off, and a thousand pounds of gold was being weighed out to him. The Roman Tribune complained of some unfairness, and Brennus threw his heavy sword into the balance with the weights. When asked the meaning of this act, he scornfully replied, 'Woe to the conquered.'

I have that picture before me as I write. It is in a book which I consider all but priceless: 'The History of France in Pictures,' by Paul Lehugeur. Only, you must ask for it as 'L'Histoire de France en Cent Tableaux.' The text is in French, but simple French which almost any one should be able to read who knows even a few words of the language. There are one hundred big pages of pictures, comprising nearly five hundred illustrations, each with a very few lines of explanation. I should love to see it made available for English readers, the pictures reproduced in a much smaller book of many more pages — the plates not reduced in size, but arranged in a volume easier to handle than the one I own, which is like a big atlas in dimensions. I bought mine at the Bon-Marché department store in Paris. I dare say you could get a copy at almost any good book department or book store in Paris. If not, try the publisher, A. Lahure, 9, rue de Fleurus, Paris. And you will find rue de Fleurus over near the Luxembourg Gardens, running north and south across rue d'Assas. The brave deed of the Chevalier d'Assas for whom the street was named is the picture on the cover of the book. Lahure is at the corner of rue de Fleurus and rue d'Assas, just a very short 'block' from that corner to which I know you go looking for the old Carmelite Convent where so much tragic history was made.

Sens Cathedral not only claims that its first bishop was a friend of Christ, sent to Sens directly by Saint Peter; but, as it comes on down the ages, vaunts itself as 'having raised to God the first monument of Gothic form,' being 'the first to conceive and execute in an imperishable work the marvellous lines of this new style.'

It was very new, and far from complete when the Great Council met here, in 1140, at which Abélard was condemned. The King (Louis VII) was present, with a glittering court — including Eleanor. The Archbishop of Sens was surrounded by his seven suffragans, the Bishops of Chartres, Auxerre, Meaux, Paris, Orléans, Noyon, Troyes. Saint Bernard, Abélard's chief accuser, had an army of monks present. There were countless great knights and lords.

Bernard was in the pulpit, with Abélard's heretical treatise in his hand, when Abélard entered, walked slowly down the nave to the pulpit, and faced his judge.

The reading of the questioned passages had scarcely begun when Abélard rose.

'I appeal to Rome,' he said. Then turned, and with dignity which held every one speechless, walked back up the nave to the main portal, and left the cathedral.

In his absence, he was condemned.

A quarter-century later, Thomas à Becket came hither, fleeing from a council of condemnation at Northampton wherein he had entered, alone, and appealed to Rome; and here and hereabouts he dwelt for some years.

At Sens, in 1234, young Louis IX was married to Marguerite of Provence (one of the four daughters of Count Berenger, each of whom became a queen) with the famous ring in which were engraved the words 'God, France, and Marguerite.' 'Beyond this ring I have no love,' said Louis.

Five years later, returning from the Holy Land with the Crown of Thorns, he brought it here for safe-keeping until the Sainte-Chapelle at Paris could be built to house it.

I think you will find Sens Cathedral interesting for many reasons. Its associations are unusually so. Its relation to Gothic architecture is full of interest. (From here, in 1175, went William of Sens to rebuild the east end of Canterbury Cathedral, five years after Becket's murder there.) Its stained glass is superb — glorious! And whatever else you may miss about its exterior, do not neglect to see that exquisite spot leading to its south transept door!

I'd make the oval circuit of the town, on the boulevards where the old ramparts were. And if I were a picture-maker, I'd be sure to have one of the Poterne des Quatre-Mares (which Becket knew) and the section of Gallo-Roman wall adjoining it.

There are some fine old houses, too — the best of them in the rue de la République which runs north and south across the centre of the city.

From Sens your way leads to Fontainebleau, where you may have luncheon — if you haven't taken it at Hôtel de Paris, in the rue de la République, at Sens — at the Hôtel de France, opposite the Palace; and thence into Paris by either one of two routes, 7 or 5. Now, how shall you undertake to do some of this by train? From Tours to Poitiers, I'd say; then Perigueux and the excursions in the Dordogne. Then, Brive to Cahors, perhaps; and Cahors to Toulouse, changing there for Carcassonne. I don't think I'd try the Gorges of the Tarn if I were not motoring — I'd probably go from Carcassonne to Nîmes, and thence to Le Puy, and on to Clermont. After this, unless you are a very leisurely traveller, you'd perhaps feel that you should get back to Paris.

V

FROM PARIS TO NICE AND MONTE CARLO, AND BACK TO PARIS

This chapter I hope to make helpful for those who are en route to or from Italy by way of the great playground of southeastern France. It is a 'main-travelled road,' and has been so for more than twenty centuries; no other in France equals it for traffic or for history.

My suggestion for the first day's objective, out of Paris, is Dijon if you are a hardy traveller and in some haste (it is one hundred and eighty-five miles from Paris), or Auxerre, by way of Sens, as on the last day of our return from Carcassonne, if you are more leisurely; and then from Auxerre to Vézelay and Avallon and Sémur to Dijon — or, from Auxerre to Tonnerre and thence to Dijon by Route 5, which we shall follow in this chapter because we followed the other route on our last 'lap' in the preceding journey.

I shall imagine that you have made a fine early start from Paris (by 8.30 at latest), have had luncheon at Sens, and are leaving by the Route d'Alsace-Lorraine (Route 60), after following which for a very short distance, to Theil, you pick up Route 5.

At Tonnerre, forty-five miles from Sens, you may care to pause long enough to visit the chapel of the hospital founded in 1293 by Margaret of Burgundy, sister-in-law of Saint Louis, whose tomb here (although it replaces the original that the Revolutionists destroyed) is classed as a national monument. Whatever the furies of '93 left of the bones of Louvois is also here. He was one of Louis XIV's

great ministers — held 'the portfolio of War,' as we say —
and among other things was responsible for the establishment of Les Invalides under whose Dome, one thinks, he
ought to lie, rather than here. He bought the countship of
Tonnerre five years before his sudden death (of apoplexy)
at the age of fifty-two. About fifteen miles farther on your
way, at Ancy-le-Franc, you may visit the superb château
he bought at the same time — a château designed by
Primaticcio, whom Francis I brought from Italy to design
the new palace at Fontainebleau. (Should you be specially
interested in châteaux, you would be well repaid for a
détour of five miles, east from Tonnerre, to Tanlay, where
there is a very fine château in two parts — an older part
begun for the brother of Admiral de Coligny — murdered
in the Massacre of Saint Bartholomew's Eve — and a
slightly newer part built by Émery, finance minister under
Mazarin. The apartments are magnificently furnished.)

A little south of Louvois' château is the boundary-mark
between the old provinces of Champagne and Burgundy;
and still a little south of that is the ruined castle of Rochefort.

Your route now reaches Montbard, where there used to
be a fine feudal castle which was largely demolished by
Buffon, the great naturalist; on the principle, I suppose,
that a little Nature is better than a lot of antiquated architecture. However, the park is so lovely that I'm sure no one
will wish to quarrel with the naturalist's choice. The upper
terraces form one of the most beautiful public promenades
in France, and there are fine walks along the Canal de
Bourgogne which was projected in Louis XII's reign (about
1500) and finished in 1832. It unites the Atlantic and the
Mediterranean, and is one hundred and fifty miles long.

At Montbard, I'd quit Route 5, briefly, for Route 80, so
as to visit Sémur, one of the most strikingly picturesque

small towns in France — a perfect Paradise for the photographer and other picture-makers.

The charming river Armançon which contributes so much to this vicinity, did its best to create an island here, and almost succeeded; it flows around three steeply escarped sides of a rosy granite rock; and then, leaving a bit of bottle-neck, turns away sharply, north and south — but not too brusquely; I suspect that it loves lingering, to reflect the beauty of Sémur and to have its picture taken.

The local guide-book, knowing that one of the prime reasons why people visit Sémur is to take pictures of some sort (mental or other) away with them, has a feature which I have never seen elsewhere: a 'tour' of the lovely old town with all its most noted picture-taking points the objectives, and information as to the hours of day when the light is best for each of them. It even goes so far as comments like these: 'The water, here, is generally so mirror-like as to give back a too-complete reflection, so the wise photographer will throw a stone into it before making his exposure'; and, 'on Saturday mornings from 7 to 8.30, the foreground, here, will show the herds of cattle' — the slaughter-house being there, and Saturday (I suppose) the day for killing.

This picture-itinerary is so admirable an idea in a guide-book that I am going to give it to you in summary, translated. It was made, a good many years ago (early in this century) by M. Viney, who was a member of the Commission of the National Society of French Clubs of Photographers.

You will enter the outskirts of Sémur by the rue de Paris, and cross the river at the 'bottle-neck,' by the Pont Joly. On the other side of the bottle-neck is the Pont Pinard, dominated by the donjon of the old castle. You should have views in both directions, here, and from both banks of the river; but the best light, M. Viney says, is from 9 to 11 A.M.

Then, turn south along the Armançon, following rue Chaude, pass the sawmill, and at the water-edge, at the corner of the bath-house, get your picture of the donjon and the mill. Light good, here, from 7 to 9 A.M., or 2 to 3 P.M. Here is where you must throw your stone.

Now, keep on going south, on what has changed its name to rue du Saussis, cross the little rivulet, and climb the very steep street leading to the viaduct. Before reaching the viaduct, go into a garden near the last house, and thence make your picture of the south flank. The time recommended for this is 7 o'clock to 8.30 — which is hard for me to understand, as I should think a south exposure would be better lighted nearer to noonday or after it. However, I'm translating, not advising; and I'm sure M. Viney knew.

Next, climb down, retrace your steps, and cross the river on the stepping-stones. From the opposite bank, you get your distance view of Notre-Dame and its towers: 7 to 8.30 A.M.

Then, leaving the stepping-stones, you follow the little path which leads north, cross rue Pertuisot, and take the Sentier des Jardins (or Garden Path) almost to its end: when you have come to some pines above a mill, look, at the left, for a stairway by which you may reach a garden whence you take (7 to 10 A.M., or 5 to 6 P.M.) what is probably the finest view of Sémur. There are several other fine viewpoints hereabouts, but I won't enumerate them all for fear of wearying the traveller who is not a camera-carrier. But, on your way back, along the river edge, you will find some good views, upstream and downstream, at their best from 3 to 5 P.M.

Still on the far side of the river, you come to the bridge

and convent of the Minims, from which there are good pictures of the old houses on the river edge.

When you have crossed the Pont-des-Minims and taken rue des Vaux, at your left, you will come, in a hundred steps or so, to a paved alley leading to the river; from the foot of this you get a very fine picture of the donjon and the Pont-Joly.

East of Pont-Joly is rue du Pont-Joly, which changes its name as it rounds the corner and leads to the Porte Guillier, a superb mediæval town gate, whose picture from the outside you must surely take.

If you stay a considerable time at Sémur you may feel inclined for a look at some interiors — church, or geological museum, or what-not — but if your stay must be all-too-short, I'm sure you cannot do better than to spend it in a circuit of the town outside the natural fortifications, and in the enchanting streets west of the 'bottle-neck.'

Should you be a picture-making enthusiast, intent upon some of those early-morning views, you will find Hôtel de la Côte d'Or just outside the Porte Guillier. It is said to be good. I cannot testify, as it has not yet been my good fortune to stay in Sémur long enough to need a hotel. I hope to, some day soon.

If you *do* stay, on pictures bent, let me entreat you to make an excursion to Époisses, eight miles west, on the road to Avallon.

The cheeses of Époisses are famous; its history is long; I dare say it has other claims upon our attention. But the magic of its name for me is its feudal château, built in the fourteenth century and still surrounded by its double ring of walls and its inner and outer moats. Many eminent associations has this château (including some with Madame de Sévigné, who visited here the ancestors of the present owners), but its charm for me is just its Sleeping Beauty

loveliness, as of something Time and the ravaging hand of
rampaging man has spared to us.

Enthusiasts on Madame de Sévigné ought, however, not
to leave this vicinity without visiting the interior of the
château; then taking the road southeast to Bourbilly (G.
C. 4) to return thence to Sémur by G. C. 9. Bourbilly,
where the little girl who was to become Madame de Sévigné passed much time in her earliest youth, has a modern
château built on feudal lines, in place of the one she knew;
but it conserves some precious souvenirs of her. We shall
have further reminders of her when we near Bussy, after
leaving Sémur.

When ready to resume your journey toward the south,
leave Sémur by the Porte Guillier, rue de la Liberté and
Route Départementale 6 toward Les Laumes; which is taking you back to your Route 5 — the great national highway from Paris to Geneva.

Les Laumes is a railway junction. But about a mile and
a half southeast of it is a village called Alise-Sainte-Reine,
near which, on the side of Mont Auxois, was the fort where
Vercingetorix is believed to have made his last resistance
against Cæsar — after which he surrendered and was carried captive to Rome. A colossal statue of the young chieftain, by Aimé Millet, marks the site; and in the village is a
little museum containing archæological objects brought to
light by the excavations. Perhaps only an antiquary can
reconstitute, in his mind, the old Gallo-Roman town that
once was here. But surely anybody can get a thrill out of
standing on the spot!

The Sainte Reine whose name is associated with the last
stand of the Gauls against Rome, was a young Christian
girl of the third century who is believed to have refused to
marry the Emperor of Rome because he was a pagan —
and to have been martyred at his command. Each year, on

September 10th, there is a mediæval mystery play enacted here by young girls, before an assemblage numbering five or six thousand peasants and townsfolk from roundabout.

The Sévigné pilgrims go some four miles northeast of Les Laumes to the Château of Bussy-Rabutin, the home of that scandal-mongering cousin of hers (it was he who told her of her husband's infatuation for Ninon de l'Enclos) who was banished from court and ordered to retire hither in punishment for his part in a particularly outrageous orgy during Holy Week of 1659. Here he beguiled his enforced leisure by writing, for the amusement of his mistress, his 'Histoire Amoureuse des Gaules,' a series of sketches of the 'affairs' of many court ladies, which circulated freely in manuscript and caused an immense amount of stir. He was sent to the Bastille, in 1665, and remained there for more than a year, being liberated only on condition that he come here to his Burgundy estate, and *stay*.

Aside from its interest through association with Bussy, the château, with its magnificent furnishings, wealth of portraits (a catalogue of the treasures fills one hundred and fifty pages!), its gardens by Le Nôtre (fine water effects), and its superb park, is well worthy of a very long détour to visit. And so is Flavigny!

There are small, winding roads that go from Alise-Sainte-Reine to Flavigny, but they are not numbered. You must ask for them, or look for signs. Flavigny is about four miles from Alise (or Alésia), south by a little east.

Chateaubriand wrote of Flavigny: 'I owe to the vale of Flavigny one of my most vivid and most moving memories: it is the aspect of the valley of Jerusalem; these old fortifications recall the desolated ramparts of the Temple. These clumps of trees, are they not the austere shade of the Mount of Olives?'

There is a fine parish church, classed among the historic

monuments of France, with superb fifteenth-century Flemish choir stalls. And there are remains of the Abbey of Flavigny, dating from the early seventh century, including a crypt which is the only bit of Carolingian architecture left intact in all Burgundy. The abbey remains now are part of a candy factory where is manufactured a bonbon, *Anis de l'Abbaye de Flavigny*, famous for more than two centuries. Each bonbon has a single anise seed in its centre; and the packets in which they are sold have been familiar to millions of persons since Louis XIV was king. This may not allure you; but if you love an old, old town, magnificently situated, I do not see how you can fail to delight in Flavigny and its superb old town gates, its narrow, winding old streets, its lovely old houses. *I* think it a gem.

From Flavigny, return (west) to your Route 5, and resume your southward way. About six miles from Pouillenay where you 'pick up' your Geneva road, is Posanges (no détour for this; it lies at your very hand) with a superb feudal château which should on no account be missed, whether your preoccupation be pictures, romance, or history. A matter of twenty miles, and you're at Dijon, where you will (I dare say) spend the night at Hôtel de la Cloche. If you enter town by the Route de Plombières, passing between the railway station, and the Botanical Garden, you have only to follow boulevard Sévigné to the Place Darcy on which the hotel stands. This square, whereon the principal cafés are situated, has an elegant public garden somewhat reminiscent of the Tuileries Gardens at Paris.

I cannot commend the hotel, unless its management has recently changed, or improved; but if you want to see Dijon you must make the best of it, or spend the night at Saulieu or Beaune, and go to Dijon in the morning.

Rue de la Liberté, the 'Main Street' of Dijon, leads from the Porte Guillaume, close to your hotel, to the Place d'Armes, an arcaded, semi-circular *place* (pronounced *plass*, or *plahs*) facing the old palace of the Dukes of Burgundy. Here, in the Restaurant Aux Trois Faisans, I think you should dine.

Remember that the Burgundian, more, perhaps, than any other provincial of France, loves the proverb: 'Better a good meal than good clothes.'

This is the place, *par excellence*, to eat snails. The ham and other pork products are famous. The fowl is not inferior to that of Bresse to which you're going (no! it isn't a mere legend about the chicken one gets in Bresse; I've eaten delicious chicken in a hundred places, but there *is* something surpassing about the *poulardes de Bresse*, the country of Brillat-Savarin!); the beef is unrivalled — and *bœuf bourguignon* is a classic dish; the game is peerless (M. Dulac opines that saddle of hare *à la* Piron, *le râble de lièvre à la* Piron, has its like only in Paradise; the truffles and mushrooms are supremely good; the vegetables are fine, and plentiful; Dijon is famed for its sweets as for its mustard. And its wines are unsurpassed, if not unequalled, in all the world.

How shall one begin to enumerate even a few of the most renowned:

Chambertin, of course; and Romanée-Conti; Clos-de-Vougeot, and Richebourg; Montrachet ——

Always ask your head waiter! He loves nothing better than to suggest. If his recommendations are of wines too costly, do not hesitate to tell him so. If there is one thing which calls for no apology to a Frenchman, it is economy. He may wonder why you spend so much money on clothes and travelling, and economize on an essential of life like fine wine. But never mind! Ask — and learn!

After dinner, and a stroll, you may enjoy finishing up the evening at a café like the Grande Taverne, 20, rue de la

Gare, on the other side of the public garden from your hotel — near the station.

I can't remember when, nor how, the name of Burgundy first laid hold on my imagination, so that it was forever leaping into prominence from many a printed page whereon, perchance, a dozen other great names stayed in an indefinite mass. Burgundy!

Had I known 'The Vagabond King' when a child, I could — perhaps — account for this. But, somehow, without that, the fascination took hold; and as time went on, I found that I was reading, avidly, everything I could find about Burgundy, and trailing Burgundian dukes all over this part of the world.

I have found it an invaluable predilection. After all, the Dukes of Burgundy who extensively interest us are only four; the rest of Burgundian history is their background or their aftermath. But any one who has a clear-cut conception of those four men and their relation to European history has the key to most of the interesting and significant situations in Europe between the battle of Poitiers and the age of Louis XIV — three hundred and fifty years.

After that disastrous battle of Poitiers, where France's King was taken captive, there went with King John over to England (in the custody of the chivalrous Black Prince) that fourteen-year-old son, Philip, who fought at his father's side until the last, and was not taken until he was desperately wounded.

The first day of his arrival at the court of England, where the royal captives were so courteously and handsomely treated, this young warrior startled the company at table in the Savoy Palace, by jumping up and boxing the ears of King Edward's cup-bearer for serving the King of England before the King of France; 'for,' he said, 'though his father, King John, was unfortunate, he was the sovereign of the King of England.'

This 'game' youngster was his father's fourth son; and he was a grandson of that blind King John of Bohemia who had died on the battle-field of Crécy ten years before, and whose crest — three feathers — and motto, *Ich dien* ('I serve'), had been appropriated by the Black Prince and have served the Princes of Wales ever since. His paternal grandmother was Jeanne of Burgundy, through whom, when fiery Philip was nineteen years old, Burgundy returned again to the possessions of the French Crown which, about a hundred and thirty years before, had bestowed it on the French King's younger brother and his descendants.

Philip's father, who was then at liberty ('out on bond,' we'd say) trying to collect money for his ransom, gave Burgundy to young Philip.

Poor King John didn't get nearly enough money, you'll remember, and went back to England and gave himself up, dying there soon afterwards and leaving the French throne to his eldest son, Charles V.

When Philip (who seems early to have deserved his surname 'The Bold') was five-and-twenty he married, at Ghent, the widow of the preceding Duke of Burgundy (the last of the old line), who was in her own right a very great heiress, and brought him a vast increase of his possessions, including Flanders and the rich *county* of Burgundy in eastern France, thenceforth united with the *duchy*. And therewith the Duke of Burgundy became the richest and most powerful vassal of the French Crown. And when Charles V died, in 1380, Philip and his elder but less powerful brothers governed the kingdom of their young nephew, Charles VI — later to be known as 'The Mad.'

If you have this much in mind, you will much the more readily comprehend the events leading up to Jeanne d'Arc's day and service.

Robert J. Casey, in his book on 'The Lost Kingdom of

Burgundy,' says that 'Dijon was a Gallic city before the coming of the Romans and a military base during the days of the empire, but not until the Valois dukes did it acquire any importance. . . . With the arrival of Philip in 1364, however, the city became aware of its destiny. . . . The brother of King Charles V had begun to dream his royal dream, and he proceeded to build a capital out of the marsh town that he had found there. From Flanders, his heritage from his wife, came the riches that were to make Dijon the envy of kings for a hundred years. Master builders, sculptors, artisans skilled in the working of wood and stone, carvers of ivory, jewellers, artists, weavers of tapestry, armorers, and needle-workers with a facile touch trooped in from Bruges and Ghent at the call of this mediæval Aladdin. And at his behest they threw up the golden tower of the fairy city. Little wonder that his widow was forced to place her keys on his coffin when he died — token of her renunciation of his debts.

'Philip began the construction of a ducal palace to replace the ruined château of the Capetian dukes. The first of the towers erected under his supervision remains to-day as the Tour de Bar. Some years later he completed the monastery of Chartreuse de Champnol, a building suited to be what he had intended it to be, the last resting-place of the ducal line.'

To write, even in outline, of Philip and his three successors were matter for a volume and not for a very few pages. But I'm sure you will wish, to-morrow, when visiting old Dijon, to have in mind at least this much about them:

Philip was duke for forty years; and when he died, his son and heir (named for Grandfather John) had already earned the surname of *Sans Peur*, the Fearless, by his conduct in the bloody battle of Nicopolis where he was taken prisoner by Sultan Bajazet.

It was this John, born here at Dijon, who struggled with his cousin Louis of Orléans for chief place in the kingdom of poor, demented Charles VI, and caused the murder of Orléans in the dark streets of Paris, in November, 1407. Twelve years later, John himself was murdered, on the bridge at Montereau, by the men of the Dauphin — later Charles VII — and there was a new Duke of Burgundy, another Philip, known to history as 'The Good.' He, too, was born here in the palace at Dijon. And in retaliation for his father's murder, he took the English side in the still-lingering Hundred Years' War, being the Duke of Burgundy whose soldiers captured Jeanne d'Arc at Compiègne and sold her to their English allies.

Philip's sister Margaret was the wife of our old friend Arthur of Richemont (or Richmond) who keeps crossing our path ever since we met him at Vannes; and another sister of Philip, Anne, was married to the Duke of Bedford, Henry V's uncle and the Regent for little Henry VI. It was Philip who founded the Order of the Golden Fleece — to commemorate, 'tis said, the glorious tresses of a lady he loved, but was not married to.

And Philip's son and successor was that Charles the Bold who fills so many fascinating pages of history. His daughter and heiress, Mary, was she whose marriage and its issue carried on the claims of Burgundy through Emperor Charles V (her grandson) and Philip II of Spain, and caused much of the warfare between France and Spain for two centuries.

Now, in the morning, when you set forth, I'd go straight back to the Place d'Armes, and lose no time getting into the palace of the Dukes of Burgundy, now part of the Hôtel de Ville of Dijon.

There are some lovely old houses at Dijon; but in journeying through France you'll see many lovely old houses.

There are some fine churches; but France is full of fine churches. If you have time for all Dijon's attractions, well and good. But if you haven't, I'd begin with the ducal palace, continue with the Palais de Justice, and see the park on my southward way.

Give more than a passing thought, when you see the Tour de Bar, to René of Anjou, Duc de Bar, who was imprisoned there; for on this journey you are to meet René more frequently than any other personage, and 'tis best to be a bit brushed-up on his relationships and why he had so many castles despite his chronic poverty.

He was of that House of Anjou-in-Sicily-and-Naples which had begun its Italian history when the brother of Saint Louis went down there, on the Pope's urging, to 'oust' Manfred.

If you consult a cyclopædia for facts about René, you will find him described as 'Duke of Anjou, of Lorraine and Bar, Count of Provence and of Piedmont, King of Naples, Sicily, and Jerusalem.' And, more or less briefly, he was all of those; but continuously he was a gentle, artistic, poetic soul, of manifold sorrows and perpetual poverty. René was the second son, and rather portionless, when he was betrothed, at ten, to a daughter of the Duke of Lorraine. His sister was married to the Dauphin, afterwards Charles VII.

Though only twenty-two years old, René was the father of four children (the youngest of them, two years old, that Margaret of Anjou who made so many tears flow in sympathy with her) when his father-in-law died and his claims to the Duchy of Lorraine were disputed by a male cousin of his wife's, backed by Philip the Good of Burgundy. They battled, at Bulgnéville (up nearer to Nancy, the Lorraine capital), and René was defeated, taken prisoner, and brought hither by the Burgundians.

His young duchess appealed to his brother-in-law, the

King of France. But Philip of Burgundy, the powerful
captor of René, was also Charles VII's brother-in-law, besides being his bitter enemy. And, somehow, Charles didn't
seem to feel called upon to 'mix in' on René's troubles.
When René got out of here, after nine months' durance, it
was by yielding up (as King John of France had done,
seventy-five years before, and Francis I was to do, nearly
one hundred years later) his two sons as hostages. Then he
went about the job of trying to scrape up his ransom. But
after nearly three years of liberty, he was forced to come
back again, and spend two more years a captive in this
tower.

The other day I heard of a young woman, touring France
(no! visiting Paris), who was suddenly seized with a desire
for information. 'What do they have over here?' she in-
quired — 'a king?'

Now, if you don't get a fair sort of start on René, before
you get down into Provence, you are going to feel yourself
almost equally in need of facts. So I pray you to regard
with sympathy his tower, where he languished for claiming
his wife's birthright; and to recall that from here the poor
soul passed on, presently, to another mess of trouble and
defeat trying to hold his own inheritance of Naples and
Sicily when it had been willed to him.

The great treasures of the museum are in the magnificent
Salle des Gardes of the dukes; they are the tombs of Philip
the Bold and his son John the Fearless, brought hither from
the Chartreuse; and the two Flemish altar pieces painted
for the abbey church there, where masses were to be continually said for the repose of their souls who had been
Burgundy's rulers.

After having seen the palace (not omitting the celebrated kitchen), I'd have a look, even if it had to be a brief
one, down rue des Forges which runs west from it a little

way, parallel with the busy rue de la Liberté; and I wouldn't be that close to Notre-Dame without at least an impression of its unique architecture — especially the triple rows of gargoyles and those exquisitely arcaded galleries on the façade — and its famous Jacquemart clock whose quaint figures have been hammering out the hours here since 1382.

North from Notre-Dame there's much delightful strolling that might be done; but you may not have time for it.

The Palais de Justice is a very short distance south of the ducal palaces.

You should lunch at Beaune; and you will be sorry to hasten away from there. Beaune is twenty-three miles from Dijon, and the way lies through those vineyards of the Côtes d'Or, or Golden Hillsides, whose names alone are almost intoxicating; Chambertin, Bougeot, Romanée, Saint-George! A little (seven and a half miles) to the east of Nuits-Saint-Georges is Citeaux, the mother house of the great Cistercian Order to which Europe, and civilization, owed so much. Saint Bernard settled there, in 1114, and went thence to found Clairvaux, up between Troyes and Chaumont. I doubt if this détour would repay many travellers. I'd keep on, to Beaune — which is truly an adorable place.

The Dukes of Burgundy regarded Beaune as the third city of their duchy; and the two huge towers at the entrance of the town are survivals of their castle.

I hope you'll buy picture-cards or something in the bookseller's shop on Place Monge, because the building, with its Gothic front, used to be the 'town house' of the Pot family, whose castle you are presently to visit, after leaving Beaune.

⊢ The great 'sight' of Beaune is its Hôtel-Dieu, or hospital, built about 1443, by Nicholas Rolin, Chancellor of Duke Philip the Good, who imported Flemish nuns from Malines

to run it. The 'hospital sisters' of to-day look much as did
the first of their predecessors — even to their white batiste
hennins (headdress); and their surroundings may well give
them cause to wonder in what century they live — the
fifteenth or the twentieth. Theirs is another world than
ours, certainly!

Few structures in Europe are more picturesque than
this, without and within. I think I won't say a great deal
about it, so that it may give you as many surprises as possible. But see if it isn't just like a collection of very lovely
old paintings in which, somehow, the figures occasionally
move.

Chancellor Rolin's daughter died in the hospital. She
was named Philipote, evidently from Philip Pot, who
shared with her father Duke Philip's favor, and her picture is in Roger van der Weyden's great altar piece, painted
for the chapel, but now hanging in the Musée of the hospital. Try if you cannot as easily 'see' the Chancellor and
his wife and son move from the painted panel to the bedside
of a patient there to-day, as to the deathbed of Philipote.
They all belong together! And to the backgrounds!

Lunch at Hôtel de la Poste. And when you can tear
yourself away from Beaune, take, not the direct road for
Chagny (Route 6), but that right-hand fork which leads to
Pommard and Volnay, more famous vineyard towns, to La
Rochepot and then bends back to Chagny.

I think you will find the Castle of Rochepot a real 'thrill.'

The story is that 'once upon a time' (and if you ever saw
a once-upon-a-time place, surely this is it!) the lord of this
castle hired a certain William Pot to dig a well. Five long
years William dug; and whenever he broached, delicately,
the matter o' money, his lord gave him a promissory note.
William had five of these when the well was finished; but
the lord of Laroche had no money to pay them.

'I cannot pay you in gold,' Mr. Casey, in 'The Lost Kingdom of Burgundy,' represents him as saying, 'because I haven't any gold. I can give you part of my estates in far Aquitaine, or my title as King of Nubia — I think it's Nubia, or maybe East Mauretania — or I can give you this castle as it stands and move to my hôtel in Dijon.'

William preferred the castle. How long after William came Philip, I do not know. That is, I know when Philip came along, but I don't know when William did his digging.

Philip was born here just before Jeanne d'Arc went to Chinon to rouse the Dauphin; just before Margaret of Anjou was born and René was made prisoner in Dijon.

And when he had grown old enough to wed, and was betrothed to Jeanne de Beaufremont, Constantinople fell to the Mohammedans, and Philip felt that he must do something about it.

So, off he went, and got captured by the infidels and clapped into a dungeon, where he beguiled himself with writing poetry until the news was broken to him that he was to furnish a Mohammedan holiday — closely patterned after the old Roman sort. He was given a sword (or dagger) one foot long, and introduced to a famishing lion in an awful hurry to meet him.

On the lion's first advance, Philip slashed one of his fore paws. The astonished and very displeased lion sat down to lick his injury. Then it was Philip's turn to make advances. That tongue which the beast was using to lick his bleeding paw, Philip cut neatly off.

The lion opened his mouth to roar with pain, and Philip rammed the dagger down the beast's throat, reaching some vital inward.

The lion died; the Moslems cheered; the Sultan descended into the arena, hung a gold chain about Philip's neck, and told him that he was free.

When Philip got back to Rochepot, everybody at the castle and all round about, had gone to Dijon to attend his funeral. Like Mark Twain's, the reports of his death had been greatly exaggerated.

So Philip rode on to Dijon, where everything was in motion toward the cathedral. A catafalque, surmounted by a suit of Philip's armor and flanked by tall candles, stood before the altar; and Jeanne de Beaufremont knelt beside it, weeping.

Philip did not spoil any of the proceedings for which so much pains had been taken until they were well over. Then he disclosed himself.

He married Jeanne, and dwelt here and hereabouts for many years, and had his tomb made before he died. I hope you know it, in the Louvre. If you don't, look for it when you go back to Paris, in the collection of mediæval and renaissance sculpture. You will find it in Salle d'André Beauneveu: Philip, in armor, lying on a slab carried by eight mourning figures.

When you have feasted your sense of romance and of the picturesque on Philip's castle (which now belongs to the family of Carnot, two of whose members lie in the Panthéon at Paris — Lazare, the Republican leader, called 'the organizer of victory' in the Revolution, and Sadi, President of the Republic, assassinated at Lyons in 1894), continue on your way through Chagny to Chalon-sur-Saône where the Burgundian kings lived away back in the sixth century; and where, in the time of the Revolution and the First Empire, there lived a physicist named Joseph Nicéphore Niepce, who, in 1813, got the idea of making 'sun-pictures,' and experimented therewith for a dozen years or so, until he learned that Daguerre was working in the same direction. In 1829 they joined forces 'to coöperate in perfecting the discovery invented by M. Niepce and developed by M. Daguerre.'

Daguerre, giving directions for the time of exposure, said that for a landscape from seven to eight hours were required, 'but single monuments, when strongly lighted by the sun, or which are themselves very bright, can be taken in about three hours.'

In the Musée Denon, at Chalon, you may see Niepce's earliest cameras and their products; and if you continue to the banks of the Saône, you may pay your respects to his memory at his statue, near the Hôtel de Ville.

As you go down Route 6, toward Mâcon, I think you'll enjoy a brief stop at Tournus, to see the abbey church and its surrounding houses: the deanery, the almonry, the treasury, the abbot's lodge, the cloister garth, etc. Students of architecture certainly ought not to neglect this group of buildings.

This was the native place of Greuze.

Twenty miles farther on is Mâcon, where I once spent two days while our automobile was undergoing repairs, and discovered sundry charms at which the guide-book does not hint — the pharmacy of the Hôtel-Dieu, for instance! In itself, that is worth a pilgrimage. And Mâcon is the place from which to visit Cluny — a pilgrimage I do not advise except for the specialist; what is left of Cluny, as we read about it and imagine it, is very little and engulfed in uninteresting eighteenth-century constructions. I'm not sorry I went; but I do not recommend the journey to travellers pressed for time. And as for to-day, you may think that you have seen enough.

You can lodge comfortably at Mâcon and eat memorably; but I advise your continuing either to Lyon or to Bourg. My choice would be Bourg. Your mileage to-day if you stop at Bourg will be about a hundred and ten miles. If you go on to Lyon, it is twenty miles farther. But Bourg, though it is a pleasant, restful little town and has a most excellent hotel (Hôtel de l'Europe), and a replica of the Westminster chime of thirty-three bells, would doubtless be a far less satisfactory stopping-place than Lyon to any one who did not care for the Church of Brou.

I think the Church of Brou is one of the architectural glory spots of Europe. So far as I know, most persons who have seen it feel the same way about it. But if you suspect that no church could interest you as much as (let us say) the collection of historic costumes of Lyon, then I'd keep straight on, on Route 6, to Lyon; and I'd probably go to the Dominion Hotel, under the same excellent management as the Dominion at Avignon and at Paris, and *both* the good hotels at Auxerre — the one I stopped at and the one I *thought* I was stopping at.

However, supposing that you have chosen Bourg, and are entering it by rue de la Citadelle, you turn left in rue Alphonse Mas, cross the Champ de Mars into rue des Casernes, and then left, again, up to the Place de la Grenette where your hotel is.

Bourg (which is pronounced *Bourk*, to distinguish it sharply from Bourges — *Boorj*) is one of those nice, restful places where we may enjoy the luxury of not needing to think about anything in particular. Of course, one may indulge in this luxury anywhere. But sometimes one feels, afterwards, a bit self-reproachful or humiliated. Nor should one 'slump' too far, even here. For this evening, however, after a day very full of things to think about, I'd take a fairly complete vacation from thinking and observing.

In the morning (and I pray it may be a sunshiny one) make your way over past Notre-Dame (where the Westminster chimes are) to boulevard de Brou which will take you directly to the church — about a mile southeast.

Where the village of Brou now is there was a Gallo-

Roman settlement wiped out by fire long, long ago, and overgrown by a dense forest in which, about the tenth century, a bishop of Mâcon died in a retreat. A priory grew up about his cell, but it was poorly supported; and meanwhile Bourg was becoming quite a place, with a popular shrine at Notre-Dame.

In 1480, Marguerite de Bourbon (mother of that very masterful woman, Louise of Savoy, who had so much to do with the affairs of her son, Francis I; and mother-in-law-to-be of that other masterful lady, Marguerite of Austria, who had so much to do with the affairs of Francis' formidable opponent, Charles V) was fearful lest her husband, Philip, Count of Bresse, might not recover from an accident he had met with; so she vowed to found a Benedictine monastery at Brou where the poor priory was.

Three years later, she died, without having done anything to fulfil her vow. And when her son, Philibert, died of pneumonia contracted while hunting, in 1504, there was still nothing done about her promise to Heaven.

It was left to her young daughter-in-law to fulfil. That daughter-in-law was Marguerite, daughter of Emperor Maximilian and Mary of Burgundy, whom Charles VIII had jilted to wed Anne of Brittany; whom the son and heir of Ferdinand and Isabella had left a widow at seventeen; and who had enjoyed only three short years of wedded bliss with handsome Philibert, when pneumonia snatched him from her.

One of her first thoughts was to entomb him worthily and to keep him in perpetual prayer. So she determined to build a monastery, with a very beautiful church.

Her councillors urged her to consider, instead, a chantry in the new Church of Notre-Dame just begun at Bourg. But to this she would not listen. She summoned hither the best skill of which she knew (even Michel Colombe, of

Tours, who had recently made that epoch-marking tomb at Nantes for the parents of Marguerite's successful rival, Anne of Brittany). Before the plans were well advanced, she had to quit this part of the world and go to Malines, to govern the Netherlands in the stead of her brother who had just died, and to bring up his children, one of whom was to be Emperor Charles V. But the work went on — largely under Flemish artists; too slowly, though, to suit Marguerite.

It was as if she had a premonition that she would not see it completed; because, in 1528, she engaged to pay her master-mason five hundred pounds if the work were finished in thirty months. She died before the thirty months were over. It was March, 1532 (Marguerite having been dead fifteen months), when the church was consecrated. And in June of that year Marguerite's body was solemnly interred here, in a crypt of the choir, beside her husband and his mother.

She had left her nephew Charles V her executor. But if she bequeathed sufficient funds to maintain this princely sepulchre, Charles must have diverted them to purposes of his own. For the church had fallen into sad decay one hundred and thirty years later, and was then repaired at great expense. Another restoration took place in 1759.

Then came the Revolution. And a deputy from hereabouts to the Constituent Assembly got a decree making this a national monument.

Under the Terror, it was used for storing hay — which saved its glorious sculptures from destruction.

Subsequently, it was a pigsty, a prison for priests, a garrison for veterans, a prison, a cavalry barracks, an alms station for beggars, and an asylum for the insane. In 1823 it became a church again. Now it is under the care of the Ministry of Fine Arts and Education — a temple of Beauty and Love for worshippers of every creed.

If you can read French, I strongly advise studying the details at least of the tombs, with Victor Nodet's booklet (which the custodian will sell you) in hand. Should it be necessary to confine your study to what you may do in a brief time, take the pages, beginning on page 55, which deal with the tomb of Philibert. It seems to me that any one who reads those few pages, and closely observes the sculpture to note the details described, must get, in brief, a delightful realization of what the intensive study of such masterpieces means. I'd love to translate it for this chapter; but I know I mustn't — except these few lines with which M. Nodet concludes his description of the three tombs:

'In the midst of woodwork darkened by time, in the splendor of marvellous windows, these beautiful marbles glow with an incomparable magnificence. The visitor goes from one tomb to another continuously charmed by a detail hitherto unnoticed; and in this setting rare in its preservation, still living after four centuries, he finds a clear vision of the splendors of that epoch of exuberant vigor as it hastened to embrace a new ideal without renouncing the old Gothic masters who were its real inspiration.'

I never enter into any discussion on art — nor, indeed, on anything; not being inclined for argument — but if I *did*, I might sometimes ask how a canvas (for instance) which seems to represent a broken kaleidoscope, but is said to represent Autumn or Spring, or some of each, can be a perfectly reputable 'art' when it has no known antecedents and no discoverable relations. And if any of these sporadic 'accidents' of to-day survive, what — I wonder — will the student of a later day think of the period when evolution stopped and a new sort of spontaneous generation began? It must be an awful responsibility to inaugurate a new species.

The superb choir stalls are in themselves worth coming far to see, and deserve study in detail. So does the reredos in the Lady Chapel, showing the seven joys of the Virgin. And if you share my interest in 'Who *Was* Who,' you'll find the windows not only beautiful but absorbing. Be sure to see the representations of Marguerite and Philibert in the lower panels of the Assumption window in the chapel of Marguerite; and to test your knowledge of heraldry on the windows of the apse which show the descent of these two who left, of their love and union, no flesh-and-blood heir, but rather this pæan of stone and glass and wood whose beauty keeps a praising choir always worshipful about their resting-place.

On Philibert's side (left) see his escutcheons of Savoy and Bourbon, and reflect on his relation to Louise of Savoy, his sister, and to her children, Francis I and Marguerite of Angoulême, grandmother of Henry IV. On the side of Marguerite of Austria see her long lines of descent, imperial on her father's side, Burgundian (with imperial pretensions) on her mother's.

Ah! it is a place for manifold reflections, this exquisite Church of Brou. To see it once is not enough. You will promise yourself a return to it, before long.

And I like to think about Marguerite's frustrations and what, in spite of them, she left to us. The crown of France was snatched from her when she was about twelve years old and had been bred from her babyhood to wear it. The crown of united Spain, which seemed secured to her, was lifted from above her head by the hand of death, when she was seventeen. The crown of happy wedlock which she had briefly worn was turned to widow's weeds before she was twenty-five.

French crowns are but mem'ries, now, and Spanish crowns but anachronisms. But Love is still regnant, and this superb shrine of his keeps Marguerite in perpetual remembrance.

You know her motto: '*Fortune, infortune, forte une.*' (In fortune or misfortune one woman is strong.)

I'm very grateful to Marguerite!

Should it be summer when you come this way (and the Riviera is a *much* more attractive place in summer — certain spots on it, at any rate — than most persons realize; with a climate more agreeable on the whole than the fashionable Normandy coast, perhaps; and out-of-season prices wonderfully attractive), you would do better to go from Bourg to Geneva, and proceed to Nice by the Route des Alpes. For the Rhône Valley can get pretty hot and dusty in July, August, and September.

Earlier than mid-June, I would go down by way of Avignon, and come back, if possible, by the Route des Alpes.

Supposing that to be your plan, you take Route 83 from Bourg to Lyon — thirty-eight miles — unless you don't mind a matter of eight extra miles; in which case I'd certainly take the slightly longer route which runs southeast from Bourg to Neuville, there joins Route 84, and takes you through Meximieux, a mile or so east of which lies Pérouges, a perfect picture town of seventy-one inhabitants dwelling in houses of the fifteenth and sixteenth centuries. The wee, lovely place is something almost incredibly charming. I doubt if you ever saw anything more irresistible than the Hostellerie du Vieux-Pérouges. To Avignon is one hundred and forty miles more; and between Lyon and Avignon there is no attractive place to stop for the night. Vienne is too near Lyon (seventeen miles) to support a good hotel. Valence, which is forty-five miles farther, might well support a good hotel (I should think), but doesn't; at least, it was a long way from being good when I was last there, in the spring of 1926. And when I say 'good,' I don't mean that a hotel of the provinces should be expected to be like a *de luxe* hotel on the Riviera. I have in mind the standard that many and many a modest inn in a small, unfrequented town manages to maintain. The Croix d'Or, or Gold Cross, at Valence is rather pretentious; it is near enough to Lyon to know something about cooking. But we thought we had seldom been in a place where 'reducing' would call for less renunciation. Indeed, good food is hard to find, except at Avignon and Arles, between Lyon and the Mediterranean coast.

So, at Lyon you must decide whether you want to linger there for a night, or to put up with what Valence can offer you, or to press on to Avignon.

There is a vast amount to think about, at Lyon, but not a very great deal to *see* except a very handsome modern city with some picturesque old quarters.

With no disparagement to the other hotels (many of which, I doubt not, are excellent), but because it is the one I happen to know, I suggest the Dominion Palace, while admitting that it is not at all 'central.' Perhaps I shall try, next time, the Royal, on Place Bellecour; or the Terminus, which, though beside the principal railway station, is attractively located on the Cours de Verdun — the Saône on its left, crossed by Pont-Kitchener, and the Rhône on its right, crossed by Pont-Gallieni. Both these latter are in that central part of Lyon which lies between the two rivers; while the 'Dominion' lies northeast — over the Rhône by the Pont-Morand and out the Cours Morand.

I'd lunch or dine (as my plan permitted) at Morateur, 3, rue du Président-Carnot — a street which begins near the Pont-Lafayette (over the Rhône) and runs southwest toward the statue of Carnot in the Place de la République. (President Sadi Carnot — whom we specially recalled at

Rochepot — was assassinated at Lyon in 1894.) And if I had two 'good repasts' to enjoy here, I think I'd look up a place that M. Dulac mentions, quoting a local authority on dining as a high art — Le Restaurant Carillon, rue Puits-Gaillot; I don't know it, but I mean to.

As to actual 'sights' to see in Lyon, aside from the beautiful city itself, I think they are not many: the Musée Historique des Tissus, in the Palais du Commerce et de la Bourse, is the principal one for most wayfarers. It is between the two rivers, close to the Pont-Lafayette, over the Rhône. That musée, and the orchids and palms in the greenhouses (the finest in France) of the Parc de la Tête d'Or — near the Dominion Hotel. The distance view from the Tour Métallique, on the heights at the western side of the city, is magnificent, on a clear afternoon. And while on the hill of Fourvière (where the tower is) you may want to see the pilgrimage church and the Hospice de l'Antiquaille on the site of the palace of the prætorian prefects, in which Germanicus was born (the father of Caligula and grandfather of Nero); and also Claudius; and Caracalla.

Many imperial associations has Lyon, and most splendid ones. But there is little here to remind us of them.

I doubt if the average traveller (like you and me) cares to go much farther back, at Lyon, than the introduction of silk-raising and silk-weaving, in the fifteenth century. It is as a silk city that we think of it, chiefly. And two men stand out among the many who have made the history of that industry.

One is Joseph Marie Jacquard, son of a Lyon weaver, who was born here in 1752. He inherited two looms from his father, and started business on his own account, but did not prosper. After the terrible days of the Revolution — which were especially terrible here — Jacquard went to work in a factory, and spent his spare time tinkering with

HÔTEL DE VILLE, LYON
From an old mezzotint

an invention by which a single workman was enabled to produce elaborate fabrics as easily as the plainest web, and by changing the 'cartoons' to make the most different textures on the same looms. In 1803 he was summoned to Paris by Napoleon, and attached to the Conservatoire des Arts et Métiers. Nine years later, there were eleven thousand of his looms in use in France. He died in 1834, having been well rewarded for his contribution to national prosperity.

Thirty years later, the silk industry was gravely threatened by a disease which was ravaging the invaluable worms; and there came hither, in June, 1865, a man who till then had never seen a silkworm — Louis Pasteur — but who, by September of that same year was able to announce results which pointed to the cause of the disease and the prevention of it.

Magnificent Louis Pasteur! To few men who have ever lived has it been given to be such benefactors of their kind. *Never* neglect an opportunity to pay homage to his memory!

Lyon has given the world many great artists, of whose achievements she is justly proud. Philibert Delorme went hence to work on the Palace of Fontainebleau, on the Louvre, on Diane de Poitiers' Anet. Coysevox was from Lyon, who did the tomb of Mazarin (now in the Louvre) and much sculpture for Versailles, and the equestrian figures of Fame and Mercury, made for Marly, but now adorning the pillars of the Tuileries Gardens terrace, at the Place de la Concorde. Facing them, across that grandest square, are the horse-tamers, also from Marly, by Guillaume Coustou, who was a native of Lyon a generation after Coysevox. Meissonier, painter of soldiers and battles, and Puvis de Chavannes of the magnificent murals, are among the others who went from Lyon to distinction in Paris and throughout the world.

But of all the children of Lyon none enjoys a wider fame

than Madame Récamier, born here on December 3, 1777; and whose most recent and most scholarly biography has been written by the most eminent of contemporary citizens of Lyon — Édouard Herriot, Mayor of Lyon during the War, and Premier of France since.

Marie Julie Bernard was the daughter of a pretty, calculating mother and — presumably — of a king's councillor and notary of Lyon. It seems probable that she was, instead, the daughter of Jacques Récamier, to whom she was married, in 1793, when she was fifteen and he was forty-two, and with whom she lived platonically for many long years; the supposition being that he wedded her when he believed himself to be in the shadow of the guillotine — that ceremony being the only one whereby he could leave her his fortune.

Lyon has a notable art museum; and even if you are too hurried a visitor to do any justice to its treasures, I think you would enjoy a glimpse within its lovely garden surrounded by the cloisters of the Benedictine abbey whose buildings now house the collections. Also, I'm sure you would like your recollections of Lyon to include one of the library, which is housed in the fifteenth-century palace of the archbishops, on the west bank of the Saône, beyond Pont de Tilsit — close to the cathedral, of course! The library is a magnificent one, especially rich in manuscripts and fine bindings, and more beautifully installed than almost any other library in France. A 'mental snap-shot' of places like these is a delightful thing to have in that album we call our memory. You may have but a very brief time for a city like Lyon, but that need not keep you from coming away with a few exceedingly fine impressions which will always 'pop to the fore' when you read or hear its name. And that, I believe, is one of the highly legitimate reasons for going a-travelling.

At Vienne you will doubtless want a glimpse of the Temple of Augustus and Livia (one of the two Roman temples left in France), which stands close to your path through the city from north to south, near the Rhône, and about opposite that square tower across the river which was built in 1349 by the first of the Valois kings (Philip VI) to guard what was then the frontier of France. And as you leave the city by the rue d'Avignon, skirting the Public Garden, you may see the arch topped by a tall pyramid which stood in the Roman circus of long ago.

As you come on down the left bank of the Rhône, you pass through (twenty-five miles south of Vienne) the town of Saint-Vallier, with a castle that belonged to the brother of Diane de Poitiers. And if you were loafing along, in no particular hurry, I might suggest that you make a little détour to the east, to Rochetaillé, and the great masonry dam which makes a reservoir for Saint-Étienne and a charming lake for us.

At Tain (four miles south of Saint-Vallier), whose vineyards produce noted wines, there are two suspension bridges across the Rhône, one of them the oldest bridge of its kind in France, built by the builder of France's first railway.

These connect Tain with Tournon on the right bank. And unless you are hurrying to Avignon, I'd cross the river, and proceed for a little way down the other shore. Five miles below Tournon is Châteaubourg, with a castle in which Saint Louis slept on his way to embark, at Aigues-Mortes, on the Seventh Crusade. In those days, and until the end of the nineteenth century, this castle on its commanding rock rose proudly above the Rhône. But that river, like our Mississippi, is subject to changes of course; and one fine day it swung away from Châteaubourg and left it — to the joy of photographers — reflecting itself in a glassy-surfaced 'lone' or dead arm.

About three miles south is Saint-Péray, whose sparkling wines are famous; and above it is the astonishing eagle's nest castle of Crussol with a superb view over the Rhône Valley.

Thence you may recross the Rhône by the Pont de Saint-Péray, into Valence, capital of that Duchy of Valentinois which Louis XII gave to Cæsar Borgia in payment for the nice divorce that Cæsar's papa, Pope Alexander VI, granted Louis — enabling the latter to put away Louis XI's lame daughter Jeanne, and marry the recently widowed Anne de Bretagne. Later, the title of Duchesse de Valentinois was borne by Diane de Poitiers.

Leaving the bridge, you are in avenue Gambetta, with the park Jouvet and the Champ de Mars on your right, and the cathedral and old town on your left.

If you turn left at the beginning of Place de la République (a continuation of avenue Gambetta), you will come, soon, to the curious Maison des Têtes, in the Grande-Rue, behind the cathedral. At number 48 in that street, Napoleon lodged when he was in his first command as Second Lieutenant of Artillery (he being the first Corsican so commissioned) with the regiment of La Fère, in garrison at Valence. He came here in November, 1785, when he was sixteen. The next year he met Caroline Colombier and began his first love affair. He was 'writing' a good deal, then — delightful finalities on Religion, and Patriotism, and pretty nearly everything else. And from here he wrote, in April, 1786: 'The Corsicans have already shaken off the yoke of the Genoese, they can do the same to that of the French.'

He was a long way, yet, from being a Frenchman at heart — that lad who was one day to write, in far exile from France: 'I desire that my ashes shall rest on the banks of the Seine, in the midst of the French people whom I have so greatly loved.'

It is for that homesick boy's sake that I go to Valence, when hereabouts. You may find other reasons.

At the top of Grande-Rue you may turn back toward the cathedral by way of rue Pérollerie, number 7 in which is the Maison Dupré-Latour which has a handsome Renaissance doorway.

South from the Place de la République runs avenue Victor-Hugo, which is the continuation of your route toward Avignon.

Twenty-three miles downstream is Montélimar, which leaves you in no uncertainty as to its claim to celebrity; the road bristles with reminders of its nougat. And of course you'll stop and buy some — even if there are sweets you like better than this, made of honey and nuts; tasty, but rather a foe to dentistry.

At Donzère, eight miles on, a road branches off, east, to Grignan, where Madame de Sévigné died at the château of her idolized daughter, and where she lies buried.

Twenty miles from Donzère is Orange, seat of the famous House of Orange, who, in the Middle Ages, used the Roman Arc de Triomphe built in Tiberius' day as part of a stronghold which they built around it and from the débris of which it was completely cleared only in Napoleon's imperial day.

As you come past it, and down rue Victor-Hugo, keep straight on to rue Saint-Martin; there, turn left, into Place de la République; and at the east end of the *place* take rue Caristie (right) to the Roman theatre, one of the finest constructions of the sort that Antiquity has left to us. More than forty thousand spectators could be accommodated in this auditorium when there was 'a Roman holiday.' The arena was close by, and probably had seats for at least an equal number. There may even have been a circus, with a capacity far greater. Doubtless there were many magnificent baths, and temples galore, and a forum, and palaces and villas. What the Visigoths failed to destroy, of all this, Prince Maurice of Nassau (son of William the Silent, founder of the Dutch Republic, and uncle of William of Orange who became William III of England) completed in the early years of the seventeenth century when he used the Roman remains as his quarry for building new town ramparts.

Maurice incorporated the theatre in his new fortifications. And later on it was filled up with hovels and stables. Very fortunate are we who see it cleared out and restored to use as a national theatre. Performances of the Comédie-Française are given here in August each year.

Now, five miles north of Orange, on the road to Valréas, is a shrine which I once visited, and which I would that many of my readers might also go to see: Sérignan, where Henri Fabre spent his last years.

I wonder if you know a lovable and illuminating book by Percy F. Bicknell, published by the Century Company, called 'The Human Side of Fabre'? Fabre, who 'had the capacity to make chemistry as dramatic as history, and biology as enthralling as a detective story'! Fabre, who was so great that he loved to enthuse the simplest, far better than to astound the erudite.

Child of the soil he was, born (in 1823) of poor and illiterate peasant stock over west of the Tarn Gorges. When he was ten, his family moved to Rodez, where the father tried restaurant-keeping — with scant success. Thence, to Toulouse, with no better luck; and presently to Montpellier, where Henri peddled lemons and worked on the railway between Beaucaire and Nîmes — and competed for a free scholarship at the Primary Normal School of Avignon, where, in the middle of his second year, he was pronounced by his teachers to be 'lazy, backward, and of only moderate intelligence'! However, he 'passed,' got his diploma, and went to teach at Carpentras, for seven hundred francs a year. There, convinced that a little knowledge of chemistry would be of practical use to the budding farmers and manufacturers he was teaching, he inaugurated a course in it; the thing was noised abroad; more pupils came. 'I was,' he wrote later, 'fairly launched on my career. Time and an indomitable will were bound to do the rest.'

Before he was twenty-one, he married a young woman of Carpentras. And though he often had difficulty in collecting his pittance of pay, he welcomed his babies when they began to come.

He seems to have left Carpentras in 1850, to teach for three years at Ajaccio (in Corsica) for eighteen hundred francs a year. It was there that he resolved to devote the rest of his life to the study of nature.

His next move was to the lycée, or academy, at Avignon, where he taught for seventeen years, at a salary of only sixteen hundred francs — even when they 'sat seven at table' in his house.

'No promotion,' says Mr. Bicknell, 'no slightest addition to his pay except as he might occasionally earn it by outside work, and no promise of better things to come or even of a retirement pension or of a pittance to his family in the event of his death, contributed to lessen his anxieties and make him more content with his lot during this period. But Fabre was a born teacher as well as a born naturalist. To teach others while learning himself was his never-failing joy.'

When Pasteur (one year older than Fabre) came down to Avignon to study the silkworm disease, he sought out Fabre. Here is Fabre's account of the visit:

'"I should like," said he, "to see some cocoons. I have never seen any. Could you get me some?"'

'"Nothing easier," I replied. "My landlord deals in cocoons, and he lives next door. Have the goodness to wait a moment and I will fetch what you desire."

'A few steps took me to my neighbor's house, where I filled my pockets with cocoons. Then I hastened back and presented them to the man of science. He took up one and turned it over and over in his hand, examining it curiously, as we should examine a foreign object from the ends of the earth. Finally he held it up to his ear and shook it.

'"It rattles," said he in great surprise. "There's something inside."

'"Certainly," I replied. "The chrysalis."

'"What do you mean — the chrysalis?"

'"I mean the sort of mummy into which the worm changes before turning into a butterfly."

'"And is there one of these things in every cocoon?"

'"To be sure there is, for it is in order to protect the chrysalis that the silkworm spins the cocoon."

'"Ah!"

'Such magnificent assurance greatly impressed me. Utterly ignorant of silkworms . . . Pasteur had come among us to set the silkworm industry on its feet again.'

But he did it, we know.

'He was,' Fabre goes on, about Pasteur, 'also about to revolutionize medicine and hygiene in general. His weapon was the heaven-inspired idea, careless of details and viewing things in their larger aspect. . . . Encouraged by the splendid example of Pasteur holding the cocoon to his ear and shaking it, I have made it a rule to follow the method of ignorance in my study of instinct. . . . I plant myself squarely and determinedly in front of my subject and stay there until I succeed in making it speak.'

In 1870, Fabre was practically forced out of Avignon by the jealousy and superstition of those who resented his teachings because they could not understand them. It was John Stuart Mill (of whom more, anon), with whom he had become acquainted at Avignon, who loaned him three thousand francs wherewith to move to Orange and start life anew. Here he embarked upon his great career as the teacher of all the world, through books.

He had long felt that school textbooks were needlessly stiff and formal and uninteresting. Why, he asked himself, should not young readers be entertained and instructed at the same time, by having their curiosity aroused and their natural eagerness to know more about the world around them gratified? Accordingly he proceeded to tell them 'stories,' as he called his simple and vivid sketches about plants and animals, the sun and the planets, the air we breathe, the food we eat, the water we drink, and the clothes we wear.

At Orange he lived from 1870 to 1879. While here, death took from him his beloved son and co-worker Jules, 'a youth of exceptional gifts and the delight of his father's heart.'

In a dedicatory note to his 'Souvenirs,' Fabre wrote:

'*To my son Jules.* Dear child, my ardently devoted collaborator in the study of insects, my clear-eyed assistant in botanical research, it was for your sake that I began to write these volumes, in memory of you I have gone on with the work, and in the bitterness of my bereavement I shall still go on. . . . Fortified as I am by my indomitable faith in a Beyond, the book seems to me to carry on the studies that we once pursued together.'

At length, when he was fifty-six, he came to haven in a home of his own.

'I have at last what I have been longing for, a patch of ground, not large by any means, but walled in and secure from the annoyances of the public highway — an aban-

doned, barren, sun-scorched patch of ground, but hospitable to thistles and to wasps and bees and other gauzy-
winged insects. Here, without fear of interruption from
passers-by, I can put my questions to the digger-wasp and
the sand-wasp and devote myself to that difficult intercourse in which question and answer take the form of experiment. Here, with no need of distant excursions, which
take up so much time, with no fatiguing tramps that leave
the attention less alert than it should be, I can plan my
methods of attack, lay my ambuscades, and watch the results from day to day and from hour to hour. . . . For forty
years I have contended with indomitable courage against
the petty ills of life and now at last the laboratory so ardently desired has come to me.'

Here he lived for thirty-five years. And here, in the village churchyard, he lies beneath the epitaph he himself
composed:

'Those whom we think to have passed away are but gone
before. This is by no means the end, but the threshold of a
higher life.'

Fifteen miles from Orange is Avignon, where I hope you
may be going to stop for several days whilst you explore the
vicinity — it being one of the greatest centres in France for
one-day excursions of the most extraordinary interest, in
every direction.

I hope you will not class me as a Philistine if I sing some
praises of the new, beautiful, and supremely comfortable
Dominion Hotel. I think you know that I like quaint,
'characteristic' small inns, if they are good. There may
be many such in the Rhône Valley, but I have not found
them. The only one I know is the Hôtel du Nord, at
Arles — of which, more anon. And I cannot find that I
think less enthusiastically of Petrarch and Laura, of

Rienzi and the Colonna, of Queen Joanna and Saint Catherine, because I have slept in a room 'done' charmingly in *toile de Jouy*, and dined excellently well on a handsome terrace. In fact, I find myself appreciatively murmuring Browning's lines:

'Nor soul helps flesh more, now, than flesh helps soul.'

You may prefer Hôtel de l'Europe, either because it is less expensive or less modern. In any case, I'm sure you will enjoy settling yourself for several nights.

Entering Avignon by the Porte Saint-Lazare, turn to your left and follow the line of the ramparts to Porte de la République; then, turn up Cours de la République to boulevard Raspail, for the Dominion. For the Europe, take the right-hand turn on entering by Porte Saint-Lazare, and follow the boulevard to Place Crillon, above the Suspension Bridge.

Among the books you should have read coming to Provence (and will re-read with interest tenfold multiplied after your return home) is Sir Theodore Andrea Cook's classic 'Old Provence.' To this you may add a newer work, by E. I. Robson, called 'A Wayfarer in Provence' — he being likewise the 'Wayfarer' on the Loire; and Thomas Okey's 'Avignon' in the series on Mediæval Towns. Many, many others there are which the ardent lover of books will re-read before he comes and then read again after he has seen. But 'travelling light' and carrying books are far from synonymous — as I know through sad experience which does *not* teach me wisdom! — and in the event that your copy of 'Old Provence' has been left at home, I'll cull for you (knowing that these little books of mine are *not* left at home, because they are meant for travelling companions and reminders of all there is, else, to read) more than a little of Sir Theodore's work.

'There are some spots,' he says, 'in great and ancient cities of the world, which seem to resume within themselves the history, not merely of the racial centre which they represent, but of all those centuries which saw their greatest splendor. Such are the Palatine of the Cæsars, or the Vatican of the Popes, or the Kremlin of the Tsars; and such is Avignon. Within that mighty mass of architecture on the Rocher des Doms, which was palace, fortress, shrine in one, seven Popes centralized the attention of Christian and political Europe for almost a century. . . . Behind its huge buttresses have been received . . . the envoys of the Khan of Tartary [not Marco Polo's Kubla Khan, but a later] and of the Emperor of Constantinople . . . here the great tribune Rienzi chafed in his prison; here Queen Jeanne of Naples faced her accusers and bought her pardon at a price; here Urban V excommunicated Bertrand du Guesclin, and patched up peace between England and France.'

Yes — and here Petrarch came and went; hither came Sainte Catherine of Siena, and many another on whom we love to think.

Old (very old!) maps show that centuries ago the usual current of the Rhône was closer to the right (or west) bank of the river than it is to-day, and that the great rock of Avignon reared its escarpments above a sandy bank of shallow waters. The people living on the rock belonged now to one overlord and now to another (they even had a Republic for a while, modelled on that of Florence); but of those times few vestiges are left, and not many memories.

If you reach Avignon in time to permit a stroll before dinner, I suggest your going up rue de la République, through Place Georges Clemenceau and Place du Palais (with the Popes' Palace on your right), to the Promenade du Rocher des Doms, and lingering there for a while; then going back toward your hotel by the Boulevard du Rhône, looking over toward Villeneuve-lès-Avignon — a superb panorama, telling a great story!

Whether you will be most absorbed by the scenic splendor or by the remains of the old 'pont d'Avignon,' I cannot guess. Perhaps with both!

Only four arches of the famous bridge remain; there once were twenty-two. It was built in 1177–88, when Philippe-Auguste was King of France, and Henry II of England was still alive.

Those were the days of the Republic at Avignon. And the legend of Saint Benedict, or Bénézet, and the building, is so charmingly naïve that I'm sure you will be glad to recall it.

Bénézet, according to this, was a little shepherd boy of twelve who kept his mother's flocks, and had never seen the Rhône when the word of Christ came to him to build a bridge over it at Avignon, and an angel, in the guise of a pilgrim, appeared to lead him.

The Bishop was preaching to his flock, when Bénézet arrived — in that Church of Notre-Dame des Doms beside which the Popes' Palace was to rise much more than a century later. And the little shepherd from the hills stood in front of the pulpit, and in a clear voice said, 'Listen to me, all of you! Christ hath sent me to you that I may build a bridge over the Rhône.'

Thereat the Bishop was very angry and ordered the little ragamuffin dragged off and severely punished.

To the officer of the guard, Bénézet repeated what he had said to the Bishop and the people.

'What!' cried the officer. 'Can a little beggar boy do what neither God nor Saint Peter nor the Emperor Charlemagne has ever been able to accomplish? If you can move this stone and carry it to the river, I may, perhaps, believe that God hath sent you.'

Now, the stone was a fragment of a Roman building that the Saracens had destroyed, and so heavy that thirty men could not budge it. But Bénézet knelt down by it and prayed, then rose and seized it as it were a pebble, and carried it to the bank of the Rhône where the foundations of the first arch were to be laid.

Then the officer and the people worshipped him; the first day five thousand pieces of gold were gathered, and work began at once. Four years before the bridge was finished, Bénézet died, and was buried in the chapel on the bridge itself.

The building was probably done by that Brotherhood of Bridge-Builders who carried on for many centuries in many lands the old Roman connection between bridges and religion, which the Christian Church adopted from its pagan predecessor: the title of the head of the Church being that of Pontifex Maximus, or Head Bridge-Builder.

In the Middle Ages (perhaps earlier) these Brothers wore a white dress with two arches of a bridge in red upon their breast, and above them a cross.

You may like to picture them at work on the bridge; and burying Bénézet in the chapel. You may like to see Louis VIII marching against Avignon for her Albigensian heresy, demanding passage across the bridge and when this was refused settling down to starve her into submission.

Is it perfectly clear to you why the Popes came to Avignon? You have read a lot about it, doubtless; but if I may venture to judge you by myself, nothing makes you realize as travel does how vague a good many of your impressions have been. 'The Popes at Avignon? Oh, yes — certainly!' we murmur, when we are many leagues away; and it seems to suffice. But when we stand at Avignon, that great palace on one hand, and across the river that bastide of the French kings under whose protection we had sort of imagined the exiled Popes to be! Well — ! Could you explain it all, very clearly, to a fellow traveller of ten or twelve (let's say) who might ask you about it?

If you were home, where your books are — yes, of course! But on the terrace at Avignon? Perhaps I may help you. As I write these lines I am expecting to be, before they are published, again in Avignon, with a dear comrade of ten and one of twelve. And *if* they ask me (but *only* 'if'!) how came the Popes to Avignon, I shall tell them something like *this:*

'Well, it all sounds pretty much like a good many people we know — that everybody knows; there's nothing about it that's very "different" or far away or hard to understand.

'Popes have a kind of power, but not like that they used to have; they used to have so much that whoever "stood in with them" got about what he wanted, and whoever fell out with them was out o' luck. Popes are elected, you know, like Presidents. And everybody who wanted things to go *his* way, tried to get a Pope elected who would be "for" him and against his enemies or competitors. I say "everybody" not because people voted for the Popes — only cardinals vote for them — but I mean all those who were kings or emperors or others who had plans that they wanted the Pope to help them with.

'The French Kings had been getting the Popes to do a lot for them, and the other countries were "sore" about it. But by and by there was a Pope elected that the French King *thought* he could "boss" — but found he couldn't; so he got some more men who were "sore" against that Pope, and they made the Pope a prisoner and he was so furious that pretty soon he died — not in prison, but in his own Vatican where nobody paid any attention to what he wanted. There wasn't anybody strong enough to help him.

'After that, the French King was able to get a Frenchman elected Pope; and that Frenchman thought it would be safer and easier to be Pope if he came here to Avignon, instead of staying in Rome where there wasn't any real government and everybody fought everybody else.

'Avignon wasn't in France — France ended at the opposite side of the river. This side belonged to the King of Naples — who was French. You know the story that's always cropping up — in London, at the Savoy; in France wherever we find Saint Louis and his Queen Marguerite; in Naples — about the four sisters who all became queens. Well, they lived around here when they were girls — in Provence. And Beatrice, who was the oldest and was the Queen of Naples, married to Saint Louis' brother, Charles of Anjou, inherited Provence, when her father died; so it belonged to the Kings of Naples for a while.

'Then there came a Queen of Naples, named Joanna, who has a story very much like Mary, Queen of Scots; and Joanna sold Avignon to the Pope. The Popes were all Frenchmen for a while, and they stayed here. Then Saint Catherine of Siena came, and persuaded the Pope that was here then to go back to Rome. But Avignon belonged to the Popes until the French Revolution — they owned it for about four hundred and fifty years.

'But though the French Kings had a lot to say about what the French Popes did, there was always a chance that they might disagree, or a Pope might be elected who was not French. So the French Kings kept their end of Bénézet's bridge well defended.'

After your visit to the terrace of Rocher des Doms, and your walk back along the boulevards, and dinner (at which you should pay your respects to Châteauneuf-du-Pape, the celebrated local wine, and to the superb fruits and vegetables for which this district is noted), I think you'll enjoy an hour or so at one of the cafés along cours or rue de la République or the Place Clemenceau.

In the morning, when you go to visit the palace, bear in mind that there are two 'rounds' of it, one of which you must (in all probability) join: 9 o'clock, and 10.30. Should you be too late for the 10.30, you may have no other opportunity until 2.30. I have known travellers to miss seeing the palace within, because they arrived just too late to join a group going through, and were unable or unwilling to wait for the next one. Visiting hours may change. Ask your hotel concierge.

The first Pope resident at Avignon was that Bishop of Bordeaux who became Clement V, and joined with Philip IV of France (Philippe le Bel) in condemning the Knights Templars and seizing their wealth. When Jacques de Molay, the Templars' head, stood at the stake on the Île de la Cité, Paris, in March, 1314, he said: 'God will avenge our death. Woe will come ere long to those who condemn us.'

A month later, Clement V was dead; and in November of that year the French King was called to his accounting.

There was no Pope for more than two years. Then came John of Cahors, who had been Bishop of Avignon. John continued to live in the Bishop's Palace, but he projected the great Papal Palace and collected a good deal of the money to build it.

Benedict XII who was the chief builder of the palace was Pope from 1334 to 1342.

Then came Clement VI (also for eight years) whose tomb you may have seen at La Chaise Dieu. It was he before whom Queen Joanna of Naples was tried for the murder of her first husband, and acquitted. He who bought Avignon from her. He before whom Rienzi and Petrarch appeared. During his pontificate King John came to the throne of France and soon afterwards paid a visit to his palace at

Villeneuve, across the river, when there were splendid fêtes given — water-festivals on the Rhône, pageants and dances on the island of Barthelasse over which Bénézet's bridge led from the Pope's city to the King's. It was probably at this time that the nursery rhyme originated which so many millions of children have sung since. Only, instead of '*sur le pont d'Avignon*,' as we now sing it, it was probably '*sous le pont*' (*beneath* the bridge, not *on* it) that the dancing was done.

I doubt if you care to recall all the Popes of Avignon, much less all that happened here under them. But I think you will wish to see beautiful, fascinating young Queen Joanna pleading her cause before Clement VI, in the great audience hall and winning her vindication from him, to the great rage (no doubt) of her accusers from Hungary who charged her with complicity in the murder of her husband who was her co-heir to the throne of Naples.

And I think you will wish to be conscious of Rienzi coming here, after his first downfall and absence from Rome, to be thrown into a dungeon and sentenced to death because he had said it was his mission to reinstate the Pope at Rome and establish the Emperor there at the same time. And to recall that Petrarch, who was an ardent advocate of Rienzi's, couldn't help resenting Rienzi's deliverance from death being attributed to his being a poet. 'This man,' said Petrarch, 'has never that I know written a single line.'

And I dare say you will not wish to leave the palace without trying to visualize there Catherine of Siena pleading with the Holy Father to return to Rome — and persuading him to do it.

Don't neglect the Cathedral of Avignon (either before you visit the palace or after you leave it), 'for more than seventy years the premier church of Christendom' — its site scarcely surpassed by that of any other cathedral.

And it may be that you would be sorry to leave Avignon without having seen that dining-room of the Hôtel du Louvre which is said to have been an old hall of the Templars, in the thirteenth century. (It is on rue Saint-Agricol which runs from rue de la République toward the Rhône just south of Place Clemenceau.)

I would certainly see something of the walls of Avignon from their base, outside, looking up. And I can tell you of a little pilgrimage I made on my first visit to Avignon which gave me profound satisfaction — and that was to the resting-place of John Stuart Mill and his wife, in Avignon cemetery.

Do you know their story?

She was a woman of brilliant mind and frail, suffering body, the wife of a worthy but unintellectual wholesale druggist in London, named Taylor, and the mother of several children. For twenty years she was, with her husband's full consent, regularly visited by Mill, who credited her with an enormous influence on his thought and writings, and who loved her with a great devotion. It was *her* housemaid who threw into the fire the manuscript of Carlyle's 'French Revolution,' which Carlyle had loaned to Mill to read, and Mill had taken — as he took everything that interested him — to Mrs. Taylor. And Carlyle, to save some tongue-buzzing for his friends, let his own housemaid carry the blame.

In 1851, Mrs. Taylor, then a widow, married Mill, and they accomplished much together. He was, you doubtless know, one of the first great philosophical and political thinkers to champion women's suffrage.

In 1858 the East India Company, for which he had worked for thirty-six years, was dissolved, and Mill retired with a pension of £1500. Thereupon he and Mrs. Mill set out upon a long-dreamed-of Continental tour. But her

frail health was unequal to the strain of journeying as it
was then done; and she died here at Avignon.

So great was his sorrow that thereafter he seldom left her
grave. He rented a little villa from whose windows he
could look out on her resting-place, and there, with her
daughter Helen, he established himself for his remaining
years, regarding that as his home and returning to London
only when obliged to.

'His little cottage,' says Minto, 'was filled with books
and newspapers; the beautiful country round it furnished
him with a variety of walks; he read, wrote, discussed,
walked, botanized. He was extremely fond of music, and
was himself a fair pianist. His stepdaughter, Miss Taylor,
was his constant companion after his wife's death.

'"Helen," he wrote to an old colleague in the India
House, "has carried out her long-cherished scheme (about
which she tells me she consulted you) of a 'vibratory' for
me, and has made a pleasant covered walk, some thirty
feet long, where I can vibrate in cold or rainy weather. The
terrace, you must know, as it goes round two sides of the
house, has got itself dubbed the 'semi-circumgyratory.' In
addition to this, Helen has built me a herbarium, a little
room fitted up with closets for my plants, shelves for my
botanical books, and a great table whereon to manipulate
them all. Thus, you see, with my herbarium, my vibratory,
and my circumgyratory, I am in clover; and you may imagine with what scorn I think of the House of Commons,
which, comfortable club as it is said to be, could offer me
none of these comforts, or, more perfectly speaking, these
necessaries of life."'

He died at Avignon on the 8th of May, 1873, and shares
the grave of his loved companion.

I went from the grave to the cottage, and while standing
at a respectful distance from the latter was most courteously

bidden within by one of the household who came out to greet me.

You may not care as much as I do for recalling Fabre and Pasteur and Mill, in the shadow of the Papal Palace. But in case you *do* —— !

Now, then —— ! In no case must you miss the King's bastide across the river, Villeneuve-lès-Avignon, where picturesque poverty has made itself a roosting-place in the ruins of the Chartreuse which was so dear to Pope Clement VI, and decaying palaces look like old cronies of whose youth and belleship we hear tales that are hard to believe.

Villeneuve-lès-Avignon comes in the circuit that most visitors make from Avignon to Uzès, Nîmes, and the Pont-du-Gard.

There are four circular tours from Avignon two or more of which most visitors make, whether by private motor or by the autocars of the P. L. and M. railway. Three of them at least, I would that every one might take. The Vaison–Orange circuit may be missed by those who have seen Orange en route to Avignon; its other points are for rather special students of Roman antiquities and have not the general interest of Arles, Les Baux, and other places.

The Arles–Les Baux Circuit, covering sixty miles, takes all day (over ten hours) by autocar, and gives a very fair amount of time for sight-seeing: three and a half hours at Arles, two at Les Baux.

The Nîmes–Pont-du-Gard circuit is seventy-seven miles, takes ten hours, gives four hours at Nîmes and an hour at the Pont-du-Gard.

Each of these runs daily from Avignon between mid-March and late September.

Thrice a week there is the longer circuit to Tarascon, Saint-Gilles, Aigues-Mortes, Les Saintes-Maries, and Arles — a hundred and twenty-four miles, in ten hours.

None of them includes Vaucluse.

If you have your own car, or hire one to serve your will at Avignon; and if four days are more than you can spend there, I suggest this disposal of your time:

After your morning in Avignon, and luncheon there, give that afternoon to Vaucluse (twenty miles from Avignon) and thence, through Saint-Rémy, to Les Baux, and back to Avignon for dinner.

Then, for a long day see Villeneuve-lès-Avignon, the Pont-du-Gard, Nîmes, Aigues-Mortes, Les Saintes-Maries, Saint-Gilles, and back by way of Beaucaire and Tarascon — but not making your stop, then, at Tarascon.

Presuming that you are en route to Nice or thereabouts, you may well take Tarascon as you go, and Arles; then, on to Aix-en-Provence for the night, or to Marseilles if you prefer.

Few travellers care to make the journey (by motor) between Avignon and Cannes or Nice in a single day — not that it can't be done (though it's more than two hundred miles), but that there is so much en route to see. And if you are making a night stop en route, Aix is a good place to do it, and leaves a fair time for Arles. Should Marseilles be your choice for the night, you may have a glimpse of Martigues on your way to it.

The reason I do not include Les Baux in this day is that I think it makes the day a bit too 'stiff'; and I know of my own experience how practicable and delightful that half-day motor tour from Avignon to Vaucluse and Les Baux may be.

The 'higher critics' now believe that the note in Petrarch's copy of Virgil, which says that Laure 'first appeared to my eyes ... in the Church of Santa Clara at Avignon,' was written after Petrarch's death, by his secretary, and is a pious if not a poetic fiction. Some of them believe he saw her first, and always, in this 'closed valley' called Vaucluse of which Sir Theodore Cook says:

'The syllables of Petrarch and the sighs of Laura are on every breeze. Theirs are the images reflected in the crystal surface of that mysterious pool which wells from the deep heart of the mountain and pours forth its everlasting streams through the cascades of the young river toward the village of Vaucluse. It is a symbol of love and life; of love deep-seated in the elements that make the world, rising with strength irresistible toward the sunlight; foaming through the first years of youth and ardor, flowing at last with ordered stillness, turning the water-wheels of traffic and of commerce, but never losing the heaven-blue of its source, the undying, fundamental power that shapes and sways the universe.'

Sir Theodore does not believe that Laura was married. He thinks she lived all her life here in this valley; that she was not rich, and came of no famous family.

'Petrarch,' he says, 'first met her at six in the morning on a Good Friday, when he was twenty-three (1327). His heart took fire like tinder as her golden hair was twisted by the breezes into a thousand pretty knots, while she walked about in the grass and talked, wearing a green dress with violets at her bosom.'

Isn't that a charming picture?

'The little that I am,' wrote the Father of the Renaissance, 'she made me. Whatever reputation or glory be mine would never have come to me if the weak seedling of virtue placed by nature in my heart had not grown up and blossomed in that noble love of hers. . . . She drew me from the society of the base; she guided me in all my ways; she spurred my tiring Muse, and roused my fainting spirit.'

As you make your way by small roads from Vaucluse to-

ward Saint-Rémy, you will doubtless wish to stop at Maillane, where Mistral was born and lies buried.

How much Mistral is read by English-speaking readers, I
do not know. But I doubt if many of us know his books at
all intimately — though we probably all know, more or less
vaguely, on what his fame is founded. If we do not know
this, we shall feel almost as strange in Provence as a traveller would feel in Warwickshire who did not know that
Shakespeare wrote for the stage.

Mistral is adored in Provence, not only for what his own
poems do to set forth the beauty of Provençal scenery and
humanity and folklore, but for what he accomplished as the
greatest of a group of writers who banded together (in 1854)
to revive the Provençal dialect, to write in it and make it
read, and to make the history, the lore, the life of Provence
cherished throughout the province and familiar to the world
beyond.

The greatest of Mistral's poems and the one of which we
should be most conscious on our journeyings hereabouts is
'Mireio,' the simplest sort of a tale of a rich girl kept by her
ambitious parents from her poor lover. Mireille goes to the
Church of Les Saintes-Maries to pray for their aid, but has
exhausted her strength, and she dies. But into this simple
web Mistral has woven a rich tapestry of Provençal
scenery, character, customs, legends, that makes it an
epitome of what an ardent poet of Provence desired the
world to feel about the land of his nativity.

Gounod, when writing music for the opera 'Mireille,'
lived at Saint-Rémy; and halfway between Maillane and
Saint-Rémy is the big farm of Mireille's parents.

At Glanum, near the little town of Saint-Rémy, was the
place Julius Cæsar chose to set up 'the earliest Triumphal
Arch in existence outside Italy,' to commemorate the surrender of Vercingetorix at Alésia. Near this, is the beauti-

ful monument usually called 'the Mausoleum,' because it was appropriated to that use some time after Cæsar's day, but erected by him to the memory of his aunt's husband Marius, on the spot where Marius had had his camp when he planned his victorious campaign against the Barbarians who were threatening again to march against Rome, in 102 B.C. Note, on the north side of the arch, Julius Cæsar with his hand on his tall captive Vercingetorix; and on the southeast, Vercingetorix chained, and beside him Gallia, weeping.

Seven miles from Saint-Rémy you come to Les Baux of which, says Sir Theodore (still our guide! with each move we make I consult some six or eight or ten others, but come back to his 'Old Provence' as the meatiest and best), 'we shall never know either the real origin or the primeval glories. But it is the tomb of many mighty memories, of warriors . . . who traced their descent and took their arms (the star with sixteen rays) from that Balthasar, the wise King of the East, who came with his two comrades to worship the infant Christ in Bethlehem.

'It is a squalid little village that nestles to-day in the centre of the old robber-stronghold "like a rat in the heart of a dead princess," feeding, apparently, on "Gaulish tibias, skulls of Roman soldiers, dead cats of the Stone Period, and a miscellaneous assortment of rusty iron"; . . . a confusion of ruins . . . a mediæval Pompeii, a Herculaneum without its lava, set among the scarred boulders of the Alpilles, in a melancholy landscape all of cinder-gray, as might be imagined in some far-off and extinct planet of the frozen interstellar space . . . its ruins have an effect of nightmare exaggeration even in broad daylight. Huge masses of grey stone lie scattered here and there, indistinguishable from the thick walls and towers which were themselves hewn deep within the living rock. Staircases wind upwards to end in

gaping caverns. Cellars yawn hungrily for food beneath.
The shattered columns tremble on the verge of shaking
walls. The fierce wind of Provence seems to have revelled
in its task of utterly demolishing what was left; for the walls
and rocks are honeycombed and worn so deep with the fury
of the blast that the very earth seems ready to give up its
dead through every crack and crevice in its wounded surface.'

Now, as for me, both times that I have been at Les Baux
have been in the month of May, in rather late afternoon,
when only zephyrs were blowing, and all the place and
country round about was full of golden light; and *thus* my
every thought of it persists in being — just as Henry
James's persisted in being full of rain.

This is one reason why I hesitate to indulge in much
description in a little book of this sort — there is always the
very great likelihood that the weather or the light or the
flora or fauna or the costumes or customs or something-or-
other may have been entirely different when I saw them
from what they are when you're seeing them, book in
hand!

Nevertheless, Sir Theodore's descriptive writing in his
chapter on Les Baux is so rich in fine pictures that it stirs
my admiration, greatly, and I know I cannot do better for
you than give you more of it.

He is describing your approach from Saint-Rémy:

'Above the rocky amphitheatre from which the road
seems to have emerged, the silver line of the Rhône shows
like a glittering thread in the morning sunlight, just where
the elephants of Hannibal crossed it so long ago, just where
Nicolette first saw Aucassin coming downwards from the
castle gate. Through towering walls of white, a way has
been cut for the carriage road sheer down into the limestone, and quarries begin to gape on every side, until sud-

denly upon the right a little slip of green valley pushes its way into this rocky desolation, and from some hidden building in it a bell rings slowly, like the dirge for a dead world that has already turned to stone.'

I shall not pretend to you that I find myself much interested in the mediæval history of Les Baux and its lords, as Sir Theodore has so painstakingly written it. There is, in truth, none of it with which I feel acquainted, nor to become acquainted with which I am much moved, until we come to that Count Raymond Bérenger (the Fourth of that name) and his four daughters, each of whom became a queen. How much of their time those up-and-coming damsels spent here, I do not know; but as it was one of the possessions of their father, I dare say they had some associations with Les Baux, and I can imagine them here.

Beatrice, the eldest, who married Charles of Anjou, younger brother of her sister Marguerite's husband (Louis IX of France), inherited Provence; Charles bought Les Baux and thus it came, with Provence, to their great-great-granddaughter, Joanna I of Naples and Provence, whom we met at Avignon, before the Pope, and shall meet many other places hereabouts. Joanna is, I think, a fairly vivid person in my mind, and I could visualize her here if any one told a definite story of her at Les Baux; but if any one does I haven't found it.

Joanna had four husbands (one more than Mary, Queen of Scots, whose story hers rather resembles), yet left no child, and bequeathed her territories to one of the sons of King John of France. Of these there was Charles who became King Charles V; and Philip who became Duke of Burgundy; and John, the splendid Duke of Berri; and Louis, Duke of Anjou. Louis got Joanna's possessions; and thus they descended to his grandson, good King René, the father of Margaret of Anjou, and the ancestor of all the

Guises and of Marie-Antoinette, and the late Emperor Francis Joseph, and countless personages more.

René spent a good deal of time here, and is the most realizable of Les Baux's ghosts. But if he had any enjoyment, in this castle on a crag, in writing and painting and like pursuits, he had need of the solace — poor old man! — for in the last decade of his life, his son, the Duke of Calabria, died of poison at Barcelona; his daughter Margaret was a prisoner and her young son was dead at their field of defeat, Tewkesbury; these were but outstanding ones among his sorrows.

The year after René's death, Louis XI added Provence to the kingdom of France.

Sir Theodore says that he likes to 'leave Les Baux with the memory of Alexandre Dumas, who leaned over its escarpment and looked out along the plain for those pale hedgerows that the Provençal farmers made out of the bones of Marius' battles. He wondered at the little church, as you will wonder too, for it is the only building with any pretence to being weather-tight in the whole place. Its charming entrance, its altar for the sheep-shearers, its dark and massive arches, its little presentment of the Holy Maries in their boat — all are in sombre keeping with these silent ruins. Dumas, I regret to say, took away with him the little wooden figure of a saint; but it caused him such pangs of conscience that he said before it, when he got back to Arles, one of the heartiest prayers he had offered for many a long day, and maybe he has long ago atoned for a theft which was a loss to no one. For as he entered the little, cold, dark building, he heard a sound of sorrow at the eastern end. Upon an open bier, before the high altar, lay the dead body of a little girl. Her two tiny sisters knelt on either side. Her mother sat crying in a corner, and continued sobbing after the good Alexandre had thrown her his whole purse. Her little brother tried to toll the bell for a service at which no priest was present. A dozen or so of beggars had looked in to see the sight. They comprised the whole population of Les Baux.'

Now, for that long day which you're to start with crossing the bridge to Villeneuve-lès-Avignon, and going thence to the Pont-du-Gard!

About fifteen miles west of the Rhône is this magnificent fragment of an aqueduct that carried good spring water for more than twenty-five miles, from the Eure at Uzès to the Roman baths and public buildings of Nemausus — which we call Nîmes. This was built about 19 B.C. probably by Agrippa, son-in-law of Augustus, and there is nothing about it to suggest that it may not endure for another two thousand years, or more.

The lowest arches, six in number, support a second row of eleven smaller arches which in turn hold up thirty-five others that are smaller still. The enormous blocks of golden-yellow stone, quarried near by, are fitted together without cement, and form incomparably the finest Roman aqueduct not only in Provence, but in the world. And to get the full glory of the splendid thing you must see it from down in the gorge it spans, so you can glimpse blue sky through its fifty-two golden arches.

Then, on you go, fourteen miles, to Nîmes, which you will find one of the most beautiful small cities you have ever seen. She is a little sister of Lyon, in the silk industry and in her favor with Roman emperors. But Nîmes retains, better than any other city of France, the souvenirs of her imperial past; yet she does not live on them — so to speak; she is far from being one of those who rely on ancestors and ancient prestige, to press their claims to consideration. She takes dignified, elegant care of her heirlooms, but seems to wear them with a consciousness of deserving them. I like Nîmes. I wish some one would build a good hotel there.

You will enter by rue d'Avignon, leading toward the Porte d'Auguste which was the Arles gate in the old Roman wall.

If you turn to your left after you have passed the Protestant Temple (Nîmes has had many Protestants, since 1533, and much religious warfare), you will reach rue Crémieux which will take you to the Maison Carrée, built under Augustus, probably in the year one of our era, and dedicated to the 'Princes of the Imperial Youth,' those grandsons whom the Emperor had adopted as his heirs: Caius and Lucius, sons of Julia and Agrippa. No sooner were these youths consuls-elect than their grandfather sent them abroad to the government of provinces and the conduct of armies. And Caius died in Lycia, Lucius at Massilia (Marseilles), so Augustus had to find an heir in their stepfather who was also his stepson — Tiberius.

It is said that Colbert wished to have the Maison Carrée taken down and reërected in the park at Versailles; but the nearest that Paris or its neighborhood comes to enjoying this classic beauty is in the inspiration it lent to the Church of the Madeleine.

This little building is not only the most perfect example of Greek architecture that is left to us anywhere in the provinces of the Roman Empire, but in the opinion of many is 'the finest outside Hellenic territories, and one of the most elegant in the Roman world.'

It now houses a museum of antiquities.

South of the theatre, on the opposite side of the Place de la Comédie, is the beginning of rue des Chassaintes, leading to the Rond Point in boulevard Jean Jaurès, a handsome thoroughfare, long, wide, and straight, and beautifully planted.

Here, turn north (right) toward the Jardin de la Fontaine, one of the most beautiful public gardens in France, not surpassed (I think) by the Luxembourg or the Tuileries: in *size*, of course! but not in elegance, and certainly not in survivals of ancient splendors.

The fountain, which may have been a prime attraction of this site to the water-loving Romans, flows from beneath Mont Cavalier (on your right) into a series of basins which the water-gardening of the Romans must have used with fine effect — to judge from the vestiges that remain; notably the steps in hemicycle, which are not now visible except when the basin is almost dry.

The Temple of Nemausus and Diana, on your left as you enter, was 'constructed, with its marble columns, its statues, and all its ornaments, by the munificence of the Emperor Augustus' in B.C. 24, eight years before he built the town walls — including the Porte d'Auguste. It is on the site of a far older shrine to the fountain-god, set up by the Celtic tribes — Sir Theodore Cook says — and close to it has been found an altar to Isis. The Roman baths here were of great magnificence and great extent.

The bath was one of the most important functions in a Roman's day, and was no solitary ablution such as it has become with us, but a social and generally recreative institution. If you didn't take frequent baths in those days, you *certainly* were not 'in the swim.'

Now, drive down boulevard Jean Jaurès as far as rue de l'Hôtel-Dieu, and when you have reached the Hôtel-Dieu, turn, left, toward the arena, or amphitheatre, which probably dates from about 100 A.D., a few years after the completion of the Colosseum at Rome.

This magnificent structure has been cleared of 'barnacles' and again serves as an arena, seating some twenty-four thousand spectators for bull-fights and a wide variety of other attractions.

North of the arena and facing it is Durand's Restaurant, which has some reputation in the Midi, but I am not able to report more enthusiastically on it than to say that it is the best place in Nîmes that I *know*. Our Blue Guide speaks well of the cooking at Hôtel du Midi, in Square de la Couronne — to reach which you would skirt the *south* side of the arena, follow the esplanade, pass the Hôtel Luxembourg (reckoned the best at Nîmes), and pay your respects to the memory of Alphonse Daudet at his statue (reminding you that Nîmes gave him to the world), then come to Hôtel du Midi, which must have reformed since I knew it in 1914. I am a hopeful person; I shall try it again.

Wherever you lunch, don't be too slow about it. But if you love 'my Lady Nicotine,' remember that Nicot, who introduced tobacco into France, was born here.

Another child of Nîmes was François Guizot, who was born in 1787, of Protestant parents who could not, because of their faith, be publicly or legally married, but only by a private ceremony. When François was in his seventh year, his father perished on the guillotine at Nîmes, and the little boy was taken to Geneva, by his mother, to be educated. She is said to have been 'a living type of the Huguenots of the sixteenth century' — that mother who formed the character of her illustrious son and shared every vicissitude of his life — 'stern in her principles of her faith, immovable in her convictions and her sense of duty.'

In the days of her son's power, 'her simple figure, always clad in deep mourning for her martyred husband, was not absent from the splendid circle of his political friends. In the days of his exile in 1848 she followed him to London, and there at a very advanced age closed her life and was buried at Kensal Green.'

Guizot himself lived to an advanced age (eighty-seven), his mental vigor and activity unimpaired to the end. It was

AMPHITHEATRE AT NÎMES
From a print published in 1833

in those last years that his lessons to his grandchildren, on the History of France, resulted in the work by which many of us best know him.

Your way out of Nîmes is by rue de Montpellier, which begins at the Place des Arènes and runs southwest toward boulevard Jean Jaurès. Just as it leaves the Hôtel-Dieu, Place Montcalm reminds you that the defender of Quebec came from hereabouts—between Nîmes and Aigues-Mortes.

Aigues-Mortes is twenty-five miles from Nîmes, but they are quickly covered. The author of 'Old Provence,' writing in the early years of this century, found the road inferior to the railway; but I can testify that in 1926 it was much better than most of the roads in Provence.

There is food for thought in the fact that Saint Louis, though he was married to a daughter of Provence, had to buy the site you are now approaching, in order to have a Mediterranean harbor for his Crusading fleet. Beatrice, his sister-in-law, would let him use her Marseilles harbor for the occasion. But he had need, he thought, of another concerning which there could be no discussion; so he bought this swamp, in 1248, from the Abbot of Psalmodi, a monastery near by; and in the summer of that year he came hither with all the flower of his chivalry. His young wife Marguerite was with him; and his two brothers — Charles of Anjou, not yet King of Naples, and Robert of Artois, who was to die in Egypt; and a great company of noble lords. For six weeks the camp was pitched here; and then, on the 20th of August, the great fleet put slowly out to sea, the lion of Saint Mark floating at some mastheads, the leopard of England at others, and at many the fleur-de-lys of France; and from one ship and another came the deep-throated prayer-hymn, 'Veni, Creator Spiritus,' while the winds 'thundered in the canvas,' as Joinville tells us, and drove the fleet from sight of land.

More than twenty years later, Saint Louis again sailed from here, on that Crusade from which there was, for him, no returning. In the meantime, a town on the bastide plan had come into being, but it was not walled until Louis' son, Philippe le Hardi (or Bold), brought a Genoese here to construct the mighty ramparts that we see.

A century later, the town was as dead as it is to-day. The great fortifications 'guard nothing that we know as modern. The shadows and the ghosts of old Crusaders are the garrison they hold, and it is a shrunken population, in a withered chessboard of haggard-looking streets, which seems to struggle into the semblance of activity and life.'

Make a partial circuit of the ramparts. And visit the Tour de Constance, where, suffocated by the dead air which perpetuates the memory of Huguenot women languishing there, you may like to recall the Chevalier de Boufflers' account of his visit here, when he was nine-and-twenty and had not yet seen Eleanor de Sabran. He came — that gay, brilliant darling of courts and salons — to Aigues-Mortes with his uncle, the Prince de Beauvau, in 1767.

'We found at the entry of the tower,' he wrote, 'an eager guardian, who led us through a dark and twisting passage, and opened a great clanging door on which Dante's line might well have been inscribed: "All hope abandon, ye who enter here." I have no colors in which to paint the terrors of the picture which gradually grew upon our unaccustomed eyes. The scene was hideous yet pathetic, and interest in its victims struggled with disgust at their condition. Almost without air and light, fourteen women languished in misery and tears within that stone-walled chamber. As the commandant, who was visibly touched, entered the apartment, they all fell down together at his feet. I can still see them, bathed in tears, struggling to speak, unable at first to do anything but sob. Encouraged by our evident sympathy they all began to tell us their sorrows at once. Alas! the crime for which they were thus suffering was the fact that they had been brought up in the same religion as Henri Quatre. The youngest of them was fifty, and she had been here since she was eight years old. In a loud voice that shook with emotion the marshal said, "You are free!" and I was proud to be his servant at that moment.'

From Aigues-Mortes, your way leads to Les Saintes-Maries.

Tradition hereabouts has it that the three Marys, Martha, and Lazarus, after the death of Christ, were sent out to sea in an open boat and landed on these shores. They were Saint Mary Magdalen, Saint Mary, mother of James and John, and Saint Mary, sister of the Virgin. And with them was their servant, Sarah, who is believed to have died here, as ('tis said) did the latter two Marys. Martha's tomb you'll find at Tarascon, Lazarus is specially venerated at Marseilles, and you know how Vézelay grew mighty while it was believed to have the Magdalen's remains. You shall hear further of this little band as you pursue your way from Aix to Nice.

The holy Marys are venerated at this spot where the strange fortress-church rises beside the sea, but its special interest for the traveller is its picturesque pilgrimages, in May and October each year, particularly that on May 24–25, when the gypsies come from all over Europe to mount a guard of honor over the tomb of Sarah, represented as of swart color and claimed by the Romany as one of their own. Here they elect their queen. And here, following on the solemn ceremonies when the ark of the relics is lowered so that reaching, straining hands may touch it and be miraculously blessed, and the pageantry of the procession to the sea, come jousts and tourneys, bull-fights and horse-races, the piping of ancient tunes and threading of the farandole, juggling and sword-throwing, and hawk-ing of trifles, and love-making. A sight to see, indeed! If it is not a part of the landscape when you arrive, then you must set the stage, with your imagination.

The Camargue, which is close by, is a great salt delta enclosed by the Greater and the Little Rhône — no longer swift, as at Avignon and Tarascon, but like a wearied gray-beard, as Mistral puts it, who shrinks from his approach-ing end when he shall merge his name and being in the limitless sea.

'Sometimes,' says E. I. Robson, in 'A Wayfarer in Provence,' 'it is hard to realize one is in Europe. The delta, with its wild black oxen and white horses, suggests some western pampas, while its birds, chiefly its flamingoes, must remind us rather of Egypt. Certainly it is a unique part of France, and breeds unique men, women, oxen, and horses. There is, I suppose, hardly a finer type in Europe than the 'gardien' (cowboy), young or old, mounted tri-dent in hand on his white Camargue horse — rather stubby, and rather stupid-looking, but equal to every endurance, and perfectly trained to round up the black cattle of the marshlands; there is hardly a more beautiful or graceful woman than his sister, sweetheart, or wife, who sits behind him on the crupper. . . .

'It is a land of *rodeo*, of steer-roping and branding . . . and the chief mark of Camargue sport is that nobody is left out; the spectators form the barrier of the ring,' and when the bull gets really mad — which doesn't always happen in this mild form of the sport — and charges the barrier, 'every one must get behind or on top of something with all speed.'

It was on the Camargue that Mireille received the sun-stroke of which she died at Saintes-Maries. And all this region roundabout is full of her, because she is (they love to think) a type. Yet one thinks, looking at the girls on the cruppers of these Arab-descended 'broncos,' that the sort of fight they would put up for a lover would be somehow-different from Mireille's. Perhaps that is why she's their Ideal.

However, your way now lies northward to Saint-Gilles, where (the story goes) an anchorite named Egidius, or Gilles, was living in a cell, in the spring of 673, when Wamba, the King of the Visigoths, came, chasing a stag. (Some say a tame doe of Gilles'.) The hunted animal dashed into Gilles' cell, and one of Wamba's men hurled a javelin after it. This javelin pierced the hand of Gilles, and the regretful Wamba made what amends he could by giving Gilles a large tract of land here, and money to build a monastery — of which Gilles became the first abbot.

When the Saracens came, in 719, Gilles fled to Orléans, taking with him the sacred relics he had collected and the holy vessels; and Charles Martel protected him until the danger was past.

Gilles died in his own monastery here, and was canonized in the ninth century. The church that you are going to see has had more vicissitudes even than most churches, but retains some features that are among the most remarkable in France.

In the eleventh century the crypt beneath the present church was constructed to house the tomb of Saint Gilles, and Pope Urban II, in the year before he preached the First Crusade, at Clermont, came here to consecrate the high altar. Shortly afterwards, Raymond IV of Toulouse founded here the first priory in Europe of the Knights of Saint John, and began the great church of which portions only are left, built into the present structure.

The favorite secretary of Saint Louis, Guy de Foulkes, who became Pope Clement IV, was born at Saint-Gilles, and he got much favor shown to the town and to the church.

It may be getting late, and you may be growing tired, but I think you will be disappointed if, when your sight-seeing of to-day has become part of the tapestry of your memory, you have not woven into it a thread or two from Saint-Gilles — a not-too-hasty look at the wonderful portal, whose statues are of extraordinary beauty and interest, and a glimpse of the famous Vis de Saint-Gilles, or Screw Staircase, celebrated throughout the world for the skill of its stone-cutting. To see this latter, you must get into the enclosure at the back, where are the ruins of the original choir.

From Saint-Gilles to Beaucaire is fifteen miles; and from Beaucaire to Avignon is about the same distance.

Beaucaire may not detain you long; but it is on your homeward way, and I know you'll want to 'pretend,' as you approach it, that you are en route to one of its famous fairs held, year after year during century after century, from the 22d to the 28th of July, and attended by all the merchant-princes of the world, bringing leather from Morocco, furs from Russia, cloth from England and France, velvets from Vienne, soaps and perfumes from Grasse, sardines and anchovies from Perpignan, wines from Bordeaux and Burgundy, silks from the Levant.

And of course you'll choose your fair at a time when you may call on Aucassin and Nicolette. Will you have it after Aucassin had 'wedded her, made her lady of Beaucaire'? Or earlier, when his proud, stern father is still Lord of Beaucaire, and lovely Nicolette, daughter of the King of Carthage, but not knowing who she was nor whence the Saracens had stolen her, lay in the upper chamber which was her prison because young Aucassin loved her and his father would not hear to the supposed mésalliance?

THE LEGEND OF ST. GILLES
By an unknown French master of the Fifteenth Century

How old this story is, we do not know; but it probably comes down to us from about the time of the Second Crusade (1148) — that one on which gay Eleanor and her gallivanting ladies went. And if that be so, the present castle, with its triangular donjon and its pretty chapel which are ascribed to Saint Louis, who stopped here on his way to Aigues-Mortes in 1248, are not those the much-tried lovers knew.

But what do you care?

Across the Rhône is Tarascon, which you'll pass through (crossing by the suspension bridge, where Hannibal crossed — with his elephants) on your way back to Avignon for dinner; but I wouldn't try to visit it until you're en route to Arles, continuing your journey to the Riviera.

When you leave Avignon to go on to Nice, you are (presumably) making toward either Aix-en-Provence, or Marseilles. In either case, your course is the same until after you have left Arles.

Now, the merest mention of Tarascon at once sets half the world to chuckling; and Tarascon doesn't like that. Tarascon has a great many reasons for taking itself seriously, even reverently, and it doesn't relish our coming there in the jovial frame of mind that 'Tartarin' has induced in us; it does not wish us to believe that any considerable number of its citizens are at all of the sort that Daudet described. Misguided Tarascon! If it could persuade me that Tartarin has a successor, and that Tarascon still claims him when he's not hunting lions, I'd be tempted to 'hang around' there in the hope of meeting him. Now, 'lion-hunters' are not scarce in any community that I know; and they are usually my *bêtes-noires*. I've a distaste so strong for them, and so great a fear of being taken for one of them, that I go to silly lengths, sometimes, and must seem more or less rude to the poor 'lions' whose path

I scuttle across. Why do I love Tartarin on his perspiring trail of a tawny African lion, and turn disgustedly away from Mrs. Leo Hunter with whose sort my way is thick? Perhaps because she lacks her Daudet, and I am not 'big' enough to see, unaided, beyond her absurdities to something intrinsically human, if not fine, in her pursuit of Big Game.

In any event, I hope Tartarin is a very real person to you as you approach Tarascon. If you are a real epicure in travel you have a pocket-size, paper-covered copy of his adventures with you. Oh, the blessed *humanness* of him! And the side-shaking, tear-rolling humor of him! I hope I'm not lacking in appreciation of Mireille; but it is the delicious absurdity of Tartarin to which I feel *akin*, and which makes me smile understandingly at Provençals of his sort, as at brothers.

What Tarascon encourages us to think about when we go there a-visiting is Saint Martha and the Tarasque from which she delivered the town. This is interesting — if not as Tarascon cherishes it, then as it probably grew:

Marius, the great Roman general whose high-born wife (he was plebeian) was Julius Cæsar's aunt, was superstitious even beyond the average of his time and of fighting men in most all times; and he carried with him on his campaigns a Syrian prophetess named Martha, transporting her in a litter with great reverence, as Plutarch says, and making sacrifices as she ordered. She foretold his victory over the Cimbrians and Teutons, near Saint-Rémy; and the tradition of a woman named Martha, from the East, who played a supernatural part in the destruction of the terrible Teuton army, easily became Martha of Bethany, sister of Lazarus, routing a writhing, snorting, fire-breathing dragon — as the stone at Les Baux, which has figures of Marius, his wife Julia, and Martha, came to be taken for a memorial of the Three Marys instead of the Three *Mariuses*.

It may have been as early as the third century, some students think, that Martha the prophetess became metamorphosed into Martha the saint. At any rate, she seems to have been worshipped here at least from the fifth century. And you should go into the venerable crypt of her church, and see her lovely tomb carved at Genoa in 1653.

It was good King René who did most to propagate the belief that the Bethany household came hither — René, whose castle reared its formidable bulk on this, the Provence, side of the Rhône to keep Brother-in-Law Charles's minions over in Beaucaire well in mind of where their dominion stopped. To King René is ascribed the Festival of the Tarasque which commences on the Sunday before Ascension, when, the Order of the Knights of the Tarasque leading, the procession goes to fetch the statue of Our Lady of the Castle and instate it in the church, to the accompaniment of great noise of guns and pipes and drums. The following Sunday there is a great feast, to which people come from all the neighboring towns and countryside, everybody in his or her bravest finery. On Whit-Monday the Tarasque comes to writhe and wriggle through the streets, led by a girl representing Saint Martha. She has a vessel of holy water in her hand and leads the Tarasque by a silk thread — so tame has he become! Behind them come many groups: shepherds with the Holy Family; porters, with Saint Christopher bearing the Child Jesus; and so on. There is fun, and fireworks, and everybody is glad Saint Martha came and started such a jolly festival. The celebration had lapsed, but Mistral revived it in 1861. Ask to 'meet the Tarasque.' I have forgotten where they keep him, but I'm quite sure he is amiable about being seen almost any day.

As you go from Tarascon to Arles, there is a cross-roads about a mile and a half before you come to Arles, where you turn, left, if you wish to see Montmajour, the ruined abbey of the Benedictines which Childebert founded in the sixth century above the cell wherein Saint Trophime, a disciple of Saint Paul, is said to have preached the Gospel. The cloister of Montmajour is famous, and the ruins are picturesque in almost every detail; but I dare say this détour is for those with a special interest in abbeys, in architecture, or in picture-making.

Arles has so much to offer that it may be you ought not to linger on the way.

Coming in from the avenue de Montmajour through the Porte de la Cavalerie, keep straight ahead to the arena, drive around it on your right, and make your first stand in Arles at whatever vantage-point you may choose for the ruins of the Greek theatre — so-called, though the Romans built it, because the Greek influence was still dominant at Arles as it had been for centuries.

'One of the sweetest legacies of the ancient world,' Henry James called this theatre, 'one of the most charming and touching ruins I had ever beheld. . . . Here the human voice, the utterance of a great language, had been supreme; the air was full of intonations and cadences.'

It was a Greek architect who designed this theatre of Arles; they were Greek actors who left those lovely, lingering cadences. A theatre, as Cook reminds us, 'was as important a part of the life and religion of a Greek town as was its temple.'

Here was found, in 1651, the exquisite Venus of Arles, now in the Louvre, which may have come from the hand of Praxiteles in his youth. Here, almost at the same time, was discovered a beautiful Greek head, now in the museum here — that Musée Lapidaire opposite Saint-Trophime,

ARLES

From an old mezzotint

installed in the former Church of Sainte-Anne, and containing one of the richest collections in France of Gallo-Roman antiquities.

The theatre was built in the first century. So, probably, was the amphitheatre. And so, too, was Saint-Trophime's first little church.

When Saint Paul left Greece, in 59 A.D., to return through Macedonia to Syria, there accompanied him, among others, Trophimus of Asia, and Timothy. And, writing to Timothy, at Ephesus, from Rome at the time of his second appearance before Nero, Saint Paul tells him 'Trophimus have I left at Miletum sick.'

It is believed at Arles that before the death of the Virgin Mary, Trophimus had dedicated an oratory to her here. At any rate, there was a church, very early, where the present Saint-Trophime stands; and in it was consecrated Saint Augustine, the apostle to England.

In 1152, the body of Saint Trophime was brought from Les Aliscamps (Elysian Fields), the Roman necropolis outside the city, to a more fitting shrine in the new church then begun to his memory.

About this church, and its marvellous cloister, at least a chapter should be written here. But though the space were not lacking, still the ability would be. If you are a student of such things, you probably have 'Old Provence' with you, and could ask for no better guide than its ninth chapter. All I can say to you is that I think you will find Saint-Trophime uncommonly interesting, and its cloister one of the most impressive you have ever seen. The last time I was there was on a beautifully sunshiny afternoon, and the light and shade were making entrancing patterns on the ancient walks. The guardian had two or three old cronies in to pass the afternoon with her. Being French women, they all had ceaselessly busy hands; and their tongues were not resting. A nice, dignified cat seemed perfectly at home there. I liked it all, immensely: the comfortable, productive ease of the elderly women; their homely, wholesome tasks; the way the sculptured saints seemed to regard them; and the unconcern of the pussycat for the saints as against her jungle-hunting in the agreeably unkempt grass of the cloister garden. I hope you may find it as pleasantly domestic as well as thrillingly beautiful.

The Arena of Arles is the largest north of the Alps. Of course it's interesting! But if your time is short, I think you'll be better satisfied if you spend it largely at the Muséon Arlatan and the Musée Lapidaire.

The latter is directly across the Place de la République from Saint-Trophime. Be sure to note there, besides the woman's head referred to, the delightful head of a little boy; the sarcophagus called that of Phèdre et Hippolyte; and the other called the 'Tomb of the Trees,' whereon, between each tree and the next interlacing one, is depicted one of the miracles of Christ; also, the Dancing Girl.

Rue de la République, running northwest from the *place*, will take you, in a minute's walk, to Muséon Arlatan, at the corner of rue de la République and rue Frédéric Mistral, in an old mansion of the Renaissance. Here is an old-fashioned farm kitchen of the Camargue at Christmas — perfectly delightful! And to the enthusiast on furnishings, even more than that. Here is another room illustrating life on a Provençal farm. A third shows an Arlésienne mother receiving symbolic gifts on the birth of her first child. And so on. One of the most interesting museums I know.

Mistral was largely responsible for this collection, and it is a more eloquent monument to his memory than the one on the site of the old Roman Forum, near which you must eat your lunch and pitch your tent, if you are not a hurrying pilgrim.

The Hôtel du Nord has the caves beneath the old Roman Forum for its cellars. Above these there is abundant creature comfort (shining spotless rooms, downy beds, up-to-date bathrooms, and excellent food) seasoned with such sauce of hospitality as to make it forever memorable. The proprietor, M. Bessières, is an archæologist of no mean sort, and a perfectly delightful gentleman. I shall always urge my friends to make a stay with him, knowing that they will reckon it among their pleasantest experiences in France. He is an enthusiast on Provence, and will interpret it to you most illuminatingly. And when you leave — unless you are going back to Avignon — ask Madame Bessières to order a luncheon put up for you to carry. Be sure that it includes sandwiches made with their delicious croissants. No mere hotel — this — but a real haven.

On your way out of Arles, follow the southern ramparts to the avenue des Aliscamps which was the main approach to Arles by the Roman road, the Aurelian Way, and was lined with imposing tombs in the same way as the Appian Way outside Rome. After Saint Trophime was buried here, so great was the ardor to lie near him in death, awaiting the Last Trump, that the people of towns far up the Rhône used to send downstream on rafts the coffins bearing their dead and money to pay for their burial here.

'As where Rhône stagnates on the plains of Arles
. . . .
The place is all thick spread with sepulchres' —

wrote Dante, drawing one of his descriptions of Hell from this place, as he is said to have drawn others from the Val d'Enfer between Les Baux and Saint-Rémy.

And now, as you take your eastward way, toward Salon, twenty-five miles, you skirt the vast stony, sunny plain

called the Crau, about eighty square miles in area, and
strewn with boulders great and small. Except on the
irrigated oases where there are a few farms, not much grows
on the Crau except a thin grass, grazing for great flocks of
sheep. And the shepherds who tend those flocks are great
astronomers, great conservators of lore and legend which
seems to make them not of an age but of all time. Provence
is full of persons who pursue immemorial vocations — the
cultivation of vine and olive, the tending of flocks, and
bringing in the catch from the sea — in conditions which
seem to make them like continuations of antiquity, like
living links with those far yesterdays when our religion and
our literature were shaping the poetry and imagery of all
times to come.

Your eye may not be ravished as it roves over the Crau;
but if you could know something of the everlasting types
which find their sustenance there beneath the friendly
stars, you would be more 'at home' than ever before with
the great old stories of the world's dewy dawn. And were
you on the Crau (where, indeed, mirages are sometimes
seen, 'tis said) at a time when he was needed, you might
even catch a glimpse of the Golden Goat who guards the
ancient monuments of Provence and helps to preserve them
for us.

It seems fitting that Provence should have nurtured
Nostradamus, the celebrated astrologer of Catherine de
Médici's time, so startlingly many of those prophecies were
fulfilled. He was born at Saint-Rémy, and his grandfather
was astrologer to King Réne. Michael Nostradamus died
at Salon in 1566 and is buried there in the Church of Saint-
Laurent. Astrology has still so many adherents (eminent
and intellectual ones, too!) that I am sure they would not
wish to pass through Salon without a thought of Nostradamus.

Are you bound for Martigues, 'the Venice of Provence,' at the mouth of the great salt lagoon called the Étang de Berre? Then you must turn south at Salon, and follow the road which curves along the east and south shores of the Étang. But if you want a glimpse of the extraordinarily picturesque Flavian bridge at Saint-Chamas, you must make a little détour to the west on the road which crosses yours at La Fare. This bridge has a fine triumphal arch at each end.

Martigues, which Joseph Pennell thought he had discovered and then learned it was a favorite of French painters, is full of picture potentialities. Ziem, whose canvases are familiar in so many galleries, found at Martigues subjects scarcely inferior to those he found at Venice. Read Pennell's 'Play in Provence.'

Were you to sail out of the harbor of Martigues in one of those 'tartanes' that the painters love, and go along the coast-line of the Gulf of Fos, to the little old town of Fos, you might land there 'pretending' that you had come with Scipio in pursuit of Hannibal then (mayhap) crossing the Rhône from Beaucaire to Tarascon. There has recently been completed, here, after fifteen years of effort and a vast expenditure of money, the Rove water tunnel, nearly five miles long, connecting Marseilles with the Étang de Berre and the Rhône.

If your course is from Arles to Marseilles, I think I'd go on through Salon to Aix, and then down on Route 8 — though you might have time for a glimpse of Martigues and then go into Marseilles by way of L'Estaque, twenty-six miles.

I wouldn't take time for Marseilles on a brief visit to Provence, unless I had to! There are a few things one may enjoy at Marseilles if obliged to be there before sailing to Algiers or Corsica or further ports. But I can't see why any one should make a special effort to get there just for the city's own sake, unless he dearly loves a port. Its interesting ancient history is as easy to recall elsewhere as there; few memorials of its past remain. It is a handsome city, and its harbor is interestingly cosmopolitan. Also, there is the Château d'If, of Monte Cristo fame. The Promenade de la Corniche is a beautiful drive, and at the Hôtel de la Réserve, on the Promenade, one eats memorably, especially of sea-foods. And on that drive one may visit the Musée du Vieux-Marseille which is in the Parc Amable Chanot. Here is, perhaps, as good a place as any in Provence to study the delightful Santons — the little colored plaster figures used in those groups called Crèches which the churches, and homes, show at Christmas-time, reproducing in effigy the scene of the Nativity at Bethlehem.

Whole families throughout this region work, evenings, on the production of these little figures, which are formed in moulds often of great antiquity — precious heirlooms from one generation to another — and charmingly colored.

To the original group of the Nativity have been added a great number of local types, so that at the Fair of Santons, which takes place each year as the Christmas season approaches, there are said to be many thousands of different objects from which to choose for the setting-up or amplification of your Crèche. There are not only the Holy Family and the kine, the shepherds and their flocks, the Three Kings and their camels, the angels and cherubim, but the fishmonger, the woodcutter, the miller, the knife-grinder, the drummer who is also a flutist — and even the funny old man who holds his newspaper upside down.

Collectors prize these 'local types' highly, and well they may. I think young travellers hereabouts should be encouraged to start their own collection, and taken (if possible) into some of the homes where the Santons are made.

Christmas in Provence is a memorable experience. All
the churches have midnight mass, and are brilliantly illuminated. Then the Crèche is seen in all its wealth of
story-telling interest. And the organs are fitted with a
special attachment which enables them to imitate the
nightingale.

Nowhere is Christmas quite so impressive as at Les
Baux, where the Corporation of the Shepherds of Les Baux,
created in the sixteenth century, still faithfully reproduces,
each year, the ceremony of the Offering of the Lamb.

Shepherds and shepherdesses, priors and prioresses are
the characters in this scene, the shepherds wearing long
woollen cloaks and the shepherdesses white dresses with
artificial flowers. The prioresses wear a hennin-shaped
headdress the peak of which is trimmed with fruit and
candies.

A peasant hidden behind the altar represents an angel
come to tell the glad tidings to a shepherd standing at the
back of the church. Then the procession comes, preceded
by the flute and drum players. First, the little rustic cart
made of hand-carved olive wood, adorned with flowers, and
all lit up with little wax candles. On it is a banner bearing
the arms of the Princess of Baux. The cart is drawn by a
goat with long horns, and in it rides a quite terrified wee
baby lamb all dressed up in ribbon bows.

Before the communion rail, at which the priest is standing, one of the priors takes the lamb and pretends to offer it
up; then passes it to his prioress, who does the same. When
all have made the Offering, the lamb is returned to the
cart, and the recessional begins. The impressiveness of this
ceremony in those surroundings may be imagined.

The Pastorals still, as in centuries long past, take place
in the weeks following Christmas, and are derived from the
old Mystery of Bethlehem which the churches used to

present in the Middle Ages. But colloquial humor almost predominates now over sacred story.

Aix-en-Provence has a long, long history, and more to show for it than Marseilles. It seems to have been quite a town and a 'spa' when Marius came, and he liked the place so well that when his legions were not occupied with military matters he employed them in building and beautifying this colony. Cæsar liked it, too, and furthered its fortunes. And the first Bishop of Aix was Saint Maximinus, who is believed to have come with the group from Bethany.

But I think that most of us, at Aix, are more concerned with King René than with Cæsar. The Good King dominates his capital, as is his due.

You will see his statue in the handsome Cours Mirabeau, the main thoroughfare of Aix; and you will feel, before you have been long in town, almost as if you had come to visit René and his Queen Jeanne de Laval.

If the time of your arrival is fairly well before five o'clock, it may be that you would like to turn, right, just beyond King René's fountain, down rue d'Italie, for a brief stop at the old Church of Saint-Jean-de-Malte and at the Musée des Beaux-Arts, next door, in buildings that were once the priory of the Knights of Malta. Even if you have not time nor inclination for a careful survey of the art and archæological treasures here, I think you will wish to see the buildings of this group, and the reconstruction (in the church) of the tomb of the Counts of Provence, with statues of Raymond Bérenger IV and his wife, Beatrice of Savoy, the parents of those four daughters each of whom became a queen and one of whom (Beatrice) was progenitress of René.

Should it be too late for this when you arrive, you can stop here on your way out of town to-morrow.

It may be that you will choose to stop at the Hôtel

Nègre-Coste on the Cours Mirabeau. If not, take the left-hand turn opposite rue d'Italie, which is rue Thiers, to the Place du Palais, in front of the Palais de Justice which occupies the site of the old palace of the Counts of Provence; follow the north side of the Palais and of the prison, to the Place aux Herbes; then past the Hôtel de Ville, with its charming belfry; and straight ahead to rue du Bon Pasteur (street of the Good Shepherd) which will take you to the Établissement Thermal (with a Roman bath in the central hall) and the Hôtel des Thermes-Sextius, named in commemoration of the Consul Sextius whose name has been contracted out of recognition in Aix — i.e., Aquæ Sextiæ.

You could reach this hotel much more directly by turning to your left, as you enter town, up Cours Sextius. But I think it is pleasant to see Cours Mirabeau at the earliest opportunity, and get an impression of the dignified old town before spending a night in its hospitality.

The cathedral, which you had almost passed when you turned off on the Good Shepherd's street, is exceptionally interesting. Its west doors are very fine; the choir tapestries are superb; you must not fail to see the triptych called 'The Burning Bush,' with its portraits of King René and Queen Jeanne; and the little cloister is charming.

The old palace of the archbishops, next door, has splendid tapestries and furniture.

And as you take your leave of Aix, I wonder if you wouldn't like, better than anything else I could offer you, Sir Theodore Cook's tribute to René with which he concludes that 'Old Provence' of his which I trust you will read 'from kivver to kivver' between your first glimpse of Provence and that leisurely visit you must certainly have promised yourself to make here some day.

Sir Theodore has just described that 'Missel du Roi

René' which is in the Bibliothèque Méjanes, and has marginal annotations in René's own handwriting:

'His character comes more clearly before us as we read these notes he wrote; and we see a man who, in the best sense of the word, was versatile; who was ignorant of nothing great, or useful, or beautiful in his time; a prince whose honorable loyalty led him in his early years to stand in arms by the side of Joan of Arc; who, in maturer life, fought the battle of France in stubbornly struggling to preserve his own inheritance; who gave a queen to England, and to Lorraine a princess, whose blood still lives upon the throne of Austria. [It did, when this was written.] Through all the mischances of his life he never lost the privilege of creating his own happiness in his own way. [What finer tribute could be paid to any man?] Full of charity and loving-kindness, not only to his own subjects, but to all the poor and the oppressed, he carried out strictly in his own life the principles on which he founded his chivalrous Order of the Crescent. Nor were the claims of a larger humanity forgotten. His love for women sometimes led him into paths where Kings are best unseen. But his tenderness and affection to both his wives were unassailable and unchallenged. He built wisely and well; he encouraged the arts of painting and of manufacture; he instituted many religious ceremonies and many festivals which lasted in their full force into the nineteenth century, and will never be forgotten in Provence. He was full of interest in history, in geography, in the natural sciences; the friend of Charles d'Orléans, the protector of François Villon, he knew what good literature was; he gave us of his best; and some of his writing still remains to testify to his enduring charm of thought and manner. He held a great place in the world of his own day, as great, at one time, as either the Duke of Burgundy [Philip the Good, and Charles the Bold] or the

King of France [Charles VII — and Louis XI]. He escaped
the terrible fate of the first (Charles the Bold, killed at
Nancy); he never deserved a hint of the ignominy which
some writers have too plentifully bestowed upon the second
[Louis XI]. Above all, he stands out, in an age which was
rather too prone to that Machiavellian intrigue so praised
by its historian Comines, as an honest politician. That is one
reason why his material successes were not so great as those
obtained by more unscrupulous players in the game of
kings. His claim upon posterity lies rather upon artistic
and intellectual grounds; upon the serenity he showed in
evil fortune, the dignity with which he faced defeat; the
constancy with which he died, at Aix, on July 10, 1480, still
in possession of his titles of inheritance and knowing that
he possessed them for the good of France.'

You have met King René often, in these pages; from
Angers, where he was born, to Aix, where he died. You
have encountered his kind ghost at Laval, where he won
his second bride; at Dijon where he was in a prison that he
beautified; at Les Baux, and Tarascon — all up and down
Provence. I'm sure you find him good to know. The stage
whereon he played his part was set with fascinating backgrounds and peopled with most wonderfully picturesque
and romantic personages. But our interest in him never
lags.

Salute his statue affectionately as you pass it on your
way toward rue d'Italie and the route for Brignoles — a
man who 'through all the mischances of life [and they were
many and sore, for René!] never lost the privilege of creating his own happiness in his own way,' and that way a fine
one! And don't forget that there is a great deal to be
learned about him in E. I. Robson's 'A Wayfarer in Provence.'

Your route for Brignoles (where you should lunch, at

the Hôtel Garrus) is Route 7, and the distance is about
thirty-six miles. So, if you make a détour or two you need
not feel pressed for time — though you may not have got
away from Aix before eleven.

On your left, soon after you leave Aix, is the Montagne
de Sainte Victoire (but to go to this, you should leave Aix
by avenue des Vauvenargues at the northeast of town)
above the plain whereon Marius won his great victory. In
the convent on this mountain, Scott lays the scene of the
interview between Margaret of Anjou and the Earl of
Oxford's son, in 'Anne of Geierstein' — which I can't remember having read; can *you?* If I didn't, it was because
I had no reason to suspect that Margaret of Anjou was
'in it'; because I read avidly, in those years when I most
read Scott, everything that I knew touched her. Those who
love climbing and views will be well rewarded by the ascent
of this mountain, which can be made in about two hours.

A little less than twenty-five miles from Aix on Route 7
is Saint-Maximin, the traditional burial-place of Mary
Magdalen, Lazarus, Martha, and three others of their
group, including Maximinus, the first Bishop of Aix. In the
crypt of the fine church there you may see what are believed
to be their sarcophagi. And from here you may make a
pilgrimage to the Sainte-Baume, where there is a grotto in
which the Magdalen is said to have spent her latter days;
and, high above it, a seemingly inaccessible chapel marking
the spot whither the angels daily conveyed her to pray.

When you have lunched at Brignoles (have trout, and
écrevisses — the latter in a *bisque*, perhaps), you have
thirty miles to go if your destination is Hyères, and sixty-
two if it is Cannes. (Nice, twenty miles farther.)

Now, were I, in dealing with the French Riviera, to
attempt anything like an enumeration of its resorts with
even a brief description of each, and a few suggestions as to

the popular excursions thereabouts, it would be matter for
a book and not for a dozen pages.

Always I have to keep in mind that this book cannot
possibly be for the sojourner in any part of France, but
must content itself with serving the traveller and giving
him something for his needs as he wings his way through,
and some direction as to where he may find fuller storehouses when he alights, not for rest only, but to make himself a nest for a season.

Mr. Robson covers the coast resorts rather completely,
if sketchily; Sir Frederick Treves, Bart., late Serjeant-Surgeon to His Majesty the King, in 'The Riviera of the Corniche Road,' has done a more leisurely, gossipy chronicle of
the towns between Nice and Mentone. Herbert Adams
Gibbons writes with his usual vigorous, correspondent's
interest in the world about him, on 'Riviera Towns.' And
the Riviera volume in the Picture Guides series, published
by The Medici Society, is, like its companion volumes of
the series, written out of the fullest knowledge and charmingly and copiously illustrated from fine photographs. The
authors of 'The French Riviera' for the Medici series
are Pierre Devoluy and Pierre Borel, and their book has a
preface by Arnold Bennett, who says:

'In whatever fashion you prefer to be alive, the Riviera is
capable of suiting your taste. If you desire to burn money,
to startle the righteous, to turn night into day, to exist
as you would in Paris or London, — only more so, — the
Riviera gives all the facilities. If you have to look twice
at a ten-shilling note before spending it, the Riviera will
eagerly meet you — so much so that within a radius of a
couple of hundred yards you can live just as cheaply or just
as expensively as you wish. Again if your notion of being
alive is to devote yourself to outdoor games and sports, the
Riviera will provide you with everything to that end —

except possibly foxes. Again, if for you the ideal existence is the regular, monotonous, correct . . . the Riviera can offer you exactly what you need. Again, if you are historically curious you can, within the limits of a short motor drive on the Riviera, pass from the most modern race-course and totalisator right back to the authentic Roman coliseum where men fought their fellow beasts, or from a twentieth-century water-main to an aqueduct that is nearly as old as sin. Again, if your caprice is to live in different civilizations on the same day, you can stroll out of the hotel where you may regulate the temperature of your bedroom on a dial, climb a hill on your own feet, and enter a village where in all essentials life is endured as it was endured five hundred years ago in the dwellings and round about the keeps of five hundred years ago. . . . The truth is that nobody could believe the Riviera who has not seen it.'

Travellers, as distinguished from sojourners, usually concern themselves with the Riviera between Fréjus and Mentone — or Genoa — and follow the coast-line from Marseilles or from Toulon, only if their route has necessarily embraced one of those ports.

But Hyères is the oldest favorite among the winter resorts of Provence and is still in high regard with English visitors. And once-upon-a-time a Scotchman went there — a very sick Scotchman, who wrote afterward: 'I was only happy once, that was at Hyères.'

He took a house there, La Solitude, a chalet built after the Swiss fashion, 'with a garden like a fairy-story and a view like a classical landscape.'

There he received a check for £100 for a story called 'Treasure Island' whose publication (in the autumn of '83) brought him his first breath of popular applause and caused him to write: 'To live reading such reviews and die eating ortolans — sich is my aspiration.'

From there he wrote to his mother about 'Fanny' (his marriage with whom he was contemplating when we left him — and Modestine — at Saint-Jean-du-Gard): 'I love her better than ever and admire her more ... my marriage has been the most successful in the world ... she is everything to me: wife, brother, sister, daughter, and dear companion; and I would not change to get a goddess or a saint. So far, after four years of matrimony.'

From there he wrote to Henley: 'If mine anchorage lies something open to the wind, Sciatica, if the crew are blind, and the captain spits blood, we cannot have all; and I may be patched up again, who knows? "His timbers are yet (indifferently) sound and he may float again."'

In May, 1884, he lay here between life and death, in the half-dark because his eyes were bad, his right hand tied to his side and speech forbidden, to prevent the recurrence of hemorrhages, sciatica racking him with pain, and with his left hand wrote some of 'The Child's Garden of Verses'! Perhaps the one that says:

> 'The world is so full of a number of things
> That I'm sure we should all be as happy as kings.'

And here 'in the valley of the shadow, unable to move, speechless, blind,' he composed the poem we call the 'Requiem.':

> 'Under the wide and starry sky
> Dig the grave and let me lie.
> Glad did I live and gladly die,
> And I laid me down with a will.
>
> 'This be the verse you grave for me:
> *Here he lies where he longed to be;*
> *Home is the sailor, home from the sea,*
> *And the hunter home from the hill.*'

What allure that tenant of La Solitude may lend Hyères for you, I cannot guess; but for me it is very great. I might

make shift to content myself with other palm-trees than
those majestic ones which line the avenues and squares of
this resort; I might, because 'the world is so full of a number of things' that are beautiful, forego the sub-tropical
Îles d'Hyères, since some of that 'number of things' must
always be foregone; I might manage without seeing the
much-pictured rue Paradis or the view from the thirteenth-
century castle. But where else may I get such rebaptism
for a glad and not a merely patient courage in life, as at
La Solitude?

Twenty-three miles east of Hyères is Cavalaire, with one
of the most beautiful beaches of the whole Mediterranean
and a summer as well as a winter popularity. Pine,
eucalyptus, mimosa, cork-oak, and live-oak grow right
down to the great crescent of fine sand and gentle surf.

Near by is Saint-Tropez, with a House of the Corsairs.
And presently one comes to Fréjus — contracted from
Forum Juluii or Julius, founded by Julius Cæsar in 50
B.C., to be a rival to Marseilles, which had taken sides with
Pompey (50 B.C. was the year before Cæsar crossed the
Rubicon and made Pompey flee from Rome).

Fréjus claims the distinction of having given to the world
and to the stage Roscius, from whom Cicero took lessons
in delivery and with whom he often engaged in friendly
rivalry to see whether an orator or an actor could express
a thought or emotion with greater effect. But there is also
some probability that Roscius was born much nearer
Rome. At any rate, if he was born here, it was not only
before the Forum Julius, but considerably before 'Uncle
Marius' came, Roscius having come upon the scene of life
about 126 B.C.

A Roman notable who was undoubtedly born here, however, was Agricola, who became Governor of Britain in
79 A.D. and succeeded in reconciling the Britons to Roman

rule and inducing them to adopt the customs and civilization of their conquerors. He was the father-in-law of Tac-
itus the historian.

The Roman town was much larger than the one we see —
five times as large. The arena could contain ten thousand
spectators; its remains are on your left as you come in, by
the avenue de Verdun. If you keep straight on, you will
presently have the cathedral on your left; and you may like
to see its seventh-century baptistery which either was a
Roman temple or employed granite monoliths from one.
The cloisters are worth seeing, too.

'There are two hotels in Fréjus, side by side on rue de la
Liberté, both unpretending. I can't remember in which
one it was that I encountered the Fury — the only one I
ever met in all my experiences of hotels in France — who
came screaming into the street after my mother and me because (not seeing any one about of whom we might ask
permission) we had ventured into her hotel unbidden.
But her rage was so terrifying that it rather spoiled our
ardor for thinking about ancient Rome, and we got out of
Fréjus as hastily as we could, although we had thought of
trying to lunch there. We went on, instead, to Saint-
Raphael; which was much pleasanter, of course, but we
didn't see the ruins of the aqueduct, which are on the other
road to Cannes. I shall do better, next time; I shall, 'on
leaving the town,' come 'all of a sudden to a place from
which the whole beautiful countryside lies spread out before
us, bathed in the full glory of the setting sun . . . a view at
once romantic and Virgilian, enhanced as it is by the high
arches of the Roman aqueduct' — some of them sixty feet
in height.

The road from Fréjus to Saint-Raphael leads us past the
beautiful estate of the late General Galliéni.

Saint-Raphael, less than two miles from Fréjus, is where

the rich Romans of Forum Julius are believed to have had their handsome villas, on the Gulf of Fréjus, famed for the deep blue of its water and the vividness of its skies. It, too, has a sandy beach, and is frequented all the year round.

It was here that young General Bonaparte arrived, triumphant, from Egypt in 1799, when he was in his thirtieth year. And it was from here that Napoleon, lately abdicated as Emperor (in that room at Fontainebleau where it is so easy to see him signing his abdication, as it is, in an adjoining room, to see him saying what was to be his last farewell to the little King of Rome), embarked for that first exile, on Elba, fifteen years later. Fifteen little years! And think of what he had packed into them!

At Saint-Raphael, in 1866, Charles Gounod composed 'Roméo et Juliette,' in a villa called 'Oustalet dou Capelan,' on the picturesque road to Cannes (twenty-seven miles) known as the Corniche d'Or or Corniche d'Estérel. This road along the Estérel offers a succession of surpassingly fine views, and takes us at last to Cannes, perhaps the most elegant of all the Riviera resorts, with its palatial hotels and sumptuous villas, its magnificent casino and smart shops, its tennis courts and polo grounds, its horse-races and regattas, its balls and fêtes and theatres and gambling, its continual whirring of motors and its great fleet of white yachts at anchor, its dazzling display of wealth almost dwarfing the prodigality of Nature. There are many, many hotels at Cannes — perhaps the most luxurious hotels in Europe are there. There is the Carlton, and the Majestic. There is the Continental, of the same supremely good management as the Continental at Paris and the Lion d'Or at Reims. And there's the beautiful Californie, in its glorious grounds, managed by the Armbrusters (father and son) of the Plaza-Athénée, Paris, who are almost unique in their art of running a great hotel without sacrifice of that personal hospitality which makes their guests feel like invited friends.

At Le Cannet, above Cannes, Rachel, the great tragédienne, died in 1858. At Golfe Juan, three and a half miles on the route from Cannes to Antibes, Napoleon landed on March 1, 1815, at the beginning of the Hundred Days before Waterloo.

Between the Golfe de la Napoule, on which Cannes lies, and the Golfe Juan, are the islands called the Lérins, including the Île Sainte-Marguerite with a fort in which the Man in the Iron Mask was a prisoner before he was taken to the Bastille, where he died; and the Île Saint-Honorat, with a monastery, founded in 410, by Saint Honorat, who found only snakes living there. He was, presently, joined by Saint Patrick, who must have had practice here in that facility which was so to endear him to Ireland.

Of course you must visit Grasse, from Cannes; and I think you will be better satisfied with your visit if you don't let the matter of perfume crowd out every other interest that Grasse has to offer — although Grasse and perfumes have been synonymous for many centuries. 'In the twelfth century,' says one writer on Provence, 'this town supplied the whole of France, Italy and Spain with its famous leather, soap and oil skilfully purified'; and another writer says that 'the whole of Europe obtained its soap from Grasse.' Some allege that it was Catherine de Médici who established the perfume industry there.

Sir Frederick Treves poured out his scorn upon the 'trippers' who 'are deposited at a scent factory by a not disinterested driver, and there they purchase soap with eagerness, as if it were the bread of life. Ninety-nine per cent of these soap-questing pilgrims do not go beyond the factory which they appear to regard as a sort of shrine,' though soap (that same soap, even!) may be bought many places elsewhere, but 'in few places can there be found an old French city so full of picturesque memories and possessed of so exquisite a cathedral.'

Among those 'memories' is one I'm sure you'll like to have with you as you climb such a street as rue de l'Évêché, which looks like a bit of the oldest Italy that Dante knew.

It is Treves who gives us this:

Count Raymond Bérenger IV (father of those four famous daughters), 'when walking one day through the streets of Grasse came upon a pilgrim.' I am sure it was in rue de l'Évêché, and that everything in it looked, seven hundred years ago, just as it does now. The count, struck by the nobility of the pilgrim's appearance, questioned him and was much pleased by 'his intelligence, by the gentleness of his manner and the graceful sentiment that accompanied his talk.' He asked the pilgrim to come into his service; and speedily they became friends.

'Many a time the two would sit in a corner of the terrace when the heat of the day was over and Romée (the erstwhile pilgrim) would tell of the wonders of the Eternal City, of the street fighting he had seen in Florence between the Amidei and the Buondelmonte, of the new Church of San Giovanni at Pistoia, of the wonderful bell tower they were building at Pisa, and of the ruins of the palace of Theodoric the Great that he had wandered among at Ravenna. He would talk, too, of strange things, of the savage, mist-enveloped island of England where the cliffs were white; of the flight of birds; of wondrous flowers that bloomed among the snow; of the hiving of bees; of the curious ways of women.'

Romée became the Count's most trusted counsellor and beloved friend, and was made his prime minister and seneschal of Grasse.

This aroused intense jealousy among the courtiers, who

determined to destroy Romée. They told Count Raymond that Romée was robbing him; that in his room he kept a mysterious coffer which no one was allowed to touch. They goaded the Count into entering Romée's room and commanding him to open the chest.

'My lord, since you no longer trust me,' said Romée sadly, 'I will open the box.'

He did so — and disclosed his dusty, tattered pilgrim's frock, two worn sandals, a coarse shirt, and a weather-stained hat with a cockleshell in it.

'Can you ever forgive me?' Count Raymond implored, when he had driven forth the 'scoundrels too mean to live.'

'I forgive you a thousand times over,' Romée replied; 'but you have broken my heart.'

There and then he took off his robes of office, donned his pilgrim's dress, made his way out of the castle and into the open road. And Raymond Bérenger never saw him again. But many a time the Count of Provence, whose four daughters Romée had done much to set on thrones, 'would be found standing alone in a certain deserted room, gazing at an empty coffer.'

Dante called Romée one of the greatest poets of his time. You remember his lines in 'Paradise':

> 'Within the pearl, that now encloseth us,
> Shines Romeo's light, whose goodly deed and fair
> Met ill acceptance. But the Provençals,
> That were his foes, have little cause for mirth.
> Ill shapes that man his course, who makes his wrong
> Of other's worth. Four daughters were there born
> To Raymond Berenger; and every one
> Became a queen: and this for him did Romeo,
> Though of mean state and from a foreign land.
> Yet envious tongues incited him to ask
> A reckoning of that just one, who returned
> Twelve fold to him for ten. Aged and poor
> He parted thence: and if the world did know
> The heart he had, begging his life by morsels,
> 'Twould deem the praise it yields him scantly dealt.'

Modern historians tell us that Romeo or Romée was not a poor pilgrim, but the son of a powerful baron — his name was Roumieu, which is Provençal for 'pilgrim' — who was never slighted, though he may have been doubted by Count Raymond; who, after the latter's death, became regent of his estates; and who, when he died, an octogenarian, at his castle of Villeneuve, near Cagnes, was Governor of Nice.

I hope these findings do not in any way jeopardize his place in Paradise where Dante put him! And, like my very young niece, who is 'glad Dumas didn't know who the Man in the Iron Mask really was' — else we should not have had 'Le Vicomte de Bragelonne' — I am glad that Dante's great learning included some things that 'ain't so.'

Other memories of Grasse besides those of Romée are of Queen Joanna (who sold Avignon), of Mirabeau and his lively sister, the Marquise de Cabris (whose house is now the Fragonard Museum), and of Fragonard, who was born here in 1732. He had studied, at Paris, under Chardin and Boucher and Van Loo before going to Italy with the Prix de Rome. And it was when he was only two-and-twenty that he painted 'Christ Washing the Feet of the Apostles,' which you will see in the Grasse Cathedral. But it was his summer's sojourn at Villa d' Este, Tivoli, that most profoundly influenced his art. Those entrancing gardens, with their fountains, grottoes, temples, and terraces, did more toward forming his style than all the training at the various schools. That, and the taste of those who were paying most for pictures when he returned to Paris — the end of Pompadour's reign and the beginning of Du Barry's. Do you know his 'Coresus,' at the Louvre? Diderot praised it so highly that Louis XV bought it and had it reproduced at the Gobelins' factory. That set the vogue. When the Terror made Fragonard flee Paris, he took with him to Grasse a series of decorative panels he had painted for Madame du

Barry's pavilion at Louveciennes, and with them he embellished the house of his friend Maubert, at number 15 in what is now boulevard Fragonard.

Scant comfort he must have had at Grasse while the Terror lasted. For, thirty victims perished on the guillotine set up where his statue now stands in the Cours; and he who had enjoyed the favor of Louis XV and Du Barry may well have shivered in his shoes until the Terror was over. Next time you see those panels in the Metropolitan Museum, New York (where they are through the munificence of the late J. Pierpont Morgan), you may imagine them here at Grasse, and Fragonard's apprehension each time he heard the roll of the drums at the scaffold's foot. He died, neglected and almost forgotten, in 1806; and for many years was buried in oblivion. Then he came into his just meed of fame; and a century after his death a small and relatively unimportant canvas of his fetched nearly $100,000 at auction in Paris.

The flower harvest around Grasse lasts nearly the whole year round. It begins in February with the violet, which lasts till April. In March and April, hyacinths and jonquils are also picked. May is the month of roses and orange flowers — May and June — and mignonette and carnations come in June, also. Then comes jasmine in July and until October (something like ten billions of these flowers are picked every year to provide the world with that popular perfume) and the tuberose is 'harvested' in August and September.

There are good hotels at Grasse, and many visitors to the Riviera find it a most attractive place to stay. (I was strongly attracted, when re-visiting Grasse just before this book went to press, by the Grand Hotel there, where one may live in supreme comfort for about five dollars a day.) But most travellers stop there briefly, and go on; if, indeed, they do not make Grasse the last stop in a circuit including the famous Gorges de Loup, Vence, Cagnes, and Antibes. This is a wonderful drive, and should on no account be missed by even the most hurrying visitor to the Riviera. It includes the eagle's-nest village of Gourdon; the ravines and waterfalls of the river Loup; Vence, which was once the capital of Roman Gaul; Cagnes, which is one of the most entrancing of ancient towns, topped by the crenellated castle of the Grimaldi; and Antibes, said to be that part of Provence which most resembled Greece and therefore specially attracted the colonizing wanderers of that great race — people who could scarcely camp in a spot without leaving some trace of imperishable beauty. On this day of manifold delights, mind that you take your luncheon at Restaurant du Pavillon des Touristes at the Pont du Loup, whose proprietor — Pierre Coste — used to be at the Carlton in London.

Vence was ancient when the Romans came; and 'he who strolls alone through the city of Vence,' as Treves says, 'may find himself carried back into the past by some nightmare witchery, and imagine that he wanders . . . amid the scenes of a half-forgotten tale.' While Captain Leslie Richardson writes of it, in 'Things Seen on the Riviera,' that it is 'a city of pure delight, a town of narrow streets, of dark archways, of many fountains, and shops open to all the winds of heaven, with the mist playing about the naked mountain-tops.'

Near Vence and Cagnes is Saint-Paul-du-Var, in whose streets one might expect to meet such persons as Giotto painted. Its circle of ramparts is unbroken; there are still the old gates, the towers, the bastions and the barbican. 'The path along the parapet that the sentry patrolled is undisturbed. One almost expects to hear his challenge for the password. The town is as ready to withstand the attack of an army of bowmen or of halberdiers as it ever was. It might even defy cannon if they were as small and as weak as the old piece of ordnance that still occupies the battery by the main gate.' In almost every street are examples of the little shops of the Middle Ages. 'No wonder the walls of the Paris salon are hung with pictures of Vence and Saint-Paul!' At Cagnes, Renoir died.

Near Cagnes, at Villeneuve-Loubet, is the Castle of Romée (or Roumieu) with a tablet in the courtyard testifying to Count Raymond's appreciation of him.

It doesn't seem to me that Nice (any more than Cannes) calls for much comment. It is an agreeable place of sojourn, a good centre for excursions. I like Nice; I enjoy it, for a while, but I don't think about much while there except creature comforts and watching the pleasure-seekers, and things of such sorts; and an occasional stroll in the old town, which is seldom seen by visitors to the new. As for hotels, there are the Negresso and the Ruhl, both very expensive. There's the Westminster, as well located and *not* expensive. And there are dozens — scores! — more. I have tried a good many of them without having developed enthusiasm for any. I am afraid that too many of them are run in that spirit which does least to endear to the traveller this locality. For motor hire on the Riviera I can commend Emile Paris, 7 rue Croix-de-Marbre, and Captain Mitchelson, 6 rue du Congrès.

If you have time, go up to Cimiez where Queen Victoria liked to stay. It was an important Roman town, but I don't believe you'll care about that as much as about the glimpses you may get of the splendid villas of to-day, and the view from the terrace beside the Franciscan monastery, where the marble cross is, and the glorious old oaks. And if you are thinking of making a sojourn at Nice, pray consider the Regina Hotel, at Cimiez, where Queen Victoria used to stay, and where you may live for about one fourth what you would pay for equal comfort down on the Promenade des Anglais.

And of course you'll go to Monte Carlo and Mentone by the Grande Corniche.

'Till the time of the First Empire,' write the authors of 'The French Riviera' in the Picture Guides, 'it was not easy to go from France to Genoa by the coast. The traveller who was not dismayed by the thought of sea-sickness, generally hired a felucca at Marseilles or at Antibes; for what is now known as the Route de la Corniche or Grande Corniche, was then nothing but a rough track, all that remained of the old Aurelian Way between Nice and San Remo.'

It was Napoleon who commanded the Grande Corniche to replace that rough track.

Some six miles from Nice, on the Grande Corniche, one looks down upon the ancient and picturesque village of Eze, on the Middle Corniche, which is one of the most fascinating places on the Riviera. 'People lived within its ramparts of rock,' Treves says, 'before the dawn of history.' Many masters it had, in turn, and its vicissitudes were manifold. It was one of the last strongholds of the Saracens on these shores.

'It was visited by plague and devastated by fever. It had a varied experience of assassination, of poisoning and of modes of torture; while its information on the subject of sudden death and its varieties must have been very full. . . . Every type of scoundrel that Europe could produce, during the Middle Ages, must, at one time or another, have rollicked and drank and sworn within its walls. The strange troopers who strutted up and down its astonished lanes in the spring would often be replaced by still stranger blusterers before the winter came.'

Eze had her troubadours, especially in the time when she owned Raymond Bérenger and his lady Béatrice as her lieges; and one of them wrote plaintive ditties about his polite passion for the Countess. Treves thought that 'the sound of these songs as they floated — like a scented breeze — down the lanes of the putrid town must have been interrupted, now and then, by the shriek of a strangled man in a cellar or the shout of the trembling watchman on the castle roof.'

Treves wrote his book only in 1920, and called Eze a chamber of death and desolation. Since then it has captured the fancy of some romantic souls who have reprieved the doddering ancient, given her a new lease of life, and set up within her venerable dwellings household altars of yet another race: beauty-lovers and history-worshippers, who lead an idyllic existence in these haunted streets above that sapphire sea.

Five miles farther, the Grande Corniche reaches La Turbie, hanging above Monte Carlo on the summit of those hills which 'crowd down to the sea with such menace as to threaten to push the light-hearted town into the deep.'

Here was a Roman town, the highest on that Aurelian way (begun in 241 B.C.), nearly eight hundred miles in length, which led from the Roman Forum to the Forum of Arles. And when once the traveller from Rome into Gaul had passed through the gate of Turbia, 'he could sit himself down on a cool bench in its shady street, wipe his brow, loosen his pack, let drop his staff and feel that the worst of the journey was over. He had crossed the frontier into Gaul and was almost within sight of the comforting city of Cemenelum (Cimiez) of which old travellers, gossiping in the Forum, had told so much.'

'La Turbie' — it is still from Treves that I am quoting — 'was a posting town that marked a critical stage in the

journey from the Eternal City. It was a place of great
bustle and commotion in the spacious Roman days; for
companies, large or small, were constantly arriving or leaving. . . . Sometimes it would be a body of Roman soldiers,
marching in rigid column, under the command of a dignified
centurion. At another time some great patrician, with his
retinue, would mount up to the town. He would grumble,
no doubt, at the steepness of the hill, but would be coaxed
by the bowing governor to come to the edge of the cliff and
look down upon Monaco Bay and upon the glorious line of
coast spread out upon either side of it. The patrician lady,
alighting from her litter, would thrill the little place with
curiosity and excitement . . . the last new *mode* of Rome,
and the way in which her hair was "done." . . . The suite at
the patrician's heels would be accosted by the young men
about town, eager to glean the latest news from men who
but a month or so ago had strolled about the Forum or
viewed some amazing spectacle from the galleries of the
Coliseum. . . . On occasion, too, a party of gladiators would
swagger along on their way to the arena at Cimiez, splendid
men, perfect in form, firm of foot, alert in carriage they
would swing down the street with a rhythmical step, followed by the children and followed, too, by the eyes of
every young woman.'

I wish I might quote more copiously, for I can think of
few things you'll enjoy more in La Turbie. But a very little
more must suffice.

This was, indeed, in those times 'a great caravanserai, a
halting-place on the march of civilization, a post by the side
of the inscrutable road that led from the wonder-teeming
East to the dull, unawakened land of the West; a road that
carried with it the making of a people who would dominate
the world when the power and the glory of Rome had passed
away.'

Of that Roman Turbia practically nothing is left but the ruins of the Tower of Victory raised by the Roman Senate to commemorate the victories of the Emperor Augustus over the tribes of southern Gaul and to record the final conquest of that tract of country. It was completed in 6 B.C., and was a colossal structure of supreme magnificence, a lofty tower very richly ornamented with a colonnade of pillars and statues, and on the top was a statue of Augustus eighteen or more feet high.

The great structure has been subjected to every imaginable violence, has furnished materials for buildings as far away as Genoa, yet is still majestic and, apparently, as long as the world endures will crown the everlasting hill.

The existing town of La Turbie, enveloped by its walls, sits strangely above Monte Carlo. And to it Sir Frederick paid this lovely tribute:

'Let such as are tired of this Vanity Fair (Monte Carlo) and of its make-believe palaces, climb up to the hill town. As they pass through the old gateway they enter into a world that was, into a town where the streets are silent and the houses homely and venerable. . . . The bold, imperious purple of the sea is changed for the tender forget-me-not blue of a strip of sky above the roofs. The dazzle of the sun is beyond the gate, but within are shadows as comforting as "the shadow of a rock in a weary land." Such light as enters falls upon an old lichen-covered wall, upon the arch of a Gothic window and upon simple things on balconies — a garment hanging to dry, a bird-cage, a pot of lavender. To those who are surfeited with riot and unreality La Turbie is a cloister, a place of peace.'

It is indeed! And as your way descends from that belvedere which gives you the far-famed panorama of the Azure Coast, you pass below another little old town, Roquebrune, which Sir Frederick Treves called 'The City of Peter Pan.'

'It is a cheerful little town, clean and trim . . . undoubtedly curious, and as one penetrates further into its by-ways
it becomes — as Alice in Wonderland would remark —
"curiouser and curiouser." It is largely a town of stairs, of
straight stairs and crooked stairs, of stairs that soar into
dark holes and are seen no more, of stairs that climb openly
to the outside of houses, of stairs bleached white, of stairs
green with weeds, and of stairs that stand alone — for the
place that they led to has gone. . . . The streets are mere
lanes and very narrow even for lanes. They appear to go
where they like, so long as they go uphill. . . . The houses
are old . . . they can hardly be said to have been designed.
. . . Some few are inclined to be gay in color, to be yellow or
pink, to have little balconies and green shutters and gar-
lands painted on the walls. . . . There are intense contrasts
of light and shade in the by-ways of Roquebrune, floods of
brilliant sunshine on the cobble stones and the walls alter-
nating with masses of black shadow. . . . There are suspi-
cious-looking doors of battered and decaying wood, stone
archways, cheery entries in the wall that open into homely
sitting rooms, as well as trap-like holes that lead into
mouldy vaults.

'One small street, the rue Pié, appears to have lost all
control over itself, for it dives insanely under another street
— houses, road and all — and then rushes down hill in the
dark to apparent destruction.'

He tells of the church and its 'dear little garden,' with
'many roses in it, a palm tree or two, and beds bright with
iris and hyacinth, narcissus and candytuft and with just
such contented flowers as are found about an old thatched
cottage. There is a well in the garden and a shady bench
with a far view over the Mediterranean, while many birds
fill the place with their singing.'

He tells of the old castle of the Lascaris.

'Roquebrune, as a town,' he says, 'belongs to the country of the story book. It is a town for boys and girls to play in. It is just the town they love to read about and dream about and to make the scene of the doings of their heroes and their heroines and their other queer people. . . . It is full of funny places, of whimsical streets and of those odd houses that children draw on slates when one of them has made the rapturous suggestion — "let us draw a street." It has an odd well too — a real well with real water — but it is bewitched and haunted by real witches . . . the people are afraid to come to it for water. Now a well of this kind is never met with in an ordinary town. . . .

'The garden of the church is a child's garden. . . . Nothing that happens in any story-book would seem out of place in Roquebrune. Indeed one is surprised in wandering through its curious ways to find it occupied by ordinary people, men with bowler hats and women who are obviously not princesses. One expects to come upon blind pedlars, old women in scarlet capes and pointed hats, mendicants who are really of royal blood, hags — especially hags with sticks — ladies wrapped in cloaks which just fail to conceal their golden hair, servants carrying heavy boxes with great secrecy, and mariners from excessively foreign ports.

'There is a steep, cobble-paved lane in Roquebrune up which Jack and Jill must assuredly have climbed when they went to fetch the pail of water which led to the regrettable accident. . . . By the parapet in the Place des Frères there is a stone upon which Little Boy Blue must have stood when he blew his horn; for no place could be conceived more appropriate for that exercise. There are walls too without number, walls both high and low, some bare, some green with ferns, which would satisfy the passion for sitting upon walls of a hundred Humpty Dumpties.

'The town itself is — I feel assured — the kind of town

that Jack reached when he climbed to the top of the Bean-stalk, for the entrance to Roquebrune is precisely the sort of entrance one would expect a beanstalk to lead to. One kitchen full of brown shadows, in a side street near the rue Pié, is that in which, almost without question, Old Mother Hubbard kept that hypothetical bone . . . while in a wicker cage in the window of a child's bedroom was the Blue Bird, singing as only that bird can sing.

'As there are still wolves in the woods about Roquebrune and as red hoods are still fashionable in the Place des Frères it is practically certain that Little Red Riding Hood lived here since it is difficult to imagine a town that would have suited her better. As for Jack the Giant Killer it is beyond dispute that he came to Roquebrune, for the very castle he approached is still standing, the very gate is there from which he hurled defiance to the giant as well as the very stair he ascended. Moreover there is a room or hall in the castle — or at least the remains of it — which obviously no one but a giant could have occupied.

'As time goes on archæologists will certainly prove, after due research, that Roquebrune is the City of Peter Pan. There is no town he would love so well; none so adapted to his particular tastes and habits, nor so convenient for the display of those domestic virtues which Wendy possessed. No one should grow up in this queer city, just as no place in a nursery tale should grow old.

'Peter Pan is not adapted to the cold, drear climate of England. He stands, as a figure in bronze, in Kensington Gardens with perhaps snow on his curly head or with rain dripping from the edge of his scanty shirt. He should be always in the sun, within sight of a sea which is ever blue and among hills which are deep in green. He could stride down a street in Roquebrune clad — as the sculptor shows him — only in his shirt without exciting more than a pleasant nod, but in the Bayswater Road he would attract attention. He is out of place in a London park in a waste of tired grass dotted with iron chairs which are let out at a penny apiece. Those delightful little people and those inquisitive animals who are peeping out of the crevices in the bronze rock upon which he stands would flourish in this sunny hill town, for there are rocks in the very streets among which they could make their homes.

'Then again Captain Hook would enjoy Roquebrune. It is so full of really horrible places and there are so many half-hidden windows out of which he could scream to the terror of honest folk. The pirates too would be more comfortable in this irregular city, for it is near the sea and close to that kind of cave without which no pirate is ever quite at ease. Moreover, the Serpentine affords but limited scope to those whose hearts are really devoted to the pursuits of piracy and buccaneering.

'So far I do not happen to have met with a pirate of Captain Hook's type within the walls of Roquebrune; but, late one afternoon when the place was lonely I saw a bent man plodding up in the shadows of the rue Mongollet. He was a sinewy creature with brown, hairy legs. I could not see his face because he bore on his shoulders a large and flabby burden, but I am convinced that he was Sindbad the Sailor, toiling up from the beach and carrying on his back the Old Man of the Sea.'

Did His Majesty, I wonder, have to become a surgical subject in order to retain by him that adorable person who wrote thus of Roquebrune? Could a Serjeant-Surgeon of such sort have anything to answer for in the recklessness of one Royal Highness with his life and limb? 'What care I for a collar-bone if its fracture fetches me Treves?' Was it to enjoy Treves that King Edward postponed his coronation to have appendicitis? We know it was Treves who cured him. Sir Frederick has wandered on now. What a happy adventurer he must be There!

I have owned his book since its publication, and have used it a goodish deal. But I have got better acquainted with it in writing this chapter than ever I was before, and I pay whole-hearted tribute to it as a model of its kind: scholarly and whimsical, historical and fanciful, delightful descriptions and a nice instinct for what to describe, catholic in the scope of its interests, genial in the treatment of them all. I wish that the publishers would reissue it in a handbook size that travellers to the Riviera might carry about with them. The ninety-two illustrations are all from photographs of Sir Frederick's own making. And don't think that because I have quoted freely from it I have given you its cream. I haven't skimmed it at all; I have merely given you a spoonful.

Some three miles after passing below Roquebrune, the Grande Corniche enters Menton which, like Nice, has an old town (though not nearly so old as Nice) and a new, 'resort' section spreading out for a mile or a mile and a half, or so, in each direction from the promontory on whose steep slopes the picturesque little old town is built. The east extension, known as Garavan, is believed by its ardent advocates (and if you stay at Menton more than a few minutes you become an advocate of the East Bay or of the West) to be more sheltered than the west, which is much more widespread and reaches to Cap Martin. All along the waterfront of both bays, and back from the water, and up on the hill slopes, are hotels almost innumerable and of nearly every grade; and *pensions* and lodgings and restaurants and tea-rooms and clubs, and shops — and British spinsters on 'stated' incomes. I'm not prepared to say that they wear 'elastic-side boots' (or Congress gaiters) as has been alleged; but they are sufficiently loyal to their Queen to maintain some individuality in dress, uninfluenced by the sumptuous displays at Monte Carlo, and to present an imposing mass of decorum which makes the respectability of Menton 'commendable, but at the same time almost awe-inspiring.'

Menton has so mild a climate that lemons, the most 'delicate' of citrus, are favored by it, and its oranges are of notable quality; yet one may mount from there (or from Nice, or Cannes) on a drowsy, balmy morning, to Peira Cava, spend some hours 'ski-ing' on the glistening snows, and 'back a favorite number at Monte Carlo in the evening.'

The gardens of Menton are among the most noted of this region of magnificent gardens; and if you cross the Italian frontier to visit the exceedingly interesting caverns of prehistoric man at Baousse-Rousse, I'd go on, three miles farther into Italy, and see the very famous gardens of Sir Thomas Hanbury — that is, if it were Monday or Friday, which are 'visiting days.'

That row of caves beside the Aurelian road is of extraordinary interest, and gives those who know how to read its 'evidence' a really great deal of information about those earliest known ancestors of ours who lived here fifty thousand years ago. But on a brief visit to Menton it is, I think, difficult to forego sunshine and flowers and focus thought upon Palæolithic progenitors.

Most wayfarers will prefer a tour of Cap Martin, 'through its dark shady woods and among the villas of crowned heads where Empresses loved to dwell.' And if time for some excursions be available, you'll doubtless climb to Sospel to see the ancient bridge and the mediæval town; though even that (to say nothing of Gorbio, and of Saint-Agnes — which can be reached only by mule-path or balloon) is for the sojourner, I should say, and not for the wayfarer.

From Cap Martin, your way along the shore, the Route

de Littoral, soon reaches Monte Carlo — which too many travellers associate only with the gambling at the Casino, though one might live in Monte Carlo almost oblivious of the Casino, as one lives in Paris oblivious of the Montmartre resorts.

Our Sir Frederick, who wrote with such child-heartedness and exquisite fantasy about Roquebrune, also liked Monte Carlo and waxed a bit scathing about the generalizations which are made of it by lurid writers who are none the less penny-a-liners even though they may receive a shilling a word. It was his opinion that 'those who wish to live the plain, unemotional life of a French country town will find that Monte Carlo fulfils their needs. They will meet with neither shocks nor distractions unless they seek them; for the circle within which the florid society of the town revolves is — like the roulette wheel — extremely small; whereas the quiet streets of Monaco, the olive groves, the hill paths, the lonely walks form a world that opens far.'

I have spent, at Monte Carlo, more time than it was worth, discounting the descriptions of the lurid confraternity as they fail to apply to the gaming-tables, or, rather, to their depressing habitués. The next time I go, I shall try the other 'game,' and see if I can learn to think of Monte Carlo apart from the dreary folk about the green baize, who seem to be getting so little fun out of their expensive pastime. Perhaps I shall make my sojourn at Beausoleil, on the hill above, which is a French commune.

Monaco has no hotels; but between it and Monte Carlo, on the Monaco roadstead, is La Condamine, with hotels of every class.

West of Monaco, on the coast road back to Nice, is Beaulieu, of tropic vegetation and villas rather oppressively magnificent; and the long narrow tongue of tree-covered rock which splits at its south or seaward end into Cap de

Saint-Hospice and Cap Ferrat. Then comes Villefranche, on its big, deep bay, 'capable of receiving the fleets of Europe'; and, six miles farther, the quais of Nice.

When you start north from Nice, your route will, in part, depend on the season. Only in late June, July, and August would you attempt the most spectacular reaches of the Route des Alpes which lie by way of Barcelonnette and Briançon.

At other times you go via Digne, Sisteron, and Gap, to Grenoble; thence, via La Grande Chartreuse, Chambéry, Aix-les-Bains, Annecy, to Geneva; or from Grenoble to Lyon.

What is usually meant when the Route des Alpes is spoken of is the journey from Évian via Briançon, a distance of four hundred and seventy miles which the autocars of the P. L. M. railroad system cover in six stages. The first stage, a hundred miles, is to Barcelonnette; the second, seventy-five miles, is to Briançon; the third, seventy-five miles, is to Grenoble; the fourth, about seventy-six miles, is from Grenoble, via the Grande Chartreuse, Chambéry, Aix-les-Bains, to Annecy; the fifth, only about sixty-four miles, is to Chamonix; and the sixth, about eighty miles, is to Évian on the shores of Lake Geneva.

There are several alternative routes, but I will not attempt to particularize them here. They are, perhaps, matter rather for specific working out with each traveller, and depend on whether he is using the P. L. M. cars or driving his own, on the season of year and the idiosyncrasies of that particular season, and on whither he is bound — on his way north — to Paris, to Switzerland, to eastern France, to the Netherlands, to a channel port.

This being in no sense a 'road book,' I shall not try to describe the risings and fallings of that superb route. The P. L. M. Company distributes, gratis, a very satisfactory booklet on it — two, in fact, one by Sir Martin Conway, former president of the Alpine Club. And the Picture Guides include an excellent volume, 'Nice to Évian, by the Route des Alpes,' by Henri Ferrand. While the Automobile Association (London) issues 'The Alps for the Motorist,' by Charles L. Freeston, F.R.G.S., author of 'France for the Motorist,' published by Cassell in England and Scribner in the United States.

For those who do not like high altitudes, I suggest a return north by way of the right bank of the Rhône (that is, if the left bank were followed coming south), or going to Nîmes, thence to Carcassonne, and Toulouse, and north through Cahors and Brive and Limoges.

VI
TO BIARRITZ AND THE PYRÉNÉES
AND BACK

For rail travel and excursions from centres, most persons will probably make Avignon their first stop; then Arles; then Cannes or Nice.

The choice of routes to Biarritz is a wide one, and your selection will, naturally, depend on whether you want to get there as directly as possible, and make your necessary stops at the highest-grade hotels available, or whether the journey is as important as the destination, and you want to see the most interesting things en route. Then, the latter being the case, what you have already seen would determine how you may chart your course to cover the utmost of what gives you greatest pleasure.

For the most direct and 'best hotel' route, I'd say: First day, Orléans for luncheon, Tours for the night; second day, Poitiers for luncheon, and probably Angoulême for the night; third day, Bordeaux for luncheon, and Biarritz for the night.

This same route, stretched to seven days, would enable you to visit the châteaux of the Loire, spend a half-day at Poitiers, and have a night at Arcachon.

If you have seen the châteaux, and have not seen lower Brittany, takes Chartres, Le Mans; Laval, Vitré, Rennes; Josselin, Vannes, with an excursion to Quiberon and Carnac; Guérande, La Boule, Nantes; Les Sables-d'Olonne, La Rochelle; Saintes, Royan; Bordeaux, Arcachon; Biarritz. This is, after the first two days, a seashore trip. And as

Biarritz and the Pyrénées should be visited from May to
September (and are not in any sense a place for winter touring, though the winter sports in the Pyrénées are fine for
the sojourner), this is 'an approach' that should be specially
agreeable in summer. To make it include Mont-Saint-
Michel, follow the route of our Chapter One for two days;
then go from Mont-Saint-Michel to Saint-Malo, Dinard,
Dinan; then, Vannes, and as before.

Another possible route is: Orléans, Bourges; second
night at Limoges; third day, Périgueux, Bordeaux — or
Arcachon; fourth night, Biarritz.

When I am en route in a country like France, every alluring place that I pass reasonably near to and cannot stop to
make or to renew acquaintance with, is so much loss.

That this point of view is not a universal one, I am reminded sometimes by reading other books on Touring in
France. I have, for instance, just read one by a 'F.R.G.S.'
who says that 'the only interesting sight of these 188 kilometres (from Bourges to Limoges) is the old Château
Raoul at Châteauroux.' Yet that is, in part, through the
Valley of the Creuse and other country George Sand has
endeared to many; and there are a score of things to see, if
not on the highway, at least in close proximity to it. Much
depends, I realize, on one's theory of touring; and mine may
be sheer folly for many tourists. But to me the delight of
travel is not merely to change, as Darwin said, the names
of places on the map to pictures one can carry in the mind,
but to make the names of places in great books, great deeds,
great lives, a part of my personal experience, my memory.

Many travellers find delight, and diversion, in observing
people and customs which seem strange and 'different' to
them.

I may as well admit that strangeness doesn't interest me
nearly as much as feeling familiarity; recognizing a kind of

kinship; finding people to be just as some great interpreter has described them — and great interpreters are never more than picturesquely and incidentally concerned with the 'differentness' of people; they are primarily concerned, always, with the fundamental likeness of humans in widely separated places and ages, beneath strangely diverse styles of rooftrees and waistcoats.

There is the kind of travel writer whose forte it is to describe the unknown. The greatest travel books of the ages have, I dare say, been written by that kind of writer, who is also explorer, discoverer.

I am, as you well know, no explorer, nor discoverer, nor adventurer; but a pilgrim, visiting shrines of certain sorts; and loving them not because I unearthed them, but because of who led me thither; not because I alone can tell about them, but because they have been gloriously told about for ages past; not because I have a unique feeling for them, but because so many persons have had it before me, so many have it with me, and so many will have it after me. I don't often like to be at a shrine in company with many fellow worshippers — as you know — but I do like shrines which many have sought and worshipped at.

Biarritz in itself would never lure me seven hundred and eighty miles from Paris; but the Pyrénées and the Basque country would; and even were there no Pyrénées at the end of those miles, I'd rate the trip there and back a great experience.

Suppose you make your own choice of routes as far as Angoulême or Limoges or Saintes.

The route to Angoulême would probably be as in our Chapter Four; to Limoges it might be the same, including Poitiers, and thence by Route 147 to Limoges, or by way of Orléans, Vierzon, Châteauroux, and Argenton-sur-Creuse.

The route to Saintes might be from Nantes and La

Rochelle, or from Angers and Niort, or from Saumur by
way of Montreuil-Bellay, Thouars, Parthenay, then Niort.
Each route has its attractions.

Suppose (since we must start somewhere) that we assume you have reached Limoges, and are, I dare say, at the
Hôtel de La Paix, in Place Jourdan on the east side of town.

The principal things to *see* in Limoges are the Musée
Adrien Dubouché, for the collections of Limoges enamels
and china; the cathedral, and perhaps Saint-Pierre-du-
Queyroix and Saint-Michel-des-Lions; the Pont-Saint-
Martial, over the Vienne, a thirteenth-century bridge on
Roman foundations; and the rue de la Boucherie and its
neighborhood.

But, before *seeing*, the thing to do, always, is to *recall*.
And the things to recall at Limoges are, perhaps, these:

There was a large force from here standing by Vercingetorix as he tried to hold Alésia. The Roman masters,
when established, not only built palaces and baths and
an arena, but created a senate here, and authorized a 'mint.'
The pretty tradition is that Saint Martial, who introduced
Christianity here, was the little boy on whose head Jesus
laid His 'kind hand when He said, "Let the little ones come
unto me."' Whether this is an historical fact or a charming
story is immaterial; what *is* material is that a community
believed it for centuries — probably a goodly portion of it
still believes this — and must surely have been influenced
by it in some lovely ways. The head of Saint Martial is in
his shrine behind the high altar of Saint-Michel-des-Lions;
and even if it happened to be somebody else's head, I don't
see how people could venerate it, thinking of the 'kind
hand' and the tender gospel proclaiming 'of such is the
Kingdom of Heaven,' without being made kinder and
tenderer thereby. Do *you?*

Then there's Saint Éloi, who was born hereabouts toward

the close of the sixth century, and was a goldsmith so skilled that he became artificer to the kings, Clothair II and Dagobert. From this, he turned to the Church, and became a great bishop. But to his influence Limoges liked to think that it owed its fame and fortune as a goldsmiths' town in the Middle Ages.

In the twelfth century Limoges began to be celebrated for its wonderful enamels on metals which were eagerly sought by all Europe. And just about the time, in the eighteenth century, when this art was dying out, temporarily, a country doctor, who had doubtless been reading his scientific journals, scraped some sticky white clay from a neighbor's shoe heels, and wondered if it might not be that kaolin, essential ingredient of china or porcelain, samples of which had recently been sent to France by a Jesuit missionary to China. It was! The clay was traced to Saint-Yrieix, twenty-five miles from Limoges on the way to Brive, whose quarries have since yielded the china-clay for Limoges and for Sèvres. There have been serious labor troubles among the porcelain-workers in Limoges, of recent years, and I do not know the present status of the industry; but about 1910, it employed some thirteen thousand persons in Limoges and vicinity, many of whom painted those Limoges 'sets' no prideful housekeeper would be without. The Havilands, of Vermont and New York, who founded a factory at Limoges in 1849, are said still to be American citizens in the third generation.

Limoges has sent into the world a number of eminent sons, on many of whom it would be good to reflect if we had time and space. But there is one upon whom we shall do well to concentrate, I think — we who are on our way to Bordeaux: Pierre Vergniaud, who was born at number 10, rue du Clocher, just about the time the doctor discovered the kaolin pits at Saint-Yrieix. Pierre went to the college of the Jesuits here, and attracted notice for his verses and his eloquent declamation. Hence he went to Paris for further education, especially in the law, and returned to this part of the country to practice.

In August, 1791, he was elected to the National Legislative Assembly, and returned to Paris toward the end of September. On October 25th, he made his first speech before the Assembly, and so impressed it that he was almost immediately elected its president. At that time, Vergniaud advocated a constitutional monarchy. But the flight of the royal family, in June, 1791, filled him with distrust of Louis XVI and he was won over to the side which favored a republic. He was presiding, in the National Assembly, when the royal family took refuge there after the storming and sacking of the Tuileries on August 10, 1792. To the request of the King for protection, he replied in dignified and respectful language. An extraordinary commission was appointed: Vergniaud wrote and read its recommendations, which were that a National Convention be formed; that the King be provisionally suspended, a governor appointed for his son, and the royal family consigned to the Luxembourg. But he was not strong enough to hold back those who had been waiting for such an opportunity as this to let loose their violence. With all his tremendous power, Vergniaud denounced the September Massacres. But even then he must have seen that the Revolution was sweeping whither he would not, could not, follow.

On the last day of December, '92, he made before the Convention an oration which was 'probably one of the greatest combinations of sound reasoning, sagacity, and eloquence which has ever been displayed in the annals of French politics. He pronounced (in the matter of the King's trial) in favor of an appeal to the people. He pictured the consequences of that temper of vengeance which animated

the Parisian mob and was fatally controlling the policy of
the Convention, and the prostration which would ensue to
France after even a successful struggle with a European
coalition, which would spring up after the murder of a King.'

Nevertheless, when his great effort had failed and the
Convention made itself the tribunal, Vergniaud voted for
the death of the King; and to him fell the exceedingly pain-
ful duty of announcing the result of the vote.

He vehemently opposed the institution of a revolutionary
tribunal, declaring that he and his party would all die
rather than consent to it. And die they all did! — Vergniaud, the last to mount the scaffold, singing the 'Marseillaise' till silenced. You paid your tribute to them in the
Chapel of the Conciergerie at Paris, where they banqueted
that last night on earth; and in the Place de la Concorde,
where they sang unfalteringly as their number dwindled on
that chill October day a trifle over two weeks after the execution of the Queen, and a trifle over one week before Madame Roland came; and in the little burial plot beside the
Chapelle Expiatoire, where they lie at rest. At Bordeaux
you are to see the thrillingly fine monument to these
Girondists and salute a section of the country whose name
they carry through history as a synonym for lofty, courageous moderation in a frenzied and demagogic period.

To reach Vergniaud's birthplace, go west from your hotel
without turning; the street changes its name several times,
but not its direction, and eventually becomes rue du
Clocher. Just beyond, is Saint-Michel-des-Lions, where
rich, warm light from fine fifteenth-century windows filters
down in jewel-radiance on the shrine where Saint Martial's
head may be.

On the other side of the Place de la Motte from this
church is the Market Hall, and from the southeast corner
of this begins the curving lane called rue de la Boucherie

lined with butchers' stalls belonging to the powerful Guild
or Corporation of Butchers, founded in the tenth century
and long since become by intermarriage a family as well as
a trade clan. There probably is not a better street in France
in which to consider the industrial corporations of the
Middle Ages; but if your stop at Limoges be in warmish
weather, it may well be that you will do your looking a little hurriedly, and your reflecting at some distance.

The evolution of a castle community, with its manu-
facturing workers of every sort, into a town, is absorbingly
interesting.

First of all, the lords of certain castles, being good business men or having such as their stewards, are able to produce more than their own households, numerous though
they be, need; and begin to be captains of industry as well
as 'patriarchs' or seigneurs; they form associations for the
promotion and extension of trade.

Then, the artisans of a castle group themselves together
in a fraternity — doubtless with the idea of profiting by
their labor beyond the old compensation, which was simply
their 'keep.' And as time goes on, we see them, in the larger
communities into which the castles have expanded, in work-
shops which are open to all comers. They continue to serve
their lords, in a degree; but they have begun to serve themselves as well. And by and by those whose first bond was a
common household where each worked for all the others,
find that they have a closer bond — in the larger community — with those who do the same kind of work as themselves. So the fraternities of workers become closer and
closer corporations of weavers, of fullers, of butchers and
bakers and candlestick-makers, which gradually assume the
regulation of their craft and trade. Mighty interesting
reading — those regulations! But I daresay we ought not
to go into detail about them here. If you want a brief

résumé of them, you have it in Chapter XVI of Funck-Brentano's book on 'The Middle Ages.'

A stone's throw northeast of the rue des Boucheries is the Place des Bancs with some picturesque old houses. All this part of the present city of Limoges is what used to be called the *ville* or the *château;* it began to group itself, in the tenth century, around Saint Martial's tomb, in a rivalry with the cité, grouped around the cathedral; each had its own ramparts, its own overlord, its separate system of administration — the cité under the Bishop, and the ville or château under the Viscounts of Limoges — and this survived until the Revolution. In the Hundred Years' War, the Bishops sided with the French, while the Viscounts yielded a grudging allegiance to the English. That must have made things interesting for the inhabitants!

When you leave Place des Bancs, walk up rue Haute Vienne toward the Hôtel de Ville and thence into Boulevard Louis Blanc which is on part of the Viscounts' ramparts. Then, walk northeast in rue des Charseix to boulevard de la Cité, which was part of the Bishops' ramparts. Their cité was of small extent, and it won't take you long to explore it all, to the river and the Pont Saint-Étienne — which is a thirteenth-century construction on Roman foundations. The cathedral has many beautiful sculptural features, and good stained glass.

The Musée Adrien Dubouché is on the other side of town, west of the Viscounts' walls. It contains more than eight thousand objects, constituting a complete history of ceramics from the earliest times, and a very important chapter in the history of enamels. Beside it is the National School of Decorative Arts where the thousands of porcelain-painters and enamel-workers are trained.

Leaving Limoges, you might take that west side of the

triangle we spoke of in Chapter Four as having Limoges for
its apex and Périgueux and Brive for its base corners; and
go through Périgueux to Bordeaux. Or you might (if you
were a zigzagging person like me) follow that Route 21
only as far as Chalus; then, cut across to La Rochefoucauld,
and into Angoulême to 'pick up' Route 141 for Cognac and
Saintes; and spend the night at Royan.

Chalus is where Richard of the Lion Heart got his death-
wound. But it wasn't a 'battle-field' in the ordinary sense,
as some writers rather loosely refer to it — hoping, perhaps,
to make the episode a little more romantic. Richard, who
was chronically 'broke,' heard that a peasant on the land
of his vassal Vidomar, Viscount of Limoges, had ploughed
up a Roman treasure hoard. Richard demanded half, and
was furious when offered *all* — or what Vidomar said was
all; which was a handful of old coins. The story had grown
rapidly on its way to Richard, and by the time he got it, the
unearthed treasure was a great lot of solid gold statues
sitting around a solid gold table. And Vidomar was trying
to put him off with a few mildewed coins! So Richard, taking Berengaria with him (or, perhaps, not exactly *taking*
her, so much as accepting her wifely company and care),
came to see about those gold statues. Obviously, the thing
to do was to take the castle and all it contained — as a
lesson to vassals who 'held out on' their lieges. This
Richard — with a small force of men — proceeded to do.
And when he had taken it, he hanged to its walls all the
garrison except one man, Gourdon, who had shot the arrow
which pierced Richard's shoulder. This man he pardoned.
There seems to be some doubt as to where Richard died.
At Chinon, they tell us his last sigh was there. The
last we know of him in life, is here at Chalus. If you have
your 'Histoire de France en Cent Tableaux,' you have a
picture of that arrow striking Richard. There isn't much

to see at Chalus now — just a ruined bit of the castle that Richard took. I dare say one must be a sentimentalist, of sorts, to feel rewarded for a visit to it. But have I ever tried to plead 'not guilty' to the charge of being sentimental? What were the defects of Richard's qualities and the short-comings of his age, I know pretty well. But who that has learned anything of life puts aught away from him because it isn't perfect? Faults teach us at least as much as flawless-ness. Richard, I hold, is part of everybody's Golden Age; to thrill about him, whether he deserved it or not, is our birthright. And having thrilled about him in one's Golden Age, how can one be cold toward him when the days are no longer suffused except by recollection? Crimes of sorts I may be brought to book for; but snatching the Lion Heart from youth shall not be one of them. If you have done with youth, you may ignore Chalus.

West of Angoulême, on Route 141, you come (in a trifle over twenty-six miles) to Cognac, which is — as Anita Loos' 'blonde' found the Place Vendôme — 'full of his-torical names,' like Hennessy and Martell. One of the least convivial recollections of all my travel days has to do with stopping at Cognac about three o'clock one afternoon in May, in company with two or three friends who felt that an appropriate thing to do would be to partake of some Hennessy or Martell *at* Cognac. Now, I like my brandy in plum-pudding sauce and in egg-nogg, and on crêpes su-zette; but I don't 'hanker for it *neat*,' unless I'm sick. So the effort to be properly commemorative at Cognac, in mid-afternoon, sitting out in front of an otherwise-unpat-ronized café on a glaring but somnolent square, was — for me — a total failure, even when my co-celebrants charged me to reflect how often, after my return home, I would think regretfully of that five-star or ten-star or whatever it was which I couldn't drink at Cognac. If your errand

to Cognac is to pay your respects to some of those 'historical names,' I trust you may find conditions more con-
ducive.

Francis I was born at Cognac, but it seemed to me his
name was less 'historical' there now than others.

The ride along the Charente, from Cognac to Saintes, is
a most beautiful one. And Saintes is worth going far to see,
I thought — though you may feel quite otherwise. I recall
that we paid respectful interest to the Abbey-Church of
Notre-Dame, but at this moment I can't tell you *why;* because we were much diverted from architecture and antiquity by a wedding which was taking place in the vicinity.
What we had come principally to see was the amphitheatre and the Arch of Germanicus. You have the latter
on your left as you enter Saintes from Cognac, just before
you cross the Charente; also, a statue of Bernard Palissy,
the great potter, whose house you visited in the rue du
Dragon at Paris; he produced some of his first enamel-ware
here.

The amphitheatre is on the other side of the river. To
reach it, you drive straight on, after crossing the Charente,
along Cours National to the Place du Bastion; then turn
south, past the fair grounds, and west to the grass-grown
ruins of the arena, which is about the age of the one at
Rome — perhaps a generation younger. When I saw it,
children were playing — some of them with puppies —
where the 'nigger heaven' or 'peanut gallery' must have
been when gladiators fought to the death there below, or
Christians died for the faith that was in them. Mothers
were sewing homely things. Wild flowers blew, on their
slender stems, among the uncut grasses, ruffled by a
languorous May breeze. And overhead, the most lamblike
and straggling little fleecy cloud flocks pastured on the vast
blue uplands of the southern sky. I didn't count the arches

that are left. But in a half-waking and half-dreamful reverie I was vaguely conscious of the generations which have played about this 'bowl' since Rome's Empire crumbled, and Charlemagne's after it (Saintes is on the road that the paladins of Charlemagne knew well), and Eleanor's sons saw her Aquitaine dismembered, and Saint Louis made her grandson (Henry III) sign a treaty here abandoning his claims on Normandy.

Twenty-three miles from Saintes, west by a little south, is Royan, next to Biarritz the most popular watering-place in this part of France. Its beautiful beaches of fine, firm, white sand are fringed by dark pine woods which in places almost come down to meet the water; there are many excellent hotels (for instance, you will find the Palace and the Paris side by side, and offering a choice in the matter of price); the sea-and-pine air is delicious; the sea-foods ditto; and there are tennis courts, a casino, etc. For those who love tennis, a good game in the late afternoon of a day of travel, followed by a dip or swim in the surf, and a chance to see something of a lively casino after a good dinner, 'seasons' sight-seeing delightfully.

And this is an interesting locality — this mouth of the Gironde. The first known lighthouse is the Phare de Cordouan on a rock at the entrance of this estuary; it was built by the Black Prince, and the one which replaces it is the work, in part, of the architect of the Escorial. It stands five miles from La Pointe-de-Grave where Lafayette embarked, in 1777, to come to America; and a monument there commemorates the coming to France of American troops in 1917: 'Lafayette, we are here.' Near there is where Zaccheus is believed to have landed — he who became Amadour — along with Veronica his wife, and Martial (I suppose the one on whose head the Kind Hand was laid). The church built to commemorate their landing was buried by the shifting sands; and after one hundred and fifteen years it was dug out and restored to service.

These places are at the tip or land's-end of the Médoc, that triangle of land between the Atlantic and the Gironde, which is world-famed for its vineyards; they lie nearer to the estuary than to the sea. Should you feel moved to make a pilgrimage in the Médoc, I think you'd better do it from Bordeaux; for I believe motors are not transported from Royan across the mouth of the Gironde. Otherwise, you must just *look* over, as best you can, toward Pauillac, where Château-Latour and Château-Lafite come from. For a short ride from Bordeaux to a celebrated vineyard, you might go as far up the Médoc as Margaux (fifteen miles) where Château-Margaux comes from.

In the event of your liking Royan so well that you decide to stop there for a day or two, you could make it a base for excursions at least as far afield as Rochefort (twenty-five miles), which gave Pierre Loti to a grateful world. And at Fouras, eight miles beyond Rochefort, you could hire a boatman to take you to the tiny Île d'Aix where Napoleon spent his last week on French soil. He was taken on board the Bellerophon from this island on July 15, 1815. You may visit the room that was his last French lodging.

Or you could go on (twenty miles) from Rochefort to La Rochelle, and perhaps visit the Île de Ré, devoted to horticulture and (I'm told — I haven't seen them!) to donkeys that wear trousers.

Much, hereabouts, for the picture-maker and seeker for material to write about.

If you are very keen about seeing quaint living conditions, I suggest that you take the coast road, in the morning as you leave Royan, down (seven miles) to Meschers, where there is a cliff-dwelling community living in holes of rocks that rise sheer out of the sea. These privileged persons are able to fish without leaving home, and seem to do a fair business, letting down their big nets from in front of their own 'doors.'

Your most direct route to Bordeaux, however, is by Cozes and Mirambeau and Blaye.

Blaye is situated, Ramon de Loi says, 'on the crossroads. The pagan tripper travelling south in search of war and booty, the Roman legions travelling north on the same honorable quest, the mediæval pilgrim from Normandy or Anjou who eased both his soul and his body by a vacation pilgrimage through the pleasant country of Gascony, as well as the mediæval merchant travelling from the supercivilized and sybaritic south north to London, all passed through the city of Blaye.

'The road to the north begins at the base of the hill which now bears the citadel which once bore the city. It leads north through Saintes, Poitiers, Tours, and Paris or Normandy. Eleanor of Aquitaine, Bernard de Ventadour, Charlemagne, Pepin, Roland, William of Aquitaine — to name only a few of the thousands of illustrious people who followed this trail — all passed Blaye and stopped there for a night or two. . . .

'Roland and Olivier, the followers of Charlemagne who founded France . . . had taken an army south into the Pyrénées — they followed the old trail, via Blaye and Bordeaux — and joined the army of Charlemagne and defeated the Saracens at Roncesvalles. On their return, they were caught in a narrow pass, and their rear-guard was completely destroyed. . . . The bodies of Roland and Olivier were brought to Blaye for burial, and the mediæval tourists could see not only the tombs but the sword of Roland, the sword Durendal that had drunk of the blood of many pagans.'

Not much that is remindful of all this can be seen now at Blaye. But with a retrospective eye, what may you not enjoy!

Eight miles nearer Bordeaux is Bourg-sur-Gironde, at the confluence of the Dordogne and the Garonne, which unite to form the Gironde — not really a river at all, but rather a long inlet of the sea or outlet of many rivers into the sea.

Bordeaux is the third largest port in France, but it is sixty miles from the sea, on the left bank of the Garonne about fifteen miles before it joins with the Dordogne to make the Gironde. Until the day of leviathan ships, even the biggest of ocean-going craft came up the river and docked at the quays. It is said that there is room for twelve hundred ships; but the monsters of the deep cannot get up there — which is a pity, because it would be such a delightful port by which to enter France. We heard much, for a while, of what Americans were going to do to make Bordeaux a more completely efficient port. But it would seem that their Aladdin ideas did not work well with the slow, substantial growth of this southern city where the Romans had a university and things have been evolving quite satisfactorily ever since. We 'jazzed 'em up for a coupla years,' as Dr. Gibbons reminds us, and then left them to do things in their own way — which must have been a considerable relief to them, although they were genial hosts to our men during the War.

Now, what your plans may be with regard to Bordeaux, I cannot guess. The 'attractions' are:

The handsome city itself, and particularly its water-front.

The cathedral and one or two of the churches.

An excellent museum of art, and a sumptuous theatre.

The tomb of Montaigne.

BORDEAUX

From an old lithograph

And two of the best restaurants in the world.

So celebrated throughout the epicurean world is one of these latter that to go to Bordeaux and not worship at least once at its shrine is an unthinkable calamity.

I recently met a lady who had motored in this part of France last year and spent two days at Bordeaux. When she got home, and spoke of Bordeaux, all that was asked her was: 'And *how* was the Chapon Fin?' To which she had to reply that she didn't know what the Chapon Fin was. The pitying looks her friends gave her, made her feel like bringing suit for damages against the touring company which prepared her itinerary without mentioning the Chapon Fin and sent her forth with a chauffeur-courier who made no suggestion about it.

Never let it be upon my head that I let any one go to Bordeaux ignorant of the Chapon Fin and also of the Chapeau-Rouge!

You could, were you bent upon spending the night at Arcachon, by the pine woods and the sea, lunch and dine at Bordeaux and get on to Arcachon after dinner. It is thirty-seven and a half miles, but the route is a veritable boulevard and you could cover it in about an hour.

But it may be that you want to make an excursion into the Médoc, or cannot bear to be so close as this to Montaigne's home and not visit it. In that case, you would spend this night at Bordeaux; and you could choose between a hotel like the Bordeaux on Place de la Comédie, or the Montré on rue Montesquieu and Place Grands Hommes.

Entering Bordeaux from Blaye and Bourg, you cross the Garonne by the Pont-de-Bordeaux, from the middle of which there is a notably fine view, downstream and up, but especially the former.

The porte facing you near the bridgehead is Porte de

Bourgogne at the entrance to the Cours Victor Hugo; the
heaven-piercing spire on your left is the belfry of Saint-
Michel, built in the late-fifteenth century; the elegant
Gothic gateway a little way downstream is the Porte de
Caillau, erected in 1495 as an arch of triumph in honor of
Charles VIII — Bordeaux having rather recently become
French again after three centuries of belonging to the Eng-
lish — at the entrance of the old palace of the Dukes of
Aquitaine and of the English Kings; and beyond this,
following the noble curve of the river, you have the Place
de la Bourse, designed by Gabriel, to whom is due, also, the
Place de la Concorde at Paris.

Should you be thinking of luncheon above all else, turn
to your right on leaving the bridge and follow the quais,
past the Porte de Caillau, and the Custom House (Douane)
and the Bourse (Stock Exchange) to the Place Richelieu.
Turning up here into Cours Chapeau Rouge, you soon
come to the restaurant of that name, at number 32. If it is
the Chapon Fin you seek first, continue, past the Place de
la Comédie (where the great theatre is, and the Hôtel de
Bordeaux), turn, right, at rue Voltaire and up to Place
Grands Hommes. The Temple of Epicurus is on the north
side of the circular *place*, at the corner of rue Montesquieu
and opposite to the rue Montaigne — two of the 'great
men' for whom the circle is named; the others being Voltaire, whose *rue* you came up, and Rousseau whose *rue* runs
from the circle toward Place de Tourny.

I thought I might make a few suggestions about food to
eat and wine to drink at Bordeaux; but I quail before the
responsibility. Best choose, as always, after conference
with your head waiter; and don't hesitate to ask what are
the component parts of any dish he commends — don't
order, at random, something you may not like, when a little
further discussion will help you to select a meal that is
ravishing.

After luncheon, take rue Montaigne to the Allées de Tourny, and see the Fountain of the Girondins and the Place des Quinconces.

Cours du Maréchal Foch, beside the fountain, will lead you to Cours de Verdun. And if you turn left there along the Public Garden, you must soon turn right at Place de Tourny if you want to see the Palais Gallien, the ruins of a Roman amphitheatre of the third century. Otherwise, continue, along Cours Georges Clemenceau, to Place Gambetta, where the guillotine stood on which three hundred persons perished in the Revolution. You'll recall how Tallien was sent down here to speed up the work of the executioner; and how he found in one of the prisons of the Terror the beautiful marquise he had adored since he, an inky printer's devil, saw her sitting to Madame Le Brun for a portrait: Thèrézia Cabarrus; and how he freed her and took her back to Paris; and how, when she was imprisoned there and again in the shadow of the guillotine, he made the frantic attack upon Robespierre which led to the latter's arrest and death and the end of the Reign of Terror.

A great deal in Bordeaux is as the Girondists knew it, and as Tallien and Thèrézia saw it.

Rue Dauphine, on the other side of Place Gambetta, may be followed to its angle with Cours d'Albert; and almost at the angle you have the musée, which has among its collections a number of pictures which are doubtless familiar to you through frequent reproductions, and many more with which you'll be glad to make acquaintance if your time permits. (Carle Vernet and Rosa Bonheur were natives of Bordeaux.) But if I had to sacrifice much, in making a hasty survey of Bordeaux, I'd omit the museum rather than the theatre; because scarcely anywhere else in Europe can you see so beautiful a theatre. Architects have imitated it for a hundred and fifty years without improving on it.

And, for historical interest, I know you'll wish to see where the National Assembly of 1871 sat at its great task of extracting France from the humiliating position in which she found herself as the result of the Franco-Prussian War.

Behind the museum is the Hôtel de Ville, which was Napoleon's palace and then the residence of the restored Bourbons. And across from this is the cathedral, in the nave of which you may see Eleanor of Aquitaine twice married. The first occasion, August 1, 1137, was an occasion indeed; for on that day Eleanor was not only married to the heir of France, but was made Duchess of Aquitaine by the abdication of her grandfather, crowned as such, and — before the eventful day was over — learned that she was also Queen of France. The next occasion was on May-Day, 1152, when Eleanor, in her thirty-second year, was married to Henry Plantagenet aged nineteen — she having been divorced but six weeks, and being almost on the eve of bearing Henry's first child — or at least her first child to Henry. Therewith Bordeaux becomes, if in no sense an English city, a possession of the English Crown; and continues so to be until late in the reign of Charles VII.

The choir of Bordeaux Cathedral was begun in the bishopric of Bertrand de Got, a native of this region (Uzeste is his birthplace and burial-place), who left here in 1305 to become Pope Clement V; who established the Papacy at Avignon, persecuted the Templars, and soon followed Jacques de Molay into the other world.

One of the most gorgeous pageants the cathedral ever witnessed was the 'joyous entry' into Bordeaux of another Eleanor — the sister of Charles V of Spain, forced by him in marriage upon his late captive, Francis I.

They were married at 2 A.M. in the monastery of Captieux; and Francis, who was polite, but made no pretence of concealing his repugnance for the marriage, conducted his

bride to within thirteen miles of Bordeaux, then left her to
make her entry alone, as regal etiquette seemed to demand.

Eleanor was travelling down the Garonne by barge. And
as a roar of artillery from the harbor announced to the sumptuously decked and expectant city that the royal galleys
were approaching, a state barge with thirty-five *grandes
dames* of France set out to meet them, preceded by a barge-
ful of musicians and followed by a procession of four hundred galleys, boats, vessels of every description. Among the
thirty-five ladies who went to receive the new Queen, were
Diane de Poitiers on whom the bridegroom had already —
'tis said — looked with a more than favoring eye; and
Mademoiselle de Heilly, his reigning mistress, who was in
effect the Queen of France (she was not yet Duchesse
d'Estampes). And it was on this occasion that Diane de
Poitiers first saw Henry, Duke of Orléans, returning with
his brother from their captivity in Spain, where they had
been held as hostages after their father's release. (We shall
have more of this captivity, as we near the Spanish border.)
Diane was in her thirty-second year, had a married daughter with her, but was not yet a widow. Henry was a sad
little boy of fourteen, motherless and not very appealing to
his gaiety-loving father. Diane felt tender sympathy for
him — so the story goes — and won his hungry heart, to
hold it forever.

The new Queen was very gorgeous. Her fair hair, we're
told, rippled to the ground, and she wore it floating that
day, confined only by a net of gold thread, surmounted by a
cap of crimson velvet bordered with pearls and ornamented
with a small white plume. Her robe was of crimson velvet,
its many slashings bordered with bands of jewels. Over this
she wore a mantle of white satin bordered by strings of rubies, emeralds, and diamonds. Her earrings were diamonds
each the size of a small nut; and round her neck she wore

the King's gift to her, a necklace of diamonds and rubies with a centre diamond of immense size. Her fingers were covered with jewels, among them a priceless ruby which had belonged to Queen Claude.

When she landed, the firing of cannon, pealing of bells, and shouts of the populace, continuing for upwards of an hour, was so great that had it thundered (we are told) no one could have heard it.

Bordeaux's present to its new Queen was an exquisite ship-model in fine gold, filled with gold crowns. After the presentation of this, the procession moved toward the cathedral.

'First marched the different trades and guilds with banners and emblems; the archers and the town sergeants following, played merrily on flutes and drums. Next rode the Archbishop of Toulouse, followed by a train of ecclesiastics. The Provost of Bordeaux appeared next, immediately preceding the captain of the King's Swiss guards, who was attended by three hundred soldiers of his band. Then came a very full band of musicians, playing most delectably. Next marched the Parliament of Bordeaux, the members clad in their robes of ceremony. A group of noblemen followed, carrying their wands of office.' Then a group of great notables and ambassadors. Then the Dauphin and the Duke of Orléans, surrounded by a hundred gentlemen of the chamber. And after them, the Queen, in an open litter, surrounded by another hundred gentlemen with their battle-axes raised. After her, the great cortège of court ladies, French and Spanish; and lastly, the archers of the King's guard, armed with halberds.

I hope you can see this glittering pageant entering the cathedral, and catch a glimpse of the magnificently decorated streets through which it passed.

Late that night Francis came to rejoin his Queen. And of

the continuous festivities which marked their progress toward Paris you have had some taste at Blois and Chambord.

From the cathedral I'd go down Cours Pasteur to the Faculté des Lettres et des Sciences, where Montaigne's tomb is. He was twice Mayor of Bordeaux; but it is not as such, I'm sure, that you wish to recall him.

Down Cours Victor-Hugo, running beside the Faculté, you'll come, presently, to the Grosse-Cloche, a tower of the old fifteenth-century Hôtel de Ville, and beautifully picturesque — with its pepper-pot towers and its great bell hanging in an archway above the clock.

If you want to see more of what Abadie could do to a venerable church, you may gratify this desire by turning, right, out of Cours Victor-Hugo at rue des Faures, past the Church of Saint-Michel and down rue Sainte-Croix to the church of what was the richest abbey in all of this rich Bordeaux. This lies close to the river, and from there you could reach the quais and drive along them past the Place des Quinconces and the Fontaine des Girondins. Back of the fountain is the rue Tournon leading to Place de Tourny, where you will find rue Fondaudège which will take you to the Palais Gallien, or ruins of the Roman amphitheatre.

I wouldn't like to leave Bordeaux without a look at these ruins, because they lay the foundation, as it were, for the quite modern city that we see; and because they were a part of the Bordeaux that Charlemagne knew, and the Plantagenets, and Montaigne, and Montesquieu.

For the same reason I'd see Saint-Seurin (to which rue de la Trésorerie leads from the Palais Gallien); Charlemagne didn't know this edifice, but the others did, and he knew its predecessor. Saint Seurin, it seems, was sent here by Saint Martial, and his successors might have been expected to remember that their founder was, after all, only a dis-

ciple of him on whose head the Kind Hand had been laid;
but they were aggrieved by the greater popularity of Saint
Romain's abbey at Blaye, where some of Saint Martial's
relics were. So they not only went to Blaye, one night in
the dark o' the moon, and stole Roland's staff from his
tomb, but they did a more devastating deed of competition:
they advertised their discovery that Christ had, while on
earth, personally dedicated and consecrated the cemetery
of Saint-Seurin (now called Les Allées Damour); and the
world with money to bequeath in exchange for sepulture so
extraordinarily sacred flocked here with gratifying results
to the treasury and fame of Saint-Seurin.

If you spend the night at Bordeaux, and go to the theatre
(or if you only go for an after-dinner stroll thereabouts),
note rue Esprit-des-Lois which runs parallel with Cours
Chapeau-Rouge, behind the theatre. There are many
streets in Bordeaux commemorating her great natives and
the grand men of France; but here is one bearing the name
of a book, of her association with which Bordeaux is justi-
fiably proud: Montesquieu's great work whose title is so
difficult to render in English that, apparently, nobody tries
to do it. I wonder if it could be conveyed by 'The Spirit of
Law' (as distinguished from the Letter of Law)? or, by
'How Laws Have Grown'?

But, for your reflection on that stroll, after a dinner forever memorable, let us refresh your memory (if you need it)
with regard to Montaigne and Montesquieu.

Michel de Montaigne was born on February 28, 1533 —
less than three years after that 'joyous entry' of Francis I's
unwanted Spanish Queen into Bordeaux. In all probability
Michel's father was somewhere in that sumptuous procession accompanying Eleanor to the cathedral. He had a
lucrative if somewhat unpoetic business (he was a herring-
merchant), but he was also a soldier who had served under

Francis I in Italy, and a city councillor (he became Mayor of Bordeaux when Michel was eleven), and we may be sure he wouldn't be left out of that procession. Michel's mother was of a family of Spanish Jews. The Château de Montaigne, where Michel was born, is nearly thirty miles west of Bordeaux, on a hill at whose foot flows the Lidoire on its way to join the Dordogne. Here, where so many of his later years were spent, Michel led a peculiarly happy childhood until he was six and was sent into Bordeaux to school — which he called a 'jail of captive youth.' The contrast between his father's method of education and that which he found among the pedagogues of his day was one of the most determining things in his life and work.

The profitable sale of herring had not so engrossed the elder Montaigne that he left his little son's early education to proceed according to the routine of the day. He had the child wakened each morning by music; he encouraged him to play in the fields and woods with the peasant children of the estate; he employed for him a tutor with whom he must talk Latin, since the tutor could not speak French; so that 'without art, or a book, or grammar, or precept, without whipping or tears, I learned a Latin as pure as my teacher himself possessed, and which I could not have spoiled or altered.'

Affectionate veneration for his father must have come as easily to this lad as to Virgil for like reasons.

Here are some sentences from Montaigne's 'Essays,' carrying a few hints of his creed on education:

'We work only to fill up the *memory* [of children], leaving the understanding and the consciousness empty.'. . . 'To know by heart is not to know.'. . . 'What we gain by study is to become by its means better and wiser.'. . . 'We must inquire who is best instructed, not who is most instructed.'

There should be no punishment for lessons not learned, in

his opinion. The purpose of learning is to form the *judgment;* and the child should be encouraged to examine, to discern, to express his estimates and opinions; he should be welcomed into 'the school of social intercourse,' and learn by observation and experience how to take his place in it; and he should enlarge the sphere of his experience by reading and by travel.

When Michel was twenty-one he was made a councillor in the Bordeaux Parlement, and during the next sixteen years of his life he 'just lived,' as we might say. He did a little soldiering and was more or less at court (the court of Charles IX); he married a well-dowered wife who was intelligent, discreet, and didn't expect too much; he became a father; he lost his own father, and entered upon the proprietorship of the Château de Montaigne; he did more or less as a councillor of Bordeaux.

Then, he gave up his councillorship, and retired to his estate to live a country life which might rectify his unsatisfactory health and give him leisure to read and to reflect on what he had seen. Charles IX gave him the order of Saint Michel about that time. And five years later, Henry III made him a gentleman-in-ordinary to his court; whereupon Henry of Navarre named him to the same office about his person.

In his study at Montaigne, he read, wrote, dictated, annotated, meditated, and edited the works of his deceased friend Étienne de la Boétie, who lived at Sarlat.

In 1580, when he was forty-seven, the first two books of his 'Essays' were published, introducing to the world not only a manner of thinking which has influenced it profoundly, but a manner of writing which until then it had never known. 'The essay as he gave it had no forerunner in modern literature and no direct ancestor in the literature of classical times. . . . Beginning with the throwing together of a few stray thoughts and quotations linked by a community of subject, the author by degrees acquires more and more certainty of hand, until he produces such masterpieces of apparent desultoriness and real unity as the essay "On the verse of Virgil."'

After the publication of these books (at Bordeaux; perhaps if your evening stroll takes you into some of the little quiet streets of what was the old town, you'll hear some of Montaigne's contemporaries discussing these essays and planning to elect him Mayor), he went on a 'grand tour' — first to Paris, where he presented a copy of his book to Henry III; thence to Plombières, where he took the waters; then to Switzerland, Bavaria, the Tyrol, and from Innsbruck over the Brenner to Verona; then Padua and Venice and Florence and Rome. He stayed five months at Rome, had an audience with the Pope, was made a Roman citizen, and was taking the cure at the baths of Lucca (he was tormented by 'stone and gravel') when he got news of his election as Mayor of Bordeaux, and a command from the King to come home and attend to the job. And as Mayor he gave sufficient satisfaction to be reëlected. It was during his second term that Henry of Navarre visited him at Château de Montaigne.

In 1588 he had a third book of essays ready, and had revised the former books; so he took them all up to Paris to arrange for publication there; and on his way back he stopped at Blois for the meeting of the States General which was in progress when Guise was murdered.

His death occurred at Montaigne in 1592.

He had been in his grave for nearly a hundred years when another château near Bordeaux saw the birth of Montesquieu.

La Brède, where Montesquieu came into the world, is about sixteen miles from Bordeaux in the direction of

Toulouse. And the Montesquieu family belongs to the old nobility of France.

Like Montaigne, Charles, Baron de la Brède et de Montesquieu, studied law and was made a councillor to the Bordeaux Parlement when he was twenty-one. Two years later he was elected president for life.

Like Montaigne, he married an heiress who did not interfere with him in any way. Like Montaigne he had an independent fortune. He lived and listened and looked about him, seeing a great deal that called, he thought, for comment — or, better, for 'airing' by discussion amongst the persons who might be doing something to improve conditions that needed improving. There was 'something rotten in the state' of France (under the Regency!) and Montesquieu knew that the way to get people talking about it was to amuse them.

So he imagined two Persians of distinction travelling in Europe and writing home to their friends their impressions of what they saw. These 'Persian Letters' were published anonymously in 1721, and had an astounding success.

The authorship soon ceased to be a secret. So Baron Montesquieu sold his parliamentary office and went up to Paris to bask in the favor of the salons. He was elected to the French Academy, and took up a residence in Paris, maintaining La Brède as his country estate.

Then, like Montaigne, he went a-travelling. He went through Austria to Hungary, and down to Italy (where he met Lord Chesterfield), and up through Verona and Innsbruck, and through Germany to Holland, and over to England, where he stayed two years, becoming very Anglophile, so that when he settled down to write at La Brède (where his study is sixty feet long by forty feet wide) he lived as much as possible like an English lord instead of as a French baron.

There he wrote his book on 'The Causes of the Grandeur and of the Decadence of the Romans,' which also had a great and deserved success. And there he slowly developed that work for which the street was named, 'one of the most important books ever written and almost certainly the greatest book of the French eighteenth century.' When the manuscript of this book was ready for publication, Montesquieu summoned a group of his literary friends to tell him, candidly, what they thought of it. And they were unanimous in urging him not to do anything with it!

To visit Montaigne's château, you would leave Bordeaux by the Pont-de-Bordeaux and avenue Thiers, and go to Libourne, where the Black Prince had a favorite residence and where his ill-fated son, Richard II, was born; and then to the quaint old town of Saint-Émilion, where I think you'll like to stop long enough to see the monolith church hewn out of the rock in the eighth century. There are only two others like it in France. Six miles farther on is Castillon, where John Talbot, Earl of Shrewsbury, was killed in the final defeat of the English in Guyenne. Then you have some four miles more to go to the Château de Montaigne where you may see many things as Michel knew them nigh on five centuries ago.

La Brède also conserves some apartments as Montesquieu left them. It may be visited on your way south, if you like.

And if you have not time to go to a further vineyard, there is Château Haut-Brion, where one of the most superb of red wines comes from, just outside Bordeaux by the Cours Maréchal Galliéni, the route for Arcachon.

The vineyards producing *Graves* begin about Haut-Brion; and shortly after leaving Château Montesquieu or La Brède, you come to Barsac and the Sauternes section, culminating in the marvellous Château Yquem. And, by the way, Cadillac is not far from Barsac (across the Garonne), and it is a bastide, with ramparts well preserved.

Talk about 'historical names'!

Now, Biarritz is about one hundred and thirty miles from Bordeaux — depending on the route you take. If you go to Arcachon, which is thirty-six and a half miles, you add nearly thirty miles to your 'run.' But it seems to me it would be a *very* great pity to be so near Arcachon and not visit it; it is such a delightful rest spot, spicy with pines and bracing with the salt tang of the sea; marvellous oysters; great still-water boating and swimming. Both the Grand-Hôtel, on the water-front, and the Hôtel des Pins, up among the pine woods, are excellent; and so, I doubt not, are some of the others that are even less expensive.

If, on your way eastward from Biarritz, it is your intention to follow the Route des Pyrénées, which passes fifteen miles to the south of Pau, I should think you would do well to take the old Route 10 out of Bordeaux, down by La Brède and Barsac and Langon and Bazas (a lovely old Gaulish town, with ramparts and ancient houses and an arcaded square), whence you could easily make the little détour to Uzeste where Pope Clement V was born and is buried, and beyond to Villandraut to see the ruins of his great moated castle and Roquetaillade whose castle looks now much as his looked then; thence there is a road to Captieux on Route 10. This is the place where Eleanor of Spain and Francis I were married, at 2 A.M.

At Roquefort, Route 10 bends southwestward in the direction of Bayonne; but you could continue due south toward Pau by Route 134. Here you have a run of from a hundred and ten to a hundred and twenty-five miles (depending on whether you make the détour) which doesn't offer any good luncheon place that I know of; so if you can't make the run to Pau in time to reach there for a late lunch,

I'd continue on Route 10 as far as Mont-de-Marsan, some thirteen and a half miles farther, and lunch at Hôtel Richelieu, which is noted for its cooking. You'll find it in the centre of town, just to your left as your Route 10 reaches the Church and Place de la Madeleine. Should you, however, be going straight through on Route 10 to Bayonne and Biarritz, I'll remind you that at Dax there is a restaurant which I have not yet tried, but which an eminent gastronomic authority describes as 'the establishment in France where I have been on many occasions the best served.' It is Restaurant Folin père, 37 rue Vincent-de-Paul, close beside your route, on the right, as you approach the Adour. On the other side of the river are the hot springs and mud baths which since Roman times have been celebrated for the cure of gout and rheumatism. The Fontaine Chaude gushes forth at a temperature of 147° Fahrenheit, steaming in its fine open basin in the centre of the town. About four and a half miles from Dax is the birthplace of Saint Vincent-de-Paul, founder of the Little Sisters of the Poor. And from Dax it is thirty-six miles to Bayonne, or forty-eight to Pau.

A motoring wayfarer who was not pressed for time might consider another and longer route to Pau, taking him through a section of France which Stendahl thought 'as beautiful as Italy.' This route leaves the one just mentioned (Route 10) at a point just before Langon, and takes Route 127, which almost immediately passes through the village of Saint-Macaire which has an immensely picturesque arcaded square and a thirteenth-century gateway.

Then this route goes meandering on with the Garonne, through La Réole (where there is much that is ancient and picturesque) to Marmande. I once stopped at Marmande for luncheon; and I do *not* recommend it for that purpose.

The principal reason for going to Marmande is that it is on the road to other places more beguiling.

Route 133 goes from Marmande to Mont-de-Marsan and Dax and Bayonne; and it goes through Castlejaloux which has some fine old wooden houses.

But I'd stick to Route 127 until I had passed Tonneins where the Lot joins the Garonne and there is a crossroads among the most charming in all the province. 'It would be criminal,' says Pierre Benoit, 'not to halt there.' Some day you must turn east from here, along the Valley of the Lot, to Cahors. But not now when you are on your way to the Pyrénées. Even *I* would hardly take so roundabout a route! I'd keep on to Aiguillon and Porte-Sainte-Marie (which has some nice old streets), and then I'd go back a tiny way to the crossroads where Route 130 starts south for Nérac and Condom.

Do you remember Xaintrailles who fought with Jeanne d'Arc? His château is in the triangle between Route 130 and Route 133. But you would hardly turn out for it unless you were specializing on the Maid. Nérac, where Marguerite d'Angoulême used sometimes to hold her simple almost austere court when she was Queen of Navarre, and where she sheltered Calvin and Marot, has only one wing of its castle left, but that is one which picture-makers should not miss; they have had nothing quite like it elsewhere.

The little river, Baise which runs through Nérac about parallel with your Route 130, separates the main town from the ancient suburb of Petit-Nérac, which looks almost exactly as it did when Marguerite knew it, and even before she was born.

If you delight in the unique, you should take the road west from Condom toward Montréal, and look out for Larresingle (three and a half miles), a village built in the ruins of an ancient castle. The photographers and sketchers will love this. But your more direct route for Pau runs a bit more southwesterly, toward Eauze, which isn't much of a place now, but used to be the capital of the Roman province of Aquitania Tertia comprising all this great country between the Garonne and the Pyrénées. Thence you continue, twenty-three miles, to Aire on the Adour, and take Route 134 south, thirty-one miles, to Pau.

But if you go to Arcachon, you would almost certainly take the route (132) through Les Landes, that great region of lakes and dunes and pine forests which has a character so peculiarly its own. The district lies between the Garonne and the Adour and the Atlantic Ocean and points almost as far east as Nérac, an area of 5400 square miles, most of the soil in which is naturally sterile, composed of fine sand resting on an impermeable tufa. There is a great deal of rain, especially near the coast; and this rainfall (sometimes nearly five feet in a year) used to lie on the flat tufa in unwholesome marshes which the few wretched inhabitants had to traverse on stilts.

About the middle of the eighteenth century a French engineer instituted a system of draining and planting which transformed the district. Hundreds of miles of ditches were dug to carry off the water into the lakes along the coast or into the streams; and hundreds of thousands of acres have been planted with maritime pines and cork-oaks.

Then there was the danger from the sand to overcome. Fringing the shore for a depth of about four miles are sand dunes from a hundred to three hundred feet in height. The prevailing wind here is from the ocean, and year by year the dunes were slowly advancing landwards, burying the cultivated lands that lay in their lee, and even the houses. So Nicholas Brémontier, toward the end of the eighteenth century, began planting the dunes with maritime pines and cork-oaks, and building a palisade, twenty to thirty feet high, behind the existing dunes to prevent their spreading.

Back of this palisade lie the lakes from which the salt water has escaped by defiltration, so that they are now quite fresh — and marvellous for duck-shooting.

Sheep are numerous in Les Landes. A well-known breed of horses is raised there. But the chief industry is furnished by the trees: resin (for turpentine, and for varnish, sealing-wax, lubricants, etc.); pine timber; tar; charcoal; and cork.

The cork-trees are toward the south — as one draws near to Spain. And if you have a young traveller with you, be prepared for questions about cork!

There will be some about resin, of course; the little cups hanging to the pine-trees will insure that. But not like the cork!

'Does it hurt the cork-trees to pull their bark off?' 'How often do they "skin" them?' 'What else do they have to do with the bark to make it into corks?' etc.

The first stripping takes place when the tree is from fifteen to twenty years of age, and the bark is rough and can't be used for anything but making ferneries, or grinding up for tan-bark. In about eight or ten years the tree is stripped again, and this time the bark is a little better, but still good only for making floats for fishing nets, and such things. Each time it is stripped (at intervals of eight to ten years) the cork is finer, more even in quality, more elastic; and the trees thrive under these period strippings (in July and August) for a hundred and fifty years and more.

After the curving pieces of bark are very, very carefully stripped from the tree, the pieces are scraped and cleaned, then heated and flattened out, and are ready to have corks cut out.

These are some of the interesting practicalities of Les Landes. Their poesies are also many, and have made strong appeal to many eminent writers and painters. Perhaps you know Rousseau's 'Étang dans Les Landes' in the Louvre. Years before the War, Gabriele d'Annunzio came here 'to work, to dream, to study in detail the most hidden nooks of this marvellous coast.'

Pierre Benoit writes in a lyric strain of Les Landes. One may, he says, wander all day long in continuous adventure among the pines, without encountering a person or a habitation, without hearing another sound than the rapping of the green woodpecker or the golden oriole, until the murmur of the ocean reaches him, and the sea-breeze sets the silent pines to talking, while the great red globe of the sun drops down into the sea beyond the white dunes with their wind-bent trees making fantastic, goblin silhouettes against the evening sky.

There is a zigzagging route from Arcachon to Biarritz which I very strongly commend to the lovers of such things as I have suggested. It is a hundred and thirty miles in length, and Michelin allots two days to it; but it can be done in one. I know — because I've done it. Take a good, hearty picnic luncheon with you from Arcachon. To supplement, or rather to complete, ours, we had the *Barsac* we had bought the day before *at* Barsac, asking for their choicest *cru* and getting something indescribably exquisite.

This route retraces the route to Bordeaux for a short distance (nothing like so far as the great wireless station, but only just beyond La Teste) and then turns south toward the largest and most northerly of the lakes, de Cazaux et de Saguinet. This you touch at its eastern edge, and go on to the second lake, below which there is a bit of boating you may like to do down the little Courant de Sainte-Eulalie, from Sainte-Eulalie-en-Born to the bridge at Mimizan which was an important port in the Middle Ages, but was buried by the shifting sands two centuries ago. There is a good bathing beach here.

The route is through the forests now (as, indeed, it has been practically all the way) to Léon, on the lake of that same name; and from here there is another boat trip recommended, down the Courant d'Huchet, as far as Moliets-et-Maâ. Thence you go on, past three more lakes, the last of them a favorite resort of French novelists, to Capbreton, whose hardy mariners first landed on Cape Breton Island, Canada; and to Bayonne.

If you are to spend but one night hereabouts, I dare say you'll wish to spend it at Biarritz. But even in such necessary haste as that I pray you not to slight Bayonne any more than you have to. For Biarritz is a *nouveau-riche*, whilst Bayonne is an aristocrat of very ancient lineage and many splendid memories. Biarritz is all the world's playground, and Bayonne is an old Gascon city. Biarritz is like many of the young women one sees there, almost burdened with jewels, swathed in the costliest of 'summer furs,' driving in the most expensive motor cars — toys that cost a pretty penny, they obviously are; and yet so lacking in personality, not to mention distinction, that one wonders how they can seem of any individual importance to anybody; if they all perished in a poison-gas attack, there could be a new squad the next day, to wear their diamonds and ride in their cars, without suggesting loss. Whereas Bayonne is a Personage; and if anything happened to her, we should say, 'I shall not look upon her like again.'

It isn't that she has so many 'sights,' but she is in herself so full of charm. And what ghosts she has!

You will, I daresay, enter by Route 10, going toward Pont-Saint-Ésprit which crosses the Adour close to where the Nive, flowing up through the middle of Bayonne, empties into it. On your right, before you reach the bridge, is Vauban's citadel, one of his thirty-three great forts, and one that has never surrendered.

Long ago, before gunpowder days, Bayonne (which in the Basque language means 'port') was a rival of Toledo in the manufacture of steel weapons. When the arquebus came to replace the sword, a citizen of Bayonne thought of a weapon combining the two: he fixed a sharp blade to the muzzle of a gun, and we got the bayonet.

Bayonne was under English rule for three hundred years, and has been under French rule for nigh on five hundred. But always she has been distinctively Basque; and one of her great charms for many admirers is the Basque flavor of her population. You will be among the Basques as long as you stay in the vicinity of the Pyrénées; and no small part of the pleasure of this visit, during its extent and afterwards, in retrospect, will be in the impressions you have got of these interesting people. So, if you can do only one thing in Bayonne — if you have to neglect the cathedral which has been building for seven centuries and is still in process of completion, and the old castle which has seen so much history — I'd say, 'See the Musée Basque.'

They are mystery folk — the Basques! One theory is that they are descended from the tribes the Greeks and Latins called Iberi. Another is that they belong to some of the fairer Berber tribes. A third makes them the survivors of a lost Atlantic continent. And a fourth brings them from nowhere, but believes that they have lived in this region 'since time began.'

Their language is absolutely unrelated to any other in Europe. They have lived under political rulers of other nations, for centuries, without sacrifice of their proud self-respect; they have forced kings and emperors to swear fidelity to the old Basque laws; in their legislative body, neither priest nor lawyer was allowed to vote, yet their respect for church and law is very great, though never abject.

They are an agricultural people, and also splendid seamen. They played their full part in the colonization of America, and were the first to establish the cod-fishing off the Newfoundland Banks. As soldiers they are remarkable on the march, but better in defence than in attack.

Their tenaciousness of their traditions has made them conserve many customs which the rest of the world that has succumbed to standardization finds delightfully picturesque and interesting. Students of folk-dancing, for instance, will find that the Basques have preserved specimens of almost every class of dance known to primitive races: animal or totem dances in which the men personate animals; harvest and vintage dances; dances of the domestic arts, like weaving; war dances, including the sword dance; religious dances; and ceremonial dances.

The national game, *pelote*, is much in evidence — almost as much as the beret, the rope-soled shoes called 'espadrilles,' and the walking-stick or makhila.

There are about 600,000 Basques on both slopes of the Pyrénées, fewer than a quarter of them on the French side.

Loyola was a Basque. Basque is our name for them, not theirs for themselves. It is a form of *Wascones*, the same from which *Gascons* is derived.

If you reach Bayonne by four o'clock or so, drive down the quais on the right (east) bank of the Nive to the second bridge, Pont Marengo, beside which the Musée Basque stands. I shall not attempt to catalogue its exhibits. But if your time is limited, concentrate on the rooms illustrating Basque costumes, industries, amusements, and living conditions.

After this, take tea (or Bayonne's famous chocolate) and Bayonne's equally famous cakes, at Durand's, on rue Porte-Neuf — cross Pont-Marengo, go up rue Gambetta past rue Victor-Hugo, and turn right in rue Porte-Neuf, a delightful arcaded street whose extension on the other side of rue Gambetta leads to the cathedral; while a few steps farther, up rue Gambetta, is the castle, some of its foundations those of the Roman citadel.

Bayonne has also a good art musée recently bequeathed to her by her distinguished son, Léon Bonnat, for so many years Director of the Beaux-Arts, at Paris. It is near the Musée Basque — on that side of the Nive called Petit Bayonne; the side where the cathedral and castle are is Grand Bayonne.

You may find yourself, at Bayonne, thinking of the days of June, 1565, when Catherine de Médici came, with Charles IX and their court, to meet her daughter Elizabeth, Queen of Spain, the third wife of Philip II. You will recall that it was at the tournament celebrating young Elizabeth's marriage (she was fourteen and her bridegroom was thirty-two) that Henry II was mortally wounded.

Elizabeth, who had never known her mother as anything but the neglected, submissive wife, the parvenu Florentine, must have had many surprises at this Bayonne meeting. For now Catherine was all-powerful. For more than a year she had been touring France with the young King, her second son, and a court of over eight hundred persons, accompanied by an enormous retinue of servants. And when they reached Bayonne, and were joined by the Spanish Queen and her ceremonious court, the old town must have been full indeed of splendor. For three weeks there were balls and tournaments and other festivities.

Brantôme tells how Queen Elizabeth made her entry into Bayonne 'mounted on an ambling horse most superbly and richly caparisoned with pearl embroideries which had formerly been used by the deceased empress and were thought to be worth one hundred thousand crowns, and some say more.'

It is funny, fulsome Brantôme who tells us that 'in Spain the courtiers dared not look upon her for fear of being taken in love and causing jealousy to the king, her husband, and, consequently, running risk of their lives. The Church people did the same from fear of temptation, they not having strength to command their flesh to look at her without being tempted.'

At this Bayonne meeting, Catherine is supposed to have plotted with the Duke of Alva (accompanying her daughter) the massacre of Saint Bartholomew's Eve, which took place more than seven years later. But the recent publication of the Spanish State Papers, including Alva's secret dispatches to Philip II, show that everything he had agreed to try to get Catherine to do, he failed of; and he reported that he found the Queen Mother 'more than cold for the holy religion.'

The parting between mother and daughter was very affecting. It was as if Catherine had a premonition that she would not see Elizabeth again. Three years later the young Queen of Spain was dead, 'leaving this world with firm courage, and desiring much the other,' Brantôme says; and hints dark things about how she came to go.

Biarritz has a brief 'season' at Easter, and is in full festival from mid-July to late September. There is a winter colony, too, but it is residential, in villas, rather than transient.

It was Empress Eugénie who gave Biarritz its vogue, and it has had many royal favors ever since.

As you come from Bayonne, toward the Grande Plage, past the golf course and tennis courts, you have, first the Regina et du Golfe Hôtel, much liked by discriminating friends of mine; then the sumptuous Grand-Hôtel du Palais, occupying, in part, Eugénie's villa; then, on the avenue Edward VII, near the Russian Church, the Carlton Hotel, perhaps the most ultra of them all.

There are two casinos, the Municipal and the Bellevue, and between them are numerous hotels. I like the Bellevue-Palace, on Place Bellevue; and I like the Angleterre, west of Casino Bellevue. But Biarritz is full of good hotels. I dare say it would be difficult to find a poor one. And of course the shops are wonderful, and tempting.

I hope no one will get the impression that I don't like Biarritz because I can't find much to say about it. I like brief stops in places of this sort; but I find them all so much alike that they don't seem to call for any comment — as is true also of many of their habitués.

Creature comforts and high luxuries you may certainly have at Biarritz in abundance; and Vanity Fair, for which you must have a *flair* if it is not to get tiresome after a day or so. But when you tire of it, there is much you may turn to. And.I should say it were a great pity not to make at least a brief excursion into Spain. San Sebastian is only a little over thirty miles along the coast; and even on the way to San Sebastian (which is of the universal fashionable seaside type) there are charming bits of real Spain. But don't stop with San Sebastian. Go on to Bilbao, along the Corniche de Biscaye. You may do this by an auxiliary service of the Route des Pyrénées in autocar; but if you have your own car, I'd do it in the reverse direction to theirs: I'd go by way of Tolosa, Loyola, and Durango, and return via the Corniche.

This takes you, as far as Saint-Jean de Luz, over the first stage of the Route des Pyrénées, which we shall describe later.

Then it crosses the Nivelle, at its mouth, and mounts rapidly, passing — on the right — the old manor of Uturbie where Louis XI, in 1462, came to meet the Kings of Castile and Aragon — not yet united in Ferdinand and Isabella.

From Urrugne (in whose church there is a gigantic

wooden Samson whose nose, if you can climb up and tweak it, will, 'tis said, make you very strong) you cross a little chain of arid hills, get a superb panorama of the sea, and descend to Behobie. On the other side of the Bidassoa is Spain. And as you look across, I'm sure you'll see a strange spectacle.

It is early on the morning of Saturday, March 17, 1526. In the middle of the little river Bidassoa, a barge has been moored. About seven o'clock, there appears on the left bank of the river a group of fifty mounted cavaliers escorting the captive King of France, attended by the Viceroy of Naples and the Constable of Castile. On the right bank appears a similar escort, and two little boys who are to go into captivity in Spain in exchange for their royal father.

Francis I, the Viceroy, the Constable, the Governor of the garrison of Madrid (who has been the King's jailer), with eight soldiers, enter a boat and row toward the barge. The little boys, with an exactly equal number of attendants, do likewise. Francis is not even permitted to embrace his little sons, but is hurried into the French boat at the moment they are hustled into the Spanish boat he has just quit.

On French soil again, Francis mounts a fleet horse waiting for him; and, waving his hat and crying, 'Once more a King!' he rides off at full gallop to Saint-Jean de Luz, where he dines before proceeding to Bayonne to be received with transports of joy by his mother, his sister Marguerite, and the whole court — but not till after he has gone to the cathedral to assist at a solemn service and Te Deum.

The little boys, meanwhile, are on their way to Vittoria, where their new stepmother-to-be is sojourning, awaiting the completion of those preliminaries which must be settled before she journeys to her bridegroom and takes back to France his little sons.

No impatient bridegroom is Francis! And none-too-anxious a father! It is more than three years before that barge does duty again in the Bidassoa, and on Sunday evening, July 3d, between six and seven, a boat leaves the Spanish side with Eleanor, the two princes, the same Constable of Castile, and another Spanish nobleman; while from the French side comes the Maréchal de Montmorency with forty-eight cases of gold coins.

When Eleanor and the princes reach French soil they are greeted with the rolling of drums, the shrill notes of trumpets and clarions, and with shouts of welcome from the multitudes. Then they take their way to Saint-Jean de Luz, to spend the night.

And if, now, you glare resentfully at that memorable island because its miasmas caused the death of Velasquez, I am certainly not the one to blame you. For the festivities and ceremonials attendant upon the marriage of young Louis XIV and his first-cousin, Marie-Thérèse (her mother and his father were brother and sister — children of the Gascon Henry IV), Velasquez, as court painter to the bride's father, Philip IV, was charged with the whole scenic display of the Spanish court, and was doubtless bidden to 'show those French what *real* royal splendor is.' And one likes to know that in all that glittering assembly of the two courts, the great painter attracted as much attention for the nobility of his bearing and the splendor of his attire as for the effects he had achieved. Almost immediately on his return to Madrid, he was stricken with what we, I suppose, call malarial fever, and died in a week — followed, a week later, by his wife. He was sixty-one years old and in full possession of his great powers; so, except for that fever-breeding island, he might have painted on and on for a dozen or a score of years.

At the Bidassoa's mouth there are two towns: Hendaye

on the French side, with its near-by beach, one of the finest
in France, its grand hotel and golf course, and its French
custom-house; and Fontarabie (or Fuentarrabia), one of
the most curious and quintessentially Spanish of cities, although it lies on the frontier. 'It is the Spanish town *par
excellence*, with its housetops almost meeting above the
narrow streets, its habitations weather-stained, the
enormous escutcheons weighting its doors, its wrought balconies and grilled windows behind which one glimpses
enigmatical faces.' In its gloomy castle, Eleanor and the
two French princes passed four weary months waiting the
arrival of those forty-eight cases of gold coin. It is, however, not to Fontarabie, but to Irun that the international
bridge crosses, and at Irun that one meets the Spanish
customs officers. To visit Fontarabie, one usually takes a
boat from Hendaye.

(A word as to those customs, at Hendaye and Irun.
They may at times be troublesome, but I have not found
them so, although travelling in an English motor-car. I
had heard tales of the long waits and other annoyances. I
found nothing but courtesy and surprising expeditiousness.)

I fear we mustn't get too detailed about this excursion
into Spain. But it takes us presently to San Sebastian,
which is both city and resort, and has a magnificent beach
fringed with great hotels; and to the picturesque old town
of Hernani; thence to Tolosa, and to Azpeïtia, where is the
Church of San Sebastiano in which Ignatius Loyola was
baptized, and a mile or two beyond to the great church enshrining the Santa Casa or Holy House where Loyola,
founder of the Jesuit Order, was born, in 1491.

Then, Durango, and Bilbao for the night. (There are
excellent modern hotels at Bilbao, and I think the city will
interest you as a type of what Spain is striving toward: a
standardized commercial city which might be anywhere.)

From Bilbao back (through San Sebastian again) you have the glorious Corniche de Biscaye, which vies, I think, with the Amalfi Drive and with the Grand Corniche of the Riviera, in magnificent road-building and in scenic beauty.

I may be quite wrong in my decided preference for taking this drive eastward, toward San Sebastian, instead of westward on the first day of the journey. The reverse direction may be better; I haven't tried it.

The 'King's Highway,' the one good road into the heart of Spain, goes from San Sebastian through Vittoria and Miranda-de-Ebro, to Burgos and thence via Aranda-de-Duero to Madrid. This can be covered in a day. But who could bear to skurry through Burgos? No matter how many times I went up and down that road, I would always (I believe) stop for a night at Burgos.

There is a second two-day excursion from Biarritz, which goes to Pampeluna and returns by Roncevaux.

When you leave Biarritz to take the regular Route des Pyrénées, in whole or in part (the autocars of the Southern Railway take seven days for the five hundred and twelve miles), it is still by Route 10 that you travel — called, within the city, avenue de la Négresse; La Négresse being the nearest station to Biarritz (two miles) on the through line of the railway from France into Spain.

And here, as on the Route des Alpes, I must not take space for too much detail, because if you are contemplating this route you may have, for a few cents, from any office of The French Railways (New York, 701 Fifth Avenue; London, 56 Haymarket) or from almost any well-equipped travel agency, a copy of the Route des Pyrénées in autocar by Georges Rozet, well translated into English, published for the Southern Railway Company. It is admirably written, beautifully illustrated, and a perfect guide. I have read a great many books on the Pyrénées; but I have got out of this 'railway guide' more of what I wanted for my travelling in this region than from all the other books together.

It is, however, not every tourist who has time and inclination for the whole route; and many there be who want to combine with parts of it a visit to Pau, and Lourdes, and Carcassonne.

So I shall tell you, briefly, what the Route des Pyrénées comprises; and then, how you may vary it and curtail it.

The first stage, or day's run, is from Biarritz to Saint-Jean de Luz, and then to Saint-Jean Pied de Port, for luncheon, and to Eaux-Bonnes for the night. Eaux-Bonnes is a health resort with sulphur springs resorted to for maladies of the chest and lungs, for grippe and its after-effects, for anæmia and auto-intoxication. It has good hotels, a casino, and is beautifully situated and 'laid out.' Five miles from it is Eaux-Chaudes with hot springs esteemed for the cure of rheumatism and eye-diseases. This is a 'run' of a hundred and twenty-seven and a half miles.

The second day, from Eaux-Bonnes to Cauterets, you ride only thirty-eight miles, but have an afternoon to spend at Cauterets.

The third day (ninety-one miles) takes you by way of the Cirque de Gavarnie and the Col du Tourmalet (nearly seven thousand feet) to Luchon, where two nights and a day are spent.

The fifth day (ninety-eight miles) is from Luchon to Ax-les-Thermes, crossing two 'cols' or high passes. The sixth (seventy-seven and a half miles) halts for luncheon at Font-Romeu and goes on to Vernet-les-Bains. And the last day (seventy-seven miles) finishes at Cerbère on the Vermilion Coast of the Mediterranean, twenty-three miles below Perpignan.

Parts of this magnificent route are practicable for motors only from about July 1st to late September.

For those who visit the Pyrénées at other seasons, and for those who dislike high passes, I offer an alternative route — shorter, and including Pau.

This follows the first stage of the regular route to within less than twenty miles of Eaux-Bonnes, then turns north to Oloron and Pau. I have left Saint-Jean de Luz after luncheon, and reached Pau in comfortable time for dinner (and done no speeding, either!), but I strongly advise a much earlier start, if possible, because there are many things en route to tempt you to linger.

Saint-Jean de Luz is a delightful place for a sojourn, or for a brief visit. I know the Golf Hotel to be most excellent, and I'm told the Angleterre is also very good. Between them, on the water-front, is a celebrated restaurant, La Réserve.

It was at Saint-Jean de Luz, June 9, 1660, that Louis XIV was married to his cousin, the Infanta Marie-Thérèse.

'Here,' says Rozet in that admirable booklet, 'interest in the picturesque is augmented by historic emotion. These young girls who cross your path, their heads covered with mantillas of fine black lace, their carriage supple and grace-ful, are the descendants of those who saw the Great King, then in the splendor of his youth, in costume embroidered in gold and hat garnished with diamonds, lead to the altar the Spanish Infanta, "blonde, fat, very short, almost dwarf, and not beautiful," but sumptuously clothed with a gown of brocade starred with precious stones and a mantle of violet velvet embroidered with fleurs de lys. She had been lodged in this house called the House of the Infanta which we see on the quai beside the port. He was lodged in this Château Lohobiague, built in 1635 and to-day called Château Louis XIV.'

This is on the Place Louis-Quatorze; and in the Mairie, adjoining, you may see the marriage contract. Back of it a little way, on your right as you follow your Route 10 to the port, is the church where the religious ceremony took place. You must see at least the main portal which was walled up after the wedding party left, so that no lesser folk might ever again make use of it. But if you can, do see the interior as well.

What absorbs me about this occasion is Anne of Austria, the 'groom's' mother, who had come, a Spanish bride, to France forty-five years before. If she were retrospectively inclined, what a lot she must have had in her mind as she sat here and saw her son married!

Less than five miles from Saint-Jean de Luz is Ascain, 'the perfect Basque Village,' where Pierre Loti wrote his Basque novel 'Ramuntcho.'

Near Cambo, a little farther on our way, is the Basque mansion and estate of Edmond Rostand — who may have written there parts, or all, of 'Cyrano de Bergerac,' 'L'Aiglon,' 'Chanticleer.'

Then we come to Ixtassou, an archaic Basque village which is the nearest point on the route to the Pas de Roland, a cleft in the mountain said to have been made, with a swing of his mighty sword, Durandel, by Charlemagne's celebrated knight. And soon we are at Saint-Jean Pied du Port, for a luncheon (which is sure to include *écrevisses* and trout) at the Central Hotel on the Place du Marché or at Restaurant de la Paix on the Place Floquet, close by. Should it be market-day, you will see a most interesting throng of Basques — so dense a throng that movement is difficult. In any event, you will see an enchanting little town which will set the picture-makers quite wild with delight. It was fifty-one miles from Biarritz to Saint-Jean Pied du Port by way of Saint-Jean de Luz; and if you are en route to Pau, you have sixty-seven and a half miles to go. I give you these figures, and a hint or two, so they may help you to decide how long you dare linger here. The 'hints' are that you will certainly wish to make at least brief stops at Mauléon and Oloron; and another thing to consider here is the advisability of making the trip (eighteen miles each way) across the Spanish border to Roncesvalles and back. The historic interest of that valley is very great, but I was counselled not to attempt the trip; so I can't report on it to you. You couldn't make it and get on to Pau that night; that's certain.

Saint-Jean Pied du Port was founded in the eleventh century and belonged to Spain until that treaty which preceded Louis XIV's marriage ceded it to France, after which time it was the capital of French Navarre for a hundred and thirty years — until the Revolution.

When it became French, Louis XIV commissioned Vauban to fortify it, enclosing the old fifteenth-century ramparts with others of the latest type, suitable for a frontier. Vauban made it his 'gem' of military architecture; but now it is 'more charming than formidable.'

At Mauléon you may see the manufacture of the rope-soled shoes of the Basques — *espadrilles* — or catch a glimpse of a *pelote* game on the new court, or inspect the curious château. Mauléon is the ancient capital of the viscounty of Soule which, alone of the old counties hereabouts, conserves its Pastorales, curious outdoor theatrical performances which seem a survival of the Moralities or Mysteries of the Middle Ages, and are purely popular in character. That is to say, they are not 'pageants' 'put on' by a producer of such, but the naïve expression of tradition and of present feeling.

Another characteristic of Soule is the church with the three-pointed belfry, like a fork with three tines, originated by a curé who hoped thus to keep his people reminded of the Trinity. There is a notable example of this at Gotein, soon after you leave Mauléon.

Aramits, twenty-three miles beyond Mauléon, is said to have given Aramis of the 'Three Musketeers' his assumed name. And here you may leave the Route des Pyrénées for (nine miles) Oloron-Sainte-Marie, which used to be two towns until Béarn became France when Henry of Navarre united his small kingdom with the greater. Here you have many old houses, and two old churches. You have now come into the country of the characteristic house of the Central Pyrénées, with its wooden galleries. Note, too, the cattle of this district.

The height on which Oloron stands is between the Valley of Ossau (on the east) and the Valley of the Aspe (on the west). This latter is an immemorial route to Spain, across the Pyrénées toward Cæsaraugusta, which somehow got itself corrupted to Saragossa. This pass and the one at Roncesvalles (or Roncevaux) leading to Pampeluna have been for countless centuries the only practicable communications between France and Spain except those at the two seas — the Atlantic and the Mediterranean. In the Middle Ages this Valley d'Aspe was an independent republic under the suzerainty of Béarn.

The Ossolaises, of the valley east of Oloron, are noted for their exceptionally picturesque fête-costumes, and for their Madonna-like faces. You would be most wonderfully fortunate were you to see a wedding hereabouts. And in any case I should seek, at Oloron, one of the gay red flowered shawls of the Ossolaises.

Pau is (as everybody knows) one of the most delightful places into which a wayfarer ever rolls toward the close of a day's journeying. It is ideal for a sojourn. And in no case should it be quitted after a shorter stay than two nights and one full day. Moreover, if you relish (as many motorists do) having your toothbrush and dressing-gown 'settled' for several nights in one place, you will find it quite possible to make Pau your headquarters while you do a considerable amount of exploring among the Pyrénées.

One does not find greater comfort anywhere than at Hôtel Gassion (I dare say there are other good hotels at Pau; but I probably shall never try another); and to have one of its balcony rooms, on the front of the house, seems to me to be very near the summit of human bliss.

I hope you may find a concert in progress on the Place Royale when you get out there after dinner. In almost any case (unless the weather is very bad) you will find that view which Lamartine called the finest land view in the world. To stand on that terrace, looking down upon the tops of mighty trees which tower above the rushing Gave de Pau, and then, with lifted gaze, away toward the magnificent panorama of the Pyrénées, the while an excellent orchestra plays behind you, is a never-to-be-forgotten experience.

In the morning, visit the castle; and in the room where Henry IV came into the world (I hope you have in mind Deveria's picture — in the Louvre — of that event!) you may like to do a little 'piecing-together' of impressions, to see how 'straight' you've got your history.

The last of the famous princes of Foix, married to a sister of Louis XI, left an heiress, Catherine, who took as husband Jean d'Albret. Their son married, when he was twenty-four and she was thirty-five, the widowed Marguerite d'Angoulême whom her brother, Francis I, had tried to marry to Henry VIII of England in the event that Henry could get rid of Catherine of Aragon. (Henry, however, had other plans!)

The marriage seems to have been a none-too-happy one, but neither party to it advertised its failure; and it was a

bitter grief to both parents when their little son died, at
Alençon, on Christmas Day, 1530, after having lived only
five and a half months. His sister, Jeanne, was thus left
heiress of Navarre. And poor little Jeanne, when she was
twelve, was married (in spite of her courageous and very
vigorous protests made to her uncle, the King) to the Duke
of Cleves. Throughout the festivities with which Francis
celebrated this marriage so distasteful to his niece, the
bride maintained a sullen, resentful attitude. When the
feastings were over, the bridegroom returned to Germany,
and Jeanne came with her parents to this castle at Pau,
where, apparently, she had never been before. (She was
born at Fontainebleau, and not here as is sometimes stated.)
You may like to imagine that arrival at the castle!

Five years later, Jeanne was as ceremoniously freed from
the hateful bond, she never having seen her bridegroom
since she was pompously pledged to him. (They were unfortunate — those Cleveses! — for Anne of Cleves, whom
Henry VIII so hastily and heartily repudiated, was this
Duke of Cleves' sister.) Francis had forced the marriage
to insure Cleves siding with him against Charles V (Francis'
new and unwanted brother-in-law!) and when Charles V
with force of arms compelled Cleves to change his allegiance, Francis consented to the dissolution of the marriage
which had never been consummated. He had some idea of
marrying Jeanne to her cousin who was later to become the
husband of Catherine de Médici. But Jeanne seems to have
done her own picking, next time; and she did it very badly,
as far as any happiness for herself was concerned, when
she married that handsome, feather-pated light-o'-love,
Antoine de Bourbon.

Their first two babies were born but to die, and it looked
as if Navarre might pass to another house, when Jeanne —
on the eve of her third confinement — came across the

CHÂTEAU AND BRIDGE OF PAU

From an engraving after a drawing by T. Allom

whole of France, from Picardy, where her husband was
stationed, to be near her father when her third child was
born. It was his belief that her other children had died because they were too delicately nurtured; and he exacted
from Jeanne a promise that this third child, so soon as born,
should be given to him to bring up.

At one end of the bridge across the Gave de Pau where
you crossed as you got your first thrilling glimpse of the
town, there used to stand a statue of the Virgin to which
the expectant mothers of Pau sang a song of many verses
imploring aid in their hour of travail.

Henri d'Albret bargained with his daughter (who was
anxious about his will) that she should sing this song during
the birth of her child, 'so that it shall not be crying or
puny.'

And Jeanne did! Or, at least so 'tis said.

Her father was overjoyed when a little boy was born,
on December 13, 1553, and in order that the child might be
brave and hardy, he rubbed garlic on the baby lips ere they
had tasted mother's milk, and then gave the youngster a
few drops of wine from his own gold cup.

The story goes that wee Henry showed liking for the
wine, whereupon his delighted grandfather exclaimed,
'Thou wilt be a true Béarnais!'

Furthermore, it was discovered that the child had been
born with four teeth.

Grandpa turned him over to a healthy peasant woman
to nurse and to bring up as a peasant's son. And if I were
you, I'd take my way from the Castle of Pau to Juraçon,
across the bridge, on the route by which you came to Pau;
because there is where the wine came from that baby
Henry liked so early in his career; and there is a restaurant
famed for Béarnais cooking: Lesquerre, on the Place du
Junquet.

There you should have *garbure*, the very thick soup which is almost the national dish of Béarn (it is compounded of vegetables, largely — potatoes, broad beans, cabbage — flavored with a pickled or preserved meat; and served in a deep plate into which it is poured on top of some red wine); and native salmon, or a Basque omelet called *piperade*, much like a Spanish omelet. How much farther you can go for luncheon, I don't know. But be sure you do justice to the cheese, and to the Jurançon wine which is not so good when transported, as when enjoyed here.

After luncheon, you may like to drive about four and a half miles northwest of Pau to Lescar, the old Roman town where the road to Cæsaraugusta (Saragossa) started, and in whose twelfth-century cathedral both Jeanne d'Albret and her mother lie in an unmarked grave or graves. (Jeanne, you will remember, died in Paris, whither she had gone to negotiate the marriage of her son with Marguerite de Valois, sister of Charles IX, in circumstances which suggested that Catherine de Médicis might have known a deal too much about it — but actually of consumption, it seems — in time to escape being slaughtered in the Saint Bartholomew massacre.)

From Pau you may visit Laruns and Eaux-Bonnes, or Lourdes and Cauterets and the Cirque de Gavarnie, or Bagnères-de-Bigorre, and Tarbes; or all of them — though not all in one day, of course.

If you wish to keep a continuing course, I'd say:

Via Lourdes to Cauterets (for luncheon) and then to Gavarnie, and back to Cauterets for the night; or, if your time be very short, from Gavarnie through Luz-Sainte-Saveur, to Bagnères-de-Bigorre for the night. And the next day to Luchon.

From Pau to Lourdes is twenty five miles.

I'm not at all sure that we ought to go as sight-seers to

Lourdes. Certainly, if I were a pilgrim who had gone there at great expense of effort and money and in a great ecstasy of faith, I should hotly resent being stared at from the sidelines by tourists who described me as 'odd' — or with some other condescending epithet.

It is easy to be shocked (or to believe that we are) at Lourdes by the vast commercialism of the place: the tremendous organization which keeps a succession of pilgrimages coming and going, and handles them efficiently all the while; and the spectacle of a big, thriving community living and profiting on the sick and suppliant. But it would be much more shocking if the sick and suppliant, arriving in great numbers (well over ten thousand per week), were left to chance for their comfort. (A detailed chapter on 'Lourdes' may be found in Paul Wilstach's book 'Along the Pyrénées.')

If we go to Lourdes, not as pilgrims but as travellers en route to Cauterets, I trust that we shall be sedulous to hide any scepticism we may feel. In the interests of good taste and good feeling I'm sure we cannot hope to find any excuse for ourselves if we go there and show even a gleam of mockery or a shrug of 'superiority.' What we think or do when we come away is our individual affair. But while we're there, we must be respectful even if we can't be reverent.

Students of history have much made clear to them at Lourdes; and students of psychology. For the devout it is, of course, an experience second only to the pilgrimage to Rome. Even were you to refrain from visiting the shrine at Lourdes, and the new town surrounding it, you ought certainly to visit the castle, with its Musée Pyrénéen, as important to see as the Musée Basque at Bayonne and the Muséon Arlaten at Arles. Always, *always* visit a regional museum!

The country around Lourdes is very beautiful, and between the old town, dominated by its castle, and the new town, dominated by its basilica, is the Gave de Pau, whose bank we follow more or less closely all the way from Pau.

Argelès-Gazost is an old town in whose main street is the ancestral home of the Dupré family, one of whose daughters — Sophie — became the mother of Ferdinand Foch. It is nine and a half miles from Lourdes, and twenty miles south of Tarbes where Sophie's boy was born. Ferdinand, who came often to the home of his grandfather, an old soldier of Napoleon, made a Chevalier of the Empire by the Emperor, was a little boy of seven when the word began to fly through these valleys that Bernadette Soubirous, a shepherdess of Lourdes, had repeatedly seen the Virgin in a grotto beside the Gave de Pau, at Lourdes. I love to think of that little Foch boy hereabouts; and for his sake, who is so great a Soul as well as so great a Soldier, I feel myself a pilgrim in this vicinity where his early youth was passed.

Argelès is an old town and a new, the latter a pleasant little spa; and even the former is 'relatively young,' as Rozet reminds us, since the first mention of it in the archives of this very old province dates no farther back than 1270. The ancient houses with their plenitude of balconies are quaintly picturesque.

Here we regain the Route des Pyrénées.

Two miles south of Argelès is Saint-Savin, where Charlemagne is said to have founded an abbey on some considerable Roman ruins. The square on which stands the abbey church (one of the finest fortified Romanesque churches in this region) is a survival of the Middle Ages. And if you could be here on August 15th, you would see one of the most curious and picturesque sights afforded anywhere in twentieth-century France: the 'ballade,' a folk-dance of the men, clad in white with belts and bretelles of

gay colors; the dance is a farandole, strangely punctuated
with athletic leaps and capers. Toward the end, the men
are joined by girls in gay costumes and long veils, and the
dance becomes a spectacle extraordinarily picturesque.

There is a society in this Pyrenean region to which we
ought all to be deeply grateful. It is called the 'Frairia ded
Desbelh' ('Association of Revival') and has its headquarters in the Pyrénées Museum at Lourdes. Its object
is to preserve and resuscitate the old costumes, customs,
and traditions of the many races peopling the Pyrénées —
Basques, Ossolois, Béarnaise, Gascons, Catalans, and many
others — and every year the members take a solemn oath
that they will wear, whenever possible (for instance, on all
fête days), the old costumes of their region. The meeting
where this oath takes place is held at the castle at Lourdes;
and at that time a jury selects the costume which is most
perfect in all its details, and awards the wearer the title of
'Dauno' and a special cape or mantle of honor which she
wears at all functions during her term of 'office.'

A very few miles beyond Saint-Savin we begin the climb
toward Cauterets, where so many of our American soldiers
in the Great War had their rest-area. There are twenty-two
springs of sulphur water which, with the summer climate,
the winter sports, the superb excursions of the neighborhood, attract some fifty thousand visitors each year.

The Hôtel Angleterre, under the same management as
the Gassion at Pau, I know to be good; and I dare say the
Continental, next door, is also excellent.

Cauterets as we see it now is not an easy place in which
to recall Marguerite, Queen of Navarre, and 'The Heptameron.' But it is said that here she wrote, while taking
the waters, parts at least of that robust collection of tales,
'The Heptameron,' wherein she imitated (in a degree) Boccaccio's 'Decameron' which had just been translated into

French and dedicated to her. Five noblemen and five ladies, returning from Cauterets, are delayed and 'detoured' by the spring floods; and to pass the time until they shall be able to resume their journey, decide to tell stories which 'shall all be true.' Marguerite intended to have a hundred stories, but got no further than the seventh day and the seventy-second tale. Unlike Boccaccio's plague-fleeing story-tellers, her flood-bound narrators do not often draw on familiar sources, Italian or French, but describe adventures which hold the mirror up to human nature of their sort in their time. And after each tale is told, the company discusses its morality.

Francis is said to have been greatly entertained by these episodes, and it is not improbable that his adoring sister had him chiefly in mind when she wrote them. For the last years of Francis were melancholy, indeed, in spite of his desperate efforts at distraction.

(This may be as good a place as any to remind you that a book which will give you a great deal for the enjoyment of many places associated with Marguerite and Francis and their contemporaries is Edith Sichel's 'Women and Men of the French Renaissance.')

Should you be stopping at Cauterets until the morrow, you may make, this afternoon, the excursion to the lovely Lac de Gaube which lies at a height of nearly six thousand feet, a short distance south. (But you cannot go by motor.) About it rise great peaks, like splendid courtiers around the monarch Vignemale whose Pigue-Longue (nearly eleven thousand feet), the highest summit of the French Pyrénées, is the abode of chamois.

In no event, I hope, will you fail to visit the Cirque de Gavarnie. And to do this it is necessary to retrace your way as far as Pierrefitte; then continue along the Gave de Pau, through Luz and Saint-Sauveur to Gavarnie.

Be sure to visit at Luz the fortified church, built by the Knights Templars and after their suppression occupied by the Knights Hospitallers of Saint John of Jerusalem. And, absorbed though you may be with the architecture of this, and all it suggests, do not fail to look for the sealed door of the Cagots.

The earliest mention of this tragic people is in 1288. For centuries they were pariahs of these Pyrenean valleys — shunned and hated, looked upon as lepers, believed to be cannibals. In towns, they had to live in segregated quarters called *cagoteries;* in villages, their huts were grouped apart from the dwellings of other folk. They had no political or social rights, and were allowed to enter a church only by a special door, which gave access to their space apart from other worshippers. If the sacrament was offered them, it was on the end of a stick, and they had their own receptacle for holy water. So pestilential was their touch considered that it was a crime for them to walk barefoot on the common road. They were compelled to wear a distinctive dress, and their only occupations were wood-cutting and carpentry and the butcher's trade.

They were little folk (probably cretins), fair and blue-eyed, and may have been leprous. Nobody knows their origin, but many theories on it have been advanced: they are Saracens; they are Albigenses; they are Visigoths; and what-not. To-day they no longer form a class, but have been more or less absorbed in the general population.

Whisk yourself back, at Luz, through some six centuries or more, and see the tragic little people entering this strange fortress-church, where a preponderance (perhaps) of the others in the congregation are the Knights Hospitallers in their black tunics with the white Maltese crosses on their breasts. A far, tucked-away corner of Europe, this! —

with what flotsam of many human tides! To the ethnologist not less fascinating than to the geologist.

I shall not attempt to describe the Cirque de Gavarnie which Victor Hugo called 'the most mysterious edifice of the most mysterious of architects.' I shall not attempt, even, to give you a 'borrowed' description — of which I have many before me. I have read and re-read them, and they all seem futile to me. Let us be very, very humble, and humbly simple, and not try to say anything about it except that it is God's amphitheatre; and on that stage, against that curving background of precipices down which the mighty cascades fall as lightly as drifting veils, any drama of the universe might fittingly be played — even to the creation of another world or the evocation of new stars for the firmament.

You may not drive up to this awesome, this sublime place. You must walk to it, about a mile, beyond where the motor road ends. And as you walk, you should leave behind you not only the purring engine of your 'Pegasus,' but everything else of which you can momentarily strip yourself that belongs to the world man has made his own, to do his will. Gavarnie is the place to stand spiritually stark and alone before the Creator.

From Cauterets to Gavarnie it is twenty-five miles; and from Gavarnie to Luchon it is sixty-seven and a half miles, much of which is stiff climbing and slow descent. If you left Pau this morning and lunched at Cauterets after visiting Lourdes and before visiting Gavarnie, I do not see how you could possibly reach Luchon to-night. In that case I advise Bagnères-de-Bigorre for the night. I have 'done' this day, and I know it is practicable.

Bagnères-de-Bigorre, which Froissart visited, and Montaigne, and Henry IV, and Madame de Maintenon (who came twice, bringing the little Duke of Maine, Louis XIV's

BAGNÈRES-DE-BIGORRE

From an engraving after a drawing by T. Allom

son by Montespan; their journey taking nearly two months, and their sojourn lasting sixteen weeks), is a pleasant old town where we were very comfortable in the Hôtel Victoria et Angleterre — and went out, in the evening, on what proved to be almost an adventurous quest of toilet soap; this quest leading us to many places that we were glad to see, and finally to a 'bazaar' which seemed to contain all the rejections and left-overs and odd-lots of several machine-furnished generations, and to be kept by an elderly couple who were human 'seconds' of a strangely inert sort. When we had rooted through the accumulations of pathetic trash which (we judged) were seldom disturbed, and had found some cakes of soap which might be usable, we felt apologetic for offering to take them away from these old people who probably were attached to all their stock through having had it so long.

Very deeply etched in memory is that glimmer-lighted haven of things nobody wants, kept by old people whom (it seemed) nobody needs.

And with all earnestness I beg you to go there, and see if you think any one has bought from the collection since we left.

Balzac would have made a great addition to the Comédie Humaine from that strange 'bazaar.' I am almost sure it was on rue Bégoie, at the end of Promenade des Coustous, south of Place Lafayette; but it might have been on rue Maréchal Foch, the next street east.

From here to Luchon (forty-five and a half miles) you have some thrilling climbing to do; and at the end of it a superbly situated health-resort and sport centre with gaieties of many sorts and a fashionable patronage. The 'seasons' are from June to October 1st; and from December 20th to March 15th for the winter sports at Superbagnères, where there is a very fine hotel reached by cog-wheel railway from Luchon.

Earlier than mid-June you probably could not get over the passes. In that case, take the road leading east from Bagnères-de-Bigorre to Capvern, and Route 117; and follow the latter, for a little less than ten miles, to Montrejeau. Then go south for about five miles, on Route 125, to Saint-Bertrand-de-Comminges, where the great cathedral on the hill above the Garonne overlooks a valley 'all green and golden' where once lay a Roman city of half a million souls, the metropolis of all the Pyrénées. Pompey either founded it or was responsible for its founding, in 72 B.C. And six centuries later a Burgundian king, chasing thus far a rival claimant for something-or-other, destroyed not only the rival but the city that sheltered him, leaving not a living thing, not one stone upon another stone.

In the eleventh century came Bertrand, a young nobleman, who built this great church — or began it, rather — and left it a legacy of traditions and legends which kept it popular and made it rich for a very long time after his labors were done. The cloister is lovely, and the wood-carvings in the cathedral are among the finest of their period in France.

The stage of the Route des Pyrénées which goes from Luchon to Ax-les-Thermes (ninety-nine miles) is said to be one of the most varied and picturesque; but as to that I cannot testify — not having seen it. From Ax-les-Thermes the route goes down to Bourg-Madame, a frontier town, and thence to Font-Romeu, from which place you may take the route described in our fourth chapter, to Carcassonne by way of Axat. A shorter way to Carcassonne, however, is by Route 117, through Saint-Girons to Foix; then up to Pamiers, and on through Mirepoix to Carcassonne, or up to Toulouse.

Your way may lead north to Cahors and Brive; or from Montauban toward Aurillac and up through the Mont

Dore; or from Carcassonne as in our Chapter IV; or from Carcassonne to Nîmes and then up the Rhône Valley, or along the Riviera and up the Route des Alpes, as in our Chapter V. If I were travelling by train and using motors only locally, I think I'd go direct to Bordeaux and see what I wanted to in that vicinity. Then to Bayonne or Biarritz or Saint-Jean de Luz, making excursions thence, including one into northern Spain. Then, the Route des Pyrénées for as many stages of it as I felt inclined for. And back north by way of Carcassonne.

VII

EAST FROM PARIS THROUGH THE MARNE VALLEY TO THE JEANNE D'ARC COUNTRY, AND TO STRASBOURG

Visitors to France tend to incline less toward the east, the battle-field area, than away from it — in my experience, and I think mine is typical. Many persons express desire to 'take a little run out to the battle-fields,' seeing one special section which has personal association for them, or covering what ground may be gone over in the time they want to spend — usually a day or two.

The prevailing impression seems to be that there is a depressing amount of desolation; that where it has been repaired, one sees only spick-and-span newness, like a built-to-sell subdivision at home; and that, even where the destruction has not laid waste, 'there isn't much to see in that part of France.'

I don't know what gives intending travellers this impression; but I know that many of them have it. And, if I can, I want to correct it for at least a few.

So, in this chapter, I shall try to indicate what, besides battle-fields and rebuilt towns, there is for the visitor in the part of France between Paris and the frontier at Strasbourg.

Of the several possible routes out of Paris toward the east, I dare say that Route 3, out through the Porte de Pantin (or Jean-Jaurès) to Meaux, will be most generally satisfactory.

To leave Paris by this route you may go straight out rue de La Fayette and its continuation as avenue Jean-Jaurès, beyond which you have rue de Paris, the National Route from Paris to Metz. And as you pass 190 avenue Jean-Jaurès, mark it well; for thither you must go some evening when you have returned to Paris, and have a thick, juicy Chateaubriand steak grilled over grapevine embers, and served with soufflé potatoes and French fried onions, as only Dagorno knows how to do it. Notable food at the Cochon d'Or, beside Dagorno's, too!

Pantin is an industrial suburb, where the Government has large factories for matches and tobacco.

This is the road over which Gallieni's famous 'taxi-cab army' raced on September 6 and 7, 1914, when eleven thousand men came out from Paris in her more or less decrepit but valiant and adequate taxis, to reënforce General Manoury on the Ourcq. Beside this road, whose military history is at least two thousand years long, you shall see, presently, the statue of Gallieni.

There is a good deal, hereabouts, to tempt us to make détours to right and left — for instance, to look for Mildred Aldrich's 'Hilltop on the Marne,' near Huiry — but places between Paris and Meaux are better visited on a short run out from Paris; and on a longer tour I'd get on to Meaux, and Belleau Wood, so as to reach Château-Thierry, fifty-one miles from Paris, for luncheon.

At Meaux you will, doubtless, wish to make at least a brief visit to the cathedral where Bossuet was bishop; and perhaps to his palace, now a museum. German patrols entered Meaux on the morning of September 5, 1914, but got out a few hours later when Manoury's men came in.

Before leaving Meaux, let us try to decide which of several possible routes you may prefer. Probably you will choose the shorter one, to Belleau Wood and Château-

Thierry (via Montreuil-aux-Lions, branching north at La Ferté-sous-Jouarre). There is also a road from La Ferté to Château-Thierry which follows the meandering Marne; and from that same fork you may take the main road to Châlons-sur-Marne, going through Montmirail in whose château Napoleon spent the night of February 14, 1814, after inflicting a defeat on Blücher. A fourth choice from La Ferté is south to Coulommiers, and east on Route 34, through Sézanne. And for taking this latter there is a very strong reason — as there is for taking the route via Belleau Wood. To that second reason we'll come, presently. But chronologically the reason for the southernmost of these four routes comes nearly four years earlier.

The 'lay' visitors to this battle-field of the Marne cannot, obviously, hope to grasp the whole of what went on here in September, 1914, and July, 1918, and has passed into history as the First and Second Battle of the Marne. But if we get a fairly clean-cut idea of one phase of each battle, we shall — perhaps — be more intelligently reverent pilgrims than if we let our impressions get somewhat confused.

So I am inviting you to imagine that it is soon after daybreak on the morning of September 6, 1914; and somehow or other you are very close to a rather small, thin figure which has, as yet, scarcely emerged from obscurity. This man has just recently been described by one of his young soldiers, writing home to his parents, as follows:

'He is a man still young [he was almost sixty-three!], slender and supple, and rather frail; his powerful head seems like a flower too heavy for a stem too slight.

'What first strikes me about him is his clear gaze, penetrating, intellectual, but above all and in spite of his tremendous energy, luminous. This light in his eyes spiritualizes a countenance which would otherwise be brutal, with its big mustache bristling above a very prominent, dominant jaw.

'When he speaks, he becomes animated to the extent of impassionedness, but never expressing himself otherwise than with simplicity and purity. . . . General Foch is a prophet whom his God transports.'

Not until he was fifty did this man attain the rank of colonel. He has been a general for seven years, and for just about a year past in command of the Twentieth Corps of the French army with headquarters at Nancy.

Since the declaration of war he has been doing notable service in Lorraine, under General Castelnau. And on August 28th, General Joffre called him to form and head the Ninth Army, made up of units from the Third, Fourth, and Fifth Armies, which had retreated, fighting magnificently, from the north.

To help him command these weary men, Foch has, as he himself has said, 'a general staff of five or six officers, gathered in haste to start with, little or no working material, our notebooks and a few maps.' And on the third day of his new command he received orders — at once terrible and immensely flattering — that with this scrambled-together and exhausted army he was to occupy the centre of Joffre's battle line and sustain the onslaught of von Bülow and the crack Prussian Guards.

Yesterday (Saturday) morning, September 5th, Foch and all the other commanders received from General Joffre the message:

'The moment has come for the army to advance at all costs and allow itself to be slain where it stands rather than give way.'

The men to whom this order was relayed by their commander had, five sixths of them, been ceaselessly engaged, without one single day's rest of any kind and much of the time without night rest either, for fourteen days, fighting as they fell back, and falling back as they fought; the skin was all worn from the soles of their feet, and what shoes they had left were stuck to their feet with blood.

They had marched under a torrid sky, on scorching roads, parched and suffocated with dust. In reality they moved with their hearts rather than with their legs. 'Our bodies had beaten a retreat, but not our hearts.' But when, worn out with fatigue, faces black with powder, blinded by the chalk of Champagne, almost dying, they learned Joffre's order announcing the offensive, their faces beamed with joy.

The château where your general (Foch) has pitched his headquarters at daybreak this Sunday morning is near the little village of Pleurs, some six miles southeast of Sézanne. The front assigned to him runs from Sézanne to the Camp de Mailly, twenty-five miles east by a little south.

As Sunday wears on, Foch's new Ninth Army loses ground practically everywhere and falls back closer to the Aube which is their 'dead line.'

On Monday the German attack becomes even fiercer; and your general says: 'They are trying to throw us back with such fury I am sure that things are going badly for them elsewhere and they are seeking compensation.'

He is right. Von Kluck is retiring in a northeasterly direction under Manoury's blows; and even von Bülow is withdrawing part of his troops from that part of his line at Foch's left. But the attempt to break through Foch's centre intensifies, as Monday's fighting continues.

Tuesday, unable to hold, Foch has to move his headquarters eleven miles south to Plancy on the north bank of the Aube. He has retreated the last step allowable. On that stand his gallant army must 'allow itself to be slain where it stands rather than give way.'

This (Tuesday) evening, Foch sends Major Réquin to General Grossetti, in command of the Forty-Second Division, on the extreme left wing of Foch's army, with the most incredible orders! Orders to leave his position (Foch is asking General Franchet d'Espérey to stretch out his right wing so as to cover the evacuated section) and march his more-dead-than-alive men the whole length of Foch's line, to strengthen the right wing.

Now, it is (I believe) a fixed principle of war not to withdraw active troops from one part of a line, during action, to strengthen another. But in Foch we have a man who dares to establish new principles.

Only one part of his army has had any success to-day; toward evening the Forty-Second Division and the Moroccans have made an irresistible lunge and driven the enemy back to the north edge of those Marshes of Saint-Gond which your map shows you, northeast of Sézanne. And to that unutterably fatigued but somewhat encouraged fighting body, Foch sends his extraordinary command.

Roused from their sleep, the men start marching.

And while they are on their way to the rescue, the threatened right wing is smashed — the Prussian Guard, wild with joy, comes through the breach.

The Forty-Second Division is too late? Ah, no!

The man who has taught French officers for years at the Superior School of War that 'a battle won is a battle in which one is not able to believe one's self vanquished,' telegraphs General Joffre, while the Prussians are celebrating their victory and toasting their advance on Paris, 'My centre gives way, my right recedes; the situation is excellent. I shall attack.'

Immortal message!

The order to attack is given. The fate of nations — perhaps of civilization! — is in the balance. And the man who has taken such a mighty chance goes out to walk on the outskirts of the village of Plancy, taking with him one of his staff officers, with whom he discusses — the probable outcome of that bold move? Not at all! What they discuss is metallurgy and economics!

The elder man who walks the river bank is not only a soldier with an enormous weight of responsibility upon him, but a most desperately anxious father, unable to get word of his only son and of one of his two sons-in-law, both of whom have been fighting on the Belgian front.

Toward six o'clock this Wednesday afternoon, September 8th, the Prussians, celebrating their certain victory, see themselves confronted by a 'new' French army pouring into the gap they had thought their clear road to Paris.

The Forty-Second Division has arrived! More than half dead of fatigue, but their eyes blazing with such immensity and intensity of purpose as to give rise to stories that they are from the dead, that they are celestial spirits, that Jeanne d'Arc leads them and angels are their advance guard, they come — silhouetted against the strong sunshine of a blazing afternoon. It is well known to the Prussian Guard that the French have no reserves. Who, then, are these men, if not from Another World?

It is 'the Miracle of the Marne.' Two days later Foch has reached the Marne in pursuit of the fleeing enemy.

'To be victorious,' Napoleon said, 'it is necessary only to be stronger than your enemy at a given point and at a given moment.'

Not only for what was accomplished there, but for the way it was accomplished and all it has in it to 'stiffen' us, spiritually, for every sort of battle against apparently overwhelming odds, I hold that village of Plancy on the Aube well-nigh sacred soil; and I will always go there when I am anywhere in the neighborhood.

Now, then, for that most northern route from La Ferté-sous-Jouarre! And at Belleau Wood it is, I dare say, not a commander with whom you wish a rendezvous, but a lad — the one you know best of all — an American boy, typifying the best young manhood of his country — doing his best, his astonishing best, at a job he never dreamed would fall to him — a youth such as Mrs. Whitney has, alighting on eagle pinions, at Saint-Nazaire.

To keep this rendezvous, follow Route 3 until you come to Vaux, and there take the road to Bouresches. Skirting the south edge of the wood, your road goes to Lucy-le-Bocage, and then turns north, along the west edge of the wood, to Porcy; here you turn east — or southeast — back toward Château-Thierry, passing Hill 190.

I've read a great deal about the Second Battle of the Marne and America's part in it, in an earnest effort to epitomize it for you and for me as we visit Belleau Wood and the American cemetery here. But I can't do it. Statements about attacks and repulses and prisoners taken and numbers of killed don't give me what I want. No 'mass movement' accounts can tell the story.

I dare say that many pilgrims to Belleau Wood will feel about it much the same way: somewhere in the tangle of thicket and barbed wire, the deep pocking of shell-holes and dugouts, the roar of guns and shriek of shells, we see his face; his figure is not so easy to distinguish from other khaki-clad, tin-helmeted figures; but his face we visualize, not as it may have looked then — stubble-grown, perhaps, blackened by powder or dirt, running with sweat — but as we've always known it. The battle's concentrated in him.

For me, although I knew many men who were there, the one whose face I see is a young actor, son of a famous comedian. The very personification of gaiety and the love of life — that laughing youth with the merry eyes and the broad, flashing smile, and every impulse apparently trivial. How in the world he got to be a Captain of Marines, I don't know. But it seems he was! And such reports as came back about him! Yet when he was home, and 'on the boards' again, and making people laugh with him in his contagious and seemingly care-free way, never a word could be got out of him about 'over there.' 'That's yesterday's job,' he answered me; 'why do you want to talk about it?'

But when I read about American troops straining at the leash, about their 'fine confidence and disdain of danger,' it is Billy's face I see, leading his men on *that* day's 'job'! Somehow, he typifies it all, for me, as — I doubt not — another youth does for you. A youth who came back to 'the old job,' or one who went On to a new one.

You will enter Château-Thierry by the avenue de Paris. Keep straight ahead till you come to the bridge over the Marne, an American gift replacing the old one blown up in 1914. Here you turn right or left, according to your choice of a place for luncheon. Restaurant Jean de la Fontaine is well spoken of, but I have no personal knowledge of it. If you wish to try it, you turn left, up through rue du Pont, to Grande-Rue, and the restaurant is at number 54. To reach the leading hotel, Hostellerie du Bonhomme, cross the bridge, go down rue Carnot, and turn, left, into avenue de la République. But as for me, I'd stop at Les Violettes, on rue Carnot, a restaurant kept by an Englishwoman who has been at Château-Thierry since the war days, who is *most* interesting and exceedingly kind; if you get a chance to chat with her you will, I'm sure, feel truly acquainted with Château-Thierry when you come away.

After luncheon, visit the castle on the hill above the Hôtel de Ville. And up there, in the pretty little park within the castle enclosure, perhaps you'll like to recall a bit about Château-Thierry as it was before 1914.

The ancient manuscripts which hand down the town's earliest annals say that Charles Martel, the Hammer of God, the savior of France from the Saracens, the grandfather of Charlemagne, was so 'charmed by the smiling aspect and by the fertility of the country' that in 720 he built himself a villa on this hill. About ten years later the importance of this strategic position dominating a vast plain, the proximity of the Marne, and the nearness of great Roman routes restored by Queen Brunhilde, inspired in him the idea of crowning the summit with a castle which should serve as a residence for his royal ward, Theodoric or Thierry — that young man born to power but not bred to it, whom Martel shut up in Saint Wandrille Abbey, giving the kingdom to his own sons, Pepin and Carloman.

It was at this castle, in 1204, that Marie of Champagne was married to Baldwin, Count of Flanders, concerning whom there's many a good and stirring story. He went off to the Fourth Crusade, and never came home again, having been made prisoner by the King of the Bulgars; but an impostor who impersonated him stirred up no-end of excitement in Flanders.

Many and many another event there is that one might recall at Château-Thierry; and of course we ought to pay our respects here to La Fontaine.

He was born here, in the house that is number 12 on the street now named for him, on July 8, 1621. His father was Master of Waters and Forests, and Captain of the Hunt, and it was probably on the walks in the forest he took with his father that little Jean laid the foundations of his love of nature. Also, there was an ample library in this paternal home; and the boy seems to have read whatever he liked.

When he was nineteen, he thought he was called to the Church; but a year's training convinced him otherwise, and he took up law.

At twenty-seven he married a young woman of sixteen, with a large *dot*, who appears to have been a very 'slack' (not to say slovenly) housekeeper, and a poor manager, preferring novel-reading to domestic ordering. Jean was pretty 'slack' himself — but he liked orderly, well-managed surroundings. Marie's house was 'higgledy-piggledy,' the baby howled an inordinate amount — and Jean went visiting. People liked to have him visit, and he liked doing it, so he became a visitor by profession, as it were. He found the law far from congenial; and when he inherited his father's situation, he filled it very badly. If Marie was dissatisfied, she was not without cause for complaint.

It was Fouquet, young Louis XIV's Superintendent of Finances and the Mæcenas of those times, who rescued Jean from Marie's bad housekeeping and took him (of all places!) to Vaux, that château so superb that Louis XIV had to build Versailles to 'top' it! There the domestic machinery moved in a rhythm that Jean enjoyed. Vatel was the chef, you know! Le Nôtre was the landscape gardener. There he met Madame de Sévigné and other notables.

When Fouquet fell into disgrace and prison, Jean 'fell into another butter-tub,' this time with the Duke and Duchess of Buillon. Then it was the dowager Duchess of Orléans who made him a gentleman of her household and installed him in the Luxembourg Palace. When she died, there came to the rescue Madame de la Sablière, a woman of great beauty and culture and high character, whose 'guest' he was for twenty years — even after she had gone to the hospital for the incurables. And when she died, in 1693, Jean went to 'visit' M. and Madame d'Hervart, whose guest he remained until his death, two years later, after almost forty years of continuous visiting.

You probably know the story of his meeting his son, being told who he was, and remarking, 'Ah, yes, I thought I had seen him somewhere!' It may be a slight exaggeration — but it is characteristic.

Yet this manner of living seems to have been what La Fontaine needed to enable him to give literature a precious legacy.

Before you leave Château-Thierry to follow the Marne eastward, perhaps you'd like a few words about that storied river.

'Materna,' the Romans called it — 'Mother' — and gradually it became La Marne.

As the crow flies, it is a hundred and sixty miles from the source of the Marne, near Langres, to its mouth at Charenton, a Paris suburb, where it empties into the Seine.

As the river road runs, it is two hundred miles.

And as the Marne twists and turns, it is three hundred and twenty-eight.

Practically every foot of the way it waters has been the stage of great events for two thousand years past. But 'the Marne,' as the Great War has graven it on the hearts of men and on the tablets of history, begins at Vitry, ninety miles (by road) from Langres, and ends at Lagny, some fifteen miles east of Charenton.

Langres stands on a plateau so high — 1550 feet — above sea-level that there is a delightful tradition that it was one of the first places uncovered when the great flood — Noah's flood! — receded.

The Abbé de Mangin, who long ago wrote a history of Langres, very gravely referred its founding to a time shortly after 'the bold enterprise of the Tower of Babel had failed.'

A more conservative lover of antiquity could trace its beginnings no farther back than 1800 B.C.

Whatever the truth may be, the hill town of France from the foot of which the Marne sets out on its adventures has long enjoyed a reputation for extreme venerability.

After leaving Langres, the Marne journeys northward without encountering anything specially interesting or memorable until it comes to Joinville, which isn't much now but a pleasant little industrial town; but long ago it was a very story-book place indeed from which one Crusader after another set forth with banners fluttering, and whose seigneurs had a facility for the favor of kings.

By and by the Marne arrives at Saint-Dizier, where it becomes navigable. Two German invasions of long ago were responsible for the founding of this town. The first was when the Vandals came, in 264, and sacked the age-hoary hill town of Langres, some of whose inhabitants escaped and fled up the river toward the dense forests, carrying with them the remains of Saint Dizier. And when they felt safely beyond the barbarians, they built a chapel to house the precious relics; habitations grouped themselves around it; and there was quite a colony guarding Saint Dizier's shrine when, two centuries later, Gallo-Romans fleeing before Attila came there for refuge — and stayed there to begin life anew.

On leaving Saint-Dizier the Marne follows a very wavering course to Vitry which Julius Cæsar founded and left in charge of a military colony made up of picked soldiers of one of his victorious legions; it being from *legio victrix* that Vitry derives its name.

In the fourteenth century Vitry persecuted her Jewish inhabitants in a frenzy of excitement caused by a rumor that the Jews 'wished' to poison the river. And one mother in Israel, condemned, with her sons, to the stake, shrieked this malediction as the flames rose about her:

'Evil be upon thee, cruel and accursed town! These flames may seem to die down, but they shall leap up again in many reprisals and shall burn thee utterly one day.'

And many indeed were the 'reprisals'! Fifty years later a terrible fire devoured the city. And forty years after that it was put to the torch for having refused submission to the English.

But it recovered, both times, and was a proud, prosperous city with a peacock on its coat of arms, when the Emperor Charles V came and reduced it to a smouldering heap of ruins.

Francis I may well have believed the town accursed. For instead of rebuilding it on the old site, he ordered what stones were left there to be transported two and a half miles away to another location on the bank of the Marne and there utilized in the foundations of a new city to which he gave the name of Vitry-le-François, substituting his salamander (truly pertinent, here!) for their peacock.

Even with all his munificence to the new town, he found it hard to lure the inhabitants away from the old. But in course of time Vitry-le-François succeeded, and Vitry-le-Brulé (or Burned) gave up the struggle.

From Vitry the Marne, swerving abruptly away from the great chalky plains that lie between Vitry and Sézanne, turns northwest toward Châlons.

Châlons was not a new town when Attila came with his vast hordes of terrible Tartars, or Huns, and met defeat in a battle wherein — 'tis said — three hundred thousand perished in a single day's fighting.

Just where this colossal and momentous conflict took place is not definitely known. Some authorities locate it northeast of Châlons, some place it southwest. But Châ-

lons was on the edge of it wherever it was; and from these
plains that wave of eastern invasion receded. But others
came!

Saint Bernard was educated (at least in part) at the Châlons cathedral school. In 1147 he preached the Second
Crusade here in the presence of the Pope; the King of
France (Louis VII) and Eleanor, doubtless; the ambassadors of the Emperor of Germany; and an immense concourse of French and German nobles.

Great days of panoply those must have been for Châlons! What riot of color must have flowed through the
narrow old streets! What pageantry must have filled the
old gray churches! What feasts must have made the trestle-
tables groan, in the great, vaulted halls of castles and palaces! What blare of trumpets and salvos of acclaiming
voices must have hailed the Crusaders as they pledged
themselves to deliver the imperilled Christians in the Holy
Land from the avenging menace of the infidels!

When Charles VII was on his way to Reims to be crowned,
a deputation of important citizens came as far as Châlons
to meet him and invest him with the keys of their city.
And about the same time, in those early days of July, 1429,
there came along the road to Vitry, and thence to Châlons,
a group of peasants from Domrémy and Vaucouleurs who
were bent upon seeing her pass who had left them, to go to
Chinon, only a very few months ago. Whether they ad-
ventured on to Reims, I do not know. But they were at
Châlons to satisfy themselves that it was indeed their little
Jeanne who was taking the King to be crowned.

Great wedding pageantry had Châlons twice in a decade,
when Louis XIV's only brother was married here, and then
the great King's only son, the Grand Dauphin. Both
brides were Bavarian princesses.

In the campaign of 1792, Châlons became the depot of

the national army, the point at which volunteers from all the provinces of France assembled to fight off that dismemberment which their Teutonic neighbors thought they could easily accomplish while France was in the throes of giving birth to democracy. Valmy is some eighteen miles from Châlons. Valmy! which tore from Goethe, 'before the immensity of a fresh horizon,' the profound cry: 'I tell you, from this place and this day comes a new era in the history of the world!'

From Châlons there are two main roads to Paris which diverge until they are perhaps fifteen miles apart, and then converge at La Ferté-sous-Jouarre, where you did your choosing between them. The upper one, which you are probably following, takes you along the Marne to Dormans and to Épernay. Dormans is the place Marshal Foch chose as symbolic of the two battles of the Marne and as fitting as any for the commemorative chapel where thanks may be given for those victories. A road runs from Dormans to Reims, through Ville-en-Tardenois.

Épernay is thirty miles from Château-Thierry. Its wine is known as 'the wine of the river' as distinguished from 'the wine of the mountain' at Reims, and is considered the best of all champagne.

I'm sure you'll want to visit one of the famous cellars and see something of the processes that intervene during five years between the gathering of the grapes and the sale of the sparkling wine.

If you continue straight on by the route which brought you into Épernay and will take you out to Châlons, you pass some of the champagne establishments. The Caves Chandon have fourteen miles of underground galleries where millions of bottles of wine are in various stages of preparation for the market. An English-speaking guide will take you through enough of this vast labyrinth to give you

an idea of the process. Dress warmly for this visit; for it
is very chill and damp down there. And don't wear dainty
shoes; for much of the way is through the slippery, oozy
mud which this soil forms and which was such a plague to
the soldiers on the march and in the trenches.

Châlons is twenty miles from Épernay, and is sometimes
called 'the Aldershot of France.'

I dare say you'll want a glimpse of the cathedral at
Châlons, which was rededicated at the time of that great
assembly when Saint Bernard preached the Second
Crusade — although most of what we see was not then
begun — and where those gorgeous royal weddings were.
Little Marie-Antoinette paused at Châlons on her way to
Versailles to wed a later Dauphin, doubtless attended a
special service at the cathedral, and saw those glorious
windows. That was in 1770. Twenty-one years later she
was here again, with her husband and children and her
sister-in-law, on their way back to Paris after their capture
at Varennes. The Préfecture where she was lodged, a
prisoner, in 1791, is only a stone's throw from the unfinished
triumphal arch erected to celebrate her entry in 1770.
Châlons has another souvenir of her: her last prayer-book,
inscribed by her:

> 'the 16 October, 4½ o'clock in the morning.
> My God! have pity on me!
> My eyes have no more tears
> to weep for you my poor
> children — good bye, good bye!
> Marie Antoinette.'

This is in the library adjoining the Hôtel de Ville. How
it came there, I do not know.

Entering Châlons from Épernay, by the rue de Faubourg
du Marne, you have the cathedral on your right soon after

you have crossed the Marne and then the canal. South of
the cathedral lies the park called the 'Jard,' where Saint
Bernard preached, standing on a stone chair. The street by
which you entered, and which is the rue de Marne after it
passes the canal, leads to the Hôtel de Ville and the musée.
To reach the principal hotel of Châlons — Hôtel de la
Haute-Mère-Dieu, or High Mother of God — turn south
(right) before you reach the Place de la Hôtel de Ville, down
rue des Lombards to the Place de la République.

The Préfecture and that unfinished arch, the Porte
Sainte Croix, are south of the musée, by the rue Carnot.

Now here we must consider what you are to do next on
this trip eastward from Paris.

If the battle-fields call you, you may go on from Châlons
to Verdun, still following your Route 3, through Sainte-
Menehould and Clermont-en-Argonne. This gives you,
from Paris, a day's 'run' of a hundred and fifty miles. And
from Verdun you can go south through Saint-Mihiel to
Vaucouleurs and the Jeanne d'Arc country, thence east to
Nancy and Strasbourg; or you can return to Paris via
Reims, Soissons, Pierrefonds, Compiègne, Senlis, and
Chantilly.

Suppose we consider first the latter possibility.

About five miles from Châlons on the road to Sainte-
Menehould is the beautiful Gothic church built to enshrine
a miraculous statue of the Virgin said to have been found
in a thorn-bush — hence the name of the church, Notre-
Dame-de-l'Épine, or Our Lady of the Thorn. This magnificent edifice, with its wealth of late-Gothic elaboration,
stands in lonely grandeur in a bleak country and seems
incongruously out of place. But there are pilgrimage times
when it is the scene of much movement.

(The vast entrenched Camp de Châlons which Napoleon
III created in 1857 is best reached by Route 77, running

north from Châlons. It is nearly fifty square miles in area and contains manœuvre fields, aviation grounds, and other military necessities.)

Continuing by your Route 3, you have, on your left, a little farther on toward Sainte-Menehould, the oval entrenchment, sixty acres in extent, which is known locally as Attila's Camp. And presently you pass, a few miles before coming to Sainte-Menehould, just to the south of Valmy where Dumouriez with his raw recruits turned back the trained fighting machine of the Duke of Brunswick.

Sainte-Menehould is the town where Louis XVI and his family, fleeing from Paris, were recognized by the postmaster's son, Drouet, who had been on guard duty at Versailles. As a matter of fact, they had been several times recognized along their route from Paris, but always before by loyal subjects who held their tongues.

Their route was by way of Montmirail to Châlons, and then along here, as you are going, to Sainte-Menehould on the edge of the Argonne Forest. They had stopped at Meaux for a relay of horses; but Meaux was used to travellers in carriages that betokened wealth and consequence. At La Ferté they left the main-travelled road, through Château-Thierry, for the less-frequented road to Châlons. Twelve miles before reaching Châlons, at the village of Chaintrix, not only were they recognized, but they acknowledged the recognition. But they were a little uneasy about Châlons, into which their carriages clattered at four o'clock in the afternoon of June 21, 1791. The postmaster (or posting-master) there knew them, but was silent.

Beyond Châlons was lonely country where there was small chance of recognition by unfriendly folk. Moreover, in that sparsely settled section they were to find scattered cavalry detachments of German mercenaries under French Royalist commanders, waiting to escort them in safety across the frontier. The first of these, Hussars under the Duc de Choiseul, were to be looked for at Somme-Vesle where the fugitives were scheduled to be at one o'clock; but it was nearly six when they got there, and not a soldier was in sight. They had been waiting since before noon, and the people were getting too curious; Choiseul feared the royal party had not got away from Paris, or that they had been intercepted en route. The lingering presence of his German Hussars was causing comment which might be fatal to the project if it were really under way. So, about half-past five o'clock Choiseul withdrew, just as the Royal Family had got almost within view, coming from Châlons.

It was sunset when they rattled into the main square of Sainte-Menehould, where several persons seemed to recognize them, but nothing was done to detain them. After they were gone, there was great excitement at Sainte-Menehould and much discussion as to what should be done. Drouet, having been a dragoon, was delegated to the pursuit, and took with him another ex-dragoon. Thundering out of the town on the last two horses left in Drouet's posting-stable, they were soon upon the heels of the heavy travelling carriages. Toward ten o'clock, near Clermont-en-Argonne, Drouet met his own postilions returning from the end of their posting-stage, and from them he learned that at Clermont the travellers had left the main Metz road and turned northward to Varennes.

Immediately, he left that main road and took to a path through the forest, along the crest of the ridge, 'a green lane of immemorial age,' says Hilaire Belloc in his 'Marie Antoinette,' 'with high trees like a wall on either side. Three hundred feet below, upon the open plain that skirts the wood, the berline swayed at speed along the paved highroad. So the race ran. The fugitives slept unwarned and deeply as they drew on to Varennes through the silent darkness. On the hills above, with every beat of the hoof upon the turf, the two riders neared and they neared. Upon who should win that race depended the issue of civil war. On the issue of that race all the future depended: all France and all Europe. The riders had eleven miles of rough woodlands in the dark to cover, an hour at most for their ride. Below them on the highroad, with a start of two miles and more, their quarry was hurrying, rolling to Varennes. If the wheels and the smooth road beat them, it was Austria over the frontier, France without government, defeat, and the end of their new world; but if they in the woodlands beat the wheels on the smooth road, then the Revolution was saved.'

The riders in the dark wood won! Five minutes ahead of the riders on the smooth road, they reached Varennes, gave the alarm, and caused the travelling carriages to be held till morning. And at seven in the morning, the return to Paris began.

In ancient times Sainte-Menehould was considered the capital of the Argonne, that wooded plateau forty-four miles long and ten miles wide which forms a natural barrier between Champagne and Lorraine. In August, 1914, this plateau had to be abandoned to the Germans, but after the First Battle of the Marne the Allies recovered some of the southern portion, which they held in the very teeth of the German Crown Prince until, largely with the aid of the troops from America, they cleared the Argonne at the close of the war. Twenty-two American divisions, numbering 630,000 men, were engaged in that great Battle of the Argonne which lasted from September 26th till the Armistice; and their casualties totalled 119,000, or nearly twenty per cent.

Should it be your plan to go south from Verdun to the Jeanne d'Arc country, I'd advise turning north at Cler-

mont, over that 'smooth road' to Varennes; thence to
Montfaucon, and down to Verdun.

But if you are going no farther than Verdun, I'd go on to
it from Clermont, and take Montfaucon on the way back
to Reims.

Supposing the latter, I dare say your course will be direct
to your hotel. Recently there has been a new one built, the
Vauban, which is said to be excellent. The one I knew
there, after the War, is now reported to me as 'impossible.'

But in almost any case you will enter Verdun by the
Porte de France, and the last stages of your way thither
will be along the Sacred Road, the main (and ofttimes the
only) artery of communication between besieged Verdun
and the world it was defending. Some days, in the spring of
1916 especially, the stream of vehicles on this little road
only seven yards wide averaged one each five seconds, past
a given point, throughout the whole twenty-four hours.
The average frequency was one vehicle every fourteen
seconds. The daily requirements for an engagement in
which fifteen or twenty divisions are engaged, as at Verdun,
when the fighting around it was heaviest, are two thousand
tons of munitions and supplies and materials for each
division; and from fifteen to twenty thousand men. This
service had all to reach Verdun by the Sacred Way. By
that same way, the sick and wounded and war-worn thousands had to be carried back toward Bar-le-Duc. To keep
this channel of feeding and evacuation in good condition for
its constant service, repair units worked day and night, as
best they could in the ceaseless stream of heavy camions.
To enter Verdun by that road and the Porte de France
seems to me one of the great, reconsecrating experiences
which a pilgrim soul may undergo.

As we approach it, let us 'recollect' a little bit about
Verdun. It has been a city for longer than any one quite

knows. But though its name has become one of the most
sacred in all the annals of France and of civilization, there
was, in all its long history prior to 1914, scarcely any event
of a sort to endear the place to France or, indeed, to any
one.

Whoever built the first town there on the heights above
the left bank of the Meuse must have made an exceptionally good stronghold; for Syagrius, when Clovis defeated
him at Soissons in 486, and hotly pursued him, fled all the
way to Verdun (more than a hundred miles) for refuge.
And Verdun was one of the last cities in northern Gaul to
accept Clovis, who did not force its capitulation until 502.

We shall pay our respects more especially to Clovis at
Reims. At Verdun let us recall Charlemagne, who got very
wroth against Verdun, destroyed its ancient walls, and
ordered their great stones carted away to Aix-la-Chapelle
(a matter of a hundred and sixty miles or more) to build his
octagonal church there. The reason for this anger was an
Italian bishop whom the Pope wanted to place over Verdun, and the people of Verdun didn't want over them.
Charlemagne needed the Pope very much, just then. So
he resented any opposition to the Pope's wishes and plans,
and he dismantled Verdun and left it defenceless except as
Nature had endowed it for resistance.

And then he went on his way to that for which he needed
the Pope: that coronation on Christmas Day, 800, amid a
great assembly at the old Church of Saint Peter in Rome,
where the Pope crowned Charlemagne, then knelt in
homage to him whilst the multitude shouted acclaim and
allegiance to the Emperor of all the world.

Charlemagne was fifty-eight years old then; a large,
paunchy, bull-necked man, white-haired, clean-shaven,
big-eyed, animated in expression and tremendously active
in movements. He was a light sleeper, a small eater, an ex-

THE CORONATION OF CHARLEMAGNE
By Raphael

ceedingly moderate drinker, domestic in his tastes and
habits, devoted to his family, a lover of music and of hunting, an almost inordinate bather. He spoke several languages, collected books, fostered education, delighted in the
talk of learned men, but could not learn to write.

He ruled as Emperor for nearly fourteen years, and left
his vast domains to his only surviving legitimate son, Louis;
who did nothing much, for a quarter of a century, but
struggle vainly to hold that which was bequeathed to him.

Louis had four sons, of whom the second predeceased
him. Of the others, Lothair and Louis were also sons of
Louis' first wife; and Charles was the son of a second wife.

The fight of these three men for the empire of their
grandfather began long before their father's death and continued for some time after it. Lothair claimed it *all*, and
Louis and Charles leagued against him. Lothair recognized
his inability to hold out against them, after the severe defeat they inflicted on him at the Battle of Fontenoy. On
the 14th of February, 842, Louis and Charles and their
followers met at Strasbourg, and enacted a solemn ceremony in which each of these two brothers swore not to
make a separate peace with Lothair. The text of this oath
has come down to us. It was taken in two languages, German and that Romance tongue which was evolving French
out of Latin. This historic text is the earliest specimen
preserved to posterity of that speech which was to become
the French language.

Lothair seems to have been impressed by this oath, and
he consented to the Treaty of Verdun in August, 843, which
is called 'the birthday of modern nationalities.' By that
treaty Louis became master of the eastern part of the Empire, with the Rhine as his western boundary, and comes
down to history as Louis 'the German'; Charles 'the Bald'
(who bothers a great many people because he has a descrip-

tive 'sub-title' so much like Charles the Bold, six centuries later) got — roughly speaking — western France; and Lothair retained the richest part, the central strip, which extended from Rome practically to what we know as Antwerp.

Louis' heritage stood, and Charles's stood, but Lothair's was doomed almost from the first to infinite subdivision and to the extinction of all national personality.

Verdun was alternately French and German for a hundred and forty years; then German for nearly six centuries, till Henry II retook it for France.

Late in August, 1792, an army of seventy thousand Prussians under the Duke of Brunswick came marching upon Verdun, boasting as they came that by the end of September they would be wining and dining in Paris. On August 30th they arrived before Verdun and opened bombardment. After fifteen hours, the town surrendered — although the commandant, unable to endure the shame of giving up the city he could not defend, blew out his brains in the council whereat surrender was voted.

Some of the townsfolk, however, did not share his humiliation; and among them was a group of hysterical women who dressed themselves in their best to receive the conquerors and showered them with candy and kisses — the candy being the *dragées* or sugared almonds for which, even then, Verdun was celebrated.

Then came the defeat of the Prussians at Valmy, and their retreat without having given those dinners at Paris. And Verdun had the bitter experience of learning what France thought of her easy surrender. This was typically expressed in a piece successfully played in Paris theatres during the Revolution, wherein a cowardly and contemptible character bore the name of Monsieur Verdun.

As for the hysterical women, they were taken to Paris —

fourteen of them — and arraigned before the Revolutionary Tribunal which condemned twelve of them to die on the scaffold. Two were spared because they were only seventeen; but they were obliged to witness the execution of the others, among whom one of these girls had three sisters, and the other saw her mother die.

Then came 1870 — and more Prussians, marching to Paris to wine and to dine. This time Verdun resisted, gallantly enough, for three weeks, then capitulated.

After that France lost Metz, and must needs strengthen greatly the fortifications of Verdun which is forty miles west of Metz on the main road to Paris.

Accordingly, in 1875 the little walled city became the centre of a great entrenched camp. And when the Prussians came again, it was to storm a collection of sixteen large forts and about twenty smaller ones, defending a castrum thirty miles in circumference and nine miles in its greatest diameter.

The population of the town was about twelve thousand; and the eight thousand or more military who manned those forts in peace times were augmented by fighting men more numerous than any army had ever before gathered for the defence of a single point of attack.

Upon this group of forts and this little town the armies of the Crown Prince rained, for months and months, something like two hundred thousand shells a day. There were many days when eight hundred shells struck within the city.

But, though holding Verdun cost hundreds of thousands of lives, failure to hold it would have cost far more. So the due of those who made of their bodies a living bulwark in order that 'They shall not pass,' is that Verdun shall be, while time endures, one of the most sacred names in the annals of human courage.

The great sight to see within the city is the citadel. And I should think that most visitors would want to visit the cathedral. If you do, don't fail to see the lovely cloister.

The forts outside Verdun which nearly every one wants to see are comprised within two circuits, one on each bank of the Meuse. There are motor-coach tours of varying lengths, daily; one, which takes about three and a half hours, includes the right bank only; a nine-hour circuit includes the left bank also. It may be that even if you have your own car, you would do better to make one of these tours under the direction of a guide who is thoroughly familiar with the ground. If not that, I'd go into Thomas Cook's office in rue du Saint-Esprit and engage a special battle-fields guide.

The right-bank circuit, thirty-seven and a half miles, leaves Verdun by the fine old Porte Chaussée, built about 1380, its architecture much like that of the Bastille, and of the same period.

In the Military Cemetery on your left as you leave Verdun, by the Faubourg Pavé, are the graves of seven unknown French soldiers whose remains were brought here, together with those of one more, from another fighting sector, that one might be at random picked to lie beneath the Arc de Triomphe, where the Eternal Torch burns above his bones.

Follow Route 18 for three and three quarters miles, then turn, left, into the road leading to Fort Tavannes, about half a mile west of the main road. The long Tavannes railway tunnel was used as a shelter for the reserves of this sector, and as a munitions depot.

Return to the road by which the fort was reached, turn into it on the right, and about three hundred yards farther on, take the right-hand fork toward Vaux.

Fort Vaux was completed only in 1911.

Now here may be the best place to consider for a few moments what Germany's plan was in concentrating on Verdun in the early days of 1916.

About Christmas, 1915 (after some seventeen months of war), General Falkenhayn submitted to the German Emperor a report in which he urged that France had reached the limits of exhaustion; that Russia was powerless, Serbia was destroyed, and Italy was deceived. Only England, he believed, was still in need of chastening — of a reminder that the war could not be won. Unfortunately, he said, it was not easy to reach England either on her own soil, or on the Continent, or in her distant possessions. But she would be defeated if the Allied armies on the Continent were broken.

Where, then, was this to be done? Defeat of Italy would have little effect on England. Operations against Russia could not begin till April. The only possible line of attack was against France. The thing to do was to attack a position of such importance that it would have to be held to the very last man — a condition which the art of war shows to be fatal to the defender.

On the 21st of February, 1916, at quarter past seven in the morning the Germans began the bombardment on a front of twenty-five miles. It was of unheard-of intensity. Heavy shells were used in vast quantities.

At a quarter before five that afternoon, the first infantry attack was launched. The Battle of Verdun was on!

On March 9th Germany announced to the world that two of her regiments had 'taken by assault the armored fort of Vaux, as well as numerous neighboring fortifications.'

What had happened was that two battalions of one of these regiments had gained a footing on Vaux Hill, but they were mown down at close range by French fire. Three

months of costly effort were necessary before the Germans
were able to enter Fort Vaux — three months during which
no fewer than eight thousand large-calibre shells fell daily
on this one fort and its immediate surroundings.

At the beginning of June, the commander of the fort,
Raynal, and his men were imprisoned in the underground
chambers of the fort, being no longer able to hold their
ground outside.

To economize food and water, the surplus contingents
were ordered to leave the fort; and a first detachment succeeded in making its escape on the night of June 4th. The
next night a hundred more men managed to get away.

Carrier pigeons now furnished, with optical signals not
always usable, the only means of communication with the
French lines. And on June 4th the last pigeon was released
from that underground columbarium which I hope you may
see. I found it one of the most affecting things in all that
area.

After that last little messenger was gone, two signal-
men who were left volunteered to change some of the signalling apparatus in the hope of letting the command know
what was going on. And on June 5th Raynal sent his last
decipherable message: 'We have reached the limit. Officers
and men have done their duty. Long live France!'

Nevertheless, he refused to surrender. Efforts to relieve
him failed. And when, on the night of June 8th, after seven
days and nights of continual fighting, the heroic defenders
of the fort were at last overpowered, the unwounded among
them had not tasted a drop of water for two days.

On November 2d (five months later) the Germans were
driven out of the fort.

Now you retrace your way to that crossroads, turn off
toward Fort de Souville, Fort de Douaumont, and the
Trench of the Bayonets, returning via Pepper Hill and

other places whose names grew terribly familiar to us during the war.

I dare not embark upon separate comment for each of them. But Douaumont, you doubtless know, has become a sort of commemorative centre for all that Verdun symbolizes. The dead from many cemeteries have been brought there. There the great Memorial is building. And of all the soul-stirring things that one may see on any battle-field, surely none surpasses that line of rusty bayonets bristling above the trench wherein their holders stood, ready to go over the top, when they were entombed alive by a tremendous explosion. The reverence of an American pilgrim to that spot has covered them with a protection against the elements; and there they'll stand, upraised against the invading foe, for — who can guess how long?

The circuit of forts on the left bank is nearly fifty-five miles in extent. But I doubt if many visitors will have time and inclination for all of it. Those who have their own cars will probably feel satisfied to take the route leading out through the Porte de France to Charny, and Cumières (which the Foreign Legion retook in August, 1917, singing 'La Madelon' as they attacked). Thence to Mort-Homme, one of the most fiercely disputed positions on the left bank; Hill 304; Malancourt, where the Germans first made use of liquid fire, on February 26, 1915; and Montfaucon, the Crown Prince's headquarters, whose capture is such a proud page in the annals of the A.E.F. The great American cemetery, where many thousands of our dead lie, is at Romagne, about five miles northwest of Montfaucon.

From Montfaucon, take the road for Varennes (the house, wherein Louis XVI, Marie-Antoinette, and their children were detained until they started back to Paris, is still standing; American troops retook Varennes on September 26, 1918) and the Argonne Forest, and on to Reims for

the night. If the right-bank forts were visited in the morning, this section of the left-bank defences could be seen during the afternoon, en route back to Paris.

You will probably approach Reims by the road which
enters the city by rue de Cernay. At the end of this street,
turn (left) in rue du Faubourg Cérès, and follow the tramway which curves around Esplanade Cérès and runs along
boulevard Lundy, toward the Porte Mars, the Promenades
Publiques, and the Square Colbert.

On the boulevard de la République, facing the Promenades, there is Claridge's Hotel, at number 37, and the
little Savoy Hotel, at number 53. The last time I was in
Reims, the Savoy was purveying a quite superlative quality
of food (cooked by the chef-proprietor) which we ate in the
very nice little garden; and the rooms, if plain, were perfectly comfortable.

Close to the Square Colbert (on which the railway station fronts) is Place Drouet-d'Erlon on which is the most
celebrated hotel of Reims, the Lion d'Or, which used to
be beside the cathedral; now very grand, with eighty bathrooms; and in the same *place* are the Continental and the
Crystal; while around the corner from it in rue Buirette is
Hotel Degermann (number 35), which also serves notably
fine food. The Lion d'Or, belonging to the same proprietor
as the Continental, Paris, and the Continental at Cannes,
is really a superfine hotel where one may enjoy such luxury
as very few other provincial hotels afford.

While you are dining, let us think about Reims.

There's a tradition that it was founded by Remus,
brother of Romulus, and is, thus, the twin sister of Rome.
Some historians scoff at this. But if you like to believe it,
their doubts need not deter you. Romulus was a much
better authenticated personage on my latest visits to Rome
than he was when I first went there. And many another

legend seems to be emerging from the limbo of myth into the very best society of indisputable facts.

We do know that the tribes from roundabout here made excursions into Italy not much later than the founding of Rome, and that they may have made transalpine raids even earlier. Perhaps they brought Remus back with them. Perhaps he came adventuring on his own account. Perhaps he didn't come at all.

But when Julius Cæsar came he found a city rich and well governed, with equitable laws and many excellent institutions, including a mint which coined money bearing the name of Remo; it was the capital of a people who called themselves the Remi, and who offered no resistance to Rome, but on the approach of Cæsar sent out two prominent citizens to tender the city's submission. They told him how to conquer Belgian Gaul, and proved themselves such splendid allies that Cæsar showed his respect for and confidence in them in many ways.

That attitude toward Rome persisted.

Some writers say that Saint Peter himself sent the Gospel to Reims by Sixtus and Timothy — that Timothy was martyred where the fort of La Pompelle stood, which was reduced to a heap of ruins in the late war. Some others say that Christianity was not accepted at Reims until the middle of the fourth century.

In those days the city was oval in shape, and traversed from south to north and from east to west by two principal streets which intersected at the Place d'Armes, and terminated at four gates in the town wall. Each of these gates was flanked by a triumphal arch; and at the north arch, beneath which passed the road to Laon, is that Porte de Mars which you saw on your way to your hotel. It is said to have been erected by the Remi in honor of Julius and Augustus Cæsar. But if this is so, they did not do it until the third century.

Then the barbarian invasions began. Rome's Empire in the West was disintegrating. But the power of the Church of Rome was strengthening mightily.

Pagan chieftains were ruling in France; and the Church saw what could be done through them.

Clovis, chief of the Franks, treated the ecclesiastics with respect, because he was shrewdly aware of their influence over the people. But his tolerance was not what the Church needed and wanted; it wanted his coöperation.

Clotilde, the wife of Clovis, was a Burgundian princess and a Christian. She introduced at court Remi, or Remigius, Bishop of Reims, and Remi gave Clovis good counsel on affairs of state.

When entering the Battle of Tolbiac, the issue of which meant so much to him, Clovis made a vow that if the victory were his he would become a Christian.

Accordingly, after the battle was won, he and his triumphant soldiers repaired to Reims (where Clotilde and Remi waited) and not only Clovis was baptized, but three thousand of his warriors with their wives and children.

This was on Christmas Day, 495 — three hundred and five years before that other memorable Christmas when Charlemagne was crowned at Saint Peter's in Rome. And Clovis, when he entered the cathedral and saw its radiance, smelt its incense and perfumes, asked the Bishop if this was the Kingdom of God which he had been told he would inherit.

Three times the sword of Clovis was plunged into the baptistery as the chief (now king) swore to 'adore what he had burned, and burn what he had adored.'

Then Remi stood awaiting the holy oil which a priest had gone to fetch; but the cleric was caught fast in the throng outside. Whereupon a dove, whiter than snow, descended from heaven and laid on the altar a vial filled with divine balm. Sceptical historians say that this pretty tale of the dove was invented by the illustrious Hincmar, Archbishop of Reims, nearly four hundred years after Clovis's day. At any rate, belief in the straight-from-Heaven-ness of that crystal vial and its tawny oil brought upwards of thirty kings to Reims to be anointed and crowned.

In 1210, the cathedral was destroyed by fire. And two years later a new cathedral was begun. When the people of Reims set about the building of this new cathedral, they had many things in mind: they were going to build not only a house of God, and the mother house to all the other churches of a diocese; they were going to build the metropolitan cathedral of France, the seat of the primate of the French Church; they were going to build the coronation place of France's kings; they were going to erect in stone an edifice worthy to be all those things and commemorative, too, of that baptism of Clovis by virtue of which Reims regarded herself and was regarded as the cradle of Christianity in France.

Naturally, they wanted to exceed everything that had yet been achieved to the glory of God — in France or elsewhere.

Viollet-le-Duc placed the period of supreme importance in French cathedral-building between the years 1180 and 1240.

'Sixty years! Astounding, that in that short space of time it was possible to secure, over so great an extent of territory, results so surprising; because it was not only workers who had to be found, but thousands of artists — men whose talent is a cause of wonder to us to-day.'

Where did France develop so many master-craftsmen, mighty architects, artists of many sorts? Who knows? The Dark Ages were scarce lifted. Of popular education there was none. Travel was difficult and dangerous. Books were unknown outside the monasteries — and not very many were even there. Yet, suddenly, when some five-and-twenty towns decided, practically all at once, to signalize a new national advance by building five-and-twenty of those marvellous edifices, art and craft were available for them all — and enthusiasm!

Of all the coronations at Reims, the most interesting is, of course, that of Charles VII.

Before his day it was the custom that the prince about to become king should present himself, mounted on a white horse, at one of the principal gates of the city and there receive the keys from the municipal magistrates. But Jeanne, obeying the Voices, changed this and received Charles herself; and thereafter, in memory of her, it was always a young girl who performed this office.

Boutet de Monvel's familiar picture of Charles's coronation scene makes us all feel as if we had been witnesses of it.

Of Reims in the war there is so much to say that it is hard to say only a little.

Von Bülow's left wing — the Prussian Guard, going to meet Foch — entered Reims on September 3, 1914.

'There was no fighting either in the town itself or in the immediate neighborhood,' the mayor testified, 'and the forts have been evacuated by our troops.'

The Germans demanded — among other things — a million francs in cash; and on September 4th, while they were making these demands on the mayor, one of their batteries began to bombard the city. In three quarters of an hour thirty-five persons were killed and twenty-five wounded.

On September 12th, on their retreat from the Marne, they evacuated Reims and settled down just outside, to destroy city and people by bombardment. They began almost on the very day of their evacuation, and ceased only as the war ended. Much of the time the rain of shells averaged from five thousand to fifteen thousand daily.

There were 117,000 people in Reims when the war began. After twenty-eight months of bombardment there still remained 17,100. In the spring of 1917 what was left of the civil population was forced to evacuate.

But during nearly three years while a considerable portion of the residents stayed there, life and work went on amid the rain of bursting shells, with incredible courage.

The first school to open underground was the 'Manoury,' installed December 7, 1914, in a wine-cellar of the Pommery establishment. Subsequently other wine-cellars were put to similar use — children, relatives, and teaching staff all living in the cellars, which were within a mile, or less, of the German lines. In 1915 and 1916 the July examinations took place as usual, and prizes were awarded.

'We were never abandoned,' wrote Monseigneur Neveux, Auxiliary Bishop of Reims, 'by any trade. We never lacked bread; the butcher shops and groceries were open; the milk-women went through the streets each day ringing a bell which perhaps prevented them from hearing the shriek of the shells, but did not safeguard them from explosions. The market had its market-women, although they had frequently to seek refuge in the cellars.'

The postmen made their rounds. City officials went about their administrative affairs. The little newspaper appeared regularly. And throughout it all the people, and the soldiers in their trenches and barracks, were shepherded by an old man almost incomparably valiant: Cardinal Luçon; past his allotted span of years when this tempest broke upon him, but incredibly strong to endure and to console. His ministrations to the fighting men and to the suffering civilians are beyond all praise. His anguish and his courage and his service make him worthy to be named with Cardinal Mercier. And I'm sure that every heart in Christendom must have rejoiced that he was able to be present at the re-dedication of his belovèd Cathedral in the summer of 1927.

After the evacuation by the Germans on September 12, 1914, some seventy to eighty of their wounded were accommodated in the nave of the cathedral, due notice of this was sent to them, and a Red Cross flag was displayed on each tower.

On the 18th, the cathedral was struck with eight-inch shells which smashed some of the thirteenth- and fourteenth-century stained-glass windows, damaged some of the outside sculptures, and killed two of the German wounded in the nave.

September 19th about 4 P.M. a shell fired the wooden scaffolding round the northwest tower which had been under repair since 1913. The fire spread quickly to the roof, the molten lead from which set fire to the straw in the nave whereon the wounded Germans were laid. In spite of the rescue party who risked their lives getting out the wounded enemy, a dozen of the German soldiers perished in the flames, which spread to the Archbishop's palace and destroyed priceless tapestries and archæological collections. That afternoon and night nearly thirty-five acres of buildings were destroyed.

When the inhabitants of Reims began coming back in the fall of 1918, of the fourteen thousand houses there had been in 1914, only about sixty were left in a state which made it possible to live in them.

I strongly advise your buying the book on Reims and the battles for its possession, issued in 1919 by Michelin and Company, Clermont-Ferrand, as one of their series of illustrated guides to the battle-fields. The whole series is excellent; but I know it is not likely that the traveller will buy a number of them. In the case of the one on Reims, I'd do it, however much I was trying to resist temptations to accumulate impedimenta. For Reims as you see it is a new city, to appreciate which you must know something of the destruction out of which it grew. The text of this book is admirable, and the illustrations are invaluable.

The manifold services rendered to the travelling public by the Michelin Company keep us all so deeply indebted to them that I, for one, am glad of an opportunity to express profound appreciation and gratefulness. They do a perfectly extraordinary amount, not merely to increase travel and to facilitate it, but to make it intelligent and rewarding. If they make a great deal of money from their tires, there certainly can't be many churls who grudge it to them. For, if Michelin should 'fail,' I can't quite think what we wayfarers should do.

I hope, too, that Mr. John D. Rockefeller knows how grateful to him many of us are for his very generous contribution to the vast sum needed for restoring the sublime cathedral. What stage of the restoration may have been reached when you visit Reims is impossible to guess. But probably none of us who knew it as it used to be will live to see it fully repaired.

See, too, what is left of the Abbey Church of Saint-Rémy.

You will probably leave Reims for Soissons by Route 31, going between these points a dozen miles or so south of the Chemin des Dames of which we used to hear so much during the war.

If I start trying to suggest what you may see hereabouts — or what you may wish to recall — this chapter will be endless. So I'm sure the only thing to do is to say that Soissons is thirty-five miles from Reims by this route; and that if you leave Reims at noon, you may lunch at the

Hôtel du Lion-Rouge at one o'clock. To reach it, keep straight ahead without a turn, as you enter Soissons, until you reach Place de la République. There, ask for the hotel, which is on rue de la Gare.

German guns left us little to see in Soissons, except the ruins of its cathedral, and the still further ruins of its already-ruined Abbey of Saint Jean-des-Vignes where Thomas à Becket resided for nine years.

Soissons is very old, and has been very important for a very long time, during which it has suffered many things, but never anything to compare with the experiences of 1914–18, which all but annihilated it.

From Soissons en route to Paris by way of Compiègne, I'm sure you'll wish to stop at Pierrefonds, the superb feudal castle built by Louis of Orléans, and wonderfully restored by Viollet-le-Duc. Pierrefonds is especially interesting because it belongs to a time when castles had not yet ceased to be fortresses but had begun trying to be palaces as well.

To Compiègne is ten and a half miles through the forest, passing Rethondes where the Armistice was signed.

Compiègne Château has many beautiful furnishings and many interesting memories. The park is lovely. The Hôtel de Ville is one of the most noted in France. It was at Compiègne that Jeanne d'Arc was captured by the Burgundians and sold to the English.

It was at Compiègne that Louis XV and the Dauphin awaited little Marie-Antoinette. It was here that Napoleon had planned to receive Marie-Antoinette's niece, Marie-Louise; but his impatience to see her took him part-way toward Soissons to surprise her.

And the forest!

The rapt worshipper, holding — or seeming to hold — his noisy heartbeats so the holy silence may not be disturbed, will wonder, as a startled rabbit flees across the brown, beam-flecked path, what can have moved the little furry thing to flight. Then he will hear it also, borne on the still air from a not-distant glade: Charlemagne's hunting-horn summoning Roland and Oliver to the woodland repast where they shall hear from the lips of his own envoys of Haroun-al-Raschid the great Caliph, the great Caliph of Bagdad. And, ere that sound has gone rollicking down the forest aisles, the listener will hear a rushing as of great wings far overhead, a drumming as of some monster bird risen from the underbrush in flight.

Then he will hold his heartbeats indeed. For if he is wise he will know who rides above the treetops: it is Guynemer, peerless knight of the air, flying again over his old home on the forest's edge and cutting wild youthful capers in the zenith to make his mother and sisters look up in recognition of the only birdman who would dare such antics.

Forever and forever while hearts in human breasts beat high for heroes, the sons of men will go to Compiègne and venerate the memory of that lad whose name is on the Panthéon, whose fame is in every heart in France, and whose spirit rides the winds to all eternity.

'No man knows his resting-place'; no flowers can deck his grave. Whether God buried him, as He buried Moses, or took him heavenward in a chariot of fire as Elijah went, no one can say. Of all the glorious eaglets who flew for France and died for France, Fame marked the lad of Compiègne for legend; and with a sense of fitness truly French, she snatched him from sepulture, left no trace of his mortality. But the rustle of his rushing wings will call vision-seeing eyes aloft, in the clearings of Compiègne, for ages on end.

And as time goes on, they who walk those forest aisles will meet Foch therein, as well as Charlemagne and the

little Maid, and Navarre, and Napoleon. And over their
heads will beat the deathless wings of France's second
Roland — the knight whose charger gallops eternally 'twixt
earth and heaven: Guynemer.

It is possible to dine at Compiègne and drive to Paris
before bedtime. I have done it many times.

But if you can spend the night, I urge you to do it, at the
Hôtel du Rond-Royal on the forest's edge, and have a room
at the back of the hotel, toward the forest. It was here that
Dr. Carrel had his hospital during the war.

There's good golf close to the hotel; and sometimes there
are horse-races. Compiègne is a delightful place for a sojourn.

Your way into Paris is through Senlis; and a very little
distance added to it will make it include Chantilly also.

And, of course, it is no great matter of miles to go from
Reims to Soissons by way of Laon; nor to go from Soissons
north to Coucy, and then across to Blérancourt, and through
Noyon to Compiègne; nor to continue west on Route 31
from Compiègne to Beauvais, and thence into Paris with a
stop at Chantilly if you like.

These are but the scantiest hints I've given you about
the great possibilities of this section.

But France is so great, and my book is so small!

Now we must go back to Châlons and pick up the trail
toward Strasbourg.

On the day you leave Paris it is quite possible to spend
the night at Bar-le-Duc — it is only a hundred and thirty-
six miles — without slighting what's to be seen on the way.
The Hôtel de Metz et du Commerce is not luxurious, but
it is comfortable and serves good food. The Ornain flows
picturesquely through the lower town, where the hotel is;
and a short distance from it is the Marne–Rhine Canal,
bordered by the old Roman road. An evening stroll in the

lower town along the waterways — especially Quai Victor-Hugo — is one of the experiences which, to some of us, have so much to do with the charm of motoring in France.

It is hardly conceivable that any one travelling by train would visit Bar-le-Duc. Yet the ancient town on the heights is full of interest; and the more modern, lower town is full of pleasantness.

Bar has had a long succession of distinguished visitors; but I doubt if her present-day guests care as much about recalling them as they do about the quiet personality of the old town itself.

If you have reasons for wishing to visit Saint-Mihiel, you may go to it from Bar (twenty-one miles) and then follow Route 64 down to Vaucouleurs and Domrémy.

If you are going straight to the Jeanne d'Arc country, you take Route 66 — following boulevard de la Rochelle from your hotel southeast to the Pont-Neuf, then crossing the Ornain and taking rue Ernest Bradfer which presently becomes Route 66.

Ligny-en-Barrois is ten miles; and Domrémy is thirty-five miles farther. A nine o'clock start from Bar should give you time to visit Domrémy, Vaucouleurs, and Toul, and get to Nancy for luncheon, the afternoon and night.

Domrémy is a quiet village not notably different from what it may well have been when Jeanne knew it — except, of course, for the white monument in her dooryard.

It seems probable that Jeanne was born on January 6, 1412 — the Day of the Kings, or Epiphany. Her father, Jacques, was a rather well-to-do peasant proprietor. Her mother was probably of even better stock, and had made a pilgrimage to Rome; she taught her little girl all the household arts, and found her specially apt at plying the needle. Jeanne tended her father's flocks at times, just as any farmer's daughter would do then, and does now. And she helped her mother. She was a physically vigorous child, yet extraordinarily sensitive. The tales her mother told, of Rome and the way thither, impressed her deeply. Travellers through Domrémy were not infrequent, the village being on a main road, and Jeanne probably heard more than a little of that talk which falls flat upon dull minds, but sets eager minds to dreaming — talk of places where stirring things happen. She was a good little girl — just naturally good, as some children are — and loved to please, to be approved.

When she was ten, the baby Henry VI of England was proclaimed King of France. Charles the Dauphin, disinherited through his own mother's connivance and through his brother-in-law's superiority in arms, showed no signs of asserting himself and driving the invader forth. The English held all of France north of the Loire and a goodly bit south of it. Their encroachments (aided by their Burgundian allies) on the rest of France were certainly much discussed in this household at Domrémy. And when Queen Isabeau was execrated — as she doubtless was — there was sure to be some one to recall the prophecy of Marie d'Avignon, who had, during the lifetime of poor, mad Charles VI and the scandalous regency of Isabeau, declared that, though France was being ruined by a woman, she would be restored by a woman — by an armed virgin from the marches of Lorraine.

About the time she was twelve, Jeanne began to be imbued with the idea that God willed to use her in freeing France from the English. Saint Michael, Prince of the armies of the Lord, Saint Catherine and Saint Margaret appeared to her in visions, spoke to her, urged her on.

How much she talked of this in her home, in the village, is hard to say. Sensitive persons with visions incline to be uncommunicative, fearing ridicule. Jeanne may have realized that no one else in Domrémy was likely to play any part in this thing she was to do, and therefore it would be useless to talk to them about it. But, on the other hand, she must have known that what must be done was not only to rouse the lethargic Dauphin, but to kindle new faith and courage in despairing France; and to do this latter she must make people believe *with her* in her destiny.

And if we have no documentation on what Domrémy thought of the girl, do we need it? What would any village, anywhere at any time, think of a nice, docile girl, doing fine needlework as she kept a watchful eye on her father's sheep or kine, who said that she was chosen by the King of Heaven to lead the armies of her earthly king to victory?

Jeanne was just past her seventeenth birthday when she at last prevailed upon Baudricourt, Governor of Vaucouleurs, to send her to the Dauphin at Chinon — when she left Domrémy never to return.

We have seen her at Chinon. We have met her at Poitiers whither Charles sent her to be examined. We have been with her as she raised the siege of Orléans. We have stood beside her at Reims when she saw Charles anointed with the holy oil brought from heaven by that dove for the baptism of Clovis. We have seen her fall, wounded, in the attempt to take Paris from the English. We have witnessed her capture at Compiègne, her trial and execution at Rouen. We have met her at other places, too.

Last of all, as it happens, we come to the village of her birth, her youth. Seventeen years of placid home-keeping life lay behind her when she left here. Some months of eventful activity lay ahead of her, and a year of prison — and the stake.

No other woman of any time has writ her name so large in history. And it was all done, mind you, within less than five months; because, after Reims she accomplished nothing. Between the latter part of April, 1429, when she marched upon Orléans, and the 16th of July, when she saw Charles crowned, her work was done. In those weeks she rallied France and began the rout of the English which her captains could, and did, conclude.

Explain it as you like and can — it is an extraordinary story, and one with undiminishing power to move men, to gird them for victory.

I wish the museum in the cottage were of a different sort. What would be appropriate and impressive there would be something such as one finds in those regional museums which are becoming so rich a part of the traveller's experience in France. If there could be here a reconstituted interior such as Jeanne knew, how it would help us to enter that family life which was hers before she passed to her brief phase on the battle-field, in palaces and in prison!

I resent show-cases and souvenirs, not to mention post-cards, when there might be rooms refurnished, figures in costumes of the period and place, at occupations such as Jeanne's household was busy with. I want a group about the hearth on a winter's night when a wayfarer has been given hospitality. I want a Musée Grevin effect here, such as that extraordinary effect (in Paris) which makes us onlookers at the murder of Marat or mourners, with Bertrand, beside the dead Napoleon.

The little church has changed its axis since Jeanne knelt there (and her house, when she lived in it, fronted on the highway), but it is not hard to see her there.

I wouldn't go, if I were you, to the basilica on the site of the Bois Chénu where Jeanne first heard her 'Voices.' I think it rather 'spoils' Domrémy — or *would*, were it not possible to avoid it and ignore it.

In any case, an hour or so spent in this village is — to my way of thinking — an experience worth going far, far to get into one's memory. And if it can be done, I'd establish friendly contact, even if only for a few minutes, with a little maid of Domrémy, playing beside the Meuse as Jeanne did, more than five centuries ago.

Then, on you go, north, as Jeanne went, to Vaucouleurs, some eleven miles and a fraction over. And there you'll pause for long enough at least to see her setting forth, with her six men-at-arms, for Chinon to travel by night and hide by day. I hope you have in mind Boutet de Monvel's picture of this!

From Vaucouleurs to Toul is fifteen miles. And from Toul to Nancy is about the same. So, when you leave Domrémy you have a little more than forty miles to go, after having covered forty-five from Bar-le-Duc to Jeanne d'Arc's birthplace.

At Toul you must pause at least long enough to see the Cloisters of Saint-Étienne. And then — to Nancy!

I've been to Nancy a good many times, and have always stayed at the Grand-Hôtel, on Place Stanislas, and liked it very much. But I notice that there are two other hotels to which some lists give precedence over the Grand; and that other recommendations (like a very recent number of 'The Voyageur en France') do not include the Grand at all. So I hasten to mention the others: the Thiers, on Place Thiers, where the railway station is; and the Excelsior, at 61, rue Stanislas, near Place Stanislas. Neither of them has a situation comparable to the Grand; but they may have other qualities most commendable. I shall investigate when next I go to Nancy. And whichever you choose, remember that Nancy has at least two restaurants which are very good: Restaurant Stanislas, at 11, Place Stanislas, and Brasserie Liégeoise, on Place Carnot.

So much for the creature comforts!

Now, about Nancy, which is one of the most attractive

provincial cities of France. There's a good deal to see at Nancy, and a great deal to remember. We shall meet a number of old friends there. But I think we won't go back of a time (1407) when Louis, Duke of Orléans, declared war on the Duke of Lorraine and sent a herald-at-arms to Nancy to tell Duke Charles to prepare a grand dinner for his enemies who would soon be there. Duke Charles sent back word that the dinner would be ready at the appointed time. It was! And it was served to a large and distinguished group of enemies — only, they ate it, not in the palace hall, but in the dungeons. Louis of Orléans was 'unavoidably detained,' somewhere. But many of his friends were present.

It was this Duke Charles to whom Jeanne d'Arc came, some twenty years later, and told him that Heaven would not fail to demand a reckoning for the way he was spending his days.

Margaret of Anjou was married at Nancy to that nephew of her uncle, Charles VII, whom Jeanne d'Arc had 'put in his place.' Charles was present at the ceremony, and both he and King René appeared in the lists during the eight days of jousting and feasting that attended the ceremony. But from contemporary accounts it would seem that more interest was aroused by the presence of Agnès Sorel than by that of any one else in all the glittering assembly.

When the fifteen-year-old bride set out for England, where she was to know so much unhappiness, her Uncle Charles accompanied her two leagues on her way, and returned to Nancy, his eyes swollen with weeping. King René went with her as far as Bar-le-Duc.

King René's grandson, Nicholas, Duke of Lorraine, having died childless in 1473, the duchy descended quite naturally to that young man's cousin, René — son of King René's other daughter, Yolande. But Charles the Bold, of

Burgundy, 'no sooner,' as an old chronicle puts it, 'learned that Nicholas was gone from life into eternity, than, hoping to seize the duchy of Lorraine, which he ardently coveted, he made the young Duke prisoner.'

But Louis XI was of no mind to let Charles succeed in this high-handedness — not because Louis had any scruples against such practices; but if anybody were going to snatch Lorraine, why should it not be Louis himself rather than his great vassal?

So Louis seized the person of a young nephew of Emperor Frederick (whose vassal Charles also was) and notified the Emperor that he would release this princeling as soon as the Emperor had made Charles set René free.

Charles yielded, and young René made his solemn entry into Nancy as its Duke, on the 14th of August, 1473.

When Charles was taking the body of his father, Philip the Good, to Dijon for interment, he had to go by way of Nancy; and Duke René came out of the city in great pomp and circumstance to pay his respects.

And after Charles left, he began to be fearful that somebody — maybe that grasping Louis XI — would try to get René's duchy away from him. So Charles led an army into Lorraine!

In vain did René plead that his duchy was 'full of peace,' and beg that the Burgundians withdraw.

Charles refused to negotiate except on condition that René join with him offensively and defensively against all their enemies.

Now, René had no enemies (except Charles) and he had no stomach for being embroiled in all of Charles's quarrels. So he declined the alliance, reminding Burgundy that he was an ally of the King of France and could not make another alliance which might involve infidelity to that one.

Then Louis persuaded René to declare war on Burgundy. And the Emperor ordered René not to permit Burgundian troops to cross Lorraine.

So René, believing himself supported by the King of France and the Emperor of Germany, threw down the gauntlet to Charles the Bold.

This is a figure of speech, with us. But to René it was a reality. He sent a herald-at-arms to cast before Charles a blood-stained war-glove, emblem of defiance.

Heralds were pretty well protected by the code of chivalry. But the one who carried that gauntlet to Burgundy's great warrior Duke was distinctly nervous about it. He delivered his message as fast as he could, and was making all haste to depart when Charles called him back and gave him a well-filled purse and some of his own sumptuous wearing apparel — as reward for the good news he had brought!

'Tell your master,' said he, 'that I shall soon be in Lorraine.'

Duke René was not frightened, and promptly laid siege to a Burgundian town called Damvilliers, about forty miles north of Verdun. He had some French troops with him. But when Charles was known to be marching to the defence of Damvilliers, Louis suddenly decided that he did not care to fight Burgundy — and recalled his soldiers!

René fell back then, and put Nancy in a state of defence. And on came the Burgundians, taking all before them, and laying siege to Nancy, which they took after a month's bombardment and blockade.

On November 30, 1475, Charles made his triumphal entry through the Porte de la Craffe, took the oath as Duke of Lorraine, and lodged himself in the ducal palace. He announced to the parliament of Lorraine that he had decided to make Nancy the capital of his vast realm, to defend and beautify the city, and maintain there a court of such magnificence as Europe had never seen.

Then he set out on a campaign against the Swiss. On March 2, 1476, he sustained a great defeat beneath the walls of Granson — and a second, in June, at Morat.

This encouraged the Lorrainers, who had mustered under Duke René, to lay siege to Nancy — which was starved into submission; the Burgundians evacuating by that same Porte de la Craffe whereby they had made their triumphant entry more than ten months before. René in person assisted his enemies to withdraw in dignity and without molestation. And when the retiring Burgundian Governor was about to dismount and make his profound thanks to the young Duke, René motioned to him to keep his saddle, saying, 'Monsieur, I thank you very humbly for having so graciously governed my duchy. If you find it agreeable to remain with me, you shall have the same treatment as I myself have.'

To which the Governor responded: 'Monsieur, I hope that you do not hold against me any ill will on account of this war. I wish very much that Monsieur of Burgundy had never commenced it; and I fear that at the end of it he and we shall not live anywhere, but shall be the victims of it.'

Even then Monsieur of Burgundy was on his way back to Nancy with a formidable army; and on October 25th, a year exactly since he began his former siege, he invested Nancy.

René went to Switzerland to hire some mercenaries, but it was the 4th of January before he got back.

It was Saturday, and bitterly cold. That was one of the severest winters on record.

Against all advice, Charles determined to make an immediate attack. The battle began between ten and eleven o'clock Sunday morning, and it was not long thereafter that

Burgundy's great Duke, whose name had made all Europe tremble, realized that nothing remained to him save to die like a valiant knight, encouraging his men.

When he attempted to put on his helmet, a silver-gilt lion, which ornamented its crest, fell off.

'It is God's warning,' said the stricken Prince — and threw himself with greater abandon into the thickest of the fight. But nothing could arrest that rout; the Burgundians were in mad flight. And as Charles spurred his horse back toward the camp he had quitted so confidently only a few hours before, he was struck by a lance-thrust and unhorsed. His assailant was a Lorraine gentleman named Claude de Beaumont.

'Save the Duke of Burgundy!' Charles cried.

But Beaumont was deaf. He heard indistinctly what was said, but he thought his victim cried, 'Long live the Duke of Burgundy!' So he struck again, and cleaved the head of Charles — then passed on, not knowing whom he had killed.

That same evening René, in triumph, reëntered his capital. And whilst he was receiving the congratulations of his people, in the palace, there was brought to him a young page of Charles who said he had seen his master killed.

In the morning this boy led a searching party to the spot. There lay the most magnificent prince in Europe, one among a thick-strewn mass of dead. His corpse had been stripped stark, and was fast frozen in the slime at the edge of a small pond. Beside it lay the body of that courteous and foreboding Burgundian whom René had thanked for the gracious government of his duchy.

The two bodies were carried, with great ceremony of respect and regret, into Nancy, where Charles lay in state for six days. René went often to look upon his dead enemy, and on one of those visits took the cold hand of the great

Duke, saying: 'Dear cousin, would to God that your misfortunes and mine had not made you thus.'

On Sunday, January 12th, a week after the battle,
Charles's body, embalmed and enclosed in a double coffin
of wood and lead, was carried to Saint-Georges Church,
where, a little more than a year before, he had taken the
oath as Duke of Lorraine. There, with all the magnificence
due his state, he was interred. The other dead gathered
from the battle-field were buried with military honors, and
René erected near their graves a memorial chapel which he
called the Chapel of the Burgundians. The pilgrimage
church of Bon-Secours stands on that spot to-day, and in
it are the handsome tombs of the last Duke of Lorraine and
his wife — of whom more, presently.

René lies in the Church of the Cordeliers, which he built
adjoining the ducal palace to give Heaven thanks for his
victory.

And Charles, since 1550, has rested in Notre-Dame-de-
Bruges, in a superb tomb of bronze gilt erected for him by
his great-grandson, Emperor Charles V. Beside him sleeps
his lovely young heiress, Mary, upon whom burdens so
heavy fell after his defeat at Nancy.

René was the founder of the great family of Lorraine and
Guise which played so great a part in the history of the sixteenth century. His second son, Claude, was the father of
Marie of Lorraine — mother of Mary, Queen of Scots —
and of those Cardinals of Lorraine and of Guise who had so
much to do with Mary Stuart's early history.

There were Dukes and Dukes of Lorraine (we can't dwell
upon them all here, nor even mention them) and there was
still one, in 1729, though Lorraine had been practically a part
of France for many years. When this Duke Leopold died
— not at Nancy, which France was occupying as a garrison
city, but at Lunéville — his son and heir, Francis, was at

the court of Vienna. And Louis XV thought that would be a good place for Francis to stay. The Emperor of Austria had no son—only a daughter, Maria-Thèrésa. He wanted to leave his possessions and his crown to her, but he knew that her tenure of them would depend very largely on the willingness of other monarchs to leave her in enjoyment of her inheritance. Louis XV was not agreeable to this plan — but he could be made so!

Louis had an indigent father-in-law on his hands — Stanislas, deposed King of Poland — and he wanted a job for father; so he proposed that Francis abdicate his ducal throne for an imperial — marry Maria-Thèrésa and let Stanislas enjoy Lorraine.

Francis 'held out' for extra concessions, and was made Grand Duke of Tuscany as well as co-ruler of the Austrian Empire. And Stanislas moved to Nancy.

When he entered Nancy, 'the city presented a picture of desolation rather than rejoicing. Many families had walled up the windows of their mansions along the route that Stanislas would pass; nearly every one fled into the country to avoid witnessing an event which chilled all their sensibilities.' For seven hundred years the scions of one family had ruled Lorraine. And this Polish interloper was about as alien to everything over which he was arbitrarily set as any one in all the world could well have been.

But Stanislas made himself beloved here, though he lived principally at Lunéville and not in Nancy. France gave him a liberal allowance, and he used it prudently for the embellishment of his capital, which he made one of the most beautiful in Europe. He was never in debt, never in need of money, yet carried on ideas of city planning which were far in advance of his day.

His wife, Queen Catherine Opalinska, hated Lorraine, pined for Poland, and was a pretty difficult companion for

Stanislas. He, as most of us know well through the engrossing pages of 'The Chevalier de Boufflers,' by Nesta H. Webster, was agreeably consoled by the Marquise de Boufflers, who reigned not only over his heart but over his court. (Her mother, the Princesse de Craon, had been the mistress of Duke Leopold, his predecessor.)

Now, supposing that you have lunched — well, but not *too* well! — let us start out to see the sights of Nancy.

You are probably not far from Place Stanislas, surrounded by buildings of uniform design and embellished with fine fountains and the magnificent wrought-iron gates which are so celebrated.

As you stand with your back to the Hôtel de Ville, looking across Place Stanislas, you are facing the direction in which lie most of the places you will wish to see first. Beyond Place Stanislas is the Porte Royale, a triumphal arch erected by Stanislas in honor of Louis XV. It marks one entrance to Place de la Carrière where the tournaments used to be held, and where you may see King René and Charles VII doing their prettiest to impress Agnès Sorel, Queen of Beauty at Margaret of Anjou's wedding.

A little to your left as you reach the end of this old tourney field, now so handsomely embellished by the munificence of Stanislas, is the ducal palace built by Duke René — but after those events of Charles's occupation and death. The palace entrance, known as the 'Grande Porterie,' is one of the most beautiful in Europe. The musée in the palace has many objects of interest, including some tapestries said to have been in the tent of Charles. He went magnificently to war, we know — carrying four hundred tents hung with Flemish tapestries and Genoa velvets and Lyon brocades, and with much cloth of gold; and three hundred complete services of gold and silver plate. All those were his when one day's sun rose; and when it set, he was stark, even of his shift, and wolves were gnawing ravenously at all that was left of his mortality.

Next to the palace is the church that René built in thanksgiving for that victory over Charles, and where he lies buried, and his parents, and his second wife.

The Grande-Rue, on which the palace faces, ends at the exceedingly picturesque Porte de la Craffe, through which Charles came in triumph, and his garrison withdrew ten months later. Beyond it is the Porte de la Citadelle in the walls built two centuries later to enclose a larger town.

Rue de la Craffe leads from the *porte* of that name to the Porte Desilles erected under Louis XVI in 1785, in honor of the birth of the Dauphin and also of the alliance between France and the United States negotiated in 1778 by John Adams, Benjamin Franklin, and Arthur Lee, whereby France recognized the independence of the new Republic.

From this gate, come down Cours Léopold to Place Carnot and rue Stanislas.

The Place de la Croix de Bourgogne, where Charles's body was found, may be reached by turning west in rue du Faubourg Stanislas to rue Jeanne d'Arc, and following the latter a short distance southeast.

In the evening, walk in the Promenade de la Pepinière, the beautiful park connected with France's school of forestry.

There are military band concerts in the Pepinière three evenings a week.

In 1870, after Sédan, Nancy was chosen for General Manteuffel, commander of the First German Army Corps, as headquarters pending the withdrawal of the victors on the payment of the last sou in the billion-dollar indemnity they exacted, along with the cession of Alsace-Lorraine. And during the three years he stayed in Nancy, Manteuffel delighted in ordering his military bands to play the 'Retreat.'

One who heard was a young student taking his examination for the Polytechnic at Paris.

Forty-two years later — in August, 1913 — a new commandant came to Nancy to take control of the Twentieth Army Corps, whose position there, guarding France's eastern frontier, was considered one of the most important to the safety of the nation.

The first order that he gave was one that brought out the full band strength of the six regiments quartered in the town. They were to play the 'March Lorraine' and the 'Sambre et Meuse,' and to fill Nancy with those stirring airs. It was a veritable tidal wave of triumphant sound that he wanted — for it had much to efface.

Nancy will never forget that night! It was Saturday, the 23d of August, 1913. And the new commandant's name was Ferdinand Foch!

When you leave Nancy in the morning, en route to Strasbourg, you take rue Saint-Dizier through the heart of town, continuing on it after it becomes rue de Strasbourg. The Church of Bon-Secours, where Stanislas is buried, is on your right as you leave town by the road (Route 4) for Lunéville.

Lunéville, about twenty miles from Nancy, is a familiar name to thousands of Americans because near here was a training-sector for some divisions of the A.E.F. in 1918. It is still military in aspect, being a garrison town; and the palace which Duke Léopold of Lorraine built and King Stanislas embellished is now a cavalry barracks.

Do you recall Nesta Webster's description of its garden?

'Lunéville,' she says, 'must have been an enchanting place for a small boy. King Stanislas was not unlike an Indian Rajah in his passion for mechanical devices, and the garden of the Château was laid out at enormous expense to provide every kind of amusement. Here was a "Kiosque" in which to sit and listen to music, enlivened by clockwork figures representing the performer; and at every turn one encountered cascades and fountains, sham rockwork and miniature lakes, cupolas and cottages, minarets and pagodas. Most exciting of all was the famous "Rocher," on which a life-size model of a village was erected. This too moved by clockwork, and on being wound up awoke to clamorous life — cocks crowed loudly, dogs barked, cats ran after mice, and a drunkard's wife leant out of a window and poured a pail of water on the head of her returning spouse in the most realistic manner.'

It is Mrs. Webster, too, who gives us this picture of the end of poor Stanislas, in that palace which is now a barracks:

'One cold February morning the king had risen as usual at half-past six, and, dismissing his attendants, sat down before the fire to smoke his pipe, dressed in a wadded dressing-gown of Indian silk, a present from his daughter, the Queen of France. His pipe ended, the king rose and attempted to lay it down on the high mantelpiece; but, in reaching up, the edge of his dressing-gown caught fire and in a moment the cotton wadding was in a blaze. The poor old man shouted loudly for help, but by some strange misfortune all his attendants were out of hearing; he then tried to reach the bell, but in doing so he stumbled and fell forward into the fireplace. Here he lay still in flames when an old woman employed to scrub the floors heard his moans and rushed in to the rescue. Whilst calling for help she attempted herself to put out the flames, and in the effort was badly burnt. Even in his pain the king's sense of humor did not desert him: "How strange," he remarked to her, "that, at our ages, you and I should both burn with the same flame!"'

And from his deathbed he dictated a letter to his daughter, referring gayly to the dressing-gown:

'You gave it to me to keep me warm; but it has kept me too warm.'

The main routes to the east diverge at Lunéville. Route 4 curves to the north and approaches Strasbourg by way of Sarrebourg and Saverne. Route 59 starts at Lunéville and goes by way of Baccarat and Saint-Dié, to Sélestat.

Baccarat manufactures a crystal glass very highly esteemed throughout the world.

Fifteen miles farther on Route 59 is Saint-Dié, where there was published, in 1507, a geographical work in which for the first time the name of America was suggested for the New World.

Now, here we are on the borders of Alsace, with a whole world of beauty and history before us, and a few pages of our little book left in which to pay our totally inadequate tribute.

Visitors to France do not go to Alsace; at least, not many go. And it seemed best to use what space we had for those localities in which there is the largest amount of travel by English-speaking persons journeying through Europe. A good many seem now to be asking about a stop-over at Strasbourg. But scarcely any seem to consider the charms of the Vosges.

For the traveller who has from ten days to three weeks for Paris and the rest of France, and who may not go to France more than once or twice in a lifetime, I do not urge this Alsatian corner in competition with Normandy, the Château Country, Carcassonne, the Rhône Valley, and the Riviera.

But to the traveller who goes often, who has more time, and who wants 'something quite different,' I commend Alsace. Perhaps in later editions of this book I shall include more about Alsace because I have learned that more persons than I suspect are eager to go there.

For the present, I'll try to content myself with the outline of one motor tour which can be made from Nancy to Strasbourg and back to Paris, in three or four days, and which will give at least an idea of the charm of the Vosges mountain region and the exceedingly picturesque Alsatian towns.

This takes you from Raon-l'Étape, five miles beyond Baccarat, by a beautiful climb to Sainte-Odile for luncheon at the convent. (Perhaps you are so fortunate as to have in your memory pictures of Miss Frances Starr in 'Marie-Odile.' You won't see any nun or novice half so lovely as she was in the part of the little novice left alone here in the Franco-Prussian War days. But you will be rewarded by a glorious view from the terrace, although you will doubtless wish you might have had it before this place got so Coney-Island-y.)

Sainte-Odile is the patron saint of Alsace. She was born about 660, at Obernai, and her father was Duke of Alsace under Childeric II, his brother-in-law. Doubly disappointed when his first-born was not only a daughter but a blind daughter, Duke Adalric gave way to a terrible rage and ordered her either killed or carried far away where no one would know her origin. The mother's entreaties made no impression on him. So the baby was entrusted to an old servant who took her to a distant convent whose abbess was an aunt of the Duchess. For some reason the child was not even baptized; but in spite of this extraordinary omission she grew up in beautiful holiness. A Bishop of Ratisbonne had a vision in which God directed him to go to the convent where this girl was who had been born blind, to baptize her and give her the name Odile, and thereupon she would gain her sight.

The miracle happened, and Odile was told of her exalted birth. She went to her father, who at first would not receive her, but whose favorite child she eventually became. When she refused to marry the prince of his choice, however, she had to flee before his wrath. He went in pursuit of her, and finally agreed not only to let her lead a conventual life, but to give her his fortress of Hohenbourg in which to found the first convent in Alsace.

From Sainte-Odile, you descend to Obernai, her birthplace.

'Each time,' says André Hallays in his book 'The Spell of Alsace,' 'that one leaves the Vosges for the plain, in Upper Alsace, there is the same succession of pictures: forests of firs, then a cool narrow valley where a little river turns the mill wheels, then vineyards, and finally, at the foot of the last hill, the watchtowers and belfries of a little city. When we descend from Sainte-Odile, the valley is called the Klingenthal, the river the Ehn, the little city Obernai. This one is charming, even among all its beautiful sisters. . . . It has great fortifications of the thirteenth century. . . . It ravishes the ear, the eye, and the imagination.'

It does, indeed! If there were nothing to see in all Alsace but Obernai, I should still feel that Alsace was much-to-be-desired. There, more than in any other town I've ever seen, I had the feeling that Sir Frederick Treves had at Roquebrune.

'The years are many, the years are long' since I saw Maude Adams in 'Peter Pan,' and assured her that I believed in the fairies. Of *course* I believe in them! But at times I almost forget that I do. Then, one day most memorable, I rolled into Obernai on the best-possible equivalent for a magic carpet, and rubbed my eyes, and looked again —— It was still there! I was truly seeing it!

The fairy-tales are not 'made-up' at all! They're all TRUE! Those tales of Grimm's which I owned in five green-bound volumes full of enchanted princesses, errant, rescuing princes, maidens with hair and heart of gold, witches in peaked hats, storks nesting in chimneys, and other persons and things which were no part of real life in Chicago — perhaps it was inevitable that as time went on I should think of them as tales of the Never-Never-Land. Then I came to Obernai — and was ashamed. I didn't see any witches, but I saw many storks and their nests. I didn't actually see any enchanted princesses, but I saw palaces where I am sure some had lived before they got wickedly changed into something-or-other. Everything about Obernai belongs to those green-bound books. Everything in them not only could easily happen in Obernai, but would *have* to happen in such a place!

Oh, please, please, go to Obernai!

And when you know you'll never 'doubt' again, you may go on to Strasbourg.

Now, I have a terrible confession to make about Strasbourg, where I had not been since just before the war, till I went there in the summer of 1926. I didn't like it very well!

I know why! I had expected to find it much more jubilantly French — not more than it is, perhaps, but more than it seemed to me.

I didn't like the hotel — the Maison Rouge. The fact that the plumbing seemed to need a great deal of attention is more French than German, I dare say; but the 'dour' atmosphere, the indifference to requests, the lack of service (we 'toted' our own luggage, when it became evident that we must 'tote' it or do without it), all made us feel like aliens in an enemy land, tolerated because we must be, but with no pretence at welcome. We must have got into a nest of 'Irreconcilables.' In the shops there were no smiles and 'Thank Yous.' We thought the shop-folk sullen and grudging.

Ah, well! Why go on? It may change! It may never have been as it seemed to us. Places, like people, 'get on our nerves,' sometimes, because we are not attuned to their key. I am willing to admit that the fault was all mine. But I couldn't like Strasbourg.

However —— ! What difference does that make? And if, in spite of this, I could help you to like it and enjoy it, what a real triumph that would be!

It seems that once upon a time (in geological, not human 'time') the Vosges Mountains and the mountains of the Black Forest, now some seventy miles apart, were one and the same range, which a titanic upheaval split in two and spread on either side of the narrow valley, part of which has long been called Upper Alsace. Through this rift (too wide to be called a chasm) flows the Rhine and its multitude of tributaries. A turbulent current, the Rhine, all through the valley, a length of a hundred and twenty-five miles, in the course of which the swirling, oft-augmented stream flows downhill on a descent of more than four hundred and fifty feet to the hundred miles. From February to June, each year, when the mountain snows are melting and the mountain torrents are swollen till they laugh noisily at their inadequate wee beds, the Rhine (which rises near the Saint Gothard Pass in southern Switzerland, and leads a very errant life before it enters upon its boundary duties between Germany and Switzerland, then between Germany and France) is a boisterous, badly behaved river — especially between Bâle and Lauterbourg, which are respectively at the south and north extremities of Alsace; and owing to this waywardness, century after century went by without a single village settling on the whole west bank between those points. And in all that length (a hundred and twenty-five

miles) there were, until the seventeenth century, only two
bridges, both of the pontoon type, one near Bâle and one
near Strasbourg.

There was very little crossing of the Rhine at any point
in what we now call Alsace. The capricious river consti-
tuted a barrier to relations between the peoples on either
side of it, 'surer than the best walls.' And equally entrenched were the Alsatians on their western front by the
Vosges, which, for long ages, were regarded as uncrossable
and impenetrable except at Belfort (on the south) and at
Saverne (northwest of Strasbourg). At each of these places
there was a natural 'cut' in the mountains, through which
men passed if they passed at all. Thus was Alsace shut in
by Nature. Unless you keep this in mind, you cannot
understand her history.

Nor was Nature content with shutting Alsace in. She
went further: she cut the enclosed space into many little
parcels, each more or less separated by natural barriers
from the others. There was distinctness in each parcel, yet
a spirit of unity among them all. Together they produced
nearly everything requisite for their common needs, and
depended little on the world outside.

The people who settled here were Celts. When Greece was
in her Golden Age, the section of Europe we now call Alsace
was almost the centre of the vast area inhabited by the
Celts — a people who liked 'staying put.' They were tillers
of the soil, not nomads. They were democratic, and had
small use for kings. Whereas, across the turbulent Rhine
were those Germanic peoples whose essential differences
from the Celts Cæsar described for us; who were nomads,
living by the chase and by war; who were *not* democratic,
and set the glory of their chief and of the clan above the
development of the individual in ability to rule.

When Cæsar came, conquering Gaul and fixing its

eastern boundary at the estranging Rhine, he interfered practically not at all with the Celtic tribes he found in Alsace; nor did many Romans from the Tiber's banks, or elsewhere, come to mingle with these new citizens of the Empire. The Celts between the Vosges and the Rhine were so little disturbed by Roman rule that for long centuries after it ceased in their part of the world, they went on, as they had gone before Rome came, developing their Celtic institutions, cherishing their old Celtic republicanism — but with a difference! Rome had not deflected them, but she had impermeated them with new ideas, ideas essentially Latin.

The Celts of Alsace remained agricultural, peaceable, democratic. But they took kindly to the Roman ideas for good roads, facile communication, abundant water-supply brought by aqueducts, and other public works which only a rather highly organized community can effect.

In course of time the Celtic tongue disappeared and Latin took its place. Celtic law gave way to Roman law; the Druidic religion to the worship of Rome's deities. Underneath all this, though, persisted a remarkably sturdy development which was unswervingly democratic and never imperialistic; which took from Rome that which helped, and left to Rome's other citizens that which enervated and made for decline.

Alsace knew little of the earliest barbarian invasions. There were two great routes, in those days and for long afterwards, between middle Europe and Gaul. One of them led from the valley of the Danube through Switzerland and into Gaul at Belfort; the other was the northern route, into Belgium and thence to Picardy and Champagne. All the early invaders came by one or the other of these routes, crossing the Rhine either at Bâle or at Mayence or at Cologne — to the south or else far to the north of Alsace.

But in the middle of the fourth century a swarm of the devastators achieved the crossing of the Rhine near Strasbourg and pillaged this city, which had grown from a Roman garrison to a municipality. But Julian (not yet become emperor and apostate, still only commander of Rome's legions along the Rhine) defeated them with great slaughter; and those of them he did not kill or take alive, he drove back across the Rhine.

But the later invasions were not so well resisted. Strasbourg was, for instance, probably the first Gallic town to suffer at Attila's hands, and may also have been the last — on his retreat from Châlons, when he left so little of this place that even the name disappeared.

Then, one day, another battle was fought near the dust and débris that had been a city of the Roman Empire and a garrison for Roman legions — a battle remarkable in its contending forces as in its enduring results: Tolbiac, wherein one Germanic (Frankish) chieftain, Clovis, fighting nominally as a defender of Roman rule in eastern Gaul, defeated the Germanic chieftain of the Alamans, and made it clear that further incursions from east of the Rhine would be summarily dealt with.

There is a tradition at Strasbourg that in gratitude for this victory Clovis, even before he went to Reims to fulfil his vow and offer himself for baptism, laid the foundations of a cathedral in this place where he and his successors rebuilt the city and reinstituted its old Celto-Roman system of self-government.

At Verdun we recalled the Treaty of Verdun by which Alsace fell to Lothair, who, when he died, divided his share into three parts, leaving this part to his youngest son. The eldest brother coveted this, and complained to his uncles. Uncle Charles the Bald minded his own business in France (where he had a good deal to mind, much of it furnished by the Norman raids), but Uncle Louis the German came to help his nephew — and stayed to help himself. When he got there, he recalled that twenty-three years before his father had promised him Alsace. And filial piety made him feel that he ought to keep it. So, keep it he did! That is how Alsace became German.

In 1263 Strasbourg became a republic, a little state of itself, walled, armed, defended; determined to mind its own business and oblige other folks to mind theirs. And this example was soon followed by all the towns of Alsace, aided by the Emperor, who saw in this a way of reducing the power of his nobles and increasing the number and strength of places directly answerable to him.

But when the little towns began to enjoy so much security, so much wealth and power, the nobles flocked into them, from their neighboring castles, to dwell; and within a generation after the founding of the tiny republics, or free cities, many of them were entirely in the hands of the patriciate.

The struggles between burghers and nobles were bitter, in Strasbourg, but the burghers steadily won. After 1332, not more than one third of all public offices could be held by nobles. In 1397 Strasbourg made every voter classify himself, and those who claimed nobility were ordered out of the city and forbidden to return within ten years.

Then the population was divided into twenty 'tribes' which were named for as many trades: butchers, bakers, wine-merchants, coopers, etc., with the tribe of boatmen at the head. Each tribe comprised not only all the workmen of the particular calling whose name it bore, but as many other citizens as found that group most to their liking. All voting was done through the tribes. Each tribe had its own constitution and regulations. Each had a meeting-place, which was the centre of social as well as political

life for its members. In times of danger every man rushed
to his tribe's meeting-place and thence to the gates or bastions this tribe had been designated to defend.

To enter a tribe, one had to inscribe himself as an ap-
prentice to that trade, pay a certain sum into the tribal
treasury, and work three years in the establishment of a
patron or master. He then paid again into the treasury and
was designated a journeyman, after which he was free to
make, whenever he felt himself able, such a demonstration
of his craft as might win him from the experts the title of
master-craftsman. Each trade or craft could have only so
many masters. When that number was filled, no amount
of money or influence sufficed to get another master ac-
credited. Often the control of a prosperous trade was in the
hands of a few families and passed from father to son for
many generations.

A stranger could scarcely find work in a city like Strasbourg. And if he could not find work at the end of three
days, he had to leave town.

It was the tribes which elected the magistracy; and the
magistracy which made and enforced the laws.

But in 1434 'a gentleman of Mayence' who, driven from
his native town by some dissensions of whose nature we are
not very definitely informed, came to Strasbourg and managed to 'get on.'

His name was Johann Gansfleich of Gutenberg. When
he left Mayence some one there owed him three hundred
and thirteen florins which he was unable to collect. Fourteen years after he had settled at Strasbourg, he learned
that the Recorder of Mayence was in his adopted city, and
promptly had that official arrested for the unpaid debt of
one of his townsmen!

Johann lived at Strasbourg for nearly twenty-five years,
and married a young lady of very good family there. He

cut gems and polished mirrors, and experimented with movable type which he cut from wood and strung on a stout cord to keep the alignment.

While he was living here and dreaming of making books that many people might afford, there was founded at Sélestat a Latin school which rapidly became famous and attracted hundreds of students. The founder of the school had been in Italy and there had become acquainted with the Greek and Latin classics then beginning to be read and studied with tremendous results.

At Sélestat many young men became so enamoured of the forbidden literature — Homer and Virgil, Horace and Pindar, Herodotus and Pliny, Plato and Cicero — that numbers of them went to Italy to continue their studies and, incidentally, to witness the dawn of the Renaissance, of the Golden Age of our Christian era. They, when they returned, and others with them, formed at Strasbourg the first literary society of modern Europe. Nowhere outside of Italy in those days — not even at Paris — was there such culture in the classics, such zest for the new philosophy of humanism, such disposition to think, to compare, to challenge, instead of accepting without question and obeying without comprehending.

In 1538, John Calvin came to Strasbourg, married here, and preached, wrote, and taught his reformed doctrines for three years. With him, and following him, came no fewer than fifteen hundred Frenchmen, disciples of his faith.

Now, of all that might be said of Strasbourg in the sixteenth and seventeenth centuries, I'm afraid we must omit everything. Because to begin on it is to be involved in a long story that cannot be briefly told.

Louis XIV, when Alsace became French again, permitted the people of Strasbourg so much freedom to develop according to their ancient preferences that, when the Revolu-

tion came and Germany urged Alsace to break away from
France, the urging was heeded only by a negligible few
whose interests lay that way.

After the Bastille fell, the citizens of Strasbourg met and
signed a declaration saying: 'We have the honor to be
French; we are of one mind, one spirit, with you; we shall
adhere to the decrees of the National Assembly.'

When war against France was declared by the Emperor
(Marie-Antoinette's brother) on April 20, 1792, one fourth
of the total adult population of Alsace rushed to arms to
defend France. Fathers took their places beside their sons.
All hearts were aflame. It was in the white heat of that fire
that the 'Marseillaise,' the great hymn of freedom, was
born.

Lieutenant Rouget de Lisle was a frequent visitor at the
home of Friedrich de Dietrich who had been the Royal
Prætor at Strasbourg and was now its elected Mayor. The
young officer, well born, socially well dowered, was a
favored intimate of the little group that gathered often in
the salon of the Mayor's house, for conversation, music, and
other fireside pleasures.

On the evening of April 23, 1792, nothing was talked of
in that gathering except the war news just come to Strasbourg. Austria was going to put down the Revolution in
France, was she? Nowhere was her intention learned with
fiercer indignation than at Strasbourg, for so many generations a Hapsburg fief. The men of Strasbourg were clamor-
ing for places with the other defenders of France. They
were to march almost immediately.

In the Dietrich home, where music was deemed the only
adequate expression for such emotions as were hastening all
heartbeats then, they talked that night of what strains the
soldiers of liberty might march to as they went to meet the
invading foe.

Men going to battle in such glorious conditions could not be voiced by any of the old songs made for soldiers of a king. This warfare must have a new hymn, a new chant of consecration.

Whether some one suggested to Rouget de Lisle that he write a marching song for the departing army of the Rhine, or whether the urge came to him from within his own heart after he left the Mayor's house that night, we do not know.

He was a violinist of some talent, wrote verses, and occasionally composed airs. When he returned to his lodging that night, it was not to sleep; and before dawn he had completed words and music of what he called 'The Chant of Departure of the Army of the Rhine.'

At a very early hour he presented himself at the home of Dietrich, where he found the Mayor in his garden tending his lettuces, which he gladly left to go indoors and hear the new composition.

'Great!' he cried. 'Just the thing! This evening we will reassemble all who were here last night; and you shall sing your song for them.'

(I hope you know the picture of that scene, in the Louvre Museum!)

Next time you hear this song, note that it contains not a suggestion of aggressive warfare, of battle for possessions; it is to defence that this great hymn calls the children of the country. The sentiments it expresses are identified with the growth of liberties. No country is mentioned. No special 'tyrant' is designated. It is the hymn of free men ready to fight in defence of their human rights and liberties; and it was born in Strasbourg in the depths of an April night when the tread of Austria's advancing hosts must have been all but audible to an ear that listened while the world slept.

(The hymn was called 'La Marseillaise' because it was

the men of the Midi, marching on Paris in July and August, to attack the Tuileries and depose the King, who sang it with such effect that it fired France.)

During the wars of the Revolution and of the Empire, Alsace gave sixty-two generals to lead the armies of France — among them Kellermann and Kléber — and on the Arc de Triomphe in Paris are the names of twenty-eight who aided Napoleon in his victories. Alsace remained ardent for him until the Bellerophon had carried him away to exile.

If you try the Hôtel de la Ville de Paris, which I tried before the war and which I remember as satisfactory (you will find it in rue de la Mésange, leading to Place Broglie), you will be but a step from the house of Dietrich, which is number 2 Place Broglie. From the west end of this *place* (nearest to your hotel), rue de Dôme leads straight to the rose-red cathedral standing in the midst of a wealth of ancient and most picturesque houses, including the Maison Kammerzell whose ground floor dates from 1467, its ornate upper stories from 1589; this is on the north side of the cathedral square; on the west side, at the corner of rue Mercière, is the former Hôtellerie du Cerf mentioned as early as 1268.

East of the cathedral is a school occupying the site of an old hostelry where Gutenberg is said to have made his first experiments with printing.

And south of the cathedral is the Frauenhaus, or house of the cathedral architects, with a wing built in 1347 and another built in 1589; and the palace of the Cardinals de Rohan, of whom Strasbourg had four in succession between 1704 and the Revolution — none of them remarkable for his virtues, but all of them remarkable for their pride and their magnificence, the last of them the Cardinal de Rohan of the diamond necklace affair, the dupe of Cagliostro and the Motte woman (see 'So You're Going to

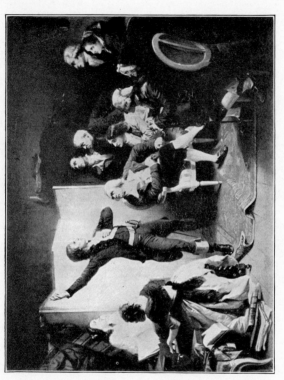

ROUGET DE LISLE SINGING THE MARSEILLAISE
By A. A. P. Isidore

Paris,' pp. 251-56). A visitor to his episcopal court here says: 'His household expenses were ruinous and unbelievable. I will tell only one thing, which will give an idea of the rest: he had no less than fourteen stewards and twenty-five valets de chambre.' She tells how he received her, wearing a cassock of scarlet watered silk and a surplice of English point lace of incalculable value, and carrying in his hand an illuminated missal, a family heirloom of unique antiquity and magnificence; he would not deign to carry a printed book!

In this palace little Marie-Antoinette was a guest on her way to marry the Dauphin. She had left Vienna on the morning of April 21st. On the evening of May 6th she could see, far off against the sunset, 'the astonishing spire' of Strasbourg — her first glimpse of France.

'She bore upon her person during this last night on German soil a last letter of her mother's which had reached her but the day before yesterday,' says Belloc in his 'Marie Antoinette.' 'It was the most intimate and the most searching she was to receive in all the long correspondence which was to pass between them for ten years, and it contained a phrase which the child could hardly understand, but which, if texts and single phrases were of the least advantage to conduct, might have deflected her history and that of Europe: "The one felicity of this world is a happy marriage; I can say so with knowledge; and the whole hangs upon the woman, that she should be willing, gentle, and able to amuse!"'

'Next day at noon she crossed in great pomp to an island in mid-river, where a temporary building of wood had been raised upon the exact frontier for the ceremony of her livery.

'It is possible that the long ritual of her position — she was to endure it for twenty years! — was already a burden upon her versatility, even after these short weeks. Here, on this island, the true extent of the French parade first met her. It was sufficient to teach her what etiquette was to mean. The poor child had to take off every stitch of her clothes and to dress, to a ribbon or a hair pin, with an order strictly ordained and in things all brought from Versailles for the occasion. Once so dressed she was conducted to a central room where her German household gave her to her French one, and the Archduchess entered forever the million formalities of her new world.'

At the Cardinal's palace, she saw his nephew, a handsome man of thirty, standing by his side. He was the man who was to play, as the next Cardinal de Rohan, so sinister a part in her undoing.

Napoleon was also a sojourner beneath this roof, as were both his empresses. The Musée des Beaux-Arts, the Musée of Decorative Arts (especially fine), and the Musée Préhistorique, are among the present tenants of the palace.

Everybody visits the cathedral and sees the astronomical clock, so I am saying nothing about them. Too few visit the Rohan palace and the historical museum of the city in the old Grande-Boucherie and facing the fourteenth-century custom-house on the other side of the Pont-Corveau. Across the latter (from the predecessor of which criminals used to be thrown into the river) is the Musée Alsacien — one of those provincial museums illustrating the life of the district, which ought not to be neglected by any intelligent traveller; they are invaluable, and fascinating, too.

The quai which occupies the north bank of the river Ill west of the covered market which used to be the custom-house is Quai Saint-Thomas, at number 7 on which is the old Hôtel de l'Esprit where the Emperor Maximilian I lodged (Mary of Burgundy's husband), and, much later, Jean-Jacques Rousseau, Goethe, and other notables. In the

Church of Saint-Thomas, behind the quai, is the elaborate tomb, by Pigalle, of the Marshal de Saxe, owner of Chambord, lover of Adrienne Lecouvreur, and progenitor of George Sand.

Between this church and the cathedral lie the principal things of interest to the lovers of the ancient and picturesque; and practically every foot of these old streets, as well as the length of Grande-Rue to the north of this section, should be explored on foot.

In any case, be sure to see the Gutenberg statue in the Place Gutenberg, a very short distance west of the cathedral; and to walk down rue des Tonneliers to see the lovely old houses, including the richly sculptured one at number 23 known as the 'Brasserie de Pigeon'; and the one at number 13 called the 'house of the bear.'

From the rue Mercière, flanking Place Gutenberg on the south, there is a fine perspective of the cathedral. And at number 36, rue Vieux-Marché-aux-Poissons (or old fish market) is the house wherein Goethe lived, in 1770–71, whilst he was a student at the University. He was here when little Marie-Antoinette came. It was while he lived here that the idyl with Friederike occurred. There is a very great deal one would love to recall about Goethe's stay at Strasbourg. But that, I dare say, must be for the further detail on Alsace which we may include, some day.

When you have wandered to your heart's content about the Old Town, drive through Place Broglie and across Pont-du-Théâtre to the New Town — the Kaiser Town, built between 1870 and 1918. And it may be that you will want to drive to the Pont-de-Kehl which crosses the Rhine between France and Germany. To do this, follow rue des Vosges, back of Place de la République, until it becomes rue de la Forêt-Noire (street of the Black Forest) leading direct to the bridgehead.

Don't forget that Alsatian cooking is among the best in France, and that the wines are worthy of it. (Who was it said that the districts which produce good wines usually produce good cooks?)

Valentin Sorg's, 52, rue du Vieux-Marché-aux-Vins, is the most celebrated restaurant; it is west of your hotel, along the same street which does not change its direction, though it changes its name. It is expensive, but notable. You may not be encouraged to eat sauerkraut there, though it is a famous dish in Alsace. But you'll get the best of pâtés and terrines de foie gras, and other Alsatian specialties; and a fine cellar of Rhine and Moselle wines, also of the fruit brandies which are a specialty of Alsace. *L'eau-de-vie-de framboises* (raspberry brandy) is the most noted. To my way of thinking it is like liquid fire. Good beer at Strasbourg, too! I wish I had liked the people better — and the hotel.

When you leave Strasbourg, take Route 83 for Sélestat, and thence (by a détour to the west) to the castle of Haut-Königsbourg, which I think you will find of great interest for a variety of reasons.

Charlemagne gave this forested mountain to the Abbey of Saint-Denis, near Paris; and it seems to have belonged to the abbey until the Hohenstaufen family came to rule Alsace. They saw the military value and crowned the crest with a stronghold which had varying fortunes of little interest to us. The castle fell into picturesque ruins and in 1865 it was bought by the town of Sélestat — probably for its 'excursion values' — which found the cost of upkeep so heavy that, in 1899, when Emperor William II came to visit the ruin, somebody had the bright idea of presenting him with the castle — and the upkeep.

Then it was William's turn to have a bright idea. He thought it would be nice to have the castle rebuilt as it was in feudal times — and to let Alsace pay for it, or at least pay half the cost. Alsace protested; but in vain.

The work was done; the Kaiser was provided with a stage-setting wherein, once a year, he could play (for the duration of a lunch hour) the rôle of a mediæval suzerain with his vassals about him; and the 'trippers' were furnished with something theatric and imperial, to keep them in mind of their War-Lord and his direct descent from the old War-Lords of storied times.

There is an excellent guide-book of the castle on sale at the entrance; it has many fine photographs showing the place as it was, before 1899, and as it is now. What your conclusions about it all may be, I cannot guess. But I feel quite sure you will enjoy drawing them.

Lunch at Colmar at the restaurant called La Maison des Têtes, at 19, rue des Têtes. If you duplicate my experience there, your luncheon will be a most memorable one — one of the best you've had in touring France.

Colmar is a picturesque old town which numbers among its illustrious sons Auguste Bartholdi, sculptor of the Lion of Belfort and of the Statue of Liberty in New York Harbor.

The musée of Colmar is a notably good one; even if you have scant time to do justice to its contents, don't fail to see the building, particularly the cloister; for it is housed in a thirteenth-century convent.

Colmar is rich in lovely old houses, sculptured and painted. Be sure to see the Maison Pfister, close to the cathedral. And here, as everywhere in Alsace, keep a sharp lookout *behind* the picturesque exteriors, for the most enchanting courtyards in the world and the greatest variety of fine old wells.

From Colmar you may continue to Belfort (forty-five miles), the natural and immemorial passage between the Vosges and the Jura; and thence via the famously lovely

Valley of the Doubs, to Besançon (fifty-five miles farther), a delightful old town and the centre for many very beautiful excursions.

Or, you may cross the Col de la Schlucht, one of the most beautiful mountain passes I know, and spend the late afternoon and the night and as much more time as you have to give, at lovely Lake Gerardmer where there is a surpassingly good hotel (Grand-Hôtel du Lac) at which you are sure to wish you could linger indefinitely.

And when you must leave Gerardmer, lying more than two thousand feet above sea-level, you may return to Paris by way of the great spas at Vittel and Contrexéville, or by way of Chaumont and Troyes.

The latter is one of the most interesting towns in France, very, very rich in beautiful old architecture and sculpture and stained glass. I have found its Terminus Hotel comfortable, and the food there excellent. And of the treasures of Troyes I dare not speak in detail — for they mean a chapter in themselves.

En route from Troyes toward Paris, you pass through Payn, where Hugh de Payn, founder, or at least first Master, of the Knights Templars was born.

By another route (77) you may go to Arcis-sur-Aube, which was Danton's native place, and thence to Plancy, where Foch walked the river bank after sending that historic message.

In either case you may return to Paris through Provins, which our picture-makers must on no account miss.

I have scarcely hinted at a tithe of the possibilities on this eastward-from-Paris journey. But if I have induced even a few more travellers to consider the attractions of that section of France comprising the Vosges and the Jura, I shall be glad indeed.

INDEX

INDEX

THE CLARA LAUGHLIN
TRAVEL SERVICES

EVERYTHING that can serve you in foreign travel, steamship tickets on every line, at tariff rates, hotel reservations everywhere, motors, guides, shopping addresses, couriers to meet you and see you to your train or boat.

The same sort of helpfulness that these books have, you will find in these offices, and the same spirit of friendly interest in the success of your trip abroad.

See what we can do to help you get the most enjoyment for the money you want to spend.

Ask about The Clara Laughlin Motor Tours in England, France, Italy, Spain, Switzerland.

Offices of The Clara Laughlin Travel Services:

410 S. Michigan Ave., Chicago.

Bush House, Aldwych, London, c/o Globe Travel Co.

Via Partenope, Naples.
(All Italian offices those of Pisa Brothers)

1 Piazza Santa Trinità, Florence.

18 East 53rd St., New York City.

4 Avenue de l'Opéra, Paris. c/o Globe Travel Co.

123 Via Torino, Rome.

2345 Fondamenta Ostreghe, Venice.

You are invited to make use of our American offices for all your requirements in ocean transportation (same prices as over the company's own counters) and to enjoy our planning and counsel.

You are invited to use our offices abroad for all your travel needs while there: tickets, motors, reservations, guides, etc.

Extemporized that can serve you in foreign travel.
Steamship tickets on every line, at lowest rates; hotel
reservations everywhere; courier guides, shopping,
addresses, couriers to meet you and see you to your
train or boat.

The same sort of helpfulness that the Cook here
you will find in these offices, and the same spirit of
thoughtfulness in the service of your trip abroad.

See what we can do to help you and the rest the
moment for the money you want to spend.

*Ask about The Clark Lumpini Major Tours in this
book. France, Italy, Spain, Switzerland.*

Offices of The Clark Lumpini Travel Services

410-5 Manufacturers' Bldg. — US Trust East 64, New York.

Raisi House, Alfa-el; Inn,   Exposee de la France; Tour-
den, 400 Clark; Travel,   on (Haliet; Plunet.
Via Bellaman, Laghem.
All Eastern often Travel of.   234 Eta's Paris, Paris.
Flea Programs.
1 Reaux, Baazac, Italia.   CRIL Frateinse el Voyage,
Florence.   (lance.

YOU are invited to make use of this American
offices for all your requirements in future transportation issue presents over the minor in their own quiet-
ley, and to enjoy our planning and change.

You are invited to use our office abroad for all
your travel needs, and to there resolve anxious assets,
various galleries, etc.